RENEWALS 458-4574
DATE DUE

WITHDRAWN
UTSA Libraries

Soft Power and Its Perils

Soft Power and Its Perils
U.S. Cultural Policy in Early Postwar Japan and Permanent Dependency

Takeshi Matsuda

Woodrow Wilson Center Press
Washington, D.C.

Stanford University Press
Stanford, California

EDITORIAL OFFICES
Woodrow Wilson Center Press
Woodrow Wilson International Center for Scholars
One Woodrow Wilson Plaza
1300 Pennsylvania Avenue, N.W.
Washington, DC 20004-3027
Telephone: 202-691-4010
www.wilsoncenter.org

Order From
Stanford University Press
Chicago Distribution Center
11030 South Langley Avenue
Chicago, Ill. 60628
Telephone: 1-800-621-2736

© 2007 by Takeshi Matsuda
All rights reserved
Printed in the United States of America on acid-free paper ∞

2 4 6 8 9 7 5 3 1

Library of Congress Cataloging-in-Publication Data

Matsuda, Takeshi, 1945–
    Soft power and its perils : U.S. cultural policy in early postwar Japan and permanent dependency / Takeshi Matsuda.
      p. cm.
    Includes bibliographical references and index.
    ISBN 978-0-8047-0040-5 (cloth : alk. paper)
    1. Japan—History—Allied occupation, 1945–1952. 2. Government missions, American—Japan. 3. Japan—Civilization—American influences. 4. United States—Foreign relations—Japan. 5. Japan—Foreign relations—United States. I. Title.
DS889.16.M38 2007
952.04′4—dc22

                                                                                         2007010419

Woodrow Wilson International Center for Scholars

The Woodrow Wilson International Center for Scholars, established by Congress in 1968 and headquartered in Washington, D.C., is a living national memorial to President Wilson. The Center's mission is to commemorate the ideals and concerns of Woodrow Wilson by providing a link between the worlds of ideas and policy, while fostering research, study, discussion, and collaboration among a broad spectrum of individuals concerned with policy and scholarship in national and international affairs. Supported by public and private funds, the Center is a nonpartisan institution. It establishes and maintains a neutral forum for free, open, and informed dialogue. Conclusions or opinions expressed in Center publications and programs are those of the authors and speakers and do not necessarily reflect the views of the Center staff, fellows, trustees, advisory groups, or any individuals or organizations that provide financial support to the Center.

The Center is the publisher of *The Wilson Quarterly* and home of Woodrow Wilson Center Press, *dialogue* radio and television, and the monthly newsletter "Centerpoint." For more information about the Center's activities and publications, please visit us on the web at www.wilsoncenter.org.

Lee H. Hamilton, President and Director

Board of Trustees
Joseph B. Gildenhorn, Chair
David A. Metzner, Vice Chair

Public Members: James H. Billington, Librarian of Congress; Bruce Cole, Chairman, National Endowment for the Humanities; Michael O. Leavitt, Secretary of Health and Human Services; Condoleezza Rice, Secretary of State; Cristián Samper, acting Secretary of the Smithsonian Institution; Margaret Spellings, Secretary of Education; Allen Weinstein, Archivist of the United States. Tami Longaberger, designated appointee of the President from within the federal government

Private Citizen Members: Robin Cook, Donald E. Garcia, Bruce S. Gelb, Sander R. Gerber, Charles L. Glazer, Susan Hutchison, Ignacio E. Sanchez

For the late Mr. Robert W. Arthur and Mrs. Irma M. Arthur

Contents

List of Illustrations	xi
Foreword, by John W. Dower	xiii
Preface	xvii
Introduction	1
1 Occupation Reform as an American Cultural Offensive	15
2 The Cold War, the "Reverse Course," and the Rise of Nationalism	41
3 The Making of a "Soft Peace" and Japan's "Proper Place"	64
4 John D. Rockefeller III in Tokyo: Cultural Exchange versus Cultural Imperialism	95
5 The Rockefeller Report: Countering the Communist Menace	113
6 The U.S. Cultural Offensive and Japanese Intellectuals	138
7 Making Japanese Pro-American: The 1950 American Studies Seminar in Tokyo	161
8 The Kyoto American Studies Seminar and American Soft Power	185
9 Occupation Reform, "Shallow Democracy," and Consumerism	214
Conclusion	244
Appendix A The State of Scholarship on U.S.-Japan Relations	257
Appendix B The Tokyo-Stanford Seminars in American Studies	263
Appendix C The Kyoto Seminars in American Studies	265
Notes	267
Bibliography	337
Index	359

List of Illustrations

Following page 160

1, 2. Daily necessities of the occupation forces
3. Cartoon of General Douglas MacArthur
4. Cartoon of Ginza Post Exchange
5. Tokyo-Stanford American Studies Seminars, 1950
6. Tokyo-Stanford American Studies Seminars, 1950
7. The International House of Juapan
8. Matsumoto Shigeharu in front of the International House
9. Matsumoto Shigeharu and John D. Rockefeller III at the International House, 1972
10. President Dwight D. Eisenhower meets with Secretary of State John Foster Dulles, 1956
11. Dean Acheson, 1965
12. President of Tokyo University Nambara Shigeru
13. President of Tokyo University Yanaihara Tadao
14. Charles B. Fahs, 1958
15. The Rockefeller family visiting Prime Minister of Japan Nobusuke Kishi's house, 1958
16. John D. Rockefeller III in Japan, 1952
17. President of Tokyo University Nambara Shigeru presenting a diploma, 1950

Foreword

John W. Dower

In popular U.S. commentary on the world since World War II, it has become a cliché to describe the American-led postwar occupation of Japan as a great success story. The reasons why seem obvious. Since the war and occupation ended, Japan has become a democracy governed by rule of law. Its political system may sometimes seem ossified and dysfunctional, but no more so than in most other contemporary democracies. Its postwar economic accomplishments are impressive, and have spread prosperity quite equitably throughout the Japanese populace. Unlike the militarized state prior to 1945, postwar Japan has not threatened its neighbors and the peace of the world. On the contrary, despite an ever-increasing military capability, it has remained attentive to the "no-war" strictures laid down in the drastically revised constitution that was adopted under strong U.S. pressure in 1947. And, of course, ever since 1945 Japan has proven itself to be a loyal friend and ally of the United States. Takeshi Matsuda would argue that it has, indeed, been loyal to a fault.

Democracy, prosperity, military restraint—these are admirable accomplishments by almost any reckoning outside the extremist fringes of Japanese neo-nationalism, where the putative lost virtues of the prewar state are still revered. Still, the rosy scenario of an easy and enormously successful occupation can be misleading. This certainly bedazzled and blinded war planners in the administration of President George W. Bush, who beginning in 2002 repeatedly evoked defeated Japan (and to a lesser degree Germany) as reason for being sanguine that the war of choice against Iraq also would have a happy ending. Such analogies were flawed from the start: almost everything that contributed to the eventual success of postwar reconstruction and democratization in Japan was patently missing in Iraq and in President Bush's America as well. Still, such misuses of history die hard. Even after occupied Iraq plunged into chaos, the president was still evoking Japan as a meaningful model.

Professor Matsuda approaches this same historical moment from a very different direction—as a scholar who completed his doctoral work in U.S. diplomatic history at the University of Wisconsin–Madison in 1979 and returned to Japan to become a leading figure in American Studies there. He represents a generation that knows the occupation period only "as history"— but knows the subtle legacies of the occupation in his country first-hand, both in the academic community and the more amorphous realm we call popular consciousness. Foreign policy has three legs, he argues here in *Soft Power and Its Perils*—political, economic, and cultural; and even in the "soft" last of these, the realm of so-called cultural policy, the American handlers of occupied Japan left a mixed long-term legacy. Dynamic exchange programs and enduring friendships have been one side of this legacy, "cultural corrosion" and psychological as well as structural dependency the other side.

This is a severe appraisal, particularly coming as it does from a long-time scholar of, and good friend of, the United States. "Soft power" is an appealing concept, especially among critics of the militant unilateralism of recent U.S. foreign policy. It is a concept that many Japanese officials both in and outside the Foreign Ministry have embraced as a polestar for Japan's own ideal role in a precarious world. As Professor Matsuda argues, however, the line between soft power and cultural imperialism, a more old-fashioned and pejorative term, is easily breached—with consequences that may only become fully apparent many years later.

The protagonists in this case study of occupied and early post-occupation Japan were keenly sensitive to the challenge of exercising persuasive influence short of abrasive imperialism. John D. Rockefeller III, who played a fleeting but important role in promoting U.S. cultural policy vis-à-vis Japan beginning in 1951, took care to emphasize that future interchange between the erstwhile victors and the vanquished must be a "two-way street" that avoided "the problem of cultural imperialism." In a relationship of such glaring inequality and disparity of power, however, this was easier said than done. The two-way street amounted to a multilane highway on the U.S. side and single lane on the other (accommodating, initially, mostly Japanese "cultural" products of a traditional, aesthetic sort). Certainly in American eyes, the United States was—and still remains, more a half-century later—defeated Japan's teacher and preacher, as well as supreme military commander.

In analyzing early postwar cultural policy, Professor Matsuda uncovers more than a little uncomfortable detail. Portions of U.S. policy were indeed generous, and Americans like Rockefeller were intelligent and sincere. At the same time, however, their policy prescriptions were formulated at a time of particularly intense Cold War hysteria. Soft and hard policies were promoted as a package by a homogeneous cadre of Americans who deemed themselves instant experts on the collective Japanese mind, without knowing the language or much else about Japan apart from what conservative Japanese told them. The U.S. cultural offensive involved media censorship, "Red purges" in both the public and private sectors, and a blithe acceptance of what in retrospect seem eerily Orwellian undertakings (like the official "Campaign of Truth" launched in April 1950). These concerted propaganda activities extolled the sublime virtues of American-style freedom and democracy even while Jim Crow segregation blighted the United States, women were denied equal opportunity there, McCarthyism choked off serious debate, and U.S. foreign policy supported opposition to genuine national-liberation movements in Asia and elsewhere.

In this milieu, serious Japanese reservations about American policies and practices were dismissed as irrational and dangerous, if not outright communistic and seditious. Marxism, socialism, and communism did find serious voice in Japan in these early postwar years, as they did in war-torn Europe and elsewhere in Asia. Some intellectuals and activists did toe the Soviet line. At the same time, pacifism and neutrality in the Cold War found support at all levels of Japanese society—hardly surprising in a country that had been savaged only a few years earlier by home-grown militarism and global war.

While these complex political, intellectual, and ideological currents draw the serious attention of historians today, America's cultural cold warriors bundled them together and essentially dismissed criticism of the United States and its policies as evidence of either gross ignorance or malign intent. Japanese who had lived for six years under U.S. military control were dismissed as having little or no understanding of the United States. Legitimate fears about America's retreat from early "demilitarization and democratization" policies, America's demand that Japan undertake remilitarization under the eagle's wing and acquiesce in a "separate peace" agreement (excluding the Soviet Union and China), America's detachment of Okinawa as an essentially neocolonial military base to which the "generous" peace settlement did not apply, America's irresistible insistence that Japan participate in the strict economic as well as military containment of

China—all such critical expressions of concern were brushed aside as the cant of irrational and irresponsible leftists. As we learn from the archival records exhumed in these pages, the banner of "rationality" that American cultural commissars unfurled in Japan in the early 1950s often was planted in a cultural arrogance and paucity of self-awareness that bordered on racism.

No one denies that Rockefeller's two-way street flourished over the years that followed, contributing to lively exchanges as well as enduring collegial friendships. International House in Tokyo is one notable product of these early soft-policy initiatives. Another is the institutionalization of American Studies in higher education that Professor Matsuda scrutinizes in these pages. What is most original and unsettling in *Soft Power and Its Perils* is, first, its documentation of how deeply rooted in Cold War paranoia such early "cultural" undertakings were; and second, how flawed and even pernicious they now appear in the eyes of a Japanese Americanist who entered the field a generation later. The U.S.-sponsored and generously funded American Studies agenda, in this critique, ended up reinforcing academic hierarchy and inbreeding, as well as self-censorship when it came to commenting on controversial U.S. policies—hardly an impressive model of democracy in action.

More damning yet, Professor Matsuda observes that American policymakers and cultural emissaries have never abandoned their early postwar assumption of moral, cultural, and intellectual superiority; and the Japanese elites whom the United States has so carefully cultivated, in turn, have rarely failed to acquiesce to such cultural hegemony. He is not the only observer to argue that "an abiding psychology of dependence on the United States" has gripped Japan for over six decades now as a consequence of the intricate manner in which hard and soft policies have been braided together. Few such critics, however, have developed their argument through such a detailed case study.

In the final analysis, this inhibiting psychological malady is more a Japanese than an American problem—albeit one that carries implications extending far beyond Japan per se. And in *Soft Power and Its Perils* we have the strong beginnings of a necessary diagnosis of these perils from the only place where such a critique can really be effective: from where the power falls.

Preface

Because I spent a considerable part of my life at the University of Wisconsin–Madison and embraced the so-called Wisconsin spirit of "thinking otherwise," I felt that a new history of U.S.-Japan relations was needed to ask new questions. This volume addresses a neglected and perhaps enormously sensitive issue of the U.S.-Japan relationship: how the cultural dimension of that relationship has affected its "quality." To avoid controversial and politically sensitive issues, scholars often ignore the subjects that need study the most. And on this issue, it may be worth remembering what Thomas L. Friedman, the noted American journalist, wrote on February 10, 2002, in the *New York Times*. Talking about the United States, he maintained that "whenever a people reduces all its problems to a conspiracy by someone else, it absolves itself and its leaders of any responsibility for its predicament—and any need for self-examination. No civilization has ever prospered with that approach. Only in a society that embraces self-criticism can the political process produce real facts to cope with real problems."

A specific episode is also related to the conceptualization of this book. While I was undertaking research at the Rockefeller Archive Center, I ran across a passage that inspired me so much that I felt compelled to address the cultural issues surrounding U.S.-Japan relations. Dean Rusk, president of the Rockefeller Foundation in his statement on August 3, 1954, before the Special Committee to Investigate Tax-Exempt Foundations of the Eighty-third Congress, pointed out that the charter of the Rockefeller Foundation stipulates that "its funds shall be spent for 'the well-being of mankind.' . . . An important guide toward this end has been the founder's statement that, 'The best philanthropy involves a search for cause, an attempt to cure evils at their source.'"

I thought that writing a new history of Japanese-American relations and making an attempt to define and assuage the evils at their cause might reciprocate American generosity to me, a recipient of U.S. grants and fellowships. I have taken to heart historian Charles A. Beard's thesis in his 1933 address to the American Historical Association, "Written History As an Act of Faith," and have written this volume to demonstrate my faith in my profession as a historian by practicing what I believe to be right and proper.

Democracy and Freedom of Information

From almost forty years of experience in American Studies, I have learned that democracy provides for, and protects, the vital process of subjecting the existing order of things to steady examination. As a corollary, the principle of public access to government information is enormously important in a civil and democratic society. Greater openness and access to official documents are a vital key to the goals of political reform, government accountability, and better understanding of government policy, as well as an important key to the future of democracy. Under such conditions, an informed public not only keeps democracy alive and robust, but also truly sustains the fine quality of democracy. Citizens' capability of judging public issues and questions is crucial to the openness and freedom of public discussion and the prevention of assumptions of authority against the general will.

During my stint as a Woodrow Wilson Center fellow in 2001–2002, I was fortunate to have access to U.S. government records at the National Archives and Records Administration in College Park, Maryland, those at the National Security Archive of George Washington University in Washington, D.C., and the private papers at the Rockefeller Archive Center in Sleepy Hollow, New York. This book largely resulted from my efforts to take full advantage of the openness of and access to public and private documents in the United States. Unfortunately, I was unable to use official documents in Japan's own archives for the reason that they were simply inaccessible. And I had to rely on the Rockefeller Archive Center in New York for the papers pertaining to the founding of International House of Japan (where documents in the archive were also closed to the public). Indeed, the accessibility of public and private documents in the United States and Japan presented a sharp contrast. It appears glaringly ironic in light of the fact that a Japan-U.S. symposium was held in Tokyo in 1995 on the subject of the internationalization of Japan and public access to government information (http://www.gwu.edu/~nsarchiv/japan/1995foiaconferencereport.htm). Participants in the symposium unanimously called for greater openness of Japan's official documents, and yet little seems to have been done since that time to improve Japan's situation. It is therefore my earnest hope that this book will serve not only as a reminder of the need to increase public awareness of the vital importance of expanding public access to official information in Japan, but also as a catalyst for that effort.

Acknowledgments

I could not have finished writing this book on U.S.-Japan cultural relations without the kind advice, guidance, and encouragement of many friends and colleagues. Taking this opportunity, I wish to thank them all for their support and help.

Here I would like to acknowledge the countless debts I have accumulated from those people. First, my indebtedness to the late professors Merrill Jensen of the University of Wisconsin–Madison and Imazu Akira of Kyoto University is longstanding and deep. I am profoundly grateful to Thomas J. McCormick, professor emeritus of the University of Wisconsin–Madison; John W. Dower, Ford International Professor of History at the Massachusetts Institute of Technology; Aruga Tadashi, professor emeritus of Hitotsubashi University, Tokyo; and Takahashi Akira, professor emeritus of Osaka City University, for their lasting support. I am indebted as well to the dedicated librarians and archivists serving at the following institutions: the U.S. Library of Congress, Washington, D.C.; the National Archives and Records Administration, College Park, Maryland; the National Security Archive (directors William Burr and Robert A. Wampler) at the Gelman Library, George Washington University, Washington, D.C.; the Rockefeller Archive Center (director Darwin H. Stapleton and archivist Thomas Rosenbaum for research grant 2000); the Edwin O. Reischauer Institute of Japanese Studies, Harvard University; the Special Collections Section, University of Arkansas Libraries, Fayetteville; the State Historical Library of Wisconsin, Madison; the University of Wisconsin Memorial Library, Madison; the United States–Japan Foundation (Dr. George Packard and Takuma Takeo for research grant 1999–2001); the Woodrow Wilson International Center for Scholars, Washington, D.C. (2001–2002); Wolfson College, University of Cambridge; and the Center for Pacific and American Studies, University of Tokyo. For friendship and support, I am very thankful to Robert and Mary Arthur, William S. Borden, Bruce Cumings, Michael Glennon, Robert Halstead, Robert Hathaway, Laura E. Hein, Rogers Hollingsworth, Allen Hunter, Akira Iriye, Stanley I. Kutler, Walter LaFeber, Melvyn Leffler, Rosemary Lyon, Lucy J. Mathiak, Mary B. McDonnell, Joe Moore, Patrick K. O'Brien, Lynda Pritchard, Donald T. Roden, E. B. Smith, Susan Smulyan, Han Tie, Joseph Tulchin, David Willis, Marilyn B. Young, Akita Shigeru, Higashi Julie, Hirano Ken-Ichirō, Matsuhara Ichirō, Ishikawa Taneo, Kan Hideki, Katō Yōko, Nishimura Shigeo, Ōtsuru Chieko, Sasaki Yutaka, Sugita Yoneyuki, Yolanda Tsuda, colleagues of the Green Tea Project, members of Japan–United States Forum for Intellectual Exchange, and my graduate students at Osaka University of Foreign Studies. Last but by no means least, my heartfelt thanks goes to Keiko Matsuda and the rest of my family.

A Note on Japanese Names

The author has followed the rule that the historian John W. Dower established in his book *Embracing Defeat: Japan in the Wake of World War II* (Norton, 1999). As a general rule, the Japanese practice is observed in which the family name or surname comes first, before the given or personal name (thus, for example, Prime Minister Yoshida's full name is Yoshida Shigeru). However, this rule is not observed when Japanese who live outside the country have chosen to follow the Western order.

Soft Power and Its Perils

Introduction

> Cultural interchange alone will not bring about stable and peaceful relations between Japan and the United States or other nations. Policies and actions in the economic and political fields will be equally important. It is the sum total of all three which determine what the long-range relationship will be.
>
> —John D. Rockefeller III, 1951

> Soft power came in the Marshall Plan. . . . We did the same thing in Japan.
>
> —Secretary of State Colin Powell, World Economic Forum, 2003

As the United States marched inexorably toward war against Iraq in March 2003, U.S. policy makers looked to post–World War II Japan and Germany as models of successful military occupations. In making the imagined analogy with Japan, President George W. Bush repeatedly pointed out how America's benign, "soft power" occupation had worked effectively in that country. He confidently declared that he would destroy Iraqi dictator Saddam Hussein's tyranny and then reshape Iraq. Neoconservatives—notably former Deputy Secretary of Defense Paul D. Wolfowitz and the vice chairman of the Defense Policy Board, Richard N. Perle—also talked about drawing lessons from Japan and Germany that might be applicable to Islamic Iraq. They claimed that U.S. soft and hard power permanently reshaped the future of Japan to the same extent it did that of Germany, because the Japanese were overwhelmed and completely defeated. But when it seemed that war with Iraq was imminent, the historian John W. Dower warned the hawkish Bush administration and the American people against drawing likenesses between the postwar military occupations of Japan and of Iraq. He insisted that the occupation of Japan offered no model whatsoever for the occupation of Iraq.[1]

Indeed, as of early 2007 no peace was in sight, nor was there any sign of reconstruction or a reshaping of Iraq. It was feared that the ravaged Islamic country would continue to be divided for some time, with a terrorist threat still hanging over its head. Even so, the Bush administration persisted in invoking the "success story" of the U.S. occupation of Japan despite the lack of basis for comparing Iraq and defeated Japan. Moreover, the Japan success story emphasized by President Bush was highly dubious: an unfortunate long-term legacy of the U.S. occupation of Japan was its permanent dependency and "subordinate independence" in its relationship with the United States.

In contrast to the current situation in Iraq, the U.S. occupation of Japan was a democratic experiment supported by American soft power, as well as hard power. Two factors are essential to making soft power work in an occupied country. First, a vast amount of information should be gathered about the country and its culture through a long period of sustained area studies well ahead of the occupation. Second, policymakers should make full use of the findings and expertise of the specialists and execute policy resolutely by translating the academic fruit of this expertise into concrete programs. U.S. preparation for the occupation of Japan began immediately after Japan's attack on Pearl Harbor on December 7, 1941—that is, four years before the actual occupation of the country. Indeed, during the war in the Pacific, American experts on Japan conducted detailed studies of Japan. One such effort was *The Chrysanthemum and the Sword,* written in 1946 by cultural anthropologist Ruth Benedict.[2] Prominent private think tanks, such as the Council on Foreign Relations and the Institute of Pacific Relations, and interdepartmental agencies in Washington also spent a great deal of effort defining the general objectives of the occupation of Japan and formulating programs needed to meet the specific objectives of the United States.[3]

Unconditional Surrender and the Democratization of Japan

The Japanese accepted unconditional surrender in 1945 with feelings of disappointment and betrayal, but also relief. No doubt all welcomed the end of the war, because it meant their survival. Surrender also meant liberation from a premodern yoke of feudalism and the oppression of the military government under which they had suffered for more than ten years. In other words, the Japanese outlived not only the war, but also a long period of repression by a totalitarian regime. After the war, the Supreme Commander for the Allied Powers (SCAP) arrived in Japan with a variety of measures to implement drastic reforms. Most of the reform measures had emerged from the area studies, a chief component of American soft power. During their almost seven years of occupation, the Americans made the best use of American scholarship on Japan as they reshaped the country into a peaceful, democratic nation. Among the reforms pursued were the dissolution of Japan's financial industrial *zaibatsu* complexes, land reform, abolition of state Shintoism, and the drafting of a new constitution.

The Japanese were hardly bystanders, however. Although Japanese activists had ardently hoped to reform the country themselves, they had been for the most part unsuccessful, both before and during the war.[4] Thus, during the occupation the Japanese did not sit idly, watching the Americans carry out important reforms. Rather, the occupation reform was a U.S.-Japan joint undertaking, according to a noted Japanese historian.[5]

Japan's surrender and the subsequent U.S. occupation of Japan provided the Japanese with a golden opportunity to rebuild their country as *heiwa bunka kokka* (a nation of peace and culture) and start anew.[6] Japanese intellectuals, particularly specialists on America, after reflecting deeply on Japan's military past, which had ended tragically, pledged not to make the same mistake again. They were determined to construct a new Japan by making the best use of their expertise to democratize their country. Most scholars regarded the United States as a model of what the most advanced nation ought to be; they believed it to be the embodiment of a genuine revolution.

Sociologist Robert N. Bellah stressed the importance of American Studies as a step toward the materialization of modernization. In a paper presented at International Christian University in Tokyo, he maintained that "America is by no means a perfect society, but in looking over the world today I think it is clear that it is closer to whatever is meant by modern society than any other. It is the most radical departure from traditional society and I believe the most genuinely revolutionary society in existence. . . . I think it is incumbent on those involved in the modernization process to make a serious study of the nature of American society."[7] What Bellah meant by "revolutionary" was the process of gradualist rationalization and industrialization[8]—not necessarily the attributes commonly recognized in "democratic" revolutions such as the seventeenth-century Puritan revolution and the eighteenth-century French Revolution. Whatever the differences in the shades of meaning, Japanese scholars were eager to learn from the United States. The Japanese perception of America was so positive that scholars pursued American Studies earnestly at the initial stage of the U.S. occupation and found its interdisciplinary breadth pragmatic and rewarding. Many even sought to win Fulbright scholarships or grants from the Rockefeller Foundation so that they could study in the United States for lengthy periods of time and upon their return to Japan make constructive contributions to Japanese society.

Six years after Japan's surrender in 1945, President Harry S. Truman sent John Foster Dulles to Japan to serve as his special envoy. The dispatch of the "Dulles Peace Mission" on January 25, 1951, was widely perceived as an important preparatory step toward making peace with Japan and putting an end to the occupation. Dulles recognized the importance of protecting U.S. security and economic interests, but at the same time he was fully aware of the importance of long-term cultural relations for U.S.-Japan relations. He believed that "the peace treaty, no matter how intelligent its provisions, cannot of itself assure that Japan will remain within the orbit of the free world."[9] Dulles asked prominent philanthropist John D. Rockefeller III to join the peace mission as a consultant on cultural affairs. Since his visit to Kyoto in 1929, Rockefeller had become interested in Japan and intrigued by its culture, and so he accepted Dulles's offer.[10] Rockefeller took the view that politics, economics, and culture were the three major components of American foreign relations. Based on that view, he believed that a lasting friendship and mutual understanding between Americans and Japanese would blossom "as the result of the sum total of all types of relations, one of the most important of which was the cultural."[11]

Dulles characterized the peace mission as unique, because one member of the U.S. delegation was specifically charged with finding ways to promote cultural and educational cooperation with the Japanese people.[12] He regarded that step as an important beginning in America's wholesale effort to institutionalize better cultural relations with Japan after the war. Indeed, the U.S. occupation policy as a whole fit into the U.S. grand-scale cultural offensives in Japan and elsewhere. At that time, the United States was in the midst of fighting a bitter cold war against the Soviet Union and communism throughout the world. Because occupied Japan was a crucial battleground in the cultural cold war, Rockefeller exercised American soft power discreetly in postwar U.S.-Japan relations. He clearly recognized that the American strategy of employing soft power could be problematic—in a form that later would be called "cultural imperialism." But more than four decades would pass before historians and scholars of international relations, such as John Tomlinson and others, would pay attention to this controversial issue and popularize that notion in the early 1990s.[13]

Rockefeller carefully and cleverly avoided being branded an American cultural imperialist. Perhaps with such a goal in mind, he astutely invented the idea of a "two-way street" when he envisioned U.S.-Japan binational cultural programs, thereby avoiding the evils of the one-way imposition of culture by a powerful country on a weaker nation.[14] In a 1951 article in the *Tokyo Times,* Chief Justice Tanaka Kōtarō pointed out that Japan had already experienced the one-way imposition of culture by a powerful country in its prewar and wartime cultural programs.[15] And based on an American cultural flow that could be measured by the volume of information and the number of people coming into Japan, it was also clear that a powerful America was "imposing" its culture on a weaker postwar Japan, despite Rockefeller's intentions. Actually, Rockefeller's ideas and behavior were far more sophisticated and complex than the concept of cultural imperialism. He practiced "cultural hegemony," a notion that Italian political theorist Antonio Gramsci had crystallized in the last century. *Hegemony* could be defined as the capacity of a dominant power, through a combination of coercion and consent, to make other nations conform voluntarily to certain norms of behavior and act as the dominant country would like them to. As one noted political scientist has explained, the term hegemony is reserved for a consensual order, an element that distinguishes the hegemonic from the nonhegemonic.[16] Hegemony, which is continually being negotiated, includes resistance as well, however. Acculturation through cultural hegemony includes push and pull, wheeling and dealing, compromises, consensus, and, above all, generosity. The fact remains, however, that hegemony as a structure of dominance is sustained by broad-based consent through acceptance of an ideology associated with universalistic principles, though not in the absence of force.

Defining *Culture* and *Cultural Relations*

Two other terms used extensively in this volume should be defined as well: *culture* and *cultural relations*. According to Jessica C. E. Gienow-Hecht, in the late nineteenth-century culture referred primarily to "high culture"—

that is, the masterpieces of art, music, and literature. In the twentieth century, however, American culture became regarded as a shared system of beliefs and customs open to anyone. Today culture embraces both popular and high culture.[17] Accordingly, in this book the term *culture* is used not in the narrow sense of intellectual or aesthetic pursuits at the higher levels, but rather in its broader sense of relating to the life of a people as a whole.[18] *Cultural relations* can be defined as the broad range of contacts through which the way of life of one people is made known to another. These contacts include both direct personal relations among individuals and groups of people from the two countries as well as more impersonal communications between the people and the media. From these contacts arise opinions and attitudes, favorable or unfavorable, about the foreign nation and its culture. In combination with existing political and economic conditions, these opinions and attitudes enter into the determination of a nation's policy.

Until recently, most studies of U.S. cultural relations with other countries assumed that the United States exercised cultural imperialism—that is, they adopted a dominance-subordination relationship.[19] Dominance refers to a nation's preponderance of material power, which results in a one-way flow of influence and relations. But this assumption does not capture accurately the interactive nature of cultural relations or the US.-Japan relationship. Although America's influence on Japan has been stronger than Japan's influence on America, the American influence on Japanese society and culture was not a simplistic process by which the United States used its dominant political and economic power to induce the Japanese to accept American cultural products and visions. Nor did the penetration of American culture into Japan result in Japan's passive acceptance of that culture. Actually, they interacted.[20] Japanese reaction to American stimuli was varied and complex, ranging from positive and avid acceptance to total resistance and even rejection. When Japanese imported American culture, they usually chose the parts of American culture they believed would suit their needs. Every Japanese social group constructed its own filtering mechanisms for taking what it wanted from the American model and rejecting the rest. It seems important to ask, then, what aspects of American culture were chosen—and by which Japanese—and what were rejected and why.

According to Emily S. Rosenberg, a leading U.S. diplomatic historian, scholars have tended to focus on nuclear shields, alliance systems, and joint military maneuvers as the substance of free world alignments during the cold war. But she argues that "the strength of political/military arrangements . . . emerged within the context of another mighty force: the semiotic power that equated America with an inevitable and desirable future that was 'modern.'" She goes on to observe that "the semiotics of America's consumer-driven, mass-mediated products also helped bind the anti-communist coalition together. Policy and business elites of the postwar era clearly understood that a 'cultural offensive' powerfully served larger geopolitical and economic interests."[21] Perhaps one could argue that the U.S. occupation of Japan and subsequent U.S.-Japan relations based on security treaty arrangements were part of a U.S. global effort to spread American society and values by exporting human, cultural, and material capital abroad.

The U.S. government and its overseas agencies have not been alone in these monumental cultural relations efforts. The private sector had always been regarded as the "senior partner" in the exchange field, but in 1956 nongovernmental initiatives received a great impetus from a speech delivered at Baylor University in Texas by President Dwight D. Eisenhower, in which he commented on what he termed "people-to-people" activities.[22] A host of nongovernmental organizations such as corporations, foundations, arts groups, universities, sports teams, labor unions, and mission boards have been among the most effective transmitters of the cultural ideals and values central to American society, but this is not to say that official U.S. government organizations have not had an influence on culture as well.[23] Among nongovernmental organizations, the ones most in the public eye have been the practical economic organizations dealing with the exchange of capital, goods, and services essential for trade. These economic organizations, together with government agencies, have also received virtually all the scholarly attention.

The Basic Themes of This Book

This book highlights three issues: (1) the government-foundation-university relationship in postwar U.S.-Japan cultural relations; (2) the institutional and attitudinal problems of individual scholars; and (3) the shallowness and superficiality of democracy in Japan. These themes are described in the sections that follow.

Government-Foundation-University Interlock

The problem of the government-foundation-university interlock pervaded postwar Japan. This volume illuminates the symbiosis among those three entities as manifested in postwar U.S.-Japan cultural relations. The Gramscian notion of cultural hegemony[24] is used to demonstrate how Japan fell into a psychological trap of permanent dependency in its relationship with the United States through the promises and perils of American soft power. This is not to suggest that a conspiracy was responsible, however.

The volume also sheds light on the nature of the immediate postwar U.S.-Japan cultural relations and the institutionalization of cultural interchange, in particular. In doing so, it focuses primarily on the activities of John Rockefeller, Charles Burton Fahs (director of the Rockefeller Foundation's Humanities Division), and other prominent Americans, while analyzing the thought of their Japanese counterparts such as Matsumoto Shigeharu and Takagi Yasaka. All of these figures contributed much to institutionalizing postwar U.S.-Japan cultural relations, which continue to bond these two countries today.[25] Rockefeller, Matsumoto, and other leaders undertook this effort with a view toward promoting mutual understanding between the two peoples. By institutionalizing U.S.-Japan cultural interchange, they hoped that ideas and people would flow regularly and steadily between the two countries across the Pacific. In other words, cultural interchange programs would provide an invaluable environment through which new American ideas, information, technology, and American intellectuals would find their ways into postwar Japanese society, and vice versa.

Thanks to the close cooperation between Japanese and American leaders, U.S.-Japan cultural relations flourished and became full blown in later years in ways that few people would have ever dreamed in the late 1940s and early 1950s. These cultural interchange programs played an exceptionally important part in making many Japanese intellectuals pro-American liberals. In this sense, it can be said that the American and Japanese pioneers in the U.S.-Japan cultural interchange succeeded in "stabilizing and perpetuating a particular kind of order" within Japan and in the Asia-Pacific region.[26]

As Japan passed into the 1960s, the 1970s, and beyond, the founding scholars of American Studies in Japan and their successors discovered that it was enormously difficult to maintain the pristine spirit of American Studies during its pioneering days. As U.S.-Japan relations grew exponentially important during the cold war years, it was recognized that American Studies was essential to maintaining amicable bilateral relations. American Studies in Japan was promoted by public and private funds that were poured inconspicuously both into the coffers of academic organizations and into the pockets of individual scholars. In 1961, for example, the U.S. government spent $2 million to carry out a U.S. government educational and cultural exchange program emphasizing political theory, law, social sciences, communication media, education, and labor. Meanwhile, American public affairs officers in the U.S. embassy in Tokyo stepped up "U.S. cultural presentation in Japan by encouraging private sponsorship and by providing U.S. financial assistance in the order of one million dollars annually."[27] Warren Obluck, a U.S. Information Service (USIS) officer, acknowledged that "USIS had regularly played a supporting role, . . . [and] had taken steps since the early 1950s that resulted in measurable effects on the development of American Studies in Japan." He further pointed out that "when a team of outstanding Japanese professors got to the United States on a mission to observe how American Studies was taught in America itself . . . , it was the U.S. embassy in Japan that organized that visit and covered its costs."[28] Indeed, the first Japanese Association for American Studies (Amerika Gakkai) received cordial blessings and favors from the Civil Information and Education Section (CI&E) of SCAP when it was established in 1947. In light of the vast amount of public funds earmarked for U.S. cultural foreign policy, it was not surprising that Japanese academic organizations and individual elites received a variety of aid from America. Most programs of Amerika Gakkai and their equivalent were supported financially either by the U.S. government or by U.S. private citizens and philanthropic foundations, or both.[29] Likewise, individual scholars were assisted by the United States in one way or another, including the awarding of research grants and fellowships enabling them to study in the United States for lengthy periods of time.

Soon, however, American soft power began to have corrosive and pernicious effects on many Japanese scholars. Historian Aruga Tadashi, one of Japan's leading specialists on America, detected unwholesome symptoms in the Japanese scholarship on American Studies, although he did not specifically attribute the problem to money. When he reviewed Japanese studies on America in 1980, he noted the prevalence of lackluster works using lackadaisical approaches. He then issued a warning to the members of the Japanese Association for American Studies: "Japanese scholars must admonish themselves, should a lax attitude toward conceptualization and the feeling of inertia toward study be found in the Japanese Association for American Studies."[30] Indeed, many scholars on America seemed to be developing a dependency on American "generosity." Correspondingly, the initial pioneering spirit of American Studies specialists was decreasing, although the programs and practice of American Studies remained basically unchanged. There seemed to be no way to prevent this deterioration of the once spirited practice of American Studies, reflecting systemic co-optation and a kind of cultural corruption. American soft power unintentionally stripped American Studies in Japan of much of its raison d'être—the role of cultural resistance as a moral critic.

The Problems of Individual Scholars

This volume also addresses the institutional and attitudinal problems of individual scholars. In doing so, it raises the question of why Japanese university professors had a strong penchant for ivory tower thinking despite their avowed commitment to contribute to society. As an American observer of Japan commented, Japanese scholars were traditionally disinclined to concern themselves intimately and genuinely with contemporary social and economic problems.[31]

In the postwar era, Japanese university professors, like those elsewhere in the world, were notoriously underpaid. For example, in 1951 a full professor at Tokyo University received an average monthly salary of about $100 (30,000–50,000 yen)—not enough to support a family without moonlighting.[32] In addition, there was a structural as well as economic incentive. For example, the International Christian University (ICU) paid full professors about 20 percent more than did Tokyo University. ICU was not able to stop the practice of professors' holding multiple teaching jobs, however, even though the university tried to discourage it, because ICU, like many other universities, was dependent on part-time teachers from other institutions for some of its subjects and because the university could not very well refuse to reciprocate.[33] Thus many scholars pursued multiple teaching jobs, engaged in lucrative editing or translating, or undertook textbook writing and compiling anthologies and collections. Writing for liberal and leftist journals and monthly magazines such as *Kaizo, Sekai,* and *Bungei shunju* provided a considerable source of income for some scholars. And many scholars of America acquired prestige by teaching the increasingly popular American Studies courses at universities.

After the war, Japanese intellectuals benefited from the huge amounts of money and materials they received from the U.S. government and private foundations. In fact, more often than not they were overcome by the American generosity that made it possible for many of them to study in the United States. As the cold war intensified in the 1950s and 1960s and the importance of U.S.-Japan relations gained greater recognition, America and

American Studies became more appealing—indeed fashionable—in Japan. When there emerged a high market demand for information and knowledge about America in Japanese academia and mass media, the products of American Studies became highly merchandisable in the form of books and articles in popular magazines as well as commentaries on TV talk shows. Japanese scholars found that the popularity of this kind of knowledge served them well if they were to seek promotions and higher status on the job.

As the years passed, many professors began turning the knowledge they had acquired in the United States into a commodity and pursuing nonacademic pursuits and enjoyment instead of discharging their responsibility as moral critics. In the 1980s, for example, when U.S.-Japan relations became increasingly tense and politicized, the Japanese government sought the counsel of Japanese specialists on America, but most Japanese scholars remained silent and were criticized for not responding pragmatically to the social need for accurate information on the United States. The critics of American Studies charged that "the American Studies community is responsible to activities other than self-cultivation in the academic sphere."[34]

Ironically, American soft power helped Japanese scholars to grow in power and influence, which flourished in the form of academic cliques and inbreeding. It also played a crucial, if not direct, role in helping to stratify and centralize Japan's system of higher education by means of generous grants to individual Japanese elites and universities. As Dean Rusk, president of the Rockefeller Foundation, once remarked, "Aid from a paternal government may sap . . . sturdy virtues and breed a race of weaklings."[35] Having witnessed the unintended consequences of American "generosity," Obluck noted with regret, "My impression is that the academic community in Japan has not been aggressive enough in exploiting USIS resources in recent years. . . . I cannot help but wonder if there are not other ways in which USIS itself could be more helpful."[36]

Democracy and Independence in Japan

This volume also raises a question about the shallowness and superficiality of democracy in Japan. Most Japanese and pro-Japanese Americans share the view that the democratic experiment of the U.S. occupation has worked in Japan and that democracy is well-grounded in that country. Few can deny that during the occupation the Japanese successfully adopted the legal and governmental framework for democracy and diligently learned the technical aspects of democracy from the United States. Both independence from authority and a willingness to question it are vitally important to nurturing and sustaining the quality of democracy in civil society. But after the occupation, those attributes seemed neither to develop nor grow as much as expected. Most of Japan's intellectual leaders, psychologically disposed toward toeing the line, failed to articulate their own independent systems of conduct and develop them fully during the occupation and beyond, as noted in the previous section. Indeed, in May 1951, soon after Gen. MacArthur left Japan, he stated before U.S. Senate Committee on Armed Services and the Committee on Foreign Relations that the Japanese behaved "like a boy of twelve."[37] No doubt, he was referring to the Japanese elite who worked with high-ranking SCAP officials on a daily basis during the occupation. It seems neither improbable nor accidental that, coupled with their subconscious patronizing attitudes toward the Japanese, American occupiers gained the impression that the Japanese were psychologically "juvenile" and less independent. If this characterization of the Japanese elite is not terribly wrong, the problems that Japan and its leaders face today are rooted more deeply than ever thought.

The Organization of This Volume

The first of the nine chapters that follow looks at the U.S. occupation of Japan as a cultural offensive. It begins by briefly introducing the world system perspective that is the conceptual and analytical framework used in this study. The chapter then analyzes occupation reform at great length as a U.S. cultural offensive with a special focus on censorship and copyright. Ironically, these "undemocratic" measures were taken by SCAP/CI&E to spread democracy in Japan.

Chapter 2, "The Cold War, 'Reverse Course,' and the Rise of Nationalism," provides the historical background against which the Rockefeller Foundation and the U.S. government launched a cultural offensive out of fear of communism, on the one hand, and Japanese nationalism, on the other. The chapter also thoroughly discusses the Japanese conservatism that brought about the rise of nationalism in postwar Japan.

Chapter 3, "The Making of a 'Soft Peace' and Japan's 'Proper Place,'" begins with a critical analysis of the worldviews of prominent American policy makers such as John Foster Dulles and John Rockefeller, who were chiefly responsible for making peace with Japan and establishing bilateral cultural relations. These leaders, who looked at U.S.-Japan bilateral relations as constituting the sum total of political, economic, and cultural relations, sought to establish lasting U.S.-Japan relations, believing that the peace and security treaties with Japan they were making should meet the needs and satisfy the desires of the Japanese on all three counts.

The fourth chapter is largely devoted to Rockefeller—his activities as a member of the Dulles Peace Mission and his vision of U.S.-Japan cultural relations in the post–peace treaty years—because he was enormously important in institutionalizing the U.S.-Japan cultural interchange. The chapter also delineates the dark underbelly of American soft power, which includes the cultural imperialism, the hegemony, and the creation of "permanent dependency" that characterize the U.S.-Japan relationship today.

Chapter 5 discusses the fundamental principles and specific policy recommendations contained in the Rockefeller report on U.S.-Japan cultural relations. It analyzes Rockefeller's specific proposals, differentiating between programs of cultural interchange and programs of information interchange. The chapter argues that his proposals were made primarily to counter the communist menace in response to the growing influence of communism in Japan. This chapter also portrays the push-and-pull process involved in the founding of the International House of Japan, a symbol of the institutionalization of U.S.-Japan cultural interchange.

Chapter 6, "The U.S. Cultural Offensive and Japanese Intellectuals," looks first at the extent to which the Japanese were made vulnerable to communism by the spiritual and ideological vacuum created by their defeat in the war. A brief description of the federal agencies of cultural diplomacy follows. The chapter then details how President Harry S. Truman's multimillion-dollar anticommunist "Campaign of Truth" was put in place in response to the growing communist challenge in Japan. It also analyzes the American perception of the Japanese, especially Japanese intellectuals, and illuminates the extent to which U.S. public affairs officers feared and became obsessed with communism. Finally, the chapter demonstrates how the cold war cast a shadow over academic scholarship and illustrates the relationship between the cultural cold war and Japanese scholarship in the humanities.

The discussion in Chapter 7 revolves around the development of the Japanese Association of American Studies. The chapter also takes up the 1950 Tokyo University–Stanford University Seminar in American Studies to analyze more closely the U.S.-Japan cultural interchange program in action. The latter half of the chapter is devoted to a sensitive issue in American Studies that had to be resolved before postwar Japanese higher education could be genuinely democratized.

Chapter 8, "The Kyoto American Studies Seminar and American Soft Power," addresses the perennial problems that have afflicted Japanese academia. The age-old rivalry between Tokyo University and Kyoto University, as well as insularity and provincialism, hindered smooth coordination and collaboration between Kyoto University and Dōshisha University in carrying out the world-famous Kyoto American Studies Seminars. The analysis of these seminars reveals not only some idiosyncrasies of Japanese professors, but also the fact that American Studies in postwar Japan depended on American money from the start. A discussion of American soft power and its perils follows.

The final chapter, "Occupation Reform, 'Shallow Democracy,' and Consumerism," critically analyzes the way in which American specialists on Japan assessed its state of democracy and the way in which Japanese received American democratic ideas and ideals. Most Americans observed that Japanese democracy was shallow and superficial, but their judgment either reconfirmed their preconceived image of an old Japan or mirrored their paternalism and condescending prejudice against Japan and the Japanese. This chapter also addresses two related issues: the modernization or Americanization of Japan and democracy versus consumerism. It argues that American businessmen successfully convinced Japanese consumers to associate consumerism with democracy by using high-pressure salesmanship to promote American goods and services.

The conclusion to this volume follows. Appendix A then critically analyzes the state of scholarship on U.S.-Japan relations for the past ten years or so. Appendixes B and C list the Tokyo-Stanford Seminars in American Studies and the Kyoto Seminars in American Studies, respectively.

Chapter 1

Occupation Reform as an American Cultural Offensive

> Merely to improve the economic strength of Japan might mean the arming of a potential enemy.
>
> —Report of the Education Exchange Survey to SCAP, 1949

> Purely material characteristics [of the United States] have been greatly overemphasized in Japan.
>
> —John D. Rockefeller III, 1951

World War II tore apart the fabric of the prewar international community, devastating it with the loss of an unprecedented number of human lives and the destruction of untold resources. Moreover, the war completely shattered the old nineteenth-century liberal world order maintained under Pax Britannica.[1] And it altered the world in unpredictable and fundamental ways. For one thing, the war accelerated the speed at which the global center of power and authority—political, military, economic, intellectual, scientific, and cultural—shifted from Western Europe to America. With this dramatic and almost complete shift in power and responsibility, the United States emerged as a hegemonic nation. Like it or not, the United States was thrown into the enviable yet challenging position of being saddled with enormous responsibilities for managing the entire world—a position that urgently demanded of Washington an enormous amount of national resources to discharge its new responsibilities as builder and keeper of a new world order.

Identifying the new responsibility with idealism and pacifist aspirations, the United States launched a grand hegemonic project to re-create a liberal, capitalist world order—that is, a kind of "open door world system"[2]—in which America's ideas of economic internationalism would not only spread but also advance in every corner of the globe. It was to be an open world in which capital, goods, and services would flow freely beyond national boundaries without undue political and geographical constraints.[3] It was the kind of world order that was dear to the hearts of American leaders as an ideal—indeed, it was precisely the one that U.S. politician Wendell L. Willkie described as "One World."[4]

The world order was to be structured in a pyramid-like shape based on universal ideas and principles such as division of labor, economies of scale, comparative advantage, free trade, and free convertibility. America would play a dominant role in this world order in which power and influence would be distributed unequally among nations.[5] It was hoped that all nations not only would be free to pursue their own destinies, but also would be able to pursue their own conceptions of common goals under such a liberal capitalist world order.[6] It was presumed that the United States would reap the lion's share from the world system as the system maker, the manager, and the keeper of the new world order.[7]

To envision such an ideal type of world order is one thing; to produce it and keep it alive and afloat is quite another. Because the world system is so grand, so diverse, and so complex, no one nation is equipped with sufficient resources and expertise to manage the world system properly and single-handedly, no matter how rich and powerful it may happen to be. Thus a peaceful and stable world can be maintained only by convincing a hegemonic country to undertake two tasks. First, that hegemonic nation must serve as the world's policeman—that is, it must confront or "contain" oppositional forces in the world if disgruntled and alienated member nations of the international community challenge its leadership directly by defying and violating cardinal rules of the world system.

Second, the hegemonic country must look for suitable core nations to co-opt and win over to its side. According to this perspective, the world system is an organic body that must depend on a hegemonic nation to create subsystems such as the North Atlantic Treaty Organization (NATO), the U.S.-Japan Alliance, and the Organization of American States (OAS). As an organic body, the world system also requires subsystems to help sustain the whole. Today, in an era of one world power, the super-dominant United States divides the globe into four major industrial centers of power—the Western Hemisphere, United Kingdom, Eurasia, and East Asia—to make them help sustain the entire system itself. Similarly, after 1945 Washington sought to make a subsystem in East Asia, the strategic center of which was Japan.[8]

In persuading the chosen core allies to carry out the job of pacifying any unruly region of the world, the hegemonic nation, with the help of the core allies, is able to manage the entire world system. Thus it is imperative that the hegemonic country be able to co-opt core nations whenever and wherever, if necessary. The cost of co-optation and the ways in which to pay it depend on the issue and the situation. At times, the cost may take the form of a military shield and assistance and economic aid. At other times, it may take the form of power sharing by conferring on a supportive ally an exalted status in the form of membership in an elite club of the world's nations. But whatever form the payment of the cost of co-optation takes, the ultimate cost will rise higher.[9]

Certainly, the case of U.S.-Japan relations after the war was no exception. At the same time, the United States had a self-imposed mission that consisted of extending its moral and political purposes abroad in the form of aid and democracy. For the sake of the world system, it was imperative to keep the world safe and stable. And, for Americans, it was important to keep the American national spirit of idealism high and to maintain the dynamism of American civilization. The projection of American power and influence abroad became both an end to and a means of foreign policy. The U.S. occupation of Japan, intended to democratize and demilitarize Japan, was part of Washington's major endeavor to translate its postwar vision into concrete foreign policy. Filled with such a grand vision and ambitious purposes, Gen. Douglas MacArthur landed triumphantly in Japan in late August 1945.

The Arrival of MacArthur, a Christian General

A military plane flew into Atsugi Airfield near Tokyo on August 30, 1945, immediately after the surrender of Japan. Gen. Douglas MacArthur disembarked proudly and triumphantly, in the manner of a twentieth-century emperor Napoleon Bonaparte. That act heralded the beginning of the U.S. military occupation of Japan, which lasted six years and eight months, until April 28, 1952. MacArthur would remain Supreme Commander for the Allied Powers (SCAP) until President Harry S. Truman removed him from office on April 11, 1951.

On September 2, 1945, on the battleship *Missouri* in Tokyo Bay, the general presided over the signing ceremony for the Instrument of Surrender. It was the official beginning of the occupation of Japan. The tall, blue-eyed American emperor proclaimed, "We are gathered here . . . to conclude a solemn agreement whereby peace may be restored." He went on to declare that "it is for us, both victors and vanquished, to rise to that higher dignity which alone benefits the sacred purposes we are about to serve . . . to make the world a better one—a world dedicated to the dignity of man and fulfillment of this most cherished wish—for freedom, tolerance and justice."[10]

On September 22, the American government announced the U.S. Initial Post-Surrender Policy for Japan to implement the Potsdam Declaration. In the announcement, Washington expressed its determination to ensure that Japan would "not again become a menace to the United States or to the peace and security of the world."[11] To achieve the U.S. objectives, SCAP strove to "bring about the eventual establishment of a peaceful and responsible government" that would be supported by the freely expressed will of the people of Japan.[12] This statement proved to be one of the most important policy pronouncements the United States ever made in carrying out self-imposed hegemonic missions after World War II.

A quick perusal of the U.S. Initial Post-Surrender Policy statement makes it clear that demilitarization and democratization were the twin objectives of the U.S. occupation of Japan. According to one American observer of the occupation, "Merely to improve the economic strength of Japan might mean the arming of a potential enemy." The same American then added, "Only if the residue from the Occupation involves a thorough democratization of the citizens of Japan can the ultimately desirable result of peace and security be obtained."[13] This American citizen understood quite correctly that the U.S. objectives of demilitarization and democratization of Japan were inextricably linked. At the same time, he revealed America's messianic fervor and his deep-seated suspicion of the Japanese and their country. From an American perspective, the democratic reform of Japan was a means of serving the security interests of the United States and the world.

The U.S. Occupation of Japan as a Cultural Offensive

Japan accepted unconditional surrender on August 15, 1945, in a gesture welcomed by virtually all Japanese.[14] Often, though, defeat stirs the flames of nationalism. This was certainly true of Prussia after the Napoleonic conquest in 1806 and of China after the Sino-Japanese War in 1894–1895. But Japan's postwar nationalism, the central focus of which should have been the "independence of the Japanese nation," did not reach its peak until the 1950s.[15] As Ishikawa Tatsuzō, a novelist, remarked in 1953, "We had already lost patriotism during the wartime years."[16]

Although August 15, 1945, marked the beginning of a new state of affairs for Japan, the surrender also left the Japanese with a general sense of demoralization and insecurity.[17] The feelings of stagnation and prostration were overwhelming. The Japanese were close to bankruptcy intellectually and culturally and sadly disillusioned with the traditions, standards, and cultural heritage that they had long deeply cherished. In particular, the abolition of emperor worship with one stroke of the pen dealt them a crushing blow. It left them in a "spiritual and ideological vacuum," further driving them into a state of profound spiritual and moral confusion.[18]

In view of this situation, it was a daunting task for the Supreme Commander for the Allied Powers/General Headquarters (SCAP/GHQ) to democratize a Japan rich in its own culture and tradition. The occupation of a foreign land required the long-term mobilization of thousands of Americans, including policy makers and officers. Motivated by soaring idealism as well as America's national interest, the U.S. occupation authorities undertook "the long-range task of strengthening in Japan constructive tendencies toward democracy and respect for human values."[19] Indeed, they made every effort to graft American-type democracy onto that country, assuming that American security and the future of U.S.-Japan relations hinged on whether their democratic experiment succeeded. Within a few months of the arrival of the Allied occupation forces, a vast array of American ideas, systems, and methods were boldly introduced into Japan, one after another. Americans justified the introduction of their ways of doing things with the claim that they were superior to whatever the Japanese had to offer and that they were essential to democratization of the country. SCAP authorities made the uncritical assumption that the best way to "reorient" the Japanese was to tell them how things were done in the United States.[20] Later, SCAP claimed that it accomplished basic and far-reaching reforms that affected almost every aspect of Japanese life.

During the occupation period of 1945–1952, the American government in Washington and the Supreme Commander for the Allied Powers in Tokyo attached special importance to the cultural dimension of the occupation in order to achieve the twin objectives of democratizing Japan and transforming it into a nation friendly toward the United States. The Civil Information and Education Section (CI&E) of SCAP was charged with that daunting task during the military occupation.

The Civil Information and Education Section

Under General Order No. 183 issued on September 22, 1945, MacArthur set up CI&E in SCAP/GHQ. Its six divisions were staffed by some 150 Americans and 900 local employees.[21] CI&E was given responsibility for exercising control over Japanese education, religion, and media of expression.[22] On October 2, 1945, MacArthur appointed Col. Kenneth R. Dyke as the first chief of CI&E, with responsibility for undertaking a thorough reorientation and reeducation of the Japanese. Dyke, a liberal reformer, worked diligently to administer assignments such as the release of political prisoners and the dismantling of the infamous secret police organization known as Tokkō.[23] But six months later, in May 1946, Dyke left for the United States and Lt. Col. Donald R. Nugent succeeded him. Nugent remained CI&E chief until April 1952, the end of the occupation. A Stanford graduate who had majored in history and pedagogy, Nugent was one of the few Japan experts in the occupation bureaucracy. He had actually taught in Wakayama and Osaka before the war.[24]

First and foremost, CI&E sought diligently to eliminate militarism and ultranationalism in doctrine and practice from all the elements of the Japanese population—that is, those customs and mores that the Americans believed had made the Japanese a menace to the rest of the world. The Imperial Rescript of February 3, 1870, for example, had proclaimed the emperor to be the living embodiment of godhood and his throne to be a holy office established by the ancestral sun goddess (*amaterasu ōmikami*) and handed down in unbroken succession to the present. Moreover, the Meiji constitution of 1890 had described the sovereign as "sacred and inviolable." Prewar ideologies such as these had served to support the emperor system with its mythology of divine origins and had underpinned emperor worship.[25] Now taboos were being lifted from the old tumuli, particularly when on January 1, 1946, the emperor was declared to be "humanity" (*ningen sengen*).

Also in the spirit of the U.S. Initial Post-Surrender Policy, the Fundamental Law of Education (also called the charter of education) was enacted on March 31, 1947. This cardinal law came into existence after the Japanese applied the spirit of their new constitution to education.[26] It proclaimed: "Education shall aim at the full development of personality and soundness of mind and body, striving for the rearing of a people who shall as builders of a peaceful state and society love truth and justice, esteem individual worth, respect labor, possess a deep sense of responsibility, and become imbued with an independent spirit."[27] These were precisely the values that the American occupiers wanted the Japanese to embrace.

The Stoddard Education Mission

To meet SCAP requests for assistance and cooperation, the U.S. government occasionally dispatched special missions to Japan on an ad hoc basis. The notion of an education mission was first floated in May 1945 during discussions on German school reform and ideological reorientation.[28] To discharge its responsibilities, SCAP, and especially CI&E, relied on the high-profile U.S. civilian leaders sent to Japan to provide professional and technical expertise.

The first U.S. education mission was dispatched to Japan on March 5, 1946. It was headed by George D. Stoddard, the commissioner of education of New York State, the president-elect of the University of Illinois, and a staunch advocate of the "reorientation" of Japan.[29] During its three-week visit, the Stoddard Education Mission surveyed Japan's education system. The U.S. education mission was composed of twenty-seven educators, including two Canadians and Gordon T. Bowles, professor of anthropology at Tokyo University.[30] The Committee of Japanese Educators, organized by Japan's minister of education to work with the Stoddard mission, was made up of twenty-nine liberal academics and teachers, including Nambara Shigeru, president of the University of Tokyo.

The U.S. education mission spent one week listening to SCAP and Japanese educators, less than one week observing schools, and one week compiling its report.[31] On March 30, it presented its recommendations to Gen. MacArthur. The Stoddard report addressed the question of "how the schools and colleges of Japan could be most effectively used to help democratize that country."[32] It recommended, among other things, discontinuance of the Imperial Rescript on Education, revision of educational content (textbooks and curricula) to emphasize the democratic principles already outlined by the GHQ, a "6-3-3" school ladder in which the education of the first nine years would be free of charge, coeducational, and compulsory; reform of higher education; and administrative decentralization.[33] Some of the recommendations reflected the most advanced liberal American educational philosophy at that time. For example, Charles S. Johnson, chair of the Social Science Department at Fisk University and the only African American member of the U.S. delegation, emphasized equality of opportunity in education and insisted on inserting a stipulation that prohibited any form of discrimination in education.[34]

As for who was responsible for the report, Theodore Cohen, Labor Division chief of GHQ's Economic and Scientific Section, was quoted as saying that members of the U.S. delegation rather than local Japanese conditions often determined the content of the final recommendations.[35] The historian Takemae Eiji disagrees, however. He argues that the Stoddard report was a joint work and that some key innovations turned out to be Japanese, not American, in origin.[36] In his view, democratization was not entirely something alien that SCAP imposed on the Japanese. Rather, it was something indigenous to Japan that also arose from the populace. Actually, it was a binational joint effort in which SCAP removed the obstacles and the Japanese gave life to the reforms. In fact, according to Takemae, in later years Gordon Bowles acknowledged that roughly 60 percent of the report's content came from the Japanese side. Be that as it may, Takemae reports that Sir George Sansom, formerly commercial counselor at the British embassy in Tokyo and after the war associated with the Institute of Pacific Relations and the East Asian Institute at Columbia University, was skeptical of SCAP educational reforms undertaken in an American way. Education in the United States, he observed, "is not of such a quality as to encourage one in feeling that it provides a good model for any other country."[37]

The Stoddard Education Mission also recommended that archaeological studies be encouraged in Japan as a step toward eliminating militaristic ideas and thoughts. Along these lines, it encouraged Gerard Groot, an American archaeologist who had been in Japan since 1931 as a missionary of the Society of the Divine Word and was then working for CI&E, to develop archaeological studies in Japan.[38] Groot believed archaeological studies were particularly important for the reorientation of postwar Japan, because they could serve as a basis for rewriting Japanese early history.[39] He argued that a good account of Japan's early history would serve as the best possible guarantee against revival of the ancient mythology. Many Japanese archaeologists were anxious to undertake work of this kind. Umehara Sueji, for example, urged that a more neutral Japanese history be written in order to help place the Japanese past in a global context.[40] Umehara was a Kyoto University professor and Japan's leading archaeologist.

Other CI&E Measures to Democratize Japan

In the field of culture broadly defined, SCAP executed the U.S. Initial Post-Surrender Policy, which stipulated that the Japanese "shall be afforded opportunity and encouraged to become familiar with the history, institutions, culture, and the accomplishments of the United States and other democracies."[41] CI&E therefore sought to democratize Japanese thought and daily behavior as the flip side to demilitarization. SCAP officers encouraged in the Japanese a desire for individual liberties and democratic processes, while imbuing them with an understanding of their roles in a democratic society, with a special emphasis on *responsibilities* as well as rights.

In fact, independently of the U.S. State Department, CI&E initiated a variety of projects "to open windows on democracy."[42] First, because both SCAP and the Japanese Ministry of Education keenly recognized the need for able leadership in the field of education, the Ministry of Education established the Institute for Educational Leadership and declared on August 13, 1948, that "in inaugurating the new educational system which in principle aims at the democratization of education, it seems to be of urgent necessity to train personnel and leaders who should have full understanding of the ideas and methods of the new educational program and acquire the technique in performing their duties."[43]

SCAP and the Ministry of Education jointly organized the Institute for Education Leadership program that gave qualified Japanese personnel an opportunity to participate in two intensive twelve-week courses that ran successively. Arthur K. Loomis, adviser to the Educational Reorganization section of CI&E, was in charge of recruiting the seventy-four outstanding American educational leaders who conducted six classes under the program of the Institute for Educational Leadership.[44] The classes were attended by a total of 7,084 Japanese teachers and youth leaders, who then returned to their own communities to spread the influence and benefits of those sessions among millions of people.[45] One university president who attended the Institute for Educational Leadership program later wrote: "This is a very brief word to tell you how much I appreciated all the trouble you took to put so much helpful information at our disposal. One feels that you really grasp the situation in Japan, and are doing a truly constructive job."[46] Another wrote: "I assure you here that we are going to try our utmost to tide over the difficulties and bring about the great objective of this epoch-making reformation program of the Japanese educational system by making the most effective use of the knowledge obtained in this Institute."[47]

As for the effects of the program, CI&E officers later reported that participants in the first session took an active role in introducing democratic procedures at the prefectural and local levels.[48] Indeed, judging from what was reported, participants in the Institute for Educational Leadership apparently returned to their homes, inspired to carry on a program of education based on democratic ideals. In this sense, then, the Institute for Educational Leadership was effective in developing a realization that the decentralization and democratization of education meant that the responsibility for what took place in the schools rested with those who had local control of the schools.

Second, thirty-four American teachers served in leading Japanese universities under two-year contracts to advance the objectives of the entire program of CI&E. This project was arranged through cooperation between CI&E and Japanese educational institutions.[49]

Third, a library training school, staffed with American experts, was established under SCAP auspices at Keiō Gijuku University. The Japanese participants were taught the most advanced U.S. techniques and methods in library science. The lack of trained librarians in Japan was a critical obstacle to the goal of making books readily available to students and other readers.[50]

Fourth, some eight hundred students were selected through highly competitive examinations for one or more years of study, training, and observation in American colleges and universities. This program, which was conducted under the Exchange-of-Persons program for Japan, also brought to the United States for shorter periods of intensive training and observation almost five hundred prominent Japanese concerned with youth leadership in various ways.[51] The program was designed under the assumption that democracy could better be understood and appreciated when seen in action. Educational exchange was indeed "one of the processes that proved valuable as a means of practical instruction in the ways of democracy."[52]

U.S. "Missionary" Diplomacy by the Book

With the specific goal of spreading information on the United States and democracy, the CI&E set up its first information center in a small one-floor building in Tokyo in November 1945. It appointed Philip Olin Keeney CI&E libraries officer on February 1, 1946.[53] The CI&E information center (library) contained about three thousand books—virtually the only American books printed since 1941. The Japanese response was fantastic. An estimated 125,000 people made use of the facilities in the twelve-month period beginning March 17, 1946.[54] The average number of daily visitors was 575, even though the library had seats for only 175 persons. According to Charles B. Fahs of the Rockefeller Foundation, the Japanese visitors displayed the greatest interest in "know-how literature," especially the books on technology.[55] By the end of October 1948, GHQ/CI&E had established an additional seventeen information centers (libraries) in major cities in Japan. During 1950–1951, it added five more, for a total of twenty-three. Each center had at least six thousand books and four hundred periodicals, as well as several thousand documents and pamphlets covering all fields.[56] From the founding of the first center in Tokyo in 1945 until 1951, some six million persons used the centers.[57]

Tokyo was not the only place where the Japanese displayed a hunger for American books. In Hokkaidō, the northern island, and elsewhere, CI&E centers were crowded with Japanese looking for information on America. The CI&E center that opened in Sapporo in June 1948 boasted an average eighteen hundred visitors a day during the opening week and nine hundred during the second week.[58] Some 250,000 books, 100,000 pamphlets, and 70,000 periodical subscriptions were distributed to CI&E information centers beginning in 1947. About 15,000 items were distributed in 1951 and 1952.[59] By making available not only books and magazines, but also records, films, and pictorial exhibits, CI&E information centers made an excellent impression in Japan.[60]

Spreading information on America and democracy was not the only objective of the centers as the cold war began to take shape on every front; they also became attitude-forming media for the U.S. government in Japan. The American government did not want to call the centers "information centers," because such a title might carry the connotation of an intelligence program. It therefore later renamed them cultural centers.[61] They were for the most part strategically located near the greatest concentration of U.S. security forces and thus where potentially the greatest local friction might be engendered.[62] Within communities, the centers served as meeting places for university students, as focal points for research on various American subjects for journalists, and also as useful platforms for Japanese-American contacts. The U.S. embassy in Tokyo recognized that the information centers were effectively winning friends for the United States through an educational and cultural approach to which the Japanese proved to be particularly susceptible.[63] To put it differently, a war of ideas was now under way.

The CI&E Translation Programs and the Early Cultural Cold War

In an important way, the occupation of Japan provided the huge U.S. occupation army with opportunities to acquire first-hand information and knowledge of Japanese life and culture. The occupation army included military officers and their dependents, civilian employees of SCAP and their dependents, and ordinary GIs. By the end of 1945, American soldiers in the Allied occupation forces numbered about 430,000.[64] Each year of the almost seven years of occupation saw as many as 250,000 U.S. soldiers living in Japan.[65]

Meanwhile, on the other side of the Pacific an overwhelming majority of Americans had very little information about or accurate knowledge of Japan and its people. Likewise, as noted, the Japanese had little knowledge of the United States. Despite the fact that English was a compulsory subject in Japanese middle schools and a common elective in universities, relatively few Japanese read English with facility, and so there was no way to reach the great mass of the reading public other than through books in their own language. That problem called for special efforts to provide the Japanese with translations of foreign books, including American publications. But in such a situation, some misunderstandings were bound to occur.

During the U.S. occupation, the Soviet government announced the worldwide release of the copyrights for the works of Soviet leaders Vladimir Lenin and Joseph Stalin, which has enabled foreign publishers to publish their translations free of charge ever since. Meanwhile, Shimada Masao, a member of the Sino-Japan Translation Publications Council, stated, "Since the peace treaty the Sino-Japan Translation Publications Council . . . is maintaining direct contact with the National Society for Chinese Arts and Letters which has given us all the translation rights. . . . Therefore, there is no restriction at all. There are no royalty payments."[66] The American occupiers of Japan perceived these moves of the communist countries to be a cultural offensive targeting the United States. Yanaihara Tadao, a Christian economist and president of the University of Tokyo, was quoted as saying that it was easier to get Russian books and periodicals than American publications, although the United States was playing the leading role in the occupation. He explained that in the Soviet Union (and in China) copyrights were owned by the state and that the Soviets were enticing the Japanese to translate anything Russian without permit or fee as part of a campaign to fight the cold war between cultures.[67]

In fact, the June 8, 1953, morning edition of the *Asahi shimbun* aptly described the cultural cold war in the article "The Cold War between Democratic and Communist Camps in the Translation and Publication World": "The Cold War is being fought in the publishing world, too. In Japan, the camps of democracy and of communism are engaged in an active war in the field of translations. Both sides employ such means as supplying translation rights free or at very low royalty rates in order to get more and more books translated and published in Japan. This is a cultural war."[68]

Thus in the field of translations the U.S. government launched an all-out anticommunist "Campaign of Truth" in retaliation for Soviet propaganda activities in Japan. As a counteroffensive measure to "reverse course" in Japan, it appropriated $30,000 for the translation program for fiscal year 1953.[69] The program was "a top-priority item" in U.S. Information Service (USIS)–Japan plans. It had a two-pronged approach. One was to drive home the evilness and shortcomings of the communist system, and the other was to emphasize the soundness and superiority of the liberal capitalist system. The Cultural Materials Section of the U.S. embassy sponsored the formation of a committee of translations composed of a representative of the Committee for Free Asia; representatives of the two American firms publishing in Japan, Charles E. Tuttle Company and Swen Publishers; and a representative from the political section of the embassy and one from the office of the public affairs division.[70] It was widely believed that the printed word had an almost mystic appeal in the Far East. In Japan, in particular, Asia's most literate country, the book was probably the most potent and durable weapon in the war of ideas. An American public affairs officer in the U.S. embassy in Tokyo pointed out that the United States could not "afford to yield victory in this war by default."[71]

During this period, some significant anticommunist titles were published: *Real Soviet Russia* by David J. Dallin (1944; trans. 1949) and *Animal Farm* (1945; trans. 1949) and *Nineteen Eighty-Four* (1949; trans. 1950) by George Orwell.[72] Typical of the American titles in the CI&E translation program were *Abe Lincoln Grows Up* (1940) by Carl Sandburg, *Of Human Freedom* (1939) by Jacques Barzun, *Liberal Education* (1943) by Mark Van Doren, *Human Leadership in Industry* (1945) by Sam A. Lewisohn, *The Miracle of America* (1944) by André Maurois, *American Labor Union* (1945) by Florence Peterson, *The Babe Ruth Story* (1948) by Bob Considine, *Freedom and Culture* (1939) by John Dewey, and *Speaking Frankly* (1947) by James F. Byrnes.[73]

Meanwhile, the Japanese continued to regard France as the major source of Western civilization. And British and Russian literature, to a lesser extent, enjoyed continuing prestige and popularity. As a result, French and German literature was much translated, and there was great interest in Russian literature, but few American translations were available and so were badly needed.[74] SCAP/GHQ policy called for translating and publishing only those foreign books that were compatible with the general objectives of the occupation.

American Books in Japanese Translations

After the war, Japanese book publishing experienced a revival that saw the number of publishers and number of titles published rise steadily:[75]

Table 1.1 Japanese Book Publishing, 1945–1951

Year	Number of publishers	Number of titles published
1945	203	878
1950	1,869	13,009
1951	2,487	15,536

As noted earlier, the Japanese displayed great curiosity about the United States and had much interest in American culture in the months immediately after the end of the war.[76] A few definite lines of interest of the Japanese reading public can be discerned from the following list of American books and magazines published in translation from 1949 to 1951. The Japanese translations of *The Chrysanthemum and the Sword* (1946; trans. 1948) by Ruth Benedict and *Japan's Economy during and after the War* (1948; trans. 1950–1951) by Jerome B. Cohen reflected a self-conscious concern about American opinion of the Japanese and their problems.[77] At the same time, the Japanese were able to read varied American accounts of the recent war from works such as *The Last Chapter* (1946; trans. 1950) by Ernie Pyle, *Hiroshima* (1946; trans. 1949) by John Hersey, and Norman Mailer's *The Naked and the Dead* (1948; trans. 1949). They also enjoyed reading *Japan Diary* by Mark Gayn, which was translated in 1951.[78] In 1951 the Japanese translation of *Japan Diary* topped every best-seller list in Japan—153,000 copies of the first volume were sold and 137,000 of the second.[79] The theme of the book—that the army of occupation had made only a pretense of democratic reform in its primary effort to make Japan a military and economic bulwark against communism—struck a responsive chord.[80] Gayn's criticism of the U.S. occupation was something that the Japanese would hardly have dared to express.[81]

Quite naturally, books about the United States figured prominently among the translations.[82] To name only several, there was *The Republic* (1944; trans. 1949) by Charles A. Beard, *Only Yesterday* (1931; trans. 1940) and *Since Yesterday* (1939; trans. 1950) by Frederick Lewis Allen, and *American Democracy* (1948; trans. in three vols. 1955) by Harold J. Laski.

In literature, translations were published in 1951 of works by world-famous authors such as *American Tragedy* (1925) by Theodore Dreiser, *Tour of Duty* (1946) by John Dos Passos, *Soldier's Pay* (1926) by William Faulkner, *The Snows of Kilimanjaro* (1936) by Ernest Hemingway, and *Of Mice and Men* (1937) by John Steinbeck.[83] Popular novels such as *Gone with the Wind* (1936) by Margaret Mitchell and *The Robe* (1945) by Lloyd C. Douglas also attracted much attention. Coinciding with the release of the American film in Japan, *Gone with the Wind* broke the sales record for U.S. fiction.[84] According to Harold Strauss of Alfred A. Knopf Publishers, the Japanese tended to read America's best-sellers, including works such as Pearl S. Buck's *Good Earth* (1931), John Hersey's *Hiroshima,* and William Faulkner's *Intruder in the Dust* (1948).[85]

In the foreign magazine field, by December 1945 SCAP was permitting *Time* and *Newsweek* to publish English versions of their weekly magazines in Japan: 17,000 issues upon initial publication in Tokyo in 1946, which later rose to 29,900. In June 1946, *Reader's Digest* also entered the Japanese market.[86] In 1950 it boasted that with its circulation of 1.3 million Japanese-language copies it was the most popular of the magazines published in Japan.[87] By then, *Time* and *Newsweek* had Japanese editions as well. The insatiable desire of the general reading public to learn more about America largely explained the enormous publishing success of *Reader's Digest*. According to a historian of *Reader's Digest,* it mirrored U.S.-Japan cultural and geopolitical relations in the immediate postwar years, because, to the Japanese readers, access to *Reader's Digest* guaranteed the presence of a magazine in Japan that always "offered a moral to the story" and that presented itself as "guardian of American values."[88] In addition to *Reader's Digest,* the *New York Times* was published in English weekly. Also on sale were *Life, Collier's, American,* and *Women's Home Companion.*[89] In addition, in 1949, under CI&E direction, Japanese magazines reprinted 7,500 articles from U.S., British, Australian, and United Nations publications.[90]

Overall, the U.S. government cultural program helped to expand considerably the market for American books and magazines in Japan. Much of the intense interest of the Japanese in American books and magazines was met discreetly by direct gifts of materials from CI&E libraries. A U.S. Information and Education Service (USIE) Country Paper on Japan reported that "under the book donation program sponsored by the Army, thousands of books were shipped to Japanese educational institutions from American educational institutions, government agencies, publishers and private citizens."[91] At the same time, greater assistance was given to Japanese publishers in obtaining copyright clearance and in obtaining paper supplies for the publication of books essential to the purpose of the USIE program. Harold Strauss of Alfred A. Knopf publishers noted that "2,500 to 3,000 copies of a book must be sold to make it worthwhile."[92] Because Acting Councilor Niles W. Bond recognized that "subsidies to publishers, in one form or another, may also be required,"[93] the system of subsidization of book translations was actually adopted and vigorously employed to achieve the objectives of the CI&E program. The system consisted of an advance purchase guarantee to a Japanese publisher of a fixed number of copies of a first edition, usually at a price somewhat above the wholesale distribution price at which the book was being offered to retail outlets. This device had the following advantages. It avoided the need to make outright grants, while ensuring that the publisher at least would break even. Simultaneously, the system of subsidization furnished USIS with copies that it could use for placement in the centers or for individual presentation purposes.[94] Indeed, a guarantee to buy a certain number of copies often persuaded a foreign publisher to bring out a desirable book.[95] In November 1952, the Information Center Service director of U.S. International Information Administration of the State Department testified, without making a special reference to Japan, that "we spend about half as much in the purchase of materials to give away through indigenous channels abroad as we spend in the purchase of materials for our own . . . libraries."[96] Indeed, the market for American books served as a good barometer of U.S.-Japan cultural relations.[97]

Censorship that Spread Democratic Ideas Undemocratically

Based on their experience in two world wars, the American occupiers of Japan took it for granted that censorship and media guidance were extensions of U.S. foreign policy directed at replacing Japanese militaristic and ultranationalist ideas with American democratic values.[98] In fact, even before the military occupation of Japan began, the U.S. government had decided to fully utilize the mass media to achieve its goal of demilitarizing and democratizing that country. In early 1945, Eugene H. Dooman, chair of the Subcommittee for the Far East of State-War-Navy Coordinating Committee (SWNCC), had asserted, "It is our primary task in this war to change the basic thinking of the Japanese masses." The subcommittee took it for granted that to attain this objective "all possible media and channels" would be utilized. It then passionately urged the extension of wartime propaganda and psychological warfare techniques into the postwar era of peace in order to counter fascist and communist ideologies and secure America's long-term political interest in Japan.[99]

Although the occupation authorities made all-out efforts to establish democratic principles in all spheres of political, economic, and cultural life in Japan, the CI&E realized that it had to subtly feed the Japanese stimulating information and concepts about democracy through books if it did not wish to appear to be forcing democratic ideas down their throats.[100] The CI&E had a two-pronged strategy for such purposes. For the first prong, the army's Civil Censorship Detachment (CCD) performed the purgative duty by regulating the Japanese mass media through censorship. The main purpose, of course, was to prevent the media from being used as an instrument for anti-occupation activities by the Japanese and other nations. The CI&E also sought to control the free flow of damaging information about the United States and of undesirable materials printed in Japan. It believed that it was not desirable for all nations to have equal access to the privilege of having their books translated into Japanese.[101]

For the second prong, the Information Dissemination Branch (later called the Information Division) made the fullest use of the media to spread the gospel of American democracy, in addition to providing information about the U.S. objectives of the occupation. But as the American occupiers soon discovered, balancing the two parts of its strategy was easier said than done, because, paradoxically, the CI&E was seeking to spread the good news of democracy by controlling democracy. And the CI&E recognized its dilemma, which was one of protecting freedom of expression, on the one hand, and regulating and controlling the free press, on the other.

The CI&E Press and Publication Division took charge of censorship, together with the Civil Intelligence Section in the area of translation and publication. Circular 12 required that all printed materials for Japanese readers be cleared through the Information Division.[102] The Information Division was in fact the three-person team of civilian Donald Brown, Lt. Col. Donald Nugent (CI&E chief), and Nugent's secretary, Capt. (Women's Army Corps) Glenna Crew.[103] Of the three, Brown was the point person for all problems relating to getting printed materials to Japan. When deciding what publications should be translated, he took into consideration both SCAP policy objectives and the paper shortage in Japan.[104] Brown, a native of Ohio and graduate of the University of Pittsburgh, was formerly a journalist with the *Japan Advertiser,* an English newspaper published in Tokyo. He returned to Japan in December 1945 and worked for CI&E until the end of the U.S. occupation.[105] Glenna Crew was well informed on Japan, because she had been a secretary of Kobe College before the war. Together, the three decided which books should be approved for translation into Japanese based on their reading of English-language books.

In the early years of the occupation, many Japanese were as curious about the United States as they were suspicious of any information handed out by SCAP. Indeed, a reaction against America was the inevitable sequel to the U.S. military occupation. The CI&E censorship and mass media control program, in particular, tended to offend the sensitivities of certain groups of Japanese, especially intellectuals and university students. They found the SCAP policy of censorship humiliating, because SCAP directives, which usually went out without much explanation, were issued without negotiation.[106] They also felt they were not free to publish on certain aspects of recent European and American history and politics. And they had a deep feeling of revulsion toward American occupiers, although the Japanese criticism of the military occupation remained somewhat veiled. C. Nelson Spinks, a Stanford graduate in Japanese studies and political adviser to William J. Sebald, deputy for SCAP on the Allied Council for Japan and head of the Diplomatic Section in the U.S. embassy in Tokyo, sensed that anti-Americanism might well grow as the Japanese felt freer to criticize Americans and their actions.[107]

More broadly, all Japanese were frustrated by all the red tape involved in censorship. For example, private gifts and any exchange of printed materials had to be processed through CI&E censors. Even publications sent through the mail by American friends to individual Japanese as gifts were removed by censorship.[108] Japanese intellectuals were particularly bothered when SCAP censorship became more burdensome than that under the Japanese military. Matsukata Saburō, managing director of the Kyōdō News Agency, and Takayanagi Kenzō, a professor at Tokyo University and Japan's leading expert on American law, complained that the censorship policy was imprecise and unpredictable. When as many as twenty Japanese professors gathered at Kwansei Gakuin University (a mission college) in June 1947, they discussed the problems of university education and complained of SCAP censorship. One professor grumbled that SCAP censorship made objective writing of Western or Far Eastern history difficult, because SCAP censored anything it considered critical of the United States.[109]

Intellectuals and others also complained that SCAP held up publication far too long. For example, the CI&E held up publication of the journal of the American Bar Association for two weeks, because an article Thomas L. Blakemore had written in Japanese for this leading law journal was slightly critical of SCAP policy.[110] The Blakemore case revealed the contradiction of the CI&E censorship policy. The CI&E was trying to promulgate the gospel of democracy, while censors controlled it with all the power and authority of SCAP. As Charles Fahs of the Rockefeller Foundation noted, "We want the Japanese to learn freedom of speech, but the military censorship under SCAP is perhaps more severe than it was under the Japanese military."[111] Col. Harlan R. Statham, chief officer of the military government for the Ninth Corps in Sendai, charged that SCAP censorship was a mistake; it was restricting the free flow of printed materials. He believed "it would be wiser to flood Japan with material even if a few undesirable things" might happen in the process.[112]

Army Air Force Major Mark T. Orr, the third head of the CI&E Education Division, blamed most of the trouble compounded by censorship on Brown.[113] This capable expert on education was terribly exasperated by the fact that for many months he had not been able to get anything through Brown in his frequent attempts at CI&E clearance—indeed, CI&E clearance for the distribution of any texts took many months.[114] Orr was not the only one who had a low opinion of Brown's performance. Donald Typer, an expert on youth training, considered both Nugent and Brown "incompetent and scared." According to Typer, Nugent and Brown directed their energies toward devising ways in which to control their staff rather than seeking avenues of constructive action.[115] It was rumored that Brown did not trust his staff and that his staff was frustrated as a result.[116]

F. N. Kerlinger, an assistant education officer, also regarded Brown as "the bottleneck." According to Kerlinger, "The U.S. may already have missed its greatest opportunity by failing to supply printed materials in large quantities in the months immediately after occupation when the Japanese were most avid for it."[117] Herbert Passin, the CI&E analyst in charge of public information and sociological research, also attributed America's poor showing to the undue delay caused by military censorship.[118] He observed that "the Japanese gradually settled back to depend on their previous intellectual resources (France, Britain, Germany, etc), because their interest in American culture was kept unsatisfied."[119] Despite Japanese admiration of the German culture, however, translations of German titles had dropped markedly since World War II, because Japanese publishers had difficulty contacting German publishers.[120]

And then there was Robert B. Textor, a CI&E officer who charged SCAP with being inexplicably slow in extending to the Japanese opportunities to learn about democracy. Textor reported: "Thousands of volumes lay around in warehouses for periods of up to a year or perhaps longer, while during this crucial period in the democratization effort, hundreds of thousands of educated Japanese were doing without literature on the democratic world."[121] During his stay in Japan from spring 1946 to July 1948, Textor, who served as head of the CI&E of the local military command in Wakayama, south of Osaka, assiduously observed Japan being democratized. In his popular book *Failure in Japan,* Textor wrote, "During this period when books were lying round in warehouses, trained librarians, recruited from the United States to administer the GHQ chain, were lying around Tokyo."[122]

Not only the Japanese but also the foreign journalists working in Japan were frustrated by the restrictive SCAP/GHQ rules and regulations. The General Staff's G2 required foreign journalists to submit an application and obtain permission to leave Tokyo. G2 was under the command of Maj. Gen. Charles A. Willoughby, who was MacArthur's right-hand man in SCAP. Foreign correspondents, the Russians in particular, found the bureaucratic red tape of the General Staff's G2 extremely bothersome. Moreover, as a rule, G2 officers always followed them whenever and wherever they moved. Russian journalists detested the SCAP policy of escort as something humiliating and insulting. When they moved around, they were required to show a pass and abide by the ubiquitous "off-limits" signs whether the place was a Japanese restaurant, inn, or train. They could not help but feel that they were "G2 captives."[123] They were allowed to visit the Americanized parts of Japan, such as movie theaters for Americans and American bars and dance halls. In fact, the life of foreign reporters in occupied Japan was so constricted and so completely isolated from that of the ordinary Japanese that they could hardly observe the real Japan as much as they wished.[124] They felt that the "real Japan" was hidden from them and only the "Americanized Japan" was shown to them. The Soviet journalists suspected that the SCAP surveillance was intended to impress foreign reporters only with what American culture had achieved in Japan and that not all American residents of Japan were the "bearers of culture, civilization, and democracy."[125]

Copyright Complications

In carrying out its book translation program, SCAP had to obtain copyright clearances for the translation and publication of American books. But in actuality the reprinting of U.S. works in translation was impeded by copyright difficulties. Under the SCAP/CI&E program, Japanese publishers contracted for the translation and publication rights for 490 American works, but only 250 were actually published.[126] Of the total 1,174 translations published in Japan in 1952, American books in translation fell to only 103 titles.[127] By contrast, an estimated 330 French books, more than 200 British books, and 370 Russian titles were translated and published.[128] Dorothy R. Ward, cultural information program officer in the U.S. State Department, reported that the United States had only about a third as many titles on the Japanese market in 1952 as did the Russians, and she deplored the poor showing of American literary works among Japanese readers.[129] Glenna Crew insisted, however, that the stories about an influx of Russian materials into Japan were entirely false. She argued that Circular 12 prevented many Russian materials from coming in. Instead, she blamed Washington for the failure to provide more U.S. books with government funds. According to her, CI&E had asked for funds in almost every weekly teletype conference for more than a year.[130] But little had happened.

What explains America's poor showing? First, copyright problems virtually made it impossible for the Japanese to reprint or translate American works.[131] The Japanese wanted to publish such works, but they had to secure copyright approval from GHQ or the War Department. Moreover, under existing copyright agreements, copyrights on American books were valid as long as twenty-eight years, which meant that during that period no translation of U.S. books was permitted into Japanese.[132] But British and French books could be translated at no cost after a ten-year protective period of their copyrights.[133] In addition, the prevailing U.S. copyright rates placed America in a weak competitive position with all Japanese publishers. Copyright fees were usually 6 percent for French and British books, as opposed to 8–10 percent for American books.[134]

Second, the high royalty rates demanded by U.S. publishers and the complicated and dictatorial U.S. copyright brokerage practices also made it extremely difficult for Japanese publishers to buy the rights to U.S. books. Because of unrealistic royalty demands (10–20 percent), several major American houses began to lose their translation market in Japan. The most powerful Japanese publisher, Iwanami, stopped negotiating for any books owned by McGraw-Hill, which generally charged 18 percent on translations.[135] Under the U.S. occupation from 1945 to 1952, two methods of negotiating copyrights between Japanese and American publishers were used. One was the CI&E system of awarding copyrights to the highest bidders, and the other was the use of a local American copyright broker, particularly one named George Thomas Folster. Folster, who was also NBC's Far Eastern director for radio and television, was licensed as a literary agent under SCAP Circular 12 (March 1949). Folster was a "copyright salesman," buying the rights from U.S. owners and selling them to Japanese publishers. Because he had few competitors in this field, he incurred the reputation of being a monopolist. When he asked for what was considered a very high fee, publishers tended to assume that he was receiving an unreasonable profit. When Folster's exceedingly high commissions became generally known, Japanese suspicions about his alleged profiteering seemed to be confirmed.[136] Besides Folster, Charles E. Tuttle and Company, which represented Alfred A. Knopf and other publishers in Japan, maintained as of June 1953 a small U.S. copyright brokerage office in Tokyo and did a considerable business at reasonable rates (of the 150 book rights requested in 1952, about 50 were finally secured).[137]

Third, Japan's unfavorable foreign exchange restrictions and insufficient supply of paper made it equally, if not more, difficult for the Japanese to publish books and magazines. Alpheus W. Jessup of McGraw-Hill World News noted that a large number of Japanese wanted books in the original languages at prices they could pay, but that "the cost of an American book in yen was so great that some Japanese had to pay as much as one-half of their monthly salary for one American book."[138] Donald Nugent admitted that a long backlog in translation had resulted from the delay in solving the copyright problem, but he blamed U.S. publishers for having insisted on payment in U.S. dollars instead of yen, a policy that he thought was unreasonable.[139] In view of all these complications it is not surprising that the Japanese had no access to Japanese translations of U.S. books for quite a long time.

It was not until May 1948 that CI&E established procedures through which Japanese publishers could contact foreign copyright proprietors directly and obtain rights of translation and publication.[140] By 1949, at long last, Japanese publishers were able to contact foreign copyright proprietors directly.[141] In fact, by December 31, 1949, Japanese publishers had concluded contracts for 374 foreign books through the CI&E Information Division. Of these, 324 were American books that were recommended because of their value in furthering occupation objectives.[142] CI&E still checked the general lists of foreign books, but only to ensure that the resulting selection was not too one-sided in subject matter.[143]

Administrative Incompetence Besets American "Generosity"

The Government Section (GS) of GHQ advised MacArthur on demilitarization and democratization.[144] Moreover, GS, which occupied the central position in the GHQ bureaucracy, implemented substantial reforms in the realm of political democratization.[145] From December 1945 to April 1951, GS was under the command of Brig. Gen. Courtney Whitney. Whitney, a lawyer, was called one of the "Bataan boys,"[146] because he had joined MacArthur as director of guerrilla activities in the Philippines.

GS carried out one political reform after another. Immediately after the war, it released political prisoners, mostly communists, from jail.[147] On November 3, 1946, under the initiative and guidance of SCAP, the Japanese ratified the new constitution that established the principle of popular sovereignty and outlawed war as an instrument of national policy.[148] Women were promised legal equality and gained the right to vote.[149] As a result, Japanese politics was altered by the radically different constitutional system that increased mass participation in public affairs. (See Chapter 2 for a discussion of the U.S. democratic experiment in Japan and the Japanese responses to it.)

Although the administrative structure of SCAP/GHQ was rigidly hierarchical and thus supposedly efficient, SCAP suffered the organizational and administrative problems common to any colonial administration. These problems stemmed largely from the SCAP policy of indirect control of Japan. They narrowed down to poor liaison between GHQ and officers working in the field.

Under SCAP, the 8th Army headquarters in Yokohama commanded the military government headquarters of the First Corps in Kyoto and the Ninth Corps in Sendai, and it supervised directly the military government headquarters of three regions: Tokyo-Kanagawa, Chūgoku, and Shikoku. Meanwhile, the First Corps managed the military government headquarters of the regions of Kinki, Tōkai-Hokuriku, and Kyūshū, and the Ninth Corps administered the military government headquarters of the regions of Hokkaidō, Tōhoku, and Kantō. Officers of the local military government team then served as the contacts for officers working in the field.[150] Consider, example, Donald Nugent, the CI&E chief. He had no direct authority over the education officer at the prefecture level, nor could he even communicate directly with him. Communications had to be routed through the

8th Army headquarters in Yokohama, then through the First Corps in Kyoto, and from the First Corps to the local military command in Hyōgo prefecture, through the tactical commander to the military government officer and from him to the education officer. Reports climbed the ladder in the other direction.[151]

William L. Magistretti, an officer in the Civil Intelligence Section, observed that liaison was very poor between GHQ and the military government teams in the field. He attributed the problem to the unsuitability of military organization for military government purposes. He also commented that the tactical commanders of military government detachments frequently knew little and could not have cared less about the problems of Japanese reorientation.[152] A CI&E officer who was responsible for social education had an even harsher view of the American officers who worked in local areas of Japan. After a week-long visit of schools in Japan's provinces, he fumed: "It is easy to be fooled into thinking something is being accomplished when one sits in GHQ with a lot of other experts and confers with the officials of the Japanese Ministry of Education. But the real work must be done by the Military Government officers who are in direct touch with the schools. . . . Most local MG officers are only timeservers. Not more than 10% are qualified and interested."[153]

This officer also discovered from his field trip that local military government officers were often not only incompetent, but also arrogant and racially prejudiced. He finally lamented in despair, "We can't do it."[154] Lawyer Thomas Blakemore criticized SCAP and the military government in Japan for being fickle and inconsistent. To his dismay, Blakemore found that "the Provost Marshall seeks to maintain a strong centralized police force to maintain law and order," despite the fact that SCAP's political policy called for decentralizing the Japanese administration. "As a result," he ruefully reported, "decisions with regard to reform of police organization [had lasted] no more than twelve months."[155]

SCAP suffered personnel problems that were as serious and pernicious as its organizational problems. MacArthur and people around him illustrated the nature of the problems. Frank Hawley, Tokyo correspondent for the London *Times* and one of MacArthur's admirers, thought that the American general had made the soundest possible judgments on the information available to him, but, Hawley added, the information the general had received was "very poor."[156] He explained: "MacArthur, a man of strong loyalties, sticks to the Bataan gangs and is surrounded by incompetents who are almost his only informants."[157] C. Nelson Spinks echoed Hawley's opinion that the general was badly advised. According to him, MacArthur was so vain that he could not stand criticism, and he surrounded himself with sycophants.[158] Spinks also noted that "there were too many little ignorant men around GHQ enjoying bossing the Japanese." In one unbelievable story, he reported that an American he knew in the Economic and Scientific Section had banking experience that consisted solely of serving as a bank clerk for only six months just before the war, but that after the war the same man was in a position to dictate to the whole Japanese system of banks and bankers bred in a three-hundred-year-old tradition.[159]

Dean Bowman, a former OSS staff member who was serving as an officer of the Division of Japan and Korea Economic Affairs in the State Department, was equally concerned about the economic trends in Japan. He pointed out that the constant praise of MacArthur in the United States had resulted in neglect of the economic situation in Japan. He added: "The General refused to take responsibility for Japan's economy, yet occupation measures made it impossible for the Japanese to take full responsibility and the 'luxury occupation' placed an unnecessary burden on the Japanese economy."[160] For example, in 1946 the Japanese government spent as much as one-third of the entire national budget of 120 billion yen on covering the expenses of the American occupation forces.[161] After 1946 the government of Japan was obliged to allot 40 billion yen each year out of its entire national budget for covering the expenses of the American occupation army. In 1952 the amount jumped to 221 billion yen. By 1952 the Japanese had paid $5 billion (almost 2 trillion yen) to meet the expenses of the U.S. occupation of Japan.[162] Describing the nature of the occupation army, George F. Kennan wrote in his *Memoirs* that "the cumbersome occupational establishment was in many respects parasitical; and I am sorry to say that among the various purposes for which exactions were being made upon the Japanese, the personal enrichment of members of the occupation was not always absent."[163]

Moreover, the GHQ controlled practically all decisions in postwar Japan, even though it protested that it was the Japanese who were responsible for their government. The GHQ also required that there be an American adviser on the Japanese side who could respond to the GHQ.[164] Under those circumstances, as Spinks observed, it was next to impossible for Americans to expect capable Japanese leaders to come forward. In his opinion, most of the credit for whatever success the occupation achieved should go to the Japanese for their generally cooperative attitude, because even a negative attitude without active opposition would have made the occupation extremely difficult. In addition, Spinks remarked that the system created a dual bureaucracy—the Japanese one and the GHQ one—which together stifled any business initiative with multiple wrappings of shifting red tape.[165] Such an example illustrates another aspect of the "indirect" control of Japan and the complexity and double standard of the occupation.

Chapter 2

The Cold War, the "Reverse Course," and the Rise of Nationalism

> The real well-being of Japan—or her strength as a nation—was decidedly a secondary consideration—secondary to protection of ourselves against Japan, and secondary to payment of reparations to the victorious Allies.
>
> —Secretary of the Army Kenneth C. Royall, 1948

> We ought not to be so concerned about whether Japan is or is not a democracy. Democracy is, after all, only a means to an end. What we are interested in is the security and prosperity of the United States.
>
> —Elihu Root Jr., 1953

> As long as Japan was aligned with the United States, the chief dangers would come from the possibility of American influence disturbing Japan's social stability, or from a rallying of that country's social energies around the banner of anti-Americanism.
>
> —John D. Rockefeller III, 1954

As early as March 17, 1947, Gen. Douglas MacArthur declared that the objective of the Potsdam Declaration to demilitarize Japan had been met and that the first phase of the occupation was over. He urged Washington to prepare to draft a peace with Japan.[1] His version of an early peace reflected the image of a nonthreatening and weakened Japan that would primarily serve the security interests of the United States and of the Asia-Pacific region.

George Kennan, chair of the State Department's newly created Policy Planning Staff, opposed MacArthur's call for an early peace with Japan; he thought that the disarmament and demilitarization of Japan would deprive it of the power and energy it needed to withstand the threat of communism. In February 1946, Kennan had sent Washington a lengthy telegram from Moscow (in 1947 it became his famous "Mr. X" article in *Foreign Affairs*) in which he analyzed the communist view of the postwar world. He then became known as the father of the U.S. containment policy.[2] On February 26, 1948, Kennan felt compelled to visit Japan to talk with MacArthur. After their long chat one evening, the supreme commander seemed to be persuaded. Kennan apparently emphasized the urgent need for "the economic rehabilitation of Japan" to pave the way for its constructive contribution "to the stability and prosperity of the Far East region" in the post-treaty period. Upon his return to Washington, Kennan submitted to Secretary of State George C. Marshall a report suggesting that the United States not press for a peace treaty. As a result, the National Security Council adopted a resolution calling for the deliberations on an early peace with Japan to be postponed in order to give Japan time to shoulder the burdens of independence.[3] Thus Kennan's move was vindicated.

Meanwhile, the world was witnessing a growing division into two major blocs, the East and the West, under the mounting pressure of the cold war. On February 25, 1948, the communists took over the Czechoslovakian coalition government, and Moscow announced the construction of the Berlin Wall on June 24, 1948. Washington and Moscow vied eagerly for power and influence over thorny issues such as the Berlin blockade and airlift of 1948. Developing nations that had recently won sovereignty found themselves in dire need of aid, guidance, and support for the establishment of adequate political, economic, and educational institutions. The United States and the Soviet Union competed for the favor and support of the new and emerging nations of the developing world.

Triggered perhaps by that chain of events, the U.S. government adopted a hard-line cold war policy toward Japan. That policy was crystallized on October 7, 1948, in the document "Recommendations with Respect to United States Policy toward Japan" (generally known as NSC 13/2), which was based largely on Kennan's recommendations.[4] Two dramatic events in 1948–1950 also contributed to the onslaught of the cold war in East Asia: the outbreak of the Korean War in June 1950, as well as the Chinese Communist victory in October 1949. Without losing momentum, the Chinese government, led by Mao Tse-tung, concluded with the Soviet Union the thirty-year Treaty of Friendship, Alliance, and Mutual Assistance on February 14, 1950.

The U.S. government reacted quickly by deciding to follow as part of the U.S. response to the cold war in East Asia the policy recommendations in the report known as "NSC-68," which was submitted to the National Security Council (NSC) on April 14, 1950.[5] The outbreak of the Korean War also forced U.S. leaders to redefine America's policy priorities toward East Asia. Meanwhile, in the face of all of these events the Japanese keenly felt the need to grapple with the issue of the peace and security of their country within the framework of the two-superpower confrontation.

U.S. leaders such as President Harry Truman, Secretary of State Dean Acheson, Truman adviser John Foster Dulles, and Kennan believed that Moscow was seeking to dominate not only the Eurasian landmass but also the rest of the world. They feared that the needy developing countries would become subject to communist anti-American propaganda and, as a result, would become hostile to the United States. Irrevocably and almost without choice, the United States thus plunged itself into waging a bitter fight against world communism for survival. As for Japan's role, U.S. leaders concluded unanimously that the hegemonic responsibility as well as U.S. security interests demanded that Japan remain America's ally. They all agreed that the Far East should never fall under communist domination and that the U.S. government should give first priority to preventing such a defection.[6] Otherwise, the impact on the rest of Asia would be completely disastrous.

"Reverse Course": The American Version

In Japan, the U.S. government shifted policy priority from the initial goal of reconstructing a democratic, peace-loving nation to the new objective of turning the country into "a workshop in Asia" and "a bastion against communism." The Washington government changed the gears of U.S. occupation policy and decided either to slow down the execution of the occupation reforms of Japan or to stop imposing such reforms on the Japanese altogether.[7] This gear shift in U.S. policy priority, commonly known as the "reverse course," had its origin in part in the political sea change that took place in Washington after the more fiscally conservative Republican Party won a victory over the reform-minded Democratic Party in the 1946 U.S. congressional elections. It also reflected the growing awareness and fear among many Americans of a possible communist danger at home. This fear led to the rampage of McCarthyism in the United States in the early 1950s.

Some Americans had no qualms about redirecting and even sacrificing to some extent the initial objectives—democratization and demilitarization—of the military occupation of Japan. On January 6, 1948, when Secretary of the Army Kenneth C. Royall made a speech on U.S. policy for Japan, he called for modifying occupation programs originally intended to establish a democratic, peaceful government in Japan. He went on to state that "the real well-being of Japan—or her strength as a nation—was decidedly a secondary consideration—secondary to protection of ourselves against Japan, and secondary to payment of reparations to the victorious Allies."[8] Lawyer Elihu Root Jr., who supported the government's gear shift in policy priority, gave a compelling appraisal of the Japanese situation: "We ought not to be so concerned about whether Japan is or is not a democracy. Democracy is, after all, only a means to an end. What we are interested in is the security and prosperity of the United States." He went on to state, "If this objective is served, or at least not endangered, by an authoritarian regime in Japan, we ought not to be troubled by the non-democratic character of that regime. We must not engage in the doctrinaire pursuit of an ideal." He then insisted that the United States "make allowances for the Japanese, and not expect them to become perfect democrats overnight."[9] Sensing a change in the political climate in Washington, Eugene H. Dooman, the State Department's Far East expert, argued that the occupation reforms were no longer fit to serve the best interests of the United States and that many of those occupation reforms had been "postulated on illusions." He added that the reforms "could not possibly work and it would be an error to attempt to impose them permanently on the Japanese."[10] Dulles remarked approvingly, "It would be futile to attempt to compel adherence to the occupation reform."[11]

This sudden shift in U.S. policy priority first took shape in the U.S. calls for Japan to remilitarize. To follow up on the NSC recommendation of November 1948 that Japan create a 150,000-man national "police" force, Dulles visited Japan the week prior to the outbreak of the Korean War, urging Prime Minister Yoshida Shigeru to create a Japanese military of approximately 300,000 men.[12] On July 8, 1950, MacArthur directed the Yoshida government to organize the ground forces of the newly organized 75,000-man National Police Reserve.[13] It was expected to maintain law and order in Japan by filling in for the significant part of the U.S. occupation army that was suddenly dispatched to fight the Korean War on the Korean peninsula.

Another manifestation of the U.S. "reverse course" was SCAP's wholesale anticommunist campaign to repress and discredit the Japanese left. Responding to the growing tension between East and West around the world, on May 2, 1950, MacArthur hinted at the possibility of outlawing the Japan Communist Party (JCP). The "red purge" began on June 28, 1950, three days after the outbreak of the Korean War, when MacArthur banned the Japan Communist Party from publishing its party organ, *Akahata* (Red Flag), for one month, and then on July 18 the American general extended the order to a permanent ban.[14] From 1950 to 1951, a great many left-wing magazines and journals disappeared one after another, reflecting the right turn and the austerity program by the conservative "Dodge Line" of 1949.[15] Reportedly, as many as 511 journals and magazines were either suspended or discontinued from January to June 1950.[16]

In other areas, the red purge under the occupation began with the second *Yomiuri* newspaper dispute of 1946, which resulted in the firing of six union leaders, including Suzuki Tōmin.[17] The objective of the red purge was to break radical unions at the company and industry level. Occupation officials, conservative politicians, government bureaucrats, and corporation managers worked together in close cooperation to stamp out the threat allegedly posed by radical leftists and communists.

In the field of higher education, Walter C. Eelles, adviser to SCAP's Civil Information and Education Section, vigorously launched an anticommunist campaign, beginning with Niigata University in July 1949, to purge communist professors from university campuses throughout Japan. On May 2, 1950, the student protest against Eelles was so great that he had to give up the idea of speaking at Tōhoku University. In the full-scale red purges during this period, some eleven thousand activist union members in the public sector were fired between the end of 1949 and the outbreak of the Korean War in June 1950.[18] After the war began, the red purge was extended to the private sector, resulting in the dismissal of an additional ten to eleven thousand leftist employees by the end of 1950.[19]

By contrast, the wholesale "depurge" began with the government announcement of October 13, 1950. In the early postwar years in Japan, some 700,000 people had been purged from their jobs on the charge that they had had militaristic sympathies or had abetted Japanese aggression in earlier days. In the educational establishment alone, some 120,000 out of a half-million teachers had been purged or had resigned to avoid purging.[20] Of these, the government depurged 10,090 who had been purged on January 4, 1946, and in 1947.[21] Thus individuals previously purged "for all time" for having actively abetted militarism and ultranationalism were able to make a comeback to public life.[22] On June 20, 1951, the government announced the depurging of 2,958 prominent political and business leaders, including Ishibashi Tanzan and Miki Bukichi, and on the following July 2, 66,425 leaders of provinces and localities were depurged. All in all, more than two-thirds of the previously purged were depurged by April 28, 1952, when the peace treaty went into effect.[23]

"Reverse Course": The Russian Version

Communists in Moscow responded to the SCAP anticommunist campaign in Japan. On January 6, 1950, the Information Bureau of the Communist and Workers' Parties, known as the Cominform, publicly rebuked the Japan Communist Party in its effort to build a strong communist party in Japan. Cominform, organized in 1947 by the communist parties in Europe under the leadership of the Russian communists, sought to strengthen the collaboration and exchange of information among them and to impose a common political line on all of the communist parties of the six Eastern European countries and those of Italy and France.[24] The establishment of Cominform was the Soviet response to the U.S. anticommunist campaign, notable examples of which were the Truman Doctrine and the Marshall Plan. The Truman Doctrine, enunciated on March 12, 1947, called for the containment of Soviet expansion, pledging the employment of U.S. economic and military resources to aid Greece and Turkey and resist external aggression in those countries and elsewhere. The Marshall Plan (European Recovery Program), launched on June 5, 1947, by Secretary of State George Marshall, sought to revive a working economy in Europe. It declared that U.S. policy was directed not against any country or doctrine but against hunger, poverty, desperation, and chaos. Notwithstanding its humanitarian rhetoric, however, the Marshall Plan began to show its true color as the program was implemented. The Soviet Union rejected America's offer and announced its determination to block the Marshall Plan, which Moscow regarded as a U.S. ploy to prevent communist power and influence from spreading.

In Japan, Marxism had since the interwar years served as a major guiding ideology and enjoyed great authority, especially among some intellectuals.[25] After the war, particularly at the initial stage of the U.S. occupation, the communist ideology became enormously influential. For one thing, Marxism had great appeal to many Japanese now that their doctrine of unquestioned allegiance, religion of acquiescence, and ideology of the power state were all discredited and now that Marxism's nationalist competition was eliminated.[26] Besides, Marxism emphasized economic determinism, and thus it seemed to many Japanese to be the only systematic ideology that would help them find the answers to all their problems. Therefore, Marxists commanded great respect and trust from the rest of the population.[27]

For another thing, the Japan Communist Party was the only political party in which many members had maintained their antiwar position consistently and steadfastly and had refused ideological conversion even when they were jailed during the war. When Japanese communists were released from prisons after the war, they soon announced that they intended to undertake a peaceful revolution to democratize their nation. The presence of Japanese communists was dazzling to most intellectuals. Many intellectuals grudgingly acknowledged their failure during wartime to prevent the aggressive war in 1941.[28] Most of them felt ashamed, with the result that an inferiority complex toward the communists was implanted firmly in their heads.[29]

For the Japan Communist Party, however, the honeymoon period did not last long. The party's political influence began to diminish after the Cominform rebuke of January 1950. The Cominform denounced the JCP's prospects of a peaceful transition to a "People's Government" in Japan as utterly unrealistic in view of the impact of the current American "reverse course." And Nosaka Sanzō, the JCP chair, was openly criticized for his optimistic, easy-going strategy for a Japanese revolution by peaceful means. The public rebuke was followed by acceptance of that rebuke and an apology by the JCP—that is, the mainstream of the Japan Communist Party admitted its errors, toed the line, and abandoned its "lovable party" policy. Under the discipline of the Cominform, the JCP assertion of autonomy gave way to an explicitly international orientation.[30] The party's acceptance of the Cominform rebuke and its apology revealed a mentality characteristic of the Japanese, in particular a submissive attitude toward authority and a lack of independence in thought.

This abrupt change in policy exacted a high price from the Japan Communist Party. In addition to the harassment and outright oppression it faced from SCAP, the loss of face and independence cost the JCP popular support. Many Japanese leftists and communist sympathizers, including intellectuals and students, became utterly confused and alienated. As a result of the Cominform critique and the response to it, the JCP leadership split into two factions: the mainstream (Shokan) faction and the internationalist faction. Those in the mainstream faction, such as Tokuda Kyūichi, Nosaka Sanzō, and Itō Ritsu,[31] refused to accept the Cominform criticism, while the internationalist faction, such as Shiga Yoshio and Miyamoto Kenji, insisted that the JCP accept it. The Cominform rebuke also led to considerable dissension within the rank and file of the party. After experiencing a power struggle within the party, the JCP mainstream went largely underground. The JCP's embarrassment and accompanying ideological confusion then spurred the gradual decline in the popularity and influence of the Japan Communist Party and Marxism in Japan.[32]

In summary, the U.S. and Russian reverse courses confused many Japanese. Some became irritated with and angry at the United States, chanting slogans of anti-Americanism, while others were at a complete loss to explain the true American motives. Perceptive Japanese liberals vehemently opposed the revisionist "reverse course" programs of the Japanese government and defended the status quo and the system that the United States had introduced to Japan during the occupation. Many observers, Japanese and foreigners alike, felt that the occupation of Japan had changed in character from "too sweet a honeymoon" in the beginning to "too shrewd a honeymoon" at the end.[33] A Russian journalist, a keen observer of Japan, reported, "No matter how paradoxical it might sound, the policy priority that the Americans living in Japan took now shifted from Franklin Roosevelt's democratic course to the right that strengthened militaristic reactionary forces." The Russian journalist went on to add that some people in the United States conspired to establish in Japan a new "American bakufu"—a twentieth-century feudal shogunate government. Should that happen, he noted, the Japanese would serve the American master as slaves—a fate that would be far more tragic than that of being merely the vanquished.[34]

The Resurgence of Nationalism in Postwar Japan

The rise of nationalism in many parts of Asia after the war fueled a renewed sense of nationalism in Japan. The prolonged period of the U.S. military occupation inflamed Japanese feelings of nationalism as well. Sooner or later, a reaction against U.S. occupation policy seemed inevitable. By 1950 the contradictions of SCAP reform programs had become increasingly apparent to both the American occupiers and the occupied. Symptoms of discontentment toward the occupation began to manifest themselves as Japan gradually recovered from the ravages of war.

The Japanese especially directed their unconcealed annoyance and pent-up feelings at the U.S. occupation forces. The American presence, which militated frontally against the idea of an independent Japan, always reminded the people of Japan of their inferiority complex toward America. They resented the Allied occupation for the very reason that the presence of the American occupation forces represented nothing but alien interference with their way of life and their native culture.[35]

In expressing their nationalist sentiments, some Japanese openly leveled harsh criticism at the occupation reforms—criticism that was heard only rarely in the early years of the occupation. Others, as the end of the occupation neared, began to reexamine their initial attitude of blind and almost universal acceptance of everything American. In doing so, they began to struggle to get out from under the vast flood of Western cultural imports and search for what remained of Japan's own cultural background. Among other things, they questioned the mass standardized consumption of American culture with its predominantly Western character. They also gradually stopped belittling their own culture and started reevaluating their cultural heritage. Some made a very conscious effort to emphasize the spiritual and material values found in Japan's traditional life and formulate a course for their preservation. This effort to rediscover Japan's cultural heritage was most conspicuous in the fields of traditional art such as *Kabuki* (drama) and *Bunraku* (puppet theater) and folk craft where the Japanese could justly feel that they inherited unique qualities.[36]

Two events marked an important turning point in the resurgence of Japan's nationalism. One was the public announcement of SCAP's January 31 directive banning the planned general strike of February 1, 1947. Once MacArthur made his public issuance on January 31, SCAP and the U.S. occupation forces were no longer perceived by most Japanese as an unmistakable symbol of American liberal democracy or as a supporter of democracy in Japan.[37] The other event was the election of April 25, 1947—the second general election held since the end of the war. The election produced a quick revival of conservative forces, despite the fact that the Japan Socialist Party (JSP) won the greatest number of the seats in the Diet.[38]

Conservatism in Postwar Japan

Both during and after the war, Japanese conservatives experienced rough times, but they changed very little in terms of their philosophy and outlook on life. After 1945 conservatives came essentially from the top civil bureaucracy and the urban business community,[39] whereas before the war Japanese conservatism was supported largely by the government bureaucracy, civil service and military, the industrial-commercial community, and farmers. In terms of ideology, Japanese conservatives were neither progressive nor liberal; rather they were Tweedledum and Tweedledee—that is, they were affiliated politically with either the Japan Progressive Party (Nihon Shinpo-tō) or the Japan Liberal Party (Nihon Jiyū-tō).[40] The Japan Progressive Party, formed on November 11, 1945, was a disguised version of the prewar Japan Democratic Party (Minsei-tō), an ultraconservative party under the leadership of Shidehara Kijurō. He advocated anticommunism as well as the maintenance of *Kokutai* (the prewar national polity) and the emperor system. The Japan Liberal Party, formed on November 9, 1945, was the successor to the prewar Japan Political Friend Group (Seiyū-kai), which was under the command of Hatoyama Ichirō and then Yoshida Shigeru.[41]

In the election of April 25, 1947, the Japan Socialist Party failed to win a majority, which forced the party chair, Katayama Tetsu, to form a coalition cabinet in June 1947.[42] But this first Socialist-led government in Japan's history proved to be short-lived; it lasted only nine months. The Katayama government fell in February 1948, because the Socialist premier faced the political pressure of SCAP to rearm Japan[43] and because his cabinet suffered political turbulence such as the internal revolt by the left wing within the JSP and the division within the Japan Democratic Party.

The dissolution of the Katayama cabinet and SCAP pressure led to formation of the Ashida government on March 10, 1948. But this coalition government proved to be even more short-lived than its predecessor—it lasted less than seven months. To blame were political scandals such as the Shōwa Denkō bribery scandal, which involved government financing and contracts, and workers' tough resistance to government measures such as Government Ordinance 201, which sought to deprive public servants of the right to collective bargaining and the right to strike.

The signs of the resurgence of Japanese nationalism were discernible amid such political turbulence. One sign was the political comeback of the old guard politicians such as Hatoyama Ichirō and Yoshida Shigeru. Hatoyama had been purged on May 4, 1946, when he was about to form a new cabinet after the first general election of April 10, 1946. Having been absent from the overt political scene for nearly six years, Hatoyama staged a political comeback in December 1954, when he assumed the premiership. Yoshida formed the second Yoshida cabinet on October 19, 1948, after the collapse of the Ashida cabinet. In the third general election which was held on January 23, 1949, the Democratic Liberal Party under Yoshida won 43.9 percent of the vote and 264 seats out of a total of 466 seats (56.6 percent) in the Diet.[44] Yoshida's comeback as prime minister and his smashing victory in the third general election was the first in a long line of political victories for the old conservative forces for many years to come.

Sources of Conservatism in Postwar Japan

The Japanese government bureaucracy was a major source of conservatism in postwar Japan. After all, bureaucratic power remained as strong and important in the Japanese leadership after the war as before the war. Nonmilitarist Japanese elites consisted of conservative public officials, former Harvard men, "liberal" law professors, and Anglophile diplomats. During and after the occupation, they sought to connect with loyal Western allies represented by Japan experts, the "old Japan hands" in the U.S. State Department, or intelligence officers who believed that "democracy would never work in Japan."[45] Japanese government officials enjoyed great prestige and power buttressed by the presence of the American military forces stationed in Japan. More broadly, personal and institutional linkages between Japanese elites and the West, particularly the United States, served to solidify the power base of those nonmilitarist elites.[46]

The background of Japanese elites had one common denominator. According to Suzuki Gengo, deputy commissioner (*zaimukan*) of the Ministry of Finance, graduation from the University of Tokyo (known as Tokyo Imperial University before the war) was an almost mandatory prerequisite for entry to the more desirable government ministries, the diplomatic service, and the large industrial firms, because in Japan no university could compete with the University of Tokyo in prestige. Indeed, the Ministry of Finance recruited each year from the university's graduating classes in law and economics. Suzuki estimated in 1952 that 90 percent of the two thousand "top" positions in the Japanese government were held by University of Tokyo graduates.[47] Suzuki also pointed out that the "Tokyo boys," as they were called, "were, from the moment they entered the Ministry, singled out as candidates for executive positions. They were given the confidential assignments, those which enabled them to meet important people, and those giving an overall understanding of the work of the Ministry, while the graduates of other universities received the regional or more specified jobs."[48] The deputy financial commissioner also explained that "a master chart was kept of the Tokyo men with their year of graduation." "Of course," he added, "all the Tokyo University graduates of earlier classes must retire! Suitable jobs were found for them in banks or industry." In his way, Suzuki vividly revealed the secrets of how Tokyo University graduates kept monopolizing virtually all top-ranking positions in the government bureaucracy despite the SCAP occupation reforms. He explained how the top government bureaucrats—that is, the graduates of Tokyo University—were recruited and nurtured so that the bureaucracy of the Japanese government could remain alive and powerful. Suzuki also observed caustically, "One wonders what chance the Occupation has for quick changes." Having long been a teacher of economics in Formosa[49] and as the recipient of a doctorate in economics from the University of Wisconsin, he regarded himself as one of the very few exceptions to the prewar system.

Business-industrial leaders were a second important component of the new Japanese leadership and postwar conservatism in Japan. These leaders represented the urban business community and enjoyed social prestige and political influence equally in postwar Japan. Competition for key positions was intense; young executives were drawn from among the top college graduates. Although personal and familial connections were of vital importance in gaining key positions, like in every other aspect of Japanese life, merit and ability were increasingly important after the war.

Thus in the postwar years both elements of the new Japanese leadership—top-ranking bureaucrats and business-industrial leaders—interacted with the conservative political party. The farming population also continued to provide massive support. But not all of the old order was gone by any means. Tangible evidence remained of heavy dependency on government, solicitation of officials, and paternalism. But after the war, business–political party relations grew much broader and more diffuse than were the *zaibatsu*–party ties characteristic of the prewar era.[50]

A conventional view of modern Japan that is based largely on modernization theory emphasizes the successful efforts of the Japanese in modernization. The view contends that Japan is a unique and successful country and that it can be, therefore, a developmental "model" for the rest of Asian countries. According to this view, having been equipped with most advanced technology, the Japanese enjoy a technologically advanced modern life today because they established a democratic society, but they retain many of their own traditions and much of their culture as well. This pro-Japanese view also posits that Japanese and Western cultures are nicely and harmoniously blended or thoroughly hybridized in Japan. However, this rather simplistic representation of Japan as a successful nation glosses over the fact that Japanese and Western cultures, be it American democracy or Marxism, do exist side by side just like oil and water, without undergoing thorough blending or hybridization in that country. And yet all these images of Japan neither elucidate the reason why the Japanese conservatives were reluctant to embrace, if not outright opposed to embracing, the totality of Western or American culture, nor explain why the Japanese instead picked and chose the parts of that culture that they believed fit or suit their needs. The following paragraphs attempt to clarify the reasons why.

Japanese Conservative Thought

Conservatives reject progressives' stance that reason prevails in the end. They are profoundly skeptical about the human reason by which rationalists claim to reform society rationally; in fact, they regard such thinking as nothing but an expression of human arrogance. Conservative thinkers take the view that humans are more complex than most progressive thinkers assume.[51] In other words, they recognize the limits of human reason. Meanwhile, they defend the status quo and emphasize the importance of retaining traditional values, customs, and specific national traits. The perception of the past and the attitude toward history illustrate the distinct differences between progressives and conservatives. Progressives have a deep-rooted contempt for and intense hatred of the past, and they argue that the past customs and mores should be done away with by following the spirit of the great French Revolution. Conservatives such as the eighteenth-century philosopher and statesman Edmund Burke have a profound sense of love and respect for the present, ancestors, and their traditions, and they argue that society ought not to be conceived by following abstract ideas and ideals or a particularistic ideology.[52]

In the context of Japanese political history, Japanese conservatism had a little more complicated meaning than the term might imply. Conservatives wore two caps: one was forward-looking and progressive in the economic sphere, and the other was backward-looking and somewhat reactionary in the political and social realms. What is important here is that capitalism and conservatism should not be linked together too closely, because not all capitalists who belonged to "conservative" political parties were necessarily conservative. To be sure, many capitalists were conservative in spirit. But other capitalists belonged to "conservative" political parties and accepted a need for change. To borrow Austrian economist Joseph A. Schumpeter's famous concept of "creative destruction," they accepted the view that capitalism involved the continual destruction of the old to make room for the new, because many old trades and ways of life ceased to be economically viable. What they preferred was not absolute destruction but slow, well-sustained progress. In other words, they were pragmatists in political matters and rejected dogmatic ideology.

In a stricter sense, conservatives did not necessarily oppose change under any circumstances. Rather, they stressed the importance of gradual, evolutionary change, because they believed that the forces of change ought to be and could be moderated by slowly and carefully integrating new elements into time-tested institutions.[53] They were unhappy with and critical of the occupation reforms, particularly the political and social reforms, because those reforms had been carried out by outsiders so suddenly, swiftly, and forcefully in a thorough manner. This Janus-faced attitude of conservatives explains why most Japanese conservatives were linear developmentalists in an economic sense, while not necessarily keen on achieving modernization exactly in a European political sense—that is, the institutionalization of individual freedom, equality, human rights, and so on. In the political and social spheres, they, as nationalists, sought to keep the traditional institutions and arrangements of prewar Japan.

Among the conservative thinkers of postwar Japan were Yanagida Kunio, a pioneer of Japanese folklore; Tsuda Sōkichi, a historian; Koizumi Shinzō, an economist; Takeyama Michio, a scholar of German literature and the author of an antiwar novel, *The Harp of Burma;* Tanaka Kōtarō, Catholic chief justice and a legal scholar; and Fukuda Tsuneari, a literary critic.[54] Conservatives had in common their intense antipathy toward and contempt for radical movements, and they feared a revolution. They all detested the communist ideology, because the communists claimed that they had a theoretical and systematic understanding of all human activities that covered the whole range from economic structures to ideational attributes. In other words, postwar Japanese conservatives shared an anticommunist fervor.[55]

A Conservative Vision of Japan

In the opinion of a majority of the Japanese, particularly conservatives in the strict sense of the term, neither Europe nor America could serve as an unqualified model for Japan to emulate. Japanese leaders, who identified their country as an underdeveloped one, had had a dual image of the West since the beginning of the Meiji period (1868–1912). On the one hand, they looked at Europe and America as symbols of modernity, with which they should catch up. On the other hand, they regarded Europe and America as the countries from whose bad examples they could learn. In other words, they looked at the West as a source of lessons they could learn from the European and American experiences. And they were determined not to make the same errors committed by their Western counterparts.[56] That the Japanese came to embrace such a skewed dual image of the West can be explained by the fact that Japan had been forced into the capitalist world system in the middle of the nineteenth century, when the country had faced fierce competition with the West and possible military intervention that might threaten independence.

Japanese conservative leaders had a vision of Japan that was steeped deeply in the country's traditions and values. They advocated that their vision be translated into reality as an alternative to the Western model. The ultimate goal was to organize the country by maintaining a delicate balance between two value systems. One of them was economic security—that is, to attain economic self-sufficiency by enriching the nation. To achieve the goal, they adopted the policy of industrialization, as Meiji Japan's slogan "*fukoku–kyōhei*" (rich nation–strong army) indicates. The goal of Japanese leaders, both military and civilian, was to catch up with the West and then overtake it. They strove to transform the country into a modern nation by borrowing, adopting, and adapting science and technology from the West, and then they sought to maintain a competitive edge and a comparative advantage in the world. The Japanese took the values of self-discipline and hard work to heart. They embraced the idea (or the illusion) of steady upward progress in life. They also aspired to climb the rungs of the ladder of the global hierarchy and become exalted as an equal and respected member of the elite club formed by the world's most advanced nations.

Assuming that science and technology could be separated from the rest of European civilization, the Japanese learned advanced science and technology by separating them from the rest of Western culture, which included philosophy, rationalism, and humanism—important and yet inseparable ingredients of Western civilization. Meanwhile, Japanese leaders had to compromise the values associated with old Japan's semifeudalism and authoritarianism; after all, they had never experienced a genuine bourgeois revolution like that of Europeans and Americans.[57] In schooling, special importance was attached to mathematics, the natural sciences, and technology; the natural sciences and technology were thought to serve as the engine that would bring progress and riches to Japan. Thus in the field of education, competition for excellence became the rule of the game. In fact, in all fields the Japanese people were taught to become sufficiently competitive. Since their childhood, they had lived with the image of Japan as a tiny island country with a growing population and a scarcity of foodstuffs and natural resources.

The other objective for Japanese conservatives was to maintain the patriarchal-feudal pattern in social relationships—that is, harmony at home. Like most conservatives in other countries, Japanese conservatives had a pessimistic, if not entirely negative, view of human nature. They did not believe human beings were diligent enough to aspire to improve themselves, nor did they believe that people would establish order and sustain it of their volition. Instead, conservatives assumed that people were basically lazy and that they had a tendency to act egocentrically and destroy the existing order. Based on those premises, the leaders of Meiji Japan had established hierarchical order and promulgated the ideology of a traditional patriarchal family system throughout the nation.

After the war, Japanese conservatives continued to maintain the old feudalistic notion that people were not, in the absolute sense of the term, created *equal* in a society in which human networks were closely interconnected and interdependent.[58] In Japan, the concept of equality was rather relative and conditional. The Western idea of equality did not match up with the Japanese hierarchical idea, within which some people were more equal than others. As a corollary, they acknowledged differences in people. The "proper" places that people would occupy in society and the social roles that people would play were decided as soon as they were born on the basis of their family and educational backgrounds, gender, fortune, and other factors. Thus the occupational division of labor and a variety of statuses in society were taken for granted to help maintain a hierarchical order.

In such an ideal type of society, people of power and influence should behave paternalistically, in the same way that parents treat their children following the moral teachings of Confucianism and Buddhism. Under Confucianism, authority figures ranging from political leaders and business executives to fathers were expected to be benevolent and caring. Suzuki Daisetsu, a Buddhist philosopher, preached that they ought to care for the welfare of the members of organizations and of the nation by extending their helping hands to people below them, particularly the weak and unfortunate, in a homogeneous country such as Japan.[59] In turn, the weak and unfortunate, like children, were expected to accept and observe an ideology of *chūkō*, obedience and filial submission. In other words, they should defer to people in authority, obey the powerful, and follow the lead of the strong. In such a hierarchical society, every ordinary citizen was treated as a minor, no matter how much he or she matured as a human being. What is more surprising is that it was considered a virtue in Japan to remain a minor or act like a minor.[60]

In a like manner, the concept of freedom and the term *free enterprise* meant very different things to Japanese and to Americans. In the West, free enterprise implied freedom from the stultifying restrictions of the bureaucratic superstate. It suggested, in theory at least, a healthy and altogether desirable freedom for all people to work for the common good on their own initiative. But in Japan the concept of freedom and rugged individualism suggested something entirely different. Japanese took the view that an American type of "unfettered" freedom and free competition meant disregarding others and all social conscience and would therefore lead to chaos and social disorder beyond control. This Japanese interpretation of the concept of freedom indicated that Japanese did not have an accurate understanding of that concept, because in the West people took it for granted that free enterprise and individualism would find expression within the necessary limits imposed by law and custom in behalf of the common good.[61] Be that as it may, Japanese believed that freedom should not be absolute but rather relative and conditional and that it was natural and sometimes necessary to restrict individual freedom to maintain social cohesion and promote the interest of the whole society. In Japan, freedom was something not to be encouraged without putting on the brakes. Excessive, self-indulgent individualism and too much independence tended to lead to a disregard for the interest of others and society as a whole. Therefore, freedom should never be condoned in an overcrowded country like Japan.

Finally, conservatives believed that the traditional Japanese family system and the ideology behind it had long served to reinforce hierarchical order in Japanese society. The Japanese oligarchy and big industrialists of Meiji Japan had vigorously promoted the patriarchal family system and the familial values associated with it in order to legitimize social inequality and obscure the harsh realities of class exploitation under the pretext of harmony as one united and indivisible nation. These views are neatly summarized in the following passage from the *Cardinal Principles of the National Polity*:[62]

> In our country, under a unique family system, parent and child and husband and wife live together, supporting and helping each other.... [T]his harmony must also be made to materialize in communal life.... In each community there are those who take the upper places while there are

those who work below them. Through each one fulfilling his position is the harmony of a community obtained. To fulfill one's part means to do one's appointed task with the utmost faithfulness each in his own sphere; and by this means do those above receive help from inferiors, and inferiors are loved by superiors; and in working together harmoniously is beautiful concord manifested and created work carried out. This applies both to the community and to the State.

Following this line of thinking, Japanese conservatives claimed that the U.S. occupation and American democracy were responsible for the relaxation of social disciplines, thereby injuring their own vested interests in the old order.[63] A great many Japanese believed that the United States could not be a model for Japan to emulate for the following reasons. First, both American society and its historical experience were so vastly different from the Japanese counterparts that whatever lessons were gleaned from American experiences did not apply to Japan. In addition, the Japanese looked at America as a nation of change. They feared that the social change taking place in America was so swift and dynamic that Japan might not be able to cope with it or accommodate it.

Second, negative perceptions of Europe and America explain why Japanese conservatives believed that the West was not a suitable model for Japan to follow. For Japanese, the United States was a nation that was often discrepant in what it said and what it actually did. They pointed out that in the past Europeans and Americans had proclaimed universalistic ideas and ideals such as liberty, equality, and fraternity for all, and yet they colonized nonwhite peoples. Indeed, the credibility and reputation of the West as a world leader have been incurably tarnished by an incalculable number of recorded cases of prejudice and discrimination against ethnic minorities at home and nonwhite peoples abroad. Moreover, the Japanese were distrustful of the American government because U.S. foreign policy was full of vagaries and variability.[64] The U.S. government arbitrarily changed its policy priorities with impunity whenever it saw fit. The U.S. decision not to sue Emperor Hirohito as a prime war criminal was one such example, and the "reverse course" was another. Those instances demonstrated the American impulsiveness that led to a sudden shift in U.S. policy priority in Japan from democratization to anticommunism.[65] In addition, the Japanese were well aware that Europe and America were afflicted with serious social problems, which the Japanese attributed mainly to excessive freedom.

In summary, Japanese conservatives sought to realize economic progress and social harmony—their dream of killing two birds with one stone. They gave social order and harmony priority over everything else by controlling and curbing the forces of rapid change. But balancing those two competing values—progress and order—and harmonizing them internally were not as easy as it might appear. Japanese citizens were required to be competitive and individualistic and yet obedient to people in authority. They also had to conform to the norms of the organizations to which they belonged.

In short, the conservatives' image of Japan as an ideal society and nation resembles Japan's prewar slogan of *Kindai no chōkoku* (overcoming modernity).[66] The conservatives maintained that Japan's objective should be to overcome "modernity" by finding the ways in which internal contradictions in capitalism could be resolved. As Suzuki Shigetaka, a Japanese historian, describes aptly, for conservative Japanese "overcoming modernity" meant "overcoming democracy, capitalism, and liberalism in the realms of politics, economy, and thought respectively."[67]

This analysis tells much about Japanese conservatives' thinking and their reasoning for refusing to embrace entirely Western- or American-type democracy. It also explains why a democracy grafted during the U.S. occupation did not take root deep in Japan; rather, it remained skin-deep. At the same time, Japanese conservatives were emphasizing the uniqueness of their country and Japanese culture. There is no denying the fact that their view of an ideal Japan incorporates, to a considerable degree, ethnocentric overtones and self-complacency, if not entirely a superiority complex over the West. But that view reveals to an equal degree Japanese conservatives' sense of insecurity, defensiveness, and inferiority complex toward the West. A superiority complex and an inferiority complex are either the head or the tail of the same coin after all.

Conservatives Take Action

As the U.S. occupation came to an end, Japanese conservatives began to express openly and publicly their dissatisfaction with the new political and social order they thought had been imposed by SCAP.[68] Moreover, the imminent end of the U.S. occupation provided them with additional fuel for their feelings of nationalism. Conservatives, middle-of-the-road liberals, and radical leftists, who included communists, sought to reshape Japan's course after the occupation by mobilizing the energies of the masses to their respective camps. They never lost a chance to take advantage of the growing estrangement and resentment of the ordinary people against the occupation, and a bitter, highly competitive fight soon erupted.

Conservatives disapproved of the land reform imposed by the occupation, because it dispossessed some of the most worthwhile social elements —members of the professional classes who had been absentee landlords.[69] They criticized other economic measures as well. They regarded the shift in Japanese business behavior from reliance on personal trust to reliance on a written contract as tangible evidence of the deterioration in social morality.[70] And they attributed the noticeable lack of family discipline and a deterioration of standards in sexual behavior among young Japanese to the forced replacement of the traditional patriarchal family system with an individualistic social order.[71]

Actually, conservatives sought to retake power and influence from the American occupiers as soon as they made a political comeback. They strove to reestablish and stabilize the "Japanese way of life" by using selected aspects of the nation's tradition in an effort to contain or slow down the process of change initiated by occupation reforms. Hoping to make the process of change orderly, gradual, or minimal, they worked hard to avoid the destructive social consequences arising from the purely mechanical transfer of foreign ideas and institutions such as American democracy. For that purpose, Japanese conservatives sought to find ways to apply the brakes to too much democracy and to maximize those built-in forces within Japanese culture that could serve the cause of economic development after some redirection.[72] Specifically, conservatives began a full-scale drive to revise or readjust the occupation reforms in an effort to emasculate most of them. Four major political issues represented such moves: Japanese rearmament, constitutional revisions, the introduction of minor electoral districts, and the centralization of education.

The American Response to Japanese Nationalism

Conservatives' political moves worried many American reformers. Hugh Borton, an astute American specialist on Japan, found the resurgence of postwar Japanese nationalism ominous in character.[73] American reformers who belonged to the Government Section of the General Headquarters bureaucracy were as annoyed by the rise of Japanese conservatives as they were concerned about the growing communist influence among the Japanese.

Thomas A. Bisson, a GS officer serving GHQ from March 1946 to May 1947, quickly grasped the full meaning of the new political developments in Japan. The prolific editor of *Pacific Affairs* and the author of *Prospects for Democracy in Japan,* Bisson was very prescient in describing what the old ruling conservatives sought, either by themselves or with the tacit understanding of and sometimes in cooperation with their loyal Western allies. According to Bisson, it was almost inevitable that the established nonmilitarist Japanese elite would seek to either frustrate all the measures that had been designed to limit their power, or at least to relax the restrictions on them, once they were given an opportunity to administer SCAP directives.[74] He clearly perceived a gradual shift in the Japanese temperament toward the United States.

Other American occupation officers suspected that Japanese conservatives might turn back the clock to the days of old Japan. Those concerned Americans tried to make better sense of the subtle but unmistakable changes taking place in Japan. They wondered what attitude the Japanese government and people would take toward occupation reforms in the postoccupation period—that is, how many reform measures would be continued and how many abandoned. They also wondered whether those Japanese proposals for change represented their genuine intention to abandon occupation reforms entirely or merely to readjust these reforms to suit Japanese needs. There was every reason to suspect that many of the SCAP reforms might be seriously modified, because the conservative government might use the budgetary device of denying funds to accomplish these objectives. Thus it appeared to be incumbent upon the Americans to attempt to channel a revival of Japanese nationalism into constructive endeavors by resorting to all means available, including psychological warfare programs, and to ensure that nationalism would not lead to a return to the more independent-minded, militarist Japan that they had seen in the prewar years.

Along the same lines, American officers in SCAP and the U.S. embassy in Tokyo feared that the rise of Japanese nationalism and the desire for equality with the West might lead to Japan's detachment from the United States. Indeed, Japan might move away from America some time soon unless something was done quickly to stop the process.[75] John Rockefeller, the president of the Rockefeller Foundation, recognized correctly that the forces of nationalism were at work behind all the changes in the Japanese political climate. He then observed that "as long as Japan was aligned with the United States, the chief dangers would come from the possibility of American influence disturbing Japan's social stability, or from a rallying of that country's social energies around the banner of anti-Americanism."[76] Rockefeller realized that the Japanese "need us but they want to stand on their own feet." He recognized, however, that "Japan's relations with the United States are frustrating."[77] According to a congressional commission report, the Japanese wanted the United States to be "a partner, not a tutor, but a somewhat indulgent partner who would not demand complete reciprocity."[78] Such a Japanese understanding of "equality" with the United States was, however, perhaps naïve, somewhat warped, and not necessarily correct, because it did not reflect a U.S.-Japan power relationship.

Tristan E. Beplat, a member of the Council on Foreign Relations Study Group, agreed with Rockefeller: "Their [Japanese] concern is to expand their freedom of action and thereby become less dependent on the United States. . . . They accept help from the United States, because they need it, but they are making but conscious effort to detach themselves from us."[79] Beplat, a representative of Manufacturers Trust Company, explained Japan's situation by saying that "today the Japanese sense that they are not the master of their own destiny." He added that the Japanese might "start to play us off against one another," because he suspected that Japan's ties with China inevitably would be strengthened and that its ties with the United States would be reduced.[80] Lt. Col. Amos A. Jordan Jr. of the U.S. Military Academy concluded, "Japan is moving away from us." But Hugh Borton quickly interjected, "That is, toward independence."[81]

Many Americans also predicted that difficulties would increase in the near future in enlisting Japanese support and cooperation in the execution of U.S. global policy should the communist influence continue to grow in Japan as fast as it appeared. Besides, the prospect of an improvement in Japan's economic conditions was not necessarily bright in light of the scarcity of Japan's natural resources and its dependence on many external factors, a U.S. country paper reported.[82] To strengthen the basis of U.S.-Japan relations, Americans attached special importance to the cultural aspects of U.S. diplomacy. Robert S. Schwantes, an American Japan specialist, believed cultural relations with Japan were especially important. He called for concrete action to resist communism: "To the long-range task of buttressing the process of reform and re-education begun by the military occupation is now added the urgent need to combat the propaganda and subversive influence of communism."[83] Indeed, anticommunism was precisely the psychological as well as the historical background against which the U.S. government launched an all-out cultural offensive against communism in Japan.

Schwantes seemed embarrassed by the abrupt shift in the U.S. policy priority that had become increasingly noticeable in the wake of the Korean War. He was afraid that the U.S. "reverse course" might let down Japanese liberals who had looked up to America as a source of inspiration. Unlike Americans who considered world communism as more of a threat to Japan than the revision of occupation reforms, most Japanese liberals regarded the quick revival of old conservative forces and the revision of occupation reforms as more dangerous to Japan than communism.[84] According to Schwantes, "We may be throwing the baby out with the bath if we now try to disassociate ourselves from the basic goals of the Occupation. If we now become embarrassed or scornful in using terms like 'democracy,' 'individualism,' and 'human values,' we may be shattering the only concepts in which Japanese liberals can express their idealism. . . . Much of our talk about the about-face on Japanese disarmament seems to me much too cynical. . . . We forget to emphasize that the ultimate goal of a peaceful world without fear of aggression remains despite the necessity for changes in means.[85] Schwantes candidly admitted a slowdown in reform in Japan during and immediately after the Korean War: "Unfortunately, the chances of continuing reform in Japan are in some respects weakened by our need to enlist her active opposition to the forces of world communism."[86]

In summary, the swift change in the geopolitical configuration in East Asia in 1948–1950 led Washington to make a peace with Japan. Americans came to the realization that an overly long military occupation would not necessarily serve the interests of the United States, and so when Secretary of State Dean Acheson and British foreign minister Ernest Bevin met in Washington in September 1949, they agreed that the time had come to proceed once more with efforts to conclude a treaty with Japan.[87] It was clear that America's objective in making a peace treaty with Japan was to inhibit that country from drifting into the Soviet orbit.[88]

Chapter 3

The Making of a "Soft Peace" and Japan's "Proper Place"

The lessons of Versailles should be remembered. . . . We must not make the same mistake with Japan.

—John Foster Dulles, 1950

How can we help the Japanese to work toward desirable goals without seeming to dominate or compel them?

—John D. Rockefeller III, 1955

In 1950 President Harry Truman realized that the time had come at last to settle the terms of the peace treaty that would formally terminate the U.S. military occupation of Japan and the state of war. The Japanese government was also ready to negotiate a peace treaty with the U.S. government. On June 1, 1950, the Ministry of Foreign Affairs in Tokyo formally announced that Japan "should embark on a program of . . . concluding peace treaties with nations willing to award it independence and equality."[1] On September 14, 1950, Truman announced publicly his intention to initiate preliminary discussions on a peace treaty with the government of Japan.[2] It is reasonable to surmise that the swift change in the geopolitical configuration in East Asia during 1948–1950, especially the outbreak of the Korean War in June 1950, served as a major catalyst for Japan and the United States to speed up the peace process. Truman hoped that all countries concerned would sign the treaty, but by then he had already made up his mind that his country was prepared to proceed on a bilateral basis, even if the Soviet Union chose to oppose and try to insert the Chinese Communists into the negotiations.

The Appointment of John Foster Dulles, the Man of the Hour

U.S. Secretary of State Dean Acheson assigned longtime Washington figure John Foster Dulles to negotiate a peace with the Japanese. The secretary was convinced that "Dulles would do a good job and get the treaty through the Senate . . . with the necessary bipartisan support."[3] Acheson explained later that the main reason for appointing Dulles was political; he wanted bipartisan cooperation in the treaty making.

Dulles was widely known as an internationalist lawyer. After serving briefly as a Republican senator from New York, he became a consultant to Secretary of State Acheson in 1951 and served for two years in that capacity until he was appointed President Dwight Eisenhower's secretary of state in 1953. As a pious Christian, Dulles shared, with many other devout Presbyterians of his time, a kind of Manichean view of the world in which the forces of good were fighting against the forces of evil. Guided by his firm religious convictions, he was deeply committed to fight the cold war with the Soviet Union and world communism to the bitter end. In his holy crusade against communism, he believed that Germany and Japan held the key to ensuring America's victory in its worldwide struggle with communism. He once noted that "the future of the world depends largely on whether the Soviet Union will be able to get control over Western Germany and Japan by means short of war."[4]

Dulles never forgot, not even for a moment, that one of the U.S. global objectives was to keep Japan within the orbit of the West. He regarded Japan as the most vital area accessible to the United States to protect American national interests and security in the Far East. For Dulles, a Japan under Soviet control meant that the Soviet Union could "effectively challenge" U.S. control of the Pacific and, eventually, the U.S. West Coast.[5] In such an event, he feared that "the risk of a global war, and of American defeat in it, would have become much greater."[6] This astute, moralistic cold warrior also noted that by keeping Japan within the orbit of the West, the U.S. government would be able to maintain "the active support of Japan for both the United States and United Nations policy of preventing any aggressors from dominating the world."[7]

Other American leaders, especially the elite who participated in the Council on Foreign Relations, shared much of Dulles's worldview and his analysis of Japan's place in the U.S. global strategy. John D. Rockefeller III, for example, took the view that Japan held substantially the same position in

East Asia that Germany did in Europe.[8] According to Rockefeller and Dulles, to prevent Soviet Russia from dominating the rest of the world, it was essential to keep its vast Asian forces bottled up helplessly in a neutral corner. But that scenario, Dulles argued, would depend on Japan serving as an armed barrier to a Pacific thrust of communist forces.[9] From this point of view, therefore, the building of Japanese military forces—if built strong enough to defend Japan's homeland and Okinawa, but not strong enough to act independently—was thought desirable and necessary. Particularly after the outbreak of the Korean War, Japan's rearmament made much better sense to Dulles and other American leaders, but only so long as Japanese military forces would not hurt Japan's economic position. Dulles also preferred that Japan's military forces be not quite independent of outside support so that they might not have full freedom of action.[10]

Frederick S. Dunn was even more emphatic about the importance of Japan's geographical location in the general setting of U.S. global strategy.[11] The Princeton professor of international studies and founder of the quarterly *World Politics* remarked, "If we did not hold the good will of the Japanese people, the whole situation in the Far East would be lost."[12] John Rockefeller agreed with him: "Today the free world cannot afford to lose the industrial capacity and skilled labor of Japan." Then he asked himself a harder question: "How can we help the Japanese to work toward desirable goals without seeming to dominate or compel them?"[13] Dulles and others believed that all of the requirements—security, economics, and culture—related to U.S.-Japan bilateral relations had to be fulfilled to keep Japan within the orbit of the West. When Japan achieved a pro-U.S. orientation and an anticommunist orientation, as Dulles, John M. Allison, representative of the U.S. Mission to the United Nations, and others envisioned, the second phase of the U.S. objective in Japan would begin. It called for the materialization of Japan's contribution to the promotion of military, economic, political, and social stability in the Far East.[14]

In a similar vein, American leaders sketched the worst-case scenario in the event Japan fell under Soviet domination. If Japan's skilled and trained manpower were added to the Soviet Union's resources, the communists would be able to develop a second center (adding to the first center in the West) of top-ranking military strength in the East. This was precisely the worst-case scenario that would force the United States to reckon with the equivalent of a two-front war. With such a prospect in store, the United States would no longer be able to treat communist advances in the Far East as a secondary danger. Worse still, the United States would be forced to throw into the Far East as much effort and strength as it was devoting to Europe.[15]

Conversely, U.S. leaders believed that as long as Japan was effectively denied to the Soviet Union, the communist strength would be rooted in western and central Russia, and the Soviet Far Eastern Command and Communist China, either singly or in combination, would not be able to mobilize, in the foreseeable future at least, sufficient strength to threaten U.S. national security in the Pacific. Economically in this bipolar world, the industrial capacity and technical skill of Japan would become a valuable prize for either side. In short, the United States would be able to treat the Far Eastern thrust of communist forces as a matter of secondary importance as long as Japan remained friendly to the United States and as long as it was kept sufficiently armed.[16]

Moreover, in fighting the cold war American leaders recognized that Japan's internal stability would be a valuable asset in achieving U.S. objectives in Asia. They expected Japan to serve as a role model for many newly independent countries in Southeast Asia. As one study report of the Council on Foreign Relations pointed out: "Here is a people that has been able to absorb Western influence . . . without abandoning its own traditions. . . . Japan has demonstrated unusual stability in the sense of being able to maintain a well-functioning structure of government. This inner stability . . . may well be one of our main assets in the Far East."[17] The same report also observed that in view of the chronic political and social instability that afflicted many parts of East and Southeast Asia, Japan's influence on order and relative equilibrium through its domestic stability and foreign trade could very well serve the interests of the United States in that particular part of the world.

Finally, making peace with Japan also meant that the United States recognized the need to reestablish Japan as a national power that would fill "the power vacuum in the Far East."[18] Dulles and other American leaders believed that Japan's defeat in the war had created a power vacuum in East Asia, and that no vacuum should remain unfilled. They hoped that a peace treaty and its concomitant U.S.-Japan security treaty would forestall Japan from entering a power vacuum and thus tempting aggression.

Maintenance of the U.S.-Japan friendship was therefore not the only basis for U.S. foreign policy toward Japan after all. U.S. strategic self-interest in Japan and in the Far East was not necessarily incompatible with Japan's self-interest in national security and in reconstructing the Japanese economy.

It can be argued that at this particular juncture in the history of U.S.-Japan relations, U.S. self-interest as a hegemonic nation and Japan's interest as a client state was congruous during the U.S. occupation and beyond.

The Basic Principles of a Soft Peace

As the days of the Allied occupation of Japan became numbered, U.S. leaders, both in government and in private organizations such as the Council on Foreign Relations, the Rockefeller Foundation, and the Ford Foundation, probed what goals should be fulfilled by the peace pact. They not only studied the specific conditions that must be met to ensure the pact's success in the years beyond the military occupation, but also deliberated long-range U.S. foreign policy objectives and examined the far-reaching implications of the peace for future U.S.-Japan relations and the rest of East Asia.

As for the terms and conditions of a peace with Japan, the U.S. government faced the problem of whether it should make a "hard peace" or a "soft peace" when it restored Japan's independence. It recognized that a victor in a war must choose between the two methods of dealing with the vanquished: the "soft" approach consisted of treating the defeated former enemy well to win friendship; the "hard" approach consisting of treating the enemy harshly to prevent its resurgence. American leaders recognized that adopting a compromise between the two courses would be fatal.[19] Dulles, who had helped to negotiate the Treaty of Versailles after World War I, was cautious: "The lessons of Versailles should be remembered. . . . We must not make the same mistake with Japan."[20] Learning a lesson from history, the American leaders such as Dulles and others came up with the idea of a "peace of reconciliation" as the first and most important principle to guide a peace treaty with Japan.

The American government's decision to pursue a liberal peace—that is, "peace of reconciliation"—was aimed primarily at winning the Japanese over to the West.[21] In part, this decision represented America's recognition of its responsibility for managing the world system. Because of its far-flung responsibilities, the U.S. government correctly recognized that the United States could not maintain sufficient power within Japan to control Japan's development unless it won the hearts and minds of the Japanese people. Dulles believed that the voluntary assent of the Japanese was the first step in winning them over to and keeping them in the free world, and so the peace treaty with Japan must be a soft one.[22] It was particularly true in view of the fact that this island country was situated several thousand miles away from the United States and close to the Soviet Union. He was firmly convinced that if the Japanese did not fall into the Soviet camp, it should be because the Japanese did not want to.[23]

The second principle, corollary to the first, was the restoration of "complete and untrammeled" sovereignty to Japan.[24] In other words, the peace treaty should contain no restrictions on the freedom of action of the Japanese. The U.S. government believed a lenient, unrestricted peace treaty with Japan was the only feasible way in which Japan would become a voluntarily cooperating and reliable member of the free world. At the same time, incorporating Japan into the free world's Pacific security arrangements was the only feasible way of keeping Japan's future military potential under control.[25]

The Conditions Underlying a Soft Peace

Based on these basic principles, American leaders defined the conditions of peace under which Japan would remain within the orbit of the free world in the post-treaty period. These conditions were (1) maintaining the security and safety of Japan, (2) ensuring the economic viability of Japan, and (3) expanding cultural relations with Japan. These conditions are described in the sections that follow.

The Security and Safety of Japan

In the final days of the occupation, Japan's security was the first and foremost concern of both Americans and Japanese, and it was the first condition under which peace was made. The United States recognized, first, that Japan had been reduced to a military vacuum after World War II; second, that most Japanese had neither well-informed nor well-founded opinions about what security measures might be needed for their country; and, third, that the Japanese had little confidence in the United States. To a large extent, the lack of confidence the Japanese had in America was attributed to the vagaries and variability they saw in U.S. foreign policy, as demonstrated by two incidents that took place over the period 1949–1951.[26]

The first shocking incident took place on February 6, 1949. In the reported declaration, former secretary of the army Kenneth C. Royall was quoted as saying that American troops would be withdrawn from Japan in the event of war and that the United States might unilaterally forsake the Japanese any day now.[27] Royall's less than discreet statement was taken to mean that America might abandon Japan to its fate if the United States ever found itself in extreme trouble.[28] The Japanese feared that the United States might make a strategic withdrawal from Japan in the face of a determined Soviet invasion, because they knew that America had followed a Europe-first policy during World War II.[29] In 1951 Dulles learned in Japan that the Japanese had never recovered from their shock at Royall's statement.[30] Rockefeller also discovered that the Japanese were thus very much concerned that the United States might abandon them and leave them in the cold should the world situation become more serious.[31]

The second disturbing incident, on April 11, 1951, only added fuel to Japanese anxieties. It was the abrupt recall of General MacArthur from the highest office of SCAP in Tokyo. The general had been bitterly critical of the Truman administration's views of the situation in the Far East and the tactics being used to carry out the Korean War. On March 20, 1951, MacArthur had sent a telegram to House minority leader Joseph Martin of Massachusetts openly challenging the constitutional authority of the president to direct the nation's foreign policy.[32] Truman suspected that in taking this extraordinary action the general was entertaining his overzealous presidential ambitions, and so the president relieved MacArthur of all his commands in the Far East by invoking the fundamental principle of the supremacy of the civil over the military.[33] The removal of MacArthur further undermined Japanese confidence in the United States. The incident seemed to confirm the anxiety of the Japanese that a similar fate would likely befall them. The general feeling of the Japanese was that "if such a thing could happen overnight to so great a personage as General MacArthur, what might happen to Japan in the future? Might not Japan also be thrown overboard overnight?"[34] The MacArthur affair was a new blow to Japanese confidence in the United States.

Japanese liberals were seriously worried about whether the United States would stand by Japan if the situation got rough in Europe. For example, political science professor Takeuchi (Sterling) Tatsuji characterized the current feelings of the Japanese as "helplessness." The Japanese feared their country might become a battleground in a third world war should the United States desert them militarily and economically. Takeuchi revealed his deep-seated fear that if there was a war and Japan was held by the communists for several years, the Japanese would not survive to see the liberation, even though the United States might eventually liberate their country. He thus believed that there was an urgent need for Japan to decide on its political orientation, either East or West.[35] Kishimoto Hideo, a professor of history of religion at Tokyo University, unequivocally expressed the same kind of anxieties. He suspected that the United States might not choose to defend Japan in the event of a hot war and that America might not be able to do so even if it chose.[36] In view of these perceptions of Japanese intellectuals, American leaders felt they must assuage the Japanese fear of an external attack—especially after the Korean crisis broke out.

Dulles believed some sort of security system was needed in Japan to meet the challenge of communist countries, and he hoped the Japanese, once understanding the objectives of an American military presence in Japan, would voluntarily and spontaneously request that the United States maintain garrisons in their country for security reasons.[37] Dulles favored an agreement on garrisons that would be either short term and renewable if both parties desired it or terminable at any time by either the United States or Japan. He hoped the Japanese would not object to a continued U.S. military presence if they felt free to rid themselves of American garrisons at any time. On the day after the first meeting at the Council on Foreign Relations on Japanese peace treaty problems, George S. Franklin, Jr., director of meetings, wrote Dulles that the Japanese should have this freedom. Franklin believed the garrisons might well become festering sores, thereby threatening the whole policy of friendship, if the Japanese did not have the freedom to close them, and especially if it appeared that the American garrisons had been imposed.[38] Dulles seemed to agree with him.

In the end, Dulles adopted a subtle, realistic approach to presenting the idea of American garrisons in Japan. With pro-peace and antiwar, if not anti-American, sentiment rampant throughout Japan, he decided not to include the provision on American garrisons in the peace treaty itself but to include it in a side agreement on security. He feared that if the provision were included in the peace treaty, it might give Japanese the impression that the provision was imposed on them and it would later be criticized as an infringement of sovereignty.

The Viability of the Japanese Economy

The second condition for a soft peace and for keeping Japan within the orbit of the free world during the post-treaty period was just as important as the security and safety of Japan; it was U.S. assurance that Japan would develop a healthy economy. Dulles believed that a liberal democracy was nurtured and developed only in a civil society supported by a large, prosperous middle class highly aware of individual rights and duties. Development of such a democracy demanded that Japan have a robust economy. But the country was practically on the verge of starvation, and Japan's postwar economy was a far cry from meeting even the minimum requirements for survival.

According to the most sweeping of material calculations, the Allied assault on shipping and the bombing campaign against the home islands during the war destroyed one-quarter of Japan's wealth.[39] The SCAP bureaucracy calculated early in 1946 that Japan had "lost one-third of its total wealth and from one-third to one-half of its total potential income." Rural living standards were estimated to have fallen to 65 percent of prewar levels, while urban living standards, which were harder hit by the bombing campaign, had fallen to about 35 percent.[40] In 1946 the Japanese had an average dietary intake of only 1,449 calories a day, which had risen to only 1,851 calories a day in 1948, as opposed to 2,135 calories a day in 1938.[41]

In part, people's poor health was a reflection of the low wages earned by the average Japanese. For example, male cotton spinners at the Kanegafuchi Cotton Spinning Company, one of the oldest and largest spinning companies in Japan, earned 480 yen ($192) a month in 1945. Their female counterparts usually earned 240 yen a month, half as much as the men, although women worked at the same type of jobs. Child laborers under fifteen years of age earned 60 yen a month, or one-quarter of the wage received by female cotton spinners.[42]

In 1947 the average monthly salary of a college-educated, white-collar public employee was about 1,240 yen ($496).[43] Even as late as May 1950 when the Japanese economy began to recover, government officials earned only 10,800 yen ($30) a month on average, including allowances, while business executives earned 25,200 yen ($70) a month. In manufacturing establishments, the average monthly wage was 11,520 yen ($32) in 1951.[44] Day laborers in Tokyo, who filled the menial jobs such as leveling the ground for construction and repairing streets, received daily wages of 243 yen (or about $16 a month) in 1950, while day workers in rural areas received 140–160 yen a day (or about $9.30–$10.60 a month). The wages they received were far from sufficient to survive, because a new suit cost 15,000–20,000 yen ($41.60–$55.50) and a pair of shoes 3,000–5,000 yen ($8.30–$13.80).[45] (Differences in the yen-dollar conversion can be attributed to the Dodge Line of March 1949, which fixed the new single exchange rate at 360 yen to the U.S. dollar, as opposed to the previous exchange rate of 1 yen to $0.40. The 1949 change in the exchange rate explains the discrepancy between the 1947 figures and those for 1950–1951.) Further aggravating the situation for the average Japanese was the wild inflation until 1949. By 1946 commodity prices were 16.3 times higher than those of 1934–1936, while real wages went down to 13.6 percent of those of the prewar years.[46] Low levels of industrial production, scarce food, lack of raw materials, and a flourishing black market and rampant inflation and speculation characterized the postwar Japanese economy.

And yet the dilapidated state of the immediate postwar Japanese economy could not be explained away simply by the country's military defeat. Other factors—geographical, historical, and structural—must be taken into account as well to fully appreciate the pitiful condition of Japan's economy.

Geographical Factors

Japan, like Britain, is an island country—a beautiful archipelago made up of over three thousand islands, four of which are major mountainous ones. After the war, only 16 percent of the entire Japanese territory was arable, and the country had a high population density—3,596 persons per cultivated square mile, as opposed to 1,639 persons for China, 1,763 for Britain, and 213 for the United States. Because of its topography, the country lacked the productive capacity to feed 85 million people and thus had to import more than 20 percent of its food. Before the war, Japan's food deficiencies were supplied by its empire, mainly Korea and Formosa. But in the postwar period, the country had to import close to three million tons of foodgrain annually. In 1950 food imports totaled $337 million or one-third of total imports, and in 1951 they amounted to $558 million or one-quarter of a larger volume of total imports.[47]

Japan also suffered from an extreme paucity of the raw materials essential to a modern industrial power. Of the thirty-three metallic minerals used in industry, Japan had only six in large enough quantities to meet minimum requirements. For example, it had to import 100 percent of its raw cotton, raw wool, phosphates, rubber, nickel, tin, and bauxite; 82 percent of its iron ore; 88 percent of its crude oil; and 70 percent of its coking coal.[48] The overwhelming lack of natural resources as well as the constant pressure of an increasing population on the land made Japan heavily dependent on foreign trade to make ends meet. How then could the Japanese generate sufficient commercial exports to pay for essential imports?

Historical Factors

From a historical vantage point, Japan's loss of its empire because of the war not only led to a decline in Japan's postwar foreign trade, but also drastically changed the character of its exports in the postwar period. According to the sixth economic white paper issued by the Japanese Economic Stabilization Board (Keizai Antei Honbu) on July 1, 1952, exports at that time, including special procurement, were only 36 percent of the prewar (1934–1936) levels (30 percent excluding special procurement), and imports were only 49 percent of the prewar levels. Japan's share of world trade fell from 5 percent of both exports and imports in 1937 to 2.5 percent of world imports and 1.8 percent of world exports in 1951. Of total Asian exports, Japan accounted for 26.2 percent in 1937 but for only 11.8 percent in 1951. Its share of Asian imports dropped from 33.1 percent in 1937 to 18.7 percent in 1951.[49]

One of the most striking aspects of Japan's postwar international economy was the abnormal and unusual sources of foreign exchange income. From the end of World War II to July 1, 1951, Japan received $2 billion in aid from the United States. The outbreak of the Korean War provided Japan with $634 million—the result of the UN procurement of goods and services from Japan from June 1950 through June 1952. Thus through June 30, 1950, Japan's consistent excess of imports over exports was "balanced" by U.S. aid and by the surplus in invisible receipts attributable mainly to special procurement for Korea. In calendar year 1951, Japan had an excess of foreign exchange receipts of $335 million despite a trading deficit of $428 million. But no one expected the U.S. aid and the benefit of "special procurement" to last long and to not taper off over time.

Another distinctive feature of Japan's postwar trade pattern was that the country depended heavily on imports from the United States in contrast to its dependence on its empire before the war (see Table 3.1). Table 3.1 also shows Japan's great dependence in the postwar years on exports to Asian countries other than Japan's former empire (Korea, Formosa, Manchuria, and China).[50]

Historically, Japan enjoyed close trading ties with China. From 1902 through 1935, goods sent to China had made up about 20 percent of Japan's total annual exports. Imports from China had not dipped lower than 10 percent during the same period.[51] Before the war, 35 percent of Japan's trade had been with the mainland of East Asia.[52] Shortly before the U.S. occupation of Japan ended, SCAP economists undertook a comparative analysis of Japanese trade, using calendar year 1935 and U.S. fiscal year 1951.

Table 3.1 Geographic Pattern of Japanese Trade, 1935–1951 (percentage distribution of total value)

	Imports[a]					
	1935–1937	1947	1948	1949	1950	1951
Korea, Formosa, Manchuria, China	32.7	1.5	4.3	5.4	9.6	4.0
Other Asia	17.5	4.3	10.1	12.7	22.3	27.5
United States	25.1	91.9	64.7	64.2	44.1	35.1
Europe	10.2	2.2	3.3	7.6	4.2	8.1
Mexico, Central and South America	3.1	—	12.5	1.5	6.9	14.4
Rest of world	11.4	0.1	5.1	8.6	12.9	10.9
Total	100	100	100	100	100	100

	Exports[b]					
	1935–1937	1947	1948	1949	1950	1951
Korea, Formosa, Manchuria, China	42.5	16.8	8.5	5.4	9.2	5.2
Other Asia	20.8	40.2	43.2	45.3	36.9	46.3
United States	16.1	11.6	25.4	16.4	22.4	13.6
Europe	8.4	23.2	12.2	15.6	11.8	10.7
Mexico, Central and South America	3.5	0.2	0.4	1.3	5.7	6.9
Africa	5.7	5.0	7.7	11.5	9.0	8.2
Rest of world	3.0	3.0	2.6	4.5	5.0	9.1
Total	100	100	100	100	100	100

Source: Jerome B. Cohen, "Foreign Trade in the Japanese Economy and Japan's Trade with China," Council on Foreign Relations Study Group on Japanese Trade and Investment, Working Paper No. 1, October 20, 1952, folder 40, box 6, collection III 2Q, RAC.
[a] Includes U.S. aid shipments.
[b] Excludes special procurement of goods and services from UN forces in Korea in 1950 and 1951.

They discovered that in 1935, 40 percent of Japan's exports went to China, Korea, and Formosa versus only 7 percent in fiscal year 1951. By contrast, the study revealed that in 1935 Southeast Asian countries were the recipients of 20 percent of Japan's exports, but 42 percent in 1951.[53] These statistics indicated that Japan would have to start down the road to economic recovery by first replacing the markets it lost because of the war.

Also for geopolitical reasons, Japan needed to find markets to replace the ones on the Asian mainland. After World War II, the U.S. government had imposed international export controls on communist countries as part of

U.S. tactics to fight the cold war and to reconstruct noncommunist regions of Asia in order to obtain an equilibrium in Asia favorable to the United States.[54] The U.S. government set the first guideline for U.S. trade policy toward Communist China by making NSC-41, a February 1949 document, official policy. The consensus on trade controls that emerged after the onset of the Korean War reflected most of the military's demands. During the war years, the Truman administration had tightened international export controls. In May 1951, for example, the United States obtained UN passage of an embargo resolution against North Korea and Communist China. The Mutual Defense Assistance Control Act, also called the Battle Act, made export controls by foreign aid recipients a condition of American assistance. Under pressure from the Defense Department, in particular, the Truman administration applied an increasingly stricter embargo against Sino-Japanese trade in the wake of the communist victory in China in October 1949 and the outbreak of the Korean War.[55]

The Japanese also hotly debated the issue of whether trade with Communist China should be resumed. Prime Minister Yoshida Shigeru was committed to cooperating with the U.S. government in stopping the flow of critical and strategic goods to the Soviet bloc and Communist China. Within the Liberal Party, Yoshida was challenged by Hatoyama Ichirō, who favored resumption of trade with Communist China, as did large elements of the Japanese business community, particularly in Osaka and in the cotton spinning industry. Japanese businessmen were determined to push through a reopening of trade with China. In a news note in late May 1952, *Tōyō keizai shimbun* declared:

> Moves for reopening of trade with China and the Soviet Union are apparently getting active among industrial circles much interested in this question. Business talks are proceeding for importing 200,000 MT of Saghalien coal; representatives of 20 odd trading firms have recently discussed the matter with members of the House of Representatives; sales offers of iron ore, soybeans, etc. are coming increasingly from Chinese Export Corp.; fat and oil interests are studying counter-measures for China trade resumption with steel makers; and such influential men as Ayukawa Gisuke [Aikawa Yoshisuke] and Sugawara Tsūsai are planning to invite to Japan the British Mission now visiting Peking after the Moscow conference. MITI and Foreign Office authorities are planning to ask the U.S. government to modify the strict restrictions on trade with China, reports the *Sangyō Keizai*.[56]

Premier Yoshida argued back by emphasizing that Japan was benefiting substantially from UN procurement and from troop spending in Japan. He was supported in his arguments by correspondent Walter Simons of the *Chicago Tribune,* who boasted that special procurements, thanks to the Korean War, were enriching the entire nation of Japan. And the *New York Times* was quoted as reporting that "American soldiers stationing in Japan spend one million dollars a day."[57] Yoshida also pointed out that Japan could not have these windfall benefits and trade with China simultaneously. Put differently, according to Yoshida, Japan could not have its cake and eat it too.[58]

Structural Factors

In addition to the critical need to develop alternative markets, structural change in Japan's economy was absolutely imperative for the country to survive. Japan needed to develop its capital goods industry to produce reasonable value-added goods for export at competitive prices and to enlarge its market for such products in Southeast Asia.

But the prospects for Japan's economy appeared bleak in the post–peace treaty period. The first reason was that the temporary UN special procurement was not sufficient to put all of Japan's industrial potential to work, nor was it adequate to permit Japan to plan its import requirements or its role in the development of Southeast Asia.[59] In a report for the Foreign Policy Association, Robert A. Scalapino, a professor of political science at the University of California, argued that Japanese trade with China was inevitable, despite U.S. efforts to control exports to Communist China: "American aid must remain uncertain in terms of type, amount, and duration. In addition, the China trade in particular has been so traditional, so logical, and previously so profitable that its permanent abandonment on a large scale is almost inconceivable to Japan."[60] The problem was whether Japan should succumb to the economic temptation of trade with China, thereby putting itself at grave risk of becoming economically dependent on that country. Should that happen, it was feared that Japan would be forced to make economic and later political concessions to China and eventually would be drawn into the Chinese orbit. American experts on Japan's economy believed that consequence should be avoided at all cost. To escape this dilemma, Japan simply had to develop trade elsewhere.[61]

The second reason for the bleak future of Japan's economy was that Southeast Asian markets were not as promising as they appeared. The following factors had to be considered if Southeast Asian markets became a substitute for East Asian markets for Japan: (1) the British might offer stiff competition; (2) poverty-stricken Southeast Asia had not developed sufficient purchasing power for Japanese exports; (3) Southeast Asia was so politically unstable that it would attract few Japanese businessman; and (4) the problem of reparations might complicate diplomatic relations between Japan and the countries in Southeast Asia.[62] At a Council on Foreign Relations Study Group meeting, Eugene Dooman, former counselor at the U.S. embassy in Tokyo, ventured the opinion that it would be enormously difficult for Japan to replace the vast East Asian market in the postwar period.[63]

All said, then, Japan's future trading position seemed to be largely contingent on how well the Japanese would meet competition in world markets. In view of the state of the Japanese economy, John Foster Dulles believed the Japanese government could not undertake the welfare measures being advocated by the socialists. The socialist policies not only would further diminish Japan's economic status, but also would lead to a loss of foreign exchange that could produce chaos and possibly advance communism. From a geopolitical viewpoint, Dulles believed it was enormously important for Japan to become a self-supporting nation. With that idea in mind, he argued that the U.S. government should neither insist on reparations nor impose economic limitations of any kind on the Japanese. The imposition of reparation payments on Japan would undermine the economic recovery thus far achieved and ultimately redound to the disadvantage of the rest of democratic Asian countries.[64] In keeping with these beliefs and his understanding of the fragility of Japan's economy, Dulles shuttled back and forth between Tokyo and Manila to persuade the government of the Philippines not to demand reparations from Japan.[65]

Dulles received support for his views from various onlookers and participants in the peace process. Among them, was Ernest F. Penrose, Johns Hopkins University professor of economics, who was in complete agreement with Dulles about the U.S. approach to Japan's economy. Penrose believed SCAP was crippling Japan's economy in its effort to guarantee security, but security must be attained by political measures, not by economic means. Specifically, he was vehemently opposed to limiting production or the import of key materials for civilian needs. Penrose felt the restrictive measures would not only harm the Japanese economy but also pose other difficulties as well. He maintained that the SCAP measures would never serve as complete insurance against the appearance of new military weapons, because future technological developments would outdate checks imposed at the present time. Those types of economic measures would lead to the slow starvation and decimation of a large segment of the Japanese population.[66] The end result was that the control clauses were omitted from the Japanese peace treaty, largely because it was feared that the Japanese would feel they had not achieved national equality if the clauses were included.[67]

John M. Allison, representative of the U.S. Mission to the United Nations and soon to be appointed U.S. ambassador to Japan (1953), also concurred thoroughly with Dulles. Allison insisted that the U.S. government recognize "its responsibility for assisting in the development of new patterns of trade for Japan," if the United States wished to avoid the situation in which Japan had too dependent a relationship with China.[68] Arthur H. Dean of Sullivan and Cromwell was even more specific on this particular issue of Japan's trade pattern: "The underdeveloped areas of Southeast Asia offer a great potential market to the Japanese. It is difficult to see how such countries as India, Burma and Indonesia can ever develop their economies unless they are willing to regard Japan as the natural workshop of Asia and trade with it."[69]

No one seemed more knowledgeable about the current state of Japan's economy and the structure and the working mechanism of inter-Asian regional trade than Harvard-educated Sherwood M. Fine, director of economic planning of GHQ's Economic and Scientific Section. In his policy recommendations, Fine emphasized complementariness as a key concept in an ingenious scheme to organize and develop a triangular, regionally integrated Asian economy.[70] Fine underscored that the United States had an important role in his proposed scheme: providing financing in the form of long-term developmental capital loans at reasonably low interest rates. He maintained that U.S. participation would allay the fears of other Asian nations that Japan might reemerge as a dominant power in Asia.[71] Finally, Fine earlier had expressed his deep conviction of the soundness of his scheme, pointing out that it was foolish to even pursue a peace treaty with Japan without giving thought "to how the Japanese economy can be fitted into that of other parts of Asia."[72] Later, he pointed out to Rockefeller that "Japan, because of the complementary nature of her economy with that of Asia, can count on providing an increasing market for the enhanced export capabilities of her neighbors. The realization of such trade at a high level would constitute a significant stabilizing force in the entire world trade pattern."[73] Everybody seemed sufficiently persuaded by his logical analysis and argumentation.

U.S.-Japan Cultural Relations

The third condition for a soft peace was expanding cultural relations with Japan. Shortly after World War II, federal government agencies and many private foundations began to recognize the need to expand Americans' knowledge and understanding of other countries. In fact, the U.S. government realized that cultural relations with foreign countries were no less important than U.S. security and economic interests. Thus the U.S. government, for the first time, systematically wove cultural foreign policy into the whole fabric of U.S. strategy, in keeping with its recognition that cultural diplomacy was indispensable to achieving the objectives of U.S. foreign policy. From 1945 to 1953, the government's cultural diplomacy, sometimes called public diplomacy, and its cultural and information activities were conducted under the aegis of the State Department's assistant secretary for public and cultural affairs. After 1953, the cultural and information work was handed over to the U.S. Information Agency, which was created by Reorganization Plan 8 to follow up on President Truman's "Campaign of Truth" of 1950, aimed at dealing more effectively with the psychological dimension of the cold war. The USIA was responsible to the president through the National Security Council.[74]

In 1946 the Fulbright program, created by an amendment to the Surplus Property Act of 1944 sponsored by Sen. J. William Fulbright, began to encourage American scholars to spend time in foreign countries to undertake research and teaching. The Fulbright fellowships also were intended to provide the rest of the world with U.S. cultural emissaries who would serve as living examples of American values of democracy and capitalism. Moreover, the program enlisted foreign scholars and brought them to the United States so they would have opportunities to be directly inculcated into the American way of life.[75] Private programs similar in nature were offered by the Rockefeller and Ford Foundations.[76]

Dulles recognized that a peace treaty with Japan would not alone solve all the problems, nor would it be a panacea for U.S.-Japan relations in the post-treaty period. He believed that America's objectives could never be achieved just through signing a treaty (politics), stationing troops in Japan (security), or making trade agreements (economics). A "more continuous effort than is required in the usual bi-national program of relations" would be needed.[77] By a "continuous effort" he meant cultural interchange. The Japanese had to realize that the United States had a deep and continuing interest in their country, and that some of their basic values were shared by the United States and other free nations.[78] Dulles was convinced that a program of cultural interchange would serve this particular purpose.

Saxton E. Bradford, who was in charge of the State Department's U.S. Information and Education Service in the U.S. embassy in Tokyo, was in complete agreement with Dulles on the merits of cultural interchange. He defined his assignment as encouraging Japan "to develop her own form of government along non-totalitarian lines congenial to her people" and "to strive for as pattern of life which is consistent with the well-being of the Japanese and with the emergence of Japan as a peaceful member of the family of free nations." Therefore, he believed it was not his job to "advocate a democracy American in styles, or even Western in style, but one which is practicable in Japan."[79]

Bradford recognized that USIE programs would be limited if public programs alone were relied on to achieve U.S. objectives: "The Fulbright program just inaugurated, the Rockefeller survey with its promise of privately-financed cultural programs for the years ahead, the Grew Foundation, the International Christian University and the many other private efforts to create American-Japanese understanding and cooperation all have an important part to play."[80] Thus Bradford devised a variety of cultural activities to promote Japanese understanding of the United States.

In cooperation with Bradford, Dulles examined three methods for accomplishing the U.S. objective of cultural interchange:[81]

- *Method 1.* Persuade the Japanese by employing rational arguments and better information. This approach was thought to be useful, but its effectiveness was limited because not all people were entirely persuaded by rational arguments. Thus the first option was dropped from serious consideration.
- *Method 2.* Alter the political, social, and economic conditions in Japan that might foster a hostile attitude toward the United States. This method would require the implementation of a security system and economic conditions that would give the Japanese hope. It was grander in scale than the first method, but it would require more energy and resources from the United States. Dulles did not believe, however, that use of this method alone would be sufficient to keep the Japanese within the orbit of the free world, although U.S. assurance of Japan's security and economic recovery seemed indispensable.
- *Method 3.* Introduce other measures designed to change the culture-bound attitude of the Japanese and their subconscious motivations, something that could not be achieved by rational appeal.[82]

It was precisely the third method that Dulles thought should be adopted to make U.S.-Japan bilateral relations lasting. The focal point, of course, was on cultural relations.

John Rockefeller agreed with Dulles on the merits of cultural interchange. Rockefeller believed that the long-term relationship between Japan and the United States rested, in turn, on a combination of political, economic, and cultural relations. He broadly defined the term *culture* as relating to the life of a people as a whole—that is, covering their interests and activities other than in the fields of politics and business. It included the arts, sciences, philosophy, religion, entertainment, health, sports, literature, and education.[83] But, again, in his report on U.S.-Japan cultural relations submitted to Dulles in April 1951, he observed that "cultural interchange alone will not bring about stable and peaceful relations with Japan and the United States or other nations. Policies and actions in the economic and political fields will be equally important."[84] Robert Schwantes, a Japan specialist, was even more unequivocal and outspoken: "We cannot separate our cultural relations with Japan . . . from general goals of foreign policy."[85] More specifically, he found cultural relations with Japan particularly important in the ongoing struggle against communism.[86]

Race as an Underlining Factor in a Soft Peace

Race played an important role in helping both American and Japanese leaders define a "soft peace" and in harmonizing U.S.-Japan relations in the post-treaty years by putting Japan in the "proper place" of the postwar U.S. hegemonic project. Racial stereotypes and prejudices are the products of people and the times in which they live. Such stereotypes are used for many different reasons and purposes, depending on the issues at hand. Race was not the one and only determining factor of a soft peace, nor were American leaders fundamentally and incorrigibly racist. Rather, they made the best use of their racial thinking and perceptions of Self and Other in order to achieve their political ends.

Japan had made strenuous efforts to catch up with the West since the Meiji restoration, upholding the twin national goals of *fukoku kyōhei* (rich country and strong army) and *Datsu-A-nyū-Ō* (Quit Asia and join Europe). Meiji leaders such as Fukuzawa Yukichi, the founder of present-day Keiō University who advocated Westernization of the country, had a burning desire to have their country associate on an equal footing with the West. At the same time, they had only contempt for other Asians and a deep-rooted fear and distrust of the Soviet Union. By modernizing Japan, they sought to survive in what they perceived to be the internecine jungle in which the strong devoured the weak.

Dulles recognized that historically the Japanese wanted to be counted among the members of the Western world, but only if they were received on terms of approximate equality. At the Paris Peace Conference of 1919, Dulles had seen the Japanese struggle to achieve adoption of a racial equality clause in the Covenant of the League of Nations, but they had failed dismally. It was President Woodrow Wilson's "Fourteen Points" that had sparked Japanese agitation over the issue of racial equality in Japan. The Japanese were still smarting from the California legislation of 1913 that had banned Japanese residents in California from owning land in that state.[87]

Having witnessed what happened at Versailles in 1919, Yanagida Kunio, a pioneer in the study of Japanese folklore, harshly criticized the Japanese government for trying to achieve what was beyond its power—that is, placing Japanese on the same level as the white race of the world. At the same time, the Japanese folklorist charged his countrymen with having little interest in establishing solidarity with other Asians who had experienced racial discrimination similar to that faced by the Japanese. In fact, he blasted Japan's dishonesty in approaching the race issue, likening his country to a crow trying to closely associate itself with a peacock.[88]

Dulles shrewdly realized that the United States could achieve its objectives of co-opting Japan into the Western world as a junior partner by taking full advantage of such Japanese idiosyncrasies and double standards on race. He was disposed "to capitalize on the Japanese feeling of racial and social superiority to the Chinese, Koreans, and Russians, and to convince them that as part of the free world they would be in equal fellowship with a group which was superior to the members of the Communist world."[89] In a conversation with Sir Alvary Gascoigne, a political representative of the British Liaison Mission to SCAP, Dulles observed that the people of Japan had an intense desire to be treated as a full-fledged member of "an elite Anglo-Saxon Club."[90] Members the U.S. Council on Foreign Relations went so far as to say that the anti-American and anti-British attitudes found in Japan's recent past were rather exceptional and so were not really representative of Japan's true feelings. The formation of the 1902 Anglo-Japanese Alliance attested to that fact.[91]

Americans were aware that Japanese were particularly sensitive to the assumption that they were "backward" or "undeveloped," because Japanese felt that their own advancement was beyond the general levels of civilization in Asia. And yet most white Westerners believed the little Japanese were inferior to them in every physical, moral, and intellectual way. The problematic theory of social Darwinism which had become prevalent at the turn of the nineteenth century served to confirm their biases against nonwhite peoples. Among Americans, racist sentiments against the Japanese, along with paternalism and condescension, were widespread and often graphic. For example, in February 1945, a few weeks after being posted to the Pacific after years of covering the war in Europe, Ernie Pyle, the most admired of American war correspondents, told his millions of readers that "in Europe we felt that our enemies, horrible and deadly as they were, were still people. But out here I soon gathered that the Japanese were looked upon as something subhuman and repulsive, the way some people feel about cockroaches or mice." He went on to describe the Japanese prisoners of war: "They were wrestling and laughing and talking just like normal human beings, and yet they gave me the creeps, and I wanted a mental bath after looking at them."[92]

On this complex issue of racism and imperialism, Dulles and the Japanese, especially Japanese conservative elites such as Yoshida Shigeru, were not too far apart in the way they looked at the world. Frequently invoking the rhetoric of realism, both men shared the idea of racial hierarchy. They assumed that the whole world was made up of diverse peoples who were classified and stratified in racial terms. Dulles never questioned the superiority of the Anglo-Saxon "race"; perhaps he took it for granted that Anglo-Saxons were ensconced at the top of the racial hierarchy.

Japanese held a similar view toward foreigners, especially their Asian neighbors. Toward Europeans and Americans, the Japanese response was one of admiration as well as fear, mistrust, and hatred. Toward all others—that is, toward nonwhites, including Asians other than themselves—the Japanese attitude was as arrogant and contemptuous as the racism of the Westerners.[93] During the expansion of the Japanese empire in East Asia, the ideology of the emperor system had served to inculcate the mystique that the Japanese were unique and superior. They were the sons of the emperor, a living God on earth, and they had been charged with a special mission "to liberate other Asian brothers from the yoke of European-American imperialists" and create a Greater East Asia Co-Prosperity Sphere.[94] Under the U.S. occupation of Japan, however, Emperor Hirohito was "demystified" by means of his renunciation of divinity. As a result, the chain of racist thought surrounding the emperor ideology ought to have been critically scrutinized and discredited. And yet the U.S. government decided to retain the Japanese emperor system and use it to its advantage. Perhaps it is too much to expect people to change overnight their minds and their value systems about the emperor system simply because the emperor voiced the "declaration of humanity" (*ningen sengen*). Rather, it is reasonable to assume that nothing much changed, especially in the Japanese attitude toward their Asian neighbors.

Dulles believed that only if the Japanese felt they were equal to Westerners would Japan remain a member nation of the West. "If we persist in treating them [Japanese] as inferiors . . . and thus deny to them that sense of equality which they so ardently desire," warned Dulles, "the [peace] treaty will have been useless." With that in mind, he called for early abrogation of discriminatory immigration legislation in the United States as tangible evidence of the American will to treat the Japanese equally.[95] The year before, in 1950, Dulles had cautioned that "any failure of ours [to provide equal treatment] will only serve to drive the Japanese into the arms of the Soviets, for the Russians will offer equality." Dulles conceded that "it is true that this may be wishful thinking, but we have to take certain risks." It appeared to Dulles that it was "at least a good gamble" to take. "If properly handled, the Japanese can be brought to prefer association with the West to subservience to the Soviets," Dulles insisted.[96] Perhaps being overly obsessed with his commitment to fight against Soviet communism, Dulles used Japan's proclivity toward racism to America's fullest advantage and left it unquestioned when he negotiated a peace with the Japanese.

Japan's Alternative to the Proposed U.S. Peace Initiative

Immediately after the war, Japan suffered an acute shortage of leaders; the old leadership, be it military or civilian, was discredited by defeat and therefore gone. But various intellectuals stepped forward to comment on the U.S. peace proposals. Although everyone from academics to primary school teachers and university students claimed to be intellectuals, Japan's intellectuals, in the genuine sense of the term, were actually very small in number.[97] The significance of this finding is that intellectuals—university professors, professional writers, and thinkers—have long occupied a special place in Japan's neatly classified society.[98] They have regularly expressed their political convictions in Japan's reputable journals of opinion.[99]

The critical issues surrounding the proposed peace settlement stirred the flames of nationalism throughout Japan, especially among intellectuals.

From mid-1948 through 1952, Japanese intellectuals grappled with the contemporary problems of vital importance. They discussed the pressing questions of peaceful coexistence and Japan's independence and security in relation to the peace treaty with the United States and its allies and in relation to the rising nationalism in the neighboring Asian countries.

The Iwanami Publishing House played an important role in following and recording what intellectuals had to say about Japan's pressing problems. It also provided various scholars of various ideological persuasions with an opportunity to express their opinions freely. At the time of its first public appearance, *Sekai* was widely regarded as a liberal conservative periodical among the journals and magazines that made their debut after the war such as *Kindai bungaku, Tenbō, and Chōryū*.[100] From 1949 to 1952, Iwanami successively published special issues of *Sekai* featuring critical issues such as world peace and the proposed peace treaty.[101] In doing so, the House of Iwanami served as a "caretaker" in forming academic organizations such as Heiwa Mondai Danwakai (Peace Study Group).[102]

The Peace Study Group

In November 1948, Japanese scholars began serious discussions on peace by forming informal study groups in Tokyo and Kyoto. They responded to the call of the United Nations Educational, Scientific and Cultural Organization (UNESCO), which had put forth the proposition that war began in the minds of people. The UNESCO statement had been made public on July 13, 1948, by a group of eight world-famous social scientists, who, for the cause of peace, had appealed to the world to transcend differences in ideologies and socioeconomic systems.[103] On December 12, 1948, Japanese scholars held a plenary meeting in Tokyo and made the first of three statements on war and peace.[104] On the basis of the list of signers of the first statement, the Peace Study Group was formally organized in March 1949.[105]

The group held regular monthly meetings during the 1950s, at which it discussed the critical issue of peace and war until it dissolved in 1960.[106] The Peace Study Group was made up of Japan's leading intellectuals, young and old. They included philosophers Abe Yoshishige, Kuno Osamu, and Amano Teiyū (later minister of education); economists Ōuchi Hyōe, Yanaihara Tadao (later president of Tokyo University), Arisawa Hiromi, and Tsuru Shigeto; sociologists Shimizu Ikutarō and Tsurumi Kazuko; legal philosopher Tsunetō Kyō; social psychologist Minami Hiroshi; political scientists Maruyama Masao and Takagi Yasaka (also a historian); and historian Takeda Kiyoko.[107]

As the issue of a peace settlement for Japan attracted ever-greater public attention in the fall of 1949, scholars of the Peace Study Group hotly debated whether Japan should settle on a *zenmen kōwa* (complete and overall peace), or whether the country should conclude a *tandoku kōwa* (separate peace) with the United States and its allies from which it would exclude the Soviet Union and China. On January 15, 1950, the Peace Study Group issued its second statement, "Kōwa mondai" (The problem of the peace settlement for Japan). In the statement, which was signed by fifty-six prominent scholars, the Peace Study Group announced the following four principles, which they considered irrefutable:

1. Japan must achieve a complete and overall peace.
2. Japan must refuse to make a partial or separate peace settlement, because it would sever normal relations with China and other countries and could lead to Japan's economic dependence or subjugation to a specific country (implying the United States).
3. On constitutional grounds, Japan's "inviolable neutrality" and its membership into the United Nations are the only option for security.
4. No country should be allowed to keep military bases in Japan on a permanent basis.[108]

The scholars insisted that the complete and overall peace would surely pave the way for the peaceful coexistence of "the two worlds," believing that there would be no complete and overall peace without neutrality, because the denial of neutrality meant the denial of the possibility of the complete and overall peace.[109]

Of course, both the government in Washington and the one in Tokyo found the four principles incompatible with the line of policy under which the peace settlement was being negotiated. As a result, both political pressure and harsh criticism were directed at the members of the Peace Study Group, one after another, but the scholars held firm.[110] Against the backdrop of formulating those four principles, Japanese intellectuals felt deep regret that they were not able to prevent the Pacific war. Now they were more firmly determined than ever to avoid repeating the same mistake.[111] Maruyama Masao, a leading political scientist, called the group of scholars who shared the profound regret *kaikon kyōdōtai* (community of remorse), and he argued that it existed in Japan only temporarily after the war.[112] The group's pacifist sentiment, fed by actual fear of war as well as fear of trade stagnation, was coupled with reluctance to be hurried by the United States into a military alliance.[113] The scholars maintained that any military agreement militated against the spirit of the preamble and Article 9 of Japan's constitution and that any military arrangement would contribute toward the ruination of Japan and the world.[114] The intellectuals of the Peace Study Group were so deeply committed to pacifism and antimilitarism that pacifism and neutrality seemed to them the only practical way out for Japan. Without losing momentum, the House of Iwanami published the October 1951 special issue of *Sekai* on the subject of "Kōwa mondai" (The problem of the peace). It sold like hotcakes—about 150,000 copies.[115]

In September 1950, three months after the outbreak of the Korean War and exactly one year before conclusion of the peace treaty with Japan, the scholars of the Peace Study Group issued their third statement, "Mitabi heiwa nitsuite" (On the problem of peace for the third time).[116] Even though the Japanese government flatly rejected the idea of peaceful coexistence as being unrealistic and nonsensical and therefore unworthy of serious consideration, the third statement challenged the common sense of the day and suggested that there was a strong possibility that peaceful coexistence was a realistic way to lessen the tension between East and West. The third statement made it clear that the problem of ideological conflict and that of confrontation between nation-states were of a different order. Thus, the Peace Study Group insisted, it was a gross error to treat the two problems, ideological conflict and confrontation between nation-states, on the same level when the issue of peace was discussed. Scholars of the Peace Study Group took the view that the cold war was not entirely an ideological conflict; rather, it was a conflict arising from the differences in national interests. They believed that, unlike in an ideological conflict, nation-states could find some room to compromise with each other in negotiations so long as they dealt with national interests, even though conflicting national interests might appear irreconcilable. By placing an equal emphasis, the third statement proposed that Japan adopt a policy of unarmed neutrality, like a new nation born again after the war.

Other Views

Nambara Shigeru, the president of Tokyo University and considered to be a scholar of independent thought, insisted that neutralism was essential to Japan because it had no defense forces and needed trade with Asia in order to live.[117] More specifically, he argued that Japan must trade with China or perish and that a separate peace settlement without the concurrence of the Soviet Union and China was dangerous. According to Nambara, the Soviet

Union and China could maintain a peaceful relationship, from which Japan would be able to secure the benefits of trade and access to raw materials without endangering its independence or security. He urged the United States to make adequate efforts to reach some sort of agreement with the Soviet Union.[118]

Matsumoto Shigeharu, a journalist and lawyer, also insisted that the United States not attempt to make a peace treaty without inviting the Soviet Union and China to the negotiating table. He argued as well that perpetuation of the U.S. military presence should be avoided at all cost. He called permanent bases "garrison points."[119]

With their earnest pacifism and the memory of the scourge of war still fresh in their minds, the Japanese took an ambivalent attitude toward the critical issue of rearmament that the United States seemed to be pushing. For most of them, rearming their country had many negative connotations, such as a return to militarism, the police state, higher taxes, and higher prices; a loss of foreign markets and sources; a provocation for external attack; and a hidden American occupation. Many Japanese recognized that independence required some rearmament, but rearmament was too heavy an economic burden for them to bear. Therefore, the general attitude about the issue of rearmament could be summed up as "better to let America do it—and pay all the costs."[120]

American experts on Japan such as Charles Fahs of the Rockefeller Foundation did not share the views of the Peace Study Group on the issue of peace and war, although Fahs was impressed with idealism and honesty of Japanese scholars such as Nambara.[121] Nor did Rockefeller and Dulles understand the genuine desire of the Japanese for neutralism. Dulles firmly believed that Japan could neither hide in neutrality nor isolate itself from the worldwide struggle against Soviet-centered communist aggression. He insisted that there was not much promise in a policy of "neutralism," as many Japanese advocated.[122] Niles W. Bond, a diplomat in the U.S. embassy in Tokyo, also emphasized the same point in a USIE country paper on Japan when he argued that "the role of ostrich would be fatal" for Japan.[123] The USIE paper contended that the people of Japan had to understand that the peace treaty they wanted was possible only in a world in which the balance of power was on the free side. A USIE confidential memorandum called for Japan to actively cooperate with the free world in collective defense efforts. In return, the same memorandum added, the United States would do everything it could to guarantee Japan a respected place among nations.[124]

In 1952, in addition to the peace treaty that constituted the "soft peace," the United States concluded a bilateral security treaty with Japan that called for the ongoing presence of U.S. military forces in that country. Dulles clearly understood that the presence of American forces in Japan would serve the following purposes. First, the U.S. military presence would not only forestall the development of a power vacuum in Japan, but also work as a deterrent and protect that country from an external attack.[125] Second, the U.S. military presence would keep Japan dependent on an American military shield and restrain the Japanese from engaging in reckless behavior. After all, many people did not believe that the occupation of Japan had instilled in the Japanese a true spirit of democracy and international cooperation. The U.S. military presence was also thought to be the only feasible way to keep Japan's future military potential under control, and it would lead to the incorporation of Japan in the free world's Pacific security arrangements. Third, the U.S. military presence in Japan would serve as an insurance policy for the United States and Asian countries. It would help to diminish any fears raised by the steps taken by that country to secure its own defenses and thus help to quiet the fears of those Asian countries that had suffered from Japanese militarism. Asian countries had every reason to worry about a resurgence of militarism in Japan, and some of them feared a rebirth of Japan's economic domination and exploitation as well, because Japan was still widely regarded as an aggressive nation.[126] In Dulles's view, the U.S.-Japan security treaty was designed in part to control a potentially "berserk" Japan by keeping the country from running amok in Asia both then and in the future.

Of course, Dulles considered U.S. policy toward Japan to be part of the larger U.S. policy of building up the political, economic, and military security of the Asia-Pacific area. He regarded the U.S. military presence in Japan as one important means of helping Japan continue to develop as a democratic and peaceful nation.[127] He understood as well that the objective of the U.S. military presence in Japan was to prevent Japan from falling prey to Soviet-centered communism by incorporating that country politically and economically in the free world.[128]

The Peace and Security Treaties with Japan as "Consensual Contracts"

In 1952 the two treaties finally signed in San Francisco in September 1951 —the Treaty of Peace between Japan and the Allied powers and the separate security treaty between Japan and the United States—went into force. A hegemonic order, whose main feature is consensus rather than coercion, functions mainly by consent between the hegemon and the lesser powers in accordance with universalistic principles. In seeking cooperation from the lesser powers to keep world order, "the dominant power makes certain concessions or compromises to secure the acquiescence of lesser power to an order that can be expressed in terms of a general interest."[129] In concluding a security treaty with Japan (the lesser power), the United States (the hegemon) made power arrangements with Japan so that Japan would remain in the orbit of the West to fight communism. In doing so, the United States "generously" made a variety of concessions and compromises to Japan in order to persuade the Japanese into accepting such a bilateral agreement. Postwar Japan and the United States shared many common interests and objectives under the aegis of America's liberal capitalist world order. Most essential among the shared interests was survival. For Japan, survival meant maintaining its physical security; for the United States, it meant keeping peace and order in East Asia.

As for specific features of the "soft peace" represented by the peace treaty, one example was Article 14, which waived Japan's reparations. The article recognized that the resources of Japan were not sufficient if it was to maintain a viable economy, make complete reparation for all the damage and suffering it had caused, and at the same time meet its other obligations.[130] The article therefore permitted Japan to reconstruct its economy and the nation. The United States felt that every resource available was needed to build a strong Japan that would function as a bulwark against communism and serve as a stabilizing force in the Far East, which, of course, served the American strategic interest in East Asia as well. Article 14 demonstrated clearly that "the dominant power makes certain concessions or compromises to secure the acquiescence of lesser power to an order" that the hegemonic nation seeks to maintain.

Another feature of the "soft peace" was Article 5 of the peace treaty. This article stipulated that the Allied powers recognized that Japan was a sovereign nation possessing the inherent right of individual or collective self-defense. Thus both in theory and in practice, the article enabled Japan to conclude a security treaty with the United States—-that is, the article made it possible for the United States, with the "desire" and by the consent of the government of Japan, to maintain and dispose U.S. armed forces in and about Japan.

To be sure, the San Francisco arrangement with Japan was not entirely a one-sided imposition produced by U.S. arm-twisting; it was a contract based on mutual agreement. Appealing to and counting on Japan's self-interest and the Japanese sense of reason, the United States presented the government of Japan with a set of options from which Tokyo had to choose, although there was little room for the Japanese to make a free choice in view of the roiling international circumstances at that time. The important point here is that Washington took the trouble to persuade the Japanese and to let Tokyo choose, within limits, the course of its own history. This kind of tactfulness represented one of the essential features of American diplomacy of a hegemonic nature.

Although the United States saw a peace treaty as a worthy goal, it considered a security pact the foundation for future relations between the United States and Japan. Both the peace and the security treaties were considered to be one unit of the power arrangement between the United States and Japan. In undertaking such an arrangement, the United States retained most of the important rights and privileges that Washington had gained from Tokyo during the U.S. occupation. When John Foster Dulles arrived in Tokyo in January 1951 to discuss the terms of a peace settlement, he spoke generously in public, describing Japan as a "party to be consulted," not a nation to be "dictated by victors." In private, however, he told aides that the principal question to be answered was "do we get the right to station as many troops as we want where we want and for as long as we want or do we not?"[131] Indeed, Washington succeeded in retaining a U.S. military base system on Japanese soil. The Japanese, by contrast, chose to swallow the bitter pill at San Francisco. In fact, that was the reality of American "generosity" and soft power.

To be more specific, in order to fight communism the United States realized it had to bolster ties with Japan, place U.S.-Japan relations on a durable basis, and, equally important, keep satisfying Japanese needs for years to come. Indeed, the communist giants made tempting offers to Japan such as territorial concessions, relaxed fishing restrictions, and access to Siberian and Mainland China development. American concessions to Japan thus had to be far more attractive than anything the Soviet Union or China might offer. In other words, if Japan was to remain firmly aligned with the United States, not only should the United States provide Japan with a military shield for its defense, but also U.S. trade policy should give Japan access to a fair and reasonable share of the vitally important U.S. market. And the United States needed to exert its influence to open markets of other industrial countries to Japan on a nondiscriminatory basis.

No one knew how expensive it would eventually become to co-opt Japan at that time, but history shows that the ultimate cost of co-optation is bound to rise whatever form payment might take.[132] Astute American policy makers looked beyond the immediate cost of co-optation policy, however, and focused on the long-range interests of the United States and the positive side of co-optation policy. According to their logic, Japan's continued dependence on security and trade, particularly with the United States, would give America considerable leverage in relation to Japan. Not only was the strategic position of Japan as one of the four major industrial complexes in the world important, but also the U.S. military base structure on Japan's soil would make it possible for the United States to deploy U.S. forces in proximity to the area of threat. At the same time, the U.S. government looked at Japan more broadly after the war, not from the perspective of the U.S.-Japan bilateral relations alone, but from the wider view of the whole world system. As one American observer commented, "Our relations with Japan can now be placed in a broader framework than was ever possible before World War II. What really counts is Japan's relation to the free world, not exclusive ties to the United States."[133]

But there should be no mistake or confusion about U.S. motives and "generosity" in light of the harsh reality of world politics at that time.[134] American "generosity" was codified in the peace and security treaties in the context of real U.S. concerns about Japan's political and geopolitical inclinations toward independence and neutralism. Despite the enticements offered by the United Sates, it must have been hard for the Japanese to swallow the U.S-Japan security arrangement, because the peace and security treaties represented an unequal power arrangement that the United States practically imposed on the Japanese. In fact, American "generosity" came at a severe cost. It was symbolized, for example, by American retention of the U.S. military garrison system on Japanese soil and of direct control in Okinawa—not only of the military bases but also in the form of a variety of sacrifices that were inexorably forced on the people in Okinawa.

Ten years after the San Francisco peace treaty was concluded, Japanese prime minister Ikeda Hayato was reminded in the strongest terms by Secretary of State Dean Rusk that the United States considered its alliance with Japan "as utterly fundamental, not based on philanthropy or amiability but essential to the United States in its own defense and in relation to the defense of the Free World."[135] In other words, it can be argued that Okinawa was the price paid for American "generosity."[136]

To recapitulate, the United States had a clear vision of the need to reconstruct and maintain a liberal capitalist order in East Asia after the war. Soon after the war, however, Washington discovered that the Soviet Union and Communist China were vehemently opposed to the American hegemonic project. The U.S. government was concerned about the weakness and vulnerability in the Far East, particularly about local hostilities in Korea, Vietnam, and the tension-ridden Taiwan Straits area. In addition, it was concerned about the weaknesses in Japan's social and political structure. With the onslaught of the cold war in Asia, which was dramatized by the outbreak of the Korean War in 1950, American leaders such as Acheson, Dulles, Kennan, and others came to the full realization that it was in the interest of the United States and the free world to stimulate Japan's resurgence as a major Far Eastern power and that a U.S. military base system would be needed to serve as a point of strength for fighting communism. With single-minded determination, the United States decided to squarely confront the communist countries and prevent the communist influence from spreading throughout East Asia. To do so, Washington chose to build up Japan and accelerate its development as a major Far Eastern power.

Chapter 4

John D. Rockefeller III in Tokyo: Cultural Exchange versus Cultural Imperialism

> Institutions will be primarily Japanese in leadership . . . so that they will not be subject to a charge of American cultural imperialism.
>
> —Charles B. Fahs, 1951

> If too much emphasis is placed on one side of the picture, we are faced with the problem of cultural imperialism.
>
> —John D. Rockefeller III, 1952

On January 22, 1951, President Harry Truman dispatched the Dulles Peace Mission to Japan; it was headed by John Foster Dulles, Truman's special representative.[1] The purpose of this presidential delegation was to lay the groundwork with Gen. Douglas MacArthur and the Japanese for a peace treaty to be concluded between Japan and the nations directly involved in the war against the Empire of Japan. The peace treaty would signal the end of the occupation and therefore the rationale for having American troops and bases in Japan. The U.S. State Department responded to this situation by suggesting that the peace treaty be accompanied or followed by a mutual security treaty that would allow an American military presence in Japan under much better conditions than occupation.[2] The suggestion was, in part, a compromise solution to satisfy the U.S. Department of Defense.

Dulles was quoted as saying that he regarded the peace treaty as only the starting point in U.S.-Japan relations. He believed the treaty would be valid and effective as long as the relations between the Americans and Japanese were good and as long as the relations between the two countries continued to develop and strengthen. Only then could the peace treaty have lasting meaning.[3] Because he was trying hard to develop a treaty that would be fair, workable, and enduring, he placed a high premium on cultural relations in such a broad context.[4]

In early December 1950, Dulles had asked Rockefeller if he would be interested in going to Japan as a member of the Dulles Peace Mission.[5] Dulles, who had been a trustee of the Rockefeller Foundation since 1935 and who was appointed chair of the board of trustees in 1950, served the Rockefeller Foundation until he became President Dwight Eisenhower's secretary of state in 1953. While working for the foundation, Dulles and the younger Rockefeller (by eighteen years) saw a great deal of each other, and so an affectionate relationship sprang up between them.[6] Dulles characterized his peace mission to Japan as unique in the history of peace missions, because one of its members was specifically charged with finding ways to promote cultural and educational cooperation.[7] Indeed, Dulles invited Rockefeller to join the mission as a consultant on cultural affairs so that the Japanese might understand that the United States was not thinking entirely in military and economic terms, but also hoping to strengthen long-range cultural relations between the two countries.[8] In his view, the appointment of Rockefeller would reduce the emphasis on the military side of his mission by broadening the basis of the peace delegation.[9]

Rockefeller seemed to be the perfect choice, because he was known as a philanthropist keenly interested in the Far East and educational and cultural programs. He was thus charged with responsibility for the cultural, educational, and informational aspects of U.S.-Japan relations. Rockefeller was the eldest of the five sons of John D. Rockefeller Jr. Since his boyhood, he had been frail, excessively serious, almost pathologically shy and self-conscious, and overburdened with a sense of responsibility. In his long struggle to overcome these handicaps and liberate himself from his father's domineering influence, Rockefeller had been looking for the right outlet for his energy, ideas, and enthusiasm.[10] The Dulles Peace Mission to Japan seemed to be just the right outlet, and so he accepted the post with zest.

Among the American specialists on Japan Rockefeller consulted prior to his departure for Tokyo were Charles Fahs, new director of the Humanities Division of the Rockefeller Foundation, and Edwin O. Reischauer, associate professor of Japanese history at Harvard.[11] Rockefeller was particularly impressed with Fahs, who, he noted, had "an amazing fund of knowledge about Japan and a very imaginative approach in relation to his assignment."[12] Reischauer gave Rockefeller a list of people whom he thought Rockefeller should contact in Japan.[13]

Rockefeller also spent four days in Washington consulting with high-ranking government officials on his assignment. They included Secretary of State Dean Acheson, Dulles, Assistant Secretary of State for Far Eastern Affairs Dean Rusk, and other Far Eastern experts in the State Department such as Joseph C. Grew, former American ambassador to Japan, and John K. Emmerson, planning adviser in the Bureau of Far Eastern Affairs.[14] As background for his planning, they briefed Rockefeller on the types of assistance the State Department had already given to binational cultural centers, primarily in Latin America.[15] Dulles then explained that Rockefeller had two important assignments in Tokyo: "the matter of the transition to State from SCAP" in cultural operations in Japan and the "long-range projects" of U.S.-Japan cultural relations.[16] Rockefeller felt that to fulfill those challenging assignments he would badly need "the wholehearted and active support" of Dulles.[17] Meanwhile, Dulles gave him carte blanche, telling to make of his assignments whatever he wanted.[18]

Rockefeller recognized that the Civil Information and Education Section of SCAP had already undertaken much work in the educational and cultural field. But he regretted that it had all been on U.S. initiative. Rockefeller believed it was important to emphasize the two-way nature of the cultural relationship—that is, how both countries could benefit from it. He also realized that the success of such an effort depended on ongoing support by the Japanese.[19] Rockefeller deplored the fact that the CI&E targets had been too vague and general and that they had missed the intellectuals and many of the younger leaders in Japan. He thus decided to adopt the approach of talking "primarily with Japanese—to find out from them their ideas as to such relationship."[20]

Settling into Toyko

On January 22, 1951, the Dulles party left Washington for Tokyo on a specially fitted out military air transport plane, a Constellation, provided by the U.S. government for the mission. The trip was quite long (sixty-three hours and fifteen minutes) because of strong head winds, but not unpleasant. Rockefeller described the flight as a two-and-a-half-day house party.[21] Upon their arrival at Haneda Airport in Tokyo on January 25, the American delegation was greeted by General and Mrs. MacArthur and a very large group of newsmen. It was Rockefeller's third visit to Japan—his earlier trips were in 1929 and 1947. Rockefeller was to stay in Tokyo about a month, until February 22.

On the morning after their arrival, the members of the peace mission went right to work. All of them made a courtesy call on MacArthur in his office in the Dai Ichi Building. Among other things, they talked about the plans for treaty discussions with the Japanese. All who were present at the meeting were very much impressed by the general—with his knowledge of the problem, his forthright and hard-hitting approach, his clarity and forcefulness of expression, and his devotion to his assignment.[22]

Rockefeller received considerable publicity from the press during his stay in Japan. His popularity was explained by the fact that not only was he a member of the Dulles mission, but also his name was well known to the Japanese through the extensive work of the Rockefeller Foundation in Japan and the Far East. Although the Japanese directed their interest primarily toward the political, economic, and security aspects of the Japanese peace settlement in the work of the Dulles mission, they paid just as much, if not more, attention to Rockefeller's task of building a U.S.-Japan cultural exchange.[23]

But the American visitor soon learned that the Japanese had built up excessive expectations about the help they might receive from the Rockefeller Foundation.[24] For example, Yamamoto Yūzō, one of Japan's most distinguished novelists and a member of the House of Councilors, put in a plea to Rockefeller for a fellowship program that would take Japanese students to the United States at an early stage in their studies and for long terms of study.[25] Rockefeller explained to the Japanese press that the purpose of his visit was to learn more about ways in which the Japanese would like to develop and strengthen long-range cultural relations between the United States and Japan.[26] The press warmly welcomed Rockefeller's initiative in the field of cultural interchange. Most Japanese editorials stressed the desirability of nurturing shared values in order to promote the friendship of the two peoples across the Pacific. They not only expressed appreciation of America's material achievements, but also recognized that the Japanese needed to be acquainted with the "spiritual assets" of the United States.

Rockefeller was assigned to the difficult but important task of achieving both a short-term objective and a long-range goal during his month-long stay in Japan. The short-term objective was to facilitate a smooth and orderly transition of cultural relations programs from SCAP/CI&E to the State Department's U.S. Information and Education Service.[27] Responsibility for administering the cultural activities of CI&E was to be transferred to USIE after Japan won independence.[28] In Washington, two separate offices, the Office of International Information (OII) and the Office of Educational Exchange (OEX), were established in the State Department in 1948.[29] Known jointly as USIE, the two offices began to oversee U.S. cultural foreign policy that year. It was understood that the services of USIE would begin no later than March 1952, one month before the peace treaty was to go into effect.[30] The long-range goal for Rockefeller was to lay the foundation for the institutionalization of a cultural interchange that would promote mutual understanding between Japan and the United States in the post-treaty years.

Rockefeller and the Cultural Offensive

The U.S. State Department separately dispatched Saxton E. Bradford from Washington to work with Rockefeller in Tokyo.[31] There, Bradford assumed the position of head of the Public Affairs Office of the Diplomatic Section in the U.S. embassy. Both Rockefeller and Bradford were keenly aware that after the conclusion of the peace treaty USIE could depend on nothing more than the power of persuasion.[32] By contrast, CI&E had the advantage of working in the context of the enforceable power of the military occupation.

Bradford recognized that radio programs, publications, motion pictures, information centers, book translations, exchange programs, and the use of American teachers might be the usual standard USIE activities, but he believed that the success of USIE would depend instead on how well the Americans were able to convince the Japanese themselves to spread American ideas.[33] The American Studies program abroad (as discussed in detail in the chapters that follow) was another important aspect of the USIE cultural program. "American Studies Conferences" were held in several countries to acquaint foreign educators and others with American history, culture, and institutions. The Program for Foreign Newsmen brought journalists to the United States for a few months so they could serve as working members of American newspaper staffs. Meanwhile, the Voice of America was being broadcast over thirty-six transmitters in twenty-five languages.[34] By fiscal year 1952, the appropriations for the USIE program was $85 million and its total personnel numbered just over 12,000, some 850 of whom were American officers stationed at Foreign Service posts abroad.[35]

Many Japanese expressed concern about the possibility of American cultural exchange programs coming to an end with the termination of the occupation and the conclusion of a peace treaty. Indeed, Rockefeller discovered that many Japanese had enjoyed using the CI&E cultural facilities during the military occupation (see Chapter 1). The poor state of Japanese public libraries spoke for itself. The Public Library of Kyoto Prefecture, for example, had a sizable but completely out-of-date collection, because it had received no new American or European books for ten years and few new Japanese ones.[36] Donald Nugent, the CI&E chief, found the Japanese very apprehensive; they feared the United States might abandon them after they attained sovereignty. In one place, forty thousand signatures were collected protesting such action when rumors circulated that the CI&E centers would close.[37] The U.S. government, however, had no intention of closing all the libraries after the termination of the military occupation—a viewpoint echoed by Dorothy R. Ward, cultural information program officer of the State Department: "We cannot simply close the doors and leave." Whatever their thinking, it was disclosed that the information centers were soon converted to bilateral operations—that is, the books, building, and staff were turned over to the Japanese for administration.[38]

While Bradford and USIE were acquainting themselves with issues such as libraries, Rockefeller was meeting scores of important people, including Emperor Hirohito. On February 4, 1951, for example, John and Blanchette Rockefeller attended a duck netting party as guests of the emperor (guests netted ducks that they then cooked over a charcoal fire at their table). The Rockefellers found the netting "rather amusing but not very sporting."[39] Matsudaira Yasumasa, grand master of ceremonies of the Imperial Household, hosted the party.

On a more serious note, Rockefeller exchanged views with leaders in virtually every important domain of Japanese life and culture. These leaders included Prime Minister Yoshida Shigeru; Kabayama Aisuke, chair of the Grew Scholarship Foundation, and Kanō Hisaakira, president of the Society for International Cultural Relations. Later, these Japanese would become instrumental in institutionalizing the U.S.-Japan cultural interchange. Rockefeller also met with Japanese intellectual leaders. They included Nambara Shigeru, president of Tokyo University; Torigai Risaburō, president of Kyoto University; Takagi Yasaka, the father of American Studies in Japan; Rōyama Masamichi, a political scientist; Tsurumi Yūsuke, a novelist and an Institute of Pacific Relations member; his son Tsurumi Shunsuke, a Harvard graduate and author of *A Cultural History of Postwar Japan, 1945–1980;* and Tsurumi's daughter Tsurumi Kazuko, a Vassar and Princeton graduate.[40] (The American perceptions of Japanese intellectuals are described in Chapter 5.) Rockefeller also renewed his acquaintance with Matsumoto Shigeharu, a lawyer he had met at the third Institute of Pacific Relations conference held in Kyoto in 1929.[41] He and his Japanese friends discussed a wide range of subject matters that included, of course, the general character of cultural interchange programs between the two countries in the post-treaty period.

In his diary, Rockefeller detailed his activities in Tokyo, including how he approached Japanese. He noted that he was mainly operating on his own, "first seeing a lot of Japanese, trying to get a sense of what their feeling was, what the prospects were for the future; and having done this, beginning talks with them in terms of what steps might be initiated in order to bring our peoples closer together in a positive fashion.... The ... weeks I was there were [spent]getting background, developing my own thinking and preparing recommendation to Dulles."[42] Thus the incubation process for institutionalizing U.S.-Japan cultural relations got under way. In this sense, Rockefeller took an important step toward developing cultural interchange between Japan and the United States.

Cultural Interchange

The concept of cultural interchange, a fairly new one in the field of foreign relations, reflected the growing participation of private citizens in the field of foreign affairs and the rapid development in mass communications since the end of World War II. The object of cultural interchange was "the totality of the beliefs, attitudes, and opinions of the whole population."[43] It facilitated the exchange of knowledge between nations and dealt with the problem of trying to influence a population's attitudes so that its political behavior might change. Thus cultural interchange was not an end in itself. In the case of the United States and Japan, it was generally thought to serve four major purposes: (1) to broaden the bridge of understanding between the two countries; (2) to enrich and strengthen each culture; (3) to develop intelligent, talented persons by giving scholars from each country access to unique resources in the other; and (4) to bring together capable people from both cultures for the joint study of basic common problems.[44]

Rockefeller believed that cultural interchange was essential to world peace, because it helped to make the peoples of different countries more aware of their common origins. He recognized that cultural relations might not in themselves make peace, but that one could not envision peace without them. In his opinion, a sound and enduring relationship between countries had to be based on shared values. It was posited that broadening the community of interest among nations and peoples would lead to the establishment of a world order and the assurance of international peace and stability. Indeed, Rockefeller regarded cultural interchange as an effort to "regain a world order in which all nations were free to pursue their own conceptions of common goals, free to pursue their own destinies."[45]

The chief of the State Department's Division of Exchange of Persons, Francis J. Colligan, held a similar view. He found that kind of community of interest the "psychological groundwork upon which a stable order among free men can be achieved."[46] Japan expert Robert Schwantes joined the chorus: "Only so far as two peoples find a community of interest on basic questions will they be able to experience the rich and psychological rewards of cultural amity."[47]

Dulles, too, recognized the importance of cultural interchange; it was to create mutual understanding and respect between the peoples involved. For him, mutual understanding meant mutual respect for one another's way of life, culture, and achievement; mutual sympathy with one another's problems; and a friendly, trusting relationship. He hoped that through cultural interchange the peoples of Japan and the United States would have a sympathetic appreciation and understanding of the desires, thoughts, ideas, and aspirations of each other and of their respective ways of life.[48] Thus American leaders believed that shared values were a key concept in cultural interchange: "there is no basis for cooperative activity if no values are shared."[49]

Donald Nugent also stressed the significance of cultural interchange. The CI&E chief wrote Rockefeller, "I am convinced that this sharing of intellectual and cultural resources will be of as much importance as the sharing of economic resources and technical know-how.... Perhaps it will be of even more importance in the long run to the solidarity of the free nations."[50] Milton Eisenhower, who was President Dwight Eisenhower's brother and a distinguished university president in his own right, would have agreed with Nugent had he met him in person. Eisenhower was quoted as saying that "economic cooperation, political cooperation, and military cooperation may break down under the strain of crisis unless there is much more than superficial understanding of one another's cultures, problems, and aspirations."[51]

The Three Principles of Cultural Interchange

Rockefeller believed cultural interchange had to be based on three principles: (1) the concept of the two-way street; (2) the idea of a joint collaborative enterprise by the two nations involved; (3) public and private coordination and cooperation.

The Concept of the "Two-Way Street"

The concept of the two-way street in the field of cultural relations was basically the principle of reciprocity.[52] Rockefeller believed that Japanese culture had much to offer in its own right. In 1929, as he participated in a conference of the Institute of Pacific Relations in Kyoto, the young Rockefeller had come to appreciate the culture of Japan while wandering around Kyoto's temples and shrines. He had particularly found comfort in the ceremonial understatement of the Oriental character.[53] He thus hoped that Japan would contribute as well as receive in the two-way street of the cultural interchange from which both countries would benefit.

Rockefeller also believed that the United States needed to reexamine its image of Japan more thoroughly. In his opinion, it was not sufficient to see Japan primarily as a bulwark against communism. That kind of negative approach would antagonize the Japanese and cause even conservatives to believe that Americans were placing too much emphasis on the communist threat and therefore too much stress on essentially defensive, negative measures.[54] The success of U.S.-Japan cultural projects depended, he stressed, on mutual respect and the full and voluntary cooperation of the Japanese, which were essential in the two-way process of cultural exchange.[55]

Rockefeller favored the idea of the two-way street for different reasons as well. First, he believed it would provide a safeguard against "cultural imperialism"—that is, the use of culture as an arm of government to extend the government's national power, to rationalize its policies, and to justify its fundamental ideology.[56] A two-way exchange of culture would minimize the danger that Americans would be accused of being cultural imperialists. Rockefeller maintained that historically cultural exchange tended to become predominantly a one-way street primarily for the purpose of serving political objectives. "If too much emphasis is placed on one side of the picture," he remarked, "we are faced with the problem of cultural imperialism."[57] Rockefeller foresaw that the dominant political and economic position of the United States in relation to Japan might well raise fears among the Japanese that the United States might attempt to assert cultural dominance.[58] In other words, every effort should be made to prevent U.S.-Japan cultural relations from becoming predominantly a form of American cultural promotion in Japan.

The second reason Rockefeller favored the two-way street approach is that he feared that the latent xenophobia of the Japanese might manifest itself in an artificially stimulated and undesirable resurgence of Japanism as a reaction to the "over-Westernization" of the country if the cultural stream then flowing from America to Japan was not accompanied by some complementary outflow from that country. Cultural endeavors should never allow themselves to become "unilateral and patronizing," Rockefeller argued.[59] "Such imperialism would in the long run be as unfortunate for ourselves as for Japan."[60] Harold G. Henderson, a professor at Columbia University and a member of Council on Foreign Relations Study Group on American Cultural Relations with Japan, concurred: "If we try to influence the Japanese from above, they will resent it. We must genuinely feel an equality and be ready to learn as well as to teach."[61]

Tact was the third reason Rockefeller emphasized the idea of the two-way street. He was aware that the Japanese were basically proud, sensitive people, who required a great deal of tact. Rockefeller also learned that in the hundred-year history of U.S.-Japan relations, the feelings of national inferiority that the Japanese held toward the United States had been exacerbated by the long history of racial discrimination against American citizens of Japanese ancestry living on the U.S. West Coast. In more recent years, the Japanese had been humiliated by the defeat in war, and their pride had been hurt by the prolonged military censorship and control under the military occupation.[62] Extremely sensitive to the American assumption of superiority, the Japanese had held ambivalent feelings toward the United States ever since Commodore Mathew Perry's visit to their country a century earlier.

One episode especially ruffled Japanese feathers in their ambivalent feelings toward the United States. On May 5, 1951, in his remarks before hearings of the U.S. Senate Committees on Armed Services and on Foreign Relations, Gen. Douglas MacArthur said: "If the Anglo-Saxon was say 45 years of age in his development, in the sciences, the arts, divinity, culture, the Germans were quite mature. The Japanese, however, in spite of their antiquity measured by time, were in a very tuitionary condition. Measured by the standards of modern civilization, they would be like a boy of twelve as compared with our development of 45 years."[63] In other words, the retiring American general equated the mentality of the Japanese adult with that of a twelve-year old American.[64] Although the Japanese had respected MacArthur and regarded him as their benefactor, his less than careful remark tarnished his reputation to an immeasurable degree. Indeed, his comment has been described as *hyaku-nichi no seppō he hitotsu* (one hour's cold will spoil seven years' warming).[65] To the present day, historians and others have interpreted MacArthur's statement as an expression of his innately patronizing and condescending view of the Japanese rooted in racism.

In view of this situation, Rockefeller, who was back in the United States when MacArthur made his comments, reasoned that nothing would more effectively appeal to Japanese pride and redress their injured feelings than the fact that foreigners appreciated and respected their culture. Indeed, for Rockefeller mutual respect was "the soundest basis for mutual understanding and cooperation" in U.S.-Japan cultural relations: "We should make it known to the Japanese that there is a definite and increasing interest among Americans in the culture of Japan.... A realization on the part of Japan that such interest and understanding does exist will have a strong psychological influence upon them."[66] W. Phillips Davidson, a representative of the Rand Corporation and a member of the Council on Foreign Relations Study Group on American Cultural Relations with Japan over which Rockefeller presided, expressed his positive view of the concept of the two-way street in a different way. He was aware that the Japanese did not necessarily have a high opinion of American culture, and so he remarked concisely: "Perhaps a good way to convince the Japanese of the high level of our culture is to appreciate Japanese culture."[67]

Rockefeller discovered that the Japanese liked the idea of a two-way process of cultural interchange. Chief Justice Tanaka Kōtarō, who was highly respected by Japanese as a sound thinker and a man of great personal integrity, endorsed the idea wholeheartedly. In his article "Cultural Interchange between Japan and the United States," the chief justice criticized Japan's prewar official cultural promotion as high-pressure salesmanship to enhance Japan's national prestige by attempting to demonstrate Japan's cultural superiority. He admitted that the Japanese "had some political objects to exalt national prestige" in their cultural diplomacy,[68] but he regretted Japan's past record of cultural interchange with other countries, which he called "cultural imperialism." With that record in mind, he urged his countrymen to pay due attention lest "cultural imperialism" insinuate itself into future international cultural relations. He believed strongly that the "superior culture of a nation might be naturally appreciated by foreigners without being particularly propagandized."[69]

The Japanese press also supported the idea of the "two-way street," although editorial writers generally emphasized the difficulty of quickly achieving a genuine appreciation of foreign cultures. They warned against mistaking superficial familiarity for understanding. Meanwhile, once the Korean War boom began to trigger Japan's economic recovery, nationalism rose gradually but steadily in Japan. In connection with cultural interchange, the Japanese press published a series of nationalistic stories that reflected the gut feelings of the people. *Yomiuri,* one of the three major newspapers in the country, stressed the importance of Japanese establishing their cultural identity. The paper insisted that "if the Japanese desire a real interchange of culture with the United States, they must first of all become true Japanese, since they will not be respected merely because they are Americanized."[70] Another Japanese newspaper carried an article appealing to Japanese nationalism. The *Nippon Times* also editorialized on the subject of cultural interchange. In an understatement, the paper noted that "it must not be forgotten that Japan, too, in her little way may have a cultural message for the United States and other nations of the world."[71]

Joint U.S.-Japan Enterprise

Related to the concept of the "two-way street" was the second principle of cultural interchange: Japanese and Americans should carry out the programs of cultural interchange together. Charles Fahs of the Rockefeller Foundation wrote Rockefeller, "It is unwise to place one's hope for the development of cultural relations on such institutions maintained by one country—even privately—within the territory of another," and he went on to urge that the Americans "work as fully as possible through the institutions of the country in which the activity is carried on." Fahs also pointed out that full transfer to Japanese leadership and maintenance should be made within a five-year period once the U.S.-Japan cultural interchange programs were under way. As Fahs explained to Rockefeller, "I think that this transfer is necessary not to save money but to achieve the kind of Japanese attitudes and response which is necessary for the project to be successful."[72] Rockefeller did not have to be persuaded. Both he and Fahs strongly believed that the full development of U.S.-Japan cultural relations would require full and voluntary cooperation from the Japanese.

Public and Private Coordination and Cooperation

The third principle underlying cultural interchange was the relationship of government and private endeavors to such an effort. The problem boiled down to whether cultural activities should be under government control and management and, if so, to what extent.

On the one hand, it appeared extremely untenable to maintain that cultural activities should be left entirely in private hands. But such a view was eventually embraced, because the United States had participated in two world wars in the twentieth century, with the result that the government's power had been expanded to an unprecedented degree. Thus in the context of the cold war it seemed inevitable that cultural diplomacy had a certain political taint. On the other hand, it was feared that the use of cultural programs to meet a country's immediate policy goals and objectives might defeat the long-run purpose of mutual understanding among peoples.

Following the latter line of argument, Rockefeller maintained that direct government control or operation of such projects was not desirable in an age in which a growing number of private citizens and nongovernmental, nonprofit organizations had begun to participate in foreign affairs.[73] He feared the perception that the United States was engaging in "cultural imperialism." Saxton Bradford wrote him that Japanese intellectuals were inclined to be suspicious of any government-sponsored cultural interchange program, because there was a certain underlying fear of foreign governmental intervention in internal affairs.[74]

In fact, since 1945 U.S. private organizations and individuals had expanded their activities in Japan. For example, the Rockefeller Foundation was carrying out a limited exchange program (Committee for Intellectual Exchange) and supporting scientific and educational projects such as a University of Tokyo–Stanford University seminar in American Studies and a plan to establish an International House of Japan in Tokyo. Ford exchangees from India and Pakistan were being sent to Japan after having visited the United States. Meanwhile, the YMCA and the YWCA were conducting educational and cultural enterprises. And CARE was sending food packages, medial supplies, and books. Elsewhere, American businesses, such as banks, shipping lines, and representatives of international corporations, were participating in Japanese civic welfare projects, disseminating considerable technological information, and awarding scholarships to Japanese students in the United States. The United Mine Workers of America had sent funds to Japanese coal miner unions. Protestant and Catholic churches were maintaining 3,500 missionaries in Japan, and in 1952 they furnished teachers and a varying amount of aid to sixty-three schools with 94,177 students.[75] Politically, the privately supported Committee for Free Asia and Radio Free Asia were carrying on anticommunist work within the limitations imposed by the Japanese government. Among other things, they provided subsidies for farm publications and gave aid to student anticommunist groups. Their combined budget for fiscal year 1953 was over $400,000.[76] Radio Free Asia was founded and funded in 1950 by the U.S. Central Intelligence Agency (CIA) through a front organization called the Committee for Free Asia as an anticommunist propaganda operation, broadcasting from Manila and other locations until 1961. The Committee for Free Asia, which had its headquarters in San Francisco, was supposed to work for cultural exchange between the United States and the free nations of Asia.

Indeed, the line between propaganda and cultural relations was very thin and hard to draw in the area of cultural activities. Rockefeller maintained that institutions for cultural interchange should be privately formed and privately financed, although he recognized that private organizations and groups did not have the funds needed for extensive programs. He also contended that persons outside government and private organizations might do a better job than government agencies, because they could plan and operate cultural exchange programs with relatively more flexibility and efficiency.[77] After all, certain activities were inherently difficult for the government to carry out, whereas certain other activities were beyond the capacity of private resources. With that point in mind, Rockefeller explored the possibilities that private cultural activities could be coordinated with government ones. As for the U.S. Department of State, it entirely favored the idea of private citizens undertaking as many cultural relations activities as possible. Rockefeller was thus asked to prepare a detailed inventory of cultural activities, with the objective of working out the possible contributions of government and private agencies to those activities.[78]

The United States was not the only nation conducting informational or educational exchange programs in Japan. Britain had a reading room in Tokyo, and it published an informational bulletin. Through the British Council, it also sent distinguished British scholars to Japan to lecture and conducted a small-scale exchange program. Elsewhere, France maintained cultural centers in Tokyo and Kyoto, and the Soviet Union waived all copyright regulations, which made it possible for Japan to obtain 228 translations of Soviet works published in 1951 alone.[79]

The Three Facets of Cultural Programs

According to the U.S. State Department, U.S. government cultural programs had three facets. The first was promoting a better understanding of the United States in other countries in order to increase mutual understanding. A principal task, therefore, was to project American culture as candidly as possible so that it would become familiar to other peoples.[80] The cultural programs in this category were designed based on the assumption that peoples in foreign lands would be neither hostile to the United States nor mistrustful of American actions if they understood Americans, American culture, and the American way of life.

The second facet of cultural programs was educational in two respects. The first was academic—for example, teaching English, promoting American Studies in foreign universities, and lecturing. The second was promotional—that is, explaining American culture and American institutions to foster understanding of America. These programs were strictly educational, not political, in nature. Indeed, they were very different from the programs directed specifically at bettering the economic conditions of receiving countries and fostering political stability and democracy by helping to raise the level of literacy, technical proficiency, general knowledge, and political awareness of developing nations. But because an "educational" program alone did not suffice without a parallel program to foster cultural empathy for America,[81] both the first and the second facets of cultural programs went hand in hand.

The third facet of cultural programs was information media services, directed at achieving specific foreign policy objectives of the U.S. government, such as disarmament and the peaceful use of atomic energy. After 1953 this facet was primarily the responsibility of the U.S. Information Agency.[82] USIA utilized the media of open communication to the fullest extent possible, with a view toward demonstrating abroad that the objective of American policies was to promote the legitimate aspirations of other peoples for freedom, peace, and progress. It broadcast radio programs to other nations, maintained local information centers, and furnished foreign audiences with motion pictures, television programs, press materials, pamphlets, and magazines.

Once they were formed, the U.S. government put its cultural interchange programs to work conveying and strengthening the positive image of the United States, while seeking to correct any inaccurate images by means of its "Campaign of Truth" programs. Through its cultural programs, the government wished to stress that it was in the United States that the common man had achieved his greatest victories in the twentieth century. America was to be portrayed as a dynamic, changing society. The U.S. government also wished to send the message that the United States was a country of economic prosperity, scientific prowess, and military power. But it never believed it was sufficient for the United States to be seen wholly in those terms, and so it highlighted American art, literature, music, and the social sciences. The U.S. government dramatized as well the intense desire of Americans for peace and human progress.[83] In short, Washington provided foreign intellectual leaders with USIE materials that demonstrated America's cultural contribution to society and those that de-emphasized American materialism.[84]

In later years, Robert Schwantes of the Asia Foundation recognized the importance of cultural relations and its political relevance to the future development of U.S.-Japan relations, particularly after the signing of the San Francisco peace treaty. Schwantes pointed out that Japanese and Americans needed to better understand each other's attitudes and goals: "They want to live in essentially the same kind of free dynamic world. The problem is to expand the area of overlap in specific policy goals."[85] To drive that point home, the State Department's USIE country papers on Japan emphasized the two countries' common interests and purposes rather than the differences in their standards of living and social customs.[86]

It was more than a coincidence that after the war American and Japanese liberals on both sides of the Pacific realized the importance of the cultural dimension of foreign relations. Cultural interchange was essential to promoting mutual understanding and maintaining a lasting peaceful relationship between the two countries. When Japan regained independence in 1952, it was widely recognized that the U.S.-Japan alliance remained relatively shallow and fragile; it did not have the deep intellectual, political, and cultural roots needed to sustain U.S.-Japan relations in an era of crisis and perils.[87]

Drafting the Rockefeller Report on Cultural Interchange

By the end of February 1951, the Dulles Peace Mission had returned to the United States. Dulles was markedly optimistic that the outline of a peace settlement, on the whole favorable to Japan, had been firmly established and that substantial progress had been made toward concluding an early peace treaty. But he added that the decisions in Tokyo were not conclusive and that the wishes of the other Allies, notably the British Commonwealth nations, would have to be considered. He also had to dissuade the government of the Philippines from claiming reparations from Japan. Even so, he announced publicly that the presidential mission had dispelled uncertainties about the nature of the peace treaty and the intentions of the United

States,[88] and thus the principal objective of the mission was successfully accomplished.

Rockefeller found that the trip to Japan was "interesting and worthwhile," and he enjoyed going as part of an official mission.[89] It was widely reported in the United States that the Japanese had shown considerable interest in Rockefeller's visit and his idea of a two-way approach to cultural interchange. And yet Rockefeller was aware that the biggest part of his job lay ahead. His immediate task was to draft and submit a report containing policy recommendations on U.S.-Japan cultural relations. He recognized that these recommendations had to be "really imaginative and effective" if they were to have effects on U.S. cultural policy and thus information and educational activities undertaken by the United States in other countries.[90] This was not the first time, by the way, that Rockefeller had written such recommendations on Japan. During the war, when he had been in the U.S. naval military government, he and Merrill Shepard, a lawyer in Chicago, had prepared a paper for the State-War-Navy Coordinating Committee (SWNCC) on the reorientation of the Japanese.[91] Merrill Shepard also assisted Rockefeller in drawing up the 1951 report on U.S.-Japan cultural relations (he agreed to take a month's leave from his Chicago law firm to come to New York and work with Rockefeller on the report once the trip was over[92]). A group of Japan experts also helped to draft the report. They included Charles Fahs; Eugene Dooman; Eileen R. Donovan, an officer in the Bureau of Far Eastern Affairs of the U.S. State Department; Sir George Sansom, a British diplomat and a great and esteemed scholar on Japan and a Columbia professor from 1948 to 1953; Hugh Borton of Columbia's Far Eastern Institute; Edwin Reischauer; and Douglas W. Overton, formerly a professor at Rikkyō University in Tokyo and diplomat in the U.S. consulate in Yokohama.[93] Rockefeller characterized the drafting of the report as "a challenging opportunity" to contribute constructively to U.S.-Japan relations.[94]

In drafting the report, Rockefeller sought "original and imaginative thinking," flexibility, and recommendations based on a genuine understanding of the characteristics of the Japanese people, who lived in a "country with an unusual cultural and historical development peculiar to itself."[95] He also heeded the warning that "the great disparity between the two standards of living is a potential source of trouble, and we must play down this difference."[96] Rockefeller maintained that any program of cultural relations between the United States and Japan should be regarded as a model and as an aspect of the broader development of cultural relations among all countries of the free world.[97] The drafting team then went about its job, keeping in mind that the great majority of Japanese were still undecided about the issues of the day and that "our battle with Communist ideology will revolve around this large middle-of-the-road group."[98] The next chapter describes and discusses the Rockefeller report on U.S.-Japan cultural relations that would serve as the basis of American cultural foreign policy toward postwar Japan.

Chapter 5

The Rockefeller Report: Countering the Communist Menace

> This [early] transfer [of leadership] is necessary not to save money but to achieve the kind of Japanese attitude and response which is necessary for the project to be successful.
>
> —Charles B. Fahs, 1951

> Aid from a paternal government may sap those sturdy virtues and breed a race of weaklings.
>
> —Dean Rusk, 1954

On April 19, 1951, some two months after his return to the United States, John D. Rockefeller III submitted to John Foster Dulles the report "United States–Japanese Cultural Relations." The eighty-page "confidential" report embodied Rockefeller's unshakable conviction about the importance of cultural interchange between the United States and Japan. It was welcomed gratefully as the first comprehensive study ever made of U.S.-Japan cultural relations.[1]

The Rockefeller Report

The Rockefeller report delineated three long-range general objectives in promoting U.S.-Japan cultural interchange. The first objective was to bring Japanese and Americans closer together in their appreciation and understanding of each other and their respective ways of life. The second was to enrich the cultures of the two countries. And the third was to assist the two countries in helping each other solve mutual problems. In addition, Rockefeller proposed an elaborate program of cultural interchange of information intended to "eliminate the intellectual and spiritual vacuum" and "diminish the effectiveness of existing pressures towards communism in Japan."[2]

As for an approach, the Rockefeller report suggested that the Japanese population be divided into two general categories instead of being treated as one single entity. One category would consist of intellectual leaders—that is, in the broadest terms, scientists, government and education authorities, journalists, capitalists, military leaders, and religious leaders (largely Buddhists). Broad groups such as the farm and rural population, labor, professional groups, women, and youth fell into the second category.[3] The Rockefeller report recommended that the U.S. Information and Education Service programs target each category separately to achieve the tangible results.[4] More specifically, Rockefeller suggested that intellectual leaders be reached through long-range cumulative cultural programs such as cultural interchange and person-to-person exchanges. Another aspect of the approach recommend by the Rockefeller report was the proposal that broad groups in Japan be reached through the "interchange of information" by means of the immediate-impact media such as the press, radio, and motion pictures.[5]

Programs of Cultural Interchange Targeting Intellectuals

Although intellectual leaders made up a relatively small segment of the Japanese population, they were a very important attitude-forming group in society.[6] Indeed, Rockefeller considered intellectuals to be one of the most important groups in Japan, because they had great influence over organized labor, university students, public officials, and the like. He was convinced that they would play a significant role in molding public opinion and determining the course that Japan would take in the years ahead.[7]

Rationale for This Approach

Rockefeller thought that the U.S. government should pay much greater attention to intellectuals for the following reasons. First, Japanese intellectuals, as he had observed, were ready to absorb any intellectual influence from abroad, and they were particularly anxious to learn about the quality of American intellectual life from which they had been isolated for twenty years.[8] He envisioned the great possibility that Japanese intellectuals could become pro-American liberals if approached properly and discreetly. But in the same way, intellectuals were vulnerable to the growing communist influence in Japan and were likely to be susceptible to communist brainwashing. It was Rockefeller's view that the appropriate measures should be taken quickly to forestall the worse consequence before the situation got out of hand. Thus among social groups, Rockefeller placed a top priority on Japanese intellectuals in his proposed program of cultural interchange. The American perceptions of Japanese intellectuals and their fear of communism are discussed in the context of the cultural cold war in Chapter 6.

Second, Rockefeller thought that the most effective and efficient way to reach and influence the largest number of Japanese was to work through the Japanese leadership informally and discreetly. The Rockefeller report suggested that the U.S. government and private agencies take full advantage of the fact that Japanese intellectuals enjoyed authoritative positions in the organization and communication of groups.[9] Rockefeller's suggestion was based on his perceptions of Japan as a strongly elitist and authoritarian nation. He believed that Japanese thought and behavior tended to respond to leadership rather than an individual's sense of personal responsibility and that mass groups in Japan tended to be guided and influenced by the leadership of intellectuals. Thus because the Japanese were traditionally predisposed to follow people in authority, their attitudes could best be influenced through leadership.[10] Charles Fahs, director of the Rockefeller Foundation's Humanities Division, also maintained that the Japanese were still overinclined toward acceptance of authority.[11] Harvard professor Edwin Reischauer had a similar opinion about the deferential nature of Japanese society. At a 1949 State Department conference, he noted: "The real point I want to bring up is the problem of the special place of the scholarly classes in the Far East, particularly in the area of China, Korea, Japan—that area affected by Chinese civilization.... If we exploit the special prestige position of the scholar, the intellectual group in that area, it would seem to me that propaganda work, information aimed primarily at them would be the most effective kind of information work."[12] Fahs thought that the concepts of "prime movers" and "constituencies" seemed especially applicable to Japan. A little less than a decade later, another American report on U.S.-Japan cultural relations made a similar observation. *United States Foreign Policy: Asia,* a report prepared by Conlon Associates Ltd. at the request of the U.S. Senate Committee on Foreign Relations, recommended that one part of U.S. cultural relations programs be "directed toward Japanese leaders in every field, for Japan is still strongly an elitist society." The report went on to suggest that a program of cultural interchange targeting intellectual leaders would yield the maximum results.[13]

Japanese business leaders also shared Rockefeller's and Reischauer's views about the way to undertake cultural interchange. For example, Iwai Yūjirō, an Osaka businessman and trader, expressed his view that cultural interchange programs should target intellectual and business leaders, because the programs would not get anywhere if they targeted the Japanese people as whole as the army did. "Through top people [the programs] reach others."[14] Other Japanese leaders agreed that the Japanese were still overinclined toward the acceptance of authority. Uramatsu Samitarō, for example, maintained that Japanese always needed someone authoritative. In his critique of *The Chrysanthemum and the Sword* by Ruth Benedict, the former secretary of the Japanese Council of the Institute of Pacific Relations remarked, "The Japanese must have a *Tennō* (an emperor) and the old one will no longer do. . . . It is about time for MacArthur to go home, but you will have to send someone out to replace him."[15]

Specific Recommendations on Cultural Interchange

The Rockefeller report recommended implementation of the following initiatives to reach the intellectual leadership in Japan: (1) establishment of a cultural center in Tokyo: (2) establishment of an international house for students in Tokyo and Kyoto; (3) continuation of the exchange program for national leaders and students; (4) pursuit of an extensive program of English-language instruction; and (5) implementation of a program of material interchange.

The report recommended that the *cultural center* be established in Tokyo under a private binational board. The center would be financed directly by private American sources and indirectly by the U.S. government through donations of books and grants-in-aid for specific projects. The cultural center would maintain a complete reference library; offer advanced English-language courses and orientation courses for Japanese going abroad; sponsor lectures and meetings; assist individuals and groups in making contacts; and possibly carry out the actual administration of the Fulbright program in Japan under contract with the Fulbright board. In short, Rockefeller envisioned the center would be a general clearinghouse for U.S. cultural activities in Japan.[16]

The Rockefeller report also proposed that *international houses,* like the one in New York City, be established for students in Tokyo and Kyoto, and possibly in other cities. They, too, would be operated and financed by private binational boards, with some indirect aid from the U.S. government in the form of books and materials.

As for an *exchange program,* the Rockefeller report recommended that the existing exchange program for students and national leaders be continued in the post-treaty years. The current GARIOA (Government and Relief in Occupied Areas) reorientation program had sent a considerable number of Japanese students and leaders abroad, and the Institute of International Education had acted as agent for the U.S. Department of Army in the program. The report emphasized the great importance of maintaining a "two-way street" in the exchange of persons; it was thought to be the most effective method to infuse Japanese mind and practice with American ideas.[17] Also the "two-way street" would help to counter charges of cultural imperialism by the United States.[18]

Rockefeller also insisted that "quality rather than quantity" be the paramount guiding principle in attaining the objective of cultural exchange.[19] The Rockefeller report recommended that scholars of outstanding reputation and ability be brought to Japan, if possible, under private auspices so that they could engage directly in intimate discussions with Japanese intellectuals. Because the Japanese had traditionally perceived American civilization to be lacking "spiritual" and "cultural" dimensions, the most effective counter to this attitude, Rockefeller thought, was to bring the Japanese face-to-face with outstanding thinkers whom they respected and who were capable of making a genuine contribution to Japanese thought by bringing the Japanese up-to-date in their professional thinking in various fields. These thinkers also could play a major role in conveying understanding of the cultural dimensions of American life.[20] Rockefeller had in mind scholars such as theologian Reinhold Niebuhr, diplomat and Nobel Peace Prize winner Ralph Bunche, sociologist Karl A. Wittfogel, geneticist Herman J. Muller, and philosopher Sidney Hook.[21]

Nambara Shigeru, president of the University of Tokyo, also had a few suggestions such as chemist James B. Conant, literary critic Edmund Wilson, and sociologist Lewis Munford.[22] Rockefeller took Nambara's request seriously—he and others thought it wise to follow the Japanese lead in deciding which intellectual areas should receive priority representation in the exchange of outstanding teachers. It was believed that such a thoughtful, tactful approach would be helpful in minimizing the danger that charges of cultural imperialism would be leveled against the United States.[23]

For Rockefeller, an extensive program of *English-language instruction* in Japan was also absolutely necessary for a successful U.S.-Japan cultural exchange, although he also suggested that primary emphasis be placed on qualities such as ability, character, and leadership rather than the ability to speak English in selecting Japanese to send to the United States.[24] Echoing Rockefeller, a USIS-Japan semiannual evaluation report emphasized the potentialities of an English-language teaching program. It reported that a promising field would open for the infiltration of sound American ideas by ostensibly assisting in improving English-language teaching techniques. The report went on to state that the presence of a qualified English-language teaching specialist could have a long-term effect by making use of the opportunities for affecting textbook writing and introducing well-selected American materials and that the great potential in that field lay in the receptivity in every segment of Japanese life to the learning of English.[25] In fact, the English-language classes were held in the USIE cultural centers in part to meet the Japanese demand for English-language teaching. English classes in the centers in metropolitan areas were broken down into groups such as civil service employees, teachers, businessmen, civic organization heads, students, and government leaders.[26] It was expected, however, that the English classes in the centers could be converted into active discussion groups centered around American studies.[27] Perhaps in part thanks to such effective English teaching programs, the fifty-one Japanese leaders nominated by the end of fiscal year 1953 for grants to support three-month observation visits to the United States represented all geographic areas of Japan and many other fields. In the same year, seventy-five students and young leaders were given joint Fulbright/Smith-Mundt grants for graduate study in the United States, and 150 of them were given Fulbright/Smith-Mundt travel grants for the same purpose.[28]

Finally, the Rockefeller report suggested a program of material interchange, under which the U.S. government would provide books to Japanese schools and libraries willing to make maximum use of them. Emphasizing the two-way street of cultural relations, the Rockefeller report also suggested what the Japanese might do in the United States to foster an interest in Japan. Proposed projects included reestablishment of a Japanese cultural center in New York and exhibits of Japanese art in the United States. As to an effective way to disseminate information on America throughout Japan, the Rockefeller report recommended that every effort be made to make copyrights readily available to Japanese publishers.[29] The presentation of books and other information materials to Japanese groups or leaders was considered to be a very effective technique for strengthening American contacts with the Japanese and achieving prestige in Japan.[30] For example, the U.S. embassy in Tokyo invited top Japanese writers, critics, and dramatists (all members of the Japan PEN Club) to meet with the American public affairs staff at a tea party. At the conclusion of the party, the guests, who included Kawabata Yasunari, Abe Tomoji, and Mishima Yukio, were each presented with "a carefully selected recent American book on intellectual subjects." Kawabata received *Art Has Many Faces,* and Mishima was presented with *Ballet in America.*[31] As of January 1953, 14,219 books had been made available for presentation through the U.S. embassy staff in Tokyo and through the regional public affairs officers and the cultural centers. Of those, 13,986 were in the Japanese language and 233 were in English.[32]

Programs of Information Interchange Targeting Social Groups

In addition to targeting intellectuals, the Rockefeller report proposed that a second program of cultural interchange—the "interchange of information"—target social groups, including the farm and rural population, labor, professional groups, women, and students and youth in Japan.[33] Continuing with the idea of a two-way street, the Rockefeller report also recommended that information from Japan to the United States be made available as determined by the Japanese themselves with any assistance needed from the U.S. government and private agencies and organizations. The report insisted that the Japanese had much to offer in the field of art, which would have great appeal in the United States. Among other things, the Rockefeller report proposed the production of Japanese films that would accurately portray Japan and its way of life. It emphasized that every effort should be made to allow Japanese films to be distributed as widely as possible in the United States through both commercial and noncommercial channels. The Rockefeller report also suggested that important Japanese books and treatises on various subjects be translated into English so that the world might have the benefit of Japanese scholarship.[34]

The rural population, which at an estimated 42 million people constituted about half of the Japanese, was considered to be the most stabilizing element in Japan. SCAP land reforms enlarged the class of small landholders, who were traditionally conservative, nationalistic, and anticommunist. As a result, 87 percent of Japan's arable land was now owned by the people who toiled it.[35] Sixty percent of farmers were reported to be members of the four leading independent farm organizations.[36]

By 1950, 5.7 million Japanese workers had been organized.[37] Organized labor exercised an important influence over the domestic and foreign policies adopted by the Japanese political parties. The majority of unions were brought into the Sōhyō federation (Japan General Council of Trade Unions). Japan's labor movement was divided roughly into two groups: the right and the left. The left wing, composed of most of the labor unions in Sōhyō, had about two million members. It dominated the Left Socialist Party, which received 4.5 million votes (13.1 percent of the total) and elected seventy-two members to the Diet (the national house of representatives) in the April 19, 1953, general election. The right wing (left of the political center of the Diet) was composed of a small number of unions in Zenrō (Japanese Confederation of Labor) that together had about 750,000 members. The Right Socialist Party, which was the political wing of Zenrō, received 4.6 million votes (13.5 percent of the total) in the April 19 general election and elected sixty-six members to the Diet.[38] This party was anticommunist and friendly to the United States.

Among the socialist labor groups in Japan, the Marxists were doctrinaire, dogmatic, and extremely suspicious of capitalism and capitalist countries. The leaders of the left wing of labor were far more vigorous, dynamic, and articulate than those of the right wing, who were tempered by pragmatism.[39] The majority of labor unions brought into Sōhyō were opposed to communist infiltration. Because the majority of the left-wing leaders deeply distrusted and feared the Soviet Union, they opposed any affiliation with the World Federation of Trade Unions (WFTU), which was avowedly pro-communist. As a result, the majority of unions in Japan were affiliated with International Confederation of Free Trade Unions (ICFTU).[40] The ICFTU, an anticommunist labor organization, had withdrawn from the WFTU in 1949.

In Saxton Bradford's view, the majority of Japanese left-wing labor leaders were neutralist, pacifist, escapist, and utopian. He contemptuously called such qualities typical of an immature and inexperienced leadership.[41] Because Marxist thinking, neutralism, and pacifism pervaded the labor leadership, Americans were afraid that the socialist labor majority was susceptible to subtle manipulation for communist ends.[42] A USIE country paper on Japan suggested that Americans use the information program to seek to reach this group on the Japanese left and make it more aware of the communist danger to the working man.[43]

Women were another group targeted by the program of information interchange. Once they were gratefully liberated under the U.S. occupation and elevated to a higher social status, Japanese women emerged as a political factor. Indeed, they probably had a much greater influence on Japanese life than most people realized. Women were able to exercise their greatest influence in their households, in their communities, and in organizations of women's groups. Identified with America and American democracy, they appeared to look to the United States for guidance and leadership. The U.S. country paper on Japan recommended that women be encouraged to play a more active and decisive role in ways beneficial to the U.S. policy objective.[44]

The Rockefeller report also proposed that youth be a target group for the U.S. information program. CI&E/SCAP recognized that as many as fifty thousand university students in Japan were constantly vulnerable to communist propaganda. Indeed, communists made their greatest inroads among students, taking advantage of the postwar disillusionment, the lack of employment opportunities, and pessimism about Japan's resources and future. A small number of communists dominated student organizations, although actual communists numbered less than 5 percent of the total.[45] American Otis Cary, a professor of American Studies and director of Amherst House at Dōshisha University in Kyoto, observed that "students are rather out of touch with realities of world today. . . . [They] get their ideas as to Communism from professors, from literary magazines, from materials in the libraries."[46] Cary, a longtime resident of Japan whose family had for generations been missionaries there, was very knowledgeable about Japan and its culture. A rabid anticommunist, he was concerned about the baneful influence of communism on the Japanese.

In fact, the education and guidance of Japanese youth were of paramount importance to the United States, because it and democratic elements in Japan had to depend on the youth to carry forward the democratic reforms carried out during the occupation. CI&E officers recognized that the communist influence over Japanese youth was so strong and pervasive that they had to meet this particular danger. And, indeed, the CI&E paid more attention to this group than any other throughout the military occupation; communist propaganda activities were a constant factor in shaping the policies and actions of the CI&E.[47] A USIE country plan for Japan proposed that operations be directed at youth and university students to counter communist propaganda activities, with a concentration on providing more books, material goods, educational exchanges, and American instructors in an effort to extend U.S. influence and provide an acceptable ideology.[48] One result was that in 1951 some 1.5 million students visited twenty-three U.S. information centers.[49]

Matsui Shichirō, professor of economics at Dōshisha University and a former Rockefeller Foundation Social Science Division fellow, and Ōshimo Kakuichi, dean of Dōshisha University's Divinity School, blamed some professors of economics for the problem of communism on campus. They argued that because professors were, on the whole, unprepared to take a strong stand, the communist minority took advantage of the passivity of the majority of students to manipulate student affairs to their advantage and that they abused the student "self-government."[50] Ōshimo, in particular, attributed much of the trouble to a lack of convictions and courage on the part of the teachers. Matsui and Ōshimo pointed out that "some economic theory other than Marxian is needed—either Keynesian or anti-Keynesian would help."[51] Hugh Borton, a Columbia professor, noted that "in Japan history pretty generally is taught on Marxist pattern. It is a most unfortunate situation that young people start off with biased impression."[52]

The Rockefeller report reiterated that the immediate objective of a program of information interchange was "to encourage Japan to maintain and strengthen its position as a member of the family of free nations" and that the program should seek "to assist the Japanese in meeting their problems and needs" to accomplish the U.S. objective.[53] The report also recognized that the Japanese media were the most effective means of achieving this objective, but it recommended that existing Japanese media be utilized rather than develop competitive media.

Institutionalizing Cultural Interchange

Finally, the Rockefeller report emphasized that institutionalizing cultural interchange between Japan and the United States was as important as the program of cultural interchange itself. According to Robert Schwantes, organization should never be an end in itself, but no extensive program of action was possible without it.[54] The Rockefeller report thus recommended that two kinds of institution be established under a private binational board: a cultural center in Tokyo and an international house for students in Tokyo and in Kyoto.[55]

The cultural center was intended to play the role of a general clearinghouse for U.S. cultural activities in Japan.[56] For example, through the cultural center important visitors from America and elsewhere would be able not only to obtain access to opinion makers in Japan, but also to arrange direct personal contact with their Japanese counterparts. "Assistance should be available to specialized scholars [visiting Japan], a function which might develop into an Institute for American Studies under Japanese sponsorship," the Rockefeller report suggested. The report also suggested that those proposed institutions of cultural interchange be financed directly by private American sources and indirectly by the U.S. government.[57]

The Rockefeller report stressed the importance of establishing an international house for university students in Tokyo and in Kyoto. The purpose of the proposed international houses would be to facilitate intellectual and cultural interchange and social contact between Japanese and foreign students, scholars, and teachers. The primary function of the international houses would be to provide a common meeting place for Japanese, Americans, and other nationals, and an opportunity for Japanese students to learn firsthand something of the ideas and way of life of the Untied States and other countries. The provision of living quarters was thought to be a means to this broader end rather than an end in itself. The proposed international houses could provide a place for informal associations of Japanese, Americans, and other nationals as well.[58] According to Rockefeller, cultural and student centers would demonstrate "in specific and tangible form" America's intention to build for the long term. He believed that any tangible evidence of continuing U.S. interest in Japan was most desirable and helpful. Saxton Bradford, a public affairs officer in American embassy in Tokyo, emphasized the effectiveness of private sponsorship of such institutions in avoiding the suspicion of governmental propaganda motives that might attach to noticeable official participation.[59] U.S. consular officer Douglas Overton regarded the two suggestions in the Rockefeller report—a privately managed cultural center and international houses—as especially unique. He recommended that the U.S. government encourage Rockefeller to return to Japan as soon as possible to launch the organization of the cultural center and international houses, thereby following up on his proposal.[60]

The Rockefeller report also made specific suggestions about the point of departure for action planning. First, the report called for a realistic appraisal of the financial support that might be anticipated from both private and government sources in the United States. Second, it recommended that a qualified person be sent to Japan to further develop plans for the proposed cultural center with interested Japanese. The selected individual should also survey Japanese needs for cultural materials with particular reference to universities, colleges, and libraries. Third, the report urged the State Department to send a cultural affairs officer to Japan well in advance of the treaty to become familiar with the existing program and to make plans for continuation of those activities that might have value in the post-treaty period. The report, therefore, placed great emphasis on assigning a cultural affairs officer to the transition period, because the activities and agencies for cultural interchange developed by SCAP would end as soon as the peace treaty was concluded. The Rockefeller report suggested further that the State Department officer selected devote full time to the development and promotion of the program envisioned in the report.[61]

The U.S. Government Response to the Rockefeller Report

Dulles was pleased with the general tone of the Rockefeller report, but he feared that certain sections of the text might be misinterpreted by the Japanese, leading them to have the impression that a program had already been worked out and that they had little part in the actual preparation for the U.S.-Japan cultural relations. (In Dulles's thinking, the initiative of the Japanese in developing a cultural program was an important factor, and the active interest and support of the Japanese would be fundamental to the success of a cultural program of this type.) He thus suggested that the complete Rockefeller report be kept on a restricted basis in the State Department to prevent those particular sections from producing unfavorable reactions from the Japanese.[62]

Impressed with the Rockefeller report, Dulles sent it to Secretary of State Dean Acheson with the recommendation that it be given favorable consideration in planning and carrying out the post-treaty programs of the U.S.-Japan cultural interchange.[63] The U.S. Information and Education Service of the State Department recognized the importance of Rockefeller's suggestions and noted that the Rockefeller report contained proposals that could be incorporated into USIE programs.[64] Among the proposals in the Rockefeller report, USIE was entirely in favor of establishing a cultural center and international houses for students.[65] State Department officials felt the two proposed projects could best fulfill their purpose if they were established and operated on a strictly private basis. A privately sponsored cultural center could become a major factor in U.S.-Japan cultural relations and a valuable supplement to any government-sponsored program in Japan.[66] The State Department also thought that private sponsorship would remove the taint of government and encourage freedom of discussion.

To follow up on the action plan laid out in the Rockefeller report, Douglas Overton asked Rockefeller if he was prepared to investigate some sources of private financial support in the United States. Rockefeller said he would secure funds and support from private sources if he had "the wholehearted and active support" of Dulles. The private sources he had in mind were foundations such as Ford, Rockefeller, and Carnegie. Overton also asked Rockefeller if he could go to Japan to further develop plans with the Japanese for the proposed cultural center.[67] Dean Rusk, assistant secretary of state for Far Eastern affairs, wrote Rockefeller that some recommendations in the Rockefeller report would be followed up by USIE. Rusk reiterated that the plans for a cultural center and international houses could best be developed on a private basis.[68]

On July 30, 1951, Dulles officially asked Rockefeller to revisit Japan to develop his proposed plan.[69] Rockefeller agreed on the condition that Dulles assure him of steadfast support.[70] Rockefeller clearly recognized that the primary objective of his trip was "to tie in with the right people" in Japan, and he described the new assignment as "a rather challenging one."[71]

Rockefeller's trip was scheduled for October 13 to November 17, 1951. He asked his legal adviser, Donald H. McLean Jr., to accompany him in that capacity.[72] Rockefeller noted in his diary: "Imaginative leadership in the cultural center could, I believe, do much to develop the cultural ties between Japan and the United States and the free world generally which is so important to understanding and mutual respect."[73] Indeed, he believed that the success of the cultural center depended on its leadership. Those leaders should be "men of tact, initiative, and imagination," who would fully command the respect of those with whom they would be associating.[74]

Rockefeller spent two days in Washington before departing for Japan. There, he received full briefings from Dulles and other State Department officers for public affairs, including Eileen Donovan and Douglas Overton.[75] Rockefeller also received a long list of projects supported by both the public and the private sectors in the area of U.S.-Japan cultural relations. The projects included (1) the establishment of a Japanese-American cultural center in Tokyo and in some major American cities, as well as the establishment of an international house in Tokyo and possibly in other student centers in Japan; (2) the provision of grants to supplement Fulbright travel grants for approximately forty Japanese to go the United States, to bring twelve outstanding American intellectuals to associate with their Japanese counterparts and to lecture and develop cultural relations, and to bring twelve outstanding Japanese cultural figures to the United States; (3) the provision of fellowship funds to the cultural center for some twenty Japanese and American students in the humanities and social sciences; and (4) the support of a translation program in which American works were translated into Japanese and Japanese works into English.[76]

Rockefeller appreciated suggestions on approaches that could be used to secure maximum private participation for U.S.-Japan cultural interchange. Private participation in the interchange was believed to be not only preferable but also essential, because it would have the greatest impact and could avoid the suspicion that any governmental propaganda motives were underlying efforts. An overwhelming array of government-to-government activities, it was feared, would raise fears that such activities had ulterior political purposes. To put it differently, too much direct U.S. government involvement in civilian cultural activities—no matter how laudable—might make many people fearful of U.S. "cultural imperialism." Particularly in Japan, there was a certain underlying fear and suspicion of foreign government intervention in internal affairs. In light of this fact, it was thought better to leave the mobilization of resources to stimulate and assure nonofficial participation to private citizens, such as Rockefeller, while USIE and the U.S. embassy in Tokyo handled any relations with the Japanese government. Rockefeller seemed to be the ideal person to handle the appropriate contacts with private institutions and individuals in Japan. Other private citizens groups included universities and colleges, private foundations, the YMCA, mission groups, publishers, and cultural organizations.[77]

Although USIE favored the idea of a cultural center along the lines developed by Rockefeller, this U.S. government cultural affairs agency recognized that the project presented a sensitive problem: good judgment had to be exercised to enable maximum assistance from USIE with minimum adverse political effects—that is, any official activities that might give the Japanese people the impression that the center was an official agency had to be avoided. Overall, USIE believed Rockefeller's proposed project promised to be a major factor in U.S.-Japan cultural relations. Meanwhile, the State Department was thoroughly prepared to offer assistance to back Rockefeller up while he undertook his semiofficial assignment in Japan.[78]

Pushing the Institutionalization of Cultural Interchange in Japan

Rockefeller arrived in Tokyo on October 16, 1951, as a private individual to work out the institutionalization of a U.S.-Japan cultural interchange.[79] He was also expected to make a detailed inventory of cultural activities for which government and private cooperation and coordination could be planned in the field of U.S.-Japan cultural relations. Rockefeller hoped he would be able to secure adequate Japanese cooperation to justify the establishment of a Japanese-American cultural center in Tokyo and international houses for students in Tokyo and Kyoto. If adequate cooperation was secured from the Japanese, it was expected that these enterprises would be supported by funds provided by the Rockefeller Foundation.[80]

In Japan, Rockefeller found a group of Americans who proved to be very useful in helping him to carry out his assignment (see Chapter 1). They included U.S. Ambassador William Sebald; Saxton Bradford, head of public affairs in the Diplomatic Section; Donald Nugent, CI&E chief; Nelson Spinks, first secretary and consul; and Herbert Passin, the CI&E analyst in charge of public information and sociological research.[81] Rockefeller also met some private U.S. citizens who were helpful as well. They included Sterling W. Fisher, general manager for the Far East of *Reader's Digest;* Gordon Bowles, professor of cultural anthropology in charge of the American Studies project at Tokyo University; and Thomas Blakemore, an American attorney at law.

In Tokyo, Rockefeller wasted no time seeking "the right people" to help him further develop his plans. Among prominent Japanese leaders, he met with Matsukata Yoshisaburō (his real name, but he was widely known as Matsukata Saburō), managing director of Kyōdō News Agency; Matsumoto Shigeharu, former chief of the editorial bureau of Dōmei News Agency; Takagi Yasaka, former leader of the Japanese Institute of Pacific Relations; Kabayama Aisuke, former president of the America-Japan Society and current president of the Grew Scholarship Foundation; Kanō Hisaakira, chair of the Kokusai Bunka Shinkōkai (Society for International Relations); Nambara Shigeru, president of the University of Tokyo; Maeda Tamon, former minister of education and president of the Japan Scholarship Foundation, and Kawabata Yasunari, president of the Japan PEN Club.

Among them, Rockefeller discovered that Matsumoto Shigeharu was the most active leader and the guiding spirit, deeply committed to the promotion of U.S.-Japan cultural interchange.[82] Rockefeller found this Japanese gentleman "the very right person for the carrying forward of the project."[83] Matsumoto expressed keen interest in the cultural center project as soon as he met Rockefeller in Tokyo again. Soon, Matsumoto was so dedicated that he gave nearly half of his time to the cultural center program.[84] Matsumoto first met Rockefeller at the 1929 Kyoto Conference of the Institute of Pacific Relations where the American was the conference secretary. They quickly became conversant on a first-name basis: "Shige" and John.

Takagi Yasaka was as enthusiastic as Matsumoto about the idea of a cultural center. He was already known to Charles Fahs, director of the Rockefeller Foundation's Humanities Division, because he had served as Fahs's sponsor when he studied at Tokyo Imperial University in 1935.[85] Takagi had occupied the prestigious Hepburn Chair of American Constitution, History and Diplomacy at Tokyo University for thirty years.[86] He also had earned the reverential respect of his colleagues as the founder of American Studies in Japan.

Another prominent figure Rockefeller found helpful was Kabayama Aisuke, president of the Grew Scholarship Foundation. Kabayama was then eighty-six years old, but age did not diminish his enthusiasm about the idea of a cultural center.[87] Kabayama, the founder of Japan's Kyōdō News Agency, explained to Rockefeller why he came to support the idea of a cultural center: "A Japanese premier in the nineteen thirties had once told me how the Japanese failed in trying to improve relations with the United States by economic and political negotiation," and so he felt Japan "should try culture now." He also disclosed that his model of the cultural center was the Japan Institute in New York.[88] Having said that, Kabayama suggested that the center welcome American students, but not international visitors in general in order to "avoid its being crowded with Asians."[89] Thus despite his good intentions, Kabayama unwittingly revealed his racial bias against his Asian neighbors in his less-than-careful statement.

Although the idea of a cultural center and international houses for students in Tokyo and Kyoto was crystallized from the discussions Rockefeller had had with the Japanese in Tokyo during his last official trip, the idea of a cultural center was "a Japanese-felt need, not a reflection of U.S. interest," according to Matsumoto.[90] Very practical considerations weighed in as well on the Japanese side. Nambara remarked that a U.S.-Japan cultural center was needed to serve as a meeting place for discussion and as a facility for luncheon meetings that professors and intellectuals could afford.[91] Takagi also stressed the need for a place to meet and eat at a cost not beyond what professors could bear.[92]

After his discussions with prominent Japanese leaders and groups, Rockefeller recognized that he and the Japanese agreed on the purpose of the joint project: to provide nongovernmental foci for the healthy development of U.S.-Japan cultural relations. He was convinced that a cultural center and student international houses would make an important contribution if they were set up and led correctly. He hoped that in the long run such a project would provide centers for the encouragement of constructive Japanese participation in world affairs.[93]

The Japanese Take Action: The Cultural Center Preparatory Committee

Rockefeller discovered during this visit that the new task required much more behind-the-scenes thinking and planning than that pursued during his earlier visit to Japan. The crux of the matter seemed to be how "to move ahead with our efforts and still be sure the Japanese are really happy with what we are doing together."[94] Thus discreetly and carefully Rockefeller tried to ensure that the Japanese would feel happy in planning and executing a cultural interchange program and would assume ownership of the idea. However, Sterling Fisher advised him "to take [a] position of leadership in the beginning, otherwise [the] project would never get off ground." Fisher was confident that if the undertaking got off on the right foot, the Japanese "would pick it up and make it their own."[95]

Thus Rockefeller took the initiative. A meeting was called at the Japan Industry Club on November 12, 1951, to discuss two projects—a cultural center and an international house for students. Thirty-five prominent figures attended the meeting, representing the business, educational, and cultural communities.[96] From that meeting emerged an organizing committee, the Cultural Center Preparatory Committee; Kabayama was appointed chair and Sterling Fisher and Matsumoto executive secretaries.[97] The leadership responsibility fell primarily on Matsumoto, but he was well supported by Fisher and Gordon Bowles on the American side. Rockefeller was pleased; the activities were in "good hands."[98] Rockefeller felt particularly grateful to Fisher (calling him "a tower of strength") for his assistance and contribution to the undertaking as a representative of American business interests in Japan.[99]

Soon after the November 12 meeting, a subcommittee on program and planning was formed for the Cultural Center Preparatory Committee.[100] The subcommittee was assigned the task of basic planning, and it was to serve as an executive committee. Rockefeller seemed satisfied with the way the things had gone. After these developments, Rockefeller felt he had adequately accomplished the objective of his trip to Japan and that it was now time "to go away and let the situation develop on its own," thereby fulfilling his cardinal rule—and an ultimate aim of the cultural interchange project— to help the Japanese help themselves. However, he promised the preparatory committee that he would be glad to return if it would be helpful.[101]

Rockefeller and his party left Japan on November 17, 1951, hoping that the Matsumoto group would carry on with vigorous leadership. He noted in his diary that day: "Really don't see how things could have developed more hopefully in the short time we have been in Japan."[102] Rockefeller recognized that there was still much to be done, but at that moment he was pleased with the progress made in his proposed project.[103]

After his return to the United States, Rockefeller learned that two additional subcommittees, adjuncts to the preparatory committee, had been formed: a finance committee and a facilities committee.[104] The subcommittees not only searched for a site for the cultural center, but also raised funds to pay for the land and the cost of erecting a center building, estimated at $500,000. It was decided that the cultural center and the international house would be separate units of a single project. The cultural center would include an auditorium, a library, and rooms for music and lectures, as well as hotel-type accommodations for visiting dignitaries and for Fulbright and other educational and cultural leaders. The international student house was to be much more modest than the cultural center. It would be a suitable center for students, providing housing and social meeting space. The subcommittees also agreed to ensure that their activities would not duplicate those of the USIE cultural programs. It was hoped that the ground for the buildings would be broken by May 1952.[105]

The Public Image of a Cultural Center— A U.S. Propaganda Organ?

Undoubtedly, both Japanese and American leaders recognized the great need for some kind of some institutional arrangement that would facilitate meetings between Japanese and American scholars. But to an equal degree, they were afraid that Japanese scholars might view the proposed cultural center (and international house—the two were eventually combined) as a U.S. propaganda organ.[106] Gordon Bowles, who was a professor of anthropology at Tokyo University and who was born in Tokyo, suggested that the cultural center needed to make a major effort to convince the Japanese academic community that the center was a valuable undertaking and not merely a U.S. propaganda organ. Bowles believed that Japanese academics felt no vested interest in the cultural center and that they were standing off and watching critically to see what it would do.[107]

U.S. embassy officers participated in the conferences leading to the decision to create a cultural center. Since January 1951, the Diplomatic Section of SCAP and later the U.S. embassy in Tokyo had followed the activities of Rockefeller in Japan and had maintained close contact with him through Donald McLean, his adviser.[108] Moreover, it was the U.S. embassy that had confidentially proposed the program for the exchange of Japanese and American cultural leaders to Rockefeller in the fall of 1951 that had led to his anonymous gift to the Institute of East Asian Affairs at Columbia University, which carried out the project.[109] But Rockefeller was extremely concerned that such an official initiative by the U.S. government might be misinterpreted.[110] He was anxious to have the Japanese people view his project of cultural interchange as a strictly private undertaking that was in no way connected with official policy. Thus the U.S. embassy took "scrupulous care" to remain in the background as far as the Japanese public was concerned. All discussions that Rockefeller had with U.S. embassy officers were guarded and informal in nature.[111]

On the Japanese side as well, leaders such as Matsumoto and Takagi tried hard to avoid misunderstanding and counter any criticism of the cultural center as a U.S. propaganda machine. They held meetings with Japan's top economists, political scientists, sociologists, and others and received suggestions and comments from all the participants. Matsumoto emphasized that it was essential to the success of the cultural center to cultivate warm personal contacts between the center and scholars.[112] The directors of the cultural center went so far as to choose Tsuru Shigeto and Oda Makoto to serve on the council and on the staff of the center, respectively, with the specific goal of squelching unwarranted criticism (they feared that the value of the center would be gravely impaired if it were regarded as a propaganda agency). Tsuru, a Harvard graduate, a socialist, and a professor of economics at Hitotsubashi University in Tokyo, was director general of the Institute of Economic Research. Oda, a young freelance writer, was pro-American, but he had left-wing contacts. Apparently, the selection of Tsuru and Oda was part of careful, deliberate efforts by the directors of the center to demonstrate that the center would not be a one-sided organization.[113]

Rockefeller Grows Impatient—
One More Trip Back to Japan

Gradually, Rockefeller realized that the task of developing the cultural center and international house in Tokyo would be more complex and more time-consuming than he had anticipated. Sterling Fisher had informed him that little progress was being made, because too little time was being devoted to it by the volunteers involved.[114] Rockefeller thus recognized that he would have to work more closely with the Cultural Center Preparatory Committee if the Rockefeller Foundation was to make a substantial contribution to the center.[115] He therefore made one more trip to Japan to follow up on the work of the committee.

Rockefeller arrived in Tokyo on April 13, 1952, and he would stay for over a month, until May 18.[116] He was relieved to learn that all people concerned were "thinking pretty much in [the] same direction," but he discovered that the efforts of the program and planning subcommittee had been "disappointing."[117] He also learned that the finance subcommittee was not facing up to the question of long-range financial support.[118] As a result, the financial aspects of the proposed center were becoming an increasingly important factor.[119] The issue boiled down to what the possibilities were in Japan for financial support of an international cultural center once it was established and how the financial commitments and prospects of the institution could best be planned to ensure it would survive after the initial period of financial assistance. Rockefeller was particularly disturbed by the fact that the Japanese had not collected the detailed financial information needed to secure support from the Rockefeller Foundation.[120]

Actually, the delay stemmed in part from the huge amount of money required to undertake the proposed project. Donald McLean attributed the delay not to any lack of interest or enthusiasm but to inertia; the Japanese simply did not move into gear in the same way that the Americans did. The real problem, according to McLean, was how "to get traction on the part of the responsible Japanese."[121]

Making matters worse, Matsumoto had been laid up with a torn knee since February. Rockefeller, who had a very high opinion of Matsumoto, saw no point in having meetings of the Cultural Center Preparatory Committee without Matsumoto, the key figure. Indeed, Rockefeller's opinion of Matsumoto was so high that he wished that the Japanese would take the cultural center job on a permanent basis.[122]

Rockefeller, then, had no alternative but to exercise patience. He consoled himself with the thought that the project was being undertaken by the Japanese after all; he was simply helping them help themselves and perhaps "the final product would be a better one due to the delay." Indeed, he hoped that "it would be better adapted to Japanese needs and conditions and better received from the Japanese point of view as being more theirs."[123] Meanwhile, Rockefeller informally indicated to Matsumoto and Takagi that the Rockefeller Foundation would be willing to extend financial support to the cultural center project upon receipt of the specific plans for organization.[124]

Fund Raising and the Rockefeller Foundation

The Rockefeller Foundation was committed to developing human resources and nurturing a leadership group in a recipient country or any deserving organization. But, equally important, the foundation's assistance had a definite limit—five years. A five-year period was thought long enough to develop adequate staff and permit a gradual transfer to Japanese leadership.[125] Fahs believed an early transfer of leadership was needed "not to save money but to achieve the kind of Japanese attitude and response . . . necessary for the project to be successful." As he explained the philosophy of the Rockefeller Foundation, "the interest of the Foundation in this case was much broader. It involved basically the question of what the possibilities were in Japan for developing on a broad basis Japan's capacity for effective work in international relations." He went on to note that such work "might involve an organization such as the cultural center, but also organizations like the United Nations Association or University programs in foreign language and the foreign service." He also pointed out that institutions such as the international house and the cultural center had to be primarily led by the Japanese and "international in their interests so that they will not be subject to a charge of American cultural imperialism."[126]

The Rockefeller Foundation also expected recipients of Foundation aid to match those funds with long-term local support. It was a commonly shared view that the cultural center project had to have local roots so that it could continue under Japanese conditions.[127] Rockefeller wished no part of aid from the foundation to be used to breed people of dependency. As Dean Rusk, president of the Rockefeller Foundation, explained, the foundation believed that "aid from a paternal government may sap those sturdy virtues and breed a race of weaklings."[128] Donald McLean described fund raising as the central problem of the Cultural Center Preparatory Committee: "The true test of the program's validity would be the interest of the Japanese people in finding adequate means to support the cost of maintenance and operation of the program on a long-range basis."[129]

Thus it was agreed that American dollar funds would be raised to buy the land and to erect the center and that Japanese yen funds would be raised for the running expenses of the center. It was estimated that a fund of 100 million yen would be needed as an endowment for the latter.[130] The preparatory committee expressed its readiness to meet the challenge and declared that it would be possible "to put on a campaign for $200,000 or $250,000 from Japanese sources."[131] Upon hearing the news, Rockefeller was encouraged that the Japanese were willing to raise as much as 100 million yen. He also learned that Ichimada Hisato, governor of Bank of Japan, would head the fund-raising campaign.[132] The campaign was to begin on November 19, 1952, with the blessing of Prime Minister Yoshida Shigeru and U.S. Ambassador Robert Murphy.[133]

Initially, the preparatory committee was convinced of the advantages of having two institutions—a cultural center for scholars and an international house for students (one in Tokyo and one in Kyoto). Because of the financial constraints, however, the preparatory committee was advised to consider making two sets of preliminary plans—one plan for a center plus a single international house and the other for a center only.[134] After deliberations, the committee decided, largely because of the financial magnitude of the proposed project, that an international cultural center alone would be established in Tokyo. Also, the deadline for the grant application was fast approaching, and action needed to be taken quickly. The preparatory committee consoled itself by predicting that there would not be large numbers of foreign and especially Western students in Tokyo in the foreseeable future.[135] Thus Rockefeller and his Japanese friends abandoned the idea of building an international house for students in Tokyo, at least for the time being.

In the end, the Cultural Center Preparatory Committee submitted an application for a grant to the board of trustees of the Rockefeller Foundation in New York City just in the nick of time. The proposal for an international cultural center emphasized "the pressing necessity as well as enormous importance of cultural interchange between different peoples—side by side with political and economic relations."[136] It also highlighted the responsible position that Japan occupied between East and West. However, the proposal noted as well that a great gap remained between Japan and the rest of the world. Japanese scholars had long been kept out of touch with intellectual developments abroad. Moreover, because of Japan's limited foreign credit and the stringent financial circumstances of Japanese intellectuals, it was virtually impossible for them go abroad in significant numbers for study and mental stimulus.[137]

The application statement stressed as well the nonpolitical and nongovernmental aims of the proposed center. It proclaimed that the activities of the center would be devoted entirely to cultural relations and intellectual cooperation Thus the proposed center would (1) provide information on significant cultural activities and development in Japan and in the United States and to the extent possible in other countries; (2) develop and maintain a carefully selected and up-to-date reference library of standard works; (3) sponsor conferences, discussion groups, and education courses on current affairs; (4) provide a channel of contact between individuals and organizations in Japan and the United States and to the extent possible in other countries in the development of international cultural exchange; and (5) provide accommodations at the center for out-of-town Japanese scholars, teachers, researchers, artists, and intellectuals, as well as other American scholars who had the occasion to be in Tokyo.[138] Saxton Bradford regarded the last point as extremely important in U.S.-Japan cultural relations. He pointed out that, psychologically, it gave "more substance to the idea of cultural relations between equals than special privileges for Americans would."[139] Having such space available was considered essential to attracting persons to the center and enabling selected scholars to "live under the same roof" and thus to begin to understand one another better.[140]

At the same time, the proposal reiterated the two-way character of cultural interchange. With its high level of technical skill, image as a modern industrial nation, and rich cultural heritage, Japan was attracting the attention of an increasing number of foreign scholars, who were becoming more aware of the need to stay informed about Japan's cultural, political, social, and economic developments. The projected center would thus be in an ideal position to provide interested foreigners with help and guidance.[141] Fahs found the objectives of the proposed U.S.-Japan project to be sound and legitimate. He believed the proposed cultural center would provide a nongovernmental focus for the healthy development of cultural relations in the immediate post-treaty period. In the long run, it would provide a center for the encouragement of constructive Japanese participation in world affairs.[142]

On June 20, 1952, the board of trustees of the Rockefeller Foundation voted to donate $676,121 (or about 243 million yen) to the development of an international cultural center in Tokyo.[143] Confidentially, it was understood that the money the foundation donated to the cultural center was actually a donation from John D. Rockefeller III to the foundation with the understanding he remain an anonymous benefactor. Meanwhile, it was reported publicly that the Japanese were required to raise as much as 110 million yen in order to receive 243 million yen from the Rockefeller Foundation.[144]

Naming the Cultural Center

Once the funds were secured from the Rockefeller Foundation, the Japanese committee confronted the pleasant task of naming the new institution. Committee members had little difficulty agreeing on the Japanese name of the center—Kokusai Bunka Kaikan (international cultural house). But finding a suitable English name for it proved more problematic. They did not like the word *center* because the term *cultural center* might be confused with American cultural center, twenty-three of which were operated by USIE throughout Japan. Moreover, the term *American cultural center* might be a constant reminder of the occupation.[145] Some Japanese leaders also pointed out that the word *center* was used indiscriminately in Japan—such as pinball machine center and health center—and so they decided to avoid using the same word.[146] In the end, the committee decided on International House of Japan, even though the term *international house* had a specific meaning in the United States.[147] International houses were known widely in the United States as student dormitories where foreign students could afford to stay rather inexpensively and live together with American students. Notable examples of them were the ones in New York City, Chicago, and Berkeley.[148]

Once the name of the new institution was fixed, the preparatory committee sought a site for it. A suitable site was identified serendipitously in Azabu, a district of Tokyo. The parcel of land, which was some 3,000 *tsubo* in size (one *tsubo* equals a little less than two and a half acres), once belonged to the Iwasaki family but was under government control at that time.[149] Minister of Finance Ikeda Hayato arranged for the purchase of the property, and Minister of Foreign Affairs Okazaki Katsuo helped to authorize the incorporation of International House of Japan as a nonprofit organization.[150] The project officially got off the ground on August 27, 1952, signifying the institutionalization of the postwar U.S.-Japan cultural interchange.[151] The new International House of Japan would help foreign scholars and intellectual leaders make useful contacts in Japan, despite barriers such as language and the exclusivity that was a special characteristic of Japanese organizations; stimulate international studies in universities and other influential organizations in Japan through cooperation with foreign efforts; and direct attention to and encourage fresh ideas on issues important to Japan's interaction with the rest of the world, especially the United States and Asia. The programs of the International House of Japan were to be implemented through discussions, lectures, and publications.[152]

After completion of the new building, the International House of Japan officially opened on June 11, 1955.[153] Eighteen hundred guests attended the reception party to celebrate its opening. They included Prime Minister Hatoyama Ichirō and foreign dignitaries such as John Rockefeller, former first lady Eleanor Roosevelt, and Charles W. Cole, president of Amherst College.[154] The International House of Japan was thus now a fait accompli. It was a genuinely remarkable accomplishment, the shining symbol of U.S.-Japan cultural interchange, thanks to the untiring efforts of people such as Matsumoto, Takagi, and Rockefeller. Prof. Otis Cary at Dōshisha University called the establishment of the International House of Japan "the greatest event since the end of the war."[155] It was a historic accomplishment, even taking into account the fact that the rabid anti-American feeling triggered by the U.S. development of a hydrogen bomb reached its peak in Japan at that time. Since its opening day, the International House of Japan has served as the headquarters for cultural interchange between Japan and the rest of the world.

Chapter 6

The U.S. Cultural Offensive and Japanese Intellectuals

> If we want to try to avoid Japan's swing either to the Far Right or to the Far Left, some further thought and planning would seem to be required.
>
> —John K. Emmerson, 1951

> With the current stress on the power features of the Peace Treaty and on the bilateral Security Treaty, the broadly cultural aspects of the future Embassy operation take an added importance as a balance to the whole.
>
> —Saxton E. Bradford, 1951

By the end of World War II, the U.S. government had recognized how important a cultural dimension of foreign policy was to accomplishing its broad national objectives. International relations in the twentieth century was no longer just a matter of relations between governments; it was a matter of people-to-people contact as well. President Harry Truman clearly sensed the advent of a new age. On August 31, 1945, he proclaimed that "the nature of present-day foreign relations makes it essential for the United States to maintain information activities abroad as an integral part of the conduct of our foreign affairs."[1] In September 1945, Assistant Secretary of State William Benton articulately expressed similar beliefs about the importance of an international information program: "The development of modern means of communication has brought the peoples of the world into direct contact with each other.... Friendship between the leaders and the diplomats of the world is important, but it is not enough. The people themselves must strive to understand each other.... We must strive to interpret ourselves ... abroad through a program of education and of cultural exchange.[2]

Five years later, in 1950, Truman pointed out that the U.S. overseas information and education program was achieving results: "The task is not separate and distinct from other elements of our foreign policy. It is a necessary part of all we are doing to build a peaceful world. It is as important as armed strength or economic aid."[3] A State Department cultural affairs officer echoed Truman's words in later years in describing the character of American cultural diplomacy; "Together [programs of cultural relations, educational development, and information dissemination] comprise one leg of a three-legged stool of U.S. diplomatic relations—along with the political and economics."[4] Apparently, this State Department officer wished to draw public attention to the integration of three dimensions of American foreign policy—security, economics, and culture—into a single framework.

To Win the Hearts and Minds of the World

On April 12, 1950, about two months before the onset of the Korean War, Truman announced that the United States would undertake a multimillion-dollar "Campaign of Truth" to combat worldwide communist propaganda and to give other peoples "a full and fair picture of American life and of the aims and policies of the United States Government."[5] The U.S. cultural offensive was part of the U.S. efforts to achieve a "preponderance of power" over the Soviet Union and its communist allies.[6] This effort included carrying out psychological warfare and programs of gradual cultural infiltration throughout the world, including in key countries such as Japan, France, and Italy.[7] From a historical perspective, however, the Campaign of Truth was neither new nor the first U.S. government attempt to meet the nation's foreign policy objectives by cultural means. It was in fact part of a revival and an extension of the activities of the Office of War Information (OWI).[8]

USIE

OWI was abolished in August 1945, and responsibility for administering the overseas information program in peacetime was transferred to the new Office of International Information and Cultural Affairs in the State Department (later designated the Office of Information and Education Exchange). But the Office of Information and Education Exchange was short-lived. In its stead, two separate offices, the Office of International Information (OII) and the Office of Educational Exchange (OEX), were established in 1948 in the

State Department.[9] OII and OEX, known jointly as the U.S. Information and Education Service, or USIE, took charge of U.S. cultural foreign policy as of 1948. USIE called itself "the third arm of foreign policy" or "a basic arm of United States foreign policy."[10]

The U.S. Congress responded patriotically to Truman's request for bolstering the Campaign of Truth. Actually, the anticommunist Campaign of Truth was in line with National Security Council paper 13/2 (NSC 13/2, October 1948), which called for a hard-line cold war policy toward Japan in particular and which brought about the "reverse course" in the U.S. occupation of Japan (see Chapter 2). The Campaign of Truth was supported by the significant increases in congressional appropriations that followed the outbreak of the Korean War. Indeed, Congress almost quadrupled the budget earmarked for international information activities in 1951: from $32.7 million to $121.2 million.[11] In addition to the regular appropriation of $32.7 million for 1951, the first supplemental appropriation provided $79 million for the Campaign of Truth and the third supplemental appropriation for 1951 added another $9.5 million.[12] Thus the Truman administration received $88.5 million over the regular appropriation of $32.7 million, including substantial increases for radio operations, press and publications, motion pictures, exchange of persons, and various other cultural activities.[13] In the first half of 1951, for example, daily language programming by the Voice of America (VOA) increased more than 50 percent, from thirty hours and twenty-five minutes to forty-eight hours and twenty minutes. With the addition of daily broadcasts in nineteen new languages, forty-eight language programs were being produced by June 30, 1951.[14] As a result, the United States was able to maintain increasingly more powerful information and cultural programs abroad.

The Campaign of Truth in Japan

The Campaign of Truth in Japan had a specific objective in fighting the cold war: to create "a politically stable, economically viable nation that is capable of defense against internal subversion and external aggression and allied to the United States and the free world."[15] American leaders such as Truman, Dulles, and Rockefeller had recognized the increasing importance of a cultural dimension in U.S.-Japan relations, particularly in the posttreaty period. With U.S.-Japan relations specifically in mind, a public affairs officer in the U.S. embassy in Tokyo explained the important role that the embassy was to play in 1951: "With the current stress on the power features of the Peace Treaty and on the bilateral Security Treaty, the broadly cultural aspects of the future Embassy operation take an added importance as a balance to the whole."[16] Thus the cultural dimension of postwar U.S.-Japan relations was truly one of the three main pillars (security, economics, and culture) supporting the U.S.-Japan bilateral relationship, especially from the early 1950s on.

Target Groups of the USIE Cultural Programs

In aggressively pursuing its anticommunist Campaign of Truth against the background of the growing influence of communism in Japan, public affairs officers in the U.S. embassy in Tokyo implemented psychological programs aimed at combating "the misconceptions widely circulated by Soviet propaganda agencies."[17] Saxton Bradford understood that Japanese intellectuals could not be weaned away from their firmly held misconceptions about the United States by merely listing American virtues, disparaging the Soviet Union, and sounding a call to arms against communism.[18] The U.S. embassy in Tokyo made special efforts to reach the leaders of the press and radio who were in a position to influence the thinking of large and varied segments of the Japanese population. It recognized that the youth leaders, labor leaders, farmer leaders, women, and government officials were the most important target groups, in that order of priority.[19] This recognition of a "multiplier" factor was nothing particularly new, but it proved effective. USIE Japan redoubled its efforts to reach the leaders of young people (student and youth leaders and educators), as well as the nation's workers, with the appropriate material. Other USIE target groups were businessmen, political parties, fishermen, police and military, intellectuals, professional groups, and religious groups.[20]

The overseas information program was implemented not only through the media—radio, press, publications, motion pictures—but also through the libraries and information centers operating abroad and exchange programs.[21] For example, twenty-three information centers were in place in Japan in 1951, and at least fifty American professional librarians worked in the U.S.-run information libraries scattered throughout Japan.[22] The information centers, which used an educational and cultural approach to which the Japanese proved to be particularly susceptible, were the focal point of U.S. information activities. The centers contained a theater, a large space for exhibits, and spacious meeting rooms, as well as library facilities.[23] USIE officers, aware of the importance of reaching opinion makers in Japan, maintained contact not only with a great many city people but also with a substantial portion of the Japanese population living outside of the major cities. To interest Japanese intellectuals in the American information centers, USIE recommended that the centers send a particular professor or intellectual a postcard explaining the services of the center or inviting attention to a certain book or books.[24] Apparently as a frequent user of the information center, Saitō Makoto, a professor at the University of Tokyo, was greatly appreciative of the books available at the center: "Such a center does more for Japan than an Army battalion and costs much less."[25] As a result of efforts like this, the centers won public support from literate and attentive Japanese people.

The "Spiritual Vacuum" and Japan's Vulnerability to Communism

What were the social conditions in Japan as USIE began to carry out its information and educational programs? For one thing, the entire population was in a "spiritual vacuum" and thus extremely vulnerable to the communist influence. The confusion resulted largely from the war itself. The military defeat left the Japanese in a state of *kyodatsu* (exhaustion and despair); they were profoundly confused, indecisive, and lacking direction in their basic philosophy of life.[26] The Japanese emperor had been regarded as a living god, who had supreme responsibility for protecting Japan, the divine country, from destruction and desolation. But the indiscriminate bombings, defeat, and the subsequent military occupation abundantly demonstrated the fallibility of the supposedly infallible deities, including the emperor. Consequently, the nation's gods and goddesses of Shintō persuasion had been discredited, and the religious orientation of the people had been thrown into turmoil. The abolition of emperor worship with one stroke of the pen under the directive of the Supreme Commander for the Allied Powers dealt the Japanese an additional crushing blow, leaving American diplomats in the U.S. embassy in Tokyo unable to identify an existing religion that might fill the "spiritual and ideological vacuum" of the Japanese.[27] It thus appeared that the Japanese were extremely vulnerable to the communist enticement. And so the Japanese government found itself confronting two problems that had to be addressed immediately: how to fill the spiritual vacuum of the people and how to cope with Japan's vulnerability to communism.

Not only high-ranking Japanese government officials but also conservative leaders in business and industry were seriously concerned about the social implications of Japan's "spiritual vacuum." Among others, Mitsui Takakimi, a former member of the Mitsui *zaibatsu* family, disclosed his apprehension when he met with John Rockefeller in New York City in June 1951, telling him regrettably that there was "a real need for something to fill this void." In his opinion, democracy should replace the old imperial rule of divine order, but the Japanese people could not comprehend the full meaning of democracy.[28] Rockefeller recognized the seriousness of the spiritual crisis facing the people of Japan, and he shared Mitsui's concern. He knew that in Western democracies an underlying Christian faith gave people spiritual sustenance and fighting vigor in times of adversity, but the Japanese had lost a great source from which to draw a fighting incentive.[29] Rockefeller therefore suggested that the Japanese gain knowledge and understanding of the thinking and ways of the free world. He told them confidently, "Such knowledge and understanding will ... do much toward eliminating the intellectual and spiritual vacuum which exists as a result of Japan's defeat and recent period of relative isolation from the rest of the world."[30]

State Department officers such as John Emmerson were as seriously concerned about Japan's spiritual vacuum as Rockefeller and Mitsui. Emmerson reminded Dean Rusk that "the 'spiritual vacuum' in Japan, mentioned by a number of Japanese coming to this country, is a very real and serious problem." He pointed out as well that if the United States wanted "to try to avoid Japan's swing either to the Far Right or to the Far Left, some further thought and planning would seem to be required."[31] John Foster Dulles, America's indefatigable cold warrior, also grasped the seriousness of Japan's vulnerability to communist propaganda. Even though he was looking for an appropriate measure with which to cope with the problem, he was deeply troubled by the "mysterious Japanese elasticity"—that is, he wondered why the Japanese had become suddenly and apparently democratic in such a short period of time, even though previously they had been thoroughly controlled by military leaders. But Dulles found the answer: the Japanese were "fundamentally non-religious."[32] Dulles suspected that they did not "possess the requisite religious and spiritual qualities to withstand Communism over the long haul." And yet he was pleased to know that many Japanese were anticommunist, even though he recognized that the primary reason they hated communism was not because they were opposed to it, but because the communist ideology was connected so intimately with the Soviet Union. He also suspected that the Japanese never found the idea of subordination to a strong ruler an odd one, because they were not religious people in the Western sense of the term and they had no firm belief in the essential worth of the individual. In short, Dulles found it hard to believe that the Japanese would remain noncommunist for long.[33] Longtime Japanese resident Otis Cary had another take on the situation; he reflected that "possibly [the] Occupation had in reality opened doors of [the] country to Communism by breaking down old patterns of people and not putting anything that people could grasp in its place." In that way, the United States "may have done more harm than good."[34]

The Rising Fear of Communism in Japan

After the founding of Tokyo Imperial University in 1877, all things German enjoyed wide popularity among its students and scholars. For example, until the Pacific War of 1941–1945 German history classes constituted 80 percent of the Western history classes offered. More widely, until the end of World War II all Japanese universities had unmistakable influences of German logic, German philosophy, and German ideas of law and the state. As a result, most Japanese scholars were under the influence of the French existentialists and German Marxists. Marxism, especially theoretical Marxism, a stepchild of Hegelian dialectic, received considerable attention from Japanese intellectuals, in part because of the exclusive orientation of Japan's prewar higher learning, in both form and substance, toward German academic thinking.

During the interwar years, leftist scholars had analyzed their country's political, economic, and social systems as an important step toward mapping out a revolution. Divided in two rival groups, Kōza and Rōnō, they began in 1927 their heated, decade-long debate about the nature of the Meiji Restoration, Japanese fascism, and Japanese capitalism.[35] The Kōza, or Lectures, faction was the orthodox line of the Japan Communist Party. The Rōnō, or labor-farmer, faction broke from the party in 1927.[36] The sharp impact of Marxian economics was felt in Japan during the 1930s when the concept of a controlled economy had developed because of the war. That type of economic theory had suited the needs of the nation's war effort.

Political scientist Maruyama Masao has argued that after World War II Japanese intellectuals remained as much under the strong influence of Marxism and communism as they had been during the interwar years.[37] Immediately after the war, Marxists and communists enjoyed almost a monopoly of popularity and credibility among Japanese, because many had steadfastly maintained their ideological stance even while in prison during the wartime years. In Japanese academia as well, a scholarly debate over Japan's modern capitalism resumed among the Marxists of the Rōnō-Kōza factions after the wartime hiatus. Among controversial issues, they chose to debate vigorously the issue of dependence versus independence in Japan's relationship with the United States.[38]

In Japan, people seemed not nearly so worried about the influence of Marxism and communism as Americans. For example, Kagawa Toyohiko, a Christian activist, was heard to observe that if the economy improved a bit, the Japanese would not worry about communism.[39] Hyūga Hōsai, an Osaka businessman, pointed out that 90 percent of the Japanese were friendly toward the United States, but that a drop in the standard of living would give communists a chance to make some inroads in Japan.[40] Professor of economics Tsuru Shigeto found it more practical to put "more value to put resources into building up [the] economy to prevent Communism rather than into military needs to fight Communism."[41] Most Japanese probably took such an economically deterministic position because in a country so impoverished any improvement in the economy looked like a panacea.

In the United States, Marxism was generally understood to be an ideology that accepted the notion that one single system of thought resolved almost all problems. According to an American explanation, Marxism appealed greatly to many Japanese intellectuals not so much because of class struggle but because of economic determinism. The experts on Japan on the Council on Foreign Relations maintained that the Japanese traditionally liked to apply a simple rule to a variety of situations and that they tended to demonize their enemy by taking a Manichean view of the world in which the forces of light (we) and those of darkness (others) were fighting one another.[42] Other American specialists on Japan explained that Marxism was parallel to some of the Japanese traditional attitudes.

This American description of the influence Marxism on Japanese intellectuals may in part represent projection of the American self-image onto the Japanese. Historian Richard Hofstadter argued in his book *Anti-Intellectualism in American Life* that intellect, as a unique manifestation of human dignity, was both praised and assailed in the United States: "The man of intelligence was always and universally esteemed and praised, while the man of intellect was sometimes also praised, . . . but he was often looked upon with resentment and suspicion. The man of intellect . . . might be called unreliable, superfluous, immoral, or subversive."[43] In this sense, then, it can be argued that, in addition to their anti-Marxist biases, Americans' perception of the Japanese intelligentsia mirrored their anti-intellectualism to no small degree. Deep down in their subconscious, Americans seemed to view Japanese scholars with suspicion, fear, contempt, and even disdain.

At the same time, American leaders were so paranoid and obsessed with the fear of communism that they tended to exaggerate the degree of the communist threat—and they tended to view Japan through the lens of such paranoia and fear. Ethnocentrism and sometimes racism also added to the difficulty in seeing the country objectively. Consequently, many utterances of the Americans revealed their frustration and anxiety as well as their condescension and contempt toward the Japanese. Americans were not the only ones with contemptuous views of Japanese intellectuals, Jakev Levi, a correspondent of *Borba,* the organ of the Yugoslavian Communist Party, stopped over in Tokyo in January 1952 on his way home from covering the Korean War. After discussing a wide range of issues concerning world affairs with members of the Japanese Committee for Cultural Freedom (Nihon Bunka Jiyū Iinkai), the Yugoslavian journalist derided Japanese intellectuals for being naïve and out of touch with reality, wishy-washy about defending their own country, possessive of "no critical faculties," and ignorant of the aggressive, imperialistic, and non-Socialist nature of the Soviet Union.[44] Apparently, Saxton Bradford found much resonance with Levi's characterization of Japanese intellectuals. He sent Levi's story to the State Department, attached to his own critical commentary on Japanese intellectuals.[45] This anecdote begs the question, however, of what the Japanese thought of Americans and their cultures. The next two sections explore both the Japanese and Americans' views of each other's people and cultures.

Japanese Views of America and American Culture

American diplomats in Tokyo assumed that Japanese scholars had a low opinion of America, especially American culture.[46] For one thing, Japanese scholars described America as more materialistic and less idealistic than other countries, and they found Americans to be loud, vulgar, and short on gentleness and sensitivity.[47] In other words, Japanese professors portrayed Americans as people without much interest in cultural matters, despite all their material possessions. Japanese intellectuals also found marriage, family, and home in America to be bankrupt. In addition, they pointed out that the United States was home to racial prejudice and, in the South, the longstanding practice of racial segregation. Finally, Japanese intellectuals viewed America as a country that opted for expediency over principle and idealism. For example, during the occupation they observed an American foreign policy that was unstable and vacillating.[48]

Most Japanese shared scholars' stereotypical images of America. They believed that American civilization lacked spiritual and cultural dimensions and that American culture was shallow.[49] And they assumed that Americans tended to think only in material terms, because America was a materialistic nation without "soul."[50] They also thought that the average American was technically skillful but underdeveloped in cultural interests and intellectual capacity. As an American diplomat in Nagoya reported, "There does exist a genuine admiration for the American industrial and scientific advancements. But [there is] very little appreciation for our cultural or spiritual attainments."[51] Most Japanese also perceived America to be a violent and immoral country, with gangsters going berserk in big cities such as Chicago and New York and Americans given to intoxication and wild sprees. Of course, these Japanese views of America and Americans did not necessarily represent the reality of modern America. After all, the economics, history, and political science textbooks still used in Japanese schools gave little indication of the vast changes that had taken place in America since the New Deal period.

The truth is that American motion pictures were partly responsible for the negative images that Japanese held of American culture. Japan had over two thousand commercial motion picture theaters.[52] More than a third of the playing time in these theaters was given not to Japanese films but to pictures from abroad.[53] Indeed, American films had a tremendous influence in postwar Japan. For example, *Gone with the Wind,* a long-running American movie, opened on September 3, 1952, and turned out to be a great success. Most often than not, however, moviegoers took away negative images of America from the films or documentaries that were made largely for amusement purposes. Indeed, Hollywood movies tended to subject Japanese viewers to exaggerated pictures of America.[54] On the whole, then, the Japanese perceptions of American culture were less than flattering, if not entirely negative.[55]

Japanese intellectuals did not take American scholarship and culture very seriously until the end of World War II. Actually, most Japanese scholars had looked to Europe for wisdom and intellectual stimulation and, more specifically, to France, Britain, Germany, and Italy for intellectual leadership.[56] In the nineteenth and early twentieth centuries, the Japanese had regarded

French culture as the ideal and France as the fountainhead of Western civilization.[57] By contrast, most scholars of prewar Japan had scornfully viewed America as a nation without philosophical or moral depth. For that reason, the Hepburn Chair of American Constitution, History, and Diplomacy was not established at Tokyo Imperial University until 1918. It was the first American course offered in the history of Japanese university education.[58] The contemptuous attitude Japanese intellectuals displayed toward America was largely due to the influence of the European cultures, especially the French and German.[59] Indeed, early Japanese intellectual leaders imported a European disdain for American thinking and culture together with European Enlightenment thought and cultures.[60] The long association between Japanese intellectuals and their European counterparts made it easier for Japanese intellectuals to discuss European social concepts than American ones. For example, the idea of social discipline incorporated into the European philosophy of socialism had meaning and strong appeal for most Japanese, because it deeply touched peculiar Japanese spiritualism and experience. Conversely, Japanese scholars found the philosophy of American capitalism and individual responsibility quite difficult to understand, because American capitalism seemed to them to be something like self-interested materialism. One scholar described the intellectual milieu in postwar Japan sarcastically but quite accurately by saying that most intellectuals were obsessed with food rather than digesting American "thought."[61]

Japan and the Japanese in American Eyes

As described earlier, Americans and foreign visitors generally formed contemptuous assessments of Japan and the Japanese, but it appears that such assessments reflected their ignorance about the country and its people. How so? First, foreign visitors usually formed a problematical impression that was based on a short stay in Japan of only one or two months.[62] Second, most foreign visitors spoke little or no Japanese. While in Japan, they often remained isolated physically because of the impenetrability of the Japanese language and the tenacity with which Japanese clung to a system of cultural and social values. As a result, they had few chances to have a direct contact with Japanese. Third, sources of information were not balanced, and often they were one-sided. Foreigners, more often than not, were arrogant enough to assume that Japanese would or should be able to speak English, and so when visitors needed to communicate, they spoke to Japanese or interviewed them in English. When Japanese were approached under such circumstances, they did not feel very comfortable, nor were they in a mood to voice their opinions frankly, even if they were able to speak English. Thus foreign visitors probably had little choice but to spend time socializing the half of Japanese academics who were pro-Western, well-acculturated allies of a kind. In other words, the Japanese interviewed by foreign visitors may not have been sufficiently representative of the Japanese people as a whole. Indeed, Harvard professor Edwin Reischauer regretted that American residents of Japan made so little effort to contact the right Japanese. In his critical essay in *Foreign Affairs,* the house journal of the Council on Foreign Relations, Reischauer deplored the fact that U.S. embassy officials in Tokyo hardly attempted to establish contact with the Japanese of any political significance. He charged them with having less contact with intellectuals and oppositional elements in Japan than with English-speaking businessmen and conservative political leaders.[63]

As a result of their limited contacts with the Japanese and lack of meaningful communication, Americans often made overly hasty generalizations about Japan and its people; they liked to think they had become knowledgeable about Japan within a relatively short time. It was not surprising, then, that Westerners had a tendency to misunderstand and form misconceptions about Japan and its people. Actually, they more often than not projected their preconceived ideas upon Japan and its people only to reconfirm their stereotypical image. Thus their impressionistic observations of Japan often turned out to be either a distorted view of Japan or an illusion.

Western Perceptions of the Japanese

And what exactly were the perceptions of Japan and the Japanese? Westerners generally lamented that Japanese had a distinct psychological disposition toward being led. Americans, in particular, were afraid that Japanese were easily moved by circumstances without logical consideration and public discussion—that is, they were prone to being confused by clever propaganda, being controlled by a few leaders, and accepting newly imported movements (such as religion-based democracy, cultural movements, peace movements, and spiritual movements) promptly and yet superficially, without understanding the true meaning of them. Americans thus had a cynical disdain for the intellectual capacity of the Japanese people.[64] U.S. State Department officials feared that the moderate, gentle Japanese democracy might be attacked from both sides, communist and fascist, and nipped in the bud by these ruffians after the withdrawal of the American occupation army. In that event, the Japanese might very likely change again and become communist or return to fascism.[65] The apprehension of Westerners was based on their preconceived image that the Japanese were fickle, helpless pawns before the onslaught of the communists.

Obviously, the fear of communism reinforced such negative and effete images of Japan and its people, which necessarily reflected the Western ethnocentric and patronizing attitude toward them. Westerners seldom questioned their assumption that the Japanese were so childish and immature that they had to be taught the theory of democracy thoroughly and plainly. And yet Westerners truly believed that they were undertaking a supreme mission in which the Japanese had to be shown the true examples of advanced American, British, and Scandinavian democracy. After all, the best way to protect the Japanese from the communist threat was to explain clearly and accurately the strong points of democracy. At the same time, Westerners believed the Japanese had to be taught in the same fashion the essential spirit of Christianity, because Christianity should be the motivational power behind the anticommunist and democratic movements. Otherwise, the Japanese might begin to accept the idea that communism was not so bad after all.[66] Westerners understood that "many Japanese who are not Communists now could become Communists rather easily if they were convinced that the Communist Party was going to control Asia."[67] This fear of communism was a powerful driving force behind the U.S. cultural offensive in Japan.

U.S. Embassy's Perceptions of Japanese Intellectuals

Saxton Bradford and his colleagues at the U.S. embassy in Tokyo found certain characteristics of Japanese intellectuals quite annoying and a counterforce to the Campaign of Truth in Japan. Bradford thus called the State Department's attention to the problems surrounding "the attitudes of Japanese intellectuals towards the United States" and urged the U.S. government to address the problems immediately and resolutely.[68]

And what problems of Japanese intellectuals did American diplomats claim to have discovered? First, the distorted views of America and American culture that were generally shared by Japanese scholars annoyed the diplomats immensely. They were unable to stomach such views, they said, not so much because Japanese intellectuals' opinions were based on an unfavorable interpretation of fact, but because their views were "based on a complete misapprehension of what America was like."[69] Bradford profoundly regretted that university circles were infected with unfavorable stereotypes of American life, and that they were biased toward a Marxist orientation. He remarked that Japanese ignorance of America and American culture was "not that of a blank mind but rather that of a mind filled with [a] firmly held misconception about the United States."[70] He also criticized university professors for helping to create anti-American feeling among Japanese.

Second, American public affairs officers such as Bradford and Niles W. Bond deplored how little the Japanese knew about America and American culture, as Rockefeller discovered when he visited Japan in 1951. They held the disdainful view that the Japanese did not have adequate political, religious, or individual experience to understand Anglo-Saxon concepts of human rights, democracy, freedom, and many others that reflected the idea of American democracy. They suspected, therefore, that the Japanese confused the substance and form of many occupation-sponsored reforms because of their lack of understanding of American ideas and thought. They suspected as well that much of what was said about democratic ideas and organizations was unintelligible and rang hollow to most Japanese, because few seemed to understand the philosophical bases on which U.S. institutions rested.[71]

Third, the American diplomats in Tokyo were disturbed by the presumed naiveté of Japanese intellectuals about the nature of world politics. Bradford was especially bothered by the fact that Japanese professors seemed to apply a double standard in judging U.S. and communist conduct, imagining an ideal Marxist society that did not actually exist in the Soviet Union and a society of predatory capitalism that did not actually exist in the United States. Bradford insisted that this tendency to advance speculative interpretation without fact manifested itself clearly when Japanese scholars discussed the cold war confrontation between the Soviet Union and America.[72] He ascribed this unfortunate situation not only to the fact that a large portion of Japanese intellectuals did not have well-informed opinions of the United States, but also to the fact that they had no favorable views of U.S. foreign policy objectives.[73] Moreover, the American diplomats alleged that Japanese professors had practically no up-to-date knowledge of international affairs and that the Japanese were, on the whole, ignorant of the current world situation around them and the real nature of the Soviet state and Soviet foreign policy. On the basis of these subjective observations of the Japanese, Bradford belittled Japanese socialists for being moved by old slogans such as "class struggle," "dictatorship of the proletariat," and "economic democracy." He also criticized them for responding to those slogans without analyzing how Soviet propaganda used them. He felt that many Japanese intellectuals thought of themselves as socialists, even though they drew their politicoeconomic inspiration from primitive European socialist sources.[74]

Bradford was keenly aware that Japanese intellectuals preferred to steer a middle course and to take the neutral stance in reaction to their wartime and occupation experience for fear that a commitment to either side might make Japan once again the scene of battle. But he argued that the intellectuals' claim of a neutral stance in the sharply divided world and their much less skeptical attitude toward the Soviet Union reflected the dangerous illusion under which they were living.[75] He insisted that the intellectuals' attitudes derived not only from the philosophical idealism of Japanese academicians, but also from their communist sympathies and the impact of communist propaganda.[76] As for Japan's vulnerability to communism, Bradford maintained that the communist influence in Japan was greatest on the labor movement, the socialist movement, the intellectual class, and the students, but that Japanese vulnerability to the communist threat had little to do with the statistics of the Japan Communist Party. The Japan Communist Party was dangerous not for its numbers, but because it was the Japanese watchman, reporter, and agent for the communist world strategists who were ensuring that events in Japan could be geared to the global effort. Bradford added that this combination of communist ideological power outside Japan and domestic communist activity in Japan could pay off under many circumstances.[77]

Saxton Bradford and other American visitors to Japan also scornfully pointed out that two closely related traits characterized Japanese intellectuals: a disposition toward abstract theory and ivory tower thinking. American public affairs officers claimed that Japanese professors were too theoretical and not sufficiently empirical. According to them, Japanese scholars tended to elevate theory and the history of theory over analysis of what had actually happened.[78] It was charged that Japanese leftist intellectuals were loath to listen to anyone who would not take a theoretical position, assuming that the theoretical and abstract represented the highest form of scholarship, while observational and statistical studies, particularly those related to the contemporary period, belonged to a lower order.[79]

A group of visiting professors from Stanford University also acknowledged these characteristics of Japanese intellectuals. After participating in the first U.S.-Japan seminar, held in 1950 (see Chapter 7), they reconfirmed their preconceived image of Japanese scholars based on their conversations with Japanese participants in the seminar. Indeed, the American professors were struck by the fact that Japanese scholars were so theoretical.[80] Theodore Cohen, the Labor Division chief of General Headquarters's Economic and Scientific Section, regretted that the Japanese audience had not appreciated the lectures given by a professor from the Food Research Institute. The Japanese participants complained that the American lecturer "could not argue Marxist dialectic but had insisted on talking facts instead of theory."[81]

American scholars, especially Council on Foreign Relations experts on Japan, held a similar view of their Japanese counterparts. Princeton University professor Frederick Dunn and others pointed out that Japanese elite intellectuals preferred theory to an actual description of the world in which they lived. In fact, far too many Japanese scholars seemed content to simply add annotations to those of other annotators, which resulted in a dearth of analytical studies.[82] The American professors from Stanford observed that because there was a wide gap between pure research or scholarship and "practical affairs," Japanese intellectuals needed a great deal of mental adjustment before contemporary studies could become respectable and before there could be an easy relationship between scholars and the man in public affairs.[83] As a remedial measure, they suggested that Japanese professors learn from their American counterparts an important lesson: the content of theoretical considerations should be related to the facts.[84]

And yet the harsh criticism leveled at Japanese leftist intellectuals about their overly theoretical or abstract thinking was based too much on exaggeration, and it did not necessarily hit the mark. Testaments to their thinking were the famous seven-volume symposium proceedings *Nihon sihonshugi httatsushi kōza* (Lectures on the history of the development of Japanese capitalism), published in 1932–1933, and the eleven-volume symposium proceedings *Nihon shihonshugi kōza* (Lectures on Japanese capitalism), published in 1953–1955. Undoubtedly, leftist scholarship was under the profound influence of Marxism, but there was no question but that leftist intellectuals worked diligently. Their scholarship based on their elaborate analyses of Japanese capitalism was a product of the long-running Rōnō-Kōza debate described earlier. Perhaps because of their paranoia and rabid anticommunism, American and Japanese critics of Marxist scholarship ignored the other half of the work carried out by leftist scholars in Japan. To repeat, the fear of communism in general and the fear of Japan becoming a communist country in particular made it difficult for American leaders to see Japan as the way it was.

The second trait of Japanese intellectuals identified by Saxton Bradford was the long-standing tendency toward ivory tower thinking. Bradford did not hesitate to belittle the Japanese elite for being exceedingly withdrawn, theoretical, and of the ivory tower variety.[85] The American diplomats like him felt that university professors were prone to becoming recluses and losing contact with broad new developments by carving out small, isolated spheres for research.[86] They charged Japanese scholars with remaining aloof from direct participation in politics and business affairs. Howard S. Ellis, Stanford professor of economics, confirmed his preconceived view that Japanese scholars had "a strong penchant toward ivory tower thinking as well as a traditionally imbedded disinclination of the academic community to concern itself intimately and genuinely with contemporary social and economic problems." From his first-hand experience teaching the 1951 American Studies seminar, he acknowledged that the Japanese participants were "the cream of the crop from the numerous schools all over Japan" and that "their level of intellectual and professional sophistication . . . is very high." However, Ellis ended his commentary on a sharp note, saying that "their lack of acquaintance with America, particularly of those many subtle elements going into the American 'way of life,' is appalling."[87]

In all fairness, one response to the hostile American criticism of Japanese scholars' lack of knowledge of America and world affairs might be that SCAP censorship aggravated the hardship that Japanese intellectuals experienced after the war. As noted earlier, SCAP/CI&E carefully and severely controlled expression of opinion on occupation matters. In view of this situation, most Japanese scholars exercised self-censorship in the presence of the occupying power and kept their mouths shut altogether during the military occupation. In addition, the General Headquarters staff and American soldiers lived apart from the Japanese community for security and other reasons. Under those circumstances, Japanese intellectuals found it extremely difficult to express their views openly and freely and tended to be reticent in public discussions. Takagi Yasaka, a former student of renowned historian Frederick Jackson Turner and the pioneer of American Studies in Japan, described a situation in which "there were all too few opportunities for Japanese to discuss international problems freely with Americans or even with each other. It was difficult therefore to arrive at well-informed opinions."[88] Therefore, the Americans' harsh criticism of Japanese intellectuals should be taken with a grain of salt.

Bradford did, however, catch a glimpse of the silver lining behind the postwar Japanese development. He was encouraged to observe that Japanese public opinion was becoming articulate, even though it might not yet be completely trustworthy. Man-in-the street radio interviews and other public expressions of opinion indicated both a high degree of public awareness of foreign affairs problems and an important private dissent from official attitudes. He thought that the resumption of Japanese sovereignty might help the Japanese to release some of their long-suppressed views on international relations. But Bradford could not afford to be too optimistic, because he also saw a dangerous sign from an American perspective: an anti-American flavor to some of the dissent.[89] To win the hearts and minds of the Japanese in fighting world communism, the American realized that the U.S. government must display more adequately and systematically the intellectual and cultural attainments of America in the mainstream of Greco-Roman traditions and the Judeo-Christian culture.[90] He thus suggested that the United States use the strongest weapons in its cultural arsenal—books on history, economics, political science, psychology, anthropology, and sociology—in an attempt to compete with other Western books.[91] He observed that in these realms of scholarship the United States was in the vanguard, and American writings on these subjects could prove that the Americans, too, were able to theorize—a point on which the Japanese needed to be assured.[92]

Once Bradford accepted this difficult task, he plunged into it as his self-imposed mission. He was determined to better acquaint Japanese academicians with the reality of the world, so they might be able to realize where the true interest of Japan lay. Perhaps because of his profound fear and obsession with the growing communist influence in Japan, Bradford insisted that "a calm analysis based on simple fact [would] be more effective than a diatribe or a monotonous diet of straight anti-communist propaganda." He also took particular note of the Japanese admiration for American goods and techniques to tie in the Japanese economy and applied science with their American counterparts.[93]

The Cultural Cold War and Promoting Historical Studies in Japan

In the midst of this situation, how was the Campaign of Truth actually carried out in Japan? Public affairs officers at the U.S. embassy in Tokyo recognized that postwar Japan was in a state of flux—that is, it was a time of historical transformation when ideas and ideals played an important role in shaping people's minds and perspectives and in conditioning the pattern of human behavior. Because all Japanese, not to mention Japan's intellectuals, were determined to rebuild their nation from the ashes as quickly as possible, Americans believed that the study of history was enormously important; it would provide people with a sense of perspective without which the present would seem obscure and contemporary problems would look complex and confusing. Historians were in a position to throw light on the present through a deeper understanding of the past and of the historical process from past to present.

The U.S. embassy officers in Tokyo thus focused their utmost attention on Japanese historians, who, they recognized, had a great influence on Japanese readers. This effort was conducted against the backdrop of Japan's role as a battleground of the cultural cold war in East Asia and the U.S. government's deep commitment to fighting communism throughout the world. Actually, the Rockefeller Foundation also played a large part in fighting communism—it contributed significant funds to the humanities, of which history was an important part. For example, from 1950 to 1960 the total grants in the humanities given by the Rockefeller Foundation reportedly amounted to $37.6 million, of which about $7 million (roughly 19 percent) was earmarked for work in history.[94] Apparently, Japanese historians attracted the attention of American philanthropic foundations, including the Rockefeller Foundation.

At the time it was about to regain independence, Japan had over two hundred universities, thousands of historians, and immense library and archival resources. But American philanthropic foundations such as the Rockefeller and Ford Foundations saw Japanese historical studies rife with the growing Marxist influence over the interpretation and the writing of history. Moreover, they recognized the relative scarcity of good biography in Japanese studies in history. Those two areas were thus targeted by the Rockefeller Foundation.

Marxist interpretation of history, which had been influential in the prewar years, became dominant during the American occupation of Japan after the nationalist contenders were eliminated.[95] Japanese liberal scholars and commentators were unhappy about the situation. In his letter to the Rockefeller Foundation's Charles Fahs, Matsumoto Shigeharu lamented, "I am convinced that Japanese historiography is presently in a state of mess. And something must be done about it before it is too late."[96] He called for a more humanistic approach to the study of history and a non-Marxist approach to social sciences as well.[97] To redress the messy situation, Matsumoto recommended that biographical approaches to the study of political science and history be considered, because "Marxist analysis of politics and history reduces all great leaders to pawns of inevitable historical forces."[98] Sakanishi Shiho, a woman writer, concurred with Matsumoto. She ascribed the dominance of Marxist dialectical materialism in Japan's scholarship to SCAP's suppression of the more traditional historical teaching and its early encouragement of the Japanese left wing.[99] Paul Langer, who was in Japan studying the history of communism among Japanese students in his capacity of a Social Science Research Council researcher, agreed with these Japanese liberals. In an interview with Rockefeller, Langer remarked that "two fields of study which seem to be particularly in hands of men committed to Communist line of thinking are Russian Studies and Japanese History. . . . Most of Japanese history studied in schools of Japan has Marxist slant. What would be most constructive would be to offer [the] brightest young men in these two fields [a] chance to study in U.S., England or even elsewhere."[100]

The key historical period in modern Japanese history was the last half of the nineteenth century when the foundations of modern Japan were laid. The Meiji Restoration that overthrew the feudalistic Tokugawa regime, in particular, was the focal point of historical inquiry for many Japanese scholars oriented toward Marxism.[101] According to Fahs, "The dogmatic Marxist interpretation of that particular period provided the basis for the Communist doctrine with regard to where Japan was situated today and what the country should do tomorrow."[102] Fahs felt an urgent need to do something to counter the growing influence of Marxism in Japan. He and other officers of the Rockefeller Foundation thought it important "to support the few Japanese historians who were able and courageous enough to resist this prevailing dogmatism through new and more thorough studies of Japan's modern history."[103]

An interesting side note to this period is that Professor Sakata Yoshio, who specialized in the modernization of Japan, was selected as a Rockefeller Foundation fellow in 1956.[104] Sakata, of the Institute of Humanistic Sciences at Kyoto University, was trying to restudy Japanese intellectual history for some time, believing strongly that the restudy of Japanese history was "particularly important because of the distortions introduced by the Marxist school dominant among Japanese historians."[105] He was nominated for the honor by John W. Hall, a professor of Japanese history at the University of Michigan.[106] Fahs recognized that "Our help will enable them (non-Marxist historians) to move further ahead into the Meiji period."[107] He remarked in later years that the goal of combating the Marxist influence in Japan was an important consideration in the final selection in 1956 of grantees of a covetous Rockefeller Foundation fellowship, even though the Rockefeller Foundation declared in its mission statement that it was nonpolitical and nongovernmental.[108] This episode reveals that, notwithstanding its proclaimed principle, the Rockefeller Foundation was not necessarily above dodging its ideological neutrality at the height of the cultural cold war.

Another aspect of historical research that non-Marxist liberal scholars and the Rockefeller Foundation found peculiarly Japanese was the relative scarcity of good biography, especially political biography. Fahs identified the writings of good political biography with the development of a healthy democracy: "Biographic emphasis on the role of individuals rather than abstract social forces is healthy."[109] Accordingly, the officers of the Rockefeller Foundation looked for opportunities to encourage the writing of biography in Japan. Indeed, they succeeded in discovering Japanese candidates to suit their need. As a result, one grant-in-aid was awarded in 1955 to Tokyo University professor of political history Oka Yoshitake for his proposed work on the political biography of Yamagata Aritomo. And two grants-in-aid were made in 1958–1960 to Kyoto University professor Kōsaka Masaaki for his proposed projects in biography and nondoctrinaire interpretations of modern Japanese history.[110] There was little doubt that both Japanese scholars received fellowships from the Rockefeller Foundation on the merit of their research proposals and on the integrity of their scholarship. But it seems undeniable that the decisions of the Rockefeller Foundation were made primarily with a view toward coping with too much Marxist influence in Japan.

Promoting Area Studies in America and Abroad

The Rockefeller Foundation was equally anxious to promote area studies at home and abroad. At first, the concept of area studies was developed as a means of coordinating the many different disciplines in the social sciences and humanities with the goal of understanding a single culture or an area. According to historian Benjamin I. Schwarts, "An area is, so to speak, a cross-disciplinary unit of collective experience within which one can discern complex interactions among economic, social, political, religious, and other spheres of life."[111] Area studies presumably provided the best approach at the academic level to achieving a mutual understanding of the civilization of two or more countries and the spirit underlying their cultures.

Scholars utilized the comparative method in integrated area studies, continually drawing contrasts between the culture under study and their own cultures.[112] It was presumed that the development of an intercultural viewpoint contributed to objectivity in either direction. Thus the interdisciplinary or cross-disciplinary approach of research and teaching became a popular way in which to break down the unnecessary barriers between the "disciplines." In summary, then, area studies can be defined as an "integrated study combining the method of social sciences and the subject matters of the humanities for working out the total culture or civilization of a region."[113]

In area studies, the subject matter is usually a single culture or an area. At the risk of oversimplification, two different approaches have been proposed and practiced in area studies: the problem-oriented approach and the humanistic approach. In the problem-oriented approach, the problem may have to do with the ideas of modernization, developing economies, or democratization. This approach tends to center on the social sciences in which political science more or less plays an important part. In the humanistic approach, history and literature play a central role, with a special emphasis on the historical development of a given culture or area. This approach, because it seeks to reconstruct the total image of the culture or civilization of a given area, requires a great variety of knowledge about the area in question. Although the best approach to pursuing area studies is still being debated, whichever approach an area studies expert may choose, he or she is expected to synthesize a body of knowledge into a holistic picture of a country or area and its culture.[114]

Area studies emerged in the United States during World War II as part of the war effort. The field had grown out of the military language schools established to train young men and women in the languages of the enemy. In 1941 when the United States was at war, William J. Donovan, director of Office of Strategic Services (OSS), explained the rationale for employing the nation's best expertise in OSS, saying that it was to "collect and analyze all information and data which may bear upon national security."[115] Thus area studies developed to meet the need to gather and provide information about enemies. The purpose of training young people was to have them serve as interrogators of the Japanese—and later the Koreans, Chinese, and Vietnamese. The Research and Analysis branch was widely thought to be the most successful program in the OSS.[116] Anthropologist Cora DuBois believed that the collaborative work undertaken by the OSS during the war was the prelude to a new era of reformist thinking on an interdisciplinary basis: "The wall separating the social sciences are crumbling with increasing rapidity. . . . People are beginning to think, as well as feel, about the kind of world in which they wish to live."[117] Many scholars so trained played an important role in government activities during World War II.[118] Two decades later, in 1964, McGeorge Bundy, dean of arts and sciences at Harvard University, recalled that "it was a curious fact of academic history that the first great center of area studies . . . [was] in the Office of Strategic Services."[119]

By the end of World War II, the United States had made considerable progress in area studies. In the immediate post–World War II era, area specialists were much sought after, because American political and economic expansion around the world required informed, specialized knowledge of specific regions. Concurrently, the relatively new field of area studies was urgently promoted to meet U.S. security needs as the cold war loomed large on the horizon.

As the wartime experience demonstrated, area studies were so essential to the operation of foreign policy that the federal government and private foundations such as Rockefeller, Ford, and Carnegie were willing to provide area studies specialists with generous funds to obtain the authoritative knowledge available to them. Although the U.S. government took over the responsibility for funding area studies programs with passage of the National Education Defense Act in 1958, private foundations continued to pour money into established area studies programs in the United States.[120] As a result, large infusions of federal and private money contributed to the creation of many research and teaching programs in university area studies centers that focused on different regions of the world.[121]

Meanwhile, the American government and private foundations such as Rockefeller funded the expansion of American Studies abroad and, as a result, contributed much to founding centers for American Studies in foreign countries, including Japan. Chapters 7 and 8 will delineate the process in which the Rockefeller Foundation assisted Japanese scholars in developing American Studies in Japan with the support of the U.S. embassy as it went about conducting the Campaign of Truth in Tokyo. Ironically, however, American "soft power" diplomacy brought Japan the mixed results of solidification of the hierarchical order of Japan's centralized university system and scholars' abiding habit of dependency.

右上　進駐軍が使ったトランク式ラジオ
左上　ラッキー・ストライク　提供・たばこと塩の博物館
右　キャンプで使う固型燃料
東京・銀座4丁目角の服部時計店や松屋百貨店などが米軍に接収されてPXとなった。進駐軍には移動式のPXもあり、各地の駐留先を巡回した。PXに買物にきた米兵のまわりには子供や女性がまとわりつき、物をねだる光景が見られた。
左　ビール　米兵と酒は対語であるかのように、彼らが集まりくつろぐ場所では景気よくビールの栓が開けられ、空瓶が山をなした。

右・上・左　時流に便乗した印刷物
戦前の軍事色は敗戦とともに影をひそめ、アメリカ通を自認する知識人の著述から、映画・漫画・ぬり絵に至る広範囲な印刷物がアメリカ一色に塗りつぶされた。右は昭和21年発行のアメリカ映画の啓蒙書、上は人気漫画となった「ブロンデイ」、左は進駐軍の女性士

1. Daily necessities of the occupation forces. Reprinted with permission from *Shōgen no Shōwa shi* [A history of the Showa period of testimony], vol. 6 (Tokyo: Gakushū Kenkyūsha, 1982).

●アメリカ！アメリカ！アメリカ！

「鬼畜米英」の合唱が一転して、アメリカ賛歌に変わった。みごとというほかない変わりようであった。それはアメリカへの迎合というより、奔流のように入りこんでくるアメリカの情報を消化せねばやまないという、せっぱつまった焦燥感にかられていたというべきだろう。そうした情報から得たアメリカ風な自由で解放的な気分に、少しずつ日本的な肌合いをもったものに翻訳されて、やがて日本人の血肉に同化していくのである。

進駐軍の日用品 耐乏生活を余儀なくされた日本人からみて、PX（米軍内の酒保）には物資が豊富にあり、その横流し品は羨望の的だった。外国の品々に魅惑され、米国式の生活にあこがれる人々が大勢でた。右の写真は進駐軍が使った電気ストーブ。下はマッチ。

上 ギブ・ミー・チョコレート 米兵が無雑作にくれるガムやチョコレートに子供たちが群がった。
下「リーダース・ダイジェスト」昭和21年にアメリカ情報を満載して、日本語版が創刊された。

高まる英語熱 昭和21年2月、NHKの英会話番組がスタート。平川唯一のカム・カム英語に人気が集中した。

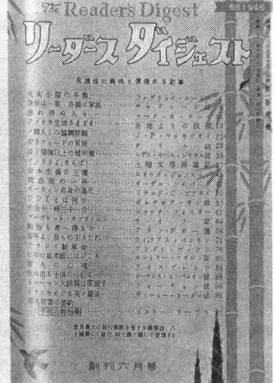

英会話の本、続々刊行 英語の必要性が声高に叫ばれ、昭和20年末までに20～30種類の類書が出た。

「日米会話手帳」終戦から1か月めに売り出され、300万部を超える大ベストセラーとなった。

2. Daily necessities of the occupation forces. Reprinted with permission from *Shōgen no Shōwa shi* [A history of the Showa period of testimony], vol. 6 (Tokyo: Gakushū Kenkyūsha, 1982).

日本のマック化
上のプラカードには〈日本の民主化〉
（デモクラチザアーチア　ヤポニイ）
となつているのを、ところどころ消し
て、〈マッカーサー化〉としている。
王座にそりかえつているのがマ元帥で
その前に天皇が座し、総理大臣がはい
つくばつている。幕張はアメリカ国旗
　　　　　　　　エフィーモフ（ソ連）

←京都の印象　　トボスキー（ポーランド）　　東京の印象→

3. Cartoon of General Douglas MacArthur. Reprinted with permission from Suyama Kei-ichi, ed., *Sekai no manga-apure nippon* [The cartoons of the world—postwar Japan] (Tokyo: Asoka Shobō, 1954).

4. Cartoon of Ginza Post Exchange. Reprinted, with permission, from *Shōgen no Shōwa shi* [A history of the Showa period of testimony], vol. 6 (Tokyo: Gakushū Kenkyūsha, 1982).

5. **Tokyo-Stanford American Studies Seminars, 1950: James Watkins, George Knoles, Joseph Davis, Claude Buss, and John Goheen with President Nambara Shigeru.** Used with permission of the University of Tokyo Center for Pacific and American Studies.

6. **Tokyo-Stanford American Studies Seminars, 1950.** Used with permission of the University of Tokyo Center for Pacific and American Studies.

7. The International House of Japan. Used with permission of the International House of Japan.

8. Matsumoto Shigeharu in front of the International House. Used with permission of the International House of Japan.

9. Matsumoto Shigeharu and John D. Rockefeller III shaking hands at the twentieth anniversary dinner of International House, 1972. Used with permission of the International House of Japan.

10. President Dwight D. Eisenhower meets with Secretary of State John Foster Dulles, 1956. Used with permission of the Dwight D. Eisenhower Library.

11. Dean Acheson at a meeting of President's consultants on foreign affairs, 1965. Used with permission of the Lyndon Baines Johnson Library.

12. President of Tokyo University Nambara Shigeru. Used with permission of The Mainichi Newspapers.

13. **President of Tokyo University Yanaihara Tadao.** Used with permission of The Mainichi Newspapers.

14. **Charles B. Fahs, 1958.** Used with permission of the Rockefeller Archive Center.

15. The Rockefeller family visiting Prime Minister Nobusuke Kishi's house during their 1958 trip to Asia. [Left to right] John D. Rockefeller IV, Blanchette Rockefeller, John D. Rockefeller III. Used with permission of the Rockefeller Archive Center.

16. John D. Rockefeller III in Japan, 1952. Used with permission of the Rockefeller Archive Center.

17. President Nambara Shigeru presenting a diploma for an American Studies degree, 1950. Used with permission of the University of Tokyo Center for Pacific and American Studies.

Chapter 7

Making Japanese Pro-American: The 1950 American Studies Seminar in Tokyo

> I would expect to proceed only in step with Japanese desires. We would never attempt to force democracy down anyone's throat.
>
> —Claude A. Buss, 1949

> The great strength of our educational system is its variety of patterns and its decentralization of control.
>
> —Dean Rusk, 1954

In early postwar Japan, very little was known about America and American culture. Both Saxton Bradford and John Rockefeller believed that the promotion of American Studies in Japan could be the answer to this problem, while serving as a weapon in the cultural cold war under way in Japan. And yet, as noted in Chapter 6, area studies in the United States, let alone American Studies, was still underdeveloped at that point.

What is American Studies? American Studies aims to produce a total understanding of the United States and American culture using a multidisciplinary approach. Such an approach seeks not only to bring about cross-fertilization in the social sciences, but also to bridge the gap between the social sciences and the humanities. American Studies concerns itself with the interpretation of America and American civilization by analyzing what makes the American people uniquely American.

Takagi Yasaka, the pioneer of American Studies in Japan, and his colleagues such as Matsumoto Shigeharu believed that one of the major reasons

Japan fought against the United States was that American Studies had not been taken seriously in prewar Japan. Both men lamented that Japanese experts on America had made so little effort to enlighten ordinary people about the United States. As a result, the Japanese people knew little about America and American culture.[1] Takagi genuinely believed that Japanese scholars needed not only to pursue American Studies seriously after the war, but also to disseminate information and knowledge about the United States throughout the nation. As he saw it, Japanese intellectuals were hardly acquainted with America and things American at the critical moment of the postwar reconstruction of Japan. That situation stemmed largely from Japan's long period of isolation from Anglo-American scholarship and also from the greater interest in Europe than in the United States before the war. Takagi associated the development of American Studies in Japan with the maturation of democracy in his country. Thus he stressed the great need "to study and grasp the essential nature of American democracy and fundamental spirit of American civilization." Tagaki went on to observe that "without the concept of individual personality, no one could hope to attain the true understanding of American Civilization, based upon the Christian ethical idea of human personality."[2] Apparently, Takagi, who was a Christian, believed that democracy and Christianity, as the most important faith and universal religion, were closely related.

Saxton Bradford, who believed Japanese scholars were lamentably lacking an adequate understanding of American life, American ideals, and American objectives in the world, regretted that Japanese intellectuals had a tendency not only to criticize the United States more on the basis of a complete misunderstanding of America, but also to react emotionally against things American.[3] He personally felt an urgent need to fill the wide information gap between his country and Japan before the communists in Japan and abroad took full advantage of this unfortunate information gap. It was thus obvious that Bradford wanted to promote American Studies in the context of fighting the cultural cold war in Japan. Rockefeller shared the same view. The Rockefeller Foundation was ready to address the potentially dangerous problems arising from this information gap in close cooperation and coordination with the American government. In fact, immediately after the war the Rockefeller Foundation resumed helping some Japanese leaders widen their views by inviting them to the United States to study. The first Japanese Association for American Studies (Amerika Gakkai) was also one of the many Japanese beneficiaries of the Rockefeller Foundation.

The Founding of the First Amerika Gakkai

In Japan, intellectuals as well as ordinary citizens have displayed keen interest in America as a nation of immigrants with ongoing processes of invention and reinvention of their new national identity. They thus have tried to grasp the essential components of American civilization and endeavored to elucidate the uniqueness that is America. Japanese have pursued American Studies not simply because their chosen subject matter is stimulating, but because U.S.-Japan relations are vitally important for their country. They have a genuine wish to contribute to maintaining amicable relations between Japan and the United States by helping to deepen mutual understandings between two peoples across the Pacific.

American Studies specialists in Japan have another specific objective in pursuing American Studies. Scholars specializing in American history have explored the American past for lessons to present to their audiences. They utilize the information and knowledge of the American past to help them define alternatives for their society and contribute to improving their own society. They have invoked the example of the United States to encourage the development of a liberal constitutional ideal in Japan.[4] Thus America specialists in Japan have made the knowledge and information gleaned from their work available to public discussions on American affairs and U.S.-Japan relations. They are expected as experts on America to participate actively in discussions on contemporary American affairs by introducing to the public their historical perspectives on America. Finally, scholars hope to gain a more accurate sense of the future direction in which humanity in general is moving, as well as to see better where they now stand.[5]

Amerika Gakkai was a group of Japanese intellectuals who were interested in studying America and American civilization. Facing the smoking ruin of their country and the prevailing confusion, these Japanese scholars shared the view that "the present day misfortune is greatly due to the lack of correct understanding of America." For them, building up Japan along democratic principles was a matter of urgent necessity, and they were firmly convinced that "the correct study of America and the dissemination of right knowledge of her" was one of the conditions indispensable to the democratization of Japan.[6] On June 29, 1946, as many as twenty-three scholars gathered in their capacity as promoters of American Studies in Japan at the Institute for American Studies on the premises of Rikkyō Gakuin University, a private university in Tokyo also known as St. Paul's University. The purpose of the gathering was to prepare for the establishment of Amerika Gakkai.[7] Rikkyō Gakuin University was the successor to the mission school that had been established by the American Episcopal Church. The Rikkyō Institute for American Studies had been founded in 1940 as a private research organization in cooperation with former U.S. ambassador Joseph Grew and other business and academic leaders. At that time, the Rikkyō Institute had three divisions, staffed by at least ten regular researchers who had pursued research on the American economy, politics, and culture.[8]

The pioneers and promoters of American Studies in Japan hoped that Amerika Gakkai would be a democratic organization free of the prewar evils of *gakubatsu* (academic cliquism), while pledging to give up the old methods. *Cooperation* became a key word.[9] On September 18, 1946, the Rikkyō Institute for American Studies solicited the Supreme Commander for the Allied Powers for his sympathetic understanding and support in behalf of a contemplated academic organization, and Gen. Douglas MacArthur responded quickly to the request with favor.[10] It was the congruence of American interest with Japanese interest that made it possible to establish Amerika Gakkai immediately after the war. On the one hand, American idealism and the traditional American sense of mission to spread democracy abroad were clearly at work. On the other hand, the genuine antimilitarist and pacifist sentiment that had grown out of the wartime experience made Japanese scholars feel it was incumbent on Japan to study America and things American with the utmost seriousness.

The first Amerika Gakkai was organized in March 1947. The organizers included Takagi; Matsumoto; Nakaya Ken-ichi, professor of the University of Tokyo; Fujiwara Moritane, director of the Rikkyō Institute for American Studies; and Shimizu Hiroshi. The opening ceremony of Amerika Gakkai was held at the Museum of Transportation at Kanda, Tokyo, in July 1947. It was open to the public and attended by nearly a hundred Japanese associated with university and academic organizations.[11] Takagi assumed the office of president of Amerika Gakkai, and Matsumoto and Fujiwara were appointed vice presidents.[12] Douglas Overton, an officer in the diplomatic service of the U.S. embassy in Tokyo and formerly a teacher at St. Paul's University, joined them. Amerika Gakkai met in Tokyo biweekly, but it was not yet a national organization, although it did have members from many parts of the country.[13]

The American Studies group tried, with difficulty, to publish *Amerika kenkyū* (Amerika Review), its monthly journal which reviewed American books and studies of contemporary trends in the United States. SCAP censorship was one of the many hardships facing Japanese scholars. Under the U.S. occupation, no statement critical of the United States was tolerated by SCAP.[14] The Civil Information and Education Section censored printed materials and raised two problems in the process of censorship related to copyright and criticism. First, it was reported that Takagi had been denied permission to republish his prewar Japanese translation of Max Farrand's *The Development of the United States,* which was published in the United States in 1918.[15] Second, Takagi learned that publication of a new edition of James Bryce's *Modern Democracies* in Japanese translation had been held up for a year. The reason for the delay was that the book in question treated too much the corruption of city governments in America.[16] Against the charges that CI&E had prevented the publication of Takagi's translation of Farrand's work, Donald Brown, chief censor of CI&E, defended his decision, arguing that the Takagi case had been primarily a copyright problem and had nothing to do with censorship. He flatly denied that there had been a delay at CI&E.[17] Brown admitted, however, that censorship had raised the question of certain passages deemed critical of the United States in the Bryce book. The main cause of the problem, he insisted, was that the Japanese publisher had not applied for permission to publish the Bryce translation until one month earlier. Be that as it may, Japanese scholars felt constrained. They regarded SCAP and the United States as the real obstacle when the publication was held up in censorship.[18]

Most articles that appeared in *Amerika Review* were on American history, mainly because scholars had little access to current materials on more recent developments in the United States. Fifty thousand copies of the first issue of the journal were printed, but that was not enough to make it self-supporting. Financial difficulties stemming from deflation and a lack of paper were the major obstacles to expansion, which forced the journal to suspend publication. But Matsumoto hoped that publication of the journal would resume after the signing of the peace treaty, when scholars would be able to write freely about the United States without fear of censorship.[19] Meanwhile, the membership of Amerika Gakkai shrank to only ten to fifteen.

The good news was that the principal members of Amerika Gakkai continued to work on the project to publish the seven-volume *Documentary History of the United States* (Genten Amerikashi) with annotations in Japanese. Beginning on February 10, 1948, they met almost every Wednesday at Tokyo University Library.[20] The series was published by Iwanami, a prestigious Japanese publishing house. The first volume, which treated the colonial period, came out in September 1950 and sold 2,500 copies.[21]

To keep the momentum going, Matsumoto asked Charles Fahs of the Rockefeller Foundation for foundation support for the promotion of American Studies in Japan.[22] But he was discouraged to learn that virtually no financial assistance was available, except for a $600 grant-in-aid appropriated for the Huntington Library in September 1948 (the library provided Amerika Gakkai with books about America).[23] The Rockefeller Foundation was, however, keenly interested in a long-range project to develop American Studies in Japan. Indeed, this American philanthropic foundation was seeking to determine what the possibilities might be for developing on a broad basis Japan's capacity for effective work in international relations.[24] Specifically, the Rockefeller Foundation sought to promote area studies in Japan not only on the United States, but also on many other parts of the world as its broad, long-term objectives.[25] Fahs explained that the Rockefeller Foundation was looking toward "the earliest possible firm establishment of American Studies within the regular framework of Japanese university education—American Studies as one of the several programs in foreign area studies which were necessary for intelligent Japanese participation in world affairs."[26] In the end, the Rockefeller Foundation chose to support American Studies programs that introduced American thought and life to Japanese in a similar way to its support of Japanese Studies programs in the United States, because the American foundation already had prewar experience supporting programs on Japanese thought and life in several American universities.[27]

The Road to the 1950 American Studies Seminar in Tokyo: The American Initiative

In July 1947, the first Salzburg Seminar in American Studies was held in Austria under the aegis of the University of Chicago and with the financial help of the Rockefeller Foundation under a special rehabilitation program. Encouraged by the successful seminar in Salzburg, Claude A. Buss, temporarily a professor at the National War College and later a Stanford professor of diplomatic history, explored the possibility of having a similar seminar in Japan. In his opinion, the time had come to encourage in Japanese scholarship a wide acquaintance with American life and institutions. Because Japan was under the U.S. occupation, Buss wrote MacArthur on October 19, 1949, hoping to secure a positive response to the idea of a seminar from the head of SCAP. Buss described the contemplated project as one of "helping the Japanese progress in their knowledge of American Studies," and he found MacArthur sufficiently receptive to the idea of having a seminar in Japan.[28] He also discussed the proposed project with Donald Nugent when the CI&E chief visited the United States.

A short time later, on November 4, 1949, Buss contacted Fahs about the possibility of a seminar and financial support for it from the Rockefeller Foundation, because he knew that the foundation was interested in developing area study programs in Japan and other countries.[29] Buss placed special emphasis on the private character of the proposed undertaking in a scholarly field that had hitherto been exclusively an area of government development: "We believe that it would be well for a private organization to be in action during the transition period, in order to lend prestige and weight to Japanese scholars who may be called upon then to argue in favor of a permanent place for American studies in the Japanese university curricula." Equally emphatically, Buss stressed the timeliness of his proposal; U.S. cultural diplomacy would soon change hands, from CI&E in SCAP to the U.S. Information and Education Service in the State Department. "As the influence of military occupation is relaxed, some reaction is to be expected," Buss reasoned.[30]

In making his arguments, Buss also emphasized the unique position of Stanford University and gave three reasons why Stanford should assume initiative and be responsible for the proposed project. The first reason was geographical. Stanford, one of the finest private universities in America, was located on the West Coast and thus closer than most other institutions to Japan. The second reason was historical. Stanford University had a Japan connection. In fact, one of the first academics of Japanese ancestry in the United States, Ichihashi Yamato, had been educated at Stanford in 1903–1908 (and Harvard in 1910) and later served on the faculty there beginning in 1914.[31] The third reason was political and humanitarian. Buss emphasized that his university was committed to "a general program of helping Japan in its search for democratic practices and ideals."[32]

In explaining his proposal to hold a six-week seminar with five or six outstanding "American scholars," Buss called for "the three-way cooperation"—among Stanford, SCAP, and the Rockefeller Foundation—that he also expressed as three requirements: (1) American professors must be persuaded to go to Japan; (2) SCAP/GHQ should provide for the selection of students, make the necessary housing and living arrangements, and provide for transportation; and (3) the Rockefeller Foundation should aid materially, as it did in Austria to defray the operating expenses of a seminar.[33] In an interview with Fahs, John E. Wallace Sterling, president of Stanford University, went so far as to say that his university was even prepared to donate $5,000 toward covering the operating expenses.[34] Buss never forgot to mention that delicate tact and diplomacy would have to be employed in dealing with the Japanese. He wrote, "I would expect to proceed only in step with Japanese desires. We would never attempt to 'force democracy down any one's throat.' I would want to be very careful that Japanese themselves assume a large measure of responsibility and display a degree of intellectual curiosity that only American assistance could satisfy."[35] Indeed, he was tactful.

Apparently, Buss's forceful argument and hard sell impressed the officers of the Rockefeller Foundation. Fahs replied, "A Seminar on American Studies for Japan would certainly be within the range of possible consideration."[36] He suggested that Buss immediately contact Takagi Yasaka, the towering professor of American history and diplomacy, who was scheduled to retire from the Tokyo University in March 1950. Encouraged by the Rockefeller Foundation's virtual assurance of support, Buss contacted Takagi on December 1, 1949, in the hope of starting a discussion on the possibility of a joint seminar in Tokyo. The American professor reminded his Japanese counterpart that a similar seminar had been an unqualified success in Austria.[37] Although on the Japanese side Nambara Shigeru, the president of Tokyo University, took the lead, Takagi laid almost all the groundwork to make the American proposal acceptable to Japanese professors.[38] Nambara, the intellectual leader of Japan and a Christian, was committed to enlightening the Japanese about democratic life after the war. He had been a professor of history of European political philosophy before he became president of prestigious Tokyo University in October 1947.[39]

The Japanese Response to the American Initiative

On October 12, 1948, the *Nippon Times,* an English-language newspaper in Japan, published an article on the appalling defects in Japan's advanced studies in the social sciences and humanities. It declared that "there is hardly any really scientific and solid social science research worthy of the name."[40] The social sciences was thus a field of study in which the United States could be of great assistance. It was sad but true that empirical study in any field of the social sciences had been underrated in Japanese universities; theory was associated with far greater prestige in Japanese academia. Allegedly, Japanese professors were still thinking in terms of nineteenth-century theory, even in the field of international relations.[41] Fahs learned from Yoneyama Keizō, a professor of political science at Keiō Gijuku University, that even students in Japan tended to think that a professor who bothered "grubbing for facts must be inferior."[42]

Matsumoto admitted that political science was one of the weakest social sciences in his country.[43] Nambara associated the development of political science in Japan with the maturation of democracy in his country. He believed that an increase in the number of experimental and empirical studies in political science was essential to sound thinking on political problems.[44] After all, he recognized, as he declared in an address delivered on October 2, 1948, that "the American scientific approach based on positivism and empiricism has hitherto not been quite 'fashionable' except among a limited circle of students specially interested in America."[45] Japanese scholars like him also felt strongly that factual study based on empiricism was essential to achieving a higher level of sophistication in the analysis of political processes and a democratic life as well. Through the leadership of Nambara and others, the Japanese Association of Political Science was organized in November 1948, and Nambara became its first president.[46] He hoped the association would encourage the development of experimental and empirical studies in political science.[47] Japanese scholars believed that the most effective way to catch up with the rest of the world was to establish in a leading graduate school a small research center where they could not only share the knowledge of the American members of the university, but also study their research methods. The Tokyo University president spearheaded area studies programs as part of a campaign to promote international cultural understanding.

In December 1949, Nambara visited the United States as a member of the U.S.-Japan Education Mission to attend the first All American Conference on Education concerning the Occupied Areas, held in Washington, D.C.[48] On December 14, he met with Charles Fahs and asked him whether the Rockefeller Foundation was still interested in assisting Japan—more specifically, whether the foundation was prepared to help establish an American institute in his country. The director of the Rockefeller Foundation's Humanities Division replied in most unequivocal terms: "The Foundation has been interested in foreign area studies both in this country and abroad.... We are interested in the possibility of development of American studies in Japan."[49] Referring specifically to the proposed seminar in American Studies that Buss was pushing, Fahs said he hoped such a seminar would contribute to the development of American Studies in regular university programs, and he urged Nambara to pay attention to area studies programs at the various institutions he visited in the United States. Fahs also hinted that when Nambara returned to Japan information gained from the United States could be the basis for his thinking on the problems of building up American Studies in Japan. Fahs added that any plan developed would "have the cooperation of Nambara, Takagi, the personnel in American studies at Rikkyō

[University], and other institutions."[50] He also made it clear that an American Studies seminar of the Austrian type was perceived to be within the established parameters of the Rockefeller Foundation's objective of institutionalizing American Studies in regular university programs in Japan.

On his way back to Japan, Nambara stopped by Stanford University and met with its president, John Sterling.[51] He also discussed a proposed joint seminar in American Studies with John D. Goheen, Buss, and other faculty members.[52] Among the problems they discussed, the central issue was the way in which cooperation could be achieved on a nongovernmental basis. To proceed with a plan, it was proposed that a Committee on American Cooperation in Tokyo be convened in Japan to maintain contact with a similar committee at Stanford.[53] Stanford had been considering for some time the need to develop new bases for intellectual cooperation between the United States and Japan. Clearly, then, Stanford was enthusiastic about accepting the invitation from the University of Tokyo to sponsor a series of seminars on American Studies in Japan in the summer of 1950.[54]

Nambara proposed that five Stanford professors teach their particular specialties on various aspects of American Studies such as government and politics, intellectual ideas, and diplomacy and the American role in world affairs for a six-week period. He was thinking that the Japanese participants would be graduate students and scholars who would be invited from several universities throughout Japan. Buss replied that "drawing on the traditional prestige of the former Tokyo Imperial University, seminars on American Studies would be in strong position to attract desirable cooperation and support among the several leading public and private institutions throughout Japan." As for the desirable transition of the initiative to Japanese leadership, the Stanford professor observed that the traditional conservatism that had governed relations among public and private institutions in the old hierarchy of Japanese scholarship could only be modified gradually. Thus "the quality of our offerings in the first year [1950] should be such that prestige will attract cooperating scholars and institutions, paving the way towards desired establishment of permanent studies in the American fields in Japanese universities."[55] The American professor could not have been more optimistic about breaking down the wall of the old hierarchy of Japanese higher education.

Seeking MacArthur's Support for the Proposed Tokyo Seminar

SCAP officers, including Donald Nugent, were pleased that talks were under way between the University of Tokyo and Stanford about a joint seminar to be held in Tokyo. Nugent promised Buss that CI&E would extend its good will and cooperation in carrying out the Stanford project as a private endeavor. But as a condition for cooperation, he hastened to add that a program of American Studies should be a long-term one.[56] As part of occupation privileges, the CI&E chief secured approval from the GHQ to billet the American professors sent to Japan to teach the seminar, thereby facilitating implementation of the project.[57]

As for the Rockefeller Foundation, Fahs indicated that he was not prepared to limit the interest of the foundation exclusively to the University of Tokyo: "I have the highest regard for Tokyo University—having been a student there myself—and for Dr. Nambara, but, there is such need for decentralization of educational developments in Japan that the needs of other institutions must always be borne in mind."[58] On a different occasion, he commented in similar vein that the foundation "did not think it wise at this time to fix a pattern of operation through either Stanford or Tokyo University."[59] Nugent had the same idea about the need to decentralize Japan's system of higher education. Embracing soaring idealism, Nugent and other CI&E officers associated decentralization of Japan's national organizations with the democratization of Japan. Nugent maintained that area studies as well as other educational developments should be decentralized if possible and that Tokyo University could not be expected to plan for the whole country. He seemed somewhat annoyed that Tokyo University was "a center of educational conservatism."[60]

Forming the Steering Committee

In April 1950, Fahs attended a meeting in Japan in which Nambara and several other Tokyo University professors discussed tentative plans for the proposed Tokyo-Stanford seminar in American Studies.[61] One of the problems in developing area studies programs was the difficulty in developing an interdepartmental organization. Among the participants in the meeting, Buss observed that Prof. Kishimoto Hideo seemed to have a clearer idea of what was involved in such programs than did other professors. Impressed with his leadership, the American professor described Kishimoto as "a first class 'driver.'"[62] Fahs emphasized that full Japanese participation was essential to make the seminar a success. He especially stressed the need for Nambara's leadership on the Japanese end.[63]

At the same meeting, the Committee on the Seminar in American Studies (CSAS) was formally organized for Tokyo University, with Nambara as chair. But the major responsibility for carrying out the seminar was assigned to a subcommittee—the Executive Committee on the Seminar in American Studies (ECSAS)—with Kishimoto at its head.[64] A Technical Committee on the Seminar in American Studies was formed under ECSAS to attend to the technical matters associated with executing the seminar. Seminar organizers decided that the Tokyo-Stanford Seminar in American Studies would be held on the campus of Tokyo University, and it would be led by five leading American scholars, who would be invited each year from 1950 through 1956. Over the seven-year period, the seminars attracted 598 Japanese specialists on America.[65]

The 1950 Tokyo-Stanford Seminar in American Studies

Because the need for university-based American Studies was felt so keenly in Japan, the first seminar in American Studies was held in the summer of 1950. The University of Tokyo received from the Rockefeller Foundation financial aid of $10,000 (plus $1,000 as reimbursement of the operating costs) for hosting the 1950 seminar, as well as a supplement of $5,000 from Stanford University.[66] Stanford also provided Tokyo University with the American professors. Over the entire seven-year period, the Rockefeller Foundation gave the University of Tokyo financial assistance of $200,000. In turn, the University of Tokyo contributed a small part of the expense— about $1,000 a year.[67]

The 1950 Tokyo-Stanford Seminar in American Studies was held during the transitional period from CI&E/SCAP to USIE in the State Department as part of the long-term U.S.-Japan cultural interchange. The seminar was the first attempt to test the idea of binational cooperation for cultural interchange since the end of the war. In his opening remarks at the reception on July 15, 1950, President Nambara declared that the purpose of the seminar was to "help to promote the mutual understanding between the Americans and the Japanese."[68] In a note to Fahs, the Japanese host characterized the binational gathering as "the first trial for the East and West meeting systematically under the academic atmosphere."[69] Calling the seminar "an unprecedented, historic event," the Tokyo University president also called it a very significant occasion "both for the promotion of American studies and cooperation of American and Japanese universities" and perhaps "one of the milestones on the road to the eternal peace not only of Japan and the Orient but also of the world at large."[70] The visiting professors from Stanford were John Goheen, professor of American philosophy; George H. Knoles, professor of American social and intellectual history; Joseph S. Davis, director of the Food Research Institute at Stanford; James T. Watkins, associate professor of political science; and Claude Buss, professor of diplomatic history.[71] Meanwhile, the summer seminar garnered much public attention.[72]

The nongovernmental, private character of the seminar was especially emphasized, even though it enjoyed the blessing and assistance of CI&E. The American visiting professors were astute enough to recognize that "the Free Enterprise nature of our undertaking has had favorable repercussions; yet we must be constantly alert for those forms of public support which would multiply the good fruits of cultural exchange."[73] In fact, the American professors maintained cooperative relationships with GHQ not only in connection with their billets and travel orders but also in dealing with the many unforeseeable eventualities in Tokyo and elsewhere in Japan.[74] In particular, they kept Donald Nugent and CI&E informed about their activities and problems. Even MacArthur received the American professors for an hour-and-a-quarter interview.[75] Meanwhile, the Korean War was being fought fiercely nearby. On the day the seminar started, Buss reported to Fahs in writing that "the Korean situation has not had too much influence on our project."[76]

Seminar Schedule and Content

The 1950 Tokyo-Stanford Seminar in American Studies was held for six weeks, from July 10 through August 20. Five preliminary conferences called specialists' conference were held July 11–14 by the five American visiting professors and Japanese specialists in the respective fields. Thus each day about twenty-five different specialists discussed the curricula in Japanese and American universities in the disciplines of economics, political science, history, philosophy, and American Studies.

The actual class seminar was held from July 17 to August 4, a period of three weeks. Each morning the entire group assembled in a general lecture hall where, over the course of the seminar, each American professor gave two lectures and four Japanese professors delivered a lecture. The lectures were delivered in English and interpreted. Some examples of general lecture titles are "Materialism and Idealism in the United States," "Pragmatism and Positivism in the United States," "Recent Social Change in the United States," and "Springs of Economic Progress in the United States." The American lecturers explained that the seminar was set up in this way to give "a feeling of solidarity" to the group and "a kind of unity and coherence" to the entire program. Participants were also divided into five small groups—

philosophy, history, diplomatic history, political science, and economics—in accordance with their disciplines. These groups met in the afternoons.[77] The average number of participants in each group was about twenty-five.[78]

In the fifth week, August 7–12, five sessions of roundtable conference were held, with the participation of about twenty-five well-recognized experts on some aspects of American Studies.[79] They discussed the "Forces Shaping American Culture," "The Changing Character of American Capitalism," "America's Role in World Affairs," "Recent American Historiography and Methodology of Area Studies in the Cultural Studies," and "Development of Area Studies in America."[80]

In the sixth and last week, August 13–20, public lectures and roundtable conferences were held at the University of Hokkaidō in Sapporo, located on the most remote northern island of Japan.[81] The public lectures, which covered the same topics presented in Tokyo, were delivered to audiences that numbered about four hundred in total attendance.[82]

The Participants

About 120 participants attended the regular three-week seminar, despite the midsummer heat and the heavy financial burden imposed by staying away from home so long.[83] Their financial hardships were exacerbated by the deflationary measures of the economic stabilization plan called the Dodge Line.[84] The participants, who represented more than fifty institutions of higher learning throughout the country, ranged in age from the twenties to the sixties and in status from graduate students to deans.

The American professors and the Japanese participants worked diligently each day from eight-thirty in the morning until five o'clock in the afternoon during the seminar weeks. In addition to the lectures, Japanese participants made many requests for outside lectures and meetings, including office hours and special programs.[85]

In the course of the seminar, the American professors were struck by how theoretical Japanese scholars tended to be. They also learned how devoted their Japanese counterparts were to historical subjects.[86] When the American professors asked a group of students in the Faculty of Law at the University of Tokyo what topics interested them for special research, the answers they received were the "Origin of the Monroe Doctrine," "John Marshall and United States Constitutional Law," and the "Philosophy of Thomas Hobbes." The American visitors found in Japan a great gap between pure research or scholarship and "practical affairs," and they detected a certain "uneasiness and insecurities" in Japanese scholars. The American professors gained the strong impression that Japanese scholars seemed to avoid deliberately either contemporary developments or applications of theoretical considerations to Japanese realities. Thus the Japanese needed to learn from them the importance of relating the content of theoretical considerations to the facts.[87] But they also felt that it might require a great deal of mental adjustment before contemporary studies would become completely respectable.[88]

And yet Buss was quite impressed by a deep store of knowledge of the Japanese participants. He wrote Dean Rusk, assistant secretary of state for Far Eastern affairs, "Many of them are profound in their thought processes and we are getting an unusually clear insight into the thinking of Japanese intellectuals."[89] Apparently, Rusk was pleased with the report from the Stanford professor. The assistant secretary replied, "I feel that this is the type of activity that should pay real dividends."[90] On the other side, Japanese participants were impressed with "the informality of American seminar methods and also at the fast pace and industry of American scholarship."[91]

Follow-up

Once the first U.S.-Japan seminar was over, Nambara pronounced the seminar a success and thanked the visiting Stanford professors, whom he praised as "admirably serious and sincere." Nambara attributed much of a success to four factors: (1) "the excellent personality and ardent efforts" of the Stanford professors; (2) the sincerity expressed by the visiting professors toward the Japanese students and especially "their genuine academic enthusiasm, frank open-mindedness, and wholesome friendship"; (3) the "beautiful harmony and cooperation" among the visiting professors; and (4) the seriousness and "keenness and liveliness" of the Japanese students.[92] The Tokyo University president never forgot to give the Japanese participants the credit they richly deserved. Each participant received a diploma at the seminar's graduation ceremony.

After the close of the seminar in Tokyo, Davis, Goheen, and Knoles visited the Kansai (Kyoto) region August 23–25 to explore the possibilities of future seminars at Kyoto University or perhaps Dōshisha University. Kyoto was an intellectual center in western Japan, comparable in importance to Tokyo. Among Japanese national universities, Kyoto University was regarded as second only to the University of Tokyo. Founded in 1897, the former imperial university boasted of having 350 faculty members and 8,000 students. The research-oriented university had seven departments: law, economics, arts and literature, agriculture, science, engineering, and medicine. Dōshisha University was one of the oldest private and Christian universities in Japan. It was founded in 1875 by Joseph Hardy Neesima, as he was called in the United States.[93] He had left Japan in 1864 to study at Amherst College and reportedly became the first Japanese to graduate from that American institution of higher learning. He eventually became one of Japan's first modern Christian leaders. Dōshisha University thus had American connections and a substantial amount of mission help.

Okamoto Harumi of Dōshisha University, a Stanford alumnus (1919), and Abe Osamu of Kyoto University, both of whom had participated in the Tokyo seminar, arranged a meeting between the American professors and the representatives of Kyoto and Dōshisha Universities.[94] At the meeting, the scholars from Kyoto and Dōshisha Universities displayed a keen interest in having a separate seminar in Kyoto in 1951—that is, a seminar similar to the one carried out in Tokyo. Or, if the University of Tokyo and Stanford planned a seminar for the summer of 1951, they hoped at least to host the American professors for perhaps a two-week period. The American visitors were struck by the obvious desire of the professors from Kyoto and Dōshisha Universities to cooperate in such a venture. The visiting Americans suspected that perhaps the interest of the Kyoto group was stimulated by its desire to share in the prestige now associated with Tokyo University for the seminar held there. They also saw no reason why the precedent set in Tokyo by the University of Tokyo and Stanford should prevent Kyoto University or Dōshisha University from arranging with some other American university for an exchange of professors or seminar project. Besides, all of the parties in the 1950 seminar—Stanford, the University of Tokyo, and the Rockefeller Foundation—regarded the Tokyo seminar as an experiment.[95] Little did anyone know that a Tokyo-Kyoto rivalry over American Studies seminars would eventually become an annoyance for the officers of the Rockefeller Foundation.

In the end, it was decided to hold the 1951 American Studies seminar at Tokyo University, with Nambara at its head.

Reviews of the 1950 American Studies Seminar

In the aftermath of the 1950 seminar, Nambara used his personal experience as leader of the seminar as the basis for significant remarks on the long-term implications of such seminars for U.S.-Japan cultural relations. First, in terms of maintaining amicable U.S.-Japan relations, Nambara expressed his conviction that American Studies seminars would make a significant contribution to the cause of peace and harmony between the two countries. In a letter to the Rockefeller Foundation, he wrote: "We will be able to render some real significant service to the people of both countries—promoting the understanding [of] the American culture in Japan, and also some day reciprocally the Japanese culture in the United States."[96]

Second, Nambara emphasized that the Tokyo-Stanford Seminar in American Studies had set the pattern for future projects of a similar nature that could be carried out elsewhere in the country, because "the workability of this kind of scheme is firmly established."[97]

Third, Nambara pointed out that interest in American Studies was widespread throughout Japan. Indeed, evidence of the popularity of American Studies in the country was the more than 150 applications received by the University of Tokyo for the seminar in the summer of 1950.[98] Nambara believed the seminar proved valuable not only for Japanese scholars themselves, who after a long period of isolation were given a rare opportunity to understand American culture directly from the visiting American scholars, but also for the promotion of American Studies in Japan. When those participants returned to their colleges and universities, the knowledge they acquired in the seminar would be further transmitted and scattered to their students. It was expected that the ensuing results would be "wide and penetrating," perhaps stimulating the establishment of chairs in American Studies in Japanese universities.[99] In other words, the seminar went far in putting American Studies on a new footing in Japanese universities. Nambara wrote Fahs: "It looks like the time for the American studies in Japan is getting ripe. It is turning out to be increasingly important to promote serious and scholarly study of America and American culture, which would be more fundamental and would not be so easily fluctuated by the sentimental feeling of the populace."[100] Obviously, Nambara was upbeat about the future development of American Studies in the country. But his less than careful use of the phrase "sentimental feeling of the populace" revealed that this Christian president, like many of his peers at that time, had an elitist attitude toward common people.

The Rockefeller Foundation was apparently pleased with the first round of the Tokyo-Stanford American Studies Seminar. The five participants from Stanford in the 1950 seminar recommended that the American Studies seminars be continued for three to five more years.[101] They pointed out that "a continuation of this idea promises cumulative results." The Stanford scholars also suggested that it was important to extend "our ideas beyond Tokyo and Stanford so as to achieve the widest possible basis for long-range intellectual cooperation between Japan and the United States."[102]

After reviewing the recommendations submitted by the Stanford professors, the Rockefeller Foundation indicated its willingness to extend financial assistance to Stanford and the University of Tokyo for five more years, until 1956, provided that the request for renewal was found to be reasonably justifiable. In doing so, the Rockefeller Foundation expected the proposed five-year program of American Studies to make noticeable contributions in three areas: (1) training Japanese teaching personnel; (2) developing the library on the United States at Tokyo University; and (3) spreading interest in American life and culture throughout Japan. Should such contributions materialize, the Rockefeller Foundation went on to state, the results would lead to the development of plans for a more permanent place for American Studies in the Japanese higher education system.[103] The Rockefeller Foundation and Stanford urged the University of Tokyo to assume vigorous leadership and control of the project immediately, independently of Stanford.

The Tokyo University professors were not anxious to do so, however; they wanted help from Stanford for three or more years. Nambara insisted that his university was not yet ready to assume the entire responsibility for directing the development of American Studies in Japan; it needed to learn more from the Americans. In fact, he feared that the American Studies "program, if placed in the hands of the Japanese now, would be a flop."[104] (Nambara may have adopted this approach because he knew that he would retire as president of Tokyo University in only one more year.) The Stanford professors supported Nambara's decision.[105] Thus the Rockefeller Foundation had no alternative but to accept Nambara's plea that the transfer of leadership to Tokyo University was premature, and so it decided to continue to support the University of Tokyo in 1951 and beyond.[106] The foundation hoped that the Japanese staff would have developed enough by the end of the five-year program that far less American help would be needed.[107]

Following up on the suggestions of Nambara and the Stanford professors, Fahs set the guidelines under which American Studies seminars would be held in Japan in the future. First, the summer seminars should be considered a temporary pumping measure and not a permanent project. Second, the seminars, for which Tokyo University would gradually assume greater responsibilities, should be given for the whole academic community of Japan and the United States, with Tokyo and Stanford acting as trustees.[108] Third, longer-term American Studies projects might develop in individual Japanese institutions under the stimulus and help of these seminars, but no single Japanese committee or organization should dictate what other Japanese institutions do.[109] The last guideline seems enormously important in the context of an overly centralized Japan. Perhaps the Rockefeller Foundation formulated this important principle so that it would embody the foundation's disposition toward decentralization.

American Studies and Democratizing Japanese Higher Education

In Japan, overcentralization was the rub in the bureaucracy of any organization. Indeed, in higher education as in many other fields there was a tendency toward overcentralization and regimentation that the Japanese had treated as something unavoidable since the days of the Meiji Restoration. Centralization versus decentralization was also hotly debated in considering the American Studies programs, even though the programs were carried out under private auspices. Specifically, the issue was whether the seminars should continue to be centered at the University of Tokyo. As an officer of the Rockefeller Foundation saw it, a bitter fight was being fought against "the old pattern of academic hierarchy and institutional pride attempting to assert itself in a new postwar world."[110]

Actually, the issue involved was twofold. One issue was the relations between the University of Tokyo and other prestigious national universities, notably Kyoto University. The other issue was the relations between the University of Tokyo and other universities in the Tokyo metropolitan area, on one hand, and in the provincial cities, on the other. A brief look at the larger picture of U.S. occupation reforms of the Japanese educational system may illuminate these issues.

The Japanese educational system was one of the most entrenched systems in the country. The Japanese Ministry of Education had not only a wide range of power and responsibilities for the organization and general control of the lower educational system as well as the power to control matters relating to art, science, literature, and religion, but also considerable authority and control over the universities. Likewise, each prefectural governor had on his staff a chief of the Division of Educational Affairs, who had responsibility for all educational matters.

Responding to the demand at the beginning of the occupation that considerable power and responsibility be returned to the hands of local people, CI&E acknowledged that "the principle is accepted that, for the purposes of democratic education, control of the schools should be widely dispersed rather than highly centralized," and so it recommended that the direct control of the Ministry of Education over local schools "be greatly curtailed."[111] It also recommended creating popularly elected educational agencies at both the local and the prefectural levels that would wield "considerable power in the approval of schools, the licensing of teachers, the selection of textbooks—power now centralized in the Ministry of Education."[112]

With a view toward studying and making recommendations on educational matters, the Japanese Educational Reform Council was established on August 9, 1946, as an outgrowth of the Committee of Japanese Educators, which was set up to work with the U.S. Education Mission headed by George Stoddard (see Chapter 1). On December 27, 1946, the Educational Reform Council submitted recommendations to the Japanese prime minister calling for reform of educational administration. The recommendations stressed the importance of matters such as correcting traditional bureaucratic standardization and formalism and securing independence of education and decentralization of educational administration. Among other things, the Council proposed that "in each village, town, city, and prefecture an education committee composed of members elected from among citizens should be organized to make decisions concerning education."[113]

Following the recommendations of the Education Reform Council, the Fundamental Law of Education was passed by the Diet on March 31, 1947. Article 10 of the law stipulates: "Education shall not be subject to improper control, but it shall be directly responsible to the whole people. School administration shall, on the basis of this realization, aim at the adjustment and establishment of the various conditions required for the pursuit of the aim of education."[114]

In 1947 CI&E sent the Japanese Ministry of Education a directive demanding that all Japanese universities except the ten large prestigious universities (former imperial universities), which were to remain national universities, be placed under the jurisdiction of the regions and provinces. CI&E argued that any system in which control stemmed directly from a purely bureaucratic organ was dangerous in a country with a long record of governmental restriction and even suppression of academic freedom. It was hoped that the CI&E scheme of decentralization would permit the regional universities to assert their distinctive local features and accommodate students not able to afford the expense of studying in a large city.[115]

As anticipated, CI&E's demand for a radical change in Japan's higher education establishment met vociferous opposition from government bureaucrats and scholars all over the country.[116] Conservative Hatoyama Ichirō and his government bureaucrats called for further centralization of the educational system. They justified the move toward centralization as a counterbalance to the rising power of the Teachers' Union, which was dominated by radical leftists.[117] Moreover, Japanese bureaucrats and scholars opposed to decentralization insisted that more localized control organs might include unworthy appointees of corrupt local bosses and some representatives of the public who would be unable to appreciate the true functions of a university. CI&E rebutted, however, that the dangers that such people might bring seemed far less serious than the dangers of regimentation and suppression by an all-powerful central government. And yet in the face of a violent opposition from government bureaucrats and scholars, CI&E had no alternative but to withdraw the demand.

In 1949 the Ministry of Education adopted under duress a token policy of decentralization in compliance with the CI&E administrative guidance and founded a *national* university in each prefecture by consolidating 250 institutions of higher learning into 68 national universities.[118] Four-year universities became the norm. Following the lead of the central government, prefectural and municipal governments also established public universities alongside private four-year institutions.[119] The new policy adopted by the government resulted ironically in placing Japan's new university system under the more stringent control of the central government.

Another difficult problem closely associated with overcentralization and regimentation was the traditional (and notorious) practice of the Japanese Ministry of Education of treating Japanese universities unequally in terms of both money and personnel. As of 1956, 35 billion yen out of the total Ministry of Education budget of 130 billion went to the 72 national universities, (and Tokyo University got 10 percent of this amount). Only one billion went to support of all kinds of private universities, although of the total number of Japanese students in universities, 290,000 were in private universities and only 180,000 in the national and other (municiple and prefecture!) publicly supported schools.[120] The prestige of Tokyo and Kyoto Universities was already well known throughout the country, and that prestige translated into more replete staffs and equipment for the two universities over the outlying regional or provincial universities. Tokyo University had substantial advantages and research funds, although salary scales at the various national universities were uniform. Another complaint, therefore, was that subsidies for research gravitated more toward the large national universities. In addition, Tokyo professors held the edge in getting renumerative magazine writing assignments, and they got more opportunities for government work and travel.[121] The consequence of the entrenched prestige of the large national universities was the ability of these centers to attract the abler scholars. Accordingly, it was harder for universities less favorably situated to retain the more qualified personnel. In this connection, Dr. Hiratsuka Masunori of Kyushu University strongly believed that "greater decentralization in the Japanese educational system was desirable."[122]

Although the SCAP idea of decentralization included the establishment of locally elected boards of education with much delegated power and authority, and although forty-six cities, towns, and villages, in addition to forty-six prefectures and five major cities (Yokohama, Kyoto, Osaka, Nagoya, and Kobe), elected boards of education on October 5, 1948, the idea of locally elected boards was short-lived because the fears expressed by Japanese bureaucrats and scholars proved to be not entirely unfounded.[123] Large numbers of teachers served on the boards that hired and fixed their salaries, thereby creating obvious conflicts of interest. And many board members, lacking a clear sense of public service, used their position to enrich themselves. With the rise of postwar nationalism, the Japanese Ministry of Education reasserted its influence over the locally elected boards, which tended to look to Tokyo for guidance.[124] Thus the new experiment was abandoned in 1955, three years after the end of the military occupation.[125]

This brief overview has revealed that the controversial issue of centralization versus decentralization pervaded many areas of Japan. Even the Tokyo-Stanford University American Studies seminar could not escape this problem. Like many projects of this kind, the seminar could hardly claim that it had been carried out perfectly and impeccably. Among the knotty problems left unresolved, one had to do with the larger issue of centralization versus decentralization. This issue emerged when scholars began discussing where American Studies seminars should be held in the future. Tokyo University president Nambara set the tone by making the general statement that such projects should be carried out on a nationwide basis and should not be monopolized narrowly by one particular institute. Having said that, he insisted that seminars be held at the University of Tokyo in the immediate future, citing cost efficiency to justify his proposal. The seminar "would not work efficiently unless some concrete institute takes real responsibilities and makes itself a dynamic pushing force," Nambara argued. "It would not be unfair and unreasonable for the University of Tokyo to take the role of caretaker of such [a] nationwide scheme in Japan."[126] No one present at the meeting challenged Nambara's statement by saying that what he said actually amounted to the University of Tokyo claiming monopolistic patronage of the American Studies seminars. Few seemed to doubt his sincere motives and his genuine good will because he was such a man of integrity. And, of course, his statement was made at a meeting in which all the participants were connected with the University of Tokyo in one way or another.

Although this particular problem about the location of the American Studies seminar was neither unique to Japan nor the Japanese academic world, it proved troublesome for both the Stanford and Tokyo committees on American Studies seminar.[127] The Tokyo University committee tried hard to find sufficient rationale to justify Nambara's position on cost efficiency. For one thing, it maintained that there was always considerable risk in shifting responsibility for the seminar from an efficient organization with experience and success to an unknown administrative committee in order to move the seminar from year to year.[128] Presumably, this argument made good sense, because more than a hundred people participated in the project every year. Second, the committee pointed out the important role a university library played during the seminar and thus underlined the indispensability of a university library being located nearby. It argued that university facilities such as a central library were essential to making the seminar effective and successful, because participants in the American Studies seminar often needed to use books in the university library in addition to the ones provided by the American professors. The University of Tokyo library was already considered substantial, containing over five hundred well-chosen works in American Studies. Besides, in 1950 CI&E did a good job in making books available in its information centers in Tokyo.[129] Indeed, the library proved to be one of the key factors in determining the location of where future seminars would be held. In addition, Japanese students had great respect for the University of Tokyo.[130]

Because the Tokyo University committee was undoubtedly sensitive to the criticism that the University of Tokyo was monopolizing American Studies seminars and that the students attending the American Studies seminars were Tokyo-centered, it was careful to choose applicants on the basis of wide geographical distribution, so that the benefits of the seminar might spread beyond the confines of the University of Tokyo.[131] But, in part because of the jealousy involved and in part because the former imperial university wielded enormous influence, criticism continued to be leveled at the University of Tokyo. Many of the graduates of this prestigious national university were scattered throughout Japan, teaching at various universities. It was reported that the conferences and roundtable discussions held in Hokkaidō in connection with the 1950 seminar had been arranged by a "very active, very capable" assistant professor of politics "reputed to be one of the four best students President Nambara ever had."[132]

CI&E officers such as Donald Nugent and Donald Brown were not entirely persuaded by the arguments of the Tokyo University committee, however. It was hard for Americans to accept those arguments at face value, because they already saw a tendency toward centralization in Japan. Brown viewed Tokyo University as "unprogressive" and wished the seminar to be more decentralized.[133] Nugent remarked, "The plan envisages only one location for the seminars. I can understand the feeling that the seminars should not be moved away from Tokyo University. On the other hand, I am convinced that two seminars, operating simultaneously in two locations, would result in far greater benefit to the over-all objectives."[134] Three years later, in 1954, Dean Rusk, president of the Rockefeller Foundation, testified before a special congressional committee: "The great strength of our educational system is its variety of patterns and its decentralization of control. We believe that it is not for government, nor for foundations, nor for any other group, to attempt to impose conformity upon this variety."[135]

In the end, after much wheeling and dealing a compromise was reached. It was recommended that the American Studies seminars be centered at the University of Tokyo with a short conference to be held at location distant from Tokyo after the close of the main session.[136] On the issue of centralization, Fahs asked Japanese scholars whether it would be possible to work toward a more nationally representative American Studies organization through the alumni of the American Studies seminars in Tokyo and Kyoto.[137] Apparently, his suggestion was made with the hope of solving the knotty problems of overcentralization. To Fah's dismay, however, Tokyo University's ambition did not stop in the field of American Studies alone. Several years later in 1958, when the issue relating to President Yanaihara's proposal for establishing an Institute of International Relations was brought up, Fahs tried to put a brake on Tokyo University's seemingly limitless ambition. He suggested that Tokyo University not attempt to do everything and urged the professors of Tokyo University to consider the possibility of a division of labor in foreign coverage among Japanese universities.[138] Fahs had strong opinions about the disadvantages of overconcentration at Tokyo University, and he thought that it might be better in the near future to continue help to Indonesian Studies at Waseda University and to look into possibilities for the Middle East (Arab) at Keiō University or Chūō University.[139] Be that as it may, the compromise of 1951 over the location of the center of American Studies seemed not to help much in solving the entire problem surrounding American Studies. Ironically, it ended up aggravating the equally, if not more, complicated problem of the Tokyo-Kyoto rivalry—that is, relationship between the Tokyo seminars and the Kyoto seminars. Nambara's assertion of monopolistic patronage of the American Studies seminars by the University of Tokyo roused ill feelings among many scholars on America, especially those in Kyoto, which resulted in a flare-up of the age-old Tokyo-Kyoto rivalry. This rivalry is described in detail in the next chapter.

Chapter 8

The Kyoto American Studies Seminar and American Soft Power

> I am also disappointed that the cooperation between Kyoto University and Dōshisha has not been worked out as fully as Goheen and Dangerfield led us to believe.
>
> —Charles B. Fahs, 1952
>
> Not even the collaboration of Kyoto University and Dōshisha, let alone the Kyoto seminar in the present form, could survive without some American money.
>
> —Virgil C. Aldrich, 1956

The Kyoto summer seminar in American Studies originated, in part, from the earnest wishes of professors and institutions in Kyoto. The Kyoto seminar was unique in the history of American Studies seminars held abroad in the sense that it was held every year but one (1953) for thirty-seven years (1951–1987).[1] The Kyoto seminar maintained such a high standard of quality for so long that it became widely known as the Kyoto American Studies Summer Seminar to many scholars of America not only in Japan, but also in the United States and the rest of the world. And yet the organizing process of this world-famous seminar was not as smooth as one might think; rather, it was quite rough and bumpy indeed.

From August 15 to August 24, 1951, a seminar in American Studies was held at Kyoto University as an extension of the Tokyo-Stanford seminar under a grant from the Rockefeller Foundation (see Chapter 7).[2] Stimulated by the successful experience of the 1951 seminar, Kyoto University and Dōshisha University decided to offer their own summer seminar in Kyoto in 1952—and not as an extension of the Tokyo seminar.[3] A joint committee was formed to organize the seminar. Scholars in Kyoto were so enthusiastic about holding a seminar of their own that they went ahead and made plans without help or even clearance from the Tokyo group. No one foresaw then that their actions would sow seeds of discord with the Tokyo group in light of established Japanese manners and etiquette.

On August 24, 1951, Torigai Risaburō, president of Kyoto University, and Ōtsuka Setsuji, president of Dōshisha University, jointly submitted a proposal to the Rockefeller Foundation for a grant to support the seminar project. Their document proposed that a Kyoto seminar in American Studies be given every summer beginning in 1952 with the financial assistance of the foundation for the benefit of students and scholars in western Japan. The proposal also requested that the Kyoto seminar be held for the same length of time as those held in Tokyo.[4] The wish of the scholars in Kyoto to achieve equal treatment with their counterparts in Tokyo was more than apparent in their proposal.

The Stanford professors who had already lectured in Tokyo gave a full and enthusiastic endorsement of the Kyoto proposal. In unequivocal terms, they expressed their willingness to help the scholars in Kyoto just as they had done with the professors in Tokyo. John Goheen wrote: "I shall be glad to do anything I can to contribute to the success of the Kyoto seminar." He added that it would be ideal if the Kyoto seminar were held on a trial basis for one year, like the one in Tokyo.[5] The philosophy professor believed that the Kyoto-Dōshisha seminars would be "the next and perhaps most constructive step" in placing American Studies in Japan "on a sound intellectual basis."[6] He recommended that the Rockefeller Foundation support a seminar in Kyoto for a month in 1952, independent of the one in Tokyo.[7] The Stanford professor also observed optimistically, "There is no doubt that American Studies in Japan will reach a climax with the establishment of the seminars in Kyoto."[8]

A Quick Response from the Rockefeller Foundation

On September 25, 1951, Charles Fahs at the Rockefeller Foundation asked Donald Nugent for a comment on Goheen's remarks. On October 11, the CI&E chief replied that the recommendation merited careful and favorable consideration. "Of lesser importance, but not without merit, is the advantage of 'decentralizing' culture interchange—that is, modifying to some degree the Tokyo monopoly."[9] Nugent thought the Kyoto seminar might have the salutary effect of helping to decentralize Japan's higher educational system if it were carried out successfully. Besides, the indirect benefit of the seminars would be increased geometrically rather than arithmetically, he added.[10]

Rockefeller Foundation officers viewed the proposed Kyoto seminar as a "constructive step" in developing American Studies in Kyoto and the nearby cities of Osaka and Kobe on an autonomous basis with Japanese leadership. The Kansai (Kyoto–Osaka–Kobe) area, a considerable rival of Tokyo with strong local feeling, was the second economic center of Japan. Its port cities of Kobe and Osaka represented a combination of trade and industry. Kyoto, perhaps the most important city in Japan in terms of cultural transition, was traditionally strong in philosophy and cultural studies. The Kansai was also the second most important area in educational institutions. It supplied Japan with many of its foremost writers and artists, and its Kabuki and Bunraku puppet plays were nationally renowned. Next to the Tokyo area, the Kansai area was the most exposed to foreign influence, and yet traditionally it had the reputation of being less open to modern ideas. Therefore, the maintenance of intellectual contacts with the United States was thought to be of real importance in the development of Japanese intellectual life over the next few years.[11]

Both Fahs and Roger F. Evans, director of the Rockefeller Foundation's Social Sciences Division, displayed genuine interest in having American Studies seminars held in Kyoto, so long as the proposed Kyoto-Dōshisha plan appropriately met the specific needs of the two universities in Kyoto. With a special emphasis on the division of labor in promoting American Studies in Japan, the Rockefeller Foundation officers insisted that the Kyoto seminar not duplicate the American Studies program at Tokyo. On October 5, 1951, an officer wrote, "Our interest might be greater if the Kyoto program would emphasize the humanities, including those humanistic subjects that might not be included in the Tokyo program." The same officer also suggested that some American institution other than Stanford serve as the American university sponsor for the Kyoto group. Such a university should have a good American Studies program and some interest in Japan, and it should be willing to undertake the labor and responsibility similar to that shouldered by Stanford in connection with the Tokyo seminars.[12] He then suggested the University of Illinois, Harvard University, and the University of Minnesota for consideration as the American university sponsor for the Kyoto group.[13]

Goheen had a hard time accepting the Rockefeller Foundation's suggestion, because he did not believe that the University of Illinois was the most desirable institution to sponsor the Kyoto seminar. Instead, he repeatedly expressed Stanford's willingness to extend a "gracious" offer to act as custodian for a temporary period. Speaking from his vantage point of having already worked with Japanese intellectuals, Goheen pointed out that identifying an American university to serve as sponsor required considerable thought and must be handled with great care in dealing with the Kyoto and Tokyo groups. The Stanford professor was quite right in thinking that the problem of choosing a sponsoring university in America was "a very complicated matter" when the delicate sensitivities of Japanese intellectuals had to be taken into consideration.[14] With Goheen's help and suggestions about seminar subjects and timing, the professors in the Kyoto group revised their initial proposal into one that met the specifications and requirements of the Rockefeller Foundation. On December 31, 1951, the officers of the American foundation finally decided that holding seminars in American Studies in a second location in Japan (Kyoto) had merit in complementing the Tokyo program.[15]

Seeking a Sponsoring University on Behalf of the Kyoto Group

Scholars in Kyoto made no secret about their wish to follow in Tokyo's footsteps and install Stanford as their sponsoring institution. But to complicate matters further, the University of Illinois expressed its willingness to sponsor the contemplated Kyoto seminar.[16] George Stoddard, president of the University of Illinois, and Prof. Royden Dangerfield pledged enthusiastic support for the Kyoto project. Stoddard was chair of the 1946 U.S. Education Mission to Japan, and Dangerfield had been a member of the Tokyo American Studies seminar staff in 1951. Both Illinois men stressed that the Kyoto project fit the program of their university, because the University of Illinois had a Japan Club whose over seventy faculty members in engineering, economics, agriculture, education, political science, and other fields had experience in Japan.[17]

Goheen did not give up the idea of Stanford helping with the Kyoto seminar. He suggested to the Rockefeller Foundation that Illinois and Stanford assume joint sponsorship for the time being. The Stanford professor wrote: "To satisfy the Japanese sense of prestige and, indeed, to secure the success of the seminars, it may be necessary for Stanford to act as custodian for a temporary period."[18] Joint sponsorship, he felt, "would afford a basis for a transition to the Illinois sponsorship if the Kyoto seminar should develop as has the Tokyo one. I am quite certain that this would work and satisfy everyone."[19] He also suggested that "for the present at least, it seems desirable for the committee at Stanford . . . do everything it can to set the Kyoto seminars on their feet."[20]

The officers of the Rockefeller Foundation took Goheen's suggestions seriously. They discussed the pros and cons of "sending *two* separate teams so far for such short stays in order to have seminars in a second location."[21] They came to the conclusion that the University of Illinois should be asked to sponsor the Kyoto seminar and that the seminar should be a joint project of Kyoto and Dōshisha Universities with the 50–50 support of the Humanities and Social Sciences Divisions.[22] Apparently, the Rockefeller Foundation thought the Kyoto seminar project was "highly desirable in view of the present critical period of U.S.-Japan relations."[23]

Following the recommendation of the two divisions, the executive committee of the Rockefeller Foundation decided on January 18, 1952, to make available $19,500 to the University of Illinois and $3,000 to the Kyoto group to support the Kyoto seminar in American Studies in the summer of 1952.[24] It was understood that the Kyoto seminar was a one-year project only, with no promise of support in subsequent years. The foundation also stressed again that the Kyoto seminar should functionally complement the Tokyo seminar rather than duplicate it. And the American foundation expressed the hope that Kyoto and Dōshisha Universities would be able to shift fairly promptly to a more normal year-round program of American Studies.[25]

And yet the officers of the Rockefeller Foundation still had two problems to tackle. One problem was how to sell the idea of the Illinois sponsorship to the Kyoto group. This problem had to be resolved if the Kyoto seminar was to be offered at all, because the Kyoto scholars still preferred the Stanford sponsorship. Another problem was the "face" aspect of the Kyoto grant. The professors in Kyoto were told bluntly that, unlike the Tokyo grant, their grant covered only one year with no prospect of extension. That stipulation must have hurt their pride, because the Kyoto scholars believed they deserved the same treatment accorded those in Tokyo. In early 1952, the Rockefeller Foundation's Roger Evans decided to stop in Tokyo and Kyoto during his trip to the Far East with a view toward promoting common understanding between the two sets of scholars.[26]

Age-Old Tokyo-Kyoto Rivalry: Whirlpool in a Pond

As soon as Evans arrived in Japan, he endeavored to mediate between the Tokyo and Kyoto groups. As he feared, he learned that the groups were at loggerheads with each other over the American Studies seminars. He also discovered that the tension was still mounting because of the unconcealed rivalry between them.

On the one hand, Nambara and Yanaihara Tadao, Nambara's successor as president of Tokyo University, were infuriated when they learned about the Kyoto plan, because they had been kept in the dark. Nambara, in particular, criticized the Kyoto scholars harshly. He felt their actions were a breach of trust and that "a patent was violated."[27] He was quoted as saying that Kyoto should have been encouraged to adopt an entirely different line of approach.

On the other hand, the Kyoto scholars had been interested for some time in developing their own plan so that they could have a seminar in the Kansai area. Apparently, the "uncalled-for" criticism leveled at the Kyoto plan irritated the Kyoto scholars considerably. They insisted that the Rockefeller Foundation not confine its attention to the Tokyo area. Scholars in Kyoto interpreted Nambara's statement as an ambitious attempt by Tokyo University to assert monopolistic patronage of American Studies seminars in Japan and hog them all.

Stanford professor George Kerr happened to be in Tokyo at the time of Evans's visit. Observing the quarrel between Tokyo and Kyoto, the Stanford professor described it as "part of the old pattern of academic hierarchy and institutional pride attempting to assert itself in a new postwar world," and he characterized the attitude of Tokyo University as "juvenile."[28] Indeed, Nambara's response may have appeared arrogant and absurd, but it is surprising in light of the great stature of Nambara, a man of integrity. To be sure, Kerr's remark may sound harmless, and yet it does reveal how American scholars looked at their Japanese counterparts. His comment "juvenile" resonated with Gen. Douglas MacArthur's gratuitous remark before a U.S. Senate committee in 1951 that the Japanese were "like a boy of twelve" (see Chapter 4).[29] Kishimoto Hideo, one of the leaders of the Tokyo American Studies group, expressed hope that with the retirement of President Nambara the American Studies seminars would become a more impersonal interest, by which he meant more of a university-wide interest. In a friendly manner, Kerr also suggested that the Tokyo group minimize or abandon its criticism of Kyoto plans for the good of all the American Studies seminars.[30]

By talking directly with the leaders of the two rival groups, Evans sought to iron out misunderstandings and promote a common interest in the development of American Studies in Japan. First, he explained that the Rockefeller Foundation's "basic interest is in looking toward area study leadership by Japanese in Japan." Second, he candidly told the Japanese that the Rockefeller Foundation had "not contemplated more than the Tokyo set-up preliminary to the building in of personnel and sources."[31] He also made it clear that any second grant to the Japanese would be limited to one year without promise of renewal. In this connection, Evans stressed once again that the Kansai area seminar should be joint (Kyoto-Dōshisha) and that it should be different from and complementary to the Tokyo-based activity to the maximum extent possible. The director of the Social Sciences Division ended the meeting by expressing hope that the two groups would "keep in close touch and 'go the limit' to make the ventures within this year complement and not duplicate each other."[32]

Goheen was able to anticipate the difficulties that rose from the Tokyo-Kyoto rivalry. In his opinion, the challenge to Tokyo's claim of exclusive right was obvious and "desirable."[33] Fahs viewed the dispute between the Tokyo and Kyoto groups as totally unnecessary. He wrote Evans: "I am a little disappointed, although not entirely surprised, that the group at Tokyo resented the Kyoto grant. It is very fortunate that you were able to be in Tokyo and Kyoto at this time to help to iron out some of the misunderstandings. I am inclined to believe, however, that it is just as well that we made the additional grant. I have tried repeatedly over the last two years to remind Tokyo that we were not giving them control over American studies in Japan and proposed to act independently. The Kyoto grant was perhaps needed to convince them."[34] Evans agreed with him. In reply, he said, "I am inclined to feel that some subsequent aid to the Kyoto group may be both necessary and desirable if both investment and goodwill are to be conserved."[35]

In April 1952, Fahs had a chance to go to Kyoto and talk with a group of professors of American Studies at Kyoto and Dōshisha Universities. From Kyoto University, he met with Ariga Tetsutarō, professor of theology; Taniguchi Yoshihiko, professor of economics; and Matsui Kiyoshi, junior professor of economics; and from Dōshisha University Matsui Shichirō, professor of economics. Ariga represented the planning committee for the Kyoto seminar. Taniguchi was Fahs's professor when the American studied at Kyoto University as a Rockefeller Foundation fellow. Matsui Kiyoshi was his former classmate under Taniguchi.

During the discussion, Fahs disclosed that the Rockefeller Foundation had the greatest interest in longer-term planning for interinstitutional cooperation or a division of labor in area studies.[36] The idea of interuniversity cooperation had grown out of the foundation's experience in extending grants to the German Association of American Studies and for a summer conference held at University College, Oxford, at which the British Association of American Studies was organized.[37] Fahs placed a special emphasis on wider intercollegiate cooperation to promote American Studies in the Kansai area.[38] At another meeting with new Kyoto University president Hattori Shunjirō, Dōshisha University president Ōtsuka Setsuji, and other scholars in the Kyoto group, Fahs discussed the ways in which arrangements could be devised for a regional division of labor in promoting American Studies. In doing so, he raised a question about the future of the Kyoto seminar: "How could cooperative arrangements or a division of labor in [the] area studies field be worked out among the universities in Kyoto and the Kansai?"[39] In fact, this issue of interinstitutional cooperation between a prestigious national university and a private university would soon prove to be a big problem for Kyoto scholars, despite the fact that they were so anxious to develop American Studies in the area.

Reviews of the 1952 Kyoto American Studies Summer Seminar

After all the twists and turns, the Kyoto seminar in American Studies was offered from August 4 to August 26, 1952. Seventeen seminar sessions were held under the auspices of the University of Illinois, Kyoto University, and Dōshisha University, with $22,500 in support from the Rockefeller Foundation.[40] Five professors from the United States—three in the humanities and two in the social sciences—were invited to teach at the seminar, which attracted 106 Japanese professors, instructors, and graduate students.[41]

On behalf of the American faculty members, Dangerfield reported that the 1952 Kyoto seminar was very successful.[42] He especially praised Matsui Shichirō and Takeuchi (Sterling) Tatsuji for contributing much to the success of the seminar. In fact, he called them the seminar's "kingpins."[43] Takeuchi, professor of international law and diplomacy at Kwansei Gakuin University located near Kobe, was American scholar Quincy Wright's protégé and the author of *War and Diplomacy in the Japanese Empire* (1936). The Illinois professor had so high an opinion of Takeuchi that he called him "a greater potential asset than even Takagi."[44] Dangerfield also reported that all the American lecturers were unanimous in recommending that the Kyoto project be continued.[45] He maintained that the outstanding lesson of the summer seminar was that "such seminars must not be an end, but a means to something more significant." But he went on to warn that "the point of diminishing returns is quickly reached. Repetition kills interest. Once the novelty is off, the Seminar is a 'dead end.'"[46]

Basking in their success, the Kyoto scholars were anxious to secure support from the Rockefeller Foundation for their grand long-range program, aimed at establishing an Institute of American Studies, presumably at Kyoto University, and an Institute of Japanese Studies at an American university, preferably in the Midwest. The Kyoto committee explained that the Japanese Institute of American Studies would facilitate the exchange of information and particularly research studies with American scholars and institutions. More specifically, it would serve as a clearinghouse for studies of Japanese society of interest to American institutions and scholars. Likewise, the scholars on the Kyoto committee explained that the American Institute of Japanese Studies would foster the study of Japanese subject matter at American institutions. More specifically, the American Institute of Japanese Studies would serve as a clearinghouse for making available to scholars and institutions in Japan the best studies of American society.[47]

The ambitious proposal presented by the Kyoto group also included holding an eight-week workshop in American Studies in Japan each summer, as well as a workshop in Japanese Studies by the American university that would sponsor the American Institute of Japanese Studies. It was hoped that such a system of dual workshops would do much to promote Japanese and American Studies in the two countries and would result in the introduction of new material into the existing curricula—a step that obviously the Rockefeller Foundation wished to promote.[48] The Kyoto proposal was indeed a cultural interchange program or a "two-way street" in the genuine sense of the term.

The officers of the Rockefeller Foundation were not very enthusiastic about the long-range program of the Kyoto group. Despite Dangerfield's positive-sounding report of the 1952 seminar, Fahs had serious doubts about the feasibility of the Kyoto group's proposed plan, especially the scale of the project.[49] Takeuchi had Fahs's confidence, because he minced no words when he asked for his opinion about a variety of proposed projects. Takeuchi was thoroughly convinced of the importance of the Kyoto seminar in the context of U.S.-Japan cultural relations (although he was dismayed at the level of anti-American sentiment emerging among Japanese intellectuals). And he was favorably inclined to think that every effort and encouragement should be given to putting American Studies in place in western Japan. He did scathingly observe, however, that for the Kyoto seminar too much money had been spent on nonessentials such as entertainment and not enough on matters directly connected with the efficient running of the seminar. Apparently, he believed the people of Kansai were too prone to seeking entertainment compared with the people of Tokyo.[50]

The University of Illinois Drops Out of the Picture

While the Kyoto project appeared to be moving down a bumpy road, Dangerfield of the University of Illinois dropped a bombshell about the pending issue of sponsorship. He announced that his university wished to be dropped from the list of candidates for university sponsor. He also revealed that Illinois might have been bypassed anyway because it had little to offer in the field of Japanese Studies. He recommended instead that the University of Michigan assume sponsorship; he thought it was much better equipped to participate in such a project.[51] Moreover, Dangerfield disclosed that President Stoddard was more interested in building a program in Near Eastern Studies than the one in Far Eastern Studies. Dangerfield hastened to add, however, that his university was still willing to act as an American cosponsor for the Kyoto seminar of 1953, if desired.[52] Fahs was not particularly surprised about this development, because he personally had wanted Illinois to become involved in a program in India rather than another one in Japan. Thus he had discreetly advised Stoddard that Japan might not be the most appropriate area for his university to pursue.[53]

To make matters worse and more complicated, George Stoddard left the presidency of the University of Illinois. Dangerfield explained that the change in the presidency would make it extremely difficult for the university to serve effectively as an American sponsor for the Kyoto committee. Because Stoddard had not yet been replaced, Illinois was virtually standing still educationally, which Dangerfield described as retrogression. Perhaps adding insult to injury, Dangerfield also divulged that if Illinois concentrated on area studies, it would be on the Middle East and certainly not Japan.[54] The University of Illinois was prepared and willing to defer to the University of Michigan or other universities with an interest in Japan.

Thanks to Dangerfield's impassioned pleading, the final decision of the Rockefeller Foundation on the Kyoto seminar was postponed until after

Fahs had frank discussions directly with the Kyoto scholars when he visited Kyoto in April 1953.[55] Takeuchi suggested that Fahs meet with Ariga Tetsutarō at Kyoto University. Takeuchi made no secret of the fact that he held a low opinion of a professor who had no experience teaching at any university other than Kyoto. In his opinion, such a professor was most likely to be too bureaucratic to be comfortable.[56] But he regarded Ariga as the best man to act as coordinator among the several institutions in the Kansai region.[57]

Accompanied by his secretary, Flora M. Rhind, Fahs arrived in Tokyo on April 10, 1953. The American visitors soon discovered that scholars in the Tokyo group, including Yanaihara and Kishimoto, were not very happy about the Kyoto program. They also learned that the Tokyo group wanted any Kyoto program to be different from that in Tokyo.[58] Five days later, Fahs and Rhind had a pleasant train ride down to Kyoto on the Tsubame (Swallow) express. On the following day, they called at Kyoto University. Fahs expressed his hope once again that the Kyoto scholars would work out something less imitative of the Tokyo program. He also told them that the Rockefeller Foundation had decided not to give the Kyoto seminar financial support for the summer of 1953 because of the impracticability of the seminar. He pointed out that adequate plans could not be worked out even with sufficient time. The American director reminded the Kyoto committee as well that a suitable cooperating institution in America had to be found. In addition, the Rockefeller Foundation must receive a real working plan and budget before it could make a decision on help for 1954.[59]

While Fahs was in the Kansai area, he was approached by several professors from Kwansei Gakuin University. Takeuchi, in particular, then proposed that professors from several institutions instead of just one (referring to Kyoto University) be placed either to serve on the general committee for the seminar or lecture in the American Studies program at Kyoto or both. In response, Fahs promised that the various possibilities for using Japanese talent in the Kansai area would be considered to ensure the quality of the Kyoto seminar.[60]

A New Proposal for the Kyoto Seminar of 1954: A Turning Point

After returning to New York City from Japan in the early summer of 1953, the officers of the Rockefeller Foundation found that the Kyoto committee had submitted a proposal for the 1954 seminar that incorporated a new idea. Under their proposal, two visiting professors were to be invited from the United States. One was to arrive in Japan in the early spring of 1954 and remain through the summer; the other was to arrive at the beginning of the summer and stay until mid-winter. In this way, at least one American professor would be in residence through most of the Japanese academic year. During the summer, when both American professors were present, they would give a cooperative seminar in American Studies jointly with perhaps three Japanese professors in the American Studies field recruited from local institutions. During the regular school year, the American professors would give regular courses in the faculties of law and of literature at Kyoto and Dōshisha Universities, so that they could have the advantage of contact with the regular student bodies and faculties. The University of Illinois offered to cooperate in administration and in the recruitment of American professors, as it had done in the program of 1952.

When Evans studied the application of the Kyoto group, he discovered a curious fact; the $32,000 that the Kyoto group was requesting for a grant was virtually the same amount Tokyo was receiving for its American Studies seminar.[61] Aware of the serious age-old rivalry between Tokyo and Kyoto, the director of the Social Sciences Division suspected that the Kyoto scholars felt they should receive as much as the Tokyo group for reasons of prestige.[62] Fahs also detected some envy in the countercriticism that the Kyoto group leveled at the Tokyo group. He wrote wryly, "This really involves envy and is in effect a compliment to the Tokyo program."[63] But Fahs was disappointed to find that there was no indication of a local contribution in the application, because he assumed that local support would be required in about the same proportion contributed by Tokyo to the same work there.[64] It was apparent that obsession with prestige and an acute rivalry with Tokyo scholars persisted among professors in Kyoto.[65]

In spite of all that, the Rockefeller Foundation officers were receptive to the Kyoto proposal. They assessed it as a constructive step in developing American Studies in Kyoto and nearby cities such as Osaka and Kobe on an autonomous basis with Japanese leadership. Such a development, they thought, was a logical counterpart to the assistance the Rockefeller Foundation had given over the last twenty years to the development of Japanese Studies in the United States.[66]

Thus after a one-year hiatus, the Kyoto seminar was held at Dōshisha University from July 19 to August 13, 1954, as part of a newly established year-round Kyoto American Studies seminar. The Kyoto seminar was sponsored by the University of Illinois, Dōshisha University, and Kyoto University under a two-year grant from the Rockefeller Foundation. The directors of the 1954 American Studies seminar were Charles M. Allen, professor of education at the University of Illinois, and Rodney L. Mott, professor of law at Colgate University. Five of the ten lecturers were Americans who had been teaching at Japanese universities, and the five others were Japanese scholars. Four fields were represented: education, American literature, political science, and economics.[67]

It was reported that the Kyoto American Studies seminar of 1954 was successful, but that only eighty-one out of the one hundred applicants participated. Reportedly, the seminar had "an average of quality, maturity, and evenness, lower than was conducive to optimum results."[68] The officers of the Rockefeller Foundation felt that the caliber of students in Kyoto had "not been quite equal" to that of the ones attracted to Tokyo. They also came to the conclusion that the program in Kyoto had been "somewhat less successful" than the one in Tokyo in securing stable sponsorship on the American side.[69] Despite such a lackluster performance, however, the Kyoto committee was able to secure a three-year grant from the Rockefeller Foundation in June 1955.

The University of Michigan as a Sponsoring Institution

The major problem the Kyoto-Dōshisha committee now had to solve was to find a cooperating university in the United States with a long-term institutional commitment to U.S.-Japan cultural interchange. The chosen institution was the University of Michigan. The committee talked with William Frankena, the Michigan philosopher who participated in the 1954 Tokyo seminar, and had hoped to reach conclusions about Michigan's sponsorship with Robert B. Hall, a political scientist at the University of Michigan, when he came to Kyoto for the Institute of Pacific Relations (IPR) conference.[70] At Evans's suggestion, Matsui Shichirō and law professor Rodney Mott set up an appointment with Robert Hall to discuss the ways in which an institutional arrangement could be made. The University of Michigan, with its Center of Japanese Studies, was a major base in the United States for work on Japan. It also maintained a center of field research in Okayama, Japan.[71]

After meeting with Matsui and Mott, Hall indicated that he favored his home university assuming sponsorship of the American side of the Kyoto American Studies seminar.[72] In his opinion, the work of the Kyoto seminar was quite in line with the work of the Center of Japanese Studies at the University of Michigan. Thus he wrote his home university to recommend that it sponsor the Kyoto seminar.

Back in the United States, Fahs found Marvin L. Niehuss, vice president of the University of Michigan, quite interested in the proposed work in

Japan. Fahs told Niehuss that it appeared to be a sound idea for Michigan as well as for the Kyoto program to have an institution with a long-term commitment to Japanese Studies assume sponsorship of the Kyoto seminar. He also explained that the University of Michigan was expected to be responsible for recruiting lecturers and handling payments to the American personnel should it assume sponsorship of the Kyoto seminar in American Studies.[73] The university answered the Rockefeller Foundation affirmatively. It agreed to sponsor the Kyoto American Studies Center and the American Studies seminar for one year, from February 1, 1955, to January 31, 1956.[74]

Scholars in the Kyoto group were pleased to learn that the University of Michigan had accepted sponsorship. In appreciation of the support of the Rockefeller Foundation, Ueno Naozō, acting chair of the Kyoto executive committee, pointed out the salutary effect of America on Japanese scholarship and the growing number of courses in American Studies at various universities in the Kansai area. He also called special attention to the fact that not only half of the newly established courses, but also curriculum, teaching activity, and guidance, were based on American ideas.[75] He regarded them as the tangible influence of the Kyoto American Studies seminars.

The summer seminar in American Studies held at Kyoto University from July 18 to August 12, 1955, offered twenty seminar sessions with the joint sponsorship of the University of Michigan, Dōshisha University, and Kyoto University under a Rockefeller Foundation grant. The directors of the seminar were Fritz Machlup, professor of economics at Johns Hopkins University, and Virgil C. Aldrich, professor of philosophy at Kenyon College. Six fields were represented: education, American literature, law and political science, economics, philosophy, and anthropology.[76]

After successfully holding the new year-round Kyoto American Studies seminar in 1954 and 1955, the scholars of the Kyoto group were able to point to its spreading influence in the Kyoto area. In doing so, they succeeded in persuading the Rockefeller Foundation officers to agree that the existing program was worth continuing.[77] Thus the Kyoto-Dōshisha committee secured an additional three-year grant for the period ending March 31, 1959.[78] This development underlines how much the Rockefeller Foundation officers expected from the Kyoto group. The American philanthropic foundation had a genuine interest in encouraging local initiative and support in the development of American Studies in foreign countries. The foundation's officers understood that it would take several years to complete the training of foreign scholars and the acquisition of library materials and to develop competence for planning and directing American Studies programs in foreign institutions. They also understood that collaboration between Kyoto and Dōshisha Universities was essential in executing the Kyoto program so that it would make the best use of American visiting professors and also increase the academic contact between scholars in the Kansai area and those in the United States. With the completion of the transfer of sponsorship from Illinois to Michigan, it was hoped that American Studies would develop as a normal and integral part of the educational programs of the universities in the Kyoto area.

The Effect of Provincialism on Kyoto-Dōshisha Collaboration

The Tokyo-Kyoto rivalry in American Studies and the lack of coordination it provoked between the two rival groups were not the only problems annoying the Rockefeller Foundation officers. Two additional problems had to be solved immediately. One was associated with the exclusivity, excessive cautiousness, and provincialism of the scholars in Kyoto. The other was the lack of genuine cooperation between the scholars of Kyoto University and those of Dōshisha University. Like the scholars in the Tokyo group, the general committee on Kyoto American Studies possessed the recognizable attributes of exclusivity and provincialism. They took the view that no professors other than Kyoto and Dōshisha professors were qualified to be on the general committee, even though, as noted earlier, Professor Takeuchi of Kwansei Gakuin University had appealed for professors of universities other than Kyoto and Dōshisha either to be placed on the general committee for the seminar or to be allowed to lecture in the American Studies program in Kyoto or both. Clearly, then, a more liberal opening of membership on the general committee for the seminar to other scholars in the Kansai area was needed, because it was feared that the excluded professors would withhold full cooperation because of lack of such recognition.[79]

One incident reveals how exclusive, parochial, and snobbish the general committee on Kyoto American Studies could be. Suekawa Hiroshi, a law professor, was president of Ritsumeikan University, a private university in Kyoto with seventeen thousand students. Ritsumeikan was known as a major center of leftist strength in Kyoto. Commenting on the problem of communism or Marxism in the universities, Namba Monkichi, president of Kobe College, considered the influence of communism on campus still serious, particularly in the faculties of economics—even at Dosihsha University—although he considered Kyoto University and Ritsumeikan particularly bad.[80] Suekawa asked Rodney Mott to give an entire course at his university. Mott, a visiting Fulbright professor for the first semester of 1954–1955, who was working to develop Fulbright cooperation with the 1955 summer seminar in Kyoto, agreed to give three lectures at Ritsumeikan. When Mott raised this matter with the general committee on Kyoto American Studies, he was told that any such action might seriously strain relations and common understanding between Kyoto University and Dōshisha University in the whole arrangement of the Kyoto seminar. To put it differently, the general committee practically forbade Mott to give lectures at Suekawa's university. Ritsumeikan took the committee's decision as an unwarranted rebuff. As a result, only four professors from Ritsumeikan attended the summer seminar of that year. Gregory Henderson, a U.S. Information Agency officer in Kyoto, regretted what had happened in Kyoto; he felt that a real opportunity was "muffed" by the decision of the general committee, because seventeen thousand students at Ritsumeikan were kept isolated from the American influence. The USIA officer went so far as to say that any future Rockefeller Foundation grants (1956 or later) to the Kyoto seminar should be conditioned on a willingness to cooperate more generously with other institutions of the area. From that experience, Mott gained the strong impression that deep-seated provincialism, even jealousy, persisted among scholars of the Kyoto group.[81]

It was anyone's guess whether Henderson's suggestion had any impact on the subsequent decision of the Rockefeller Foundation. But it is interesting to note that in 1955 lectures were given by visiting American scholars at the request of other universities and institutions in the Kansai area. Mott, for example, gave lectures before the Organization of University Professors and at the American Cultural Center in Kyoto. Machlup lectured at Kobe University, Osaka University, and some other institutions.[82] These facts inescapably point to the conclusion that a handsome grant from the Rockefeller Foundation had the powerful effect of cracking the wall of exclusivity and provincialism erected by the intellectuals in Kyoto. The membership of the general committee on Kyoto American Studies was opened up in 1955, the year in which Namba Monkichi, president of Kobe College, joined the committee. Fahs was pleased with the participation of Namba in the general committee.[83]

The second problem that afflicted the Kyoto seminar was the lack of genuine cooperation between the professors of Kyoto University and those of Dōshisha University. The Rockefeller Foundation sought to promote interuniversity cooperation as an innovative way to develop American Studies in foreign countries. In this sense, then, collaboration between the two universities was essential to accomplishing such an objective. The officers of the Rockefeller Foundation quickly learned, however, that the collaborative work between the Kyoto University, a prestigious national university, and Dōshisha University, a private university, would not proceed as smoothly as they had expected. National universities as a rule enjoyed higher prestige than private universities, and they were better staffed on the whole. In an interview, Ueno Naozō, former president of Dōshisha University, recalled his difficult dealings with his counterparts at Kyoto University: "I was told such a terrible thing that professors of a national university could not do things together with professors of a private university. But actually most administrative matters were taken care of by the Dōshisha side."[84] Although not all professors of Kyoto University were as arrogant and snobbish as the ones with whom Ueno presumably dealt, his statement does, nevertheless, seem to represent fairly accurately the general attitude that professors of the national universities usually adopted.

The lack of smooth coordination between the two universities in Kyoto resulted in part from the fact that the postwar American Studies seminars depended "almost completely on the Americans financed by the Rockefeller Foundation, because the Japanese were quite unable to pick up this dollar cost." In the same interview, Mott also ventured the opinion that the Kyoto seminar might merit continued support from the Rockefeller Foundation for a period long enough for the seminar to take root in the Japanese universities concerned. Otherwise, he was afraid that "the Kyoto activity is to die aborning."[85] Virgil Aldrich, an American participant in the 1955 Kyoto seminar, shared Mott's concern. He felt that not even the collaboration of Kyoto University and Dōshisha University, let alone the Kyoto seminar in the present form, "could survive without some American money."[86] Aldrich attached great importance to the role of the Kyoto seminar in spreading American culture in Japan. The American philosophy professor explained that the American influence "has already done its work, or much of it in Tokyo, almost to the saturating point. If you want to touch and influence the Japanese mind, Kyoto ought to be the very city, because it is situated in the strategic spot in between Osaka-Kobe and Tokyo."[87]

It was under these circumstances that a lack of genuine cooperation manifested itself between Kyoto University and Dōshisha University in the educational field. For example, Kyoto University did not formally allow Dōshisha students, or indeed any outside students, to attend lectures given at Kyoto University.[88] Thus Mott was forced to give the same lectures twice, once for Kyoto University students and once for Dōshisha students.[89] American Studies in Kyoto should have been more fully integrated into the regular academic programs of Kyoto and Dōshisha Universities.

The Kyoto seminar library also suffered from the poor collaboration between the two universities. Aldrich feared that the library might become unavailable to the scholars of the other universities if the Kyoto seminar did not continue in its present form, or if the seminar library became part of the permanent library of either university. It appeared to the American professor that only the soothing influence of a large financial grant could preserve the Kyoto seminar as an entity. And, indeed, that was precisely what Aldrich meant by no Kyoto seminar in the present form "could survive without some American money."[90]

In New York City, Fahs was quite unhappy to learn about the poor record of collaboration between the two Kyoto institutions over the past few years. The director of Rockefeller's Humanities Division hated to admit that the Kyoto seminar was "unable to survive in the present form without American funds."[91] But Fahs knew that the Rockefeller Foundation had no interest in extending the arrangement with the Kyoto program beyond March 31, 1959: "There is no reason why we should maintain it if it is not worthwhile and cannot justify support from a Japanese point of view."[92] He suggested, therefore, that the Kyoto group work out a plan to establish an Institute of American Studies with eventual government financing, just as the Tokyo group was proposing. He wrote Aldrich: "Thus far I think that the Kyoto group has been much less effective in their planning than has the group in Tokyo."[93]

Irreducible Rupture and Relationship of Inconvenience

The poor collaboration between Kyoto University and Dōshisha University eventually deteriorated into a rift. In the spring of 1957, John Hall, director of the Michigan Center for Japanese Studies, sent Fahs a bombshell: Kyoto and Dōshisha Universities were on the point of agreeing to go their separate ways on American Studies. Hall was quite annoyed by the development, because it was likely to present Michigan with some problems. In his view, Dōshisha University seemed to have more funds for American Studies, but Michigan was more anxious to retain contact with Kyoto University, which was more prestigious.[94]

Representatives of Kyoto University met on October 9, 1957.[95] In the presence of both Fahs and Evans, they discussed whether they should go their separate ways in developing American Studies programs. They also discussed the disposition of the American Studies collection. They came to the following conclusions. First, the present joint activity should not continue after expiration of the present Rockefeller Foundation grant on March 31, 1959. Second, the American Studies collection, housed at Rakuyū Kaikan of Kyoto University, would become part of the Kyoto University library.[96] The American Studies collection had grown considerably through the collaborative efforts of the American professors and their Japanese counterparts.

The arrangement appeared neither attractive nor fair from the perspective of Dōshisha University. A few months later, Dōshisha scholars disclosed their displeasure, because it was an arrangement they felt they were forced to make at Kyoto University's initiative. They complained that "they are being maneuvered into a disadvantageous position by the Kyōdai [Kyoto University] people."[97] Wendell H. Bash, Colgate professor of sociology and anthropology, described in a message to Roger Evans how the representatives of Dōshisha University believed they had fallen into such a disadvantageous position (he had received a letter from a Mr. Katsumi at Dōshisha): "The Dōshisha side, he [Katsumi] says, have tried to be good boys and wait for the resolution in Kyoto while the Kyōdai side have filled the mails with letters. Further support for three years, he feels, cannot place Dōshisha in a position to compete with Kyōdai because of their financial position as a private university. In any event, the removal of the Library to university depositories takes it away from many people who formerly were able to use it."[98]

Katsumi was quite right in pointing out how difficult and inconvenient it had become for outsiders to use the books in the American Studies collection.[99] Furthermore, Kyoto University professors of American Studies expressed their wish to discontinue the American Studies seminars. But Ueno Naozō, dean of academic affairs of Dōshisha University, thought otherwise. He maintained that his university alone was prepared to continue the Kyoto seminar. Upon learning of Ueno's unwavering commitment to keep American Studies seminars alive, the representatives of Kyoto University changed their minds and agreed to cooperate if and when the American Studies summer seminar continued in some form.[100]

By the end of 1957, it had become an open secret that the idea of interinstitutional cooperation was something like a castle in the air. Ōshimo Kakuichi, president of Dōshisha University, was shrewd enough to strengthen Dōshisha's position by turning adversity into advantage. In a letter to Fahs, he described the tense atmosphere surrounding the Kyoto-Dōshisha rift. He stressed that Dōshisha "felt no particular difficulty in cooperating from our side" with Kyoto University, but that "there seems to be considerable difficulty from their [Kyoto University] side whether the reason is that Kyoto is a Government University or some other difficulty."[101] One specific difficulty, according to Ōshimo, was the fact that Kyoto University was reluctant to part with any part of the library of the American Studies seminar. He then told Fahs about his new plan: Dōshisha University was beginning to conceptualize the idea of a Center for American Studies that would carry on the task of the Kyoto American Studies Summer Seminar after the grant expired on March 31, 1959. Ōshimo also asked the Rockefeller Foundation to provide Dōshisha University with $8,000 a year for three years for the projected Center for American Studies, which would nurture young scholars of American Studies for travel and study in the United States. He also requested $12,000 a year for three years to go largely toward the purchase of books in American Studies. Ōshimo was clever; he did not end his letter without mentioning that "we would, of course, make no claims toward any of the present Kyoto American Studies library which would naturally revert to Kyoto University"—if his request received the approval of the trustees of the Rockefeller Foundation.[102]

In May 1958, the officers of the Rockefeller Foundation formally recognized that collaboration between Kyoto University and Dōshisha University had "always been somewhat clumsy in operation" and that continued collaboration between the two universities appeared "impracticable."[103] The Americans were discreet enough not to become entangled directly in the Kyoto-Dōshisha feud, and so they endeavored to "maintain a completely impartial position and proceed only from their [Japanese] own decision and official preferences."[104] They finally reached the conclusion that the difficulties in continuing a joint program between Kyoto and Dōshisha Universities outweighed the advantages. The officers of the Rockefeller Foundation thus notified the Kyoto scholars that "we are therefore assuming that in considering any help for American Studies in Kyoto after the expiration of the present grants, we shall deal with the two Universities separately."[105]

The Rockefeller Foundation recognized that the prestige of Kyoto University was greater than that of Dōshisha University, but it believed that Dōshisha University was further advanced than Kyoto University in the development of an American Studies curriculum. In view of this situation, it concluded that the Rockefeller Foundation should "provide help directly and separately to each university."[106]

The foundation decided to assist Dōshisha University in further developing American Studies programs in order to make up for the loss that the private university had incurred from the decision on the American Studies collection. Thus the foundation decided to give Dōshisha's young scholars opportunities for travel and study in the United States and to give the university the funds it needed to improve library resources and build up the collection of basic books on America.[107] As a result, eleven promising scholars received either a full or a partial scholarship under the Dōshisha University–Rockefeller Foundation program.[108] It is no exaggeration to say that the decision of the Rockefeller Foundation paved the way for developing the human resources of the private university and also developing the present-day Dōshisha American Studies Center, whose some six thousand books and publications on America were made accessible to most America experts and graduate students in western Japan.

Legacies of the American Studies Seminars in Japan

Notwithstanding the technical difficulties as well as the awkward relations between Kyoto and Dōshisha Universities, the Kyoto American Studies seminars met a growing need for a refresher, extension-type intellectual stimulation in the Kansai area and the rest of the nation.[109] The seminars acted as an incubator in that they nurtured prospective young scholars on America—a function that Japanese universities could not fill as much as they wished. Japanese universities could not afford to offer many regular American Studies programs at the undergraduate and graduate levels, because they faced fierce competition with other branches of history and other disciplines.[110]

Otis Cary, a longtime American professor in Japan and director of Dōshisha University's Amherst House, acknowledged that the Kyoto summer sessions had been "a very effectiving [sic] ground for younger scholars," especially in the Kyoto-Osaka-Kobe area. They "have, also, slowly built up an interest in the study of America in all its phases which until recently was an untouched field in Japanese academic circles. We were doing a servicing job in American studies for the area which was essentially a pump-priming operation. I feel that cutting off the Summer Sessions will be likely to entomb the work of the Centers of each institution, especially Kyōdai, but also Dōshisha [University]."[111] In 1996 he left for the United States and never returned to Japan.[112]

Cary was not exaggerating. The Kyoto seminar served as a pilot program for area studies, a concept that was totally new in Japan. As of 1959, the American Studies summer sessions had been held for seven years, settling into a pattern of twenty sessions offered by American scholars for four weeks in a half-dozen disciplines.[113] The Kyoto seminar was a rich, eye-opening, rewarding experience for everyone who participated in it, be they Americans or Japanese, teachers or students. The officers of the Rockefeller Foundation concurred. Julian H. Steward, a professor of cultural anthropology at the University of Illinois and participant in the 1956 seminar, wrote, "The American Studies Seminar has been extremely successful not only in its more formal and planned aspects but also in its unanticipated by-products. I am convinced that somewhat more tangible results will follow. . . . I feel sure that the Seminar can achieve a unity in its diversity of subjects and find a solution to the cooperation of a national and private university." The American professor concluded in an optimistic tone by saying, "Even if the Seminar were to end completely when the Rockefeller grant expires, there is now no doubt in my mind that the grant will have paid off extraordinarily well."[114] Wendell Bash, professor of sociology and anthropology at Colgate University, echoed Steward. He regretted seeing the joint American Studies program come to an end on March 31, 1959. He wrote Roger Evans: "Personally, I would like to see the Seminar continue for a few more years. . . . I gleaned some facts about the future hopes of Kyoto University and the Dōshisha, . . . They would need books for their programs, and it is possible for the future of American studies in Kyoto that it would be necessary to provide each with a Library . . . [and] it might still be a good investment for the future."[115]

Japanese scholars such as Kyoto University president Takikawa Yukitoki and Iwamura Shinobu, Kyoto University's representative on the Executive Committee for the Kyoto American Studies Summer Seminar, maintained that "we should not let die away the interest in . . . [and] the enthusiasm for American study, which has been aroused during these six years of the Seminar."[116] Matsui Shichirō of Dōshisha University summarized the contributions of the Kyoto American Studies seminars as follows: "It is gratifying indeed that, unlike the past, a considerably greater number of people have come to pursue American Studies and gained a deeper understanding of America. It is my belief that the war could not have happened if such a situation as we see today had existed before the war." Matsui concluded on an optimistic note: "It is my sincere hope that American Studies will be studied more and harder in Japan, while at the same time Japanese Studies will be pursued in America to an equal degree so that a better understanding and friendship will be promoted between the two countries."[117]

The staff of Tokyo University also appreciated the contributions made by the Japanese American Studies seminars, and they were as committed as the Kyoto scholars to the development of American Studies in Japan. A total of 598 scholars and graduate students participated in the seven years of seminars offered at Tokyo University under the Rockefeller Foundation grant.[118] Tokyo University president Nambara acknowledged that the basis for promoting American Studies in Japan was firmly secured, even though the American Studies Association was not yet developed as a genuine national organization. Thus the prospects for developing area studies in Japan appeared to be healthy thanks to the arrangements with Stanford University and the financial assistance from the Rockefeller Foundation. Hideo Kishimoto summarized the effects of the seven years of work as follows:

> In the field of American history, eleven new chairs were established with participants in the Tokyo–Stanford University seminars as incumbents. In the area of philosophy, Waseda University, a prestigious private university, Osaka Municipal and Shiba [sic] Universities, both of which were public universities, had new chairs held by seminar participants. Additionally participants formed a new association to promote the study of philosophy in the American mode. In the field of economics, two important results were attributed to the influence of the Seminars. One was that previous emphasis on Marxian doctrine was shifting to more orthodox theories, and the other was that government and banking offices were making more use of the new (more orthodox) theories discussed in the Seminars.[119]

A professor of Keio University by the name of Dr. N. Sawada echoed Kishimoto's statement observation by saying that the series of American Studies Seminars at Tokyo had an "important influence in the field of philosophy."[120] He went on to say that the seminars "have been responsible for the growing interest on the part of young Japanese philosophers in logic and analysis and the gradual retreat of Marxism."[121]

A survey conducted in 1949 by the Rikkyô Institute for American Studies corroborated the observations of two professors about the effect of American Studies Seminars. It revealed that only 33 out of 144 Japanese universities offered courses related to America. Twenty-five years later, in 1974, research conducted by Amerika Gakkai on behalf of the Fulbright Commission in Tokyo disclosed that 208 out of 263 Japanese universities offered a total of 1,912 courses related to America. The courses were taught by 1,280 instructors.[122] These statistical figures indicate that most of the Japanese participants in the American Studies seminars were genuinely enthusiastic practitioners of the concept of U.S.-Japan cultural interchange with a burning desire to learn about the United States.

The Americans who participated in the seminars held in Japan also reaped benefits. The participating professors from Stanford University found it valuable to meet with Japanese scholars and react to their interpretations of American traditions and culture. They admitted that they gained many penetrating insights from a Japanese perspective on American history, thought, and current affairs, although they frequently found themselves in disagreement with Japanese interpretations. Those insights, they added, served as a constant stimulus for discussion and a reconsideration of American assumptions. Indeed, the Stanford professors demonstrated that the cultural interchange was reciprocal. They commented that their influence exceeded their expectations and that future teams of American professors could expand enormously the benefits and opportunities stemming from that effort and direct it toward international understanding.[123]

The cumulative effects of the American Studies seminars led to the creation of the Center of American Studies on the Komaba campus of Tokyo University in 1957.[124] As of 1950, the Rockefeller Foundation had been urging Tokyo University to incorporate the subjects offered in the summer program into its regular curriculum courses, but it was not until 1957 that the university took a decisive step in that direction. Under the new plan, American professors were invited to teach for six-month periods at Tokyo University, and Japanese scholars from other universities were allowed to study for a fixed period of time at Tokyo University.[125]

Besides the establishment of the International House of Japan was added impetus in the effort to further develop American Studies in postwar Japan (see Chapter 5). The International House served as a clearinghouse through which American scholars visiting Japan could share knowledge and information about the United States with their Japanese counterparts. The International House and the American Studies seminars worked hand in hand to help U.S.-Japan cultural interchange take root in Japan.

Promoting American Studies: Americans Working behind the Scenes

Even after Kyoto and Dōshisha Universities decided to go their separate ways in 1959, the Rockefeller Foundation continued to give individual grants to Kyoto and Dōshisha Universities in the hope of further strengthening American Studies in the Kansai area. Eventually, the persistent policy and generosity of the Rockefeller Foundation appeared to have an effect. The foundation grants permitted junior faculty members from the universities to study in America for two-and-a-half-year periods, thereby contributing to greater interest in American Studies at Kyoto University. The grants also enabled the universities to continue to expand their libraries. In August 1957, Kyoto University established a committee on American Studies to develop a separate program for the university. The coordinating and planning committee was composed of the deans of the four faculties of the humanities and social sciences—that is, the Faculties of Letters, Education, Law, and Economics.[126]

Kyoto University recognized, however, that a bottleneck in the realization of the American Studies program was the tight financial policy of the Japanese government. The government was more concerned with developing the natural sciences and technology than the social sciences and the humanities. Kyoto University sought the involvement of the Rockefeller Foundation in their negotiations with the Japanese Finance Ministry "to pull the government authorities toward approving our budget request sooner."[127] Kyoto University felt that the Rockefeller Foundation had already invested such a large amount of funds in the promotion of American Studies in Kyoto that it would not mind using its not insignificant voice in helping Kyoto University to persuade the Finance Ministry authorities to create chairs of American Studies at Kyoto University.[128]

To help Kyoto University build its programs of American Studies, broadly defined, the Rockefeller Foundation officers ingeniously invented a pattern of grant making that essentially acted as the yeast for the development of American Studies at Kyoto. As one example, the Rockefeller Foundation officers persuaded the Kyoto University Law Faculty to pledge a once-dormant law chair and the full professorship that came with it to a promising young assistant professor Kōzai upon his return from study in the United States. Kōzai was then studying in the United States with a Rockefeller Foundation social sciences fellowship for special work in that field. As a result, a pioneering chair in international relations and politics was established within the Faculty of Law at Kyoto. An understanding was also reached that another dormant chair in English law would be converted to American law and then awarded to Prof. Michida Shin-ichirō, who had just returned from two years' study in the United States divided between Michigan and Harvard under a Ford grant. Thus American grants like those of the Rockefeller Foundation effectively served as catalysts to permit the faculties of Kyoto University to convert dormant chairs into pioneering, active chairs in American Studies at that university, thereby strengthening Kyoto's interdisciplinary American Studies programs.[129]

American Soft Power and Its Perils

"Soft power" is a concept introduced and popularized by the political scientist Joseph S. Nye Jr. more than a decade ago.[130] It means the ability of a country to co-opt rather than coerce others in order to achieve the outcomes it wants.[131] Simply put, soft power is the ability to entice and attract. The intangible resources of soft power are attractive culture, ideology, and institutions.[132] In this sense, the philanthropy that has been an essential part of U.S. soft power is different from the act of simply giving alms or handouts. Soft power is an intangible, incalculable form of power that is usually accompanied by broad visions, self-restraint, and generosity.

After World War II, American leaders such as John Foster Dulles, John Rockefeller, Charles Fahs, and public affairs officers of the U.S government had not only a clear vision of what was expected of America as a hegemonic nation, but also a clear understanding of what could be accomplished by American soft power. In terms of U.S. relations with Japan, they sought to achieve the long-range objectives of the United States by taking the present and future of U.S.-Japan relations into consideration. One of the long-range U.S. objectives of the U.S. use of soft power was none other than to develop human resources in Japan, especially a leadership group friendly to the United States. These Americans sought to nurture pro-American Japanese who understood America and its broad foreign policy objectives in the world. The American elite thus linked up with moderately conservative Japanese elite in the hope of managing U.S.-Japan relations and other important issues in cooperation with them. The Japanese elite were expected to enlighten the Japanese population and lead it to support the United States in the cold war and hot wars.

Hidaka Daishirō, who in 1953 was vice president of International Christian University located at Mitaka near Tokyo, deplored the superficial character of the postwar "democratization" of the Japanese educational system. From 1946 to 1949, Hidaka had served as director of the Ministry of Education's School Education Bureau and then as vice minister under Education Minister Amano Teiyū from March 1951 to August 1952. Hidaka believed Japanese universities simply had to overcome the problems associated with pernicious practices such as old-school ties and academic inbreeding.[133]

In Hidaka's view, the vices resulted from the university chair system. In general, the relationship of a professor and a student was staunchly patriarchal in character; as an old saying goes, "Students still fear to walk on master's shadow."[134] Tenured professors often exercised patriarchal control over their students through the chair system. Students were expected to be docile, though professors did not admit it publicly. Students who chose to work under a given scholar of established reputation usually followed closely in that scholar's footsteps. Thus much of a student's training lay in those channels in which his master had specialized, which meant that students might pass up opportunities for broadening their courses of study.[135] This peculiarly dynastic system in which an aging professor trained the disciple who would carry on his tradition after he retired naturally perpetuated the more mysterious aspects of the Japanese university system. In this way, much of Japan's cultural heritage was transmitted from master to disciple in accordance with familial procedures that could hardly be called academic in the ordinary Western sense of the term.[136] Such a personalized chair system was highly likely to beget inbreeding of both the chair and the institution. It also produced factionalism (the "old boy" system) and elitism.[137]

The system of recruiting faculty members contributed to the tendency of Japanese universities to be indifferent to the outside world. It also contributed to their remaining isolated from each other both physically and mentally, thereby creating a unique culture. Indeed, the universities took great pride in being independent of each other. Therefore, if one university had to go to another university to fill its faculty requirements, it was usually looked upon as a loss of face. Such a method of filling academic posts led to an unusually high degree of inbreeding within Japanese universities and acted as little inducement for contact among Japanese educators throughout the nation.[138]

Many Japanese saw American soft power bring with it unintended consequences. First, American soft power, in effect, facilitated the restoration of the hierarchical order in the postwar Japanese academia similar to that evident in the prewar years. It helped the University of Tokyo to ensconce itself once again at the top. And American soft power even helped to sustain and solidify the traditional chair system. To put it differently, American soft power helped to entrench even more the Japanese system of higher education and to solidify the evil system of academic clique and inbreeding. The exclusivity and provincialism of Japanese universities, as well as their authoritarianism, went hand in hand with the evils of academic clique and inbreeding, as was demonstrated by the intense rivalry between Tokyo University and Kyoto University over the American Studies seminars. It was, then, a great irony that American soft power played a crucial if not direct role in stratifying and centralizing Japan's system of higher education.[139]

Second, American soft power contributed to the development of the habit of dependency in Japanese scholars, because American Studies in postwar Japan relied heavily on American money. After the war, many aspiring young Japanese were anxious to study abroad for a long period of time, but their country was poverty-stricken and no funds were available for such travel. Young scholars interested in America found American foundations such as Rockefeller and Ford to be generous donors, and so they became dependent on that generosity as illustrated by the Tokyo and Kyoto American Studies seminars.

In this connection, it might be useful here to recall the public statement that Dean Rusk made before a congressional hearing in 1954 in his capacity as president of the Rockefeller Foundation. He maintained resolutely that "aid from a paternal government [or from any organization for that matter] might sap . . . sturdy virtues and breed a race of weaklings."[140] And yet that financial dependency of Japan's American Studies seminar on outside aid was so great that Japanese scholars kept asking for American money. At the same time, the American foundation felt it had to continue extending a helping hand to them in order to keep Japan in the orbit of the West. This U.S.-Japan chain of dependency seems to militate against an avowed principle of the Rockefeller Foundation that Rusk had proclaimed in 1954. Indeed, was it not something akin to discordant irony and contradiction? It can be argued that Japan's overdependency on American funds inevitably influenced the Japanese scholarship on America in the years that followed. In other words, "excessive" American generosity not only colored Japanese scholarship on America but also had a corrosive effect on the academic freedom of Japanese scholars as historian Aruga Tadashi, a recipient of a Rockefeller Foundation grant in 1955, so pointedly observed in 1980.

It was assumed that scholars of American Studies would make a constructive contribution to important areas of Japanese society when they returned home after a lengthy stay in the United States. The experience of studying there often served not only to establish them as scholars, but also to help build their careers by lending authority to their scholarship. Upon returning to Japan, they were expected, more often than not, to find an attractive post at a university or its equivalent awaiting them. As a result, the Japanese institutions of higher education, especially the universities that offered American Studies programs, would become restructured. Universities would be filled mainly with the Japanese elite who had enjoyed access to American power and influence under the shelter of American authority.

The reality, however, was that if scholars got a job after returning from the United States to Japan they were lucky indeed. Soon or later, many returnees found themselves extremely frustrated. They discovered they were surrounded once again by a group of conservative Japanese such as their superiors and colleagues who took an unsympathetic view of whatever they had learned while in the United States. For example, a former Fulbright scholar who had studied at Tulane University and at University of California, Los Angeles, complained about the coldness with which his superiors received him. He said, "When I came back from the States, I switched my teaching system to discussion and began to require short reports." Apparently, his superiors did not appreciate the innovation in his teaching technique. When he changed his system to discussion, he found that his "colleagues would say: 'All you do now is talking and talking.'"[141] A young assistant professor at Dōshisha University in Kyoto who had come back with "American ideas" of teaching had an even more disheartening experience. He told an American interviewer that he had been banished to the sphere of English composition as a sort of punitive measure.[142]

It may well be that such unfortunate incidents did not occur often, but it can be safely said that they exemplified how difficult it was to change the conservative system of Japanese higher education from within. Therefore, when Japanese scholars went to America to study, they seemed to understand distinctly that when they returned they were not to bring back any foreign ideas. Since Japanese scholars continued to have a peculiar ambivalence toward Western culture and did not go beyond their superficial eagerness to adopt everything Western, a large portion of Western civilization, and American culture for that matter, remained either miscomprehended or undigested or both. Thus there seems to have been a serious cultural obstacle to the effectiveness of American soft power. Perhaps this problem may explain some of the reasons why Japanese scholars of American Studies failed to respond adequately to the societal need for much sought-after information on America at the critical point of U.S.-Japan relationship in the 1980s.

Chapter 9

Occupation Reform, "Shallow Democracy," and Consumerism

> Democracy must be a development from the people themselves, if it is to have meaning and to become a reality. It is by necessity a gradual and evolutionary process requiring many years.
>
> —John D. Rockefeller III, 1951

> After the war Japanese looked to Americans as coming of Messiah.... The Messiah gave them democracy and so they took it . . . [instead of growing it] from within the people.... More and more commercialism [has] gotten mixed up with democracy.
>
> —Ōhara Sōichirō, 1952

> The American-Japanese alliance is still relatively shallow; it does not have the kind of intellectual, political, and cultural roots needed to sustain it in an era of perils.
>
> —The Conlon Report, 1959

This chapter analyzes the state of democracy and the influence of Christianity in postwar Japan. In doing so, it describes how the American intellectuals affiliated with the Council on Foreign Relations analyzed and assessed the complex issue of the democratization of Japan, a major legacy of the SCAP reforms that had been instituted during the nearly seven-year U.S. occupation. It also addresses why American observers of Japan thought that Japanese democracy was shallow and superficial despite the great efforts of the American occupiers. Finally, the chapter describes the ways in which the Japanese were prone to associate democracy with commercialism.

During and immediately after the occupation, American experts on Japan, many of whom were former SCAP officers, assessed the occupation reforms in order to determine the full meaning and impact of that democratic experiment in postwar Japan. The keen-eyed Americans who gathered at the Council on Foreign Relations also discussed the U.S.-led reforms and attempted to grasp their historical significance and their lasting legacies. It was difficult enough to gain a clear understanding of the full meaning of the reforms; presenting an objective assessment of them was even more difficult. The results of the reforms could perhaps be analyzed relatively easily if the reforms covered only areas that treated tangibles and facts such as economics and public health. In the more abstract realms, such as the ones that covered people's values and thought, it was enormously difficult to evaluate the worth of reforms properly. More often than not, the occupation authorities congratulated themselves on postwar reforms, tending to overrate their immediate accomplishments in Japan and take an overly optimistic view of the reforms. Others took a less optimistic, if not totally skeptical, view of the prospect of democracy in Japan. Meanwhile, the vast majority of Americans took an affirmative stance on the democratic reforms and looked at Japan as an asset rather than a liability as America's Far East ally. They were genuinely optimistic about the future of U.S.-Japan relations.

The Council on Foreign Relations

The Council on Foreign Relations was established in New York City in 1921 for the purposes of embracing internationalism and overcoming the handicaps imposed by isolationism. With the generous financial assistance of the Rockefeller and other foundations, it served (as still does) as an important provider of knowledge and information on international affairs, with the conscious aim of helping government officials in the formation of foreign policy. Tempered by the bitter experience of World War II and the cold war, the Council on Foreign Relations came to be recognized as "the most important single private agency conducting research in foreign affairs."[1] During those years, this think tank served as a source of personnel and recruitment center for middle- and upper-level positions in the new and expanded foreign policy institutions of the United States such as the State and Defense Departments. *Washington Post* columnist Joseph Kraft once described this organization as "an incubator of men and ideas."[2] Other writers portrayed the Council on Foreign Relations as "the select professional association of the country's foreign policy community."[3]

The Council on Foreign Relations carried out its work within a structure that consisted of three tiers of discussions on foreign affairs.[4] The first tier was the dinner-forum, at which members convened in a general meeting and heard a formal address by a leading statesman such as the U.S. secretary of state or a foreign dignitary visiting Washington. The second tier was the smaller evening meeting, always strictly off the record, where a distinguished guest engaged selected Council members in more informal discussions. The third tier of discussion was a study group that consisted of a small group of members with expertise in a particular area. Study groups would meet periodically to examine international issues of critical importance. The study group on Japan comprised university professors with a broad knowledge of a specialized field, U.S. government officials, and intellectuals drawn from private organizations such as the Rockefeller Foundation and the Institute of Pacific Relations. This tiered approach to world problems made it possible to bring into contact those with knowledge about business (based on their first-hand experience in the business world), government policy and policy making, and the results of larger scholarly investigation and analysis.[5] It is the perceptions of the Japan experts in the third group that this chapter will analyze.

The Council's Study Group on Japan

The Council on Foreign Relations study group on Japan, already in operation during the war, began to meet more frequently after the war. It discussed Far Eastern affairs in 1945–1946 and in 1946–1947, and in 1947 it dealt with the Japan problem. In 1948–1949, the study group picked up the problem of the revival of Japan. In the early 1950s, the group undertook an extensive follow-up study of the U.S. occupation of Japan. It analyzed the sociopolitical and cultural influences of the sweeping SCAP reforms on Japan, while scrutinizing the lasting legacies of those reforms in the country. The study group also explored critical issues such as Japanese peace treaty problems and American cultural relations with Japan. The latter two studies were part of an attempt to determine in which direction U.S.-Japan relations should move after Japan regained its independence. Everett Case of Colgate University acted as chair of the two-year project (1950–1951) "Japanese Peace Treaty Problems," and Hugh Borton, professor of Japanese history at Columbia University, served as secretary.[6] The research project on "American Cultural Relations with Japan" was launched in 1952–1953. John Rockefeller acted as chair of the discussion meetings, and Robert Schwantes, a research fellow affiliated with the Council on Foreign Relations, served as research secretary.[7]

The Definition of Democracy

Although a clear and proper definition of the term *democracy* was essential to assessing the outcome of the democratic experiment in occupied Japan, defining this term turned out to be the most vexing problem, and it overshadowed the discussion meetings of the Council on Foreign Relations study group.[8] As for the participants' knowledge of Japan, some had learned much about Japan before the war, but most had their first contact with the Japanese either through fighting the Pacific War or through living in Japan and working for SCAP/GHQ in Tokyo during the occupation. In other words, they had in common their awareness of the pressing problems facing Japan whether they were SCAP/GHQ reformers or lifelong experts on Japan.

After exchanging views on democracy freely, the American experts on Japan agreed on the concept of a free and open society. They apparently drew references and lessons of democracy from the United States and other Western democracies. They envisioned the ideal democracy as a regime that grows out of the will and spontaneity of its citizens.[9] It is a sort of body politic that provides for and protects the vital process of subjecting the existing order to regular examination in an open society. These democratic ideas were predicated on the assumption that citizens participate actively in the civic affairs of their society and share in determining its goals. In a democracy, every potential citizen must be intelligently alert to the importance of events for the ultimate realization of human well-being and should be able to act to prevent assumptions of authority against the general will. Public opinion is considered essential to keeping democracy alive and robust. Moreover, citizens must sometimes stand up and fight against oppression to protect their rights and freedom.[10]

Such democratic ideas as government as the servant of the people and the individual's freedom of thought, expression, and scientific investigation were assumed to be essential components of democracy. Democracy recognized the potential dignity and integrity of every human being. In the American context, people cherished the notions of supremacy of the individual and faith in free inquiry as sacrosanct and dear to their hearts.[11] American experts on Japan also believed in the notion of fair opportunity for everybody regardless of creed or color. Those ideas and ideals were thought to be an integral part of American democracy.[12] Archibald MacLeish, a poet and political activist who also served as assistant secretary of state for public and cultural relations from 1944 to 1945, once remarked, "Freedom of communication, freedom of exchange of ideas, is basic to our whole political doctrine."[13] That was the common denominator when the members of the study group on Japan defined the concept of democracy. No doubt, it was an ideal type of democracy, not necessarily the reality of democracy. Democracy as an ideal body politic and democracy as the reality were quite different things in America and elsewhere.

Assessing the Democratic Experiment in Occupied Japan

The Council's experts on Japan discussed the outcome of the U.S. democratic experiment in that country extensively. They believed that future U.S.-Japan relations hinged on the results of that experiment. Although they acknowledged the achievements in some areas, they discovered that the outcomes in others fell short of their expectations. These American specialists on Japan displayed their expertise on Japan and the Japanese culture during their discussion meetings, but when they did they tended to apply their own definitions of American democracy. At the same time, they often revealed their stereotypical biases against the Japanese, as well as their preconceived ideas of Japan and the Japanese culture.

As for their general views, members of the study group on Japan agreed that the effect of democratic reforms on Japan was only skin-deep despite America's zealous efforts. Moreover, most were pessimistic about the future development of democracy in Japan. The reasons behind their views varied. Robert Schwantes observed that the general example of American democracy had had little influence in Japan, although the Japanese had accepted some guidance from America in terms of the technical details of administration.[14] Hugh Borton expressed a similar opinion; he argued that democracy had not penetrated very far in Japan. Borton, who had served as assistant chief of the State Department's Division of Japanese Affairs and special assistant to the director of the State Department's Office of Far Eastern Affairs in the late 1970s, was a professor at Columbia University.[15] Eugene Dooman, former counselor of the U.S. embassy in Tokyo and special assistant to the director of the State Department's Office of Far Eastern Affairs, echoed Borton's seasoned view.[16] Their observations of democracy in Japan were clearly less than flattering, if not totally negative. The discussion meetings, therefore, centered on the problem of why democracy did not take root in Japan as deeply as they had expected.

Divided in two groups, the American experts on Japan debated the reasons for the shallowness of democracy in Japan. One group was made up of conservative State Department Japan specialists such as Joseph Grew, Dooman, and others. They were sometimes called the "old Japan hands." With few exceptions, the "old Japan hands" attributed the superficiality of democracy in Japan largely to the *ketsujo riron* (deficiency theory). According to the deficiency theory, Japan and its people dismally failed to develop the principles of democracy, egalitarianism, individualism, and individual liberty that characterized modern Europe. Therefore, such attributes of modernism have been either nonexistent or almost nonexistent in Japan's philosophical and spiritual tradition.[17] The "old Japan hands" clung to ethnocentric stereotypes of Japan and the Japanese culture and belittled the capacity of ordinary Japanese to govern.[18] The second group consisted of American liberals and former New Deal progressives, most of whom actually planned and implemented democratic reforms in Japan during the U.S. occupation. They attributed the shallowness of Japanese democracy to the relatively short period of time since its introduction and Japan's lack of political experience with a democratic government.

The Conservative "Old Japan Hands"

On behalf of the "old Japan hands," Dooman explained the reason for the superficiality of Japanese democracy from the cultural and theological points of view. He maintained that the concept of democracy was foreign and utterly incomprehensible to the Japanese, because Japan was a non-Christian country. He argued that "democracy was linked to the idea of certain rights inseparable from the nature of a human being," and that one reason democracy had developed and thrived in the West was that "Europe had been exposed to the concepts of Christianity and the realization of the divine spark in man."[19] Dooman insisted that Japan possessed none of those democratic ideas. To make his point absolutely clear, he called attention to the fact that all the Japanese statutes and codes had expressed the idea of rights *in rem*, but not *in personam*. *In rem* refers to an act, proceeding, or right available against the world at large, whereas *in personam* refers to an act, proceeding, or right done or directed against or with reference to a specific person. A right of property is a right *in rem, whereas* the right of a beneficiary is primarily a right *in personam* against his trustee.[20] Even the modern laws of the Meiji period expressed qualified rights—that is, self-assumed limitations upon the state bestowed from above. Dooman concluded that the democratic reforms in Japan were weak for the very reason that there was no natural basis within that country.[21]

The Americans in the first group forcefully maintained that Japanese democracy was superficial and skin-deep, because occupation reforms had been postulated under the entirely erroneous illusions that Japan could be democratized. They regretted that the United States had made a gross error in carrying out thankless reforms to graft democracy onto such a culturally exotic country as Japan. Exaggerating differences in the American and Japanese cultures, they underrated the Japanese ability to understand the American type of democratic ideas and the political dynamics of democracy. The conservative experts on Japan believed that the concept of democracy was so totally alien to Japan culturally and historically that they entirely dismissed, and even laughed at, the possibility of democratizing Japan. They then pointed specifically to three factors that had affected the democratization of Japan: (1) the differences in decision-making procedures between the West and Japan; (2) Japanese national traits, and (3) the social conditions in Japan immediately after the war.

Differences in Decision Making

The American conservatives placed special emphasis on the differences in decision-making procedures between the West and Japan. They deplored the fact that Western-style democracy had not been sufficiently integrated in Japan, even though the legal and governmental framework for a democratic government had been introduced. They argued that Western democratic procedures did not sit very well with Japanese social customs.[22] In Western-style democracy, they explained, parliamentary procedure depends on the principle of majority rule, which could be confrontational. Parliamentary procedure refers to the ways in which business is transacted in a deliberative body in accordance with established rules, usages, and precedents. The principle of majority rule means that decisions supported by the greater number should prevail.

The Japanese, by contrast, practiced the social custom of consensus, or the rule of unanimity, as a means of approving measures and of solving problems. Even though this custom of reaching a consensus usually takes a longer time, it is accepted in Japan as the price for greater social harmony.[23] The conservative specialists on Japan pointed out that, according to the rules of the game of consensus, the minority opposition might be placed in a position to enjoy disproportionately greater power and considerable sympathy from the Japanese public. In an extreme case, the opposition might choose to adopt obstructive tactics in proceedings such as filibustering. They might even exercise a virtual veto in the decision-making processes that might result in political gridlock. The resulting confusion could produce a general lack of public faith in the parliamentary process and bring about a crisis in democracy, they insisted.[24] Thus conservative specialists on Japan tried to make the case that the social practices sanctioned by the Japanese custom of consensus made it extremely difficult to establish an effective democracy in Japan.[25]

National Traits

The same American specialists in the first group imputed the superficiality of democracy to the Japanese national traits—that is, they pointed to the lamentable deficiency of genuine independence and conspicuous lack of individual character (*shutaisei*) or personality at the popular level. They argued that the Japanese had not worked out democracy by themselves, but rather that it had been inspired by *outsiders*—the U.S. occupation authorities. In other words, the Japanese were forced by SCAP to destroy an old feudalistic order and establish a new democratic regime. The U.S. military government in Tokyo introduced the legal and governmental framework for a democratic government, and the Japanese took it as a given. It was democratization by heteronomy. Dooman, in particular, remarked that the occupation reforms had merely given the Japanese the mechanistic processes of democracy. Borton echoed the former American diplomat's remarks.[26]

The conservative American specialists on Japan also ascribed the shallowness of democracy in Japan to the Japanese people's noticeable lack of understanding of democratic values and their total inability to produce a working democracy—as if they possessed no intellectual capacity worthy of mention to govern democratically. However, anyone even a little familiar with modern Japanese history might recognize instantly that a powerful tradition of commoners' democratic movements has existed in Japan since the Meiji (1868–1912) and Taishō (1912–1925) periods. One example of such movements is the Popular Rights movement (*jiyūminken undō*) of the

1870s and the 1880s led by Itagaki Taisuke and Nakae Chōmin, who called for popular control of the government and chanted "no representative, no taxation."[27] Other examples are the Blue Stocking women's movement of the 1910s led by Hiratsuka Raichō and the political movement "Taishō democracy" of the 1920s. The contemptuous remarks of those conservative Americans revealed either that they were uninformed about one of the important aspects of modern Japanese history or that they disregarded it consciously and intentionally.

Postwar Social Conditions

Finally, the conservative "old Japan hands" attributed the artificiality of democracy to Japan's social conditions immediately after the war. Once again, Dooman pointed out the complete breakdown in social morality in the vanquished country. He maintained that the absence of a *social* basis for democracy was one of the causes of the failure of democracy to take root in Japan. According to him, democracy could not be effective without social morality, because it was, he insisted, an essential component of any effort to foster and advance democracy.[28] The former counselor of the U.S. embassy in Tokyo also explained the dual nature of liberty, saying that "being glad to have the right to liberty was not enough and that the people must be willing to assume the social obligations that liberty demanded of them." Dooman insisted arrogantly that the Japanese needed to acquire a sense of responsibility and a sense of fighting for their rights before democracy could grow in their country. "It would be a mistake to assume," he cautioned, "that this [referring to the introduction of the so-called democratic hardware only] would lead to democracy since the inner being of the Japanese has not been changed."[29]

In response to Dooman's remark, Frank B. Gibney Sr. commented that whenever an established code had broken down in Japan, a period of pronounced irresponsibility had been expected.[30] Gibney was an American journalist, who formerly had been in charge of the Tokyo Bureau of Time-Life (1949–1951). He was one of the four foreign correspondents in Tokyo who could use the Japanese language.[31]

In his prize-winning book *Embracing Defeat,* historian John W. Dower argues that such negative views of Japanese democracy reflected in part the disdain with which the American elite and Japan experts looked at the Japanese masses and also mirrored their racist views toward the Japanese.[32] By associating almost exclusively with the upper-class Japanese, the American elite came to share their bias against the ordinary Japanese, whom the elite uncritically assumed were unable to govern themselves. Just like a chemical chain reaction, the bias of the Japanese elite was further reinforced by their close association with such Americans. In this manner, the elite of both Japan and America portrayed ordinary Japanese as the "obedient herd" possessed of an abiding psychology of dependency.[33] Simply put, they viewed the Japanese as disposed to respond to authority submissively and behave in accordance with situational or particularistic ethics. It is extremely difficult, if not entirely impossible, to measure scientifically in statistical numbers, but one can only surmise that such negative thinking of these scholars on both sides of the Pacific might have been affected by the residual bitterness from the war, given the fact that only years earlier Japan and the United States had been at war, with heavy casualties on both sides and a horrendous conclusion to the conflict.

The New Deal Progressives

The second group of the Council's Japan experts consisted of some American liberals and former New Deal progressives who had actually planned and implemented democratic reforms in Japan during the U.S. occupation. In terms of a belief in the superficiality of democracy in Japan, the experts of the second group had much in common with the specialists in the first group, but they differed from the first group in an important way: they were ardent optimists. They thought that if the Japanese were given the appropriate opportunities to be reeducated properly Japan could be changed—not only the Japanese "hardware" (the Japanese legal system and institutions), but also the country's "software" (Japanese thought and behavioral patterns). These American experts on Japan clung to such optimism that they rejected the view of the first group that the Japanese were innately incapable of governing themselves.[34] The American liberals believed, therefore, that it was possible to graft democracy onto Japan, provided that certain conditions were met. Nevertheless, they were disappointed to discover the extent to which Japanese democracy was shallow and superficial.

This second group of Americans ascribed Japan's superficial acceptance of democracy to the relatively short period of time since its introduction and Japan's lack of political experience with a democratic government. One American public affairs officer in Nagoya, Japan, recognized that "democratic ideas are still new to many" Japanese.[35] A decade after the occupation, American observers of Japan, in trying to explain why democracy was not working well in Japan, asserted that Japanese conservatives simply ignored the need to mobilize public opinion to keep democracy alive. The conservatives depended too much on their strong parliamentary majorities, the Americans lamented. The American observers found that the Japanese public preferred a greater degree of order and that they did not sufficiently realize the importance of mobilizing public opinion to protect or to enhance their interest in a democracy.[36]

Perhaps the Japanese did find that the almost seven-year U.S. military occupation was too short to digest democratic ideas. A 1951 report of the U.S. State Department Information and Education Service recognized that the Japanese did not have sufficient time to absorb American democratic ideas and institutions—and certainly not long enough to develop a widespread understanding of democratic values, to master the democratic technique, to diffuse education and political enlightenment to the underprivileged classes, or to develop sufficiently strong vested popular interest in the new order.[37] Thus American observers of Japan in the second group were left with the impression that the Japanese as a whole were politically inexperienced because of a shortage of time.[38] In their view, the Japanese not only failed to digest the major political and social reforms of the occupation, but also failed to develop a solid sense of national purpose. They argued that in addition to how little the Japanese understood about American political ideas, postwar scandals such as the "concealed and hoarded goods scandal" and the Shōwa Denkō scandal of 1948 contributed to making many Japanese feel apathetic or cynical about democratic procedures.[39]

Others blamed the shallowness of democracy on the fact that Americans and Japanese had minimal contact with each other during the occupation and that the Japanese were not able to learn much from the Americans. They argued that very few Japanese had direct, personal contact with American residents in Japan in any meaningful sense, although the U.S. occupation lasted almost seven years. SCAP officers and American soldiers in the occupation army were prohibited as a general rule from contacting the Japanese freely. The Japanese were also ordered not to contact American GIs without any particular reason. On September 6, 1945, *Mainichi shimbun* reported that a cavalry colonel in the U.S. occupation army stationed in the Tachikawa District of Tokyo had issued orders forbidding anyone from walking outside from sunset to sunrise. SCAP/GHQ adopted these orders to prevent trouble between the occupiers and the occupied.[40] For example, in the first year of the occupation 1,929 crimes, including murder and robbery, were reported in Kanagawa Prefecture alone, but criminals were arrested in only fifty-one cases.[41] American military officers and soldiers stationed in Japan committed two murders a month and about ten other felonies on average, according to one calculation.[42]

Because most Americans lived in isolation from the Japanese community, Japan and the Japanese appeared alien to many Americans, except for those who frequented the special and exclusive "comfort facilities" for the occupation army and except for a small number of American Japan experts who were already fluent in Japanese and knowledgeable about that country.[43] A Russian correspondent learned from American informants that segregation was adopted to prevent Euro-Americans from becoming infected with dangerously contagious diseases such as venereal disease and tuberculosis. The Japanese Ministry of Health and Welfare's white paper on venereal diseases in postwar Japan reported 84,026 such patients in August 1948. Using a sarcastically twisted pun, the Japanese called syphilis *bei-doku* (America-poison) instead of the correct *bai-doku*.[44] Other Americans were more candid and outspoken about SCAP's seclusion measure; they said it was based on racism. They confided to the same Russian reporter that because the Japanese were such an inferior race with their great pride and self-conceit, foreign occupiers might feel ashamed to be close to them no matter what the circumstances. It was therefore necessary to drive home to the Japanese that they could never be equal to civilized people by segregating them from Euro-Americans.[45]

In fact, the American occupiers constituted a privileged caste, class, and race during the occupation. Together, they made up a "little America" in Japan and practiced clear-cut segregation.[46] Donald Keene, an American Japan expert in comparative literature at Columbia, spoke of the difficulties that American soldiers and their dependents had experienced from living in isolation in Japan. Their only contacts were with the "worst Japanese," who learned English for personal gain.[47] Those Japanese, the *panpan* prostitutes, reportedly communicated in a polyglot form of English—a mix of the hooker's Japanese and the GI's native tongue, which was humorously identified as "panglish."[48] Keene was quoted as saying that the Americans were, in fact, unpopular among the Japanese. Keene, who had obtained his doctorate in Japanese literature at Cambridge University in England, went to Japan at the age of thirty-one to study at Kyoto University graduate school with financial assistance from the Ford Foundation. During his stay in Japan, he had made friends with several prominent Japanese writers, including Tanizaki Jun-ichirō, Kawabata Yasunari, and Mishima Yukio.

In the midst of harsh criticism of "shallow democracy" in Japan, several

American specialists recognized the important contributions made by the occupation reforms. Theodore Cohen, an analyst in the State Department's Economic and Scientific Section (ESS), appreciated the positive effect of U.S. occupation reforms. He argued that they helped to prevent Japan from returning to the old system by holding back some of Japan's traditional forces while new movements got under way.[49] Brooks Emeny, a former member of the Foreign Policy Association, a nonprofit organization dedicated to encouraging Americans to learn more about the world, also took note of the restraining effect of the occupation reforms. He observed that the movements toward rearmament, constitutional revision, minor electoral districts, and centralization of education were tangible changes made with the intention of revising or readjusting the occupation reforms. He maintained, however, that too many new forces were at work as the result of the reforms to permit a complete reversion immediately after the occupation ended. Indeed, Emeny was optimistic, despite some forces that appeared to be pushing Japan back into its old days. He believed that whatever developed in Japan, it would not revert to the old type of centralization because some factors were resisting its revival.[50]

William J. Jorden, a member of the Council on Foreign Relations Study Group on Japan and a Carnegie newspaper fellow, expressed a similar view. He insisted that the occupation legacies of the democratic experiment "might very well repress a recurrence of the pre-war dangers."[51] In addition, he appreciated the liberating effects of SCAP reforms, which took shape in the development of unionism and the high voter turnout in elections in Japan. Indeed, Japan's voting percentage exceeded that of the United States. Jorden argued that the Japanese did not completely disregard social responsibility—their attitude toward crime, for example, had resulted in a lower crime rate in Japan than in other countries. In assessing the SCAP democratic experiment, Jorden conceded that the occupation reforms might appear too modest and too qualified by American standards. Perhaps it was because the SCAP officers thought they had accomplished more with the occupation reforms than they actually had done or could have done. Whatever the case, he believed there was little reason Americans should feel too pessimistic about the future of democracy in Japan.[52]

Other American experts on Japan were fair-minded enough to acknowledge that some of the traditional features of Japanese society were democratic, irrespective of U.S. occupation reforms. Henry Bovenkerk, a Presbyterian missionary, insisted that the Japanese communal village pattern of living offered a certain degree of democracy. His observation was based on his work in rural Japan since about 1930. He was prepared to concede, however, that the Japanese version offered less opportunity and protection for the individual than the American version. Bovenkerk, secretary of the Inter-Board Committee for Christian Work in Japan, found that democracy existed even in those Japanese villages entirely without Christianity.[53] Looking at what was happening at the riceroots (as opposed to the grassroots) level, Ardath Burks, professor of Rutgers University recognized another democratic aspect of Japanese life—the town meetings that the Japanese conducted in their rural communities, though not exactly in the same way that such meetings were conducted in America. Those meetings, he explained, were not conducted on the basis of "stand-up" votes for fear of disturbing the traditional Japanese process of rice collecting in which the members of whole rural communities cooperated. Therefore, they did not particularly want their stances on particular issues known publicly, because such revelations might militate against the rule of the game of consensus. The Rutgers professor also pointed out that the people of Japan had cooperative organizations for their agricultural processes.[54]

Judging from these observations, it seems reasonable to think that the traditional life of the Japanese in occupied Japan had other democratic features as well. F. Hilary Conroy, professor of Japanese history at the University of Pennsylvania, suggested that "Americans ought to be more willing to learn from Japan."[55] Harold G. Henderson of Columbia University also pointed out that "Americans could learn some of the real religious feelings that a lot of the Japanese had."[56] Henderson, born in New York, was educated at Columbia and had a profound knowledge of Japanese culture. He had served under Col. Kenneth Dyke as the first head of the Education and Religions Division of the Civil Information and Education Section of SCAP.[57] Bovenkerk suggested further that Americans might profit by learning from non-Christian Japanese religions, such as "respect for the aged, the natural moving into mystical experiences, the graciousness with which the Japanese moved into prayer, and the sense of close affinity to natural life."[58]

William L. Holland of the Institute of Pacific Relations and William Jorden were also clearly aware of the relativity of the value of cultures. They believed that the nature of democracy was conditioned by the country's history, culture, and tradition. Holland realized that America's "particular form of democracy might not be synonymous with democracy in Japan."[59] Jorden agreed. He recognized that the concept of democracy that the occupation authorities had normally used and spoken of was the American one. "Applied to Japan," he argued, "the concept [of democracy] might result in a far different system. . . . This might be very satisfactory for Japan."[60]

No doubt, the ultimate success of the occupation depended as much on developments in Japan as on events in the world outside of that country. Officials in the U.S. embassy in Tokyo also recognized the indigenous nature of democracy, and they quickly pointed out the danger in directly exporting American democracy to Japan: "An acceptable democratic system can be built in terms of Japanese traditions, culture, and social objectives and need not be an Anglo-Saxon or other 'foreign' version of democracy."[61] John Rockefeller similarly noted: "In Japan, as in any country, democracy must be a development from the people themselves, if it is to have meaning and to become a reality. It by necessity is a gradual and evolutionary process requiring many years."[62] Interestingly, his remark resonates with Joseph Stalin's assertion that a revolution could not be exported like a commodity and that a revolution could not succeed unless the people were thoroughly convinced that revolution was the only course they could follow to live their own lives and had the determination to act accordingly.[63] Rockefeller assumed, however, that the Japanese would not able to develop democracy by themselves; "its development can, however, be fostered and aided from the outside by example and by friendly understanding and cooperative effort."[64] That Rockefeller was friendly toward the Japanese could not be doubted, but his remark unwittingly revealed that he had a patronizing and condescending view of the people of Japan.[65]

On the whole, Theodore Cohen had a positive view of the occupation reforms, but he regretted that the U.S. occupation authorities tried to impose American methods where they did not fit.[66] Ardath Burks contended that it was improper and arrogant to export American social systems to Japan without taking sufficiently into account the social conditions of a foreign land: "You cannot expect the occupation-imposed reforms to be readily accepted" by the Japanese.[67] Hilary Conroy agreed with him: "We, the Americans, have made the mistake of assuming we could teach the Japanese everything."[68]

Undoubtedly, the Japanese genuinely admired America and its industrial and scientific advancements, but they had only fragmentary information on the United States and they tended to have little appreciation of American cultural or spiritual attainments. Americans tended to think that perhaps the lack of information was one of the major reasons for the superficiality of democracy in Japan. Rockefeller also noticed that the Japanese tended to overemphasize the material aspects of American civilization and lack a deep understanding of the nonmaterial aspects of American culture.[69]

Democracy and Christianity

This assessment of the democratic experiment cannot be completed without discussing the influence of Christianity—or lack thereof—on occupied Japan. No doubt the defeat in the Pacific War was a very unnerving, bewildering experience for the Japanese, and it struck at the very roots of their personal beliefs.[70] The defeat in war created a spiritual vacuum in the minds of most Japanese. It is no wonder, then, that a considerable number of American policy makers and Japanese Christian leaders thought Christianity might very well fill in that vacuum. They thought as well that Christianizing the whole nation might be a shortcut to its democratization. They believed that Christianity and the spread of democratic values went hand in hand.[71] Some leaders hoped that Christianity would serve as "an invincible spiritual barrier against the infiltration" of communism—the ideology that appeared to seek by suppression the way to power and advancement.[72]

Gen. Douglas MacArthur sought to bring the Japanese both democracy and Christianity.[73] On February 24, 1947, he told the U.S. Congress in a radio message that "through the firm encouragement . . . of this frail spearhead of Christianity in the Far East lies hope that to hundreds of millions of backward peoples . . . may come a heretofore unknown spiritual strength."[74] Associating Christianity with democracy, MacArthur frequently urged Protestant leaders to send ten thousand missionaries to convert the Japanese and gave them privileged access to the country.[75] President Harry Truman believed that "if Japan is to evolve into a peaceful nation, with an international against a nationalistic outlook, she must understand and appreciate the religious forces of the world."[76] Some Americans were outspoken about their self-imposed mission in Japan: "The ultimate sanctions of democracy are spiritual sanctions. The only sure way to help Japanese achieve democracy . . . is through the inculcation of Christian spiritual principles among an increasing number of Japanese leaders."[77] This statement leaves one with the unmistakable impression that American missionaries were self-confident and optimistic, moved by the burning spirit of their mission in Japan.

Indeed, Christianity enjoyed an enviable position and great prestige in the early years of the occupation. The "spiritual vacuum" created by the abolition of emperor worship presented ideal conditions for the spread of Christianity throughout Japan. On their part, the Japanese responded to Christianity as the religion of the conquerors.[78] There was a great curiosity and interest in Christianity, particularly among the younger generation, along with the glorification of everything "American" that swept the country. Christian churches had little difficulty filling their pews.

Gen. MacArthur contributed much by endorsing the distribution of Bibles and calling for more missionaries ("Make it ten million"). He also made frequent public statements in praise of Christian principles.[79] According to Frank Hawley, Tokyo correspondent for the London *Times,* MacArthur had two basic convictions: first, that the Japanese were basically good and that a Christian revival in Japan was important, and, second, that Christianity had the essential qualities that were needed to maintain and foster an egalitarian, democratic society.[80] Moreover, MacArthur believed strongly that Japan needed to become a Christian nation before democracy could take root in that country. In May 1947, MacArthur was elated by the ascension to power of Katayama Tetsu, a socialist and a Presbyterian: "Three great oriental countries now have men who embrace the Christian faith at the head of their governments, Chiang K'ai-shek in China, Manuel Roxas in the Philippines and Tetsu Katayama in Japan."[81] Prime Minister Katayama seemed to be in complete agreement with McArthur. He announced that the Japanese government "must be guided by a Christian spirit of morality." The Japanese prime minister also called for a Christian Round-Table Conference on Culture and Peace to give advice on public problems.[82]

Tokyo University president Nambara Shigeru believed Japan needed a spiritual revolution, by which he meant primarily "more Christian influence."[83] Takagi Yasaka, the father of American Studies in Japan, acknowledged the close relationship between democracy and Christianity as the world faith and universal religion. Takagi, a Christian, argued that the Japanese tradition that stressed the virtue of obedience had failed to nurture the concept of individual personality under the Buddhist and Confucian influence. He strongly believed that no one could hope to attain the true understanding of American civilization without the concept of individual personality based on the Christian ethical idea of human personality.[84]

Otis Cary, who taught U.S. history at Dōshisha University, had a different opinion. He was pessimistic about the prospects for the growth of democracy in Japan.[85] He maintained that it was "hard for democracy to exist in an area without Christianity."[86] His profound pessimism derived from his judgment that the Japanese could not understand the basic fundamentals of Christianity. The concept of human dignity for the individual—an ideal on which Christianity was based, according to Cary—was especially hard for the Japanese to comprehend. He attributed it to the analogy that Japanese society was developed along the lines of a pyramid, and so "it would take a long time to break it down to a point where their society was based not on a pyramid so much as on a straight horizontal line."[87] A few years later, Maurice Valency, the professor of comparative literature at Columbia who visited Japan in 1958 to determine how the humanities were being taught, expressed a similar view: "Theological questions have very little interest for the Japanese and their interest in Christian problems is absolutely minimal." He went on to point out that "so light indeed is their knowledge of Christianity that considerable portions of Western thought and Western literature are completely incomprehensible to them."[88]

Cary's opinions, which were often mixed with pessimism and cynicism, perhaps reflected his less than satisfactory achievement of his missionary activities in Japan.[89] He even argued that "to try to impose Western culture upon [the Japanese] people was a mistake."[90] Cary thought the Japanese were a rather fickle people, who liked to do things their own way. In 1952 he published *Nihon kaigan* (Opening of Japan's eyes), which sarcastically recounted his "eye-opening" experiences with Japanese during and after the war.[91]

Actually, Cary was not the only one who believed that Christianity and forming a democratic society were closely interrelated. Leading theologians such as Reinhold Niebuhr and Henry Bovenkerk openly argued that Christian principles and democracy were intrinsically related. Bovenkerk, a Presbyterian missionary, believed Christianity had long been associated with democracy and that the two moved along very close paths, and, indeed, may even be inseparable. Although he stressed that Christianity had advanced the most in democratic countries, he did concede that he would not go so far as to say that democracy was *the* Christian political institution. He insisted that people often deified individuals where monotheism did not exist, thereby diminishing the possibility of the existence of a working democracy.[92]

Many Japanese also thought democracy was closely associated with Christianity, whether they were Christians or not. Non-Christian leaders such as Ichimada Hisato, governor of the Bank of Japan, doubted whether Japan could maintain democratic institutions without the foundation of Christian thought and ethics that existed in the West. Christianity taught that all men were equal before God, and that each was responsible for his own salvation and personal conduct. Ichimada recognized that Christianity had certainly served as preparation and support for democracy over the years through its emphasis on individualism and equality. He was afraid, however, that Christianity and democracy could not coexist in Japan. He feared that individualism and equality might "open great possibilities of conflict in a country like Japan where most people were closely bound by group responsibility and social convention."[93] And yet Ichimada spearheaded a campaign to raise some 180 million yen (almost $500,000) to establish International Christian University (ICU) at Mitaka, near Tokyo.[94] It was Ichimada's act of faith to rebuild Japan in democratic and Christian terms. He was also committed to fortifying the country against disaffection and communism. Harada Tasuku, president of Dōshisha University from 1907 to 1920, and Ichimada shared a similar concern. Harada believed the very notion of sin as a basic inward unworthiness was completely new to the Japanese and that Japanese standards of conduct were determined by etiquette or social duty. He also believed that the central doctrine of Christ's atonement for man's sin was something his countrymen found difficult to accept.[95]

The Influence of Christianity in Postwar Japan

Actually, certain Christian customs had already penetrated Japanese society well before the postwar rush of American missionaries. The Western (Gregorian) calendar with its seven-day week was one of them. Japanese society, as a rule, revolved around the seven-day, twelve-month cycle, although Sunday, the seventh day, was not as carefully observed as in the West. Compulsory education, which had certain Christian attributes, was another development—the first kindergarten in Japan was a Christian institution. Linguistic devices such as the Hepburn system of Japanese-English transliteration, the popularity of classical music, the development of the Red Cross, and the more recent organization of the Community Chest—all had some connection with Christian concepts.[96]

Interest in Christianity did not necessarily mean, however, acceptance of the Christian faith. There was no definitive trend among the Japanese toward acceptance of the Christian faith in spite of the great curiosity and interest in Christianity. As a Japanese Christian minister pointed out, many of the Japanese who went to church did so to satisfy their curiosity about the Christian faith and perhaps to hear good moral teaching, but they had no apparent widespread desire or demand for membership in the church itself.[97] No one knew exactly how many Protestant missionaries were in Japan, but Robert Schwantes calculated about 2,000.[98] Schwantes also indicated that as many as 30,000 out of 125,000 church members might not be actively participating in their churches, and that 1 Japanese in 250 (0.4 percent) was Christian at that time, compared with 1 in 200 (0.5 percent) in 1927. Schwantes concluded that the notion that Christianity would pour in to fill the "spiritual and moral vacuum" in Japan had proved to be an illusion.[99] Henry Bovenkerk confirmed Schwantes's observation as "quite correct."[100]

Christianity did not penetrate deeply into postwar Japan for three reasons. First, according to an American diplomat, the Japanese found themselves ill at ease with Christianity, because subconsciously they viewed Christianity as a foreign religion and the agency of foreign powers. Second, American missionaries were highly sectarian and largely fundamentalist. The Japanese sometimes found American missionaries antagonistic to them. Few American missionaries had an adequate understanding or knowledge of basic Japanese patterns of behavior. It was neither surprising nor accidental that many missionaries reported that there were certain open suspicions and even resentment against Christianity in the rural areas. Third, Japanese Christianity was itself faced with a tremendous task of reconstruction. The war had destroyed one-fourth of all Protestant churches and over half of the Catholic churches. Despite the significant contributions made by Protestant missionaries and Catholics, Japan remained primarily a Buddhist country, claiming upwards of forty million believers.[101]

Moreover, the Japanese found that the basic tenets of either Shintō (The Way of Divinity), with its emphasis on nature worship, or Buddhism, with its promise of deliverance in the afterlife, still held satisfaction for them. Shintōism, Japan's indigenous religion, existed before the arrival of Buddhism in 538, and it has survived with little change until today. As one authority put it, "Buddhism has formed most of its flesh and blood for over a thousand years, though Shintō has remained the backbone of Japanese religion."[102] Thus it appears that Christianity was not able to offer a religious program able to satisfy the religious desires of the Japanese after the war; it remained a transplant in Japan in spite of the American occupation, as a U.S. embassy officer in Tokyo ruefully admitted. Put differently, during the early years of the occupation the Japanese had a great curiosity about and interest in Christianity, but Christianity failed to take full advantage of the golden opportunity presented by the war and the occupation.[103]

Japanese Perceptions of Democracy in Japan

Meanwhile, Japanese leaders were coping with the critical issue of how Japan should adapt to modernity in the face of American culture and embrace democracy. According to Osaka businessman Ōhara Sōichirō, "After the war Japanese looked to Americans as coming of Messiah—was real inspirational factor. . . . The 'Messiah' gave them democracy and so they took it—[but democracy did] not grow from within the people so [the Japanese were able to] understand its form more than its content."[104] Like Eugene Dooman and others, Ōhara regretted that the Japanese lacked "independence" and that democracy in Japan was shallow and superficial because the Japanese did not work it out by themselves.

Saitō Makoto, a professor at Tokyo University, who had just returned to Japan in 1953 after two years' absence at Harvard University, was appointed Hepburn Chair of American Constitution, History and Diplomacy at Tokyo University to succeed Takagi Yasaka, who had occupied the chair for thirty years. When Saitō was asked by an American cultural attaché the reasons for the poor showing of democracy in Japan, he responded that the Japanese desire to become democratic was genuine, but he pointed out the enormous difficulties that Japan faced before democracy took root deep in his country. His pessimism stemmed largely from what he described as "the 'ingrained' Japanese tradition." He explained that the Japanese tended to take responsible action and make moral decisions on the basis of the obligation to one's superiors or the thinking of one's father or teacher or superior. Thus the Japanese would have to undergo a far more difficult change than the mere promulgation of a new constitution and the passing of new laws.[105]

Apparently, Saitō was referring to the tendency of the Japanese to refuse or to hesitate to take a stand independently. Instead, they choose to remain uncommitted as much as they can until they feel abundantly secure and feel assured of the official endorsement from the person in authority above them. The Japanese take to heart the old saying that "a good tree is a good shelter." Such a behavioral pattern is based on their time-tested wisdom in life, and it has served them well. The sociologist Max Weber once said about the behavioral pattern of people of less independence, "The subjective assimilation of culture remained weak because it took place primarily by means of a passive absorption of what was authoritatively presented."[106] Undoubtedly, Weber was talking about the distinct German responses to the foreign cultures that were introduced to Germany prior to World War I. But such an observation also makes good sense in the Japanese context, because independence seems to be a barometer by which to measure the maturity of democracy in any given country.

Uramatsu Samitarō, the former secretary of the Japanese Institute of Pacific Relations and a writer for *Asahi shimbun* (which had a daily circulation of three million after the war), also admitted that the occupation reforms had resulted in little change; the Japanese still operated on the basis of *giri* (the system of obligations), the Japanese norm of conduct codified at the beginning of the seventeenth century. According to Uramatsu, only the surface had changed under the U.S. occupation despite SCAP publicity, and underneath the same old feudalism prevailed.[107] Matsukata Saburō, the managing director of the Kyōdō News Agency, also regretted that his country had changed little despite the unflagging zeal of SCAP for democratic reforms. Matsukata, in a somewhat exaggerated way, pointed out that the people of Japan did not necessarily practice ideas imported from abroad: "The Japanese kept in their minds, as in their houses, a foreign-style room in which foreign ideas could be segregated and kept sterile."[108]

Still others were cautiously optimistic about the prospects for democracy in Japan. Sakanishi Shiho, adviser to the Japanese Diet's House of Councilors Committee on Foreign Relations, appreciated that the Japanese had learned much from American occupiers. In her opinion, there might be a reaction in which some of the occupation reforms were swept away, but the Japanese now knew enough to stop the reaction before the occupation reforms returned to the sort of political system in place before the war.[109] Sakanishi was a little caustic on some aspects of the U.S. occupation, but she was basically friendly to the United States.[110] Until 1941, she was a librarian in the Japanese Section of the U.S. Library of Congress in Washington, D.C.

Prof. Matsui Shichirō at Dōshisha University was a cautious optimist as well. He believed that the newly adopted coeducation and the rise in Japanese labor organization would have important and lasting effects. But Matsui insisted that more time was needed to make Japan thoroughly democratic: "That's why some of us hope occupation will continue a long time."[111] Before the war, Matsui had spent several years in the United States, where he earned his Ph.D. in economics at the University of Wisconsin in 1927. After the war, he worked for about a year and a half as adviser in the Labor Division of the Economic and Scientific Section of SCAP.[112] Kondō Rinji, vice president of the Tokyo No. 1 Bar Association, shared Matsui's view. He believed that a long occupation was desirable both politically and culturally.

"To be sure, it is expensive," Kondō conceded, "but the cost could be cut by reducing the number of the occupying forces."[113]

Traditionally, the Japanese have tried to solve their internal problems by taking advantage of *gaiatsu* (external forces). After the war, they attempted to democratize their country either by taking advantage of external power and authority (the U.S. occupation army) or by depending on other external forces. Perhaps this factor accounts for Maruyama Masao's argument that "Japan's post-war democratization went no further than institutional and legal reform in the State machinery" and that "it did not reach the social structure or the people's way of life, much less the mental constitution of the people." This Tokyo university professor and towering historian of Japanese intellectual history went on to warn, "So long as democracy remains for Japan a lofty theory, an edifying doctrine, it will continue to be an indigestible import."[114]

Irrespective of how the Japanese understood the notion of American democracy, the fact remains that they embraced the machinery of democracy installed by American occupiers. Perhaps it is true that not all Japanese became genuine democrats overnight, but there is no denying the fact that American influences were at work at many levels of Japanese society and that the process of democratization did get under way. Evidence of these developments is that many Japanese intellectuals negatively responded to the gear change in U.S. policy priorities known as "reverse course" after 1947–1948 (see Chapter 2). It appeared to these intellectuals that the U.S. government was abandoning its initial objective of democratizing Japan and placing a new emphasis on remilitarizing the country.

With the rise of Japanese nationalism and the flare-up of anti-American feelings, the Japanese actually responded to American initiative and culture in the ways that demonstrated a surprising level of sophistication and at times extraordinary resilience. They picked and chose parts of American culture and digested those parts to suit their immediate needs. The Japanese sought to attain two objectives simultaneously: progress and law and order. Obsessed with progress, Japanese leaders were driven to move up in the hierarchy of nations, while maintaining order and tranquility at home and keeping their people in their proper places. To outsiders, this Japanese behavioral pattern sometimes seemed unique, somewhat contradictory, and difficult to understand. Meanwhile, Japanese leaders tried to contain or slow down the destructive processes of change that they thought American initiatives brought to their country. To smooth the processes of change and minimize the negative repercussions of change, they selected and utilized only useful aspects of the Japanese tradition such as the ideology associated with the family system.

By contrast, the U.S. occupation authorities were confident and proud of their cultural value system. They tended to assume that what was good for America was also good for the Japanese.[115] Consequently, they tended either to miss entirely the ambivalence and subtleties in a variety of Japanese responses to the American initiatives or to hardly discern them. Moreover, they projected their self-righteousness onto the Japanese, assuming that Japan's traditionalism was backward. They sometimes even displayed a patronizing and condescending attitude toward the Japanese. Meanwhile, they tended to judge the democratization of Japan by applying the absolute yardstick of American-type democracy. So many reforms were implemented in so many areas in so short a time that it was too early to draw definitive conclusions about the retention of many of the newly acquired instruments of democracy in Japan. The Council on Foreign Relations Study Group on Japan advised Americans against becoming too impatient for the tangible results of the democratic reforms in Japan. Harold Strauss of Alfred A. Knopf Publishers mildly cautioned Americans that they "may be expecting too much too soon."[116] No doubt, the American specialists on Japan discussed the legacies of democratic reforms in Japan at great length. Applying the supposedly scientific jargon of the social sciences, they ended up, however, reconfirming their stereotypical images of old Japan and their biases against that country and its people.

"Democracy" versus Consumerism in Postwar Japan

The smashing U.S. military victory in Japan in 1945, especially the atomic bombs dropped on Hiroshima and Nagasaki, overwhelmingly convinced the Japanese of American superiority in the science and technology that produced that superweaponry.[117] Actually, they saw and felt America's greatness in material civilization. Following the premise that victorious nations proven to be superior in arms must have a superior culture, most Japanese clung to the belief that any reconstruction of Japan could be facilitated by adopting the material and cultural ways of the United States. In response, they developed an extraordinary propensity for accepting things American, and many Japanese displayed an exceedingly adaptable attitude toward life. Such an attitude contributed much to making them strongly pro-American.[118]

Actually, it is sad but true that after the war the Japanese hardly took a stand on the United States and the U.S. government. Indeed, they showed a proclivity to accept everything American, which indicates the degree to which the Japanese were resigned to American culture, because it was often presented "authoritatively" by U.S. occupation forces. To put it differently, the Japanese resigned themselves to a passive and submissive acceptance of authority and developed an abiding psychology of dependency. They therefore failed to work out their own articulate system of conduct by which they could assimilate American culture subjectively and independently.[119] If the case can be made that the Japanese were made increasingly less independent and less critical of the authorities, is it not possible to argue that the U.S. occupation paved the way for the identity crisis—a lack of independence—that the Japanese had to face in the 1970s and 1980s and are still facing today?[120]

In the eyes of many Americans, after the war ordinary Japanese did a quick and remarkable about-face, transforming themselves ingeniously into a group of pro-Americans. They looked extremely adaptable, and yet they also appeared too fickle. This development was not only surprising but also incomprehensible to many Americans in light of the fact that the Japanese had been their bitter enemies until only recently. This "peculiar" behavioral pattern of the Japanese fascinated and captivated cultural anthropologist Ruth Benedict. She argued that the Japanese behaved in accordance with situational or particularistic ethics, as opposed to the so-called universal values in the Western tradition.[121]

Meanwhile, there seemed to be no reason why Americans should not take advantage of this sudden change in the Japanese attitude toward the United States. In fact, American businessmen busied themselves selling "progress," which was of great interest to the potential Japanese consumers.[122] At the same time, Americans were hard at work on advertising to whet the Japanese appetite for American goods. In fact, American businessmen took full advantage of this Japanese xenophile proclivity, and were not only skillful but also successful in creating "wants" among Japanese consumers. To that end, many branches of U.S. firms in Japan—including Coca-Cola, National City Bank of New York, Bank of America, Northwest Airlines, and American Shipping Lines—used high-pressure salesmanship to promote the sale of American goods and services, especially in motion pictures, magazines such as *Time, Newsweek,* and *Reader's Digest,* and other media. The material aspects of American culture were most apparent in the contracts for goods and services negotiated during the occupation.[123] As a result, Japan was flooded by American cultural imports and found itself under the constant pressure of a mass, standardized civilization predominantly American in character.[124]

The advertising and promotion paid off; the Japanese developed a strong desire to either possess or consume anything that came from the United States, ranging from progressive ideas and institutions such as coeducation and democracy to material goods such as cosmetics and kitchen gadgets. In fact, anything from the United States looked acceptable to them, whether it was a package of American cigarettes or the latest theory of popular government, simply because theirs was either nonexistent or regarded as being of grossly inferior quality.[125] The tendency of the Japanese to accept things American may be understandable in light of the dearth of material things and enormous psychological difficulty they faced immediately after the war.

As noted, the high-pressure advertising and the hard-sell tactics of American businessmen helped to stimulate the intense desire of many Japanese to adopt the American material and cultural way of life in the 1950s, especially after the Korean War boom. C. Martin Wilbur, a Columbia University professor, found that the Japanese craved the American image, as portrayed in the advertising for lipstick, clothing, and the like.[126] Another Columbia professor, Donald Keene, found that the Japanese taste in life, at least the taste of those living in big cities, was extraordinarily and fanatically xenophilic.[127] Keene pointed out that the best-selling cigarettes and many other products in Japan were those with labels in English. Even leftwing Japanese turned to American-style houses.[128]

A Russian journalist in Japan after the war reported that it was American "civilization" in the Ginza, the busiest section of downtown Tokyo, that foreign visitors noticed instantly and that made them rather dizzy and deaf. To the Russian, the Ginza appeared so Americanized that it gave people the impression that no vestige of the former flavor of the Ginza remained. Things such as the gaudy advertisements for Coca-Cola and Hollywood movies, the lurid covers of detective stories and obscene books, and the drunken brawls of American GIs represented American "civilization," according to this Russian critical of American culture.[129] Although it seemed to him that the entire country had embraced and adopted the bourgeois "civilization" of the United States, in reality the Ginza represented neither the whole of Tokyo nor the real life of the Japanese at large. Moreover, the Ginza was not suddenly Americanized after World War II; it was already Americanized in the 1920s and the 1930s.[130]

But not all American residents or Japanese were entirely comfortable about the way in which American consumer goods were introduced to Japan.

In fact, some were bitterly critical of the hard-sell tactics of American businessmen. Wolf I. Ladejinsky, a major SCAP adviser on land reform, was one of those critics. He harshly lashed out at U.S. publicity policies in the Far East for placing too much emphasis on selling the United States and doing too little to be helpful.[131] In later years of the 1950s, Ōhara Sōichirō, president of the Kurashiki Rayon Company in Osaka and a philanthropist, spoke caustically about the rise of commercialism and consumption in his country.[132] He regretted that Americans were spreading the notion that democracy meant consumption, as represented by items such as cars and refrigerators.[133] Ōhara warned his countrymen of the potential dangers in imitating U.S. consumption patterns, because, in his view, Japan badly needed to encourage production, not consumption. Along those lines, he emphasized the importance of Osaka as a production center, as opposed to Tokyo, which had become more of a center of consumption. He believed the Kansai (Kyoto–Osaka–Kobe) area was important, because it represented a much more independent and individualistic aspect of Japanese life.[134]

Those critical comments on consumerism were not made in a vacuum or in total isolation from the reality in which Japanese lived. By the 1950s, it was increasingly obvious that significant changes in Japanese living patterns were under way. Especially in the years after the Korean War and the resultant boom, the health of the Japanese economy improved significantly.[135] In April 1950, two years after his previous visit, Charles Fahs recorded how much he was impressed by the rapid and remarkable improvement in Japan's economy. He saw "better highways, more cars, including new Japanese-made busses and motored tricycles, better clothes," as well as new buildings under construction.[136] Theodore Cohen, an adviser to ESS, also noticed the general progress in Japan's economy. Commenting on the expansion of Japan's foreign trade, he singled out the country's exports, which approached $700 million in 1950.[137]

A Consumer Revolution in the Making

What was actually happening in Japan in the 1950s and afterward was a consumer revolution in the making—a revolution of rising expectations and material aspirations that every single Japanese cherished. This development, which represented a dynamic, changing quality of postwar Japan, resulted from several factors that included the expansion of mass communications; the diffusion of knowledge, information, and technology; shifts (stimulated by advertising) in the propensity of the Japanese to consume; and, above all, the latest cultural impact of the West, particularly the United States. Indeed, many of the changes in diverse areas such as popular music, fashions, and even household gadgets seemed to originate in the United States. Also, many new kinds of exotic and addictive foodstuffs such as Coca-Cola and hamburgers were becoming not only available but also easily accessible to many Japanese consumers.

As Japan moved into the 1960s, the consumerism trend in Japan became all too real, particularly after Japanese prime minister Ikeda Hayato proclaimed his vaunted income-doubling program in 1960, fifteen years after Japan's surrender. In a show of patriotism, the people of Japan worked harder and longer in order to reconstruct their war-torn economy as quickly as possible. The harder and longer they worked the more reward they thought they deserved. And, in fact, they gradually but steadily received an appropriate reward for their everyday toil, and so they began to satisfy their material needs and desires by purchasing new goods and services, most of which came from the United States. In this way, the rise of the material and mass consumption culture in Japan increasingly was linked with trade with the United States, manifested in the great variety of American consumer goods and services imported by Japan in the 1960s and the 1970s. The American material influence thus grew quickly.

This development brought about changes in the Japanese patterns of consumption, savings, and investment. For example, the Japanese adopted and then adapted the system of installment payments after the "new economics" was introduced from the United States. New economics extolled the "virtues" of consumption and the merits of immediate gratification by driving home to potential buyers that buying meant saving. By doing so, it sought not only to put consumers off their guard, but also unburden them of their sense of guilt about overspending. In later years, after Japan had accumulated a greater surplus of U.S. dollars and liberalized foreign money, the Japanese began to use credit cards and then purchased even more goods made in America and elsewhere.[138] The virtue of deferring happiness, which had once been considered a traditional value in Japan, seemed to be eroding. However, the Japanese people did not have a monopoly on the virtue of deferring happiness; it had been a traditional cardinal virtue in the United States as well before consumerism became rampant after World War II. And yet it could be argued that the forceful introduction of those American innovations and goods affected the entire political, economic, and social structure of Japan.

No doubt the Japanese took pride in the rise of commercialism and consumerism as tangible evidence that their steadfast efforts to recover the national economy had borne fruit. After all, they committed themselves to the early reconstruction of their country with the deep conviction that an early economic recovery would provide their poverty-stricken countrymen with a secure livelihood and thereby stabilize the whole nation. But the Japanese leaders found themselves in a dilemma, because they were profoundly concerned about certain influences that these rapid changes would bring with them—that is, they were worried about the effects of modernism and mass consumerism on the thoughts and behavior of ordinary people. Indeed, it was feared that epicurean hedonism would undermine and even replace the traditional Japanese virtue of deferring happiness and the Japanese work ethic. At the same time, consumerism stressed individualistic egalitarianism, at least in theory, at the expense of the traditional Japanese sense of communitarian obligation and respect for the hierarchical order of society. Japanese conservatives, in particular, were afraid that the Japanese social class system, the family system, and other aspects of the Japanese traditional way of life were being altered by the advent of consumerism (also see Chapter 2). Gradually, then, they felt the need to confront the intractable problems associated with it. The problems boiled down to (1) to what extent this seemingly baneful American influence could be tolerated; (2) how the poisonous effects of consumerism could be curbed; and (3) how the effects could be harnessed to Japan's advantage.

Actually, the Japanese were struggling with the central question of how to deal with occupation reforms and the American culture that was introduced to them directly and authoritatively. Indeed, although the Japanese sought and eagerly bought American goods, their purchasing behavior indicated neither a love of America nor a deep understanding of American democracy. William Jorden, the shrewd American observer of Japan mentioned earlier in this chapter, explained that the Japanese bought things made in America mainly because goods made in the U.S.A. implied something better to the Japanese.[139] In other words, the Japanese tended to associate the United States with American material goods rather than its core values embodied in human rights and democracy. John Rockefeller wryly recognized that the Japanese tended to overemphasize the purely material characteristics of American culture.[140]

Soft Power and American "Generosity" in Postwar Japan

A closer look from today's broader perspective leaves one with the impression that the Allied occupation of Japan was a constructive, enlightening experience for the great majority of Japanese. Few could doubt the high ideals and unflagging zeal of the occupying Americans. The SCAP authorities seemed to have convincingly demonstrated generosity, sympathy, and goodwill toward the Japanese.[141] Robert Schwantes, an American specialist on Japan, believed the SCAP program was built on laudable ideals, despite its obtuseness and bungling.[142] This view of the U.S. occupation of Japan has contributed in large part to the "success story" image of the seven-year military occupation. Perhaps the Japanese responded with goodwill toward the United States most of the time and numerous friendly relationships developed between the two peoples as a result of American goodwill and assistance during the occupation. But, in fact, most Japanese responded to the SCAP reforms both positively and negatively, depending on the specific issue involved, because the U.S. occupation as a whole was both benevolent and onerous.[143] What is important is that some problems underlay the success story image of the occupation, particularly in the cultural field—that is, American "soft power." Much of the emerging U.S. soft power thinking about Japan was ideological and time-dated; it largely derived from a fear of communism. The anticommunist "reverse course" was a case in point. Censorship was the source of some of these problems, which were simply antidemocratic. Indeed, a certain aspect of soft power was beset by the incompetence of GHQ officers and the ideology of the American occupation of Japan. American "generosity" was shaped by ideology (fear of communism). It is enormously important to note, however, that the American generosity observed in occupied Japan did not extend to Okinawa and Korea, the two other areas occupied in Asia. In fact, Okinawa was the price paid for America's "generosity" in Japan's four major lands—Hokkaidō, Honshū, Shikoku, and Kyūshū—and elsewhere.

Robert Schwantes recognized such flaws and failings in the occupation reforms and SCAP administration, and yet he praised the positive contribution the reforms made to the development of democracy in Japan. Theodore Cohen of ESS also gave SCAP high marks. He thought the function of the occupation was to hold back some of the traditional forces in Japan while new movements got under way. He described the occupation as "a man holding a bear trap open while the bear escapes."[144]

Conclusion

Soon after World War II, the U.S. government discovered that the wartime spirit of U.S.-Soviet cooperation was rapidly degenerating into hostility in areas in which the interests of the two nations came into conflict. The Soviet Union was vehemently opposed to any American hegemonic projects. At the same time, the U.S. government was apprehensive about the vulnerability of the free world in the face of impending Soviet expansionism.

In postwar Japan, the U.S. government was concerned about the internal weakness of a Japanese social and political structure that was emerging from a "spiritual vacuum." From the viewpoint of U.S. self-interest and national security, Japan was the most vital area in the Far East accessible to the United States. The American government found it utterly unacceptable for communists, together with radical leftists in labor unions, to seize power from the pro-American moderate conservatives in Japan. A Japan under socialist rule would not only irrevocably jeopardize U.S.-Japan relations, but also precipitate a major power shift in Asia in favor of the communist bloc. Such a situation, the U.S. government feared, would spur other Asian nations to swing toward communist-oriented neutralism.

Therefore, Washington chose to build up Japan and accelerate its development as a major Far Eastern power. Japanese military forces were thought desirable from an American point of view if they were built up sufficiently to defend Japan's homeland and Okinawa. This view became even more credible after the outbreak of the Korean War, but it was conditioned on not allowing Japanese military forces to hurt Japan's economic position and keeping those forces in check. The American government ensured that Japan would not gain full freedom of action, however. It was enormously important for the United States to prevent Japan from running amok as the country had done in the 1930s. In the eyes of most Americans, the Japanese were still unstable, unreliable, and unpredictable, requiring constant care and attention. Indeed, the paternalism and condescension exhibited by American leaders was on full view in 1919 when American banker G. K. Weeks, who was negotiating with his Japanese counterparts over the terms and conditions of Japan's entry into the New Chinese Consortium, an international banking syndicate organized to help modernize China, stated: "I look upon the Japanese as I would upon a small boy who possessed the same extraordinary energy and ambition which they possess. To attempt to suppress him, or to let him run wild, would be equally dangerous. The wise thing to do would be by sympathetic and intelligent direction, to reasonably control and mould the exercise of his energy. I believe this could be done in the case of the Japanese, but the job of course requires a man who is both strong and diplomatic."[1] And those perceptions of the Japanese did not change over time. It was thought better that Japan's military forces remain not quite independent of outside support. The U.S. government was single-mindedly determined to confront the Soviet Union and Communist China in order to prevent their influence from spreading throughout Asia and elsewhere and to maintain the geopolitical balance in East Asia.

Fighting Communism by Establishing Cultural Relations with Japan

In pursing their goal, U.S. leaders instinctively recognized that they could draw on lessons from history. In fact, the American government used its valuable insights from past U.S.-Japan relations in devising the U.S. policy guidelines toward postwar Japan. For one thing, government leaders recalled that interwar U.S.-Japan relations had been amicable under the system established by the 1922 Washington Naval Treaty, but that the friendly bilateral relationship deteriorated markedly in the 1930s and finally collapsed in the early 1940s. The lesson learned was that economic leverage alone was not effective enough to repress Japan's temptation to act independently or powerful enough to contain the country's expansionism. They also recognized the growing importance of the cultural dimension of foreign policy at the dawn of an age of mass communication and information technology. They thought that a postwar U.S.-Japan relationship should be multifaceted and comprehensive enough to integrate all three dimensions of the bilateral relationship—military, economic, and cultural. American leaders sought to reorient the U.S.-Japan bilateral relationship of the post-treaty years with such a historical sense and mission in mind.

The more the U.S. government intensified the campaign to combat the communists' worldwide anti-American propaganda, the more important it regarded the cultural dimension of U.S.-Japan relations. The United States clearly understood what could be accomplished by American "soft power," or the ability to entice and attract others, as Joseph Nye presented it some time ago.[2] In making U.S. policy toward Japan, American leaders took into consideration what future for Japan would suit America's policy objectives in East Asia. One of the long-range U.S. objectives in Japan was to develop human resources and nurture a pro-American leadership group that would support U.S. goals. It was hoped that American and Japanese leaders would manage the bilateral relationship and combat the communist influence together so that it would not spread throughout East Asia. It was expected that pro-American liberals in Japan would support the United States if they understood America and fully appreciated America's broad foreign policy objectives. Indeed, those liberals would act as interlocutor and mediator between the Americans and Japanese and enlighten the Japanese population so that it would understand and go along with U.S. foreign policy objectives. The United States thus assigned Japanese liberals a vital role in keeping U.S.-Japan relations on a durable basis. That was, in fact, the cultural dimension of the lesson that American leaders learned from the interwar U.S.-Japan relationship.

In attaching special importance to the cultural dimension of U.S.-Japan relations, the U.S. government and private organizations such as the Rockefeller and Ford Foundations never doubted the propriety of making use of soft power, nor did they hesitate to utilize America's soft power to the fullest extent to achieve political ends. Indeed, during the U.S. occupation of Japan, the Civil Information and Education Section of SCAP carried out a variety of educational reforms in an attempt to democratize Japanese traditional thought and behavior. During and after the occupation, Washington also endeavored to institutionalize cultural interchange to ensure that U.S.-Japan relations would be lasting and strong. John Rockefeller and Japanese leaders such as Kabayama Aisuke, Matsumoto Shigeharu, and Takagi Yasaka played an important role in institutionalizing the U.S.-Japan cultural interchange in cooperation with their American counterparts. American public affairs officers in the U.S. embassy in Tokyo also helped those Japanese leaders from behind the scenes. As described earlier in this volume,

Japanese and American leaders were responsible for establishing the International House of Japan and also were instrumental in developing American Studies after the war.

The U.S. Cultural Offensive and Its Unintended Consequences

In 1947 the U.S. government changed gears in its foreign policy priorities for Japan, and it even made sacrifices in the initial objectives of democratization and demilitarization.[3] On April 12, 1950, President Harry Truman announced that the United States would undertake a multimillion-dollar Campaign of Truth to combat worldwide communist propaganda.[4] The U.S. government began to devote increasingly more time, money, and energy to information programs, while waging psychological warfare against the Soviet Union and its communist cohorts around the world. After the outbreak of the Korean War in June 1950, the U.S. Congress tripled the budget that had been earmarked for international information activities.[5] To fight the cold war, Washington widely disseminated information and knowledge that projected positive, forward-looking images of America. Ironically but almost inevitably, the U.S. cultural offensive polarized Japanese intellectuals, especially the Japanese scholars of American Studies in the 1950s and 1960s. One group was made up of the growing number of non-Marxist liberal academics, and the other was composed of a majority of Japanese intellectuals under the influence of Marxism. Robert Schwantes recognized the political effect of the gear change in U.S. foreign policy. Indeed, he candidly admitted the slowdown in reform in Japan: "Unfortunately, the chances of continuing reform in Japan are in some respects weakened by our need to enlist her active opposition to the forces of world communism."[6]

The U.S. anticommunist campaign also cast its shadow over the Japanese system of higher education. In the world of higher education, as in many other fields, there was a tendency toward the overcentralization and regimentation that appear unavoidable in the modern bureaucratic state. During the occupation, SCAP/CI&E made a quixotic attempt to reverse this presumably irreversible trend by decentralizing Japan's system of higher education. SCAP/CI&E officers also believed such a change would make Japanese education genuinely democratic. The U.S.-based liberal view was that the concentration of Japanese universities in the big cities brought with it many evils, one of which was the inbreeding that militated against the spirit of an equal opportunity education. The plan to establish a national university in each prefecture was intended to serve that purpose, but this American democratic experiment turned out to be short-lived, in part because of the vehement opposition of conservative Japanese bureaucrats and academics. These factors, in addition to the distracting influence of the cold war in Asia, contributed to leaving the U.S.-led educational reforms incomplete.

In this context, it was a great irony that American soft power played a crucial, if not direct, role in stratifying and centralizing Japan's system of higher education. After obtaining generous grants from American donors, the Japanese elite and universities, especially those universities that offered American Studies programs, were restructured. And yet the Japanese elite, who had access to American soft power, occupied many prestigious university positions and enjoyed power and influence within the shelter of America's authority. The traditional method of filling academic posts and the traditional chair system in Japanese universities were blamed for the academic inbreeding as well. Meanwhile, generous American grants and scholarships permitted selected Japanese elite to study abroad for a considerably long period of time. The experience of studying in the United States not only allowed this particular group of academics to establish themselves as scholars but also lent authority to their scholarship. The result was that upon their return to Japan, they usually had attractive promising posts awaiting them. Thus despite or because of the occupation reforms, American soft power facilitated restoration of the hierarchical order that characterized Japanese academia before the war and gave it legitimacy by ensconcing the University of Tokyo at the top of the institutional hierarchy. The Japanese system of academic clique and inbreeding was left virtually intact.

And what were the psychological effects of American soft power on the Japanese elite, including bureaucrats? As noted earlier, U.S. soft power facilitated and begot the breeding of intellectual weaklings. The Japanese elite who had been nurtured to become pro-American gained ever greater power and influence in the postwar Japanese society. The Japanese bureaucracy, too, actually attained greater authority and influence than it had possessed even at the height of the mobilization for war, in part because Gen. Douglas MacArthur and SCAP officers depended so heavily on the indigenous technocratic elite to implement their directives under the occupation policy of indirect control of Japan and its people.[7]

And yet the postwar Japanese elite were pathetically weak before authority and lamentably deficient in independence in thought and behavior.

During the occupation, the Japanese elite had access not only to top-ranking GHQ officers on a daily basis, but also influential Americans such as the officers of the Rockefeller Foundation when they occasionally visited Japan. Meanwhile, these elite often curried favor with Americans obsequiously. As historian John Dower pointedly argues, "One legacy of the revolution from above was continued socialization in the acceptance of authority."[8] Resigned to America as the source of authority, Japanese intellectuals failed to articulate their own system of conduct. Instead, they accepted many of the American initiatives that were authoritatively presented to them. Pointing to the consequences of "the revolution from above," William Leonhart, a diplomat at the U.S. embassy in Tokyo, disclosed his contemptuous feelings toward Japanese scientists: "Many Japanese scientists, despite their attainment, might be characterized as politically gullible, naïve and fuzzy-minded, as well as strongly anti-militaristic."[9] It seems, then, neither accidental nor unreasonable that Americans such as MacArthur and others formed the impression that the Japanese were "juvenile" and that they behaved "like a boy of twelve."[10]

U.S. soft power also was responsible for the Japanese elite developing an abiding dependency on American "generosity." After the war, many Japanese scholars were assisted by the United States in one way or another, including research grants and scholarships. In light of the enormous amount of public funds earmarked for U.S. cultural foreign policy objectives, it was not surprising that the Japanese elite received various forms of aid from the U.S. embassy in Tokyo as well as from American philanthropic foundations in New York. In 1961, for example, the U.S. government spent $2 million to carry out its educational and cultural exchange programs, which emphasized the areas of political theory, law, social sciences, communication media, education, and labor.[11] Following the American foreign policy guidelines, public affairs officers in the U.S. embassy in Tokyo stepped up the U.S. cultural effort in Japan by encouraging private sponsorship and providing about $1 million a year in U.S. financial assistance.[12]

The Japanese academic study groups received favors and overly cordial blessings from SCAP/CI&E. One typical example was the Japanese Association for American Studies (Amerika Gakkai), which was established in 1947. Most programs of Amerika Gakkai were sponsored financially by either the U.S. government or American private citizens and philanthropic foundations.[13] As a result, the Japanese elite developed a dependency on American generosity, especially those elite pursuing the establishment of American Studies in Japan. As Warren Obluck, an officer in the U.S. Information Service, acknowledged candidly, beginning in the early 1950s USIS had played a supporting role "that resulted in measurable effects on the development of American Studies in Japan." When a team of outstanding Japanese professors visited the United States on a mission to observe how American Studies was taught in America itself, Obluck pointed out that the U.S. embassy in Japan organized the visit and covered its costs.[14]

American soft power in the form of financial aid also helped Japanese professors to increase their power and influence at Japanese universities. On the one hand, U.S. aid helped them to build up their careers. On the other, Japanese scholars' strong tendency to engage in ivory tower thinking led them to place a disproportionate emphasis on the pursuit of knowledge. The result was that they became excessively concerned about self-cultivation. They had little moral hesitation to commodify the information and knowledge they gleaned from their scholarly work when it might lead to a promotion or a higher job status. Perhaps this result was unintended, but it was nevertheless unfortunate, even noting that Japanese university professors worked longer hours and were notoriously more underpaid than those in most countries of the world.[15]

Japanese intellectuals, of course, appreciated receiving the huge amounts of money and materials from the U.S. government and private Americans, and yet they were overwhelmed and mesmerized by American generosity. At times, in appreciation of American goodwill and generosity, they cooperated positively with the U.S. embassy in Tokyo and its branch offices scattered throughout the country. At some other times, they refrained from criticizing U.S. foreign policy even if they did not necessarily agree with it. Worse still, sometimes they confused American political action with American goodwill and generosity, and chose to keep their mouths shut even at the very time that U.S.-Japan relations were so critical that their expertise opinions and counsel were much sought.

A related problem surrounding Japanese intellectuals, notably most experts on America, was their traditionally imbedded disinclination to concern themselves with contemporary social and economic problems.[16] For example, in the 1980s when the United States and Japan were at loggerheads over economic issues, U.S.-Japan relations became extremely politicized and increasingly tense. Events that affected U.S.-Japan relations and thus a public understanding of the United States overtook the Japanese people in rapid succession. Under those circumstances, the expertise and counsel of Japanese specialists on America were badly needed, but most of these specialists remained silent and withdrawn from the heated public debate over the contemporary issues surrounding U.S.-Japan relations. In response, businessmen and the mass media in Japan, among others, harshly criticized Japanese scholars of American Studies for not providing a pragmatic response to the social need for accurate information on the United States. These critics reminded the American Studies community that it was "responsible to activities other than self-cultivation in the academic sphere."[17]

Americans shared this criticism of Japanese scholars. One American observer complained, "While activities in American Studies are definitely on the rise, they do not necessarily address these new events and the issues they raise."[18] Another joined this critic by pointing out that American Studies professors in Japan were specialists and so did not fully understand the United States, nor were they willing to deal with American society frontally as they succumbed to their own "increasing insularism" and "growing arrogance."[19] These specialists could meet the challenges facing them only by revitalizing American Studies through "extending [it] to tackle today's crucial issues." This critic also suggested that American Studies specialists in Japan increase their communication with the nonacademic community.[20] Perhaps it was no accident, then, that the U.S.-Japan Friendship Commission, one of the major U.S. financial donors to American Studies in Japan, concluded in 1986 that the American Studies initiative in Japan was no longer helping to contribute to Japanese understanding of the United States. The commission notified Amerika Gakkai of its intention to terminate financial support of American Studies in Japan.

The critics who accused Japanese scholars of ivory tower thinking charged that American Studies of the 1980s was little different from that of thirty years earlier. Their comments perhaps make better sense when they are compared with some of the observations made about the American Studies of the early 1950s. For example, as one American scholar who lectured in Japan in the early 1950s described his experience: "I have just returned from two months in Japan as a member of the five-man staff of the American Studies Seminar.... [It was] the cream of the crop from the numerous schools all over Japan.... Their level of intellectual and professional sophistication ... is very high." And yet "their lack of acquaintance with America, particularly of those many subtle elements going into the American 'way of life' is appalling."[21]

From such criticism, ordinary people inescapably formed the impression that Japanese liberals did not practice what they learned from American Studies, nor did they practice what they preached. As a result, they did not win respect or gain the legitimacy needed to continue to pursue American

Studies. In Max Weber's *The Protestant Ethic and the Spirit of Capitalism* Paul Bunyan says, "It will not be said, did you believe?—but: were you Doers or Talkers only."[22] Spirit, like fever, is something ephemeral and cannot be preserved eternally. Therefore, man attempts to institutionalize the spirit to keep it as pure as possible and to preserve it as long as possible. However, once the spirit is institutionalized and tied to the power and authority of the state, it begins to decay, although the form of it may remain. What emerges is a precarious balance between power and knowledge. It is because power necessarily corrupts and destroys people by means of "pride, anger, and the desire of the flesh, the desire of the eyes, and the pride of life." The response is to lament and ask, "Is there no way to prevent this—this continual decay?"[23] It may seem far-fetched, but could it be argued that this unavoidable process of decay applied to postwar Japanese American Studies as well? No matter how idealistic the motive of philanthropy may be, idealism is susceptible to corruption by self-interest—conscious or unconscious—because money works like a double-edged sword, being at times a facilitator and at times a poison.[24] It depends on the way money is used.

Of course, scholarship in general and American Studies in particular are not constant. They fluctuate, reflecting to no small degree changes in U.S.-Japan relations over time.[25] But if these observations of Japanese experts on America are fundamentally correct, it means that intellectuals are shirking their social responsibility to be moral critics who offer innovative policies and strategies and alternative ways of thinking about Japan's national interests and U.S-Japan relations, both immediate and long term. In a democratic society, scholarship, especially scholarship supported at the public's expense, is inevitably judged in terms of its contribution to society. But such a judgment should not be only in terms of immediate tangible benefits, nor should the more remote and less obviously utilitarian fields of study be abandoned, because scholarship in either category has its own contribution to make to society. After all, too rarely is scholarship rewarded for its contribution to society. And being relevant is harder, more sensitive, and more troublesome. The net result has been the stunting of scholars' sense of social responsibility. Therefore, it is important for individual scholars to not forget to ask wherein the value of one's work lies.

Jacques Barzun, the author of *The House of Intellect,* argues that philanthropy impedes intellectual creativity: "Philanthropy is manipulation . . . anxiously contrived, timidly eager for approval, and therefore seeking love and publicity."[26] Dean Rusk, president of the Rockefeller Foundation in 1954, extolled the virtue of self-reliance and frugality, while rejecting the psychology of dependency. Representing the foundation, he once remarked, "There is a possibility . . . that aid from a paternal government may sap . . . sturdy virtues and breed a race of weaklings."[27] It would be a great irony indeed if money were one of the main causes of the problem of dependency facing American specialists in Japan today, because the principle of good works was one of the tenets of Rockefeller's strong Baptist faith in creative philanthropy.[28]

The Future of U.S.-Japan Relations?

From my forty-year pursuit of American Studies, punctuated by occasional stays in the United States to study and teach, I have learned that America and its people are willing to take into account the views and opinions of others. Americans have tremendous courage and the ability to challenge and solve problems if they find those problems vital to themselves and the country. At the same time, they like to exchange sincere ideas and well-founded opinions that may challenge their assumptions and offer alternative ways to cope with contemporary issues, even if those ideas and opinions may be very different from their own. And Americans are willing to listen to such opinions and pay respect to such friends in foreign lands. I happen to take the view that neither Japanese nor Americans lack creative imaginations and innovative ideas. People need to engage readily in frank and genuine discussions. It is my deep-seated conviction that only then do people win respect from each other. True friendship and love grow between people in this way. A U.S.-Japan relationship is no exception.

Unfortunately, on both sides of the Pacific excessive pride, a short-sighted lust for power, timidity, and an unwillingness to confront real issues, as well as mutual suspicion and mistrust, have long prevented a genuine exchange of ideas and opinions between Americans and Japanese. And U.S. foreign policy seems unlikely to produce mutually satisfactory outcomes, no matter how generous and good intentioned Americans may claim they are, because it seeks to influence, if not control, foreign countries and peoples by keeping them always dependent on the United States. Indeed, few frank discussions are conducted on an equal footing, because foreign countries are made to feel either subservient or inferior to America. In turn, Americans feel superior and comfortable by starting diplomatic discussions with their counterparts from the position of the powerful might and money. This negotiating style of the U.S. government has distinctly colored U.S.-

Japan relations for the past sixty years, creating in Japan a psychology of dependence on the United States.

Documents from the last half-century reveal that U.S.-Japan relations have been neither genuinely cordial nor healthy during this period. As late as 1964, the American leaders who attended the secretary of state's policy planning meeting on May 5 of that year disclosed their true feelings toward Japan and its people: "It is doubtful whether in Japan there is full recognition that the occupation is really over. The Japanese are too preoccupied with U.S. reactions and not sufficiently with defining their own interests. We need to stimulate Japanese consideration of their problems from their point of view.... A clear recognition of the real identity of U.S. and Japanese interests would provide a more solid basis for our relations."[29] This document reveals how much the Japanese were afraid of the United States and how much they were concerned about the U.S. reactions to whatever action they might take.

Meanwhile, features such as ambiguity, inarticulateness, ambivalence, and lack of commitment characterized the Japanese negotiating style. During the 1960s, these Japanese traits gave American negotiators the impression that America might get away with ignoring Japan and its interests in executing U.S. foreign policy that involved Japan. The result was that Japan received too many "kicks in the teeth" from the United States, notwithstanding the oft-quoted American utterance that the United States regarded Japan as an equal and important partner.[30] A State Department officer disclosed in 1963 that "the apparent assumption in Treasury, Defense, Commerce, Agriculture, and other Departments, however, is that ... its [Japan's] security and economic dependence on us is so great, and its economy so strong that we can ignore its interests with impunity."[31]

Americans had similar problems and idiosyncrasies. Americans seem to deal with problems only when they feel they have an overpowering military and economic advantage. They negotiate with foreigners splendidly, so long as their counterparts remain conspicuously inferior to them in power and influence. When Americans see relations of power and influence tipping in a foreign country's favor, they feel less confident and less patient—that is, they begin to feel anxious and threatened and are easily irritated. Then they often behave awkwardly, high-handedly, and even abnormally. U.S. foreign relations are even more confounded when the issue involves a nonwhite race, whatever the issue may be. America's Japan bashing of the 1980s was a case in point. A high-ranking American officer acknowledged that Americans were not "well-equipped to face the fact that in economic growth terms another nation (and especially an Asian nation) has seemingly been able to organize itself and its resources more efficiently than we. For the present we feel vaguely threatened, perhaps resentful, and unsure how to deal with the situation."[32]

The ways in which U.S.-Japan relations unfold in the future depends on historical junctures created by a combination of physical factors and human actors. To borrow from William Roseberry, "There are always relationships and meanings that are excluded from the dominant order of things, but alternative meanings, alternative values, and alternative versions of a people's life and history inevitably emerge."[33] In this connection, all one can say is that the future of U.S.-Japan relations remains to be seen and that people watching it should be on guard.

Appendix A

The State of Scholarship on U.S.-Japan Relations

Much work has been done to date on the complex reality of the unique and enduring U.S.-Japan relationship, reflecting its special importance in the postwar period. The scholarship on U.S.-Japan relations, however, has been regrettably unbalanced in terms of subject matter and approaches.

The first characteristic of the scholarship on U.S.-Japan relations is that the security and economic issues of U.S.-Japan relations have attracted by far the most scholarly attention, whereas the cultural dimension of that bilateral relationship has attracted relatively scant commentary. A similar tendency was pointed out in the recent German scholarship on the occupation of Germany.[1] It is regrettable but true that cultural relations either have been treated as a subject of secondary importance or have been simply ignored altogether. This lopsided treatment seems strange and unsound in view of the increasingly important concept of the "soft power" of the United States, an idea introduced and popularized by the political scientist Joseph S. Nye Jr. more than a decade ago.[2] When one looks at the host of current works on U.S.-Japan relations, it reveals few attempts to bring more than three dimensions of the U.S.-Japan relationship together—security, economics, and culture—and integrate them into a single framework for analyzing the bilateral relations. It may be worth remembering a pertinent remark quoted by Francis J. Colligan, chief of the Division of Exchange of Persons of the U.S. Department of State: "Foreign policy today must be total. It embraces all categories of international relations. Cultural exchange is one of them."[3]

The second characteristic is historians' predilection for dichotomies and binary opposites, along with their proclivity for using a narrowly focused binational framework. This predilection characterizes the English-language scholarship on U.S.-Japan relations. Dichotomies between conversion/diversion and continuity/discontinuity, to name only two, are rife among historians.[4] For example, one school of thought, dubbed the scholars of convergence theories, came into vogue in the United States during the 1960s and in Japan a little later. At that time, both nations were wooing each other fervently as indispensable partners in the cold war being waged in Asia and elsewhere. Most of the studies conducted by the positivist, modernization theorists stressed Japan's similarities with the United States, while they either blurred or underrated the differences that existed between the two countries. Those studies were based on an optimistic assumption that Japanese society would ultimately converge with U.S. society in the future if it continued to modernize itself by learning from the experiences of America. Modernization theory provided these scholars with an attractive explanation for Japan's success story as a modern nation. The theory posited a universal, quantitatively measurable movement whereby all societies progress toward a single ideal form of organization that can be described as "modern," though "modern" might just as well be thought of as "capitalist."[5]

More recently, historians have taken a postmodernist approach that is completely relativist at heart. Recognizing the fact that Japan had grown to be one of the most advanced industrial societies on earth by the 1980s after having accomplished the goal of modernization and industrialization, Japanese scholars took such an approach to place the Euro-American values and cultures in relative terms. They emphasized the uniqueness and distinctiveness of Japan's traditional culture by way of overcoming its long-held inferiority complex in relation to the West and seeking a national identity. In Japan, postmodernism has been defined as a movement that seeks "the deconstruction of modernism or, more fundamentally, of the framework of Western metaphysics," according to the literary critic Karatani Kōjin. It involves the "disappearance of the subject, the de-centering (or 'multi-centering') of the [putative] center, and pastiche or collage for creativity."[6] In response to the "postmodern condition," historians of postmodernism contend that there are no universals, no reality, only individual perceptions.[7] They argue that every kind of expression, every kind of representation, every kind of culture are as valid as others.[8] Needless to say, the postmodernist approach corresponds largely with that of multiculturalism and has come to dominate Japanese studies in the United States since the 1990s.

The other school of thought—that is, the divergence approach, as opposed to the convergence approach of the 1960s—became fashionable during the 1980s when U.S.-Japan trade friction came to dominate bilateral relations.

With the sense of an impending clash between the two Pacific rivals, scholars sought to understand what had brought Japan an economic miracle and sustained its economic growth, which in turn produced fierce U.S.-Japan economic competition. Scholars who had been dubbed revisionists on Japan—such as Ezra Vogel, Chalmers Johnson, and Walter LaFeber, to name only a few on the American side—came to emphasize Japanese particularity, and they stressed the enduring and deep transhistorical differences that they believed existed between Japan and the United States.[9] The major institutions of Japanese society, especially government–business relations, according to the revisionists, were fundamentally different from those of the United States. These scholars argued that clash, rather than cordial entente, was the dominant theme of the history of U.S.-Japan relations. The scholars actually belonged to the "Japan uniqueness" school of essentialism in which they have argued that Japanese culture is and always has been irreducibly unique and non-Western with its own universalistic, timeless values. As a result, studies in U.S.-Japan relations have cycled around divergence/convergence theories—first, "divergence" theory in the 1930s and the 1940s, and then "convergence" theory in the 1960s, and once again "divergence" theory in the 1980s and the 1990s.[10] Some scholars of the U.S. occupation of Japan keenly felt the need to move away from this increasingly sterile debate over dichotomies, even though these problems are undoubtedly important.

The third characteristic of the scholarship on U.S.-Japan relations—mainly works in Japanese language—is that leftist/Marxist historians have taken a historical, not dichotomous, approach and attempted to place Japan in its historical and contemporary context as part of the worldwide development of capitalism. The interpretation and appraisal of occupation reforms have been one of the continuing and central problems for these scholars. They have grappled with the consequences of occupation reforms and attempted to assess the quality of the democratic experiment undertaken either jointly or separately by the Supreme Commander for the Allied Powers (SCAP) and the Japanese. The issue of continuity versus discontinuity in the context of the history of modern Japan in general, and of Japan's capitalist development in particular, became one focus in their debate over historiography. More recent leftist historians have become very aware of the importance of culture.[11] They also made an attempt to periodize the U.S. occupation and were able to elucidate certain distinct characteristics of different stages of the occupation, which lasted six years and eight months.[12] Not only did they discuss key concepts such as the "reverse course" of the U.S. occupation policy from democracy to the cold war, but they also discussed the problem of determining exactly when the "reverse course" began.

Scholarship on U.S.-Japan relations has dramatically, if not drastically, transformed itself since the 1980s. To scholars' joy and excitement, many of the public documents and records on the occupation were declassified and became available in the United States and elsewhere in the 1980s. This availability led to the publication of a great number of articles and books on U.S.-Japan relations in general and on the U.S. occupation of Japan in particular. In 1990 Iokibe Makoto, a historian of modern Japanese politics and diplomacy, attempted to break the impasse he thought had resulted primarily from the ongoing fruitless debate over the paradigm of dichotomies by raising a new question: who was responsible for occupation reforms? And he presented a hypothesis that the occupation reforms were a joint U.S.-Japan undertaking to democratize the country.[13]

Thanks to the opening of documents and records in the 1980s, the methodologies and approaches of scholars became not only variegated but also more sophisticated and mature. The U.S. occupation of Japan was more carefully scrutinized, and thus that scrutiny was followed by minute descriptions of the historical reality, a reinvention of old categories and establishment of new ones, and international comparative studies of the U.S. military occupation. As a result, the process of the U.S. occupation ceased to be simple and clear-cut. The reality of the occupation era proved far more complicated than scholars had previously thought.

The fourth feature characterizing the previous studies of U.S.-Japan relations was their peculiar myopia. An overwhelming majority of scholars of U.S.-Japan relations have been almost obsessed with focusing their scholarship within a narrow binational framework. Yoshida Shigeru, who served as a prototype of Japan's conservative political realist, became prime minister for a good part of the U.S. occupation period. Prime Minister Yoshida, unlike Ishibashi Tanzan who briefly became prime minister in 1956,[14] chose not to confront the powerful Americans directly. To put it differently, he did not choose to resist SCAP and Gen. Douglas MacArthur frontally for the purpose of upholding Japan's national interest. Instead, Yoshida chose to cooperate and even cuddle up to the American occupiers. According to the Japanese prime minister, peoples or different races of the world formed a natural hierarchy based on inherent qualities and capabilities, and each ethnic or national group had its "proper place" in the regional or global scheme of things. Based on the ideas of division of labor and racism, he used this ideology of "proper place" to rationalize and reinforce disparate status and power relationships among people, races, and countries.[15] Historian Iokibe Makoto has extolled Yoshida for his astuteness, tactfulness, and statesmanship. Apparently, Iokibe admires the Japanese premier for acting not as an unreasonable recalcitrant but as a "good loser," who proceeded valiantly in his dealings with an absolutely powerful victor. He argues that Yoshida always kept in mind his conviction that history provided many examples of losing wars and winning the peace.[16]

And why did Yoshida behave the way he did? Did he really recognize that Japan had to pay an unavoidable price for seeking protection under a U.S. security umbrella? Based on his calculation of costs and benefits, did he judge that recalcitrance would not serve Japan's or his supporting party's interest under U.S. overwhelming dominance? Yoshida's attitude and behavioral pattern in dealing with the victorious United States was neither novel nor original. Instead, it was part of the traditional tactics that the Japanese occasionally employ when they deal with superior Western powers. It was exactly the same attitude and tactic that pro-Western Japanese diplomats, such as Shidehara Kijurō (1872–1951) and Debuchi Katsuji (1878–1947), Yoshida's immediate superiors at the Japanese Foreign Ministry, had used in negotiating with American officials in Washington and elsewhere during and after World War I.[17]

In addition, Iokibe points out that a polarity of extreme harshness and extreme generosity were distinctly characteristic of the U.S. occupation of Japan. Having made that remark, he places great emphasis on the generosity and good intentions of the "American people," but he concedes that the notion of generosity and the goodness of intentions are relative and could be subjective, depending on the definition and the measurement. From the viewpoint of humaneness and political wisdom, he argues broadly and sweepingly, it is praiseworthy that the United States so generously extended a helping hand to the defeated former enemy during the occupation.[18]

Without a doubt, the historian Iokibe has made a significant contribution to occupation historiography, and his respect and admiration for Yoshida and "Americans" must be genuine. Few would quarrel with his general assumption that "Americans" are a generous people. And still fewer would disagree with his contention that "Americans" were full of goodwill and admirably generous toward many Japanese, if not all, during the occupation. Here, then, it might be useful to look at the issue of "generosity" in broad terms. Is it not true, too, that the thoughts and behavior of a people or a nation change over time? Is it not undeniable as well that a people could be generous toward others sometimes while the same people could become less generous and even harsher at other times, depending on the time and the place in which they happen to find themselves? It is often said that the United States is extremely generous either when there exists no nation that challenges America and threatens its security, or when other nations acknowledge the American preponderance of power and agree to accept American leadership by depending on U.S. protection for their national security. But, as the world of the 1980s witnessed, the United States began to feel less confident and become increasingly anxious and irritable when it found other rivals catching up with it. On the U.S. scene as well, it was observed that generosity did not always extend equally to all racial and ethnic groups even within the United States during exactly the same time period when, as Iokibe alleged, "Americans" were generous toward "Japanese."

It is hardly necessary to stress that this is not to say that "Americans" are neither generous nor humane but callous. On the contrary, they are one of the most generous and humane peoples on earth. Americans have been generous enough to offer to share material and technical resources with other countries of the world with the objective of helping others to help themselves. Rather, the central question that historians of U.S.-Japan relations need to address is why the United States acted so "generously" during the occupation, instead of starting with the assumption that "Americans" are a generous people all the time. Was it not possible that the United States executed its "generous" occupation policy because the global interest of the United States demanded that it should as a hegemonic nation? Was it not possible that the congruence of American interest in the occupation of Japan, on the one hand, with U.S. global interests, on the other hand, did exist at that particular time in history?

Iokibe emphasizes the unchanging or static national trait of Americans—that is, their generosity and good intentions—and, in doing so, takes a rather ahistorical view, an insight that he might have gained from neighboring disciplines such as cultural anthropology. In this connection, a broader perspective of world systems analysis and the concept of cultural hegemony might be helpful in elucidating the real nature and irony of U.S. occupation policy. In short, it is regrettable that today myopia remains a central characteristic of most studies of U.S.-Japan relations.

Appendix B

The Tokyo-Stanford Seminars in American Studies

Visiting Americans:

1950
Joseph S. Davis (chair), economics, Stanford
Claude A. Buss, international relations, Stanford
John D. Goheen, philosophy, Stanford
George H. Knoles, history, Stanford
James T. Watkins, political science, Stanford

1951
John D. Goheen (chair), philosophy, Stanford
Royden J. Dangerfield, political science, Illinois
Howard S. Ellis, economics, California, Berkeley
Leon Howard, literature, California, Los Angeles
George H. Knoles, history, Stanford

1952
George H. Knoles (chair), history, Stanford
Perry Miller, literature, Harvard
Lorie Tarshis, economics, Stanford
Robert Walker, political science, Stanford
Morton White, philosophy, Harvard

1953
John D. Goheen (chair), philosophy, Stanford
Alpheus Thomas Mason, political science, Princeton

Edward S. Shaw, economics, Stanford
Henry Nash Smith, literature, Minnesota
C. Van Woodward, history, Johns Hopkins

1954
William Frankena, American philosophy, Michigan
Harold Fisher, American diplomatic history, Stanford
Leon Howard, American literature, California, Los Angeles
Clyde Kluchhohn, cultural anthropology, Harvard
Lorie Tarshis, economics, Stanford

1955
Donald H. Davidson, philosophy, Stanford
Hendrick S. Houthakker, economics, Stanford
Merrilll Jensen, history, Wisconsin
Harold D. Laswell, political science, Chicago
Harry Levin, literature, Harvard

1956
John D. Goheen, philosophy, Stanford
John Hazard, comparative law, Columbia
George H. Knoles, English literature, Stanford
Wassily W. Leontief, economics, Harvard

1957
No Tokyo seminar

1958
Walter Gellhorn, law, Columbia

1959
Carl Finley Christ (spring 1959), economics, Chicago
Willard Van Orman Quine (summer 1959), symbolic logic, Harvard
Merle Curti (fall 1959), history, Wisconsin

Source: Tokyo-Stanford American Studies Seminar List, January 20, 1959, folder 13, box 2, series 205, record group 1.2, Rockefeller Foundation Archives, Rockefeller Archive Center, Sleepy Hollow, N.Y.

Appendix C

The Kyoto Seminars in American Studies

Visiting Americans:

1952
Royden J. Dangerfield, political science, Illinois
John T. Flanagan, English-American literature, Illinois
Clarence Henry Graham, psychology, Columbia
Joseph John Spenger, economics, Duke
William O. Stanley, education, Illinois

1954
Charles M. Allen, education, Illinois
Rodney L. Mott, constitutional law, Colgate

1955
Virgil C. Aldrich, philosophy, Kenyon
Fritz Machlup, economics, Johns Hopkins

1956
Norman E. Nelson, literature, Michigan
Julian H. Steward, anthropology, Illinois

1957
Wendell H. Bash, sociology, Colgate
Edward S. Bordin, psychology, Michigan

1958
Richard N. Current, history, Women's College, University of North Carolina
Rupert N. Evans, education, Illinois
Charles Hartshorne, philosophy, Emory
Jeremy Ingalls, American literature, Rockford College
Douglas B. Maggs, administrative law, Duke
Daniel Suits, economics, Michigan

Visiting Japanese:

1955
Sakata Yoshio, history, Kyoto
Sugai Shūichi, administrative law, tax, Kyoto

1956
Tasugi Kiso, economics, Kyoto

1957
Izui Hisanosuke, linguistics, Kyoto
Nobechi Masayuki, psychology, Dōshisha

1958
Hashimoto Makoto, sociology, Dōshisha
Matsui Shichirō, economics, Dōshisha

1958
Hozumi Fumio, history of socioeconomic thought, Kyoto

1959
Imatani Itsunosuke, philosophy, Dōshisha

Source: Kyoto American Studies Seminar List, January 20, 1959, folder 34, box 5, series 609, record group 1.2, Rockefeller Foundation Archives, Rockefeller Archive Center, Sleepy Hollow, N.Y.

Notes

Introduction

1. John W. Dower, "Flunking Postwar Japanese History," *Japan Times,* December 16, 2003; "A Warning from History," *Boston Review,* March 6, 2003; "Lessons from Japan about War's Aftermath," *New York Times,* October 27, 2002.
2. Ruth Benedict, *The Chrysanthemum and the Sword: Patterns of Japanese Culture* (Boston: Houghton Mifflin, 1946).
3. The War and Peace Studies of the Council on Foreign Relations were actually inaugurated in 1939. For studies on Japan, see *Studies of American Interests in the War and the Peace,* Hamilton Fish Armstrong, rapporteur (New York: Council on Foreign Relations, 1942). For studies conducted by the Institute of Pacific Relations, see *Proceedings of the Institute of Pacific Relations, War and Peace in the Pacific: A Preliminary Report of the Eighth Conference of the IPR on Wartime and Post-war Cooperation of the United Nations in the Pacific and the Far East, Mont Tremblant, Quebec, December 4–14, 1942* (New York: International Secretariat, Institute of Pacific Relations, 1943); and "Provisional Analytical Summary of IPR Conference on Japanese Character Structure," December 16–17, 1944, prepared by Margaret Mead, Papers of the Institute of Pacific Relations, Box 92, Japanese Psychiatrist Meetings, Butler Library, Columbia University, New York.
4. One example is reform of the land tenure system. On February 26, 1936, a band of young military officers of the Imperial Way (Kōdō) faction resorted to a military coup, thereby attempting at the Shōwa Restoration to carry out land reform that had been left unfinished by the Meiji leaders. The agrarian distress evident in the tenancy disputes and the rural poverty symbolized by the horrible practice of selling young daughters were attributed to one of the powerful driving forces that prompted the rebels to attempt to seize power through a top-level coup. But the military coup was squashed. Thoroughgoing land reforms had to wait until the end of the war when the Supreme Commander for the Allied Powers carried them out during the occupation of Japan. See Ronald Dore, *Land Reform in Japan* (London: Oxford University Press, 1959).
5. Iokibe Makoto claims he can identify three types of occupation reforms. The first type is U.S. reforms that SCAP either directed or dictated—that is, antimonopoly legis-

lation and dissolution of the Zaibatsu combine. The second type is reforms that the Japanese initiated and proposed before SCAP issued directives—that is, election laws and labor union legislation. The third type of reforms is a combination of the first and second types in which SCAP and the Japanese collaborated—that is, land reform and constitutional revision. Iokibe Makoto, "Senryō—Nichibei ga futatabi deatta ba" [The occupation—The place where Japan and America met once again], in *Nichibei no Shōwa* [Shōwa—Japan and America] (Tokyo: TBS Britannica, 1990), 62–82; Iokibe, "Senryō kaikaku no san ruikei" [The three types of occupation reforms], *Leviathan* 6 (1990): 97–120.

6. Morito Tatsuo, "Heiwa kokka no kensetsu" [The construction of a peaceful nation], *Kaizō* (January 1946): 3–16.

7. Robert N. Bellah, "Values and Social Changes in Modern Japan," Asian Cultural Studies 3, International Christian University, Tokyo, October 1962, 13–56, cited by John W. Dower, *Origins of the Modern Japanese State: Selected Writings of E. H. Norman* (New York: Random House, 1975), 60.

8. Dower, *Origins of the Modern Japanese State,* 62.

9. "Japanese Peace Treaty Problems, First Meeting, October 23, 1950," Council on Foreign Relations Study Group Report, Manuscript Division, Council on Foreign Relations, New York.

10. John D. Rockefeller III had been a trustee of the Rockefeller Foundation since 1931, and he and Dulles had long been acquainted through mutual work on the foundation. John Curtis Perry, "Private Philanthropy and Foreign Affairs: The Case of John D. Rockefeller, 3rd and Japan," *Asian Perspective* 8 (fall–winter 1984): 268–284.

11. "Proposal for a Cultural Center and Student International House," September 6, 1951, item: Japanese-American Cultural Relations, folder 6, box 1, series 609, record group (RG) 1.2, Rockefeller Family Archives, Rockefeller Archive Center, Sleepy Hollow, N.Y. (hereafter RAC).

12. John D. Rockefeller III diary entry, January 22, 1951, folder 62, box 7, series 1-OMR files, RG 5 (John D. Rockefeller III), Rockefeller Family Archives, RAC; John Foster Dulles to John D. Rockefeller III, draft letter, May 4, 1951, confidential U.S. State Department special files, Japan, 1947–1956 (microfilm, University Publications of America, 1990, in reel 13, lot files 54-D-423: Japanese Peace Treaty Files of John Foster Dulles, 1947–1952).

13. John Tomlinson, *Cultural Imperialism: A Critical Introduction* (London: Continuum, 1991). Also see Rob Kross, "American Empire and Cultural Imperialism: A View from the Receiving End," *Diplomatic History* 23 (summer 1999): 463–477.

14. A cultural affairs officer explained the sensitivity of the issue of cultural imperialism: "The program [the State Department's International Exchange Service, IES] has been governed by the policy of cooperation in its approach to other peoples. This is an extremely important point, especially today when a good part of the world is quite sensitive to the threat, the charge, or the propaganda regarding possible cultural imperialism. In the administration of the program, for example, in many countries we have binational commissions composed of local Americans and foreign nationals to participate in the planning and administration of the program. . . . The results of such a policy, wisely conceived at the time the United States Information and Educational Exchange Act of 1948 ([the Smith-Mundt Act] became law, is quite evident." "General Information and Problems of the Department's International Exchange Service," August 1954, Bureau of Educational and Cultural Affairs Historical Collection, U.S. Department of State,

manuscript number 468, box 301, file 34, Special Collections Section, University of Arkansas Libraries, Fayetteville.

15. Commenting on the past cultural interchange between Japan and other countries, Chief Justice Tanaka Kōtarō criticized the Japanese programs for neglecting to take in foreign culture while they placed importance on introducing Japanese culture to foreign countries. Tanaka Kōtarō, "Cultural Interchange between Japan and America," *Tokyo Times,* February 21, 1951.

16. Robert W. Cox with Timothy J. Sinclair. *Approaches to World Order* (Cambridge: Cambridge University Press, 1966), 57, 120.

17. Jessica C. E. Gienow-Hecht, "Art Is Democracy and Democracy Is Art: Culture, Propaganda, and the *Neue Zeitung* in Germany, 1944–1947," *Diplomatic History* 23, no. 1 (1999): 29.

18. The word *culture* has had complex meanings. For an etymological discussion, see Raymond Williams, *Keywords: A Vocabulary of Culture and Society,* rev. ed. (New York: Oxford University Press, 1983), 87–93.

19. Robert F. Arnove, ed., *Philanthropy and Cultural Imperialism: The Foundations at Home and Abroad* (Boston: G. K. Hall, 1980); John Tomlinson, *Bunka teikokushugi* [Cultural imperialism: A critical introduction], trans. Makoto Kataoka (Tokyo: Seido-Sha, 1993).

20. For the excellent works recently produced on cultural (sexual) interactions between Americans and Germans, see Petra Goedde, *GIs and Germans: Culture, Gender, and Foreign Relations, 1945–1949* (New Haven, Conn.: Yale University Press, 2003); and Maria Höhn, *GIs and Fräuleins: The German-American Encounters in1950s West Germany* (Chapel Hill: University of North Carolina Press, 2002).

21. Emily S. Rosenberg, "Cultural Interactions," in *Encyclopedia of the United States in the Twentieth Century,* vol. 2, ed. Stanley I. Kutler (New York: Scribner's Sons, 1996), 708.

22. Rosemary O'Neil, "A Brief History of Department of State Involvement in International Exchange," fall 1972, Bureau of Educational and Cultural Affairs Historical Collection, U.S. Department of State, file 12, box 103, Special Collections Section, University of Arkansas Libraries, Fayetteville.

23. Gienow-Hecht has attempted to assess the extent to which American values were transmitted to Germany in her study of the *Neue Zeitung* from 1944 to1947. She emphasizes the significance of cultural "brokers" or the agencies of acculturation that mediate between the United States and the foreign nations in the process of cultural transfer. See Gienow-Hecht, "Art Is Democracy and Democracy Is Art," 21–43. For further discussions of the role played by nonstate actors, see Akira Iriye, *Global Community: The Role of International Organizations in the Making of the Contemporary World* (Berkeley: University of California Press, 2002).

24. Also see T. Jackson Lears, "The Concept of Cultural Hegemony: Problems and Possibilities," *American Historical Review* 90, no. 3 (1985): 567–593.

25. Studies of the U.S. occupation of Japan have generally paid far more attention to U.S. general Douglas MacArthur and Japanese premier Yoshida Shigeru.

26. Cox defines *institutionalization* as "a means of stabilizing and perpetuating a particular kind of order." Cox with Sinclair, *Approaches to World Order,* 99.

27. "Guidelines of U.S. Policy toward Japan," Secret Policy Paper, May 3, 1961, U.S. Department of State, US-J 00098, Japan and the United States: Diplomatic, Secu-

rity and Economic Relations, 1960–1976, National Security Archive, Gelman Library, George Washington University, Washington, D.C.

28. Warren Obluck, "The Development of American Studies in Japan: As Observed from an American Point of View," *Bulletin of the Center for American Studies of the University of Tokyo* 8 (1985): 1–7.

29. Notoji Masako, "The University of Tokyo–Stanford University American Studies Seminar," *Survey of American Studies in Japan: Development of American Studies Seminars* (Tokyo: International House of Japan, 1998), 25–26.

30. Aruga Tadashi, "Kaiko to tembō: Amerika" [Retrospect and prospect: America], *Shigaku Zasshi* 90 (1980), cited in Shigaku-kai (Shinkawa Kenzaburō), ed., *Nihon Rekishi Gakkai no kaiko to tembō* [Retrospect and prospect of Japanese historical world], vol. 25 of *Amerika* (Tokyo: Yamakawa Shuppan, 1988), 172.

31. Howard S. Ellis, Department of Economics, Stanford University, to Joseph H. Willits, director for social sciences, Rockefeller Foundation, September 2, 1951, folder 6, box 1, Stanford University–American Studies (Japanese Program), series 205, RG 1.2, Rockefeller Foundation Archives, RAC.

32. Maurice Valency, "Some Observations on the Teaching of the Humanities in Japan, A Preliminary Report Submitted to the Ford Foundation, July 1, 1959," p. 17, folder 430, box 48, series 1-OMR files, RG 5 (John D. Rockefeller III), Rockefeller Family Archives, RAC.

33. Entry of April 12, 1956, Charles B. Fahs Diaries, Box 18, Record Group 12.1, Rockefeller Foundation Archives, Rockefeller Archive Center, Sleepy Hollow, N.Y.

34. Eric J. Gangloff, "American Studies and Public Responsibility," *Bulletin of the Center for American Studies of the University of Tokyo* 10 (1987): 9–11.

35. Dean Rusk (president), "Statement of the Rockefeller Foundation and the General Education Board to the Special Committee to Investigate Tax-Exempt Foundations," Eighty-third Cong., 2nd sess., August 3, 1954, 1080.

36. Obluck, "Development of American Studies in Japan."

37. John W. Dower, *Embracing Defeat: Japan in the Wake of World War II* (New York: Norton, 1999), 550–551.

1 Occupation Reform as an American Cultural Offensive

1. Karl Polanyi, *The Great Transformation: The Political and Economic Origins of Our Time* (Boston: Beacon Press, 1944); Charles P. Kindleberger, *World Economic Primacy: 1500 to 1990* (New York: Oxford University Press, 1996).

2. For further discussion of America's hegemonic project, see Thomas J. McCormick, *America's Half-Century: United States Foreign Policy in the Cold War and After* (Baltimore: Johns Hopkins University Press, 1995). See especially the preface to the Japanese translation, *Pakusu Amerikāna no Gojū Nen,* trans. Takeshi Matsuda, Takahashi Akira, and Sugita Yoneyuki (Tokyo: Tokyo Sōgen Sha, 1999), 4–18.

3. For further treatment of the world system and hegemony, see McCormick, *America's Half-Century,* 1–16.

4. Wendell L. Willkie, *One World* (New York: Simon and Schuster, 1943).

5. McCormick, *America's Half-Century,* 4–7.

6. "American Cultural Relations with Japan, Sixth Meeting June 3, 1953," Council on Foreign Relations Study Group Report, folder 42, box 6, collection III 2Q, Rockefeller Family Archives, Rockefeller Archive Center, Sleepy Hollow, N.Y. (hereafter RAC).

7. Historical sociologist Immanuel Wallerstein uses the terms *world economies* and *world system* interchangeably. He defines *world economies* as vast uneven chains of integrated production structures dissected by multiple political structures. The basic logic of world economies, he goes on to explain, is that the accumulated surplus is distributed unequally in favor of those able to achieve various kinds of temporary monopolies in the market networks. See Immanuel Wallerstein, *Unthinking Social Science* (Cambridge: Polity Press, 1991), 247.

8. "Japan: Confidential Memorandum of Conversation, April 8, 1961," sent to Douglas MacArthur from U.S. Department of State, US-J 00090, Japan and the United States: Diplomatic, Security and Economic Relations, 1960–1976, National Security Archive, Gelman Library, George Washington University, Washington, D.C.

9. For a detailed discussion of this topic of hegemony and co-optation, see McCormick, *America's Half-Century,* 4–7; and Immanuel Wallerstein, *The Capitalist World-System* (Cambridge: Cambridge University Press, 1979), 35–36.

10. Douglas MacArthur, *Reminiscences* (New York: McGraw-Hill, 1964), 275.

11. Kashima Heiwa Kenkyūsho, ed., *Nihon gaikō shuyō bunsho/nenpyō (1), 1941–1960* [Major Japanese diplomatic documents/chronology (1), 1941–1960] (Tokyo: Hara Shobō, 1983), 81–91; Hosoya Chihiro, Aruga Tadashi, Ishii Osamu, and Sasaki Takuya, eds., *Nichibei kankei shiryōshū* [Collected documents concerning Japan-U.S. relations] (Toyko: University of Tokyo Press, 1999), 27–33.

12. John W. Dower, *Embracing Defeat: Japan in the Wake of World War II* (New York: Norton, 1999), 76–77.

13. Digest of "Report of the Education Exchange Survey," September 17, 1949, folder 444, box 49, record group (RG) 5 (John D. Rockefeller III), Rockefeller Family Archives, RAC.

14. For example, Iwanami Shigeo, the founder of the publishing house Iwanami, revealed a sense of relief upon hearing the news of Japan's surrender. See Yoshino Genzaburō, "Sōkan made" [Until the first issue was published], *Sekai* (January 1966): 259–268; "Sengo sanjū nen to 'Sekai' no sanjū nen" [Thirty years after the war and thirty years of *Sekai*], *Sekai* (January 1976): 253–282.

15. Political scientist Maruyama Masao has persuasively analyzed, from a psycho-historical perspective, why Japanese nationalism did not reach a peak on August 15, 1945. See Maruyama Masao, "Nationalism in Japan: Its Theoretical Background and Prospect," in Maruyama, *Thought and Behavior in Modern Japanese Politics,* ed. Ivan Morris, trans. David Titus (London: Oxford University Press, 1963), 136, 148.

16. Ishikawa Tatsuzō, "Hanbei kanjō wa kienai" [Anti-American feelings will not disappear], *Chūō kōron* (November 1953): 34.

17. Ara Masato, "Daini no seishun" [The second youth], in *Kindai Bungaku* [Modern literature] (Tokyo: Yagumo Shoten, 1946), 2. For a detailed description of the *kyodatsu* (exhaustion and despair) condition, see Dower, *Embracing Defeat,* especially chap. 3.

18. Tokyo 1020 to U.S. Department of State, February 2, 1951, 794.00/2-251, U.S. Department of State, U.S. National Archives and Records Administration, College Park, Md. (hereafter NARA); Saxton Bradford, AMEMBASSY, Tokyo, to U.S. Department of State, "IIA: ICS: American Books in Japanese Translation, 1952," April 1, 1953, 511.9421/4-153, U.S. Department of State, NARA.

19. Robert S. Schwantes to John D. Rockefeller III, January 23, 1955, folder 42, box 6, collection III 2Q, Rockefeller Family Archives, RAC.

20. Robert S. Schwantes, "The Exchange of Cultural Materials," Council on Foreign Relations Study Group on American Cultural Relations with Japan, Working Paper No. 5, April 22, 1953, folder 42, box 6, collection III 2Q, Rockefeller Family Archives, RAC.

21. They were Plans and Operations, School and Organization, Research, Press and Publications, Radio, and Motion Pictures. See Ariyama Teruo, *Senryōki media shi kenkyū* [A study of media during the occupation period] (Tokyo: Kashiwa Shobō, 1996), 237–238; and W. Bradley Connors, Confidential Memorandum: USIE Program for Japan, March 3, 1951, 511.9421/3-351, U.S. Department of State, NARA.

22. Robert S. Schwantes, *Japanese and Americans: A Century of Cultural Relations* (New York: Harper and Brothers, 1955), 308–309.

23. Takemae Eiji, *GHQ* (Tokyo: Iwanami Shoten, 1983), 116; Takemae Eiji, "GHQ ron—Sono soshiki to kaikakusha tachi" [On GHQ—Its organization and reformers], in *Sengo Niohn: Senryō to sengo kaikau* [Postwar Japan: The occupation and postwar reforms], vol. 2, ed. Nakamura Masanori et al. (Tokyo: Iwanami Shoten, 1995), 55.

24. Shinbori Michiya, ed., *Shinnichika no Tanjō* [The birth of Japan experts](Tokyo: Tōshindō, 1986), 141; Takemae, "GHQ ron," 55.

25. See Maruyama Masao, "Theory and Psychology of Ultra-Nationalism," in Maruyama, *Thought and Behavior in Modern Japanese Politics,* ed. Ivan Morris, trans. David Titus (London: Oxford University Press, 1963), 1–24.

26. Hidaka Daishirō, "Senryōka no kyōiku kaikaku" [Educational reform under the occupation], in Yuasa Hachirō et al., *Watashi no ikita nijū seiki* [The twentieth century during which I lived] (Tokyo: Nihon Kirisutokyōdan Shuppan, 1980), 122.

27. Quoted in "Report of the United States Cultural Science Mission to Japan, January 1949," Supreme Commander for the Allied Powers, Civil Information and Education Section, p. 5, folder 444, box 49, RG 5 (John D. Rockefeller III), Rockefeller Family Archives, RAC.

28. Takemae Eiji, *The Allied Occupation of Japan* (New York: Continuum, 2002), 352.

29. Ibid., 354.

30. Born in Tokyo in 1904, Bowles held a doctorate from Harvard University in anthropology. He had taught English at Dai Ichi Kōtō Gakkō (The First Higher School, currently the Komaba Campus of the University of Tokyo) from 1925 to 1927. He served as secretary of the education mission. See Ōsaki Hitoshi et al., *Sengo daigakushi* [A postwar history of university] (Tokyo: Daiichi Hōki Shuppan Kabushiki Kaisha, 1985), 5; and USPOLAD, Tokyo, to U.S. Department of State, October 23, 1951, 894.43/10-2351, U.S. Department of State, NARA.

31. Ibid., xii.

32. Gary H. Tsuchimochi, *Education Reform in Postwar Japan: The 1946 U.S. Education Mission* (Tokyo: University of Tokyo Press, 1993), 4.

33. Ibid.; *The Report of the United States Education Mission to Japan,* trans. Murai Minoru (Tokyo: Kōdansha, 1979); Takemae, *Allied Occupation of Japan,* 352–371.

34. Takemae, *Allied Occupation of Japan,* 357.

35. Cohen was quoted in Herbert Passin, "The Occupation—Some Reflections," in *Nichibei no Shōwa* [Shōwa—Japan and America] (Tokyo: TBS Britannica, 1990), 94.

36. Takemae, *Allied Occupation of Japan,* 357.

37. Ibid., 355.
38. Entry of June 20, 1947, Charles B. Fahs Diaries, series 12.1 diaries, Rockefeller Foundation Archives, RAC (hereafter Fahs Diaries).
39. Ibid.
40. Entry of June 24, 1947, Fahs Diaries.
41. Hosoya et al., *Nichibei kankei shiryōshū,* 30.
42. Schwantes, *Japanese and Americans,* 308–309; Rosemary O'Neil, "A Brief History of Department of State Involvement in International Exchange," fall 1972, file 12, box 103, Bureau of Educational and Cultural Affairs Historical Collection, U.S. Department of State, Special Collections Section, University of Arkansas Libraries, Fayetteville.
43. Institute for Educational Leadership by General Headquarters, Supreme Commander for the Allied Powers, Civil Information and Education Section, Education Division, undated, folder 445, box 49, series 1-OMR files, RG 5 (John D. Rockefeller III), Rockefeller Family Archives, RAC.
44. Ibid.
45. Enclosure: Undated draft of a reply to Louis C. Ieradi from Jack K. McFall, assistant secretary of state, in Jack K. McFall to Sen. James H. Duff, December 17, 1951, 511.94/12-1751, U.S. Department of State, NARA.
46. Institute for Educational Leadership by General Headquarters.
47. Ibid.
48. Ibid.
49. Enclosure: Undated draft of a reply to Ieradi from McFall.
50. Ibid.
51. Ibid.
52. Digest of "Report of the Education Exchange Survey."
53. Kon Madoko, "Nihon senryō to toshokan" [The occupation of Japan and library], *Kiyō shakaigakka* (Chuō University) 2 (April 1992): 1–14.
54. Schwantes, " Exchange of Cultural Materials," 12.
55. Entry of June 5, 1947, Fahs Diaries.
56. Civil Information and Education Section, General Headquarters, Supreme Commander for the Allied Powers (hereafter CI&E), *Mission and Accomplishments of the Occupation in the Civil Information and Education Fields,* January 1, 1950, folder 444, box 49, series 1-OMR files, RG 5 (John D. Rockefeller III), Rockefeller Family Archives, RAC. The author is grateful to Prof. Kon Madoko and Ms. Bungo Reiko for providing him with valuable information on the CI&E information center libraries.
57. Niles W. Bond, USPOLAD, Tokyo, to U.S. Department of State, USIE Country Paper on Japan, August 16, 1951, 511.9421/8-1651, U.S. Department of State, NARA.
58. Entry of June 13, 1948, Fahs Diaries.
59. Bond, USPOLAD, Tokyo, to U.S. Department of State, USIE Country Paper on Japan.
60. Schwantes, "Exchange of Cultural Materials," 13.
61. "American Cultural Relations with Japan, Fifth Meeting, April 30, 1953, Digest of Discussion," Council on Foreign Relations Study Group Report, folder 42, box 6, collection III 2Q, Rockefeller Family Archives, RAC.
62. Saxton Bradford, AMEMBASSY, Tokyo, Desp. No. 1343, "Semi-annual Evaluation Report," January 23, 1953, 511.94/1-2353, U.S. Department of State, NARA.
63. "American Cultural Relations with Japan, Fifth Meeting, April 30, 1953, Digest of Discussion."

64. Takemae, *GHQ,* 45.
65. Dower, *Embracing Defeat,* 138.
66. AMEMBASSY, Tokyo, to U.S. Department of State, Desp. No. 2750, "IIA: Japanese Press Comments on the U.S. Copyright Situation," June 26, 1953, 511.9421/6-2653, U.S. Department of State, NARA.
67. Entry of June 4, 1947, Fahs Diaries.
68. Quoted in AMEMBASSY, Tokyo, to U.S. Department of State, Desp. No. 2750, "IIA: Japanese Press Comments on the U.S. Copyright Situation."
69. Bradford, AMEMBASSY, Tokyo, Desp. No. 1343, "Semi-annual Evaluation Report."
70. Ibid.
71. Ibid.
72. Bradford, AMEMBASSY, Tokyo, to U.S. Department of State, "IIA: ICS: American Books in Japanese Translation, 1952."
73. CI&E, *Mission and Accomplishments,* 4.
74. Ibid.
75. Bradford, AMEMBASSY, Tokyo, to U.S. Department of State, "IIA: ICS: American Books in Japanese Translation, 1952."
76. Entry of July 14, 1947, Fahs Diaries.
77. Schwantes, "Exchange of Cultural Materials."
78. Mark Gayn, *Japan Diary,* 2 vols., trans. Imoto Takeo (Tokyo: Chikuma Shobō, 1951).
79. Bradford, AMEMBASSY, Tokyo, to U.S. Department of State, "IIA: ICS: American Books in Japanese Translation, 1952."
80. See entry from Gayn's *Japan Diary* in Tomita Hitoshi, ed., *Jiten gaikokujin no mita Nihon* [Japan through foreign eyes: An annotated bibliography] (Tokyo: Nichigai Associates, 1992), 66–69; Bradford, AMEMBASSY, Tokyo, to U.S. Department of State, "IIA: ICS: American Books in Japanese Translation, 1952."
81. Schwantes, "Exchange of Cultural Materials," 3; Schwantes, *Japanese and Americans,* 227.
82. Schwantes, *Japanese and Americans,* 227.
83. "American Cultural Relations with Japan, Fifth Meeting, April 30, 1953, Digest of Discussion"; Schwantes, "Exchange of Cultural Materials," 3.
84. Bradford, AMEMBASSY, Tokyo, Desp. No. 1343, "Semi-annual Evaluation Report."
85. Bond, USPOLAD, Tokyo, to U.S. Department of State, USIE Country Paper on Japan.
86. Barak Kushner and Satō Masaharu, "Digesting Postwar Japanese Media," *Diplomatic History* 29 (January 2005): 36, 37, 46.
87. CI&E, *Mission and Accomplishments,* 4. The circulation number of *Reader's Digest* varies. For example, in their recent work on *Reader's Digest,* Barak Kushner and Satō Masaharu claim that it was 1.5 million copies; ibid., 27.
88. Joanne P. Sharp, *Condensing the Cold War: Reader's Digest and American Identity* (Minneapolis: University of Minnesota Press. 2000), xiv. Cited in Kushner and Satō, "Digesting Postwar Japanese Media." 27.
89. CI&E, *Mission and Accomplishments, 4.*
90. Bond, USPOLAD, Tokyo, to U.S. Department of State, USIE Country Paper on Japan.

91. Ibid.
92. "American Cultural Relations with Japan, Fifth Meeting, April 30, 1953, Digest of Discussion," 6.
93. Bond, USPOLAD, Tokyo, to U.S. Department of State, USIE Country Paper on Japan.
94. Saxton Bradford, AMEMBASSY, Tokyo, to U.S. Department of State, Desp. No. 2286, "IIA Prospectus for Japan, Enclosure: 1954–1955," April 30, 1953, 511.94/4-3053, U.S. Department of State, NARA.
95. Ibid.
96. Ibid.
97. Schwantes, "Exchange of Cultural Materials," 4.
98. For further information on civil censorship and media control in Japan by SCAP, see Marlene J. Mayo, "Civil Censorship and Media Control in Early Occupied Japan," in *Americans as Proconsuls: United States Military Government in Germany and Japan, 1944–1952,* ed. Robert Wolfe (Carbondale and Edwardsville: Southern Illinois University Press, 1984), 263–320.
99. Takemae, *Allied Occupation of Japan,* 383.
100. CI&E, *Mission and Accomplishments;* entry of July 14, 1947, Fahs Diaries.
101. Connors, Confidential Memorandum.
102. Entry of June 29, 1947, Fahs Diaries.
103. Entries of June 19 and July 2, 1947, Fahs Diaries.
104. Entry of July 2, 1947, Fahs Diaries.
105. *Asahi Shimbun,* August 24, 2005, 17.
106. The saying *shinchūgun no mei ni yori* (by order of the occupation army) became very fashionable among Japanese once *Asahi Shimbun* used it in the article "Tensei jingo" [Vox populi, vox Dei] on July 14, 1947.
107. Entry of C. Nelson Spinks, John D. Rockefeller III Diaries 1952, folder 63, box 7, series 1-OMR files, RG 5 (John D. Rockefeller III), Japan Section, Rockefeller Family Archives, RAC; USPOLAD, Tokyo, to U.S. Department of State, Mission Telegram No. 788, dated October 18, 1951, October 23, 1951, 894.43/10-2351, U.S. Department of State, NARA.
108. Entry of June 24, 1947, Fahs Diaries.
109. Entry of June 23, 1947, Fahs Diaries.
110. Blakemore, a lawyer and former Office of Strategic Services (OSS) staff member who had studied law at Tokyo Imperial University, advised on the revisions of the Civil Law and the Civil Proceedings Act. Entry of June 5, 1947, Fahs Diaries; Takemae, "GHQ ron," 2:60.
111. Entry of June 5, 1947, Fahs Diaries.
112. Entry of June 30, 1947, Fahs Diaries.
113. Orr was a capable but very young man as Fahs saw him. He had graduated from the University of North Carolina and became the third chief of the CI&E Education Division while still in uniform. Entry of June 29, 1947, Fahs Diaries; Herbert J. Wunderlich, *The Japanese Textbook Problem and Solution, 1945–1946,* trans. Gary H. Tsuchimochi (Tokyo: Tamagawa University Press, 1998).
114. Ibid.; Takemae, *GHQ,* 118.
115. Entry of June 14, 1948, Fahs Diaries.
116. Entry of June 29, 1947, Fahs Diaries.
117. Entries of June 5 and June 30, 1947, Fahs Diaries.

118. Entry of June 5, 1947, Fahs Diaries; Takemae, *GHQ,* 127. Passin, a Jewish American who was born in Chicago as and whose parents had emigrated from Russia during the Russo-Japanese War, had studied at the University of Chicago, where he majored in anthropology. After teaching at Northwestern University, he joined CI&E once he completed army courses in Japanese at the University of Michigan. Passin, who was quite proficient in Japanese, was regarded as "one of the most impressive of the young men trained during the war." Bradford, AMEMBASSY, Tokyo, to U.S. Department of State, "IIA: ICS: American Books in Japanese Translation, 1952."

119. Entry of June 5, 1947, Fahs Diaries.

120. Bradford, AMEMBASSY, Tokyo, to U.S. Department of State, "IIA: ICS: American Books in Japanese Translation, 1952."

121. "American Cultural Relations with Japan, Fifth Meeting, April 30, 1953, Digest of Discussion," 13; Robert B. Textor, *Failure in Japan,* trans. Shimojima Ren (Tokyo: Bungei Shunjū Sha, 1952), 225.

122. Ibid., 225.

123. O. Kurganov, *Amerikantsy v Yaponii, reportaz* (USSR, 1946); reprinted as *Nihon ni iru Amerika-jin: Sovieto kisha no Nippon nikki* [The Americans in Japan: The Japan diary by a Soviet journalist], trans. Takagi Hideto (Tokyo: Satsuki Shobō, 1952), 39–40.

124. Ibid., 16–17.

125. Ibid., 17–18.

126. Bradford, AMEMBASSY, Tokyo, Desp. No. 1343, "Semi-annual Evaluation Report," 19.

127. Bradford, AMEMBASSY, Tokyo, to U.S. Department of State, "IIA: ICS: American Books in Japanese Translation, 1952."

128. Ibid.; "American Cultural Relations with Japan, Fifth Meeting, April 30, 1953, Digest of Discussion," 4.

129. Ibid.

130. Entry of July 2, 1947, Fahs Diaries.

131. Entry of June 4, 1947, Fahs Diaries.

132. Bradford, AMEMBASSY, Tokyo, to U.S. Department of State, "IIA: ICS: American Books in Japanese Translation, 1952."

133. Bradford, AMEMBASSY, Tokyo, Desp. No. 1343, "Semi-annual Evaluation Report."

134. AMEMBASSY, Tokyo, to U.S. Department of State, Desp. No. 2750, "IIA: Japanese Press Comments on the U.S. Copyright Situation."

135. Ibid.

136. Ibid.

137. "American Cultural Relations with Japan, Fifth Meeting, April 30, 1953, Digest of Discussion."

138. Ibid.

139. Entry of July 3, 1947, Fahs Diaries.

140. Ibid.

141. Schwantes, "Exchange of Cultural Materials."

142. CI&E, *Mission and Accomplishments,* 4.

143. Entry of April 27, 1950, Fahs Diaries.

144. Takemae, *GHQ,* 107.

145. Ibid., 3.

146. As Frank Hawley, a correspondent of the London *Times,* noted, the "Bataan boys" were top-ranking GHQ/SCAP officers with whom General MacArthur had fought during the Pacific War. They were Brig. Gen. Bonner F. Fellers (military secretary), Brig. Gen. Courtney Whitney (one of General MacArthur's closest friends from the Philippine days and chief of the Government Section), Lt. Gen. Richard K. Sutherland (chief of staff), Maj. Gen. Richard J. Marshall (chief of staff), Maj. Gen. Charles A. Willoughby (assistant chief of staff, G-2), and Maj. Gen. William F. Marquat (the first U.S. representative on the Allied Council for Japan and chief of the Economic and Scientific Section). SCAP and General Willoughby, in particular, insisted on complete control of all channels to Washington. Entries of June 7, June 9, and July 1, 1947, Fahs Diaries; Takemae, *GHQ,* 3.

147. Hosoya et al., *Nichibei kankei shiryōshū,* 30.

148. Inoue Kiyoko, *MacArthur's Japanese Constitution: A Linguistic and Cultural Study of Its Making* (Chicago: University of Chicago Press, 1991), trans. Koseki Shōichi and Igarashi Masako (Tokyo: Karihara Shoten, 1994).

149. For anecdotal evidence, see Katō Shizue, *Aisuru 'Nihon' e no yuigon* [A will to a loving 'Japan'] (Tokyo: Shoen-Shinsha, 1995), 97–106.

150. Takemae Eiji, *Senryō sengoshi* [A history of the postwar occupation] (Tokyo: Shoshisha, 1980), 40–41, 49–50; Takemae, *GHQ,* 55.

151. Prefecture is a local administrative unit like a district. Japan is divided into Hokkaido, Tokyo, Kyoto, and Osaka, and forty-three prefectures. Each prefecture has a local government with a governor enjoying a wide range of local autonomy. Entry of July 10, 1947, Fahs Diaries.

152. Ibid.

153. Entry of July 14, 1947, Fahs Diaries.

154. Ibid.

155. Entry of June 5, 1947, Fahs Diaries

156. Entry of July 1, 1947, Fahs Diaries. Hawley had taught English at Dai San Kōtō Gakkō (the Third Higher School, currently Kyoto University) in Kyoto and had served with the British Ministry of Information in Tokyo before the war. He was then a correspondent for the London *Times* and, temporarily, for the *Christian Science Monitor.* He was very conversant in Japanese. Entries of June 4 and July 1, 1947, Fahs Diaries.

157. Entry of July 1, 1947, Fahs Diaries; Takemae, *GHQ,* 3.

158. C. Nelson Spinks had earned his Ph.D. from Stanford University and had taught English at Tokyo University of Commerce from 1936 to 1941. He had good command of the Japanese language, and he had a wide circle of cultural, educational, and political contacts in Japan. Spinks served as GHQ's director of research and analysis from 1946 to 1948. Entry of July 3, 1947, Fahs Diaries; USPOLAD, Tokyo, to U.S. Department of State, Mission Telegram No. 788.

159. Entry of July 3, 1947, Fahs Diaries.

160. Entry of June 5, 1947, Fahs Diaries.

161. George F. Kennan, *Memoirs, 1925–1950* (Boston: Little, Brown, 1967), 387; Hidaka, "Senryōka no kyōiku kaikaku," 134.

162. I. Poltavskii, *Okkupirovannaya Yaponiya* (USSR, 1952); reprinted as *Senryō ka no Nihon* [Japan under the occupation], trans. Makiyama Kei (Tokyo: Sō jusha, 1953), 40, 119.

163. Kennan, *Memoirs: 1925–1950,* 387.

164. Entry of July 2, 1947, Fahs Diaries.

165. Entry of July 3, 1947, Fahs Diaries.

2 The Cold War, "Reverse Course," and Rise of Nationalism

1. George F. Kennan, *Memoirs, 1925–1950* (Boston: Little, Brown, 1967), 375.
2. For a further discussion of Kennan's initiative, see Igarashi Takeshi, *Tainichi kōwa to reisen—Sengo Nichibeikankei no keisei* [The peace treaty with Japan and the cold war—The formation of postwar U.S.-Japan relations] (Tokyo: University of Tokyo Press, 1986), 63–124.
3. Kennan, *Memoirs, 1925–1950*, 376–383. 386, 391–392.
4. Hosoya Chihiro et al., eds., *Nichibei kankei shiryōshū* [Collected documents concerning Japan-U.S. relations] (Tokyo: University of Tokyo Press, 1999), 55–62.
5. "NSC-68: A Report to the National Security Council by the Executive Secretary on United States Objectives and Programs for National Security, April 14, 1950," *Naval War College Review;* reprinted from vol. 27(May–June 1975); Ernest R. May, ed., *American Cold War Strategy: Interpreting NSC 68* (Boston: Bedford Books of St. Martin's Press, 1993).
6. "The Far East," Working Paper No. 11, March 30, 1954, folder 55, box 8, series 1-Office of the Messrs. Rockefeller files, collection III 2Q, Rockefeller Archive Center, Sleepy Hollow, N.Y. (hereafter RAC).
7. Kennan, *Memoirs, 1925–1950*, 393.
8. Speech by Secretary of the Army Kenneth C. Royall on U.S. policy for Japan, San Francisco, January 6, 1948; reprinted in Hosoya et al., *Nichibei kankei shiryōshū*, 46–48.
9. Elihu Root Jr. was a representative of the law firm of Root, Ballantine, Harlan, Bushly, and Palmer. "American Cultural Relations with Japan, Sixth Meeting, June 3, 1953," Council on Foreign Relations Study Group Report, folder 42, box 6, collection III 2Q, Rockefeller Family Archives, RAC.
10. "Japanese Peace Treaty Problems, First Meeting, October 23, 1950," Council on Foreign Relations Study Group Report, Manuscript Division, Council on Foreign Relations, New York.
11. Ibid.
12. John W. Dower, *Origins of the Modern Japanese State: Selected Writings of E. H. Norman* (New York: Random House, 1975), 40.
13. Iwanami Shoten, *Kindai Nihon sōgō nempyō* [The comprehensive chronological table of modern Japan], 4th ed. (Tokyo: Iwanami Shoten, 2001), 378.
14. Japan Communist Party, *Nihon Kyōsantō no 60-nen* [A 60-year history of the Japan Communist Party], 2 vols. (Tokyo: Japan Communist Party, 1983), 1:213.
15. The Dodge Line is the name given to a series of economic measures adopted to curb inflation in postwar Japan. In February 1949, the American government sent the Detroit banker Joseph Dodge to Tokyo to stabilize Japan's inflationary economy. The so-called Dodge Line called for a balanced budget, severe curtailment of credit from government banks, a single exchange rate, and retrenchment of personnel in government and private industries. The Dodge Line of economic austerity aimed to put Japan back on its feet as a viable market economy by curbing inflation and domestic consumption and promoting a export sector, which resulted in Japan launching an "export drive" throughout the world during the 1960s and 1970s.
16. Figure based on Midorikawa Tōru's statement at discussion meeting on " 'Heiwa Mondai Danwakai' nitsuite" [Concerning the Peace Study Group], *Sekai* (fortieth an-

niversary edition); reprinted in *Sengo heiwaron no genryū* [The sources of pro-peace arguments in postwar Japan] (Tokyo: Iwanami Shoten, July 1985), 84.

17. Joe Moore, *Japanese Workers and the Struggle for Power, 1945–1947* (Madison: University of Wisconsin Press, 1983), 190–196.

18. Sasaki Takeshi et al., eds., *Encyclopedia of Postwar Japan, 1945–1994* (Tokyo: Sanseidō, 1995), 938.

19. John W. Dower, *Embracing Defeat: Japan in the Wake of World War II* (New York: Norton, 1999), 272.

20. Kennan, *Memoirs, 1925–1950*, 388.

21. Matsuo Takayoshi, *Kokusai kokka eno shuppatsu* [The start of an international nation], vol. 21 of *Nihon no rekishi* [A history of Japan] (Tokyo: Shūei Sha, 1993), 44.

22. Dower, *Embracing Defeat*, 272.

23. Sasaki et al., *Encyclopedia of Postwar Japan, 1945–1994*, 616–617.

24. Thomas Parrish, *The Cold War Encyclopedia* (New York: Henry Holt, 1996), 70.

25. Maruyama Masao, "Kindai Nihon no chishikijin" [Intellectuals of modern Japan], *Kōei no ichi kara* [From the position of the rearguard] (Tokyo: Mirai Sha, 1982), 71–133.

26. "Humanities Program and Relation Foundation Interests in History, 1950–1960," prepared by Charles B. Fahs, November 16, 1960, p. 6, file 18, box 3, Pro-25b, series 911 Humanities, Administration, Program and Policy, record group (RG) 3, Rockefeller Foundation Archives, RAC.

27. Based on Kuno Osamu's statement at discussion meeting on "'Heiwa Mondai Danwakai' nitsuite" [Concerning the Peace Study Group]," *Sekai* (fortieth anniversary edition); reprinted in *Sengo heiwaron no genryū* [The sources of pro-peace arguments in postwar Japan] (Tokyo: Iwanami Shoten, July 1985), 14.

28. Based on Maruyama Masao's statement at discussion meeting on "'Heiwa Mondai Danwakai' nitsuite" [Concerning the Peace Study Group], *Sekai* (fortieth anniversary edition); reprinted in *Sengo heiwaron no genryū* [The sources of pro-peace arguments in postwar Japan] (Tokyo: Iwanami Shoten, July 1985), 52.

29. Tsuzuki Tsutomu, *Sengo Nihon no chishikijin—Maruyama Masao to sono jidai* [The intellectuals of postwar Japan: Maruyama Masao and the times he lived] (Yokohama: Seori Shobō, 1995), 108–110.

30. Maruyama Masao, *Thought and Behavior in Modern Japanese Politics*. ed. Ivan Morris, trans. David Titus (London: Oxford University Press, 1963). See translator's note 1, p. 154.

31. Itō Ritsu, *Itō Ritsu kaikoroku* [A memoir of Itō Ritsu] (Tokyo: Bungei Shunjū, 1993).

32. For further information on the Japan Communist Party, see Japan Communist Party, *Nihon Kyōsantō no rokujū nen* [The sixty years of the Japan Communist Party], 2 vols. (Tokyo: Shin Nippon Shuppan Sha, 1983); Inumaru Giichi, Kobayashi Eizō, and Ishizuka Shigetarō, *'Nihon kyōsantō kenkyū' no kenkyū* [A study of 'The Study of the Japan Communist Party'] (Tokyo: Gendaishi Shuppan Kai, 1980); and Andō Jinbe-e, *Sengo nihon kyōsantō shiki* [A private record of the postwar Japan Communist Party] (Tokyo: Bungei Shunjū, 1995).

33. Saxton Bradford, USPOLAD, Tokyo, to U.S. Department of State, January 18, 1951, 511.94/1-1892, U.S. Department of State, National Archives and Records Administration, College Park, Md. (hereafter NARA).

34. O. Kurganov, *Amerikantsy v Yaponii, reportaz* (USSR, 1946); reprinted as *Nihon ni iru Amerika-jin: Sovieto kisha no Nippon nikki* [The Americans in Japan: The Japan diary by a Soviet journalist], trans. Takagi Hideto (Tokyo: Satsuki Shobō, 1952), 251–252, 253.

35. Ishikawa Tasuzō, "Hanbei kanjō wa kienai" [Anti-American feelings will not disappear], *Chūō kōron* (November 1953): 34.

36. Tōyama Shigeki, *Sengo no rekishigaku to rekishi ishiki* [Postwar historiography and historical conceptualization] (Tokyo: Iwanami Shoten, 1968), 128–131.

37. Moore, *Japanese Workers,* 229–243.

38. The results of the general election of April 25, 1947, were as follows: Japan Socialist Party: 26.2 percent of vote, 143 of 466 seats (30.6 percent); Japan Liberal Party (conservative under Yoshida Shigeru): 26.9 percent, 131 seats (28.1 percent); Japan Democratic Party (middle-right whose core was the former Japan Progressive Party): 25.0 percent, 121 seats (25.9 percent); People's Cooperative Party (Kokumin Kyōdō-tō): 7.0 percent, 29 seats (6.2 percent); Japan Communist Party: 3.7 percent, 4 seats; various factions: 5.4 percent, 25 seats; independents: 5.8 percent, 13 seats. The significance of the election lay in the fact that it virtually assured the old conservative forces successive political victories for many years to come. Matsuo, *Kokusai kokka e no shuppatsu* , 90.

39. Ibid., 93.

40. Kurganov, *Amerikantsy v Yaponii, reportaz,* 130.

41. Matsuo, *Kokusai kokka e no shuppatsu* , 40.

42. In the newly formed Katayama cabinet, the Japan Socialist Party occupied seven cabinet posts, the Japan Democratic Party under Ashida Hitoshi seven posts, and the People's Cooperative Party under Miki Takeo two posts. Miyano Tōru, *Saigono riberarisuto: Ashida Hitoshi* [The last liberalist: Ashida Hitoshi] (Tokyo: Bungei Shunjū, 1987); Matsuo, *Kokusai kokka e no shuppatsu,* 92.

43. Katayama Testsu, "The truth about the dissolution of the Katayama government," *Asahi Shimbun,* March 4, 1976; Matsuo, *Kokusai kokka e no shuppatsu,* 99.

44. The conservative Democratic Party gained 15.7 percent of the vote and 69 seats (14.8 percent); the Socialist Party won 13.5 percent of the vote and 48 seats (10.3 percent); and the JCP gained 9.7 percent of the vote and 35 seats (7.5 percent). Matsuo, *Kokusai kokka e no shuppatsu,* 125.

45. Dower, *Embracing Defeat,* 218.

46. Ibid.

47. Takemae Eiji, *The Allied Occupation of Japan* (New York: Continuum, 2002), 367; also see Kubota Akira, *Higher Civil Servants in Postwar Japan* (Princeton, N.J.: Princeton University Press, 1969).

48. Charles Fahs of the Rockefeller Foundation found Suzuki's story particularly interesting and revealing. This account is based on Fahs's diary entry of May 1, 1952, Charles B. Fahs Diaries, series 12.1 diaries, Rockefeller Foundation Archives, RAC (hereafter Fahs Diaries).

49. Entry of February 28, 1951, Fahs Diaries.

50. Conlon Associates Ltd., *United States Foreign Policy: Asia,* study prepared at the request of the Committee on Foreign Relations, U.S. Senate, November 1, 1959 (Washington, D.C.: Government Printing Office, 1959), 93 (hereafter Conlon report).

51. Progressives such as Maruyama Masao and Ōtsuka Hisao, perhaps the two leading theorists and advocates of modernism (*kindaishugi*), have profound confidence and

trust in the ability of humans to reason. Progressives are rationalists, who believe that a human's reason plays a positive role in humankind's zigzag, nevertheless steady, progress.

52. Hashikawa Bunzō, ed., *Sengo Nihon shisō taikei* [A system of thoughts of postwar Japan], vol. 7 of *Hoshu no shisō* [The thought of a conservative] (Tokyo: Chikuma Shobō, 1968), 35–36; Hayashi Kentarō, ed., *Gendai Nihon shisō taikei* [The thoughts of modern Japan], vol. 35 of *Shin hoshushugi* [Neoconservatism] (Tokyo: Chikuma Shobō, 1963), 7–42.

53. Jonathan Crowther, ed., *Oxford Advanced Learner's Dictionary of Current English,* 5th ed. (Oxford: Oxford University Press, 1995), 245; Jack C. Plano and Milton Greenberg, eds., *The American Political Dictionary,* 6th ed. (New York: Holt, Rinehart and Winston, 1982), 6; M. A. Riff, ed., *Dictionary of Modern Political Ideologies* (New York: St. Martin's Press, 1987), 67–72.

54. Arase Yutaka, "Sengo jōkyō e no shisōteki taiō" [Philosophical responses to the postwar situation], in *Kindai Nihon shakai shisō shi* [A history of social thoughts of modern Japan], ed. Furuta Hikaru et al. (Tokyo: Yūhikaku, 1971), 327–329; Hayashi, *Gendai Nihon shisō taikei,* 35:7–42.

55. Arase Yutaka, "Sengo jōkyō e no shisōteki taiō," 327–329; Hashikawa Bunzō, ed., *Sengo Nihon shisō taikei* [A system of thoughts of postwar Japan], vol. 7 of *Hoshu no shisō* [The thought of a conservative] (Tokyo: Chikuma Shobō, 1968), 6.

56. Ishida Takeshi, *Shakai kagaku saikō* [Rethinking social sciences] (Tokyo: University of Tokyo Press, 1995), 86–87.

57. Maruyama Masao, "Nationalism in Japan: Its Theoretical Background and Prospects," in Maruyama, *Thought and Behavior in Modern Japanese Politics,* ed. Ivan Morris, trans. David Titus (London: Oxford University Press, 1963), 144–146; Takeshi Matsuda, "The Coming of the Pacific War: Japanese Perspectives," *Reviews in American History* 14 (December 1986): 629–652.

58. Tōyama, *Sengo no rekishigaku to rekishi ishiki,* 9–10.

59. Suzuki Daisetsu, "Meiji no seishin to jiyū" [The Meiji spirit and freedom], in *Sengo Nihon shisō taikei* [A system of thoughts of postwar Japan], ed. Hashikawa Bunzō, vol. 7 of *Hoshu no shisō* [The thought of a conservative] (Tokyo: Chikuma Shobō, 1968), 37–38, 199–207.

60. Maruyama Masao, "Aru jiyūshugisha eno tegami" [A letter to a liberal], in Maruyama, *Gendai seiji no shisō to kodō* [Thought and behavior in modern Japanese politics] (Tokyo: Miraisha, 1964), 144; Ōtsuka Hisao, "Jiyū to dokuritsu" (1946) [Freedom and independence], in *Ōtsuka Hisao chosaku shū* [Ōtsuka Hisao collected works], vol. 8 (Tokyo: Iwanami Shoten, 1969), 176–186; Kawashima Takenobu, "Nihonshakai no kazokuteki kōsei" [The family-like structure of Japanese society], *Chūō kōron* (June 1946), in *Kindaishugi,* vol. 34 of *Gendai Nihon shisō taikei,* ed. Hidaka Rokurō (Tokyo: Chikuma Shobō, 1964), 236–249.

61. Edwin O. Reischauer, *Wanted: An Asian Policy* (New York: Knopf, 1955), as cited in John W. Dower, *Origins of the Modern Japanese State: Selected Writings of E. H. Norman* (New York: Random House, 1975), 48.

62. As quoted in John W. Dower, *War without Mercy: Peace and Power in the Pacific War* (New York: Pantheon Books, 1986), 280.

63. Niles W. Bond, USPOLAD, Tokyo, to U.S. Department of State, USIE Country Paper on Japan, August 16, 1951, 511.9421/8-1651, U.S. Department of State, NARA.

64. "Japanese Peace Treaty Problems, First Meeting, October 23, 1950."
65. For a brief discussion of the "reverse course," see Chapter 3.
66. Kawakami Tetsutarō et al., *Kindai no chōkoku* [Overcoming modernity] (Tokyo: Tomiyamabō, 1979); Hiromatsu Wataru, *"Kindai no chōkoku"* ron [A treatise on "Overcoming Modernity"] (Tokyo: Kōdan-Sha, 1989).
67. See Ishida, *Shakai kagaku saikō,* 90.
68. Bond, USPOLAD, Tokyo, to U.S. Department of State, USIE Country Paper on Japan.
69. Confidential—Security Information, USIE Country Plan—Japan, Priority III, December 4, 1951, 511.94/12-451, U.S. Department of State, NARA.
70. "Japan between East and West, Fourth Meeting, May 21, 1956," Council on Foreign Relations Discussion Meeting Report, Manuscript Division, Council on Foreign Relations, New York.
71. Confidential—Security Information, USIE Country Plan—Japan.
72. Conlon report.
73. "Japan between East and West, Fifth Meeting, May 23, 1956," Council on Foreign Relations Discussion Meeting Report, Manuscript Division, Council on Foreign Relations, New York.
74. Thomas A. Bisson, *Prospects for Democracy in Japan* (New York: Macmillan, 1949); Bisson, "Reform Years in Japan, 1945–47: An Occupation Memoir," unpublished manuscript, 1975; Howard B. Schonberger, *Aftermath of War: Americans and the Remaking of Japan, 1945–1952* (Kent, Ohio: Kent State University Press, 1989), chap. 3; Dower, *Embracing Defeat,* chap. 6.
75. Saxton Bradford, USPOLAD, Tokyo, to U.S. Department of State, September 7, 1951, 511.94/9-751, U.S. Department of State, NARA.
76. "The Far East," Working Paper No. 12, April 27, 1954, folder 55, box 8, series 1-OMR files, collection III 2Q, RAC.
77. "Japan between East and West, Third Meeting, May 7, 1956," Council on Foreign Relations Discussion Meeting Report, Manuscript Division, Council on Foreign Relations, New York.
78. Conlon report, 101.
79. "Japan between East and West, Third Meeting, May 7, 1956."
80. Ibid.
81. Ibid.
82. USPOLAD, Tokyo, to U.S. Department of State, USIE Country Paper on Japan.
83. Council on Foreign Relations Memorandum for the Committee on Studies, "Robert S. Schwantes Proposal for a Study of Japanese-American Cultural Relations," undated, Council on Foreign Relations Library, New York.
84. Dallas Finn, "What the Japanese Intellectuals Are Thinking," *American Scholar* 24 (autumn 1955): 445.
85. Robert S. Schwantes to John D. Rockefeller III, January 23, 1955, folder 42, box 6, collection III 2Q, RAC.
86. Council on Foreign Relations Memorandum for the Committee on Studies, "Robert S. Schwantes Proposal."
87. Kennan, *Memoirs: 1925–1950,* 395.
88. "Japanese Peace Treaty Problems, First Meeting, October 23, 1950."

3 The Making of a "Soft Peace" and Japan's "Proper Place"

1. "Japanese Peace Treaty Problems: Progress toward Framing a Peace Treaty with Japan," October 16, 1950, Council on Foreign Relations Study Group Report, Manuscript Division, Council on Foreign Relations, New York.
2. U.S. Department of State Bulletin, no. 23, September 25, 1950, 513; Hosoya Chihiro, Aruga Tadashi, Ishii Osamu, and Sasaki Takuya, eds., *A Documentary History of U.S.-Japanese Relations, 1945–1997* (Tokyo: University of Tokyo Press, 1999), 78.
3. Dean Acheson, *Present at the Creation* (New York: Norton, 1969), 432.
4. "Japanese Peace Treaty Problems, First Meeting, October 23, 1950," Council on Foreign Relations Study Group Report, Manuscript Division, Council on Foreign Relations, New York.
5. "The Far East (continued)," April 27, 1954, Council on Foreign Relations Study Group Working Paper No. 12, folder 55, box 8, series 1-OMR files, collection III 2Q, Rockefeller Archive Center, Sleep Hollow, N.Y. (hereafter RAC).
6. "Japanese Peace Treaty Problems, First Meeting, October 23, 1950."
7. Niles W. Bond, USPOLAD, Tokyo, to U.S. Department of State, USIE Country Paper on Japan, August 16, 1951, 511.9421/8-1651, U.S. Department of State, National Archives and Records Administration, College Park, Md. (hereafter NARA).
8. Peter Collier and David Horowitz, *The Rockefellers: An American Dynasty* (New York: Holt, Rinehart and Winston, 1976), 284.
9. "Japanese Peace Treaty Problems, First Meeting, October 23, 1950."
10. A. H. McCullum, Member, Panel "D" Japan, Top Secret Memorandum for Mr. John Allison, Chairman, Panel "D" Japan, April 28, 1952, 511.94/4-2852, U.S. Department of State, NARA.
11. Frederick S. Dunn, head of the Center of International Studies at Princeton, describes the origins of the Japanese peace settlement in 1951 in his last work, *Peace-Making and the Settlement with Japan* (Princeton, N.J.: Princeton University Press, 1963). It is a standard account of the making of peace with Japan by an author who had access to still-closed State Department records.
12. "American Cultural Relations with Japan, Sixth Meeting, June 3, 1953," Council on Foreign Relations Study Group Report, folder 42, box 6, collection III 2Q, Rockefeller Foundation Archives, RAC.
13. John D. Rockefeller III to Robert S. Schwantes, January 18, 1955, folder 42, box 6, collection III 2Q, RAC.
14. McCullum, Member, Panel "D" Japan, Top Secret Memorandum for Allison, Chairman, Panel "D" Japan.
15. "The Far East (continued)."
16. Ibid.
17. Ibid.
18. McCullum, Member, Panel "D" Japan, Top Secret Memorandum for Allison, Chairman, Panel "D" Japan.
19. "Japanese Peace Treaty Problems, First Meeting, October 23, 1950."
20. Ibid.
21. U.S. Department of State outgoing telegram to USDEL, San Francisco, September 3, 1951, 511.94/9-351, U.S. Department of State, NARA.

22. "Japanese Peace Treaty Problems, First Meeting, October 23, 1950."
23. Ibid.; "American Cultural Relations with Japan, Sixth Meeting, June 3, 1953."
24. Ibid.
25. Confidential Draft, "Special Guidance on Japan," June 29, 1951, 511.9421/6-2951, U.S. Department of State, NARA.
26. "Japanese Peace Treaty Problems, First Meeting, October 23, 1950."
27. Saxton Bradford, AMEMBASSY, Tokyo, to U.S. Department of State, "Attitudes of Japanese Intellectuals towards the United States," June 4, 1952, 511.94/6-452, U.S. Department of State, NARA.
28. "Japanese Peace Treaty Problems, Sixth Meeting, May 25, 1951," Council on Foreign Relations Study Group Report, Manuscript Division, Council on Foreign Relations; Robert D. Eldridge and Ayako Kusunoki, "To Base or Not to Base? Yoshida Shigeru, the 1950 Ikeda Mission, and Post-Treaty Japanese Security Conceptions," *Kobe University Law Review* 33, no. 1 (1999): 114.
29. Bradford, AMEMBASSY, Tokyo, to U.S. Department of State, "Attitudes of Japanese Intellectuals towards the United States."
30. "Japanese Peace Treaty Problems, Sixth Meeting, May 25, 1951."
31. Report to Ambassador John Foster Dulles, April 16, 1951, folder 446, box 49, series 1-OMR files, record group (RG) 5 (John D. Rockefeller III), Rockefeller Family Archives, RAC.
32. Telegram to Rep. Joseph Martin (1951), quoted in Lawrence S. Wittner, ed., *MacArthur* (Englewood Cliffs, N.J.: Prentice Hall, 1971), 45.
33. Douglas MacArthur, *Reminiscences* (New York: McGraw-Hill, 1964), 360–364, 389–395. For more information on the Truman-MacArthur conflict, see John W. Spanier, *The Truman-MacArthur Controversy and the Korean War* (New York: Norton, 1965).
34. "Japanese Peace Treaty Problems, Sixth Meeting, May 25, 1951."
35. Entry of May 9, 1950, Charles B. Fahs Diaries, series 12.1 diaries, Rockefeller Foundation Archives, RAC (hereafter Fahs Diaries).
36. Entry of May 11, 1950, Fahs Diaries. Kishimoto, president of the Japanese Science of Religion Association, was well acquainted with Fahs. He had been Fahs's instructor in Japanese at Harvard in 1932 in the first Far East summer seminar supported by the Rockefeller Foundation. Entries of June 7, 1947, and March 1, 1951, Fahs Diaries.
37. "Japanese Peace Treaty Problems, First Meeting, October 23, 1950."
38. George S. Franklin Jr., director of meetings, to John Foster Dulles, October 24, 1950, Council on Foreign Relations, New York.
39. John W. Dower, *Embracing Defeat: Japan in the Wake of World War II* (New York: Norton, 1999), 45.
40. Ibid.
41. Today, the Japanese maintain an average dietary intake of about 2,500 calories a day. Takeuchi Hiroshi, *Shōwa keizaishi* [An economic history of Shōwa Japan] (Tokyo: Chikuma Shobō, 1988), 93.
42. O. Kurganov, *Amerikantsy v Yaponii, reportaz* (USSR, 1946); reprinted as *Nihon ni iru Amerikajin: Sovieto kisha no Nippon nikki* [The Americans in Japan: The Japan diary by a Soviet journalist], trans. Takagi Hideto (Tokyo: Satsuki Shobō, 1952), 120–121.
43. Dower, *Embracing Defeat*, 63.

44. "Japanese Trade and Investment, First Meeting, October 27, 1952," Council on Foreign Relations Discussion Meeting Report, p. 3, folder 40, box 6, collection III 2Q, RAC.

45. I. Poltavskii, *Okkupirovannaya Yaponiya* (USSR, 1952); reprinted as *Senryō ka no Nihon* [Japan under the occupation], trans. Makiyama Kei (Tokyo: Sō Jusha, 1953), 135.

46. Matsuo Takayoshi, *Kokusai kokka e no shuppatsu* [The start for an internationalist nation], vol. 21 of *Nihon no rekishi* [A history of Japan] (Tokyo: Shūei Sha, 1993), 34.

47. Jerome B. Cohen, "Foreign Trade in the Japanese Economy and Japan's Trade with China," Council on Foreign Relations Study Group on Japanese Trade and Investment, Working Paper No. 1, October 20, 1952, folder 40, box 6, collection III 2Q, RAC.

48. Ibid.

49. Ibid., 2, 3.

50. Ibid., 7.

51. Katō (Yasuhara) Yōko, "Japan, Communist China, Export Controls in Asia, 1948–1952," *Diplomatic History* 10 (winter 1986): 81.

52. "Japanese Peace Treaty Problems, First Meeting, October 23, 1950."

53. Ibid., 9.

54. Katō (Yasuhara), "Japan, Communist China, Export Controls in Asia, 1948–1952," 75.

55. Ibid., 82–85.

56. Quoted in Cohen, "Foreign Trade in the Japanese Economy and Japan's Trade with China."

57. Ishikawa Tasuzō, "Hanbei kanjō wa kienai" [Anti-American feelings will not disappear], *Chūō kōron* (November 1953): 36, 37.

58. Cohen, "Foreign Trade in the Japanese Economy and Japan's Trade with China," 17.

59. Ibid., 10.

60. Ibid., 21.

61. "Japanese Trade and Investment, First Meeting, October 27, 1952," 13.

62. Ibid., 15.

63. "Japanese Peace Treaty Problems, First Meeting, October 23, 1950."

64. Confidential File, Tokyo 1275 to U.S. Department of State, March 15, 1951, 794.00/3-1551, U.S. Department of State, NARA.

65. For further discussion of this subject, see Itō Yūko, "Sengo Amerika no tai Firipin gunji seisaku to Nihon yōin" [Postwar U.S. military policy toward the Philippines and a Japan factor], in *Philippines-Japanese Relations,* ed. Ikehata Setsuho and Lydia N. Yu Jose (Quezon City: Ateneo de Manila University Press, 2003). A revised and translated version of this book was issued by Tokyo publisher Iwanami Shoten in 2004; see chap. 9, 327–366.

66. Council on Foreign Relations Discussion Group on Japan, Discussion Meeting Report, Japan, Fourth Meeting, April 1, 1948, Manuscript Division, Council on Foreign Relations, New York, 3.

67. "American Cultural Relations with Japan, Sixth Meeting, June 3, 1953."

68. "Japanese Peace Treaty Problems, First Meeting, October 23, 1950."

69. Ibid. The evolution of the concept of Japan as "the workshop of Asia" was persuasively analyzed by William S. Borden. See *The Pacific Alliance: United States Foreign Economic Policy and Japanese Trade Recovery, 1947–1955* (Madison: University of Wisconsin Press, 1984).

70. Sherwood M. Fine to John D. Rockefeller III, August 4, 1952, folder 422, box 46, series 1-OMR files, record group (RG) 5 (John D. Rockefeller III), Rockefeller Family Archives, RAC; also see Borden, *Pacific Alliance*.

71. Ibid.

72. Entry of April 27, 1950, Fahs Diaries.

73. Fine to Rockefeller, August 4, 1952; also see Borden, *Pacific Alliance*.

74. Robert S. Schwantes, *Japanese and Americans: A Century of Cultural Relations* (New York: Harper and Brothers, 1955), 306.

75. "Introduction: The 'Afterlife' of Area Studies," in *Learning Places: The Afterlives of Area Studies,* ed. Masao Miyoshi and Harry D. Harootunian (Durham, N.C.: Duke University Press, 2002), 3; Kondō Ken, *Mō hitotsu no Nichibei kankei: Furuburaito kyōiku kōryū no yonjū nen* [The other side of Japan-U.S. relations: Forty years of the Fulbright Program] (Tokyo: Japan Times, 1992).

76. Frank A. Ninkovich, *The Diplomacy of Ideas: U.S. Foreign Policy and Cultural Relations, 1938–1950* (Cambridge: Cambridge University Press, 1981).

77. "American Cultural Relations with Japan, Sixth Meeting, June 3, 1953."

78. Ibid.

79. Confidential Memorandum, Notes on USIE Japan, March 3, 1951, 511.9421/3-351, U.S. Department of State, NARA.

80. The Grew Foundation was started when former U.S. ambassador Joseph C. Grew contributed the Japanese royalties from the sales in Japan of the translation of his two-volume *Ten Years in Japan*. The collection of further funds, which began with a contribution from the emperor and empress, was carried out under the leadership of Ichimada Hisato, governor of the Bank of Japan. This foundation administered fellowships for the exchange of students between Japan and the United States. Entry of February 27, 1951, Fahs Diaries.

81. According to Frederick S. Dunn, professor and director of the Center of International Studies at Princeton University, "The object of cultural interchange is to foster peaceful relations and mutual enrichment. It deals with the problem of trying to influence men's attitudes so that political behavior will be changed." "American Cultural Relations with Japan, Sixth Meeting, June 3, 1953."

82. Ibid; Saxton Bradford, USPOLAD, Tokyo, to U.S. Department of State, September 7, 1951, 511.94/9-751, U.S. Department of State, NARA.

83. "Proposed Cultural and Student Centers," memorandum dated November 15, 1951 (handed conference members by Rockefeller), attachment to Confidential Memorandum of Conversation, U.S. Department of State, December 3, 1951, confidential U.S. State Department special files, Japan, 1947–1956 (microfilm, University Publications of America, 1990, in reel 13, lot files 54-D-423: Japanese Peace Treaty Files of John Foster Dulles, 1947–1952).

84. Report to Ambassador John Foster Dulles, April 16, 1951.

85. Schwantes, *Japanese and Americans,* 43.

86. Ibid.

87. See Roy Watson Curry, *Woodrow Wilson and Far Eastern Policy, 1913–1921* (New York: Octagon Books, 1968), 253–255; Russell H. Fifield, *Woodrow Wilson and*

the Far East: The Diplomacy of the Shantung Question (Hamden, Conn.: Archon Books, 1965), 158–169; and Ian H. Nish, *Alliance in Decline: A Study in Anglo-Japanese Relations, 1908–23* (London: Athlone Press, 1972), 269–271.

88. Iesaka Kazushi, *Nihonjin no jinshu kan* [The Japanese views on race], rev. ed. (Tokyo: Kōbundō, 1986), 110–153.

89. Dunn, *Peace-Making and the Settlement with Japan*, 100.

90. Note of the discussion held on January 29, 1951, between Dulles and Sir Alvary Gascoigne, political representative of the British Liaison Mission to SCAP, *Foreign Relations of the United States 1951*, vol. 6, part 1 (Washington, D.C.: Government Printing Office, 1977), 825.

91. "Japanese Peace Treaty Problems, First Meeting, October 23, 1950."

92. Quoted in John W. Dower, "Race, Language, and War in Two Cultures," in *Japan War and Peace: Selected Essays* (New York: New Press, 1993), 258. A little over a quarter of a century later, in 1971, President Richard Nixon compared the Japanese to lice. Whereas Pyle's utterance was made during the war, Nixon's was made during a time of peace. The case could be made, however, that "war" might have applied to the president's state of mind. Nixon said, "The Japanese are all over Asia like a bunch of lice. Let's look at Japan and Germany: Both have a sense of frustration and a memory of defeat. What must be done is to make sure we have a room for them." White House Special Files: POF: Memorandum for the President, beginning December 19, 1971, box 87, Memorandum for the President's File, December 20, 1971 (Government House, Bermuda).

93. Dower, "Race. Language, and War in Two Cultures," 271. For further treatment and discussion of Japanese and American stereotypes and racial prejudices, see John W. Dower, *War without Mercy: Peace and Power in the Pacific War* (New York: Pantheon Books, 1986).

94. Ishida Takeshi, *Shakai kagaku saikō: Haisen kara hanseiki no dōjidaishi.* [Rethinking social sciences: The development of social sciences in postwar Japan] (Tokyo: University of Tokyo Press, 1995), 47–48; Dower, "Race. Language, and War in Two Cultures," 277, 279.

95. "Japanese Peace Treaty Problems, Sixth Meeting, May 25, 1951."

96. "Japanese Peace Treaty Problems, First Meeting, October 23, 1950."

97. Luciano Gruppi, *Il concetto di egemonia in Gramsci* (Rome: Editori Riuniti); reprinted as *Guramushi no hegemoni ron* [Gramsci's theory on Hegemony], trans. Ōtsu Shinsaku (Tokyo: Gōdō Shuppan Sha, 1979), esp. chap. 6, sec. 6, 114–117. For further discussion of the meanings of *intellectual,* see Raymond Williams, *Keywords: A Vocabulary of Culture and Society,* rev. ed. (New York: Oxford University Press, 1983), 169–171; and Dallas Finn, "What the Japanese Intellectuals Are Thinking," *American Scholar* 24 (autumn 1955): 443.

98. Maruyama Masao analyzes the concept of intellectuals in the context of Japanese modern history. See Maruyama Masao, "Kindai Nihon no chishikijin" [Intellectuals of modern Japan], in *Kōei no ichi kara* [From the position of the rearguard] (Tokyo: Mirai Sha, 1982), 71–133.

99. These journals included Iwanami's *Shisō* and *Sekai, Chūō kōron, Bungei shunjū,* and *Kaizō,* to name only a few. *Shisō, Chūō kōron,* and *Bungei shunjū* began publication before the war and have continued publication to the present day. Tsuzuki Tsutomu, *Sengo Nihon no chishikijin—Maruyama Masao to sono jidai* [The intellectuals of postwar Japan: Maruyama Masao and the times he lived] (Yokahama: Seori Shobō, 1995), 120–121. Iwanami began publishing *Sekai* in December 1945, and it is still published

today. The first issue immediately sold 80,000 copies. Yoshino Genzaburō, "Sōkan made" [Until the first issue was published], *Sekai* (January 1966): 259–268.

100. Kido Mataichi, Kuno Osamu, Kuwabara Takeo, and Nakano Yoshio, "Sōkan no koro" [About the time of the first issue], *Sekai* (January 1966): 176–191, cited in Midorikawa Tōru's statement at discussion meeting on "Heiwa Mondai Danwaka to sono go," *Sekai* (fortieth anniversary edition); reprinted in *Sengo heiwaron no genryū* [The sources of pro-peace arguments in postwar Japan] (Tokyo: Iwanami Shoten, July 1985), 58.

101. The special issues of *Sekai* were as follows: March 1949, "Heiwa mondai" (The problem of peace); April 1950, "Sekai heiwa to kōwa no mondai" (World peace and the settlement of the peace); October 1951, "Kōwa mondai" (The problem of the peace); January 1952, "Minzoku no unmei to kōwa-go no minshuka" (The problems concerning the destiny of the nation and democratization after the peace treaty); May 1952, "Heiwa kenpō to saibusō mondai" (The problems surrounding the peaceful constitution and rearmament).

102. See Midorikawa Tōru's statement at discussion meeting on "Heiwa Mondai Danwakai to sono go," 57.

103. See ibid., 60. Yoshino Genzaburō recalls that the UNESCO statement was made public on July 18, 1948. See Maruyama Masao and Yoshino Genzaburō, "Abe sensei to Heiwa Mondai Danwakai" [Professor Abe and the Peace Study Group], *Sekai* (August 1966):125.

104. This information appeared in the March 1949 issue of *Sekai*. See Midorikawa Tōru's statement at discussion meeting on "Heiwa Mondai Danwakai to sono go," 56; and Kido et al., "Sōkan no koro," 187.

105. See "'Heiwa Mondai Danwakai' nitsuite" and "Heiwa Mondai Danwakai to sono go"; reprinted in *Sengo heiwaron no genryū* [The sources of pro-peace arguments in postwar Japan] (Tokyo: Iwanami Shoten, July 1985); and Maruyama and Yoshino, "Abe sensei to Heiwa Mondai Danwakai," 121–134. The subject of the Peace Study Group has been treated by several scholars. See Igarashi Takeshi, "Sengo nihon gaiko shisei no keisei" [The formation of postwar Japan's diplomatic posture], *Kokka Gakkai Zasshi* (Journal of the Association of Political and Social Sciences, University of Tokyo) 97 (July–August 1984); Tsuzuki, *Sengo Nihon no chishikijin—Maruyama Masao to sono jidai;* and Ishida, *Shakai kagaku saikō*.

106. *Sekai* (the fortieth anniversary edition); reprinted in *Sengo heiwaron no genryū* [The sources of pro-peace arguments in postwar Japan] (Tokyo: Iwanami Shoten, July 1985).

107. Ibid., 108–111.

108. The second statement of the Peace Study Group appeared in the March 1950 issue of *Sekai*. See "Kowa mondai nitsuite no Heiwa Mondai Danwakai seimei" [The Peace Study Group's statement concerning the problem of the peace], *Sekai* (fortieth anniversary edition); reprinted in *Sengo heiwaron no genryū* [The sources of pro-peace arguments in postwar Japan] (Tokyo: Iwanami Shoten, July 1985), 108–111. See also "A Statement by the Peace Study Group on the Problem of the Peace Settlement for Japan (1950)," in *The Japan Reader 2. Post War Japan: 1945 to the Present,* ed. Jon Livingston, Joe Moore, and Felicia Oldfather (New York: Pantheon Books, 1973), 250–253.

109. Yoshino Genzaburō, "Sengo sanjū nen to '*Sekai*' no sanjū nen" [Thirty years after the war and thirty years of *Sekai*], *Sekai* (January 1976): 262.

110. Maruyama and Yoshino, "Abe sensei to Heiwa Mondai Danwakai," 126.

111. Yoshino, "Sōkan made," 259–268; Maruyama and Yoshino, "Abe sensei to Heiwa Mondai Danwakai," 126–127; Yoshino, "Sengo sanjū nen to '*Sekai*' no sanjū nen," 261.

112. Maruyama, "Kindai Nihon no chishikijin," 114.

113. Saxton Bradford, USPOLAD, Tokyo, Desp. No. 1207, "Psychological Factors in Japan," February 28, 1952, 511.94/2-2852, U.S. Department of State, NARA.

114. See "Statement by the Peace Study Group," 250–253.

115. See Midorikawa Tōru's statement at discussion meeting on "Heiwa Mondai Danwakai to sono go," 63. For further information, see Laura Hein, *Reasonable Men, Powerful Words: Political Culture and Expertise in Twentieth-Century Japan* (Washington, D. C.: Woodrow Wilson Center Press; Berkeley: University of California Press, 2004), especially chap. 5, 114–139.

116. The third statement of the Peace Study Group appeared in the December 1950 issue of *Sekai*.

117. Entries of April 27 and May 11, 1950, Fahs Diaries.

118. Entry of December 14, 1949, Fahs Diaries.

119. Entry of May 5, 1950, Fahs Diaries.

120. AMEMBASSY, Tokyo, to U.S. Department of State, Desp. No. 542, September 16, 1952, 511.94/9-1652, U.S. Department of State, NARA.

121. Entry of April 14, 1952, Fahs Diaries.

122. "American Cultural Relations with Japan, Sixth Meeting, June 3, 1953."

123. Bond, USPOLAD, Tokyo, to U.S. Department of State, USIE Country Paper on Japan.

124. Confidential Memorandum, Notes on USIE Japan, March 3, 1951.

125. Ibid.

126. Ibid.

127. Confidential Draft, "Special Guidance on Japan," June 29, 1951.

128. In 1961, ten years after the conclusion of the peace treaty and security treaty with Japan, the U.S. State Department estimated that the U.S. military base system in Japan and on Okinawa would save the United States "hundreds of millions of dollars" each year in peacetime in maintaining the Seventh Fleet and other military forces in the Western Pacific. Besides, the State Department went on to state, if Japan's alliance with the United States and its interdependence with the West became intimate and responsive to Japanese interests, such an environment would thoroughly discourage any Japanese government, whether left or right, from reversing the course that Japan had chosen in San Francisco in 1952. This statement in support of the U.S.-Japan security system makes the whole argument that Japan was "a free rider" superficial and hollow. The so-called free-rider argument was often made with a view toward criticizing Japan for not contributing to security efforts—that is, taking a free ride. The argument became fashionable in the United States in the early 1980s during which Japan grew to be an economic giant and the U. S. economic prowess appeared in decline. Such an argument not necessarily based on facts seems to have been politically motivated for the purpose of Japan bashing and was part of the political game that was played in the United States. See "Japan: Confidential Memorandum of Conversation, April 8, 1961," sent to Gen. Douglas MacArthur from U.S. Department of State, US-J 00090, Japan and the United States: Diplomatic, Security and Economic Relations, 1960–1976, National Security Archive, Gelman Library, George Washington University, Washington, D.C. (hereafter National Security Archive). See also "Department of State Policy on the Future of

Japan," Secret Policy Paper sent to Dean Rusk from U.S. Department of State, US-J 00329, and "Guidelines of U.S. Policy toward Japan," Secret Policy Paper, May 3, 1961, Office of Northeast Asian Affairs, Bureau of Far Eastern Affairs, U.S. Department of State, US-J 00098.

129. Robert W. Cox, with Timothy J. Sinclair, *Approaches to World Order* (Cambridge: Cambridge University Press, 1966), 56.

130. See "Treaty of Peace with Japan," in Hosoya et al., *Documentary History of U.S.-Japanese Relations, 1945–1997,* 123–134.

131. Michael Schaller, "The United States, Japan, and China at Fifty," in *Partnership: United States and Japan, 1951–2001,* ed. Akira Iriye and Robert Wampler (Tokyo: Kōdansha International, 2001), 39.

132. Immanuel Wallerstein, *The Capitalist World-System* (Cambridge: Cambridge University Press, 1979), 35–36.

133. Schwantes, *Japanese and Americans,* 329–330.

134. For further discussion of American "generosity," see Appendix A.

135. "U.S.-Japan Relations: Japan-ROK Settlement Prospects," Confidential Memorandum, Office of East Asian Affairs, Bureau of Far Eastern Affairs, U.S. Department of State, US-J 00285, Japan and the United States: Diplomatic, Security and Economic Relations, 1960–1976, National Security Archive.

136. See Miyazato Seigen, *Nichibei kankei to Okinawa* [U.S.-Japan relations and Okinawa] (Tokyo: Iwanami Shoten, 2000); *Okinawa Times,* ed., *Okinawa kara: Beigun kichi mondai no shinsō* [The report from Okinawa: The depth of the problems of U.S. military bases] (Tokyo: Asahi Shimbun Sha, 1997); Asahi Shimbun, eds., *Okinawa hōkoku, 1969* [The Okinawa Report, 1969] (Tokyo: Asahi Shimbun Sha, 1996); Okinawa Prefecture, ed., *Okinawa: Kunan no gendaishi* [Okinawa: A contemporary history of sufferings] (Tokyo: Iwanami Shoten, 1996); Teruya Yoshihiko and Yamazato Katsunori, eds., *Postwar Okinawa and America: Fifty Years of Cross-Cultural Contact* (Naha: Okinawa Times, 1995); Ōta Masahide, *Minikui Nihonjin* [The ugly Japanese] (Tokyo: Simul Shuppan Kai, 1995); Ōta Masahide, *Okinawa no chōsen* [The challenge of Okinawa] (Tokyo: Kōbun Sha, 1990); Miyazato Seigen, *Amerika no Okinawa tōchi* [American rule over Okinawa] (Tokyo: Iwanami Shoten, 1966); Hiyane Teruo, "Sengo Nihon niokeru Okinawaron no shisōteki keifu" [The philosophical genealogy of discussions on Okinawa in postwar Japan], *Shisō* (December 2005): 24–41.

4 John D. Rockefeller III in Tokyo: Cultural Exchange versus Cultural Imperialism

1. The Dulles Peace Mission comprised John Foster Dulles and Mrs. Dulles; John M. Allison, deputy to Dulles; Assistant Secretary of the Army Earl D. Johnson and Mrs. Johnson; Maj. Gen. Carter B. Magruder, special assistant for occupied areas, Office of the Secretary of the Army; Col. C. Stanton Babcock, chief of the government branch under Magruder; Robert A. Fearey, Office of Northeast Asian Affairs, Department of State; John D. Rockefeller III, a consultant to the mission, and Mrs. Rockefeller; and Doris A. Doyle, secretary to Dulles. *Papers Relating to Foreign Relations of the United States 1951,* vol. 6, Asia and the Pacific, Part 1 (Washington, D.C.: Government Printing Of-

fice, 1977), 141. See entry of January 22, 1951, John D. Rockefeller III Diaries, series 1-OMR files, record group (RG) 5 (John D. Rockefeller III), Rockefeller Family Archives (hereafter Rockefeller Diaries), Rockefeller Archive Center, Sleepy Hollow, N.Y. (hereafter RAC); John Foster Dulles to John D. Rockefeller III, draft letter, May 4, 1951, confidential U.S. State Department special files, Japan, 1947–1956 (microfilm, University Publications of America, 1990, in reel 13, lot files 54-D-423: Japanese Peace Treaty Files of John Foster Dulles, 1947–1952).

2. John E. Harr and Peter J. Johnson, *The Rockefeller Century* (New York: Scribner's Sons, 1988), 505.

3. John D. Rockefeller III to DeWitt Wallace, *Reader's Digest,* November 26, 1951, folder 461, box 52, series 1-OMR files, RG 5 (John D. Rockefeller III), Rockefeller Family Archives, RAC.

4. Ibid.

5. Harr and Johnson, *Rockefeller Century,* 502.

6. Peter Collier and David Horowitz, *The Rockefellers: An American Dynasty* (New York: Holt, Rinehart and Winston, 1976), 282.

7. Dulles to Rockefeller, draft letter, May 4, 1951.

8. Memorandum by Robert A. Fearey, Office of Northeast Asian Affairs, "Mr. Rockefeller's Work," *Papers Relating to Foreign Relations of the United States 1951,* vol. 6, Asia and the Pacific, Part 1 (Washington, D.C.: Government Printing Office, 1977), 814.

9. Entry of January 22, 1951, Rockefeller Diaries.

10. John E. Harr and Peter J. Johnson, *The Rockefeller Conscience: An American Family in Public and Private* (New York: Scribner's Sons, 1991), 10.

11. Entries of January 5, 8, and 12, 1951, Rockefeller Diaries.

12. Entry of January 8, 1951, Rockefeller Diaries.

13. Entry of January 12, 1951, Rockefeller Diaries.

14. Among the other officials with whom John D. Rockefeller III met in Washington were Max Hamilton, an old Japan hand in the State Department and then chair of the Far Eastern Commission; Robert Fearey; U. Alexis Johnson, deputy director of Northeast Asian Affairs; Eugene H. Dooman; Earl Johnson; and Joe Ballantine of the Brookings Institution. Entry of January 14–17, 1951, Rockefeller Diaries.

15. Howland H. Sargeant, deputy assistant secretary for public affairs, to Saxton Bradford, undated, 511.94/11-1551, U.S. Department of State, National Archives and Records Administration, College Park, Md. (hereafter NARA).

16. Entry of January 14–17, 1951, Rockefeller Diaries.

17. Memorandum of conversation on Rockefeller Report on U.S.-Japanese Cultural Relations, August 20, 1951, 511.94/8-2051, U.S. Department of State, NARA.

18. Entry of January 14–17, 1951, Rockefeller Diaries.

19. Entry of January 22, 1951, Rockefeller Diaries.

20. Douglas W. Overton to U. Alexis Johnson, Confidential Office Memorandum on USIE Planning for Japan, March 30, 1951, 511.9421/3-3051, U.S. Department of State, NARA.

21. Entry of January 24–25, 1951, Rockefeller Diaries 1951. Also see entry of January 22, 1951, Rockefeller Diaries; and Harr and Johnson, *Rockefeller Century,* 507.

22. Entry of January 27, 1951, Rockefeller Diaries.

23. Niles W. Bond, confidential, Desp. No. 1246, "Future Implication of a Cultural

Interchange Program with Japan," March 12, 1951, 511.94/3-1251, U.S. Department of State, NARA.

24. Entry of February 22, 1951, Charles B. Fahs Diaries, series 12.1 diaries, Rockefeller Foundation Archives, RAC (hereafter Fahs Diaries).

25. Entry of March 1951, Fahs Diaries.

26. Statement by John D. Rockefeller III, January 25, 1951, confidential U.S. State Department special files, Japan, 1947–1956 (microfilm, University Publications of America, 1990, in reel 13, lot series 54-D-423: Japanese Peace Treaty Files of John Foster Dulles, 1947–1952).

27. Before the phase-out stage of the occupation began, the CI&E headquarters in Tokyo was staffed by 321 Americans; 23 information center directors (also American) were in the field, for a total staff of 344. Throughout most of the occupation, SCAP had a complement of 544 American CI&E personnel. USPOLAD, Tokyo, to U.S. Department of State, Desp. No. 370, September 7, 1951, 511.94/9-751, U.S. Department of State, NARA.

28. With the establishment of the U.S. Information Agency in 1953, the State Department was relieved of responsibility for the operation of the information program. USIA formulated U.S. information policy, but under the guidance of the State Department to ensure conformity with American foreign policy. Most information programs fell under the jurisdiction of the new USIA, whereas the responsibility for administering the exchange program remained in the Bureau of Educational and Cultural Affairs in the State Department. The mission of USIA was to influence foreign audiences and make them feel more receptive to America and its foreign policy. The United States Information Service the field arm of USIA, operated in some 300 cities in more than 150 countries during the cold war years. USIS offered a broad range of activities—press, publication, film, libraries, and radio, in addition to cultural and educational exchange programs. Psychological and information programs in Japan continued to be implemented by USIS-Japan from 1953 through July 1959. The office was located in an annex of the U.S. embassy in Tokyo. At the end of 1953, the U.S. cultural program that specifically targeted Japan was the third largest USIA field operation, as measured by total number of personnel. Richard A. Johnson, *The Administration of United States Foreign Policy* (Austin: University of Texas Press, 1971), 85, 89; Wilson Dizard Jr., "Telling America's Story," *American Heritage* (August/September 2003): 41–47; Harr and Johnson, *Rockefeller Century,* 505; Alec Dubro and Matsui Michio, "Hajimete vçru wo nugu amerika tainichi sennō kōsaku no zenbō" [Panel-D Japan: The whole feature of American operations for brainwashing Japan, now revealed], *Views* (Kōdan Sha Publishing Co.) (November 1994): 40, 44; Howard R. Ludden, "The International Information Program of the United States: State Department Years, 1945–1953," Ph.D. diss., Princeton University, Princeton, N.J., 1966, 96; Robert S. Schwantes, *Japanese and Americans: A Century of Cultural Relations* (New York: Harper and Brothers, 1955), 313–314.

29. Ludden, "International Information Program of the United States," 91.

30. At their peak during 1945–1951 the CI&E and Civil Affairs teams had about 300 personnel in the field and 244 at headquarters for a total of 544. By comparison, at the time of the transfer of responsibility in March 1952 USIE had 47 in the field and 83 at headquarters for a total of 130. Saxton Bradford, USPOLAD, Tokyo, to U.S. Department of State, Desp. No. 370, September 7, 1951, 511.94/9-751, U.S. Department of State, NARA.

31. Entry of March 1, 1951, Fahs Diaries.
32. Confidential memorandum, Notes on USIE Japan, March 3, 1951, 511.9421/3-351, U.S. Department of State, NARA.
33. Overton to Johnson, Confidential Office Memorandum on USIE Planning for Japan.
34. Ludden, "International Information Program of the United States," 38, 199.
35. William Barnes and John H. Morgan, *The Foreign Service of the United States: Origins, Development, and Functions,* Department of State Publication 7050, Department and Foreign Service Series 96, Historical Office, Bureau of Public Affairs, U.S. Department of State (Washington D.C.: Government Printing Office, 1961), 289.
36. Entry of June 25, 1947, Fahs Diaries.
37. Entry of February 23, 1951, Fahs Diaries; "American Cultural Relations with Japan, Fifth Meeting, April 30, 1953, Digest of Discussion," Council on Foreign Relations Study Group Report, Manuscript Division, Council on Foreign Relations, New York, 14.
38. "American Cultural Relations with Japan, Fifth Meeting, April 30, 1953, Digest of Discussion," 14.
39. Entry of February 4, 1951, Rockefeller Diaries.
40. Tsurumi Shunsuke, *A Cultural History of Postwar Japan, 1945–1980* (London: KPI Limited, 1987). This work was first published in Japanese, *Sengo Nihon no taishū bunkashi* (Tokyo: Iwanami Shoten, 1984).
41. For more information on the Institute of Pacific Relations, see Akami Tomoko, *Internationalizing the Pacific: The United States, Japan and the Institute of Pacific Relations in War and Peace, 1919–1945* (New York: Routledge, 2002).
42. Quoted in Collier and Horowitz, *Rockefellers: An American Dynasty,* 283.
43. "American Cultural Relations with Japan, Sixth Meeting, June 3, 1953," Council on Foreign Relations Study Group Report, folder 42, box 6, collection III 2Q, Rockefeller Foundation Archives, RAC.
44. AMEMBASSY, Tokyo, to U.S. State Department, Desp. No. 669, February 8, 1962, Attachment: Hugh Borton, "Report of the First Meeting of the Joint United States–Japan Conference on Cultural and Educational Interchange," January 31, 1962, 511.943/2-862, U.S. Department of State, NARA.
45. "American Cultural Relations with Japan, Sixth Meeting, June 3, 1953."
46. Francis J. Colligan, "The Fulbright Act: An Opportunity and a Challenge to American Educators," August 10, 1949, Bureau of Educational and Cultural Affairs Historical Collection, U.S. Department of State, manuscript number 468, box 296, file 29, Special Collections Section, University of Arkansas Libraries, Fayetteville.
47. Robert S. Schwantes, *Japanese and Americans: A Century of Cultural Relations* (New York: Harper and Brothers, 1955), 327.
48. Japanese-American Cultural Relations, Council on Foreign Relations Study Group, July 27, 1953, folder 447, box 50, series 1-OMR files, RG 5 (John D. Rockefeller III), Rockefeller Family Archives, RAC.
49. "American Cultural Relations with Japan, Sixth Meeting, June 3, 1953."
50. Donald R. Nugent to John D. Rockefeller III, February 14, 1951, folder 445, box 49, series 1-OMR files, RG 5 (John D. Rockefeller III), Rockefeller Family Archives, RAC.
51. Quoted in Francis J. Colligan, "The Government and Cultural Interchange," *Review of Politics* 20, no. 4 (1958): 564.

52. Report to Ambassador John Foster Dulles, April 16, 1951, folder 446, box 49, series 1-OMR files, RG 5 (John D. Rockefeller III), Rockefeller Family Archives, RAC.
53. Collier and Horowitz, *Rockefellers: An American Dynasty,* 280.
54. Conlon Associates Ltd., *United States Foreign Policy: Asia,* study prepared at the request of the Committee on Foreign Relations, U.S. Senate, November 1, 1959 (Washington, D.C.: Government Printing Office, 1959), 96 (hereafter Conlon report).
55. Report to Ambassador John Foster Dulles, April 16, 1951.
56. For further discussion of cultural imperialism, see John Tomlinson, *Cultural Imperialism: A Critical Introduction* (London: Continuum, 1991).
57. "American Cultural Relations with Japan, First Meeting, December 17, 1952," Council on Foreign Relations Study Group Report, folder 40, box 6, collection III 2Q, Rockefeller Foundation Archives, RAC.
58. Report to Ambassador John Foster Dulles, April 16, 1951.
59. "Proposed Cultural and Student Centers," memorandum dated November 15, 1951 (handed conference members by Rockefeller), attachment to Confidential Memorandum of Conversation, U.S. Department of State, December 3, 1951, confidential U.S. State Department special files, Japan, 1947–1956 (microfilm, University Publications of America, 1990, in reel 13, lot files 54-D-423: Japanese Peace Treaty Files of John Foster Dulles, 1947–1952).
60. "American Cultural Relations with Japan, First Meeting, December 17, 1952."
61. "American Cultural Relations with Japan, Sixth Meeting, June 3, 1953."
62. Niles W. Bond, USPOLAD, Tokyo, to U.S. Department of State, USIE Country Paper on Japan, August 16, 1951, 511.9421/8-1651, U.S. Department of State, NARA.
63. John W. Dower, *Embracing Defeat: Japan in the Wake of World War II* (New York: Norton, 1999), 550–551.
64. Saxton Bradford, AMEMBASSY, Tokyo, to U.S. Department of State, "Attitudes of Japanese Intellectuals towards the United States," June 4, 1952, 511.94/6-452, U.S. Department of State, NARA.
65. Fukuda Sadayoshi, "Hanbei shisō" [Anti-American thought], *Bungei shunjū* (September 1953): 77.
66. Report to Ambassador John Foster Dulles, April 16, 1951.
67. "American Cultural Relations with Japan, Sixth Meeting, June 3, 1953."
68. Tanaka Kōtarō, "Cultural Interchange between Japan and the United States," *Tokyo Times,* February 21, 1951, folder 445, box 49, series 1-OMR files, RG 5 (John D. Rockefeller III), Rockefeller Family Archives, RAC.
69. Donald R. Nugent to John D. Rockefeller III, March 6, 1951, folder 461, box 52, series 1-OMR files, RG 5 (John D. Rockefeller III), Rockefeller Family Archives, RAC.
70. Quoted in Bond, confidential, Desp. No. 1246, "Future Implication of a Cultural Interchange Programs with Japan."
71. Quoted in ibid.
72. Charles B. Fahs to John D. Rockefeller III, August 29, 1951, folder 6, box 1, 1.2 series 609, RG 1.2, Rockefeller Foundation Archives, RAC.
73. Report to Ambassador John Foster Dulles, April 16, 1951.
74. Saxton Bradford to John D. Rockefeller III, "Relations of Governmental and Private Endeavor in the Field of Japanese-American Cultural Relations," October 17, 1951, folder 461, box 51, series 1-OMR files, RG 5 (John D. Rockefeller III), Rockefeller Family Archives, RAC.

75. AMEMBASSY, Tokyo, to U.S. Department of State, USIS Country Plan—Japan, April 27, 1953, 511.94/4-2753, U.S. Department of State, NARA.
76. Ibid.; Saxton Bradford, AMEMBASSY, Tokyo, Desp. No. 1343, "Semi-annual Evaluation Report," January 23, 1953, 511.94/1-2353, U.S. Department of State, NARA.
77. Bradford to Rockefeller, "Relations of Governmental and Private Endeavor in the Field of Japanese-American Cultural Relations."
78. Ibid.
79. Bradford, AMEMBASSY, Tokyo, Desp. No. 1343, "Semi-annual Evaluation Report."
80. Warren M. Robbins (USIA), "Toward an American Global Cultural-Educational-Informational Program in the Framework of the Present World Scene," December 14, 1960, Bureau of Educational and Cultural Affairs Historical Collection, U.S. Department of State, Special Collections Section, University of Arkansas Libraries, Fayetteville.
81. Ibid.
82. Ibid.
83. Conlon report, 96.
84. Confidential—Security Information, USIE Country Plan—Japan, Priority III, December 4, 1951, 511.94/12-451, U.S. Department of State, NARA.
85. Schwantes, *Japanese and Americans,* 327.
86. Bond, USPOLAD, Tokyo, to U.S. Department of State, USIE Country Paper on Japan.
87. Conlon report.
88. Confidential file, Tokyo 1275 to U.S. Department of State, March 15, 1951, 794.00/3-1551, U.S. Department of State, NARA.
89. Entry of February 23, 1951, Rockefeller Diaries.
90. Ibid.
91. Entries of February 26 and February 27, 1951, Rockefeller Diaries.
92. Harr and Johnson, *Rockefeller Century,* 507.
93. Entry of March 17, 1951, Rockefeller Diaries; entry of June 11, 1948, Fahs Diaries.
94. Report to Ambassador John Foster Dulles, April 16, 1951.
95. Ibid.
96. Overton to Johnson, Confidential Office Memorandum on USIE Planning for Japan.
97. Ibid.
98. Ibid.

5 The Rockefeller Report: Countering the Communist Menace

1. Douglas W. Overton to U. Alexis Johnson, "Rockefeller Report on U.S.-Japanese Cultural Relations," April 13, 1951, 511.94/4-1351, U.S. Department of State, National Archives and Records Administration, College Park, Md. (hereafter NARA).
2. Department of State for the Press, No. 819, September 12, 1951, confidential U.S. State Department special files, Japan, 1947–1956 (microfilm, University Publications of America, 1990, in reel 13, lot files 54-D-423: Japanese Peace Treaty Files of John Foster Dulles, 1947–1952).

3. Report to Ambassador John Foster Dulles, April 16, 1951, folder 446, box 49, series 1-OMR files, record group (RG) 5 (John D. Rockefeller III), Rockefeller Family Archives, Rockefeller Archive Center, Sleepy Hollow, N.Y. (hereafter RAC); Confidential—Security Information, USIE Country Plan—Japan, Priority III, December 4, 1951, 511.94/12-451, U.S. Department of State, NARA.

4. A USIE officer was critical of SCAP for neglecting cultural programs in favor of mass information media programs. Niles W. Bond, USPOLAD, Tokyo, to U.S. Department of State, USIE Country Paper on Japan, August 16, 1951, 511.9421/8-1651, U.S. Department of State, NARA.

5. Report to Ambassador John Foster Dulles, April 16, 1951; Overton to Johnson, "Rockefeller Report on U.S.-Japanese Cultural Relations."

6. Report to Ambassador John Foster Dulles, April 16, 1951; Confidential—Security Information, USIE Country Plan—Japan. Japanese intellectuals have discussed, both heatedly and in length, what role they should have played and should play in society. Prefatory Note, "Seinen to chishikisō wa doko e iku" [Where are the youth and intellectuals going?] *Chūō kōron* (February 1946): 1–7; Hidaka Rokurō, "Dai chishikijin ron" [A great essay on intellectuals] *Kindai bungaku* 6 (February 1947): 2–12; Hayashi Kentarō, "Gendai chishikijin no ryōshin" [Good sense of modern intellectuals] *Sekai* (October 1950): 97–103; Joseph Fromm, "Nihon no chishikijin e chokugen suru" [To advise Japanese intellectuals] *Sekai* (May 1952): 131–135; Sugi Katsuo, "Fromm shi e no tegami" [A letter to Mr. Fromm] *Sekai* (June 1952): 40–44; Hotta Yoshie, "Nihon no chishikijin" [Japanese intellectuals], in *Iwanami kōza gendai shisō* [Iwanami course of modern thoughts], vol. 11 of *Gendai Nihon no shisō* [Thoughts of modern Japan] (Tokyo: Iwanami Shoten, 1957),157–183; Kato Shūichi and Kuno Osamu, eds., *Kindai Nihon shisō shi kōza* [Course of history of modern Japanese thoughts], vol. 4 of *Chishikijin no seisei to yakuwari* [The emergence of intellectuals and their role] (Tokyo: Chikuma Shobō, 1959); Takeuchi Yoshimi, "Interi ron" [An essay on intellectuals], in *Takeuchi Yoshimi zenshū* [Collected works of Takeuchi Yoshimi], vol. 6 *of Nihon ideorogī* [Japanese Ideology] (Tokyo: Chikuma Shobō, 1980), 86–105; Maruyama Masao, "Kindai Nihon no chishikijin" [Intellectuals of modern Japan], in *Kōei no ichi kara* [From the position of the rearguard] (Tokyo: Mirai-Sha, 1982), 73–133.

7. "Proposal for a Cultural Center and Student International House," September 6, 1951, item: Japanese-American Cultural Relations, folder 6, box 1, series 609, RG 1.2, Rockefeller Family Archives, RAC.

8. Bond, USPOLAD, Tokyo, to U.S. Department of State, USIE Country Paper on Japan.

9. Report to Ambassador John Foster Dulles, April 16, 1951.

10. Ibid.

11. Entry of June 9, 1948, Charles B. Fahs Diaries, series 12.1 diaries, Rockefeller Foundation Archives, RAC (hereafter Fahs Diaries).

12. Quoted in John W. Dower, "E. H. Norman, Japan and the Uses of History," in *Origins of the Modern Japanese State: Selected Writings of E. H. Norman,* ed. John W. Dower (New York: Random House, 1975), 49.

13. Conlon Associates Ltd., *United States Foreign Policy: Asia,* study prepared at the request of the Committee on Foreign Relations, U.S. Senate, November 1, 1959 (Washington, D.C.: Government Printing Office, 1959), 11 (hereafter Conlon report).

14. Entry of Iwai Yūjirō, undated, John D. Rockefeller III Diaries 1952, Japan section, folder 63, box 7, series 1-OMR files, RG 5 (John D. Rockefeller III), Rockefeller

Family Archives, RAC (hereafter Rockefeller Diaries). For further information on Iwai Yūjirō, see Iwai Yūjirō, *Osaka shōnin no tetsugaku* [The philosophy of an Osaka merchant] (Tokyo: Tokyo Nunoi Shuppan, 1994).

15. Entry of June 9, 1948, Fahs Diaries.

16. Overton to Johnson, "Rockefeller Report on U.S.-Japanese Cultural Relations."

17. Confidential Security Information from Robert D. Murphy to Secretary of State, September 5, 1952, 511.94/9-552, U.S. Department of State, NARA.

18. John L. Stegmaier to John M. Allison and U. Alexis Johnson, Memorandum on Study Group on Japanese-American Cultural Relations, January 19, 1953, 511.94/1-1953, U.S. Department of State, NARA.

19. Report to Ambassador John Foster Dulles, April 16, 1951.

20. Ibid.

21. Enclosure: Memorandum to John D. Rockefeller III from Saxton Bradford, October 17, 1951, in Charles N. Spinks, USPOLAD, Tokyo, Desp. No. 630, October 22, 1951, 511.94/10-2251, U.S. Department of State, NARA.

22. Entry of December 14, 1949, Fahs Diaries.

23. Stegmaier to Allison and Johnson, Memorandum on Study Group on Japanese-American Cultural Relations.

24. Memorandum, John D. Rockefeller III to John M. Allison, September 23, 1952, 511.94/9-2352, U.S. Department of State, NARA.

25. Saxton Bradford, AMEMBASSY, Tokyo, Desp. No. 1343, "Semi-annual Evaluation Report," January 23, 1953, 511.94/1-2353, U.S. Department of State, NARA.

26. Saxton Bradford, AMEMBASSY, Tokyo to U.S. State Department of State, "IIA Prospectus for Japan," April 30, 1953, 511.94/4-3053, U.S. Department of State, NARA.

27. Bradford, AMEMBASSY, Tokyo, Desp. No. 1343, "Semi-annual Evaluation Report."

28. Willard A. Hanna, U.S. Information Service, to U.S. Information Agency, "Semi-annual Evaluation Report," September 8, 1953, 511.94/9-853, In addition, the English Language Education Council Inc. was created in 1956 for the purpose of improving and popularizing effective theories and techniques of teaching English based on modern linguistics. It was financed by the Council on Economic and Cultural Affairs Inc. of the United States, which contributed about 17 million yen, and by Japanese business circles, which gave about 13 million yen. "Progress Report on the Recommendations Made by the First United States–Japan Conference on Cultural and Educational Interchange," September 17, 1963, folder 32, box 5, series 609, RG 1.2 , Rockefeller Foundation Archives, RAC.

29. Overton to Johnson, "Rockefeller Report on U.S.-Japanese Cultural Relations."

30. Confidential Security Information, from Murphy to Secretary of State.

31. Saxton Bradford, AMEMBASSY, Tokyo, to U.S. Department of State, Desp. No. 161, "Japan Pen Club," July 24, 1952, 511.94/7-2452, U.S. Department of State, NARA.

32. Bradford, AMEMBASSY, Tokyo, Desp. No. 1343, "Semi-annual Evaluation Report."

33. Report to Ambassador John Foster Dulles, April 16, 1951; Confidential—Security Information, USIE Country Plan—Japan.

34. Report to Ambassador John Foster Dulles, April 16, 1951; Overton to Johnson, "Rockefeller Report on U.S.-Japanese Cultural Relations."

35. Bradford, AMEMBASSY, Tokyo, Desp. No. 1343, "Semi-annual Evaluation Report."

36. AMEMBASSY, Tokyo, to U.S. Department of State, Desp. No. 2259, April 27, 1953, 551.94/4-2753, U.S. Department of State, NARA.
37. Bond, USPOLAD, Tokyo, to U.S. Department of State, USIE Country Paper on Japan.
38. Matsuo Takayoshi, *Kokusai kokka e no shuppatsu* [The start as an international nation], vol. 21 of *Nihon no rekishi* [A history of Japan] (Tokyo: Shūei Sha, 1993), 177.
39. AMEMBASSY, Tokyo, to U.S. Department of State, Desp. No. 2259.
40. Niles W. Bond, USPOLAD, Tokyo, to U.S. Department of State, USIE Country Paper on Japan.
41. AMEMBASSY, Tokyo, to U.S. Department of State, Desp. No. 2259.
42. Bradford, AMEMBASSY, Tokyo, Desp. No. 1343, "Semi-annual Evaluation Report."
43. Bond, USPOLAD, Tokyo, to U.S. Department of State, USIE Country Paper on Japan.
44. Ibid.
45. AMEMBASSY, Tokyo, to U.S. Department of State, Desp. No. 2259.
46. Entry of Otis Cary, undated, John D. Rockefeller III Diaries 1952, Japan section, folder 63, box 7, series 1-OMR files, RG 5 (John D. Rockefeller III), Rockefeller Family Archives, RAC.
47. Enclosure: Undated draft of a reply to Louis C. Ieradi from Jack K. McFall, assistant secretary of state, in Jack K. McFall to Sen. James H. Duff, December 17, 1951, 511.94/12-1751, U.S. Department of State, NARA.
48. Confidential—Security Information, USIE Country Plan—Japan.
49. Enclosure: Undated draft of a reply to Ieradi from McFall.
50. Entry of April 22, 1952, Fahs Diaires.
51. Entry of April 23, 1952, Fahs Diaries.
52. Entry of Hugh Borton, undated, John D. Rockefeller III Diaries 1952, Japan section, folder 63, box 7, series 1-OMR files, RG 5 (John D. Rockefeller III), Rockefeller Family Archives, RAC.
53. Report to Ambassador John Foster Dulles, April 16, 1951.
54. Council on Foreign Relations Study Group on American Cultural Relations with Japan, "Binational Cultural Organizations," Working Paper No. 6, prepared by Robert S. Schwantes, May 26, 1953, folder 42, box 6, collection III 2Q, RAC.
55. Report to Ambassador John Foster Dulles, April 16, 1951.
56. "Proposed Cultural and Student Centers," memorandum dated November 15, 1951 (handed to conference members by Rockefeller), attachment to Confidential Memorandum of Conversation, U.S. Department of State, December 3, 1951, confidential U.S. State Department special files, Japan, 1947–1956 (microfilm, University Publications of America, 1990, in reel 13, lot series 54-D-423: Japanese Peace Treaty Files of John Foster Dulles, 1947–1952).
57. Report to John Foster Ambassador Dulles, April 16, 1951.
58. "Proposal for a Cultural Center and Student International House"; "Proposed Cultural and Student Centers," memorandum dated November 15, 1951 (handed conference members by Rockefeller), attachment to Confidential Memorandum of Conversation, U.S. Department of State, December 3, 1951, confidential U.S. State Department special files, Japan, 1947–1956 (microfilm, University Publications of America, 1990, in reel 13, lot files 54-D-423: Japanese Peace Treaty Files, John Foster Dulles, 1947–1952); Saxton Bradford to John D. Rockefeller III, October 17, 1951, folder 461,

box 51, series 1-OMR files, RG 5 (John D. Rockefeller III), Rockefeller Family Archives, RAC.

59. Bradford to Rockefeller, October 17, 1951.

60. Overton to Johnson, "Rockefeller Report on U.S.-Japanese Cultural Relations."

61. John D. Rockefeller III to John Foster Dulles, April 19, 1951, confidential U.S. State Department special files, Japan, 1947–1956 (microfilm, University Publications of America, 1990, in reel 13, lot files 54-D-423: Japanese Peace Treaty Files of John Foster Dulles, 1947–1952).

62. Entry of April 16, 1951, Rockefeller Diaries; John D. Rockefeller III to John Foster Dulles, April 23, 1951, confidential U.S. State Department special files, Japan, 1947–1956 (microfilm, University Publications of America, 1990, in reel 13, lot files 54-D-423: Japanese Peace Treaty Files, John Foster Dulles, 1947–1952).

63. John Foster Dulles to John D. Rockefeller III, May 4, 1951, confidential U.S. State Department special files, Japan, 1947–1956 (microfilm, University Publications of America, 1990, in reel 13, lot files 54-D-423: Japanese Peace Treaty Files, John Foster Dulles, 1947–1952).

64. "Comment on Mr. Rockefeller's Suggestions for the Japan Program Contained in his Letter of April 19th to Mr. Dulles," Mr. Hulten to W. Bradley Connors, June 27, 1951, attachment to W. Bradley Connors to John Foster Dulles, July 18, 1951, confidential U.S. State Department special files, Japan, 1947–1956 (microfilm, University Publications of America, 1990, in reel 13, lot files 54-D-423: Japanese Peace Treaty Files of John Foster Dulles, 1947–1952); Bradford to Rockefeller, October 17, 1951.

65. Bradford to Rockefeller, October 17, 1951.

66. "Comment on Mr. Rockefeller's suggestions for the Japan program contained in his letter of April 19thth to Mr. Dulles."

67. Confidential Memorandum of Conversation between John D. Rockefeller III and Douglas Overton, August 20, 1951, 511.94/8-2051, U.S. Department of State, NARA.

68. Charles B. Fahs, "John D. Rockefeller, III's Memorandum on Japanese-American Cultural Relations," interoffice correspondence, September 6, 1951, folder 6, box 1, series 609, RG 1.2, Rockefeller Foundation Archives, RAC.

69. John Foster Dulles to John D. Rockefeller III, July 30, 1951, 511.94/7-3051, U.S. Department of State, NARA.

70. Confidential Memorandum of Conversation between Rockefeller and Overton, August 20, 1951.

71. John D. Rockefeller III to John Foster Dulles, August 16, 1951, confidential U.S. State Department special files, Japan, 1947–1956 (microfilm, University Publications of America, 1990, in reel 13, lot files 54-D-423: Japanese Peace Treaty Files of John Foster Dulles, 1947–1952); entry of October 13, 1951, Rockefeller Diaries.

72. Entry of August 21, 1951, Rockefeller Diaries.

73. Entry of October 13, 1951, Rockefeller Diaries.

74. Rockefeller to Dulles, August 16, 1951; ibid.

75. Rockefeller also spoke to William Johnson, number-two man to Edward Barrett, the assistant secretary for public affairs; Bradley Connors, the public affairs man in the Far East; and Jane Alden, personal assistant to Johnson on Far East matters. Entry of September 25–26, Rockefeller Diaries.

76. Ibid.

77. Bradford to Rockefeller, October 17, 1951.

78. Ibid.

79. Rockefeller and his party flew from New York City through Chicago to San Francisco (about twelve hours), then to Honolulu (nine and a half hours), Wake (nine hours and forty minutes), and finally to Tokyo (eight and a half hours in flight). Entries of October 13, 14, and 16, 1951, Rockefeller Diaries.

80. Charles N. Spinks, USPOLAD, Tokyo, Desp. No. 630, "Comments on Rockefeller Report," October 22, 1951, 511.94/10-2251, U.S. Department of State, NARA.

81. Entry of June 5, 1947, Fahs Diaries; Takemae Eiji, *GHQ* (Tokyo: Iwanami Shoten, 1983), 127.

82. Entry of November 8, 1951, Rockefeller Diaries.

83. Entry of May 1, 1952, Fahs Diaries.

84. Sterling W. Fisher to John D. Rockefeller III, February 6, 1952, folder 7, box 1, series 609, Japanese-American Cultural Relations 1950–1953 (January–June), RG 1.2, Rockefeller Foundation Archives, RAC.

85. Entry of June 7, 1947, Fahs Diaries.

86. AMEMBASSY, Tokyo, to U.S. Department of State, Memorandum of Conversation between Prof. Makoto Saito of Tokyo University and Cultural Attaché Margaret H. Williams, May 5, 1953, 511.94/5-1153, U.S. Department of State, NARA.

87. Entry of October 26, 1951, Rockefeller Diaries.

88. Entry of April 15, 1952, Fahs Diaries.

89. Entry of October 26, 1951, Rockefeller Diaries.

90. Entry of October 14, 1951, Rockefeller Diaries; excerpt from interview, John D. Rockefeller III by Charles B. Fahs, November 23, 1951, folder 6, box, 1, series 609, RG 1.2, Rockefeller Family Archives, RAC; entry of April 15, 1952, Fahs Diaries; Matsumoto Shigeharu, *Shanhai jidai* [My years in Shanghai], vol. 1 (Tokyo: Chūō Kōron Sha, 1974), 32.

91. Entry of April 14, 1952, Fahs Diaries.

92. Entry of April 19, 1952, Fahs Diaries.

93. Memo by Charles B. Fahs, folder 470, box 52, series 1-OMR files, RG 5 (John D. Rockefeller III), Rockefeller Family Archives, RAC.

94. Entry of November 5, 1951, Rockefeller Diaries.

95. Ibid.

96. Entry of November 12, 1951, Rockefeller Diaries; International House of Japan, *Kokusai Bunka Kaikan 50-nen no ayumi, 1952–2002* [A 50-year history of the International House of Japan, 1952–2002](Tokyo: International House of Japan, 2003), 8; Matsumoto Shigeharu, *Shōwa-shi eno ichi shōgen* [A testimony to Shōwa history] (Tokyo: Tachibana Shuppan, 2001), 316.

97. The following leaders in Japan were elected members of the board of directors of the Cultural Center Preparatory Committee on July 15, 1952: Kabayama Aisuke, chair and former president, America-Japan Society; Gordon Bowles, associate managing director and professor of cultural anthropology, University of Tokyo; Sterling Fisher, general manager for the Far East , Reader's Digest Association Inc.; Ichimada Hisato, governor, Bank of Japan; Ishikawa Ichirō, president, Federation of Economic Organizations (the Japanese counterpart of American Manufacturers Association); Jōdai Tano, professor of English, Japan Women's University; Kameyama Naoto, professor emeritus, Tokyo University, and president, Japan Science Society; Koizumi Shinzō, education adviser to the crown prince, member of the Japan Academy, and former president, Keiō Gijuku University; Matsukata Yoshisaburō; Matsumoto Shigeharu; Maeda Tamon; Tak-

agi Yasaka; Shibusawa Keizō, former governor of the Bank of Japan, finance minister from 1946 to 1947, and president of the Japan Ethnological Association; and E. J. Griffith, E. J. Griffith & Co., Tokyo, who was engaged in foreign trade and a prominent member of the American community in Japan. Entry of November 12, 1951, Rockefeller Diaries; Matsumoto Shigeharu to Charles B. Fahs, July 22, 1952, folder 462, box 51, International House of Japan, series 1-OMR files, RG 5 (John D. Rockefeller III), Rockefeller Family Archives, RAC.

98. Entry of November 12, 1951, Rockefeller Diaries.

99. John D. Rockefeller III to DeWitt Wallace, *Readers' Digest,* November 26, 1951, folder 461, box 51, series 1-OMR files, RG 5 (John D. Rockefeller III), Rockefeller Family Archives, RAC.

100. The following were members of the program and planning subcommittee: Maeda Tamon; Matsukata Yoshisaburō; Gordon Bowles; Sterling Fisher; Furugaki Tetsuo, president, Japan Broadcasting Corporation; Harold Hacket, vice president, International Christian University; Jōdai Tano; Kabayama Aiskue; Kameyama Naoto; Kanō Hisaakira; Koizumi Shinzō; Matsumoto Shigeharu; Nambara Shigeru; Sakanishi Shiho, a Ph.D. in philosophy and member of the Foreign Affairs Committee of the House of Councilors; Takagi Yasaka; Tagasaki Kiyoshi, president, *Nippon Times;* Tōhata Seiichi, professor of agricultural economics, Tokyo University; and Tsuru Shigeto. Entry of November 15, 1951, Rockefeller Diaries; Saxton Bradford, USPOLAD, Tokyo, to U.S. Department of State, "Rockefeller 'Centers,'" April 4, 1952, 511.94/4-452, U.S. Department of State, NARA.

101. Entry of November 12, 1951, Rockefeller Diaries.

102. Entry of November 17, 1951, Rockefeller Diaries.

103. John D. Rockefeller III to Chester Barnard, president of Rockefeller Foundation, December 26, 1951, folder 6, box 1, RG 1.2, Rockefeller Foundation Archives, RAC.

104. The finance committee consisted of James P. Duddy, second vice president, Chase National Bank, Tokyo; Fujiyama Aiichirō, chair of the Japan Chamber of Commerce and Tokyo Chamber of Commerce; Ichimada Hisato; Ishikawa Ichirō, president of the Federation of Economic Organization (a Japanese counterpart of the American Manufacturers' Association); Y. J. Johnson, vice president and manager, Bank of America, Tokyo; Kanō Hisaakira; and Charles Linton, a representative of Asiatic Trading Co. The facilities committee was composed of Tagasaki Kiyoshi (chair); Matsushita Sakae (secretary), general manager, Nippon Trading Co., and president, Japanese chapter of the International House Association; Gordon Bowles; Kanō Hisaakira; Koizumi Shinzō; Maeda Tamon; and Takagi Yasaka. Bradford, USPOLAD, Tokyo, to U.S. Department of State, "Rockefeller 'Centers.'"

105. Ibid.

106. Eldridge Sibley, executive associate, Social Science Research Council, to Joseph H. Willits, Rockefeller Foundation, October 19, 1953, folder 10, box 2, series 609, RG 1.2, Rockefeller Foundation Archives, RAC.

107. Entry of April 26, 1954, Fahs Diaries.

108. Saxton Bradford, USPOLAD, Tokyo, to U.S. Department of State, "International Cultural Center in Japan," July 14, 1952, 511.94/7-1452, U.S. Department of State, NARA.

109. Ibid.; interview with Matsumoto Shigeharu by Kunihiro Masao "Shōwashi e shōgen—sekai no naka no Nihon 26—nagai no yūjō de kokusai bunka kaikan wo set-

suritsu" [To establish the International House of Japan thanks to the friendship of people at home and abroad], *Ekonomisuto,* October 15,1985, 85.

110. Entry of April 26, 1954, Fahs Diaries.

111. Bradford, USPOLAD, Tokyo, to U.S. Department of State, "International Cultural Center in Japan."

112. Those Japanese scholars and intellectuals included Nakayama Ichirō, president, Hitotsubashi University; Tōhata Seiichi, professor, University of Tokyo; Ryū Shintarō, chief editor, *Asahi shimbun;* and Rōyama Masamichi, Oka Yoshitake, Tsuji Kiyoaki, and Maruyama Masao, all professors at the University of Tokyo. Matsumoto Shigeharu to Charles B. Fahs, November 27, 1952, folder 462, box 51, series 1-OMR files, RG 5 (John D. Rockefeller III), Rockefeller Family Archives, RAC.

113. Entry of April 26, 1954, Fahs Diaries.

114. Fisher to Rockefeller, February 6, 1952.

115. Entry of April 15, 1952, Rockefeller Diaries.

116. Entry of April 9–April 14, 1952, Rockefeller Diaries

117. Entries of April 17 and 21, 1952, Rockefeller Diaries.

118. Entry of April 25, 1952, Rockefeller, Diaries.

119. Rockefeller to Barnard, December 26, 1951.

120. Entry of May 18, 1952, Rockefeller Diaries.

121. Ibid.

122. Entry of April 15, 1952, Fahs Diaries; International House of Japan, *Kokusai Bunka Kaikan 50-nen no ayumi, 1952–2002,* 10; entries of April 18 and May 16, 1952, Rockefeller Diaries.

123. Entry of May 18, 1952, Rockefeller Diaries.

124. "Proposal for a Cultural Center and Student International House"; Rockefeller to Barnard, December 26, 1951; Donald H. McLean Jr., Memorandum for Record, April 28, 1952, folder 462, box 51, series 1-OMR files, RG 5 (John D. Rockefeller III), Rockefeller Family Archives, RAC.

125. Entry of April 18, 1952, Fahs Diaries.

126. Charles B. Fahs to John D. Rockefeller III, August 29, 1951, folder 6, box 1, series 609, RG 1.2, Rockefeller Foundation Archives, RAC.

127. Entry of May 1, 1952, Fahs Diaries.

128. Dean Rusk (president), "Statement of the Rockefeller Foundation and the General Education Board to the Special Committee to Investigate Tax-Exempt Foundations," Eighty-third Cong., 2nd sess., August 3, 1954, 1065–1213.

129. McLean, Memorandum for Record, April 28, 1952.

130. Bradford, USPOLAD, Tokyo, to U.S. Department of State, "Rockefeller 'Centers.'"

131. Rockefeller to Barnard, December 26, 1951.

132. Entries of April 21 and 25, 1952, Rockefeller Diaries.

133. International House of Japan, *Kokusai Bunka Kaikan 50-nen no ayumi, 1952–2002,* 13; Matsumoto, *Shōwa-shi eno ichi shōgen,* 319.

134. Entry of April 30, 1952, Fahs Diaries.

135. AMEMBASSY, Tokyo, to U.S. Department of State, "International Cultural Center in Japan."

136. AMEMBASSY, Tokyo, to U.S. Department of State, "Proposal to the Board of Trustees of the Rockefeller Foundation," July 14, 1952, 511.94/7-1452, U.S. Department of State, NARA.

137. Ibid.
138. Ibid.
139. Bradford to Rockefeller, October 17, 1951.
140. AMEMBASSY, Tokyo, to U.S. Department of State, "Proposal to the Board of Trustees of the Rockefeller Foundation."
141. Ibid.
142. Memo by Charles B. Fahs, undated, folder 470, box 52, series 1-OMR files, RG 5 (John D. Rockefeller III), Rockefeller Family Archives, RAC.
143. AMEMBASSY, Tokyo, to U.S. Department of State, "International Cultural Center in Japan."
144. International House of Japan, *Kokusai Bunka Kaikan 50-nen no ayumi, 1952–2002,* 14–16; *Asahi,* November 19, 1952.
145. Olcott H. Deming to U.S. Department of State, October 14, 1952, 511.94/10-1452, U.S. Department of State, NARA.
146. International House of Japan, *Kokusai Bunka Kaikan 50-nen no ayumi, 1952–2002,* 12. For more information on the International House of Japan, see Matsumoto Shigeharu, *Waga kokoro no jijoden* [An autobiography of my mind] (Tokyo: Kodansha, 1992), 181–194.
147. Takagi Yasaka and Matsumoto Shigeharu to John D. Rockefeller III and Donald H. McLean Jr., July 23, 1952, folder 8, box 1, series 609, RG 1.2, Rockefeller Foundation Archives, RAC.
148. Matsumoto Shigeharu, *Waga kokoro no jijoden* [An autobiography of my mind] (Tokyo: Kōdan Sha, 1992), 190; Matsumoto, *Shōwa-shi eno ichi shōgen,* 322.
149. Entry of May 1, 1952, Fahs Diaries; Matsumoto, *Shōwa-shi eno ichi shōgen,* 321.
150. Remarks by U.S. Ambassador Robert D. Murphy at the opening of the fundraising campaign for the International House of Japan, November 19, 1952, folder 462, box 51, series 1-OMR files, RG 5 (John D. Rockefeller III), Rockefeller Family Archives, RAC.
151. The following were members of the board of the International House of Japan: Kabayama Aisuke, chair; Matsumoto Shigeharu, managing director; Gordon T. Bowles, associate managing director; Sterling W. Fisher; E. G. Griffith; Ichimada Hisato; Jōdai Tano; Kameyama Naoto; Koizumi Shinzō; Matsukata Yoshisaburō; Maeda Tamon; Nambara Shigeru; Shibusawa Keizō; and Takagi Yasaka. The comptrollers were James P. Duddy, Fujiyama Aiichirō, and Kano Hisaakira. International House, folder 465, box 51, series 1-OMR files, RG 5 (John D. Rockefeller III), Rockefeller Family Archives, RAC.
152. Resolved Rockefeller Foundation 62099, folder 6, box 1, series 609, RG 1.2, Rockefeller Foundation Archives, RAC.
153. *Nippon Times,* June 12, 1955. For further information on the origins and a variety of the activities of the International House of Japan, see International House of Japan, *Kokusai Bunka Kaikan 50-nen no ayumi, 1952–2002;* Igarashi Takeshi, "Sengo nichibei bunka kōryū keikaku no taidō" [Fermentation of postwar U.S.-Japan Cultural Exchange Program], in *Senryō to Nihon shūkyō* [The occupation and Japanese religion], ed. Ikado Fujio (Tokyo: Mirai Sha, 1993), 119–142; Fujita Fumiko, "'Nichibei chiteki kohryu keikaku'to senkyuhyaku goju nendai nichibei kankei" ['U.S.-Japan Intellectual Exchange Program' and U.S.-Japan relations of the 1950s], *American Studies* 5 (2000): 69–85.

154. Matsumoto, *Shōwa-shi eno ichi shōgen*, 325.
155. Ibid., 319.

6 The U.S. Cultural Offensive and Japanese Intellectuals

1. Quoted in Walter L. Hixton, *Parting the Curtain: Propaganda, Culture, and the Cold War, 1945–1961* (London: Macmillan, 1997), 5.
2. William Benton, "Statement," *Department of State Bulletin,* September 23, 1945, 430, as quoted in Howard R. Ludden, "The International Information Program of the United States: State Department Years, 1945–1953," Ph.D. diss., Princeton University, Princeton, N.J., 1966, 44.
3. As quoted in Warren M. Robbins (USIA), "Toward an American Global Cultural-Educational-Informational Program in the Framework of the Present World Scene," December 14, 1960, Bureau of Educational and Cultural Affairs Historical Collection, U.S. Department of State, Special Collections Section, University of Arkansas Libraries, Fayetteville.
4. Ibid.
5. As quoted in Hixton, *Parting the Curtain,* 5. Also see Rosemary O'Neil, "A Brief History of Department of State Involvement in International Exchange," fall 1972, Bureau of Educational and Cultural Affairs Historical Collection, U.S. Department of State, file 12, box 103, Special Collections Section, University of Arkansas Libraries, Fayetteville.
6. Melvyn P. Leffler, *A Preponderance of Power: National Security, the Truman Administration, and the Cold War* (Stanford, Calif.: Stanford University Press, 1992).
7. Alec Dubro and Matsui Michio, "Hajimete vçru wo nugu amerika tainichi sennō kōsaku no zenbō" [Panel-D Japan: The whole feature of American operations for brainwashing Japan, now revealed], *Views* (Kōdan Sha Publishing Co.) (November, December 1994; January, February, March, April, May 1995).
8. Earlier efforts had been made during the Woodrow Wilson administration, which had used propaganda and culture as weapons to "make the world safe for democracy." Actually, on April 13, 1917, the Committee on Public Information was set up with the appointment of American journalist George Creel as chair. Two decades later, as World War II loomed large, a Division of Cultural Relations was established in 1938. It had responsibility for promoting friendly understanding through cultural exchange that included education and arts and sciences. During the war years, the Office of War Information and the Coordinator of Inter-American Affairs were established to plan and conduct the dissemination of information. Elmer H. Davis, American writer and radio news commentator, was appointed head of OWI in 1942. Stephen L. Vaughn, *Holding Fast Inner Lines: Democracy, Nationalism and the Committee on Public Information* (Chapel Hill: University of North Carolina Press, 1980); James L. McCamy, *The Administration of American Foreign Affairs* (New York: Knopf, 1950), 51–52; William Barnes and John H. Morgan, *The Foreign Service of the United States: Origins, Development, and Functions,* Department of State Publication 7050, Department and Foreign Service Series 96, Historical Office, Bureau of Public Affairs, U.S. Department of State (Washington, D.C.: Government Printing Office, 1961), 288.
9. Ludden, "International Information Program of the United States," 91.

10. Niles W. Bond, USPOLAD, Tokyo, to U.S. Department of State, USIE Country Paper on Japan, August 16, 1951, 511.9421/8-1651, U.S. Department of State, National Archives and Records Administration, College Park, Md. (hereafter NARA).

11. Richard T. Arndt, "Beikoku no bunka kōhō gaikō—Kiwadoi baransu" [Cultural and informational diplomacy in the U.S.: The precarious balance], *Kokusai mondai* 338 (May 1988): 46; Ludden, "International Information Program of the United States."

12. U.S. Department of State, *Secretary's Seventh Semiannual Report*, 46, cited in Ludden, "International Information Program of the United States," 157.

13. Hixton, *Parting the Curtain*, 16; Dubro and Matsui, "Hajimete vçru wo nugu amerika tainichi sennō kōsaku no zenbō."

14. U.S. Department of State, *Secretary's Seventh Semiannual Report*, Table 1, 5, as cited in Ludden, "International Information Program of the United States," 162.

15. Robert S. Schwantes, *Japanese and Americans: A Century of Cultural Relations* (New York: Harper and Brothers, 1955), 313–314.

16. Saxton Bradford, USPOLAD, Tokyo to the Department of State, Desp. No. 370, September 7, 1951, 511.94/9-751, U.S. Department of State, NARA.

17. NSC 125/2, "United States Objectives and Courses of Action with Respect to Japan," August 7, 1952, *Papers Relating to Foreign Relations of the United States 1952–1954*, vol. 14, China and Japan, Part 2 (Washington, D.C.: Government Printing Office, 1985), 1306; Confidential memorandum, Notes on USIE Japan, March 3, 1951, U.S. State Department, 511.9421/3-351, NARA.

18. Saxton Bradford, AMEMBASSY, Tokyo, to U.S. Department of State, "Attitudes of Japanese Intellectuals towards the United States," June 4, 1952, 511.94/6-452, U.S. Department of State, NARA.

19. Earl R. Linch, AMCONSULATE, Nagoya, to AMEMBASSY, Tokyo, "Semiannual Evaluation Report," December 18, 1952, 511.94/12-852, U.S. Department of State, NARA.

20. Confidential memorandum, Notes on USIE Japan.

21. Barnes and Morgan, *Foreign Service of the United States*, 288. Similar functions for the occupied areas of Germany, Austria, Japan, and Korea were performed in coordination with the Office of the Assistant Secretary for Occupied Areas. Ludden, "International Information Program of the United States," 96.

22. This information was provided by Prof. Kon Madoko with the cooperation of Ms. Bungo Reiko. An American library operated abroad under the jurisdiction of the State Department was called an American information library, whereas a library run under the jurisdiction of the U.S. Army in occupied countries such as Germany, Austria, Japan, and Korea was called an information center. In Germany, however, the American information center had been called *Amerika Haus* since October 1947. As many as twenty-seven such centers were operating in Germany in 1951. Kon Madoko, "Amerika no jōhō kōryū to toshokan" [Interchange of information on America and library], *Kiyō Shakaigakka* (Chuō University) 4 (June 1994): 38.

23. Confidential memorandum, Notes on USIE Japan.

24. Bradford, AMEMBASSY, Tokyo, to U.S. Department of State, "Attitudes of Japanese Intellectuals towards the United States."

25. American Embassy, Tokyo, to U.S. Department of State, Memorandum of conversation between Professor Saitō of Tokyo University and Cultural Attaché Margaret H. Williams, May 5, 1953, 511.94/5-1153, U.S. Department of State, NARA.

26. Tokyo 1020 to U.S. Department of State, February 2, 1951, 794.00/2-251, U.S.

Department of State, NARA; Saxton Bradford, AMEMBASSY, Tokyo, to U.S. Department of State, "IIA: ICS: American Books in Japanese Translation, 1952," April 1, 1953, 511.9421/4013, U.S. Department of State, NARA.

27. Ibid.

28. Entry of June 19, 1951, John D. Rockefeller III Diaries, series 1-OMR files, record group (RG) 5 (John D. Rockefeller III), Rockefeller Family Archives (hereafter Rockefeller Diaries), Rockefeller Archive Center, Sleepy Hollow, N.Y. (hereafter RAC).

29. Tokyo 1020 to the Department of State, February 2, 1951.

30. Report to Ambassador John Foster Dulles, April 16, 1951, folder 446, box 49, series 1-OMR files, RG 5 (John D. Rockefeller III), Rockefeller Family Archives, RAC.

31. John K. Emmerson to Dean Rusk, confidential office memorandum, May 18, 1951, 794.00/5-1851, U.S. Department of State, NARA. For more information on Emmerson's thoughts, see John K. Emmerson, *The Japanese Dilemma: Arms, Yen and Power* (New York: Dunellen Publishing, 1971); and Emmerson, *The Japanese Thread: A Life in the U.S. Foreign Service* (New York: Holt, Rinehart and Winston, 1978).

32. "Japanese Peace Treaty Problems, Sixth Meeting, May 25, 1951," Council on Foreign Relations Study Group Report, Manuscript Division, Council on Foreign Relations, New York.

33. Ibid.

34. Entry of Otis Cary, undated, Rockefeller Diaries.

35. Kojima Tsunehisa, *Nihon shihonshugi ronsōshi* [A history of the debate over Japanese capitalism] (Tokyo: Ariesu Shobō, 1976), 1, 25–44.

36. James W. Morley, ed., *Dilemmas of Growth in Prewar Japan* (Princeton, N.J.: Princeton University Press, 1971), 12, 19.

37. Maruyama Masao, "Kindai Nihon no chishikijin" [Intellectuals of modern Japan], in *Kōei no ichi kara* [From the position of the rearguard] (Tokyo: Mirai Sha, 1982), 71–133.

38. Takauchi Toshikazu, *Gendai Nihon shihonshugi ronsō* [A debate over modern Japanese capitalism] (Tokyo: San-ichi Shobō, 1973); Kojima, *Nihon shihonshugi ronsōshi*.

39. Entry of Kagawa Toyohiko, undated, Rockefeller Diaries.

40. Entry of Hyūga Hōsai, undated, Rockefeller Diaries.

41. Entry of Tsuru Shigeto, undated, Rockefeller Diaries.

42. "Japan between East and West, Fourth Meeting, May 21, 1956," Council on Foreign Relations Discussion Meeting Report, Manuscript Division, Council on Foreign Relations, New York, 1–2.

43. Richard Hofstadter, *Anti-Intellectualism in American Life* (New York: Knopf, 1962), 24–25.

44. Present at the meeting were Ōhira Zengo, professor of international law, Hitotsubashi University; Amamiya Yōzō, chief of the Science Department, Yomiuri Press; Naoi Takeo, a *New Leader* correspondent; Hazama Shinjirō, an independent socialist; Fukuzawa Ichirō, an author and critic; Tsushima Tadayuki, a painter and author of a book on Soviet economics; Okura Asahi, an executive secretary of Japanese Committee for Cultural Freedom; Arahata Kanson, a socialist leader and former member of the Diet; and Kohori Junji, an independent socialist. *Yomiuri Shimbun*, January 16, 1952; Saxton Bradford, USPOLAD, Tokyo, to U.S. Department of State, January 18, 1952, 511.94/1-1852, U.S. Department of State, NARA.

45. Bradford, USPOLAD, Tokyo, to U.S. Department of State, January 18, 1952.

46. Niles W. Bond, USPOLAD, Tokyo, to U.S. Department of State, USIE Country Paper on Japan, August 16, 1951, 511.9421/8-1651, U.S. Department of State, NARA.
47. Bradford, AMEMBASSY, Tokyo, to U.S. Department of State, "Attitudes of Japanese Intellectuals towards the United States."
48. Ibid.
49. Saxton Bradford, AMEMBASSY, Tokyo, to U.S. Department of State, "Psychological Factors in Japan," February 28, 1952, 511.94/2-2852, U.S. Department of State, NARA.
50. Robbins (USIA), "Toward an American Global Cultural-Educational-Informational Program in the Framework of the Present World Scene."
51. Linch, AMCONSULATE, Nagoya, to AMEMBASSY, Tokyo, "Semi-annual Evaluation Report."
52. Confidential—Security Information. USIE Country Plan—Japan, Priority III, December 4, 1951, 511.94/12-451, U.S. Department of State, NARA.
53. Civil Information and Education Section, General Headquarters, Supreme Commander for the Allied Powers, *Mission and Accomplishments of the Occupation in the Civil Information and Education Fields,* January 1, 1950, folder 444, box 49, series 1-OMR files, RG 5 (John D. Rockefeller III), Rockefeller Family Archives, RAC, 10; "Japan Between East and West, Fourth Meeting, May 21, 1956"; Council on Foreign Relations Study Group on American Cultural Relations with Japan, "The Exchange of Cultural Materials," Working Paper No. 5, prepared by Robert S. Schwantes, April 22, 1953, folder 42, box 6, collection III 2Q, RAC.
54. Satō Tadao, "Wareware ni totte amerika towa nanika" [What does America mean to us?] *Shisō no kagaku* 68 (November 1967): 4.
55. Bradford, AMEMBASSY, Tokyo, to U.S. Department of State, "Attitudes of Japanese Intellectuals towards the United States"; Arthur Thompson, "The Development of American Studies in Japan," *American Studies* 5 (July 1960): 2.
56. Fukuda Sadayoshi, "Hanbei shisō" [Anti-American thought], *Bungei shunjū* (September 1953): 77.
57. Saxton Bradford, AMEMBASSY, Tokyo, to U.S. Department of State, "American Books in Translation, 1952," April 1, 1952, 511.9421/4-153, U.S. Department of State, NARA.
58. See the entry "The Hepburn Chair" in *Nichibei bunka kōryū jiten* [A dictionary of Japan-U.S. cultural interchange], ed. Kamei Shunsuke (Tokyo: Nan-undō, 1988), 222–223.
59. Fukuda, "Hanbei shisō," 76; Enclosure: Memorandum to John D. Rockefeller III from Saxton Bradford, October 17, 1951, in Charles N. Spinks, USPOLAD, Tokyo, Desp. No. 630, October 22, 1951, 511.94/10-2251, U.S. Department of State, NARA.
60. Hirano Takashi, "Nihon no daigaku niokeru Amerika Kenkyū kankei no kyōiku jōkyō" [The state of offering American Studies courses at Japanese universities], *Bulletin of the Center for American Studies of the University of Tokyo* 1 (1978): 21.
61. Fukuda, "Hanbei shisō," 77.
62. George Stoddard's education mission to Japan in March 1946 lasted less than a month (see Chapter 1), while Maurice Valency's stay in Japan in the summer of 1958 to research how the humanities were being taught in Japan lasted two months. In his report, Valency acknowledged that his observations were "simply a series of impressions on the part of a sympathetic and informed observer who had an opportunity to speak at

length with some dozens of Japanese." Maurice Valency, "Some Observations on the Teaching of the Humanities in Japan, A Preliminary Report Submitted to the Ford Foundation, July 1, 1959," folder 430, box 48, series 1-OMR files, RG 5 (John D. Rockefeller III), Rockefeller Family Archives, RAC.

63. Edwin O. Reischauer, "The Broken Dialogue with Japan," *Foreign Affairs* 39, no. 1 (1960): 11–26; Edwin O. Reischauer to J. Graham Parsons, assistant secretary of state, November 8, 1960, 611.94/11-860, US-J 00079, Japan and the United States: Diplomatic, Security and Economic Relations, 1960–1976, National Security Archive, Gelman Library, George Washington University, Washington, D.C.

64. Memorandum from Round Table Conference on Christian Culture and Peace, submitted to John Foster Dulles, April 19, 1951.

65. Ibid.

66. Ibid.

67. "American Cultural Relations with Japan, Sixth Meeting, June 3, 1953," Council on Foreign Relations Study Group Report, folder 42, box 6, collection III 2Q, Rockefeller Foundation Archives, RAC.

68. Bradford, AMEMBASSY, Tokyo, to U.S. Department of State, "Attitudes of Japanese Intellectuals towards the United States."

69. Ibid.

70. Ibid.

71. Tokyo 1275 to U.S. Department of State, March 15, 1951, 794.00/3-1551, U.S. Department of State, NARA.

72. Saxton Bradford to Niles W. Bond, Top Secret Memorandum on Draft Psychological Strategy Plan for the Pro-U.S. Orientation of Japan, July 28, 1952, 511.94/7-2852, U.S. Department of State, NARA.

73. Tsurumi Shunsuke, "Nihon chishikijin no Amerika zō" [Japanese intellectuals' images of America], *Chūō kōron* (July 1956): 170–178.

74. Bradford to Bond, Top Secret Memorandum on Draft Psychological Strategy Plan.

75. Robert D. Murphy to Secretary of State, confidential security information, September 5, 1952, 511.94/9-552, U.S. Department of State, NARA.

76. Bradford, AMEMBASSY, Tokyo, to U.S. Department of State, "Attitudes of Japanese Intellectuals towards the United States."

77. Bradford to Bond, Top Secret Memorandum on Draft Psychological Strategy Plan.

78. Ibid.

79. Interview: entry of Matsumoto Shigeharu, November 4, 1954, folder 868, box 100, series 200, RG 1.2, Rockefeller Foundation Archives, RAC.

80. "Seminars in American Studies in Japan, 1950, Report of the Stanford Professors: Joseph S. Davis, Claude A. Buss, John D. Goheen, George H. Knoles, and James T. Watkins," folder 5, box 1, series 205, RG 1.2, Rockefeller Foundation Archives, RAC (hereafter "Report of the Stanford Professors").

81. Entry of March 2, 1951, Charles B. Fahs Diaries, series 12.1 diaries, Rockefeller Foundation Archives, RAC (hereafter Fahs Diaries).

82. "American Cultural Relations with Japan, Sixth Meeting, June 3, 1953," Council on Foreign Relations Study Group Report, folder 42, box 6, collection III 2Q, Rockefeller Foundation Archives, RAC.

83. "Report of the Stanford Professors."

84. Howard S. Ellis, Department of Economics, Stanford University, to Joseph H.

Willits, director for the Social Sciences, Rockefeller Foundation, September 2, 1951, folder 6, box 12, series 205, RG 1.2, Rockefeller Foundation Archives, RAC.

85. Bradford, AMEMBASSY, Tokyo, to U.S. Department of States, "Attitudes of Japanese Intellectuals towards the United States."
86. Thompson, "Development of American Studies in Japan," 2.
87. Ellis to Willits, September 2, 1951.
88. Entry of May 7, 1950, Fahs Diaries.
89. Bradford, AMEMBASSY, Tokyo, to the Department of State, "Psychological Factors in Japan."
90. Bond, USPOLAD, Tokyo, to U.S. Department of State, USIE Country Paper on Japan.
91. Bradford, AMEMBASSY, Tokyo, to U.S. Department of State, "IIA: ICS: American Books in Japanese Translation, 1952."
92. Ibid.
93. Bradford, AMEMBASSY, Tokyo, to U.S. Department of States, "Attitudes of Japanese Intellectuals towards the United States."
94. John W. Dower, "E. H. Norman, Japan and the Uses of History," in *Origins of the Modern Japanese State: Selected Writings of E. H. Norman* (New York: Random House, 1975), 1.
95. Ibid., 6.
96. Matsumoto Shigeharu to Charles B. Fahs, August 26, 1954, folder 12, box 2, series 609, RG 1.2, Rockefeller Foundation Archives, RAC.
97. Ibid.
98. Matsumoto Shigeharu to Charles B. Fahs, August 10, 1954, folder 12, box 2, series 609, RG 1.2, Rockefeller Foundation Archives, RAC.
99. Entry of April 7, 1952, Fahs Diaries. Careful readers may recognize that these cutting remarks on Japanese historiography by Japanese liberals such as Matsumoto and Sakanishi set the stage for the Shōwashi ronsō (Shōwa history debate) in the 1950s. *Shōwashi,* a short history of Shōwa Japan, was written in 1955 by three scholars of Japanese modern history: Tōyama Shigeki, Imai Seiichi, and Fujiwara Akira. An article written by Kamei Katsuichirō, a literary critic, triggered the famous debate over the writing of the modern history of Japan. This concise history of the Shōwa period, 1926–1988, captivated many historians, political scientists, philosophers, and critics, no matter their ideological persuasion, from 1955 and beyond.
100. Entry of Paul Langer, undated, Rockefeller Diaries.
101. Dower, "E. H. Norman, Japan and the Uses of History," especially the section "Politics of Scholarship: Norman and His Successors," 31–65.
102. "Humanities Program and Related Foundation Interests in History, 1950–1960," prepared by Charles B. Fahs, November 16, 1960, pp. 6–7, file 18, box 3, series 911, RG3, Rockefeller Foundation Archives, RAC.
103. Ibid.
104. Ibid.
105. Entry of April 26, 1953, Charles B. Fahs Diaries, Box 18, Record Group 12.1, Rockefeller Foundation Archives, Rockefeller Archive Center, Sleepy Hollow, N.Y.
106. Tokyo University Center for American Studies (Tokyo Daigaku Amerika Kenkyū Shiryō Sentā), ed., *Ueno Naozō sensei ni kiku* [Interview with Professor Ueno Naozō], vol. 10 of *American Studies in Japan: Oral History Series* (Tokyo: Tokyo University Center for American Studies, 1980), 28.
107. Entry of April 26, 1953, Charles B. Fahs Diaries.

108. Dean Rusk (president), "Statement of the Rockefeller Foundation and the General Education Board to the Special Committee to Investigate Tax-Exempt Foundations," Eighty-third Cong., 2nd sess., August 3, 1954, 1070.
109. "Humanities Program and Related Foundation Interests in History, 1950–1960," prepared by Charles B. Fahs.
110. Ibid.
111. Benjamin I. Schwarts, "Presidential Address: Area Studies as a Critical Discipline," *Journal of Asian Studies* 60 (November 1980): 15.
112. William N. Fenton, *Area Studies in American Universities* (Washington, D.C.: American Council on Education, 1947), 82.
113. Ibid., 22.
114. Robert Hall, *Area Studies: With Special Reference to Their Implications for Research in the Social Sciences* (New York: Committee on World Area Research Program, Social Science Research Council, 1948); Miyoshi Masao and Harry D. Harootunian, eds., *Learning Places: The Afterlives of Area Studies* (Durham, N.C.: Duke University Press, 2002); "Discussion on 'Chiiki kenkyū no arikata' " ["How area studies should be pursued"], *American Review* 6 (1972): 52–78; Tokyo University Center for American Studies, *Matsumoto Shigeharu sensei ni kiku* [Interview with Professor Matsumoto Shigeharu], vol. 9 of *American Studies in Japan: Oral History Series*. (Tokyo: Tokyo University Center for American Studies, 1980), 54–55.
115. Bruce Cummings, "Boundary Displacement: The State, the Foundations, Area Studies during and after the Cold War," in *Learning Places: The Afterlives of Area Studies,* ed. Miyoshi Masao and Harry D. Harootunian, (Durham, N.C.: Duke University Press, 2002), 264.
116. Harry D. Harootunian, "Postcoloniality's Unconscious/Area Studies' Desire," in *Learning Places: The Afterlives of Area Studies,* ed. Miyoshi Masao and Harry D. Harootunian, (Durham, N.C.: Duke University Press, 2002), 155.
117. Miyoshi and Harootunian, *Learning Places,* 268.
118. "The Program in the Humanities: A Statement by Fahs," undated. folder 33, box 4, series 911, RG 3.1, Rockefeller Foundation Archives, RAC; Robert Gordon Sproul, president of University of California, to Chester J. Barnard, president of Rockefeller Foundation, July 12, 1950, folder 5, box 1, series 911, RG 3, Rockefeller Foundation Archives, RAC.
119. Cummings, "Boundary Displacement," 261.
120. Harootunian, "Postcoloniality's Unconscious/Area Studies' Desire," 156.
121. Stanley J. Heginbotham, "Shifting the Focus of International Programs," *Chronicle of Higher Education,* October 19, 1994, A68.

7   Making Japanese Pro-American: The 1950 American Studies Seminar in Tokyo

1. Tokyo University Center for American Studies (Tokyo Daigaku Amerika Kenkyū Shiryō Sentā), ed., *Nakaya Ken-ichi sensei ni kiku* [Interview with Professor Nakaya Ken-ichi], vol. 4 of *American Studies in Japan: Oral History Series* (Tokyo: Tokyo University Center for American Studies, 1978), 13; Tokyo University Center for American Studies, ed., *Matsumoto Shigeharu sensei ni kiku* [Interview with Professor

Matsumoto Shigeharu], vol. 9 of *American Studies in Japan: Oral History Series* (Tokyo: Tokyo University Center for American Studies, 1980), 40.

2. Takagi Yasaka, "Opening Remarks at the Conference of the Stanford Visiting Professors with Members of Society of Science and Thought and America Institute," July 24, 1950, Tokyo University–Stanford University American Studies Seminars file, Takagi Bunko, Amerika Taiheiyō Chiiki Kenkyū Sentā (Center for America–Pacific Area Studies), University of Tokyo, Tokyo (hereafter Takagi Bunko).

3. Saxton Bradford, AMEMBASSY, Tokyo, to U.S. Department of State, "Attitudes of Japanese Intellectuals towards the United States," June 4, 1952, 511.94/6-452, U.S. Department of State, National Archives and Records Administration, Washington, D.C. (hereafter NARA); Bradford, AMEMBASSY, Tokyo, Desp. No. 1343, "Semi-annual Evaluation Report," January 23, 1953, 511.94/1-2353, U.S. Department of State, NARA.

4. Aruga Tadashi, "Japanese Scholarship and the Meaning of American History," *Journal of American History* 79, no. 2 (1992): 504–514; David Thelen, "Of Audiences, Borderlands, and Comparisons: Toward the Internationalization of American History," *Journal of American History* 79, no. 2 (1992): 434.

5. Matsuda Takeshi, "American Studies: History," *International Encyclopedia of the Social and Behavioral Sciences* (Oxford: Elsevier, 2004).

6. "Prospectus for Establishing the Amerika Gakkai, 1946," undated, Amerika Gakkai file, Takagi Bunko.

7. "Amerika Gakkai seturitsu keika" [The progress of the establishment of the Amerika Gakkai], undated, Amerika Gakkai file, Takagi Bunko.

8. Tokyo University Center for American Studies, ed., *Shimuzu Hiroshi sensei ni kiku* [Interview with Professor Shimuzu Hiroshi], vol. 1 of *American Studies in Japan: Oral History Series* (Tokyo: Tokyo University Center for American Studies, 1977), 1, 2.

9. "Amerika Gakkai seturitsu keika."

10. Institute for American Studies of Rikkyō University to Supreme Commander of the American Force and Staff, September 18, 1946, Amerika Gakkai file, Takagi Bunko.

11. Tokyo University Center for American Studies, *Matsumoto Shigeharu sensei ni kiku*, 41–42.

12. Tokyo University Center for American Studies, *Shimizu Hiroshi sensei ni kiku*. Five reports say that Amerika Gakkai was organized in March 1947. According to "Amerika Gakkai seturitsu keika," Amerika Gakkai was formed in April 1947.

13. Entry of February 26, 1951, Charles B. Fahs Diaries, series 12.1 diaries, (hereafter Fahs Diaries), Rockefeller Foundation Archives, Rockefeller Archive Center, Sleepy Hollow, N.Y. (hereafter RAC).

14. Tokyo University Center for American Studies, *Nakaya Ken-ichi sensei ni kiku,* 16.

15. Entry of June 7, 1947, Fahs Diaries.

16. Tokyo University Center for American Studies, *Matsumoto Shigeharu sensei ni kiku*, 36.

17. Entry of June 7, 1947, Fahs Diaries.

18. Ibid. Also see Chapter 1 on CI&E censorship.

19. Entries of July 3, 1947, June 9, 1948, May 4, 1950, and February 26, 1951, Fahs Diaries.

20. Tokyo University Center for American Studies, *Matsumoto Shigeharu sensei ni kiku*, 45.

21. Tokyo University Center for American Studies, *Shimizu Hiroshi sensei ni kiku,* 8.

22. Entry of February 26, 1951, Fahs Diaries.

23. Stanford University–Tokyo University, Resolved Rockefeller Foundation 50141, December 5, 1950, folder 4, box 1, series 205, record group (RG) 1.2, Rockefeller Foundation Archives, RAC.

24. By that time, the Rockefeller Foundation had already provided some assistance for Chinese Studies at the University of Tokyo. Interview, Claude A. Buss by Charles B. Fahs, November 10, 1949, folder 4, box 1, series 205, RG 1.2, Rockefeller Foundation Archives, RAC; entry of Hugh Borton, August 6, 1951, Fahs Diaries.

25. Entry of April 28, 1950, Fahs Diaries.

26. Excerpt from interview, J. E. Wallace Sterling by Charles B. Fahs, December 5, 1949, folder 4, box 1, series 205, RG 1.2, Rockefeller Foundation Archives, RAC.

27. Rockefeller Foundation, *Annual Report 1951* (New York: Rockefeller Foundation, 1952), 81–82.

28. Claude A. Buss to Charles B. Fahs, November 4, 1949, folder 4, box 1, series 205, RG 1.2, Rockefeller Foundation Archives, RAC.

29. Ibid.

30. Claude A. Buss to Charles B. Fahs, February 6, 1950, folder 4, box 1, series 205, Rockefeller Foundation Archives, RAC.

31. Address at reception opening the American Studies Seminar by President Nambara Shigeru, July 15, 1950, Tokyo University–Stanford University American Studies Seminars file, Takagi Bunko; Notoji Masako, "The University of Tokyo–Stanford University American Studies Seminar," in *Survey of American Studies in Japan: Development of American Studies Seminars* (Tokyo: International House of Japan, 1998), 21.

32. Claude A. Buss to Raymond Fosdick, Rockefeller Foundation, November 30, 1949, folder 4, box 1, series 205, RG 1.2, Rockefeller Foundation Archives, RAC.

33. Buss to Fahs, November 4, 1949; February 6, 1950.

34. Interview, Sterling by Fahs, December 5, 1949.

35. Buss to Fosdick, November 30, 1949.

36. Interview, Buss by Fahs, November 10, 1949.

37. Claude A. Buss to Takagi Yasaka, December 1, 1949, Stanford University File, Takagi Bunko.

38. "Part VI: The Discussion Meeting of February 6, 1997," in *Survey of American Studies in Japan: Development of American Studies Seminars* (Tokyo: International House of Japan, 1998), 93.

39. Katō Takashi, *Nambara Shigeru: Kindai Nihon to chishikijin.* [Nambara Shigeru: Modern Japan and intellectuals] (Tokyo: Iwanami Shoten, 1997).

40. "Revitalizing the Social Sciences," *Nippon Times,* October 12, 1948; "Report of the United States Cultural Science Mission to Japan," January 1949, Civil Information and Education Section, Supreme Commander for the Allied Powers, p. 10, folder 444, box 49, RG 5 (John D. Rockefeller III), Rockefeller Family Archives, RAC.

41. John L. Stegmaier to John M. Allison and U. Alexis Johnson, Memorandum on Study Group on Japanese-American Cultural Relations, January 19, 1953, 511.94/1-1953, U.S. Department of State, NARA.

42. Entry of June 16 1948, Fahs Diaries.

43. Matsumoto Shigeharu to Charles B. Fahs, August 10, 1954, folder 12, box 2, series 609, RG 1.2, Rockefeller Foundation Archives, RAC.

44. Entry of December 14 1949, Fahs Diaries. "Experimental studies in political science" refers to political economic experiments and behavioral studies that aim to find out why human behavior and political economic outcomes deviate significantly from expectations of rational choice theories.
45. "Report of the United States Cultural Science Mission to Japan," 6.
46. Katō, *Nambara Shigeru,* 164.
47. Entry of December 14, 1949, Fahs Diaries.
48. Katō, *Nambara Shigeru,* 162.
49. Entry of December 14, 1949, Fahs Diaries.
50. Ibid.
51. Tokyo University Center for American Studies, ed., *Saitō Makoto sensei ni kiku* [Interview with Professor Saitō Makoto], vol. 28 of *American Studies in Japan: Oral History Series* (Tokyo: Tokyo University Center for American Studies, 1991), 31.
52. Tokyo University Center for American Studies, *Matsumoto Shigeharu sensei ni kiku,* 50.
53. Memorandum: Conversation of Nambara Shigeru, Ichihashi Yamato, Dr. Kawai, George Kerr, and Claude Buss, January 4, 1950, folder 4, box 1, series 205, RG 1.2, Rockefeller Foundation Archives, RAC.
54. Buss to Fahs, February 6, 1950.
55. Ibid.
56. Claude A. Buss to Charles B. Fahs, February 21, 1950, folder 4, box 1, series 205, RG 1.2, Rockefeller Foundation Archives, RAC.
57. Entry of April 27, 1950, Fahs Diaries.
58. Charles B. Fahs to Claude A. Buss, January 19, 1950, folder 4, box 1, series 205, RG 1.2, Rockefeller Foundation Archives, RAC.
59. Excerpt from entry of April 27, 1950, Fahs Diaries.
60. Entry of February 23, 1951, Fahs Diaries.
61. Other professors attending the meeting were Takagi Yasaka; Yanaihara Tadao, professor of economics and dean of the Faculty of General Education; Kishimoto Hideo, professor of the history of religion and head of the Institute of Oriental Studies; and Oka Yoshitake, professor of political history. Entry of April 28, 1950, Fahs Diaries.
62. Claude A. Buss to Charles B. Fahs, July 10, 1950, folder 4, box 1, series 205, RG 1.2, Rockefeller Foundation Archives, RAC.
63. Ibid.
64. Kishimoto and six other professors constituted ECSAS: Kaji Shinzō, Hashiba Shōichi, Maeda Yōichi, Konno Genpachirō, Nakaya Ken-ichi, and Saitō Makoto. Kaji Motoo, "Tokyo Daigaku–Sutanfōdo Daigaku Amerika Kenkyū Seminā to Nihon niokeru Amerika Kenkyū [The Tokyo University–Stanford University American Studies Seminar and American Studies in Japan]," *Bulletin of the Center for American Studies of the University of Tokyo,* vol. 4 (Tokyo: Tokyo University Center for American Studies, 1981), 4; "Proposal to the Rockefeller Foundation Concerning the Seminar in American Studies in Japan," folder 6, box 1, series 205, RG 1.2, Rockefeller Foundation Archives, RAC.
65. Notoji, "University of Tokyo–Stanford University American Studies Seminar," 20–21.
66. Interview, Sterling by Fahs, December 5, 1949; Buss to Fahs, February 6, 1950; Tokyo University, Resolved Rockefeller Foundation 50099, September 22, 1950, folder 4, box 1, series 205, RG 1.2, Rockefeller Foundation Archives, RAC; Nambara Shigeru

to Charles B. Fahs, September 12, 1950, folder 4, box 1, series 205, RG 1.2, Rockefeller Foundation Archives, RAC.

67. Notoji, "University of Tokyo–Stanford University American Studies Seminar," 20.

68. Address at reception opening the American Studies Seminar by President Nambara Shigeru, July 15, 1950.

69. Nambara Shigeru to Charles B. Fahs, July 26, 1950, folder 4, box 1, series 205, RG 1.2, Rockefeller Foundation Archives, RAC.

70. Ibid.; address at reception opening the American Studies Seminar by President Nambara Shigeru, July 15, 1950.

71. Personal data of Stanford professors, 1950, Tokyo University–Stanford University American Studies Seminars file, Takagi Bunko.

72. *Asahi Shimbun,* July 11, 1950, 4.

73. Memorandum report for President J. E. Wallace Sterling prepared by Claude A. Buss, August 23, 1950, folder 5, box 1, series 205, RG 1.2, Rockefeller Foundation Archives, RAC.

74. "Seminars in American Studies in Japan, 1950, Report of the Stanford Professors: Joseph S. Davis, Claude A. Buss, John D. Goheen, George H. Knoles, and James T. Watkins," October 16, 1950, folder 5, box 1, series 205, RG 1.2, Rockefeller Foundation Archives, RAC (hereafter "Report of the Stanford Professors").

75. "Report of the Stanford Professors."

76. Buss to Fahs, July 10, 1950.

77. The following topics were covered by the seminars: *American Social and Cultural History:* Basic Forces Shaping American History; Major Patterns in U.S. Social and Cultural History; Nationalism and Sectionalism in U.S. History; Immigration and the Development of an American Type; Emergence of Social Classes in America; Role of the Cities; Christian Reactions to Urbanism and Industrialism; Impact of Modern Science on Religious Thought; Changing Methods and Objectives in the Social Sciences; American Historiography; Recent Educational Thought and Practice; Emergence of American Art; Literary Cross Currents in 20th Century America; American Political Theory; *Philosophy:* Historical Influences in Contemporary Philosophy; The Classical Tradition; The British Empiricists and Kant; Hegel and Marx; Contemporary Philosophic Schools in the United States; The Pragmatism of James and Dewey; Dewey's Influence on Education and Social Theory; Idealism of Royce and Whitehead; Materialism; Positivism and the Philosophy of Language; *The United States and International Organization:* Political Studies in the United States; International Relations in the United States; U.S. Policy and International Organization; U.S. Planning for Post-War Organization; The San Francisco Conference and the Charter of the United Nations; U.S. Policies in the U.N.; Constitutional Development of the Charter; U.S. Security and the U.N.; Regional Arrangements; Social and Economic Policies in the U.N.; Dependent Areas; UNESCO; Public Opinion and the U.N.; International Integration; *Diplomatic History of the United States:* Diplomatic Factor in American History; America's Traditional Policies; Mechanism for the Conduct of Foreign Relations; Public Opinion: The Man on the Street; The Present Position of the U.S. in World Affairs; Settling the Peace—After World War II; Quest for Security; Policies Seeking Improvement of Human Welfare; The Cold War: American-Russian Relations; Our Problems in Europe; America's Position in the Near and Middle East; The U.S. in Southeast Asia; America's Policies in China; The U.S. and Japan; *Economics:* Standards of Living: Basic Concepts;

Standards of Living: Indicators and Indexes; International Disparities in Levels of Consumption and Living; Population, Resources and Productivity; Production and Consumption; Purchasing Power in Theory and Practice; Demand in Recent Economic Thought; Income, Consumption and Employment; Secular Stagnation? Mature Economy?; Agricultural Developments and Policies; Business Cycle Problems and Policies; International Trade and the ITO Charter; International Commodity Agreements; Point Four Programs and Possibilities. Memorandum report for President Sterling prepared by Buss, August 23, 1950.

78. The number of participants reported varied. For example, Nambara recorded that 119 students attended the regular three-week seminar, whereas Buss documented that it was about 125. Kaji Motoo reported that the number was 128. Nambara to Fahs, July 26, 1950, September 12, 1950; Memorandum report for President Sterling prepared by Buss, August 23, 1950; Kaji, "Tokyo Daigaku–Sutanfōdo DaigakuAmerika Kenkyū Seminā to Nihon niokeru Amerika Kenkyū," 4.

79. They included Professors Takagi Yasaka, Maeda Yōichi, Tsuru Shigeto, Ohara Keiji, Sakanishi Shiho, and Tsurumi Kazuko. Memorandum report for President Sterling prepared by Buss, August 23, 1950; Kaji, "Tokyo Daigaku–Sutanfōdo Daigaku Amerika Kenkyū Seminā to Nihon niokeru Amerika Kenkyū," 5.

80. Ibid.

81. Kaji, "Tokyo Daigaku–Sutanfōdo Daigaku Amerika Kenkyū Seminā to Nihon niokeru Amerika Kenkyū," 4–5.

82. Memorandum report for President Sterling prepared by Buss, August 23, 1950.

83. For the roster of participants in the 1950 American Studies Seminar, see "Amerika kenkyū seminā sankasha meibo" [The list of participants in American Studies Seminar], Tokyo University–Stanford University American Studies Seminars file, Takagi Bunko.

84. Buss to Fahs, July 10, 1950.

85. Nambara to Fahs, September 12, 1950.

86. Memorandum report for President Sterling prepared by Buss, August 23, 1950.

87. "Report of the Stanford Professors."

88. Memorandum report for President Sterling prepared by Buss, August 23, 1950.

89. Claude A. Buss to Dean Rusk, July 18, 1950, 511.94/7-1850, U.S. Department of State, NARA.

90. Dean Rusk to Claude A. Buss, July 31, 1950, 511.94/7-1850, U.S. Department of State, NARA.

91. Interviews with J. E. Wallace Sterling, October 30, 1950, folder 5, box 1, series 205, RG 1.2, Rockefeller Foundation Archives, RAC.

92. Nambara to Fahs, September 12, 1950.

93. Gakkō Hōjin Dōshisha, Gendaigo de Yomu Neesima Joe Henshū Inkai, ed., *Gendaigo de yomu Neesima Joe* [Neesima Joe for today's readers] (Kyoto: Maruzen, 2000).

94. The following scholars attended the meeting: Ōtsuka Setsuji (president), Okamoto Harumi, and Matsui Shichirō of Dōshisha University; and Toyosaki Minoru, Hara Zuien, Abe Osamu, and Yokoyama Shumpū of Kyoto University. " Report of the Stanford Professors."

95. Ibid.

96. Nambara to Fahs, September 12, 1950.

97. Ibid.

98. Ibid.

99. Nambara to Fahs, July 26, 1950.

100. Nambara Shigeru to Charles B. Fahs, October 25, 1950, folder 5, box 1, series 205, RG 1.2, Rockefeller Foundation Archives, RAC.

101. "Report of the Stanford Professors."

102. Memorandum report for President J Sterling prepared by Buss, August 23, 1950.

103. Stanford University–Tokyo University, Resolved Rockefeller Foundation 51211, December 4–5, 1951, folder 4, box 1, series 205, RG 1.2, Rockefeller Foundation Archives, RAC.

104. Interviews with Sterling, October 30, 1950.

105. Ibid.; "Proposal to the Rockefeller Foundation concerning the Seminar in American Studies in Japan," December 26, 1951.

106. Stanford University–Tokyo University, Resolved Rockefeller Foundation 50141, December 5, 1950.

107. Interviews with John Goheen, September 17, 1951, folder 6, box 1, series 205, RG 1.2, Rockefeller Foundation Archives, RAC.

108. Entries of February 24, 1951, and May 2, 1952, Fahs Diaries; interviews, Stanford University professors by Charles B. Fahs, April 13, 1951, folder 6, box 1, series 205, RG 1.2, Rockefeller Foundation Archives, RAC.

109. Interviews, Stanford University professors by Fahs, April 13, 1951.

110. Roger F. Evans (Rockefeller Foundation) to Joint Seminar in American Studies Kyoto Area Steering Committee chair professor Ariga Tetsutarō of Kyoto University and American Studies Seminar Tokyo University Steering Committee cochairs professors Kishimoto Hideo and Kaji Shinzō, February 10, 1952, folder 866, box 99, series 200, RG 1.2, Rockefeller Foundation Archives, RAC.

111. Memorandum from Institute for Educational Leadership to General Headquarters, March 1954, folder 445, box 49, series 1-OMR files, RG 5 (John D. Rockefeller III), Rockefeller Family Archives, RAC. The Institute for Educational Leadership was under the joint sponsorship of the Japanese Ministry of Education and the Education Division of SCAP's CI&E Section.

112. Ibid.

113. Ibid.

114. Ibid.

115. Takemae Eiji, *The Allied Occupation of Japan* (New York: Continuum, 2002), 366.

116. Sengo Daigaku-shi Kenkyūkai (Association for Postwar History Studies in University), Ōsaki Hitoshi, Tōyama Atsuko, Bandō Kumiko, Tokiwa Yutaka, Uesugi Michiyo, Yamashita Tomio et al., *Sengo daigaku-shi* [A postwar history of university] (Tokyo: Daiichi Hōki Suppan Kabushiki Kaisha, 1985), 139, 144, 200.

117. "Japan between East and West, Fifth Meeting, May 23, 1956," Council on Foreign Relations Discussion Meeting Report, Manuscript Division, Council on Foreign Relations, New York, 4.

118. Sengo Daigakushi Kenkyūkai, Ōsaki et al., *Sengo daigaku-shi,* 139, 144, 200.

119. Takemae, *Allied Occupation of Japan,* 366.

120. Entry of April 14, 1956, Charles B. Fahs Diaries, Box 18, Record Group 12.1, Rockefeller Foundation Archives, Rockefeller Archive Center, Sleepy Hollow. N.Y.

121. Entry of April 29, 1956, Charles B. Fahs Diaries.

Notes to Pages 182–185　　　317

122. Ibid.
123. Aleksei P. Kislenko, "Nihon kyoiku-seido no konponteki kaikaku nitsuite" [On the fundamental reform of the Japanese educational system], in *Soren wa Nihon ni Naniwo Nozomu ka* [What the Soviet Union expects from Japan], ed. Kuzma. N. Derevyanko (Soviet representative of the Allied Council of Japan) et al.; trans. Nisso Shinzen kyōkai (Tokyo: Ōdosha, 1949), 105; memo from Institute for Educational Leadership to General Headquarters, March 1954.
124. Takemae, *Allied Occupation of Japan*, 371.
125. Herbert Passin, "The Occupation—Some Reflections," in *Nichibei no Shōwa* [Shōwa—Japan and America] (Tokyo: TBS Britannica, 1990), 101.
126. Nambara to Fahs, October 25, 1950.
127. The following were members of the Tokyo and Stanford committees: *Tokyo University:* Nambara Shigeru (honorary chair), Kishimoto Hideo (chair), Hashiba Masaichi, Konno Genpachirō, Maeda Gorō, Miyazawa Toshiyoshi, Nakaya Ken-ichi, Nishikawa Masami, Takagi Teiji, Tsuji Naoshirō, Ugai Nobushige, Uno Kozō, Yamada Moritarō, Yanaihara Tadao; advisers: Matsumoto Shigeharu, Nakano Yoshio, Takagi Yasaka; *Stanford University:* J. E. Wallace Sterling (honorary chair), John D. Goheen (chair), Claude A. Buss, Joseph S. Davis, Harold Fisher, Kazuo Kawai, George Kerr, George H. Knoles, James T. Watkins. "Proposal to the Rockefeller Foundation concerning the Seminar in American Studies in Japan," December 26, 1951.
128. Ibid.
129. Memorandum report for President Sterling prepared by Buss, August 23, 1950.
130. "Proposal to the Rockefeller Foundation concerning the Seminar in American Studies in Japan," December 26, 1951.
131. Ibid.
132. Memorandum report for President J Sterling prepared by Buss, August 23, 1950.
133. Entry of February 24, 1951, Fahs Diaries.
134. Donald R. Nugent to Charles B. Fahs, October 16, 1951, folder 5, box 1, series 205, RG 1.2, Rockefeller Foundation Archives, RAC.
135. Dean Rusk (president), "Statement of the Rockefeller Foundation and the General Education Board to the Special Committee to Investigate Tax-Exempt Foundations," Eighty-third Cong., 2nd sess., August 3, 1954, 1077.
136. "Proposal to the Rockefeller Foundation concerning the Seminar in American Studies in Japan," December 26, 1951.
137. Entry of February 24, 1951, Fahs Diaries.
138. Entry of April 11, 1958. Charles B. Fahs Diaries, Box 18, Record Group 12.1, Rockefeller Foundation Archives, Rockefeller Archive Center. Sleepy Hollow, N.Y.
139. Entry of April 21, 1958, Charles B. Fahs Diaries.

8　The Kyoto American Studies Seminar and American Soft Power

1. Merrill Jensen, "Kyoto Amerika Kenkyū Kaki Seminā to hito to shisō no kokusi kōryū" [Kyoto American Studies Summer Seminar and international interchange of people and thought], *Dōshisha American Studies* (Center for American Studies, Dōshisha

University) 7 (March 1972): 21; Sasaki Takashi, "Kyoto Amerika Kenkyū Kaki Seminā" [The Kyoto American Studies Summer Seminar], in *Sengo Nihon no "Amerika Kenkyu Seminā" no ayumi* [Survey of American Studies in Japan: Development of "American Studies Seminars"], ed. International House of Japan Inc. (Tokyo: International House of Japan, 1998), 54.

2. This brief seminar had eight sessions at which five subjects were offered: political science (specifically conduct of foreign policy, taught by Royden J. Dangerfield, professor of political science and director of the Institute of Government and Public Affairs at the University of Illinois), economics (specifically stagnation theory and the American economy, taught by Howard S. Ellis, professor of economics at the University of California), American literature (taught by Leon Howard, professor of American literature at University of California), philosophy (specifically contemporary American philosophy, taught by John D. Goheen, professor of philosophy at Stanford University), and American history (taught by George H. Knoles, professor of American history at Stanford University). One hundred and six Japanese scholars on America participated in the 1951 Kyoto seminar. "American Cultural Relations with Japan, Third Meeting, February 27, 1953," Council on Foreign Relations Discussion Meeting Report, Manuscript Division, Council on Foreign Relations, New York, 2, 3; Matsuyama Nobunao, "Kyoto Amerika Kenkyū Kaki Seminā" [Kyoto American Studies Summer Seminar], *Bulletin of the Center for American Studies of the University of Tokyo* 1 (1978): 27.

3. Kyoto University Social Sciences and American Studies, Resolved Rockefeller Foundation 58100, May 23, 1958, folder 34, box 5, series 609, record group (RG) 1.2, Rockefeller Foundation Archives, Rockefeller Archive Center, Sleepy Hollow, N.Y. (hereafter RAC); Kyoto University: American Studies, October 15, 1960, folder 37, box 5, series 609, RG 1.2, Rockefeller Foundation Archives, RAC.

4. Torigai Risaburō and Ōtsuka Setsuji to Charles B. Fahs, August 24, 1951, folder 866, box 99, series 200, RG 1.2, Rockefeller Foundation Archives, RAC.

5. John D. Goheen to Charles B. Fahs, October 4, 1951, folder 866, box 99, series 200, RG 1.2, Rockefeller Foundation Archives, RAC.

6. John D. Goheen to Edward F. D' Arms, October 12, 1951, folder 866, box 99, series 200, RG 1.2, Rockefeller Foundation Archives, RAC.

7. Interview, John D. Goheen by Charles B. Fahs, September 17, 1951, folder 6, box 1, series 205, RG 1.2, Rockefeller Foundation Archives, RAC.

8. Goheen to Fahs, October 4, 1951.

9. Donald R. Nugent to Charles B. Fahs, October 11, 1951, folder 866, box 99, series 200, RG 1.2, Rockefeller Foundation Archives, RAC.

10. Ibid.

11. Kyoto University and Dōshisha University, University of Illinois, Resolved Rockefeller Foundation 53129, September 25, 1953, folder 866, box 99, series 200, RG 1.2, Rockefeller Foundation Archives, RAC.

12. Edward F. D' Arms to John D. Goheen, October 5, 1951, folder 866, box 99, series 200, RG 1.2, Rockefeller Foundation Archives, RAC.

13. Ibid.; interview, Goheen by Fahs, September 17, 1951; Nugent to Fahs, October 11, 1951.

14. John D. Goheen to John Marshall, associate director, Humanities Division, Rockefeller Foundation, October 24, 1951, folder 866, box 99, series 200, RG 1.2, Rockefeller Foundation Archives, RAC.

15. Roger F. Evans, interoffice correspondence on Kyoto Seminars in American Studies, December 31, 1951, folder 866, box 99, series 200, RG 1.2, Rockefeller Foundation Archives, RAC.
16. John D. Goheen to Charles B. Fahs, December 20, 1951, folder 866, box 99, series 200, RG 1.2, Rockefeller Foundation Archives, RAC.
17. Interview, Royden J. Dangerfield by Roger F. Evans and Charles B. Fahs, January 10, 1952, folder 866, box 99, series 200, RG 1.2, Rockefeller Foundation Archives, RAC.
18. Goheen to Fahs, October 4, 1951.
19. Goheen to Fahs, December 20, 1951.
20. Goheen to D'Arms, October 12, 1951.
21. Roger F. Evans to Charles B. Fahs, December 31, 1951, folder 866, box 99, series 200, RG 1.2, Rockefeller Foundation Archives, RAC (emphasis in original).
22. Roger F. Evans to Joseph H. Willits, January 3, 1952, folder 866, box 99, series 200, RG 1.2, Rockefeller Foundation Archives, RAC.
23. University of Illinois, Kyoto University, and Dōshisha University, Resolved Rockefeller Foundation 52015, January 18, 1952, folder 866, box 99, series 200, RG 1.2, Rockefeller Foundation Archives, RAC.
24. Ibid.; George D. Stoddard to Charles B. Fahs, February 12, 1952, folder 866, box 99, series 200, RG 1.2, Rockefeller Foundation Archives, RAC. To place the amounts of Rockefeller Foundation grants in perspective, in 1952 the annual tuition and fees for a student at Tokyo University was 6,000 yen (about $17), and in 1953 a Japanese professor's monthly salary was 14,000 yen (about $40). Shūkan Asashi, ed., *Sengo nedan shi Nenpyō* [A chronological history of commodity prices in postwar Japan] (Tokyo: Asahi Shimbun Sha, 1995), 153.
25. Interview, Dangerfield by Evans and Fahs, January 10, 1952.
26. Evans to Willits, January 3, 1952.
27. John D. Goheen to Charles B. Fahs, February 15, 1952, folder 7, box 1, series 205, RG 1.2, Rockefeller Foundation Archives, RAC.
28. Ibid.
29. The following demonstrates how little Americans' perceptions of the Japanese have changed over time. In 1919 American banker G. K. Weeks, vice president of the National City Company, was negotiating with Japanese bankers over the terms and conditions of Japan's entry into the New Chinese Consortium. Weeks said, "I look upon the Japanese as I would upon a small boy who possessed the same extraordinary energy and ambition which they possess." G. K. Weeks to C. E. Mitchell, president of the National City Company, November 1, 1919, in Thomas Lamont to Breckenridge Long, December 18, 1919, 893.51/2590, U.S. Department of State, National Archives and Records Administration, Washington, D.C. (hereafter NARA), quoted in Matsuda Takeshi, "Woodrow Wilson's Dollar Diplomacy in the Far East: The New Chinese Consortium, 1917–1921," Ph.D. diss., University of Wisconsin, 1979, 297.
30. Goheen to Fahs, February 15, 1952.
31. Interview, Royden J. Dangerfield by Roger F. Evans and Charles B. Fahs, January 10, 1952, folder 866, box 99, series 200, RG 1.2, Rockefeller Foundation Archives, RAC.
32. Roger F. Evans to Joint Seminar in American Studies Kyoto Area Steering Committee chair professor Ariga Tetsutarō of Kyoto University and American Studies Seminar Tokyo University Steering Committee cochairs professor Kishimoto Hideo and

professor Kaji Shinzō, February 10, 1952, folder 866, box 99, series 200, RG 1.2, Rockefeller Foundation Archives, RAC.

33. Excerpt from Goheen to Fahs, February 15, 1952.

34. Charles B. Fahs to Roger F. Evans, February 14, 1952, folder 866, box 99, series 200, RG 1.2, Rockefeller Foundation Archives, RAC.

35. Roger F. Evans to Charles B. Fahs, February 17, 1952, folder 866, box 99, series 200, RG 1.2, Rockefeller Foundation Archives, RAC.

36. Entries of April 23, 1952, and April 17, 1953, Charles B. Fahs Diaries, series 12.1 diaries, Rockefeller Foundation Archives, RAC (hereafter Fahs Diaries).

37. Rockefeller Foundation, *Annual Report 1955* (New York: Rockefeller Foundation, 1956), 150–151.

38. Entries of April 23, 1952, and April 17, 1953, Fahs Diaries.

39. Entries of April 24, 1952, and April 17, 1953, Fahs Diaries.

40. Rockefeller Foundation, *Annual Report 1952* (New York: Rockefeller Foundation, 1953), 273–274.

41. They were William O. Stanley, associate professor of the philosophy of education at the University of Illinois who taught "philosophy of education in America"; Clarence H. Graham, professor of psychology at Columbia University, who lectured on experimental psychology; John T. Flanagan, professor of American literature at the University of Illinois, who lectured on contemporary American literature; Joseph J. Spengler, professor of economics at Duke University, who taught "industrial relations in America"; and Royden J. Dangerfield, professor of political science at the University of Illinois, who lectured on political parties and public opinion in America. Kyoto University and Dōshisha University, University of Illinois, Resolved Rockefeller Foundation 53129, September 25, 1953.

42. Interview, Royden J. Dangerfield by Roger F. Evans and Charles B. Fahs, October 7, 1952, Illinois-Kyoto American Studies Seminar, folder 866, box 99, series 200, RG 1.2, Rockefeller Foundation Archives, RAC.

43. Royden J. Dangerfield to Ariga Tetsutarō, April 4, 1952, folder 866, box 99, series 200, RG 1.2, Rockefeller Foundation Archives, RAC; Rockefeller Foundation, *Annual Report 1952*, 273–274; ibid.

44. Interview, Dangerfield by Evans and Fahs, October 7, 1952.

45. Royden J. Dangerfield to Charles B. Fahs, February 24, 1953, folder 867, box 99, series 200, RG 1.2, Rockefeller Foundation Archives, RAC.

46. Interview, Dangerfield by Evans and Fahs, October 7, 1952.

47. Dangerfield to Fahs, February 24, 1953.

48. Ibid.

49. Charles B. Fahs to Royden J. Dangerfield, February 26, 1953, folder 867, box 99, series 200, RG 1.2, Rockefeller Foundation Archives, RAC.

50. Sterling T. Takeuchi to Charles B. Fahs, March 29, 1953, folder 867, box 99, series 200, RG 1.2, Rockefeller Foundation Archives, RAC.

51. Dangerfield to Fahs, February 24, 1953.

52. Ibid.

53. Interview, George Stoddard by Charles B. Fahs and Flora M. Rhind, February 15, 1952, folder 6, box 1, series 205, RG 1.2, Rockefeller Foundation Archives, RAC.

54. Interview, Royden J. Dangerfield by Roger F. Evans, August 16, 1954, folder 868, box 100, series 200, RG 1.2, Rockefeller Foundation Archives, RAC.

55. Royden J. Dangerfield to Charles B. Fahs, March 9, 1953, folder 867, box 99, series 200, RG 1.2, Rockefeller Foundation Archives, RAC.

56. Ibid.
57. Takeuchi to Fahs, March 29, 1953.
58. Entry of April 14, 1953, Fahs Diaries.
59. Entry of April 17, 1953, Fahs Diaries.
60. Entries of April 16 and April 17, 1953, Fahs Diaries.
61. Matsui Shichirō to Charles B. Fahs and Tabata Shinobu, president of Dōshisha University, and Hattori Shunjirō, president of Kyoto University, to Charles B. Fahs, August 1, 1953, folder 867, box 99, series 200, RG 1.2, Rockefeller Foundation Archives, RAC.
62. John Marshall to Charles B. Fahs, August 14, 1953, folder 867, box 99, series 200, RG 1.2, Rockefeller Foundation Archives, RAC.
63. Charles B. Fahs to John D. Goheen, June 25, 1953, folder 8, box 2, series 205, RG 1.2, Rockefeller Foundation Archives, RAC.
64. Marshall to Fahs, August 14, 1953.
65. Matsui to Fahs, and Tabata and Hattori to Fahs, August 1, 1953.
66. Kyoto University and Dōshisha University, University of Illinois, Resolved Rockefeller Foundation 53129, September 25, 1953.
67. The professors and the courses they taught were as follows: Charles M. Allen, "Current Movement in American Educational Practice"; Stanley E. Ballinger, professor of education at Indiana State University, "Current Controversies in American Educational Theory"; Rodney L. Mott, "Courts and American Constitutional Law"; Matsui Shichirō, professor of economics at Dōshisha University, "Labor Movements and Industrial Relations in the United States"; Miyagawa Tetsuo, professor of economics of Boston University, "Contributions of Industrial Sociology"; Kodera Takeshirō, professor of economics at Kwansei Gakuin University, "Monetary Theory in the United States"; Aoyama Hideo, professor of economics at Kyoto University, "Theory of Economic Dynamics: Past and Present"; Ichimura Shin-ichi, professor of economics at Wakayama University, "Recent Topics in Economic Theory"; R. A. Jelliffe, professor of American literature at Kobe College, "On the Poetry of Edwin Arlington Robinson"; Burton E. Martin, professor of American literature at Tōhoku University, "On Robert Frost's Poetry"; Robert H. Grant, professor of American literature at Dōshisha University, "On Theodore Dreiser"; and Lindley W. Hubbell, professor of American literature at Dōshisha University, "Contemporary Tendencies in American Dramas. International House of Japan Inc., *Sengo Nihon no "Amerika Kenkyu Seminā" no ayumi;* Kyoto American Studies Summer Seminars, undated, folder 869, box 100, series 200, RG 1.2, Rockefeller Foundation Archives, RAC.
68. Roger F. Evans on Kyoto American Studies Seminar, September 16, 1954, folder 868, box 100, series 200, RG 1.2, Rockefeller Foundation Archives, RAC.
69. Kyoto University and Dōshisha University, University of Michigan, Resolved Rockefeller Foundation 54146, October 29, 1954, folder 866, box 99, series 200, RG 1.2, Rockefeller Foundation Archives, RAC.
70. Evans on Kyoto American Studies Seminar, September 16, 1954.
71. Rodney L. Mott to Charles B. Fahs, September 27, 1954, folder 868, box 100, series 200, RG 1.2, Rockefeller Foundation Archives, RAC.
72. Ibid.
73. Kyoto University and Dōshisha University, University of Michigan, Resolved Rockefeller Foundation 54146, October 29, 1954.
74. Marvin L. Niehuss to Charles B. Fahs, October 8, 1954, folder 868, box 100, series 200, RG 1.2, Rockefeller Foundation Archives, RAC.

75. Ueno Naozō to Charles B. Fahs, October 9, 1954, folder 868, box 100, series 200, RG 1.2, Rockefeller Foundation Archives, RAC.

76. Professors and the subjects of their seminars were as follows: Fritz Machlup, "Problems of Competition and Monopoly" and "Problems of International Trade Theory"; Virgil C. Aldrich, "Theories of Cognition and Valuation, Traditional and Linguistic"; Gordon W. Hewes, professor of anthropology at the University of Colorado, "Recent Trends in American Anthropology"; Emilio A. Lanier, professor of American literature at Fisk University, "The Genteel Tradition in American Literature"; Kathryn Mulholland, professor of American literature at Brooklyn College, "Dramatic Reading of Contemporary American Drama and Poetry"; Robert H. Grant, professor of education at Dōshisha University, "Tests and Measurements"; Roy E. Wanger, professor of American literature at Kent State University, "Improving the Curriculum through Audiovisual Materials"; Mavis Mann, professor of law and political science at West Virginia University, "State and Local Government"; Takahashi Teizō, professor of law and political science at Dōshisha University, "Comparative Government"; and Sugai Shūichi, professor of law and political science at Kyoto University, "Principles of American Administrative Law." Kyoto American Studies Summer Seminars, undated; International House of Japan Inc., *Sengo Nihon no "Amerika Kenkyu Seminā" no ayumi.*

77. Ōshimo Kakuichi and Takikawa Yukitoki to Charles B. Fahs, May 24, 1955, folder 869, box 100, series 200, RG 1.2, Rockefeller Foundation Archives, RAC.

78. Kyoto University and Dōshisha University, University of Michigan, Resolved Rockefeller Foundation 55104 and 55105, June 24, 1955, folder 866, box 99, series 200, RG 1.2, Rockefeller Foundation Archives, RAC.

79. Evans on Kyoto American Studies Seminar, September 16, 1954.

80. Entry of April 25, 1956, Charles B. Fahs Diaries, Box 18, Record Group 12.1, Rockefeller Foundation Archives, Rockefeller Archive Center, Sleepy Hollow, N.Y.

81. Evans on Kyoto American Studies Seminar, September 16, 1954.

82. Ōshimo and Takikawa to Fahs, May 24, 1955.

83. Entry of May 30, 1955, Fahs Diaries.

84. Tokyo University Center for American Studies (Tokyo Daigaku Amerika Kenkyū Shiryō Sentā), ed., *Ueno Naozō sensei ni kiku* [Interview with Professor Ueno Naozō], vol. 10 of *American Studies in Japan: Oral History Series* (Tokyo: Tokyo University Center for American Studies, 1980), 24.

85. Interview, Prof. Rodney L. Mott, Colgate University, regarding Kyoto American Studies Seminar, April 6, 1956, folder 870, box 100, series 200, RG 1.2, Rockefeller Foundation Archives, RAC.

86. Virgil C. Aldrich to Charles B. Fahs, February 27, 1956, folder 870, box 100, series 200, RG 1.2, Rockefeller Foundation Archives, RAC.

87. Ibid.

88. Interview, Tasugi Kiso by Charles B. Fahs and Roger F. Evans, January 25, 28, 1957, folder 34, box 5, series 609, RG 1.2, Rockefeller Foundation Archives, RAC.

89. Evans on Kyoto American Studies Seminar, September 16, 1954.

90. Aldrich to Fahs, February 27, 1956.

91. Fahs to Evans, February 14, 1952.

92. Charles B. Fahs to Virgil C. Aldrich, March 9, 1956, folder 870, box 100, series 200, RG 1.2, Rockefeller Foundation Archives, RAC.

93. Ibid.

94. Interview, Prof. John Hall, University of Michigan, March 26, 1957, folder 871, box 100, series 200, RG 1.2, Rockefeller Foundation Archives, RAC.

95. The following representatives attended the meeting: Takikawa Yukitoshi, president of Kyoto University; Nakanishi Nobutarō, professor of English literature, replacing Dean Yoshikawa, Faculty of Letters; Kōsaka Masaaki, dean, Faculty of Education; Tasugi Kiso, professor of economics; and Iwamura Shinobu, professor of Chinese and Near East history and archaeology-anthropology, Research Institute for Humanistic Sciences. Charles B. Fahs, Kyoto University American Studies, October 9, 1957, folder 34, box 5, series 609, RG 1.2, Rockefeller Foundation Archives, RAC.

96. Dōshisha University–American Studies and Social Sciences, Resolved Rockefeller Foundation 58099, May 23, 1958, folder 1, box 1, series 200, RG 1.2, Rockefeller Foundation Archives, RAC.

97. Wendell H. Bash to Roger F. Evans, April 4, 1958, folder 35, box 5, series 609, RG 1.2, Rockefeller Foundation Archives, RAC.

98. Ibid.

99. This author also felt the same way.

100. Tokyo University Center for American Studies, *Ueno Naozō sensei ni kiku,* 25–26.

101. Ōshimo Kakuichi to Charles B. Fahs, February 21, 1958, folder 1, box 1, series 609, RG 1.2, Rockefeller Foundation Archives, RAC.

102. Ibid.

103. Dōshisha University–American Studies and Social Sciences, Resolved Rockefeller Foundation 58099, May 23, 1958.

104. Roger F. Evans to Wendell H. Bash, April 21, 1958, folder 35, box 5, series 609, RG 1.2, Rockefeller Foundation Archives, RAC.

105. Charles B. Fahs to Ōshimo Kakuichi, January 30, 1958, folder 35, box 5, series 609, RG 1.2, series 609, RG 1.2, Rockefeller Foundation Archives, RAC.

106. Dōshisha University–American Studies and Social Sciences, Resolved Rockefeller Foundation 58099, May 23, 1958.

107. Ibid.

108. Ōshimo Shōichi, "Dōshisha daigaku akerika kenkyūsho" [Dōshisha University Center for American Studies], *Bulletin of the Center for American Studies of the University of Tokyo* 1 (1978): 33.

109. Kyoto American Studies Seminar's Summer Sessions, June 1, 1959, folder 1, box 1, series 609, RG 1.2, Rockefeller Foundation Archives, RAC.

110. Sasaki, "Kyoto Amerika Kenkyu Kaki Seminā," 61; Matsuyama, "Kyoto Amerika Kenkyū Kaki Seminā," 28.

111. Otis Cary to Charles B. Fahs, April 23, 1959, folder 1, box 1, series 609, RG 1.2, Rockefeller Foundation Archives, RAC.

112. Japanese newspapers reported that Cary died in Oakland, California, on April 14, 2006. *Asahi shimbun,* April 16, 2006; *Sankei shimbun,* April 18, 2006.

113. Kyoto American Studies Seminar's Summer Sessions, June 1, 1959.

114. Julian H. Steward to Charles B. Fahs, August 21, 1956, folder 870, box 100, series 200, RG 1.2, Rockefeller Foundation Archives, RAC.

115. Wendell H. Bash to Roger F. Evans, March 6, 1958, folder 35, box 5, series 609, RG 1.2, Rockefeller Foundation Archives, RAC.

116. Iwamura Shinobu to Charles B. Fahs, September 26, 1957, folder 34, box 5, series 609, RG 1.2, Rockefeller Foundation Archives, RAC.

117. Tokyo University Center for American Studies, *Matsui Shichirō sensei ni kiku* [Interview with Professor Matsui Shichirō], vol. 8 of *American Studies in Japan: Oral History Series* (Tokyo: Tokyo University Center for American Studies, 1980), 29.

118. Ōmori Wataru, Shinkawa Kenzaburō, Yui Daizaburō, and Endō Yasuo, eds., *Tokyo Daigaku Amerika Kenkyū Shiryō Sentā 30 nen no ayumi* [The first 30 years of the Tokyo University Center for American Studies] (Tokyo: Tokyo Daigaku Amerika Kenkyū Shiryō Sentā, 1997), 8.

119. The chairs were established in eight national universities—Osaka, Shizuoka, Fukushima, Ehime, Okayama, Yamaguchi, Chiba, and Kagwa Agricultural College—and in three private universities—Seijō, Fukuoka Women's, and Meiji Gakuin. In addition, twenty seminar participants were lecturing in American history (new courses) in twenty different universities. Interview, Prof. Kishimoto Hideo by Roger F. Evans, January 28, 1957, folder 12, box 2, series 205, RG 1.2, Rockefeller Foundation Archives, RAC.

120. Entry of April 26, 1956, Charles B. Fahs Diaries, Box 18, Record Group 12.1, Rockefeller Foundation Archives, RAC.

121. Ibid.

122. The Center of American Studies was formally founded on the Komaba campus of Tokyo University in 1965.

123. See Tokyo University, American Studies, in Rockefeller Foundation, *Annual Report 1957* (New York: Rockefeller Foundation, 1958), 228.

124. Hirano Takashi, "Nihon no daigaku niokeru Amerika Kenkyū kankei no kyōiku jōkyō" [The state of offering American Studies courses at Japanese universities], *Bulletin of the Center for American Studies of the University of Tokyo* 1 (1978): 21–26.

125. "Seminars in American Studies in Japan, 1950, Report of the Stanford Professors: Joseph S. Davis, Claude A. Buss, John D. Goheen, George H. Knoles, and James T. Watkins," October 16, 1950, folder 5, box 1, series 205, RG 1.2, Rockefeller Foundation Archives, RAC.

126. Fahs, Kyoto University American Studies, October 9, 1957.

127. Iwamura Shinobu to Roger F. Evans, May 6, 1958, folder 35, box 5, series 609, RG 1.2, Rockefeller Foundation Archives, RAC.

128. Iwamura to Fahs, September 26, 1957.

129. Fahs, Kyoto University American Studies, October 9, 1957.

130. Joseph S. Nye Jr., *Soft Power: The Means to Success in World Politics* (New York: Public Affairs, 2004); Nye, *The Paradox of American Power: Why the World's Only Super Power Can't Go It Alone* (New York: Oxford University Press, 2002); Nye, *Bound to Lead: The Changing Nature of American Power* (New York: Basic Books, 1990).

131. Nye, *Soft Power,* 2, 5; Nye, *Paradox of American Power,* 8–12.

132. Nye, *Paradox of American Power,* 9.

133. Entry of April 23, 1953, Fahs Diaries; Robert S. Schwantes, *Japanese and Americans: A Century of Cultural Relations* (New York: Harper and Brothers, 1955), 270–271.

134. Maurice Valency, "Some Observations on the Teaching of the Humanities in Japan, A Preliminary Report Submitted to the Ford Foundation, July 1, 1959," folder 430, box 48, series 1-OMR files, RG 5 (John D. Rockefeller III), Rockefeller Family Archives, RAC.

135. Report of the United States Cultural Science Mission to Japan, January 1949, Supreme Commander for the Allied Powers, Civil Information and Education Section,

p. 36, folder 444, box 49, RG 5 (John D. Rockefeller III), Rockefeller Foundation Archives, RAC.

136. Valency, "Some Observations on the Teaching of the Humanities in Japan," 6.

137. Takemae Eiji, *The Allied Occupation of Japan* (New York: Continuum, 2002), 366.

138. "American Cultural Relations with Japan, Third Meeting, February 27, 1953," 2, 3.

139. See Soma Hewa and Philo Hove, eds., *Philanthropy and Cultural Context: Western Philanthropy in South, East, and Southeast Asia in the 20th Century* (New York: University Press of America, 1997); Robert F. Arnove, ed., *Philanthropy and Cultural Imperialism: The Foundations at Home and Abroad* (Boston: G. K. Hall, 1980); Warren Weaver, *U.S. Philanthropic Foundations* (New York: Harper and Row, 1967); Volker Berghahn, "Philanthropy and Diplomacy in the 'American Century,'" *Diplomatic History* 23, no. 3 (1999): 393–419.

140. Dean Rusk (president), "Statement of the Rockefeller Foundation and the General Education Board to the Special Committee to Investigate Tax-Exempt Foundations," Eighty-third Cong., 2nd sess., August 3, 1954, 1065–1213.

141. Valency, "Some Observations on the Teaching of the Humanities in Japan," 15.

142. Ibid.

9 Occupation Reform, "Shallow Democracy," and Consumerism

1. The Council on Foreign Relations moved to its present home, the former Harold Pratt mansion at 58 East 68th Street and Park Avenue in New York City in 1945, but its basic mechanism has changed little over the years. It continues to publish its journal, *Foreign Affairs,* upholding the principles that it will not support any one cause no matter how worthwhile, that it will tolerate "wide differences of opinion," and that its articles will present no "consensus of beliefs." The magazine claims it can "do more to guide American public opinion by a broad hospitality to divergent ideas." Elisabeth Jakab, "The Council on Foreign Relations," *Book Forum* 3, no. 4 (1978): 444, cited by Leonard Silk and Mark Silk, *The American Establishment* (New York: Basic Books, 1980), 187–189, 193, 201.

2. Silk and Silk, *American Establishment,* 184. For further information on the Council on Foreign Relations, see Laurence H. Shoup and William Minter, *Imperial Brain Trust: The Council on Foreign Relations and United States Foreign Policy* (New York: Monthly Review Press, 1977), 14–15; Iokibe Makoto, *Beikoku no Nihon senryō seisaku* [The American policy of the occupation of Japan], vol. 1 (Tokyo: Chūō Kōron Sha, 1985), 13–19.

3. Silk and Silk, *American Establishment.* 223.

4. Ibid., 187–188.

5. Ibid.

6. The study group consisted of the following: John M. Allison, U.S. Mission to the United Nations; Martin Toscan Bennett, consulting engineer; Arthur H. Dean, Sullivan and Cromwell; Wallace B. Donham; Eugene H. Dooman, McKay's Overseas Company; William H. Draper Jr., Dillon, Read; John Foster Dulles, U.S. representative to the

United Nations; Herbert Feis, Policy Planning Staff, U.S. Department of State; Abijah U. Fox, American Thread Company; Joseph C. Grew, former ambassador to Japan; William R. Herod, International General Electric Company; William L. Holland, Institute of Pacific Relations; Charles L. Kades, Hawkins, Dalafield and Wood; August Maffry, Irving Trust Company; J. Morden Murphy, Bankers Trust Company; John E. Orchard, School of Business, Columbia University; Edwin O. Reischauer, Harvard University; Elihu Root Jr., Root, Ballantine, Harlan, Bushby and Palmer; Charles E. Saltzman, Henry Sears and Company; Francis B. Sayre, U.S. Mission to the United Nations (United Nations Trusteeship Council); Lewis L. Strauss, Rockefeller Brothers Inc.; Charles P. Taft, Headley, Taft and Headley; and Henry P. Van Dusen, Union Theological Seminary. Council on Foreign Relations Study Group on Japanese Peace Treaty Problems, 1950–1951, Council on Foreign Relations Archives, New York.

7. The study group comprised the following: Joseph W. Ballantine, Brookings Institution; Hugh Borton, Columbia University; W. Phillips Davison, Rand Corporation; Arthur H. Dean, Sullivan and Cromwell; Frederick S. Dunn, Princeton University; Russell Durgin, Japan International Christian University Foundation; Charles B. Fahs, Rockefeller Foundation; Harold G. Henderson, Columbia University; Kenneth Holland, Institute of Pacific Relations; Alpheus Jessup, Carnegie Newspaper Fellow; Kenneth S. Latourette, Yale University; Donald McLean Jr., Rockefeller Brothers Inc.; J. Morden Murphy, Bankers Trust Company; Douglas Overton, Japan Society Inc.; Carleton Sprague Smith, New York Public Library; John L. Stegmaier, U.S. Department of State; Shephard Stone, Ford Foundation; and Melville H. Walker, National Foreign Trade Council. Council on Foreign Relations Study Group on American Cultural Relations with Japan, 1952–1953, Council on Foreign Relations Archives, New York.

8. For a discussion of the definition of *democracy,* see Raymond Williams, *Keywords: A Vocabulary of Culture and Society,* rev. ed. (New York: Oxford University Press, 1983), 93–98.

9. Ōtsuka Hisao, "Jiyū to dokuritsu" [Freedom and independence], in *Ōtsuka Hisao chosaku shū* [Ōtsuka Hisao collected works], vol. 8 (Tokyo: Iwanami Shoten, 1969), 176–186.

10. Kuno Osamu, a Japanese activist philosopher, argues that citizens living under democracy have two faces. At times, "voluntary citizens" think and act in the way described in the text. At other times, "passive citizens" choose to live in peace and comfort as long as these values are guaranteed. Kuno Osamu, "Shimin-shugi no seiritsu" [The establishment of citizen-ism], *Shisō no kagaku* (July 1980).

11. Robert S. Schwantes, *Japanese and Americans: A Century of Cultural Relations* (New York: Harper and Brothers, 1955), 331.

12. Warren M. Robbins (USIA), "Toward an American Global Cultural-Educational-Informational Program in the Framework of the Present World Scene," December 14, 1960, Bureau of Educational and Cultural Affairs Historical Collection, U.S. Department of State, Special Collections Section, University of Arkansas Libraries, Fayetteville.

13. Address given by Archibald MacLeish, assistant secretary of state, before the annual meeting of the Association of American Colleges, Atlantic City, N.J., January 10, 1945, Bureau of Educational and Cultural Affairs Historical Collection, U.S. Department of State, manuscript number 468, Special Collections Section, University of Arkansas Libraries, Fayetteville.

14. Robert S. Schwantes, Memorandum for the Committee on Studies, undated, Council on Foreign Relations Library, Council on Foreign Relations, New York;

Schwantes to John D. Rockefeller III, January 23, 1955, folder 42, box 6, collection III 2Q, Foreign Policy, Index # 187.1, Council on Foreign Relations, JDRIII, American Cultural Relations with Japan, 1952–1956, Rockefeller Archive Center, Sleepy Hollow, N.Y. (hereafter RAC).

15. "Japan between East and West, Fifth Meeting, May 23, 1956," Council on Foreign Relations Discussion Meeting Report, Manuscript Division, Council on Foreign Relations, New York, 2. Also see Ōkurashō Zaisei Shi Shitsu, ed., *Amerika no tainici senryō seisaku* [American occupation policy of Japan], vol. 3 of *Shōwa Zaisei-shi* [A history of Shōwa Japan's finances] (Tokyo: Tōyō Keizai Shinpō Sha, 1976).

16. "Japan between East and West, Fifth Meeting, May 23, 1956," 2.

17. Hidaka Rokurō, "Sengo no 'kindaishugi'" [Postwar_gmodernism"], in *Kindaishugi* [Modernism], vol. 34 of *Gendai Nihon shisō taikei* [Outline of modern Japanese thoughts], ed. Hidaka Rokurō (Tokyo: Chikuma Shobō, 1964), 37.

18. John W. Dower, *Embracing Defeat: Japan in the Wake of World War II* (New York: Norton, 1999), 217.

19. "Japan between East and West, Fifth Meeting, May 23, 1956," 1–2.

20. P. G. Osborn, *A Concise Law Dictionary*, 5th ed. (London: Sweet and Maxwell, 1964), 163.

21. "Japan between East and West, Fifth Meeting, May 23, 1956," 1–2.

22. Conlon Associates Ltd., *United States Foreign Policy: Asia*, study prepared at the request of the Committee on Foreign Relations, U.S. Senate, November 1, 1959 (Washington, D.C.: Government Printing Office, 1959), 98 (hereafter Conlon report).

23. Ibid.

24. Dean Rusk to Thomas L. Hughes, September 18, 1963, US-J 00270, Japan and the United States: Diplomatic, Security and Economic Relations, 1960–1976, National Security Archive, Gelman Library, George Washington University, Washington, D.C. (hereafter National Security Archive).

25. Conlon report, 97–98.

26. "Japan between East and West, Fifth Meeting, May 23, 1956."

27. Ike Nobutaka, *Beginning of Political Democracy in Japan* (New York: Greenwood Press, 1969), 53–59, quoted in *The Japan Reader 1: Imperial Japan, 1800–1945*, ed. Jon Livingston, Joe Moore, and Felicia Oldfather (New York: Pantheon Books, 1973), 179.

28. "Japan between East and West, Fifth Meeting, May 23, 1956."

29. Ibid.

30. Ibid.

31. Entry of May 11, 1950, Charles B. Fahs Diaries, series 12.1 diaries, Rockefeller Foundation Archives, RAC (hereafter Fahs Diaries).

32. Dower, *Embracing Defeat*, 218.

33. Ibid., 219.

34. This author is indebted to the historian Dower for his insight on and analysis of American Japan specialists. For more information and analysis of American liberals and progressives on Japan, see Chapter 6, "The Experts and the Obedient Herd," in Dower, *Embracing Defeat*, 217–224.

35. Earl R. Linch, AMCONSULATE, Nagoya, to AMEMBASSY, Tokyo, "Semi-annual Evaluation Report," December 18, 1952, 511.94/12-852, U.S. Department of State, National Archives and Records Administration, College Park, Md. (hereafter NARA).

36. J. Graham Parsons to David M. Bane, "United States Policy toward Japan," Secret Memorandum, July 1, 1960, U.S. Department of State, US-J 00060, Japan and the United States: Diplomatic, Security and Economic Relations, 1960–1976, National Security Archive; "Guidelines of U.S. Policy toward Japan," Secret Policy Paper, May 3, 1961, U.S. Department of State, US-J 00098, Japan and the United States: Diplomatic, Security and Economic Relations, 1960–1976, National Security Archive.

37. Niles W. Bond, USPOLAD, Tokyo, to U.S. Department of State, USIE Country Paper on Japan, August 16, 1951, 511.9421/8-1651, U.S. Department of State, NARA.

38. Parsons to Bane, "United States Policy toward Japan," Secret Memorandum, July 1, 1960; "Guideline of U.S. Policy toward Japan," Secret Policy Paper, May 3, 1961.

39. Shōwa Denkō was a fertilizer industry involved in a major bribery scandal related to government contracts and financing. Dower, *Embracing Defeat*, 117, 535; Bond, USPOLAD, Tokyo, to U.S. Department of State, USIE Country Paper on Japan.

40. Shinbori Michiya, ed., *Shinichika no tanjō* [The birth of Japan experts] (Tokyo: Tōshindō, 1986), 138, 148.

41. Matsuo Takayoshi, *Kokusai Kokka e no Shuppatsu* [The start for an international nation], vol. 21 of *Nihon no rekishi* [A history of Japan] (Tokyo: Shūei Sha, 1993), 24.

42. I. Poltavskii, *Okkupirovannaya Yaponiya* (USSR, 1952); reprinted as *Senryō ka no Nihon* [Japan under the occupation], trans. Makiyama Kei (Tokyo: Sōjjusha, 1953), 32.

43. Conlon report, 96; Dower, *Embracing Defeat*, 123–132.

44. Poltavskii, *Okkupirovannaya Yaponiya*, 40–42.

45. Ibid.

46. Dower, *Embracing Defeat*, 206.

47. "Japan between East and West, First Meeting, April 17, 1956," Council on Foreign Relations Discussion Meeting Report, Manuscript Division, Council on Foreign Relations, New York, 5.

48. Dower, *Embracing Defeat*, 134–135.

49. Entry of July 12, 1947, Fahs Diaries.

50. "Japan between East and West, Fifth Meeting, May 23, 1956," 4.

51. Ibid., 2.

52. Ibid.

53. "American Cultural Relations with Japan, Fourth Meeting, March 30, 1953, Digest of Discussion," Council on Foreign Relations Study Group Report, Manuscript Division, Council on Foreign Relations, New York, 14.

54. "Japan between East and West, Fifth Meeting, May 23, 1956," 2.

55. "Japan between East and West, Fourth Meeting, May 21, 1956," Council on Foreign Relations Discussion Meeting Report, Manuscript Division, Council on Foreign Relations, New York, 11.

56. "American Cultural Relations with Japan, Fourth Meeting, March 30, 1953, Digest of Discussion," 16.

57. For biographical information on Harold Henderson, see Takemae Eiji, *GHQ* (Tokyo: Iwanami Shoten, 1983), 118; Takemae Eiji, *The Allied Occupation of Japan* (New York: Continuum, 2002), 352; and Dower, *Embracing Defeat*, 310.

58. "American Cultural Relations with Japan, Fourth Meeting, March 30, 1953, Digest of Discussion," 16.

59. "Japan between East and West, Fifth Meeting, May 23, 1956," 2.

60. Ibid.

61. Bond, USPOLAD, Tokyo, to U.S. Department of State, USIE Country Paper on Japan.

62. Report to Ambassador John Foster Dulles, April 16, 1951, folder 446, box 49, series 1-OMR files, record group (RG) 5 (John D. Rockefeller III), Rockefeller Family Archives, RAC, 64.

63. Suga Michi, "Tai-nichi kōwa to soren no tachiba" [The Japanese peace treaty and the position of the Soviet Union], in *Soren wa Nihon ni Naniwo Nozomu ka* [What the Soviet Union expects from Japan], ed. Kuzma N. Derevyanko (Soviet representative of the Allied Council of Japan Shinzen Kyōkai [The Association for Japanese-Soviet Friendship]) (Tokyo: Ōdo Sha, 1949), 3. In an interview by Roy Howard in 1936, Stalin reportedly said, "The export of revolution is nonsense. Every country, should it so desire, will itself achieve its own revolution, and if it does not desire it, there will be no revolution. Now, for example, our country desired to make a revolution and made it."

64. Report to Ambassador John Foster Dulles, April 16, 1951.

65. On a different occasion, the American ambassador to Japan, Douglas MacArthur II, revealed a similar type of paternalism toward Japan. The 1960 riotous demonstration that the Japanese staged to oppose ratification of the new U.S-Japan security treaty forced cancellation of U.S. president Dwight Eisenhower's visit to Japan. Apparently perturbed by the turn of the events in Japan, the frustrated American ambassador said, "We should not panic over the recent developments in Japan and must always remember that democracy in Japan is still very young and that many of the mechanisms and institutions of Western democracy that have been imported into Japan are still strange and new to Japanese who are only 80 years out of feudalism." Ambassador Douglas MacArthur II (U.S. Embassy, Japan) to Secretary Christian A. Herter Jr., Presidential Visit (Confidential Cable #004231), May 15, 1960, US-J 00053. Japan and the United States: Diplomatic, Security and Economic Relations, 1960–1976, National Security Archive.

66. Entry of March 2, 1951, Fahs Diaries.

67. "Japan between East and West, Fifth Meeting, May 23, 1956," 3.

68. "Japan between East and West, Fourth Meeting, May 21, 1956," 11.

69. Report to Ambassador John Foster Dulles, April 16, 1951.

70. "American Cultural Relations with Japan, Fourth Meeting, March 30, 1953, Digest of Discussion," 10.

71. Julie Higashi, "The Religious Occupation in Postwar Japan: The Christian Community and Educational Institutions," in *The Age of Creolization in the Pacific: In Search of Emerging Culture and Shared Values in the Japan-America Borderlands,* ed. Takeshi Matsuda (Hiroshima: Keisuisha, 2001), 100–101.

72. Quoted in Takemae, *Allied Occupation of Japan,* 377.

73. George F. Kennan, *Memoirs: 1925–1950* (Boston: Little, Brown, 1967), 384.

74. Quoted in Takemae, *Allied Occupation of Japan,* 377.

75. Saxton Bradford, AMEMBASSY, Tokyo, to U.S. Department of State, "Attitudes of Japanese Intellectuals towards the United States," June 4, 1952, 511.94/6-452, U.S. Department of State, NARA.

76. Douglas Horton, James C. Baker, Luman J. Shafer, and Walter W. Van Kirk, *The Return to Japan: Report of the Christian Deputation to Japan, October–November, 1945* (New York: Friendship, 1945), cited in Higashi, "Religious Occupation in Postwar Japan," 103.

77. Japan Christian University Foundation Inc. to Secretary of State Dean G. Acheson, "A Christian University for Japan," June 29, 1949, 894.4212/6-2949, U.S. Department of State, NARA.

78. "American Cultural Relations with Japan, Fourth Meeting, March 30, 1953, Digest of Discussion," 10.

79. Council on Foreign Relations Study Group on American Cultural Relations with Japan, "The Cultural Role of American Missionaries in Japan," Working Paper No. 4, prepared by Robert S. Schwantes, March 24, 1953, folder 41, box 4, collection III 2Q, Rockefeller Foundation Archives, RAC.

80. See Higashi, "Religious Occupation in Postwar Japan," 103. Hawley disagreed with MacArthur on both counts. He believed that the Japanese had little interest in good and bad. Entry of July 1, 1947, Fahs Diaries.

81. Quoted in Takemae, *Allied Occupation of Japan*, 377.

82. Council on Foreign Relations Study Group on American Cultural Relations with Japan, "Cultural Role of American Missionaries in Japan."

83. Entry of December 14, 1949, Fahs Diaries.

84. Takagi Yasaka, "Opening Remarks at the Conference of the Stanford Visiting Professors with Members of Society of Science and Thought and America Institute," July 24, 1950, Tokyo University–Stanford University American Studies Seminars file, Takagi Bunko, Amerika Taiheiyō Chiiki Kenkyū Sentā [Center for America-Pacific Area Studies], University of Tokyo (hereafter Takagi Bunko).

85. Dower, *Embracing Defeat*, 309.

86. Entry of Otis Cary, undated, John D. Rockefeller III Diaries 1952, series 1-OMR files, RG 5 (John D. Rockefeller III), Rockefeller Family Archives, RAC (hereafter Rockefeller Diaries).

87. Entry of Otis Cary and Donald H. McLean Jr., Memorandum for Record, May 3, 1952, folder 462, box 51, series 1-OMR files, RG 5 (John D. Rockefeller III), Rockefeller Family Archives, RAC. McLean was a former army captain and Rockefeller's staff associate.

88. Maurice Valency, "Some Observations on the Teaching of the Humanities in Japan, A Preliminary Report Submitted to the Ford Foundation, July 1, 1959," folder 430, box 48, series 1-OMR files, RG 5 (John D. Rockefeller III), Rockefeller Family Archives, RAC.

89. Endō Shūsaku, a renowned Japanese novelist, has dealt with one of the most fascinating problems surrounding Christianity and Japanese-ness. In his prize-winning novel *Chinmoku* (Silence), he successfully portrays intangible cross-cultural barriers as well as psychological agonies that missionaries from the West experience when they spread Christianity in Japan. The author seems to argue that the Japanese have no capacity to conceive of God, a supreme being that transcends humans, in the same way that the Westerners do. See Endō Shūsaku, *Chinmoku* [Silence] (Tokyo: Shinchō Sha, 1978).

90. Entry of Cary and McLean, Memorandum for Record, May 3, 1952.

91. Otis Cary, *Nihon kaigan* [Opening of Japan's eyes] (Tokyo: Hōsei University Press, 1952).

92. "American Cultural Relations with Japan, Fourth Meeting, March 30, 1953, Digest of Discussion," 7.

93. Council on Foreign Relations Study Group on American Cultural Relations with Japan, "Cultural Role of American Missionaries in Japan."

94. Entry of Ichimada Hisato, February 14, 1951, folder 6, box 1, series 609, RG 1.2, Rockefeller Foundation Archives, RAC.

95. Council on Foreign Relations Study Group on American Cultural Relations with Japan, "Cultural Role of American Missionaries in Japan," 4.

96. "American Cultural Relations with Japan, Fourth Meeting, March 30, 1953, Digest of Discussion," 2.

97. Tokyo 1020 to U.S. Department of State, February 2, 1951, 794.00/2-251, U.S. Department of State, NARA.

98. According to the most accurate figures, 1,119 Protestant missionaries were in Japan in 1951, and a slightly smaller number of Catholic ones. Bovenkerk noted that as of 1951 about 60 percent of Protestant missionaries were engaged in educational work; 25 percent in evangelical outreach—that is, working outside of institutions; and 8 percent in social service work. Ibid., 2–6.

99. In 1951 the total population of Japan was 84.54 million. Council on Foreign Relations Study Group on American Cultural Relations with Japan, "Cultural Role of American Missionaries in Japan"; ibid.

100. "American Cultural Relations with Japan, Fourth Meeting, March 30, 1953, Digest of Discussion," 6.

101. Tokyo 1020 to U.S. Department of State, February 2, 1951.

102. Ibid.

103. Ibid.

104. Entry of Ōhara Sōichirō, undated, Rockefeller Diaries 1952.

105. AMEMBASSY, Tokyo, to U.S. Department of State, Memorandum of Conversation between Professor Saitō of Tokyo University and Cultural Attaché Margaret H. Williams, May 5, 1953, 511.94/5-1153, U.S. Department of State, NARA.

106. Max Weber, *The Protestant Ethic and the Spirit of Capitalism,* trans. Talcott Parsons (London: Unwin Paperbacks, 1985), 240.

107. Entry of July 13, 1947, Fahs Diaries.

108. Ibid.

109. Entry of April 17, 1952, Fahs Diaries.

110. Entry of February 28, 1951, Fahs Diaries.

111. Entry of June 24, 1947, Fahs Diaries.

112. Tokyo University Center for American Studies (Tokyo Daigaku Amerika Kenkyū Shiryō Sentā), *Matsui Shichirō sensei ni kiku* [Interview with Professor Matsui Shichirō], vol. 8 of *American Studies in Japan: Oral History Series* (Tokyo: Tokyo University Center for American Studies, 1980), 11.

113. Entry of July 7, 1947, Fahs Diaries.

114. Maruyama Masao, "Nationalism in Japan: Its Theoretical Background and Prospects," in *Thought and Behavior in Modern Japanese Politics,* ed. Ivan Morris (London: Oxford University Press, 1963), 152.

115. Ishikawa Tatsuzō, "Hanbei kanjō wa kienai" [Anti-American feelings will not disappear], *Chūō kōron* (November 1953): 35.

116. "Japan between East and West, Fifth Meeting, May 23, 1956," 3.

117. Ishida Takeshi, *Shakai kagaku saikō* [Rethinking the social sciences] (Tokyo: University of Tokyo Press, 1995), 51.

118. Niles W. Bond, confidential, Desp. No. 1246, "Future Implication of a Cultural Interchange Programs with Japan," March 12, 1951, 511.94/3-1251, U.S. Department of State, NARA.

119. For further discussion of this subject, see Weber, *Protestant Ethic and the Spirit of Capitalism,* 240.

120. Against the backdrop of the spectacular economic progress that Japan made in a short time during the 1960s, Japanese intellectuals were engaged in a heated controversy over chimerical issues such as the uniqueness of Japan or *Nihonjin-ron* during the 1970s and 1980s. They spent much time and energy soul searching by reassessing their achievements and reexamining past records. In doing so, they sought to regain confidence and acquire a sense of direction from which they would be able to go to the next level. Whether they succeeded in moving beyond this identity crisis remains to be seen.

121. Ruth Benedict, *The Chrysanthemum and the Sword: Patterns of Japanese Culture* (Boston: Houghton Mifflin, 1946); Dower, *Embracing Defeat,* 219. For critical views, see Charles Douglas Smith, *Uchinaru gaikoku: "Kiku to Katana" saikō* [A foreign country within: *The Chrysanthemum and the Sword* revisited], trans. Kaji Etsuko (Tokyo: Jiji Tsūshin Sha, 1981); and Aoki Tamotsu, *Nihon bunka ron no henyō* [The transformation of theories on Japaneseness] (Tokyo: Chūō Kōron Sha, 1990).

122. "American Cultural Relations with Japan, Sixth Meeting, June 3, 1953," Council on Foreign Relations Study Group Report, folder 42, box 6, collection III 2Q, Rockefeller Foundation Archives, RAC.

123. Bond, USPOLAD, Tokyo, to U.S. Department of State, USIE Country Paper on Japan.

124. Confidential—Security Information, USIE Country Plan—Japan, Priority III, December 4, 1951, 511.94/12-451, U.S. Department of State, NARA.

125. Bond, confidential, Desp. 1246, "Future Implication of a Cultural Interchange Programs with Japan."

126. "American Cultural Relations with Japan, Fifth Meeting, April 30, 1953, Digest of Discussion," Council on Foreign Relations Study Group Report, Council on Foreign Relations, New York.

127. "Japan between East and West, First Meeting, April 17, 1956," 5.

128. "Japan between East and West, Fourth Meeting, May 21, 1956," 8–11.

129. Poltavskii, *Okkupirovannaya Yaponiya,* 25, 68.

130. For an excellent treatment of the "Americanization of Japanese culture," see Honma Nagayo, "Nihon bunka no Amerikaka" [Americanization of Japanese culture], in *Washington taisei to Nichibei kankei* [The Washington treaty system and Japanese-American relations], ed. Hosoya Chihiro and Saitō Makoto (Tokyo: University of Tokyo Press, 1978), 603–630.

131. Ladejinsky was an agricultural economist in the U.S. Department of Agriculture from April 1935 to July 1946 and a major SCAP adviser on land reform from December 1945 to January 1947. Entry of February 25, 1951, Fahs Diaries.

132. Entry of April 28, 1952, Rockefeller Diaries. For more information on Ōhara Sōichirō, see Inoue Tarō, *Hekotarenai risōshugisha—Ōhara Sōichirō* [An unyielding idealist—Ōhara Sōichirō] (Tokyo: Kōdan Sha, 1993).

133. Entry of May 19, 1954, Fahs Diaries.

134. Ibid.

135. Conlon report, 87.

136. Entry of April 26, 1950, Fahs Diaries.

137. Entry of May 13, 1950, Fahs Diaries.

138. Conlon report, 95.

139. "Japan between East and West, Fourth Meeting, May 21, 1956," 11.
140. Report to Ambassador John Foster Dulles, April 16, 1951.
141. Tokyo 1020 to U.S. Department of State, February 2, 1951.
142. Robert S. Schwantes to John D. Rockefeller III, January 23, 1955, folder 42, box 6, collection III 2Q, Rockefeller Foundation Archives, RAC.
143. USPOLAD, Tokyo, to U.S. Department of State, September 7, 1951, 511.94/9-751, U.S. Department of State, NARA.
144. Entry of July 12, 1947, Fahs Diaries.

Conclusion

1. G. K. Weeks to C. E. Mitchell, president of the National City Company, November 1, 1919: Enclosure in Thomas Lamont to Breckinridge Long, December 18, 1919, 893.51/2590, U.S. Department of State, National Archives and Records Administration, College Park, Md. (hereafter NARA), as quoted in Matsuda Takeshi, "Woodrow Wilson's Dollar Diplomacy in the Far East: The New Chinese Consortium, 1917–1921, Ph.D. diss., University of Wisconsin-Madison, 1979, 297.

2. Joseph S. Nye Jr., *Soft Power: The Means to Success in World Politics* (New York: Public Affairs, 2004); Nye, *The Paradox of American Power: Why the World's Only Super Power Can't Go It Alone* (New York: Oxford University Press, 2002); Nye, *Bound to Lead: The Changing Nature of American Power* (New York: Basic Books, 1990).

3. Richard T. Arndt, "Beikoku no bunkakōhō gaikō—Kiwadoi baransu" [Cultural and informational diplomacy in the U.S.: The precarious balance], *Kokusai mondai* 338 (May 1988): 46; Howard R. Ludden, "The International Information Program of the United States: State Department Years, 1945–1953," Ph.D. diss., Princeton University, Princeton, N.J., 1966.

4. Rosemary O'Neil, "A Brief History of Department of State Involvement in International Exchange," fall 1972, Bureau of Education and Cultural Affairs, U.S. Department of State, box 103, file 12, Historical Collection, Special Collections Section, University of Arkansas Libraries., Fayetteville.

5. Arndt, "Beikoku no bunkakōhō gaikō, 46; Ludden, "International Information Program of the United. States."

6. Robert S. Schwantes, "Proposal for a Study of Japanese-American Cultural Relations," Council on Foreign Relations Memorandum for the Committee on Studies, undated, Council on Foreign Relations Library, New York.

7. John W. Dower, *Embracing Defeat: Japan in the Wake of World War II* (New York: Norton, 1999), 213.

8. Ibid., 439.

9. Secret Minutes: Summary Record of Meeting, April 25, 1960–U.S. Embassy, Tokyo, US-J 00036, April 25, 1960; Secret Minutes: Summary Record of Meeting, April 26, 1960–U.S. Embassy, Tokyo, US-J 00037, April 26, 1960, Japan and the United States: Diplomatic, Security and Economic Relations, 1960–1976, National Security Archive, Gelman Library, George Washington University, Washington, D.C. (hereafter National Security Archive).

10. Dower, *Embracing Defeat,* 550–551.

11. "Guideline of U.S. Policy toward Japan," Secret Policy Paper, May 3, 1961, U.S. Department of State, US-J 00098, Japan and the United States: Diplomatic, Security and Economic Relations, 1960–1976, National Security Archive.

12. Ibid.

13. Notoji Masako, "The University of Tokyo–Stanford University American Studies Seminar," *Survey of American Studies in Japan: Development of American Studies Seminars* (Tokyo: International House of Japan, 1998), 25–26.

14. Warren Obluck, "The Development of American Studies in Japan: As Observed from an American Point of View," *Bulletin of the Center for American Studies of the University of Tokyo* 8 (1985): 1–7.

15. Maurice Valency, "Some Observations on the Teaching of the Humanities in Japan, A Preliminary Report Submitted to the Ford Foundation, July 1, 1959," folder 430, box 48, series 1-OMR files, record group (RG) 5 (John D. Rockefeller III), Rockefeller Family Archives, Rockefeller Archive Center, Sleepy Hollow, N.Y. (hereafter RAC).

16. Howard S. Ellis, Stanford University, to Joseph H. Willits, Rockefeller Foundation, September 2, 1951, folder 6, box 1, series 205, RG 1.2, Rockefeller Foundation Archives, RAC.

17. Eric J. Gangloff, "American Studies and Public Responsibility," *Bulletin of the Center for American Studies of the University of Tokyo* 10 (1987): 9–11.

18. Ibid.

19. Sharon Minichiello, "Impressions of American Studies in Japan," *Bulletin of the Center for American Studies of the University of Tokyo* 9 (1986): 1–4.

20. Ibid.

21. Ellis to Willits, September 2, 1951.

22. Max Weber, *The Protestant Ethic and the Spirit of Capitalism,* trans. Talcott Parsons (London: Unwin Paperbacks, 1985), 230.

23. Ibid, 175.

24. John Curtis Perry, "Private Philanthropy and Foreign Affairs: The Case of John D. Rockefeller, III and Japan," *Asian Perspective* 8 (fall–winter 1984): 269.

25. Richard J. Samuels, professor of Japanese political history at MIT, points out that a similar phenomenon affects American scholarship on Japanese politics and the behavioral patterns of American scholars of Japanese politics and history. See Samuels, "Japanese Political Studies and the Myth of the Independent Intellectual," in *The Political Culture of Foreign Area and International Studies: Essays in Honor of Lucian W. Pye,* ed. Richard J. Samuels and Myron Weiner (Washington, D.C.: Brassey's, 1992), 17–56; "Amerika no Nihon ron wo sōtenken suru" [A thorough examination of the theories of Japan in America], *Chūō kōron* (May 1992): 134–159; "Nihon ishitsu ronjatachi no kōzai" [The merit and the demerit of scholars of Japanese uniqueness], *Chūō kōron* (June 1992): 190–207; and Shimada Haruo, Murakami Yasusuke, and Richard J. Samuels, "Miushinawareta nichibei no zentai zō: Zadankai" [A roundtable talk on Samuels's article], *Chūō kōron* (May 1992): 124–133.

26. Jacques Barzun, *The House of Intellect* (New York: Harper's, 1961), 198.

27. Dean Rusk (president), "Statement of the Rockefeller Foundation and the General Education Board to the Special Committee to Investigate Tax-Exempt Foundations," Eighty-third Congress, 2nd sess., August 3, 1954, 1080.

28. Raymond B. Fosdick, *The Story of the Rockefeller Foundation* (New York: Harper and Brothers, 1952).

29. "Secret, Department of State Policy Planning Council, The Future of Japan. Highlights from the Secretary's Policy Planning Meeting Held May 5, 1964," US-J 00321, Japan and the United States: Diplomatic, Security and Economics Relations, 1960–1976, National Security Archive.

30. Roger Hilsman to Acting Secretary, August 9, 1963, on NSC Japan Presentation, US-J 00263, Japan and the United States: Diplomatic, Security and Economics Relations, 1960–1976, National Security Archive.

31. Ibid.

32. "Secret Policy Paper, NSSM-12, Policy toward Japan: Part One: Political, Psychological, and Security Aspects of the Relationship," National Security Council, US-J 01391, Japan and the United States: Diplomatic, Security and Economics Relations, 1960–1976, National Security Archive.

33. William Roseberry, *Anthropologies and Histories: Essays in Culture, History, and Political Economy* (New Brunswick, N.J.: Rutgers University Press, 1989), 2.

Appendix A The State of Scholarship on U.S.-Japan Relations

1. Reinhold Wagnleitner, "American Cultural Diplomacy, the Cinema, and the Cold War in Central Europe," *European Contributions to American Studies* (Netherlands) 28 (1994): 196–210.

2. Joseph S. Nye Jr., *Soft Power: The Means to Success in World Politics* (New York: Public Affairs, 2004); Nye, *The Paradox of American Power: Why the World's Only Super Power Can't Go It Alone* (New York: Oxford University Press, 2002): Nye, *Bound to Lead: The Changing Nature of American Power* (New York: Basic Books, 1990).

3. Quoted in Francis J. Colligan, "The Government and Cultural Interchange," *Review of Politics* 20, no. 4 (1958): 564, cited in William Y. Elliot et al., *The Political Economy of American Foreign Policy: Its Concepts, Strategy, and Limits* (New York: Henry Holt, 1955).

4. Laura E. Hein, "Free-Floating Anxieties on the Pacific," *Diplomatic History* 20 (summer 1996): 411–437; John W. Dower, "Nihon wo hakaru," [Sizing up (and breaking down) Japan], *Shisō* (September 1995): 65–96; (October 1995): 67–89.

5. Notable examples of studies based on modernization theory are the volumes in the Princeton University Press modernization of Japan series: Marius B. Jansen, ed., *Changing Japanese Attitudes toward Modernization* (1965); William W. Lockwood, ed., *The State and Economic Enterprise in Japan* (1965); R. P. Dore, ed., *Aspects of Social Change in Modern Japan* (1967); Robert E. Ward, ed., *Political Development in Modern Japan* (1968); Donald H. Shiverly, ed., *Tradition and Modernization in Japanese Culture* (1971); James William Morley, ed., *Dilemma of Growth in Prewar Japan* (1971).

6. Karatani Kōjin, "Ri no hihan" [A critique of Ri], *Gendaishi techō* [The notebook of modern poetry] (May 1986): 40; J. Victor Koschmannn, "Maruyama Masao and the Incomplete Project of Modernity," in *Postmodernism and Japan,* ed. Miyoshi Masao and Harry D. Harootunian (Durham, N.C.: Duke University Press, 1989), 124.

7. For a discussion of the problems as well as the promises of the postmodernist approach, see Ishida Takeshi, *Shakai kagaku saikō* [Rethinking social sciences] (Tokyo: University of Tokyo Press, 1995), 123–132; Masao Miyoshi and Harry D. Harootunian,

eds., *Learning Places: The Afterlives of Area Studies* (Durham, N.C.: Duke University Press, 2002); Masao and Harootunian, *Postmodernism and Japan.*

8. Rey Chow, "Theory, Area Studies, Cultural Studies: Issues of Pedagogy in Multiculturalism," in *Learning Places: The Afterlives of Area Studies,* ed. Masao Miyoshi and Harry D. Harootunian (Durham, N.C.: Duke University Press, 2002), 113.

9. Ezra Vogel, *Japan as Number One* (Cambridge, Mass.: Harvard University Press, 1979); Chalmers Johnson, *MITI and the Japanese Miracle: The Growth of Industrial Policy, 1925–1975* (Stanford, Calif.: Stanford University Press, 1982); Walter LaFeber, *The Clash: U.S.-Japanese Relations Throughout History* (New York: Norton, 1997).

10. Hein, "Free-Floating Anxieties on the Pacific," 411–437; Dower, "Nihon wo hakaru."

11. Nihei Satoshi, "Nihon shihonshugi no sengo saihen to kiki no shinkō" [The postwar restructuring of Japanese capitalism and the progression of a crisis], *Tochiseido shigaku* 41 (1968): 1–23; Ōishi Kaichirō, "Sengo kaikaku to Nihon shihonshugi no kōzō henka—Sono renzoku setsu to danzetsu setsu" [The postwar reform and the structural changes in Japanese capitalism—Its continuity thesis and discontinuity thesis], *Sengo kaikaku* [The postwar reform], ed. Tokyo Daigaku Shakai Kagaku Kenkyūsho (Institute of Social Science, University of Tokyo) (Tokyo: Tokyo Daigaku Shuppan Kai, 1974), 63–97; Ōshima Yūichi, "Sengo kaikaku haaku no kiso shiten" [The basic viewpoints for an understanding of postwar reform], *Rekishi hyōron,* ed. Rekishi Kagaku Kyōgikai 322 (February 1977): 84–97.

12. Nakamura Takafusa, *Shōwa shi* [A Shōwa history], vol. 1, 1926–1945 (Tokyo: Tōyō Keizai Shimpō-Sha, 1993), 3–5; Nakamura Masanori, ed. *Senryō to sengo kaikaku* [The occupation and postwar reform] (Tokyo: Yoshikawa Kōbun-Kan, 1994), 1–27.

13. See note 4.

14. Matsuo Takayoshi, ed., *Ishibashi Tanzan hyōron shū* [The collected essays of Ishibashi Tanzan] (Tokyo: Iwanami Shoten, 1991); Sataka Makoto, *Ryō Nihonshugi no seijika* [A statesman of good Japanism] (Tokyo: Tōyō Keizai Shimpō-Sha, 1994); Handō Kazutoshi, *Tatakau Ishibashi Tanzan* [A fighting Ishibashi Tanzan] (Tokyo: Tōyō Keizai Shimpō-Sha, 1995).

15. Dower, *War without Mercy,* 266.

16. Iokibe Makoto, "Senryō—Nichibei ga futatabi deatta ba," in *Nichibei no Shōwa* [Shōwa—Japan and America] (Tokyo: TBS Britannica, 1990), 74–75; John W. Dower, *Empire and Aftermath: Yoshida Shigeru and the Japanese Experience, 1878–1954* (Cambridge, Mass.: Council on East Asian Studies, Harvard University, 1988), 312–313; Dower, *War without Mercy,* 305.

17. See Matsuda Takeshi," Woodrow Wilson's Dollar Diplomacy in the Far East: The New Chinese Consortium, 1917–1921," Ph.D. diss., University of Wisconsin, Madison, 1979.

18. Iokibe, "Senryō—Nichibei ga futatabi deatta ba," 82.

Bibliography

Primary Source Materials

English-Language Publications

Acheson, Dean G. *Present at Creation.* New York: Norton, 1969.
Allison, John M. *Ambassador from the Prairie or Allison Wonderland.* Boston: Houghton Mifflin, 1973.
Bisson, Thomas A. *Prospects for Democracy in Japan.* New York: Macmillan, 1949.
———. *Reform Years in Japan, 1945–47: An Occupation Memoir,* translated by Nakamura Masanori and Miura Yōichi. Tokyo: Sanseidō, 1983.
Borton, Hugh. *Spanning Japan's Modern Century: The Memoir of Hugh Borton,* translated by Gomi Toshiki. Tokyo: Asahi Shimbun Sha, 1998.
Bureau of Educational and Cultural Affairs, U.S. Department of State. "The CU Program Concept." March 12, 1974.
———. *Our International Visitors.* Washington, D.C.: Government Printing Office, 1973.
———. "Partners in Exchange." Washington, D.C.: Government Printing Office, 1972.
Bureau of Educational and Cultural Affairs Historical Collection, Manuscript collection. 468, Special Collections Division, University of Arkansas Libraries, Fayetteville.
Confidential U.S. State Department Special Files, Japan, 1947–1956. Papers Relating to Foreign Relations. Microfilm, University Publications of America, 1990.
Conlon Associates Ltd. *United States Foreign Policy: Asia.* Study prepared at the request of the Committee on Foreign Relations, U.S. Senate, No. 5. Washington, D.C.: Government Printing Office, 1959.
Council on Foreign Relations (Papers and Reports). Manuscript Division, Council on Foreign Relations, New York.
Emmerson, John K. *The Japanese Dilemma: Arms, Yen amd Power.* New York: Dunellen Publishing, 1971.
———. *The Japanese Thread: A Life in the U. S. Foreign Service.* New York: Holt, Rinehart and Winston, 1978.
Espinosa, J. Manuel. *InterAmerican Beginnings of U.S. Cultural Diplomacy, 1936–1948.* Department of State Publication 8854. Washington, D.C.: Government Printing Office, 1976.

Fahs, Charles B. Diaries, 1947–1961. Record group 12.1, Rockefeller Foundation Archives, Rockefeller Archive Center, Sleepy Hollow, N.Y.

Gimbel, John. *The American Occupation of Germany: Politics and the Military, 1945–1949.* Stanford, Calif.: Stanford University Press, 1968.

Japan and the United States: Diplomatic, Security and Economic Relations, 1960–1976. National Security Archive, Gelman Library, George Washington University, Washington, D.C.

Johnson, U. Alexis. *The Right Hand of Power: The Memoirs of an American Diplomat.* Englewood Cliffs, N.J.: Prentice Hall, 1984.

J. William Fulbright Papers. Manuscript collection MS/F959/144 /Fulbright. Special Collections Division, University of Arkansas Libraries, Fayetteville.

Kellerman, Henry J. *Cultural Relations as an Instrument of U.S. Foreign Policy: The Educational Exchange Program between the United States and Germany, 1945–1954.* Department of State Publication No. 8931. Washington, D.C.: Government Printing Office, 1978.

Kennan, George F. *Memoirs,* 1925–1950. Boston: Little, Brown, 1967.

———. *Memoir, 1950–1963.* Boston: Little, Brown, 1972.

Occupation of Japan: Policy and Progress. New York: Greenwood Press, 1969.

Papers of the Department of State. National Archives and Records Administration, College Park, Md.

Papers Relating to Foreign Relations of the United States 1951. Vol. VI Asia and the Pacific, Part 1. Washington, D.C.: Government Printing Office, 1977.

Papers Relating to Foreign Relations of the United States 1952–1954. Vol. XIV China and Japan, Part 2. Washington, D.C.: Government Printing Office, 1985.

Reischauer, Edwin O. "The Broken Dialogue with Japan." *Foreign Affairs* 39, vol. 1 (1960): 11–26.

———. *Diaries of Ambassador Reischauer.* Tokyo: Kōdan-Sha, 1995.

———. *Wanted: An Asian Policy.* New York: Knopf, 1955.

Rockefeller, John D., III. Diaries. Rockefeller Archive Center, Sleepy Hollow, N.Y.

———. "Japan Tackles Her Problems." *Foreign Affairs* 32, no. 4 (1954): 577–587.

———. Papers. Record group 5, Rockefeller Family Archives, Rockefeller Archive Center, Sleepy Town, N.Y.

———. *The Second American Revolution: Some Personal Observations,* translated by Tada Minoru. Tokyo: Eihō Sha, 1975.

Sebald, William J. *With MacArthur in Japan.* New York: Norton, 1965.

U.S. Advisory Commission on International Educational and Cultural Affairs. *A Beacon of Hope: The Exchange of Persons Program.* Washington, D.C.: Government Printing Office, 1963.

Willkie, Wendell L. *One World.* New York: Simon and Schuster, 1943.

Willoughby, Charles A. *Shirarezaru Nihon senryō: Willoughby Kaikoroku* [The occupation of Japan nobody knows: Memoir of Charles A. Willoughby]. Tokyo: Banchō Shobō, 1973.

Japanese-Language Publications

Derevyanko, Kuzma N. et al., eds. *Soren wa Nihon ni nani wo Nozomu ka* [What the Soviet Union expects from Japan], translated by Nisso Shinzen Kyōkai [The Association for Japanese-Soviet Friendship]. Tokyo: Ōdo Sha, 1949.

Endō, Yasuo et al., eds., *Tokyo Daigaku Amerika Kenkyū Shiryō Sentā 30 nen no ayumi* [The first 30 years of the Tokyo University Center for American Studies]. Tokyo: Tokyo Daigaku Amerika Kenkyū Shiryō Sentā, 1997.

Hidaka, Daishirō. "Senryō-ka no kyōiku kaikaku" [The education reform under the occupation]. In *Watashi no ikita nijū seiki* [The twentieth century in which I lived], edited by Yuasa Hachirō et al. Tokyo: Nihon Kirisutokyōdan Shuppan, 1980.

Hosoya, Chihiro, Aruga Tadashi, Ishii Osamu, and Sasaki Takuya, eds. *Nichibei kankei shiryōshū, 1945–1997* [A documentary history of U.S.-Japanese relations, 1945–1997]. Tokyo: University of Tokyo Press, 1999.

Ishibashi, Tanzan. "Hanbei kanjō hassei no riyū" [The reasons for the surgence of anti-American feelings]. *Chūō kōron* (November 1953): 40–44.

Itō, Ritsu. *Itō Ritsu kaikoroku* [A memoir of Itō Ritsu].Tokyo: Bungei Shunjū, 1993.

Iwai, Yujirō. *Osaka shōnin no tetsugaku.* [The philosophy of an Osaka merchant]. Tokyo: Tokyo Nunoi Shuppan, 1994.

Japan Communist Party, *Nihon kyōsantō no rokujū nen* [The sixty years of the Japan Communist Party]. 2 vols. Tokyo: Shin Nippon Shuppan Sha, 1983.

Kashima Heiwa Kenkyūsho, ed. *Nihon gaikō shuyō bunsho nenpyō (1), 1941–1960* [Major Japanese diplomatic documents/chronology (1), 1941–1960]. Tokyo: Hara Shobō, 1983.

Maruyama, Masao, and Fukuda Kan-ichi, eds. *Nambara Shigeru Kaikoroku* [A memoir of Nambara Shigeru]. Tokyo: University of Tokyo Press, 1989.

Matsumoto, Shigeharu. "Kokusai Bunka Kōryū ni tsuite no Shokan" [A letter on international cultural interchange]. *Gakushikai kaihō* 686 (1976): 4–9.

———. *Kokusai Nihon no shōrai wo kangaete* [Pondering on the future of an internationalist Japan]. Tokyo: Asahi Shinbun Sha, 1988.

———. *Shanhai Jidai* [My years in Shanghai]. 3 vols. Tokyo: Chūō Kōron Sha, 1974.

———. *Shōwashi e no ichi shōgen* [A testimony to Shōwa history]. Tokyo: Tachibana Shuppan, 2001.

———. *Waga kokoro no jijoden* [An autobiography of my mind]. Tokyo: Kōdan Sha, 1992.

Matsumoto, Shigeharu, and Nakaya Ken-ichi. "Chibeishugi no Teishō" [Advocacy of pro-Americanism]. *Chūō kōron* 814 (1956): 120–28.

Matsuo, Takayoshi, ed. *Ishibashi Tanzan hyōron shū* [The collection of essays of Ishibashi Tanzan]. Tokyo: Iwanami Shoten, 1991.

Nakaya, Ken-ichi, and Robert S. Schwantes, *Nichibei bunka kyōiku kōryū no jūnenkan, 1952–1961* [The 10-year period of U.S.-Japan cultural and educational interchange, 1952–1961]. 1962, mimeograph.

Ōkurashō Zaiseishitsu, ed. *Amerika no tainichi senryō seisaku: Shōwa zaiseishi* [The American occupation policy of Japan: A financial history of the Showa period]. Vol. 3. Tokyo: Tōyō Keizai Shinpō Sha, 1976.

Shūkan Asashi, ed. *Sengo nedanshi nenpyō* [A chronological history of commodity prices in postwar Japan]. Tokyo: Asahi Shimbun Sha, 1995.

Takagi Yasaka Bunko [Takagi Yasaka Papers]. Center for Pacific and American Studies, University of Tokyo, Tokyo.

Tokyo University Center for American Studies (Tokyo Daigaku Amerika Kenkyū Shiryō Sentā), ed. *American Studies in Japan: Oral History Series.* Tokyo: Tokyo University Center for American Studies, 1977–1992.

———, ed. *Takagi Yasaka chosakushū* [The collected works of Takagi Yasaka]. Vol. 5

of *Toward International Understanding*. Enlarged ed. Tokyo: University of Tokyo Press, 1971.

Yoshida, Shigeru. *Gekidō no hyakunenshi* [A 100-year history of great changes]. Tokyo: Shirakawa Shoin, 1978.

———. *Kaisō jū nen* [Memoir of Yoshida Shigeru]. 4 vols. Tokyo: Shinchō Sha, 1957.

———. *Sekai to Nippon* [The world and Japan]. Tokyo: Banchō Shobō, 1963.

———.*Yoshida Shigeru shokan* [Yoshida Shigeru Letters]. Tokyo: Chūō Kōron Sha, 1994.

Secondary Source Materials
English-Language Publications

Ackerman, William C. "Private Support Activities in International Education." *Exchange* (fall 1970): 1–13.

Akami, Tomoko. *Internationalizing the Pacific: The United States, Japan and the Institute of Pacific Relations in War and Peace, 1919–1945*. New York: Routledge, 2002.

Arnove, Robert F., ed. *Philanthropy and Cultural Imperialism: The Foundations at Home and Abroad*. Boston: G. K. Hall, 1980.

Beasley, W. G. *Japanese Imperialism, 1894–1945*. Oxford: Clarendon Press, 1987.

Benedict, Ruth. *The Chrysanthemum and the Sword: Patterns of Japanese Culture*. Boston: Houghton Mifflin, 1946; translated by Matsuji Hasegawa. Tokyo: Shakai Shisō Sha, 1972.

———. *Patterns of Culture,* translated by Toshinao Yoneyama. Tokyo: Shakai Shisō Sha, 1973.

Berghahn, Volker. "Philanthropy and Diplomacy in the 'American Century.'" *Diplomatic History* 23, no. 3 (1999): 393–419.

Blum, Robert, ed. *Cultural Affairs and Foreign Relations*. Englewood Cliff, N.J.: Prentice Hall, 1963.

Boehling, Rebecca. "Commentary: The Role of Culture in American Relations with Europe: The Case of the United States' Occupation of Germany." *Diplomatic History* 23, no.1 (winter 1999): 57–69.

Borden, William S. *The Pacific Alliance: United States Foreign Economic Policy and Japanese Trade Recovery, 1947–1955*. Madison: Univeristy of Wisconsin Press, 1984.

Burkman, Thomas W., ed. *The Occupation of Japan: Arts and Culture. The Proceedings of a Symposium at Norfolk, Virginia, 18–19 October 1984*. Norfolk, Va.: General MacArthur Foundation, 1988.

Cherrington, Ben Mark. "Ten Years After." *Association of American College Bulletin* 34 (1948): 500–522.

Cohen, Warren I. *The Asian American Century*. Cambridge, Mass.: Harvard Univeristy Press, 2002; translated by Masayo Kotani. Tokyo: Sōshi Sha, 2002.

Collier, Peter, and David Horowitz. *The Rockefellers: An American Dynasty*. New York: Holt, Rinehart and Winston, 1976.

Colligan, Francis J. "The Government and Cultural Interchange." *Review of Politics* 20, no. 4 (1958): 546–569.

———. "Twenty Years After: Two Decades of Government-Sponsored Cultural Relations." *Department of State Bulletin* 34 (1958): 112–120.
Cook, Donald B., and J. Paul Smith. "The Philosophy of the Fulbright Program." *International Social Science Bulletin* (UNESCO) 8, no. 4 (1956): 615–628.
Coombs, Phillip H. *The Fourth Dimension of Foreign Policy: Educational and Cultural Affairs.* New York: Harper and Row, 1964.
Cummings, Bruce. "Boundary Displacement: The State, the Foundations, Area Studies during and after the Cold War." In *Learning Places: The Afterlives of Area Studies,* edited by Miyoshi Masao and Harry D. Harootunian. Durham, N.C.: Duke University Press, 2002.
Dower, John W. "Commentary: 'Culture,' Theory, and Practice in U.S.-Japan Relations." *Diplomatic History* 24, no. 3 (summer 2000): 517–528.
———. *Embracing Defeat: Japan in the Wake of World War II.* New York: Norton, 1999.
———. *Empire and Aftermath: Yoshida Shigeru and the Japanese Experience, 1878–1954.* Cambridge, Mass.: Harvard University Press, 1979.
———. *Japan War and Peace: Selected Essays.* New York: New Press, 1993.
———. *Origins of the Modern Japanese State: Selected Writings of E. H. Norman.* New York: Random House, 1975.
———. "The Superdomino in Postwar Asia: Japan in and Out of the Pentagon Papers." *The Senator Gravel Edition, The Pentagon Papers. Critical Essays,* vol. 5, edited by Noam Chomsky and Howard Zinn. Boston: Beacon Press, 1972.
———. *War without Mercy: Peace and Power in the Pacific War.* New York: Pantheon Books, 1986.
Dunn, Frederick S. *Peace-Making and the Settlement with Japan.* Princeton, N.J.: Princeton University Press, 1963.
Eldridge, Robert D., and Kusunoki Ayako. "To Base or Not to Base? Yoshida Shigeru, the 1950 Ikeda Mission, and Post-Treaty Japanese Security Conceptions." *Kobe University Law Review* 33, no. 1 (1999): 97–126.
Espinosa, J. Manuel. *Landmark Events in the History of CU. Bureau of Educational and Cultural Affairs (CU).* Washington, D.C.: U.S. Department of State, 1973.
Fenton, William N. *Area Studies in American Universities.* Washington, D.C.: American Council on Education, 1947.
Finn, Dallas. "What the Japanese Intellectuals Are Thinking." *American Scholar* 24 (autumn 1955): 443–455.
Finn, Richard B. *Winners in Peace: MacArthur, Yoshida, and Postwar Japan.* Berkeley: University of California Press, 1992; translated by Osami Iino et al. Tokyo: Dōbunshoin International, 1993.
Flack, Michael. "Cultural Diplomacy: Blindspot in International Affairs Textbooks." *Exchange* (winter 1972–1973): 11–18.
———. "The Internal Relations of Mankind—The Role of International Educational, Cultural, and Scientific Relations in Global Change." *International Association* (Brussels) (December 1973): 1–3.
Fosdick, Raymond B. *The Story of the Rockefeller Foundation.* New York: Harper and Brothers, 1952; translated by Takeo Imoto and Michizo Ōsawa. Tokyo: Hōsei University Press, 1956.
Frankel, Charles. "The Era of Educational and Cultural Relations." *Department of State Bulletin,* No. 54, June 6, 1966, 889–897.

———. *The Neglected Aspect of Foreign Affairs: American Educational and Cultural Policy Abroad.* Washington, D.C.: Brookings Institution, 1966.
———. "The Scribblers and International Relations." *Foreign Affairs* 44 (1965): 1–14.
Galinsky, Hans. "American Studies in Germany: Their Growth, Variety and Prospects." *American Studies* 13, no. 1 (1974): 3–10.
Gayn, Mark. *Japan Diary.* New York: William Sloane Associates, 1948.
Gienow-Hecht, Jessica C. E. "Shame on US? Academics, Cultural Transfer, and the Cold War—A Critical Review." *Diplomatic History* 24 (summer 2000): 465–494.
Gordon, Andrew, ed. *Postwar Japan as History.* Berkeley: University of California Press, 1993.
Hall, Robert. *Area Studies: With Special Reference to Their Implications for Research in the Social Sciences.* New York: Committee on World Area Research Program, Social Science Research Council, 1948.
Halpern, Stephen Mark. "The Institute of International Education: A History." Ph.D. diss., Columbia University, 1969; Ann Arbor, Mich.: University Microfilms, 1973.
Hane, Mikiso. *Peasants Rebels and Outcastes: The Underside of Modern Japan.* New York: Pantheon Books, 1982.
Hannerz, Ulf. "The World in Creolization." *Africa* 57 (1987): 546–559.
Hanson, Haldore. "The Cultural-Cooperation Program, 1938–1943." Department of State Publication No. 2137. Washington, D.C.: Government Printing Office, 1944.
Harr, John E., and Peter J. Johnson. *The Rockefeller Century.* New York: Scribner's Sons, 1988.
———. *The Rockefeller Conscience: An American Family in Public and Private.* New York: Scribner's Sons, 1991.
Hawkins, Esther L. "Some 'Unsung' Contributors to the Fulbright-Hays Program." *Exchange* (summer 1968): 55–58.
Heginbotham, Stanley J. "Shifting the Focus of International Programs." *Chronicle of Higher Education,* October 19, 1994, A68.
Hein, Laura E. "Free-Floating Anxieties on the Pacific" *Diplomatic History* 20 (summer 1996): 411–437.
———. *Reasonable Men, Powerful Words: Political Culture and Expertise in Twentieth-Century Japan.* Washington, D.C.: Woodrow Wilson Center Press, Berkeley: University of California Press, 2004.
Hewa, Soma, and Philo Hove, eds. *Philanthropy and Cultural Context: Western Philanthropy in South, East, and Southeast Asia in the 20th Century.* New York: University Press of America, 1997.
Hixson, Walter L. *Parting the Curtain: Propaganda, Culture, and the Cold War, 1945–1961.* London: Macmillan, 1997.
Hofstede, Geert. *Cultures and Organizations: Software of the Mind.* London: McGraw-Hill, 1991; translated by Iwai Noriko and Iwai Hachirō. Tokyo: Yūhikaku, 1995.
Hooper, Paul F., ed. *Remembering the Institute of Pacific Relations: The Memoirs of William L. Holland.* Tokyo: Ryūkei Shosha, 1995.
Hosoya, Chihiro, ed. *Japan and the United States: Fifty Years of Partnership.* Tokyo: Japan Times, 2001.
Institute of International Education. *Report on the National Conference on Exchange of Persons, February 23-25, 1955.* New York: Institute of International Education, 1955.

International House of Japan, ed. *American Values in U.S. Diplomacy toward Asia: Fifth Symposium on American Studies in the Asia-Pacific Region.* Tokyo: International House of Japan, 1995.

Iriye, Akira. *Cultural Internationalism and World Order.* Baltimore: Johns Hopkins University Press, 1997.

———. "Culture and International History." In *Explaining the History of American Foreign Relations,* edited by Michael J.Hogan and Thomas G. Paterson. Cambridge: Cambridge University Press, 1991.

———. "Culture and Power: International Relations as Intercultural Relations." *Diplomatic History* 3 (1979): 115–128.

———. *Global Community: The Role of International Organizations in the Making of the Contemporary World.* Berkeley: University of California Press, 2002.

Iriye, Akira, and Robert A.Wampler, eds. *Partnership: The United States and Japan, 1951–2001.* Tokyo: Kodansha International, 2001.

Issawi, Charles. "Empire Builders, Culture Makers, and Culture Imprinters." *Journal of Interdisciplinary History* 20 (autumn 1989): 177–196.

Jameson, Fredric, and Masao Miyoshi, eds. *The Cultures of Globalization.* Durham, N.C.: Duke University Press, 1998.

Johnson, Richard A. *The Administration of United States Foreign Policy.* Austin: University of Texas Press, 1971.

Johnson, Sheila K. *American Attitudes toward Japan, 1945–1975.* Washington, D.C.: American Enterprise Institute, 1975.

Johnson, Walter. *American Studies Abroad. Special Report of the U.S. Advisory Commission on International Educational and Cultural Affairs.* Washington, D.C.: Government Printing Office, 1963.

Johnson, Walter, and Francis J. Colligan. *The Fulbright Program: A History.* Chicago: University of Chicago Press, 1965.

Josephson, Harold. *James T. Shotwell and the Rise of Internationalism in America.* Cranbury, N.J: Associated University Presses, 1975.

Katō (Yasuhara), Yōko. "Japan, Communist China, Export Controls in Asia, 1948–1952." *Diplomatic History* 10 (winter 1986): 75–89.

Koschmann, J. Victor. "Intellectuals and Politics." In *Postwar Japan as History,* edited by Andrew Gordon. Berkeley: University of California Press, 1993.

Koshiro, Yukiko. *Trans-Pacific Racisms and the U.S. Occupation of Japan.* New York: Columbia University Press, 1999.

Kraske, Gary E. *Missionaries of the Book: The American Library Profession and the Origins of United States Cultural Diplomacy in Postwar Japan.* Westport, Conn.: Greenwood Press, 1985.

Kroes, Rob. "American Empire and Cultural Imperialism." *Diplomatic History* 23, no. 3 (1999): 463–477.

———. "Commentary: World Wars and Watersheds: The Problem of Continuity in the Process of Americanization." *Diplomatic History* 23, no. 1 (1999): 71–77.

Kuisel, Richard. "Commentary: Americanization for Historians." *Diplomatic History* 24, no. 3 (2000): 509–515.

Kuklick, Bruce. "Commentary: The Future of Cultural Imperialism." *Diplomatic History* 24, no. 3 (2000): 503–508.

Kushner, Barak, and Satō Masaharu. "Digesting Postwar Japanese Media." *Diplomatic History* 29, no. 1 (2005): 27–48.

Lears, T. J. Jackson. "The Concept of Cultural Hegemony: Problems and Possibilities." *American Historical Review* 90, no. 3 (1985): 567–593.

Leffler, Melvyn P. *A Preponderance of Power: National Security, the Truman Administration, and the Cold War.* Stanford, Calif.: Stanford University Press, 1992.

Livingston, Jon, Joe Moore, and Felicia Oldfather, eds. *The Japan Reader: Postwar Japan, 1945 to the Present.* New York: Pantheon Books, 1973.

Ludden, Howard R. "The International Information Program of the United States: State Department Years, 1945–1953." Ph.D. diss., Princeton University, 1966.

Mackinder, Halford J. "The Geographical Pivot of History." *Geographical Journal* 23 (1904): 421–444.

———. "The Round World and the Winning of the Peace." *Foreign Affairs* 21, no. 4 (1943): 595–605.

Maddox, Lucy, ed. *Locating American Studies: The Evolution of a Discipline.* Baltimore: Johns Hopkins University Press, 1999.

Maekawa, Reiko. "The Allied Occupation, the Cold War, and American Philanthropy: The Rockefeller Foundation in Post War Japan." In *Philanthropy and Cultural Context: Western Philanthropy in South, East, and Southeast Asia in the 20th Century,* edited by Soma Hewa and Philo Hove. New York: University Press of America, 1997.

———. "Philanthropy and Politics at the Crossroads: John D. Rockefeller 3rd's Japanese Experience." *Kyoto University Sōgō Ningen Gakubu Kiyō* 7 (2000): 67–82.

Matsuda, Takeshi, "Woodrow Wilson's Dollar Diplomacy in the Far East: The New Chinese Consortium, 1917–1921." Ph.D. diss., University of Wisconsin-Madison, 1979.

———, ed. *The Age of Creolization in the Pacific: In Search of Emerging Cultures and Shared Values in the Japan-America Borderlands.* Hiroshima: Keisui Sha, 2001.

McCormick, Thomas J. *America's Half-Century: United States Foreign Policy in the Cold War and After.* Baltimore: Johns Hopkins University Press, 1995.

McMahon, Robert J. "Cultures of Empire." *Journal of American History* 88 (December 2001): 888–892.

McMurray, Ruth Emily, and Muna Lee. *The Cultural Approach: Another Way in International Relations.* Chapel Hill: University of North Carolina Press, 1947.

Mears, Hellen. *Mirror for Americans: Japan.* Boston: Houghton Mifflin, 1948.

Metraux, Guy S. "Cross-Cultural Education and Educational Travel: An Historical Approach." *International Social Science Bulletin* (UNESCO) 8, no. 4 (1956): 577–584.

Mignolo, Walter D. *Local Histories/Global Designs: Coloniality, Subaltern Knowledges, and Border Thinking.* Princeton, N.J.: Princeton University Press, 2000.

Mitrovich, Gregory. *Undermining the Kremlin: America's Strategy to Subvert the Soviet Bloc, 1947–1956.* Ithaca, N.Y.: Cornell University Press, 2000.

Miyoshi, Masao, and Harry D. Harootunian, eds. *Learning Places: The Afterlives of Area Studies.* Durham, N.C.: Duke University Press, 2002.

———. *Postmodernism and Japan.* Durham, N.C.: Duke University Press, 1989.

Moore, Joe. *Japanese Workers and the Struggle for Power, 1945–1947.* Madison: University of Wisconsin Press, 1983.

Morley, James W., ed. *Dilemmas of Growth in Prewar Japan.* Princeton, N.J.: Princeton University Press, 1971.

———. *Japan's Foreign Policy, 1868–1941: A Research Guide.* New York: Columbia University Press, 1974.

Moore, Michael Hoenicke. "Feature Review: After-Hours Lessons in Democracy" *Diplomatic History* 29, no. 2 (2005): 369–373.
Ninkovich, Frank A. "The Currents of Cultural Diplomacy: Art and the State Department, 1938–1947." *Diplomatic History* 1, no. 3 (1977): 215–237.
———. *The Diplomacy of Ideas: U.S. Foreign Policy and Cultural Relations, 1938–1950*. Cambridge: Cambridge University Press, 1981.
———. *Modernity and Power: A History of the Domino Theory in the Twentieth Century*. Chicago: University of Chicago Press, 1994.
Nish, Ian H. *Alliance in Decline: A Study in Anglo-Japanese Relations, 1908–23*. London: Athlone Press, 1972.
Nye, Joseph S. *Bound to Lead: The Changing Nature of American Power*. New York: Basic Books, 1990.
———. *The Paradox of American Power: Why the World's Only Super Power Can't Go It Alone*. New York: Oxford University Press, 2002.
———. *Soft Power: The Means to Success in World Politics*. New York: Public Affairs, 2004.
Passin, Herbert. *Society and Education in Japan*. Tokyo: Kōdansha International, 1982.
Pells, Richard. "Commentary: Who's Afraid of Steven Spielberg?" *Diplomatic History* 24, no. 3 (2000): 495–502.
Perry, John Curtis. "Private Philanthropy and Foreign Affairs: The Case of John D. Rockefeller III and Japan." *Asian Perspective* 8 (fall-winter 1984): 268–284.
Plummer, Brenda Gayle. "The Changing Face of Diplomatic History: A Literature Review." *History Teacher* 38 (May 2005): 28. http://www.historycooperative.org/journals/ht/38.3/plummer.html.
Polanyi, Karl. *The Great Transformation: the Political and Economic Origins of Our Time*. Boston: Beacon Press, 1944.
Rafael, Vicente L. "The Cultures of Area Studies in the United States." *Social Text* 41 (winter 1994): 91–111.
Reich, Alan A. "People-to-People Diplomacy: Key to World Understanding." *Exchange* (spring 1973): 21–27.
Richardson, John, Jr. "Transnational Communication—What's Happening?" *Department of State Bulletin,* No. 70, May 6, 1974, 489–496.
"Rising Demand for International Education." *Annals of the American Academy of Political and Social Science* (Special Issue). (May 1961).
Roseberry, William. *Anthropologies and Histories: Essays in Culture, History, and Political Economy*. New Brunswick, N.J.: Rutgers University Press, 1989.
Rosenberg, Emily S. "'Foreign Affairs' after World War II: Connecting Sexual and International Politics." *Diplomatic History* 18, no. 1 (1994): 59–70.
———. *Spreading the American Dream: American Economic and Cultural Expansion, 1890–1945*. New York: Hill and Wang, 1982.
———. "Spreading the American Dream to Asia." In *American Values in U.S. Diplomacy toward Asia,* Proceedings of the Fifth Symposium on American Studies in the Asia-Pacific Region, edited by International House of Japan, Tokyo, June 1995.
Said, Edward W. *Culture and Imperialism*. New York: Knopf, 1993.
Samuels, Richard J. "Japanese Political Studies and the Myth of the Independent Intellectual." In *The Political Culture of Foreign Area and International Studies: Essays in Honor of Lucian W. Pye,* edited by Richard J. Samuels and Myron Weiner. Washington, D.C.: Brassey's, 1992.

Schaller, Michael. *Altered States: The United States and Japan since the Occupation.* New York: Oxford University Press, 1997.

———. *The American Occupation or Japan: The Origins of the Cold War in Asia.* New York: Oxford University Press, 1985.

———. "MacArthur's Japan: The View from Washington." *Diplomatic History* 10, no. 1 (1986): 1–23.

Schonberger, Howard B. *Aftermath of War: Americans and the Remaking of Japan, 1945–1952.* Tokyo: Jijitsūshin Sha, 1994.

———. "Peacemaking in Asia: The United States, Great Britain, and the Japanese Decision to Recognize Nationalist China, 1951–52." *Diplomatic History* 10, no. 1 (1986): 59–73.

Schwantes, Robert S. *Japanese and Americans: A Century of Cultural Relations.* New York: Harper and Brothers, 1955.

———. "Japan's Cultural Foreign Policies." In *Japan's Foreign Policy, 1868–1941: A Research Guide,* edited by James W. Morley. New York: Columbia University Press, 1974.

Schwarts, Benjamin I. "Presidential Address: Area Studies as a Critical Discipline." *Journal of Asian Studies* 60 (November 1980).

Sebald, William J. *With MacArthur in Japan* [Nihon senryō gaikō no kaisō], translated by Nosue Kenzō. Tokyo: Asahi Shinbun Sha, 1966.

Simpson, Christopher, ed. *Universities and Empire: Money and Politics in the Social Sciences during the Cold War.* New York: New Press, 1998.

Stephanson, Anders. "Commentary: Considerations on Culture and Theory." *Diplomatic History* 18, no. 1 (1994): 107–119.

Takemae, Eiji. *The Allied Occupation of Japan.* New York: Continuum, 2002.

Textor, Robert B. *Failure in Japan,* translated by Shimojima Ren. Tokyo: Bungei Shunjū Sha, 1952.

Thompson, Arthur. "The Development of American Studies in Japan." *American Studies* 5 (July 1960).

Thomson, Charles A., and Walter H. C. Laves. *Cultural Relations and U. S. Foreign Policy.* Bloomington: Indiana University Press, 1963.

Tomlinson, John. *Cultural Imperialism: A Critical Introduction.* London: Continuum, 1991.

Tsurumi, Shunsuke. *A Cultural History of Postwar Japan, 1945–1980.* London: KPI Limited, 1987.

Tucker, Nancy Berkopf. "American Policy toward Sino-Japanese Trade in the Postwar Years: Politics and Prosperity." *Diplomatic History* 8, no. 3 (1984): 183–208.

U.S. Advisory Commission on International Educational and Cultural Affairs. *Open Hearts, Open Minds.* Special Report. Washington, D.C.: Government Printing Office, 1966.

Vaughn, Stephen L. *Holding Fast the Inner Lines: Democracy, Nationalism and the Committee on Public Information.* Chapel Hill: University of North Carolina Press, 1980.

Wallerstein, Immanuel. *Geopolitics and Geoculture.* Cambridge: Cambridge University Press, 1991; *Posuto Amerika,* translated by Masaru Maruyama. Tokyo: Fujiwara Shoten, 1991.

———. *Unthinking Social Science.* Cambridge: Policy Press, 1991; *Datsu shakaikagaku,* translated by Honda Kenkichi and Takahash Akira. Tokyo: Fujiwara Shoten, 1993.

Walton, Barbara J. *Foreign Student Exchange in Perspective: Research on Foreign Students in the United States.* Office of External Research, U.S. Department of State. Washington, D.C.: Government Printing Office, 1967.

Wampler, Robert A. "Japan-United States Symposium: The Internationalization of Japan and Open Government." University of Tokyo, June 9, 1995. http://www.gwu.edu/~nsarchiv/japan/1995foiaconferencereport.htm

Webb, James H., Jr. "Cultural Attaché: Scholar, Propagandist, or Bureaucrat?" *South Atlantic Quarterly* 70 (summer 1972): 352–364.

Wolfe, Robert, ed. *Americans as Proconsuls: United States Military Government in Germany and Japan, 1944–1952.* Carbondale and Edwardsville: Southern Illinois University Press, 1984.

Wolfren, Karel van. *To the Japanese Intellectuals,* translated by Nishioka Kō, Shinohara Masaru, and Nakamura Yasuo. Tokyo: Mado Sha, 1995.

Yamamura, Kōzo, ed. *The Economic Emergence of Modern Japan.* Cambridge: Cambridge University Press, 1997.

Yasuba, Yasukichi. "Anatomy of the Debate on Japanese Capitalism." *Journal of Japanese Studies* 2, no. 1 (1975): 63–82.

Young, Francis A. "Educational Exchanges and the National Interest." *The ACLS* (American Council of Learned Societies) *Newsletter* 20, no. 2 (1969).

Zeitlin, Jonathan, and Gary Hirrigel, eds. *Americanization and Its Limits: Reworking US Technology and Management in Post-War Europe and Japan.* Oxford: Oxford University Press, 2000.

Japanese-Language Publications

Akazawa, Shirō. "Shakai no henka to sengo shisō no shuppatsu" [Social changes and the start of postwar thought]. In *Nihon Dohjidai Shi* [Japanese contemporary history], vol. 1, edited by Rekishigaku Kenkyukai. Tokyo: Aoki Shoten, 1990.

Amagi, Isao. "Dai ni Kai Nichibei Bunka Kyōiku Gōdōkaigi Hōkoku" [A report for the Second U.S.-Japan Joint Conference on Culture and Education]. *Monbu jihō* 1037 (1964): 25–59.

"Amerika teikokushugi no tainichi bunka shinryaku ni kansuru ichi shiryō: 'Nakaya–Schwantes hōkoku' bassui" [One document concerning cultural aggression of American imperialism on Japan: An extract of the 'Nakaya–Schwantes Report']. *Zen-ei* 200 (1962): 146–164.

Andō, Jinbe-e, *Sengo Nihon Kyōsantō shiki* [A private record of the postwar Japan Communist Party]. Tokyo: Bungei Shunjū, 1995.

Aoki, Tamotsu. *"Nihon Bunka Ron" no henyō* [The transformation of "theories on Japaneseness"]. Tokyo: Chūō Kōron Sha, 1990.

Ara, Masato. "Daini no seishun" [The second youth]. *Kindai bungaku* 2 (1946).

Arisawa, Hiromi, gen. ed. *Showa keizai shi* [A history of Showa economy]. Tokyo: Nihon Keizai Shimbun Sha, 1976.

Arndt, Richard T. "Beikoku no bunka kohō gaikō—Kiwadoi baransu" [Cultural and informational diplomacy in the U.S.: The precarious balance] *Kokusai mondai* 338 (May 1988): 41–60.

Asahi Shimbun, ed. *Okinawa hōkoku, 1969* [The Okinawa report, 1969]. Tokyo: Asahi Shimbun Sha, 1996.

Biburosu. "Kokusai Bunka Kaikan nitsuite: Sono mokuteki to katsudō" [On the International House of Japan]. *Biburosu* 5, no. 4 (1954): 9–11.

Borton, Hugh. "Amerika no tachiba karano tenbō—Nichibei bunka kōryū" [A prospect of U.S.-Japan cultural interchange from an American perspective]. *Jiyū* 6, no 2 (1964): 77–83.

Doi, Takeo. *Chūshaku "amae" no kōzō* [Annotated anatomy of "dependency"]. Tokyo: Kōbundō, 1993.

Dower, John W. "Nihon wo hakaru" [Sizing up (and breaking down) Japan]. *Shisō* (September 1995): 65–96; (October 1995): 67–89.

———. "Tennōsei minshushugi no tanjō" [A message from the Showa emperor]. *Sekai* (September 1999): 221–230.

Dubro, Alec, and Matsui Michio. "Hajimete vçru wo nugu amerika tainichi sennō kōsaku no zenbō" [Panel-D Japan: The whole feature of American operations for brainwashing Japan, now revealed]. *Views* (November 1994).

Etō, Shinkichi, et al. *Kokusaikankei ron* [International relations]. Tokyo: University of Tokyo Press, 1982.

Fromm, Joseph. "Nihon no chishikijin e chokugen suru" *Sekai* (May 1952): 131–135.

Fujino, Naohiko. "Ajia Kenkyū niokeru Nichibei kyōryoku to kenkyūsha no shakaiteki sekinin" [U.S.-Japan cooperation in Asian Studies and scholars' social responsibility]. *Bunka hyōron* 9 (1962): 9–22.

Fujita, Fumiko. "'Nichibei Chiteki Kōryū Keikaku' to 1950 nendai Nichibei kankei" [U.S.-Japan Intellectual Exchange Program and U.S.-Japan relations of the 1950s]. *American Studies* 5 (2000): 69–85.

Fukuda, Sadayoshi. "Hanbei shisō" [Anti-American thought]. *Bungei shunjū* (September 1953): 76–82.

Fukuhara, Rintarō. "Watashi no Nichibei bunka koryu ron" [My theory on U.S.-Japan cultural interchange]. *Chūō kōron* 886 (1962): 92–100.

Furuta, Hikaru et al., eds. *Kindai Nihon shakai shisōshi* II [A history of social thoughts of modern Japan]. Tokyo: Yūhikaku, 1971.

Gakkō Hōjin Dōshisha, Gendaigo de Yomu Neesima Joe Henshū Iinkai, ed. *Gendaigo de yomu Neesima Joe* [Neesima Joe for today's readers]. Kyoto: Maruzen, 2000.

Gendai Kyōiku Kagaku. "Dai 5 kai Nichibei Bunka Kyōiku Kaigi Saishū Komyunike" [The final communiqué of the Fifth U.S.-Japan Conference on Cultural Interchange]. *Gendai kyōiku kagaku* 153 (1970): 103–105.

Handō, Kazutoshi, *Tatakau Ishibashi Tanzan* [A fighting Ishibashi Tanzan]. Tokyo: Toyo Keizai Shinpō Sha, 1995.

Haruna, Mikio. *Himitsu no fairu: CIA no tainichi kōsaku* [The secret files: CIA operations in Japan]. 2 vols. Tokyo: Kyōdō Tsūshin Sha, 2000.

Hashimoto, Bunzō, ed. *Hoshu no shisō* [The thought of a conservative]. Vol. 7 of *Sengo Nihon shisō taikei* [A system of thoughts of postwar Japan]. Tokyo: Chikuma Shobō, 1968.

Hata, Ikuhiko. *Shiroku: Nihon saigunbi* [A historical record: The rearmament of Japan]. Tokyo: Bungei Shunjū Sha, 1976.

Hayashi, Kentarō. "Gendai chishikijin no ryōshin" [Conscience of a modern intellectual]. *Sekai* (May 1950): 97–103.

———, ed. *Shin hoshushugi* [Neoconservatism]. Vol. 35 of *Gendai Nihon shisō taikei* [A system of thoughts of modern Japan]. Tokyo: Chikuma Shobō, 1963.

Hidaka, Ichirō. *Nihon no hōso no ayumi* [A history of Japanese broadcasting]. Tokyo: Ningen No Kagaku Sha, 1991.

Hidaka, Rokurō. "Dai chishikijin ron" [A great theory on intellectuals]. *Kindai bungaku* 6 (February 1947): 2–12.

———, ed. *Kindaishugi* [Modernism]. Vol. 34 of *Gendai Nihon shisō taikei* [A system of thoughts of modern Japan]. Tokyo: Chikuma Shobō, 1964.

Higuchi, Tetsuya. "Shimin seikatsu to Amerika shihon" [Citizens' life and American capital]. *Chūō kōron* 814 (1956): 130–37.

Higuchi, Yōichi, and Osuga Akira, *Nihonkoku Kenpō shiryōshū* [Compiled materials on the Japanese constitution]. Tokyo: Sanseido, 1993

Hirano, Ken-ichirō. *Kokusai bunka ron.* [International cultural relations]. Tokyo: University of Tokyo Press, 2000.

Hirano, Ken-ichirō, et al. "Nihon no bunka kōryū no genzai" [The present state of Japan's cultural interchange]. *Kokusai mondai* 421 (1995): 1–74.

Hirano, Takashi. "Nihon no daigaku niokeru Amerika Kenkyū kankei no kyōiku jōkyō" [The state of offering American Studies courses at Japanese universities]. *Bulletin of the Center for American Studies of the University of Tokyo* 1 (1978): 21–26.

Hiromatsu, Wataru. *"Kindai no chōkoku" ron* [A treatise on "Overcoming modernity"]. Tokyo: Kōdan Sha, 1989.

Hiyane, Teruo. "Sengo Nihon niokeru Okinawaron no shisōteki keifu" [The philosophical genealogy of discussions on Okinawa in postwar Japan]. *Shisō* (December 2005): 24–41.

Honma, Nagayo. "Nihon bunka no Amerika-ka—Raifu sutairu to taishū bunka" [Americanization of Japanese culture—Lifestyle and mass culture]. In *Washinton taisei to Nichibei kankei* [The Washington treaty system and Japanese-American relations], edited by Hosoya Chihiro and Makoto Saito. Tokyo: University of Tokyo Press, 1978.

Hosoya, Chihiro. *Sanfuranshisuko kōwa eno michi* [The road to the San Francisco peace treaty]. Tokyo: Chūō Kōron Sha, 1984.

Hosoya, Chihiro, and Makoto Saito, eds. *Washinton taisei to Nichibei kankei* [The Washington treaty system and Japanese-American relations]. Tokyo: University of Tokyo Press, 1978.

Hotta, Yoshie. "Nihon no chishikijin" [Japanese intellectuals]. In *Iwanami Kōza Gendai Shisō XI: Gendai Nihon no Shisō* [Iwanami Course on Modern Thought XI: Thought in Modern Japan]. Tokyo: Iwanami Shoten, 1957.

Iesaka, Kazushi. *Nihonjin no jinshu kan* [The Japanese views on race]. Tokyo: Kohbundo, 1986.

Igarashi, Takeshi. "Sengo Nichibei bunka kōryū keikaku no taidō" [Fermentation of postwar U.S.-Japan cultural exchange program]. In *Senryō to Nihon shūkyō* [The occupation and Japanese religion], edited by Ikado Fujio. Tokyo: Mirai Sha, 1993.

———. *Sengo Nichibeikankei no keisei* [The formation of postwar U.S.-Japan relations]. Tokyo: Kōdan Sha, 1995.

———. "Sengo nihon 'gaikō shisei' no keisei" [The formation of postwar Japanese 'diplomatic posture']. *Kokka gakkai zasshi* (Journal of the Association of Political and Social Sciences, University of Tokyo) 97 (August 1984): 1–45.

———. *Tainichi kōwa to reisen—Sengo Nichibeikankei no keisei* [The peace treaty with Japan and the cold war—The formation of postwar U.S.-Japan relations]. Tokyo: University of Tokyo Press, 1986.

Ikei, Masaru. *Chunichi Amerika taishi* [American ambassadors to Japan]. Tokyo: Bungei Shunjū, 2001.

Inagaki, Takeshi. *"Akuma barai" no sengo-shi—Shinpoteki bunkajin no genron to sekinin* [A postwar history of "exorcism"—Expression and responsibility of progressive intellectuals]. Tokyo: Bungei Shunjū, 1994.

Inoue, Kiyoshi. "Nichibei Kagaku Iinkai to Gakusha no Shakaiteki Sekinin" [U.S.-Japan Committee on Science and Scholars' Social Responsibility]. *Rekishi hyōron* 139 (1962): 1–11.

Inoue, Taro. *Hekotarenai risohshugisha-Ōhara Sōichiro* [An unyielding idealist—Ōhara Sōichiro]. Tokyo: Kōdan Sha, 1993.

Inui, Takashi, and Mochizuki Mamoru. "Fuzoku—goraku" [Public morals and pastime]. *Shisō* 348 (June 1953): 120–131.

International House of Japan (Kokusai Bunka Kaikan), ed. *Sengo Nihon no Amerika Kenkyu Seminā no Ayumi.* [Survey of American Studies in Japan: Development of American Studies Seminars]. Tokyo: International House of Japan, 1998.

Inumaru, Giichi, Kobayashi Eizō, and Ishizuka Shigetarō. *"Nihon Kyōsantō kenkyū" no kenkyū* [A study of "The study of the Japan Communist Party"]. Tokyo: Gendaishi Shuppan Kai, 1980.

Iokibe, Makoto. *Beikoku Nihon no senryō seisaku* [The U.S. occupation policy of Japan]. 2 vols. Tokyo: Chūō Kōron Sha, 1985.

———. *Nichibei sensō to sengo Nihon* [The Japanese-American war and postwar Japan]. Osaka: Osaka Shoseki, 1989.

———. "Senryo kaikaku no san ruikei" [The three types of occupation reforms]. *Leviathan* 6 (1990): 97–120.

———. "Senryō—Nichibei ga futatabi deatta ba" [The occupation—The place where Japan and America met once again]. In *Nichibei no Shōwa* [Shōwa—Japan and America]. Tokyo: TBS Britannica, 1990.

———. *Senryōki: Shushō tachi no shin Nihon* [The occupation period: New Japan under prime ministers]. Tokyo: Yomiuri Shimbun Sha, 1997.

Iritani, Toshio. *Maruyama Masao no Sekai* [The world in which Maruyama Masao lived]. Tokyo: Kindai Bungei Sha, 1998.

Ishida, Takeshi. *Nihon no shakai kagaku* [Social sciences in Japan]. Tokyo: University of Tokyo Press, 1984.

———. *Shakai kagaku saikō* [Rethinking social sciences: The development of social sciences in postwar Japan]. Tokyo: University of Tokyo Press, 1995.

Ishihara, Yoshirō, and Furuya Kazuo. "Nichibei kagaku 'kyōryoku' no jittai" [The reality of U.S.-Japan "cooperation" in science]. *Bunka hyōron* 20 (1963): 32–45.

Ishii, Osamu. *Reisen to Nichibei kankei* [The cold war and U.S.-Japan relations]. Tokyo: Japan Times, 1989.

Ishikawa, Tatsuzō. "Hanbei kanjō wa kienai" [Anti-American feelings will not disappear]. *Chūō kōron* (November 1953): 34–39.

Iwama, Masao. "Nichibei kyōiku bunka kōryū no shōtai to bunkyō seisaku no handōsei wo tsuku" [The reality of U.S.-Japan cooperation in education and culture and pointing at the reactionary aspect of cultural and educational policy]. *Zen-ei* 196 (1962): 104–112.

Iwanami, Yūjirō, ed. *Iwanami Kōza Gendai Shisō XI: Gendai Nihon no Shisō.* [Iwanami Course on ModernThought XI: Thought in Modern Japan]. Tokyo: Iwanami Shoten, 1957.

Japan Communist Party. *Nihon Kyōsantō no 60 nen* [A 60-year history of the Japan Communist Party]. 2 vols. Tokyo: Japan Communist Party, 1983.

Jensen, Merrill. "Kyoto Amerika Kenkyū Kaki Seminā to hito to shisō no kokusi kōryū" [Kyoto American Studies Summer Seminar and international interchange of people and thought]. *Dōshisha American Studies* 7 (March 1972): 21–28.

"Kagaku kyoryoku nikansuru nichibei iinkai: Dai 1 kai kaigo hokoku narabini fuzoku shiryo" [U.S.-Japan Committee on Cooperation in Science: The report of the first meeting and its attached documents]. *Gakujutsu geppō* 14, no. 11 (1961): 636–641.

Kaji, Motoo. "Minkan kokusai koryu no tenkai" [The development of private international exchange]. *Kokusai kōryū* 66 (1995): 25–33.

―――. "Tokyo Daigaku-Sutanfōdo Daigaku Amerika Kenkyū Seminā to Nihon Niokeru Amerika Kenkyū" [The University of Tokyo-Stanford University American Studies Seminar and American Studies in Japan]. *Bulletin of the Center for American Studies of the University of Tokyo* 4 (1981): 1–7.

Kamei, Shunsuke. *Meriken kara Amerika e* [From Meriken to America]. Tokyo: University of Tokyo Press, 1979.

―――, ed. *Nichibei bunka kōryū jiten* [A dictionary of Japan-U.S. cultural interchange]. Tokyo: Nan-undō, 1988.

Katō, Mikio, ed. *Kokusai Bunka Kaikan 50 nen no ayumi, 1952–2002* [A 50-year history of the International House of Japan, 1952–2002]. Tokyo: International House of Japan, 2003.

Katō, Shūichi, and Kuno Osamu, eds. *Kindai Nihon Shisōshi Kōza 4: Chishikijin no Seisei to Yakuwari* [Course on Intellectual History of Modern Japan 4: The Emergence of Intellectuals and Their Role]. Tokyo: Chikuma Shobō, 1959.

Katō, Takashi. *Nambara Shigeru: Kindai Nihon to chishikijin.* [Nambara Shigeru: Modern Japan and intellectual]. Tokyo: Iwanami Shoten, 1997.

Katō, Yōko. *Amerika no Sekai Senryaku to Kokomu, 1945–1992* [COCOM and CHINCOM: Changing U.S. global strategies and Japanese trade control]. Tokyo: Yūshindō Kōbun Sha, 1992.

Kawakami, Tetsutaro et al. *Kindai no chōkoku* [Overcoming modernity]. Tokyo: Tomiyamabō, 1979.

Kawashima, Takenobu. "Nihonshakai no kazokuteki kōhsei" [The family structure of Japanese society]. *Chūō kōron* (June 1946).

Kido Mataichi, Kuno Osamu, Kuwabara Takeo, and Nakano Yoshio. "Sōkan no koro" [About the time of the first issue]. *Sekai* (January 1966): 176–191.

Kislenko, Aleksei P. "Nihon kyōiku-seido no konponteki kaikaku nitsuite" [On the fundamental reform of the Japanese educational system]. In *Soren wa Nihon ni naniwo Nozomu ka* [What the Soviet Union expects from Japan], edited by Kuzma N. Derevyanko et al., translated by Nisso Shinzen Kyōkai [Association for Japan-Soviet Friendship]. Tokyo: Ōdo-Sha, 1949.

Kita, Yasutoshi. *Shirasu jirō senryō wo seotta otoko* [The man who shouldered the occupation]. Tokyo: Kōdan Sha, 2005.

Kitagawa, Ryūkichi. "Nichibei bunka kōyū to 'daigaku jichi'" [U.S.-Japan cultural interchange and 'university autonomy']. *Bungaku* 30 (1962): 544–549.

Kobayashi, Gō. "Amerika to iu na no seijiteki muishiki" [The political unconscious called America: 'Postwar' American Studies reconsidered]. *Amerikashi kenkyū* 26 (July 2003): 17–32.

Kohiyama, Rui. "Nichibei bunkakōshō nikansuru kenkyū" [A study in U.S.-Japan negotiations on culture]. *Tokyo Daigaku Amerika Kenkyū Shiryō Sentā Nenpō* 17 (1995): 31–48.

Kojima, Tsunehisa. *Nihon shihonshugi ronsōshi* [A history of the debate over Japanese capitalism]. Tokyo: Ariesu Shobō, 1976.

Kojita, Yasunao. *Nihonshi no shisō* [Thought in Japanese history]. Tokyo: Kashiwa Shobō, 1997.

Kon, Hidemi. *Yoshida Shigeru*. Tokyo: Kōdan Sha, 1967.

Kon, Madoka. "Nihon senryō to toshokan" [The occupation of Japan and library]. *Kiyō Shakaigakka* (Faculty of Letters, Chūō University) 2 (April 1992): 1–14.

Kondō, Ken. *Mō hitotsu no Nichibei kankei: Furuburaito kyoiku kōryu no yonjū nen* [The other side of Japan-U.S. relations: Forty years of the Fulbright program]. Tokyo: Japan Times, 1992.

Kōsaka, Masataka. *Saisho Yoshida Shigeru* [Premier Yoshida Shigeru]. Tokyo: Chūō Kōron Sha, 1968.

Kōsaka, Toshio. "Henka shitsutsu aru sekai no naka de" [In the midst of the changing world]. *Chūō kōron* 814 (1956): 78–86.

Kumagai, Toshiki. "Sengo Nihon Niokeru beiseifu no paburikku dipuromashī no igi" [The significance of U.S. government public diplomacy in postwar Japan]. In *Ajia Taiheiyō Sensō no igi* [The significance of the Asia-Pacific war] Tokyo: Sanwa Shobō, 2005.

Kuno, Osamu. "Shimin-shugi no seiritsu" [The establishment of citizen-ism]. *Shisō no kagaku* (July 1960).

Macklon, Catherine. *The Japanese through English Eyes*, translated by Yanagimoto Masato. Tokyo: Sōshi Sha, 1990.

Mainichi Shimbun-Sha, ed. *Iwanami shoten to Bungei Shunjū* [The House of Iwanami and Bungei Shunjū]. Tokyo: Mainichi Shimbun Sha, 1996.

Manabe, Shunji. *Amerika no Doitsu senryo seisaku* [The American occupation policy of Germany]. Kyoto: Horitsubunka Sha, 1989.

Maruyama, Masao. *Gendai seiji no shisō to kōdō* [Thought and behavior in modern Japanese politics]. Enlarged ed. Tokyo: Mirai Sha, 1964; edited by Ivan Morris. London: Oxford University Press, 1963.

———. *Kōei no ichi kara* [From the position of the rearguard]. Tokyo: Mirai Sha, 1982.

———. "Sanfuranshisuko kōwa, Chosen Sensō, Rokujū nen Anpo" [San Francisco Peace Treaty, Korean War, and U.S.-Japan Security Treaty of 1960]. *Sekai* (November 1995).

———. *Senchu to sngo no aida* [Between the war years and the postwar years]. Tokyo: Misuzu Shobō, 1976.

Maruyama, Masao, and Fukuda Kan-ichi, eds. *Kaisō no Nambara Shigeru* [The recollection of Nambara Shigeru]. Tokyo: Iwanami Shoten, 1975.

Maruyama Masao and Yoshino Genzaburō. "Abe sensei to Heiwa Mondai Danwakai." [Professor Abe and the Peace Study Group]. *Sekai* (August 1966): 121–134.

Matsumoto, Shigeharu, ed. *Kokusai Bunka Kaikan 10 nen no ayumi*. [A 10-year history of the International House of Japan]. Tokyo: International House of Japan, 1963.

Matsumura, Masayoshi. *Kokusai kōryushi* [A history of international interchange]. Tokyo: Chijinkan, 1996.

Matsuo, Takayoshi. *Nihon no rekishi, vol. 21: Kokusai kokka e no shuppatsu* [A history of Japan, vol. 21: The start as an international nation]. Tokyo: Shūei Sha, 1993.

Matsushita, Keiichi. "Sengo sedai no seikatsu to shisō." [The life and philosophy of the postwar generation]. *Shisō* 421 (1959): 12–27; *Shisō* 424 (1959): 84–106.
Matsuyama, Nobunao. "Kyoto Amerika Kenkyū Kaki Seminā." *Bulletin of the Center for American Studies of the University of Tokyo* 1 (1978): 27–31.
Mikami, Masayoshi, and Hisagawa Kikuo, eds. "Taibei kankei wo meguru Kokkai gijiroku" [The proceedings of the Japanese Diet concerning relations with the United States]. *Chūō kōron* 814 (1956): 87–110.
Miyake, Haruteru. "Amerika no senryō seisaku" [The U.S. occupation policy of Japan]. *Chūō kōron* 814 (1956): 112–119.
Miyano, Tōru. *Saigono riberarisuto: Ashida Hitoshi* [The last liberalist: Ashida Hitoshi]. Tokyo: Bungei Shunjū, 1987.
Miyazato, Seigen. *Amerika no Okinawa tōchi* [American rule over Okinawa]. Tokyo: Iwanami Shoten, 1966.
———. *Nichibei kankei to Okinawa* [U.S.-Japan Relations and Okinawa]. Tokyo: Iwanami Shoten, 2000.
Morito, Tatsuo. "Heiwa kokka no kensetsu" [The construction of a peaceful nation]. *Kaizō* (January 1946): 3–16.
Munechika, Seiya. "Nichibei Kagaku Iinkai to Nihon Gakujutsu Kaigi" [U.S.-Japan Committee on Science and the Japanese Council on the Promotion of Scholarship]. *Kyōiku* 138 (1962): 26–29.
Murakawa, Ichirō, ed. *Daresu to Yoshida Shigeru* [Dulles and Yoshida Shigeru]. Tokyo: Kokusho Kankō Kai, 1991.
Mushakōji, Kinhide. "Amerikanizeshon to Nihon" [Americanization and Japan]. *Shisō* 483 (1964): 92–102.
———. "Kindaika Nihon no tenkaiten" [The transformation of modernized Japan]. *Chūō kōron* 906 (1964): 202–212.
Murthy, P. A. Narashimha. "Indo to tainichi kōwa" [India and a peace with Japan]. *Shisō* 703 (January 1983): 96–119.
Nagahara, Keiji, and Nakamura Masanori, eds. *Rekishika ga kataru sengo shi to watashi* [The postwar history that a historian recounts and I]. Tokyo: Yoshikawa Kōbunkan, 1996.
Nakabayashi, Shigeo. "Amerika no tainichi bunka seisaku (1)." [U.S. cultural policy toward Japan (1)]. *Rekishi hyōron* 144 (1962): 1–8.
Nakamura, Masanori. "Nihon senryō no shodankai—Sono kenkyū shiteki seiri" [The stages in the occupation of Japan—A historiography]. In *Senryō Kaikaku no Kokusai Hikaku—Nihon, Ajia, Yōroppa,* edited by Yui Daizaburō, Nakamura Masanori, and Toyoshita Naruhiko. Tokyo: Sanseidō, 1994.
———. "Nihon senryō to tennō-sei" [The occupation of Japan and the emperor system]. *Rekishigaku kenkyu* 600 (November 1989): 3–15, 80.
———. "Senryō towa nandatta no ka" [What in the world the occupation was]. In *Nihon dōjidaishi* [Japan contemporary history], vol. 2, edited by Rekishigaku Kenkyukai. Tokyo: Aoki Shoten, 1990.
———, ed. *Senryō to sengo kaikaku* [The occupation and postwar reform]. Tokyo: Yoshikawa Kōbunkan, 1994.
Nakamura, Takafusa. *Showa shi* [A Showa history], Part I, 1926–1945. Tokyo: Tōyō Keizai Shimpō Sha, 1993.
Nakano, Toshio. *Ōtsuka Hisao to Maruyama Masao* [Ōtsuka Hisao and Maruyama Masao]. Tokyo: Seido Sha, 2001.

"Nichibei futatsu no kagaku kaigi" [Two U.S.-Japan conferences on science]. *Zen-ei* 193 (1962): 133–135.
"Nichibei Kagaku Gōdō Iinkai to Nihon no Kagaku" [U.S.-Japan Joint Committee on Science and Japanese Science]. *Zen-ei* 190 (1961): 153–156.
Nihei, Satoshi. "Nihon shihonshugi no sengo saihen to kiki no shinkō" [The postwar restructuring of Japanese capitalism and the progression of a crisis]. *Tochiseido shigaku* 41 (1968): 1–23.
Nishi, Toshio. *Kuni yaburete, Makkāsā* [With the nation defeated, MacArthur]. Tokyo: Chūō Kōron Sha, 1998.
Nishimura, Iwao. "Fulbright hō ni motozuku jinbutsu kōkan keikaku" [The people interchange program based on the Fulbright legislation]. *Gakujutsu geppō* 7, no. 5 (1954): 283–284.
Notoji, Masako. "Tokyo Daigaku–Stanford Daigaku Amerika Kenkyū Seminā" [The University of Tokyo–Stanford University American Studies Seminar]. In *Survey of American Studies in Japan: Development of American Studies Seminars*. Tokyo: International House of Japan, 1998.
OECD Investigation Committee. *Nihon no shakai kagaku wo hihansuru* [To criticize Japanese social sciences], translated by Japanese Ministry of Education. Tokyo: Kōdan Sha, 1980.
Ogura, Kazuo. *Yoshida Shigeru no jimon* [Yoshida Shigeru's questioning himself]. Tokyo: Fujiwara Shoten, 2003.
Ōishi, Kaichirō. "Sengo kaikaku to Nihon shihonshugi no kōzō henka—Sono renzoku setsu to danzetsu setsu" [The postwar reform and the structural changes in Japanese capitalism—Its continuity thesis and discontinuity thesis]. In *Sengo kaikaku* [The postwar reform], edited by Tokyo Daigaku Shakai Kagaku Kenkyusho. Tokyo: Tokyo Daigaku Shuppankai, 1974.
Okamoto, Kōichi, and Tsukahara Tetsuya. "Senryōgun e no tōsho ni miru senryō makki no Nihon" [Japan seen from letters to the occupation army at the closing stage of the occupation]. In *Sengo taisei no keisei* [The formation of the postwar system], edited by Nihon Gendai Shi Kenkyū Kai [Study Group of Modern Japanese History]. Tokyo: Ōtsuki Shoten, 1988.
Okinawa Prefecture, ed. *Okinawa: Kunan no gendaishi* [Okinawa: A contemporary history of sufferings]. Tokyo: Iwanami Shoten, 1996.
Okinawa Times, ed. *Okinawa kara: Beigun kichi mondai no shinsō* [The report from Okinawa: The depth of the problems of U.S. military bases]. Tokyo: Asahi Shimbun Sha, 1997.
Ōsaki, Hitoshi et al. *Sengo daigakushi* [A postwar history of university]. Tokyo: Daiichi Hōki Shuppan Kabushiki Kaisha, 1985.
Ōshima, Yūichi. "Sengo kaikaku haaku no kiso shiten" [The basic viewpoints for an understanding of postwar reform]. *Rekishi hyōron* 322 (February 1977): 84–97.
Ōshimo, Shōichi. "Dōshisha Daigaku Akerika Kenkyūsho" [Dōshisha Univeristy Center for American Studies]. *Bulletin of the Center for American Studies of the University of Tokyo* 1 (1978): 32–35.
Ōta, Masahide. *Minikui Nihonjin* [The ugly Japanese]. Tokyo: Simul Shuppan Kai, 1995.
———. *Okinawa no chōsen* [The challenge of Okinawa]. Tokyo: Kōbun Sha, 1990.
Ōtake, Hideo. *Adenauā to Yoshida Shigeru* [Konrad Adenauer and Yoshida Shigeru]. Tokyo: Chūō Kōron Sha, 1986.

Ōtsuka, Hisao. "Jiyu to dokuritsu" (1946) [Freedom and independence]. In *Ōtsuka Hisao chosaku shū* [Ōtsuka Hisao collected works], vol. 8. Tokyo: Iwanami Shoten, 1969.

———. "Kindai-teki ningen ruikei no soshutsu" (1946) [The creation of a proto-type of modern man]. In *Ōtsuka Hisao chosaku shū* [Ōtsuka Hisao collected works], vol. 8. Tokyo: Iwanami Shoten, 1969.

Ōtsuka, Hisao, Kawashima Takeyoshi, and Doi Takeo. *"Amae" to shakai kagaku* ["Dependency" and the social sciences]. Tokyo: Kōbundō, 1976.

Passin, Herbert. "Senryō ga motarashita mono" [The occupation—Some reflections]. In *Nichibei no Shōwa*. Tokyo: TBS Britannica, 1990.

Reischauer, Edwin O. "Nihonjin-ron" [The Japanese]. *Bungei shunjū* (January 1979): 138–172.

Sadoya, Shigenobu. *Amerika seishin to kindai Nihon* [The American spirit and modern Japan]. Tokyo: Kōbundō, 1974.

Said, Edward W. *Representations of the Intellectual: The 1993 Reith Lectures,* translated by Ōhashi Yōichi. Tokyo: Heibon Sha, 1995.

Saitō, Makoto. "Nihon niokeru Amerika Kenkyū—Sono rekishi to konngo no kadai" [American Studies in Japan: Its history and perspective]. *Rikkyō American Studies* 22 (March 2000): 7–32.

Saito, Makoto, Sugiyama Yasushi, Bamba Nobuya, and Hirano Ken-ichirō, eds. *Kokusai kankei niokeru bunka kōryu* [Cultural interchange in international relations]. Tokyo: Kokusai Mondai Kenkyūsho, 1984.

Sakamoto, Kazuya. *Nichibei dōmei no kizuna: Anpo Jōyaku to sōgosei no mosaku* [The bondage of the Japanese-American alliance: The Japan-U.S. Security Treaty and the quest for mutuality]. Tokyo: Yūhikaku, 2000.

Sakata, Makoto. *Ryō Nihonshugi no seijika* [A statesman of good Japanism]. Tokyo: Tōyō Keizai Shinpō Sha, 1994.

Sakuta, Keiichi. "Sengo Nihon ni okeru Amerikanizeishon" [Americanization of postwar Japan]. *Shisō* 454 (1962): 30–39.

Samuels, Richard J. "Amerika no 'nihon ron' wo sōtenken suru" [Examining 'theories on Japan' in America thoroughly]. *Chūō kōron* (May 1992): 134–159.

———. "Nihon ishitsu ronjatachi no kōzai" [The merits and demerits of advocates of the theories on Japanese uniqueness]. *Chūō kōron* (June1992): 190–207.

Sasaki, Takeshi et al., eds. *Sengo-shi dai jiten* [Encyclopedia of postwar Japan, 1945–1994]. Tokyo: Sanseidō, 1995.

Sasakura, Hideo. *Maruyama Masao ron nōto* [The notes concerning the theory on Maruyama Masao]. Tokyo: Misuzu Shobō, 1988.

Sato, Kaoru. "Nichibei Bunka Kyōiku Kaigi no gaiyō" [A summary of the U.S.-Japan Conference on Culture and Education]. *Monbu jjihō* 1016 (1962): 79–85.

Satō, Tadao. "Wareware nitotte amerika towa nanika" [What does America mean to us?]. *Shiso no kagaku* 68 (November 1967): 2–13

Sekai (fortieth anniversary edition). *Sengo heiwaron no genryū* [The sources of propeace arguments in postwar Japan]. Tokyo: Iwanami Shoten, July 1985.

Shibasaki, Atsushi. *Kindai Nihon to kokusai bunka kōryu* [International Cultural relations and modern Japan]. Tokyo: Yūshindō, 1999.

Shigeno, Akira. "Beikoku seifu no Nihon niokeru kōhō bunka katsudō nitsuite" [On U.S. government's information and cultural activities in Japan]. *Cosmica* 14 (1984): 10–40.

Shinozawa, Kōhei. "Nichibei Bunkakyoiku Kyōryoku Gōdō Iinkai Dai Ikkai Kaigō nitsuite" [On the first U.S.-Japan Joint Conference on Culture and Education]. *Gakujutsu geppō* 22, no. 7 (1969): 8–11.

Shiraishi, Mami. *Tōdai vs. Kyōdai* [Tokyo University vs. Kyoto University]. Tokyo: Shinchōsha, 2003.

Smith, Charles Douglas. *Uchinaru gaikoku: "Kiku to Katana" saikō* [A foreign country within: *The Chrysanthemum and the Sword* revisited], translated by Kaji Etsuko. Tokyo: Jiji Tsūshin Sha, 1981.

Sodei, Rinjirō et al. "Tokushū: Senryō-shi kenkyū no kadai" [Feature: The assignments for studying a history of the occupation]. *Shosai no mado* 376 (July–August 1988).

Sugi, Katsuo. "Fromm shi e no tegami" [A letter to Mr. Fromm]. *Sekai* (June1952): 40–44.

Sugiyama, Mitsunobu. *Sengo keimō to shakai kagaku no shisō* [Postwar enlightenment and thought of social sciences]. Tokyo: Shin-yō Sha, 1983.

Sugiyama, Yasushi. "Kokusai bunka kōyū kenkyū no genjō" [The state of studies in international cultural interchange]. *Kokusai mondai* 220 (1978): 2–18.

Takauchi, Toshikazu. *Gendai Nihon shihonshugi ronsō* [A debate over modern Japanese capitalism]. Tokyo: San-ichi Shobō, 1973.

Takemae, Eiji. *GHQ*. Tokyo: Iwanami Shoten, 1983.

———. *Nihon senryō—GHQ kōkan no shōgen* [Testimonies of GHQ high-ranking officers]. Tokyo: Chūō Kōron Sha, 1988.

———. *Senryō sengo shi* [A postwar occupation history]. Tokyo: Sōshi Sha, 1980.

Takeuchi, Yoshimi. "Interi ron" [A theory on intellectuals]. In *Takeuchi Yoshimi zenshū*, vol. 6, *Nihon ideorogī*. Tokyo: Chikuma Shobō, 1980.

Teruya, Yoshihiko, and Yamazato Katsunori, eds. *Sengo Okinawa to Amerika: Ibunka sesshoku no gojū-nen* [Postwar Okinawa and America: Fifty years of cross-cultural contact]. Naha: Okinawa Times, 1995.

Tominaga, Ken-ichi. "Hoshuka to posto-modan no aida—Nihon sengo-shi niokeru 'kindai-ka' no tōtatsuten" [Between getting conservative and postmodernism—The destination of 'modernization' in postwar Japanese history]. *Sekai* 525 (March 1989): 233–248.

———. "'Sengo shakai' no maku wa hikareta no ka" [The period of 'postwar society' came to an end?] *Sekai* 513 (April 1988): 39–57.

Tomita, Hitoshi, ed. *Jiten gaikokujin no mita Nihon* [Japan through foreign eyes: An annotated bibliography]. Tokyo: Nichigai Associates, 1992.

Tōyama, Shigeki. *Sengo no rekishigaku to rekishi ishiki*. [Postwar historiography and historical consciousness]. Tokyo: Iwanami Shoten, 1968.

Toyoshita, Naruhiko. "Hikaku no nakano nihon senryō" [The occupation of Japan in comparison]. In *Nihon dohjidai shi* [Japan contemporary history], vol. 2, edited by Rekishigaku Kenkyukai. Tokyo: Aoki Shoten, 1990.

Tsuru, Shigeto. "Nichibei Kagaku Iinkai eno gimon" [A question to U.S.-Japan Committee on Science]. *Chūō kōron* 880 (1962): 56–64.

Tsurumi, Shunsuke. "Nihon chishikijin no Amerika zō" [Japanese intellectuals' images of America]. *Chūō kōron* 814 (July 1956): 170–178.

Tsuzuki, Tsutomu. *Sengo Nihon no chishikijin—Maruyama Masao to sono jidai* [The intellectuals of postwar Japan: Maruyama Masao and the times he lived]. Yokohama: Seori Shobō, 1995.

Uchino, Masayuki, *Shinpan kenpo kaishaku no ronten* [The critical issues on the interpretations of the constitution]. Rev. ed. Tokyo: Nihon Hyōron Sha, 1997.

Uehara, Atsumichi. "Nichibei no bunka-kyōiku no kōyū nitsuiteno zakkan" [Thoughts on U.S.-Japan cultural and educational interchange]. *Shisō* 453 (1962): 137–144.

Watanabe, Akio, ed. *Sengo Nihon no taigaiseisaku: Kokusai kankei no henyō to Nihon no yakuwari* [The foreign policy of postwar Japan: The transformation of international relations and Japan's role]. Tokyo: Yūhikaku, 1985.

Watanabe, Akio, and Miyazato Seigen, eds. *Sanfuranshisuko kōwa* [The San Francisco peace treaty]. Tokyo: University of Tokyo Press, 1986.

Yamamoto, Fumio, ed. *Nihon masu komyunikçshon shi* [A history of Japanese mass communication]. Tokyo: University of Tokyo Press, 1970.

Yamamoto, Tadashi. "Kokusai kōyū ni okeru minkan no yakuwari" [The role of private citizens in international interchange]. *Kokusai koryū* 66 (1995): 2–13.

———. "Minkan kokusai kōyū no atarashii igi to kadai" [The new significance and assignment of private international interchange]. *Kokusai mondai* 220 (1978): 19–30.

Yamamoto, Tadashi, and David Rockefeller. "Sugureta rīdāshippu ga hakkisareru toki shakai ga kawaru" [Society changes under good leadership]. *Kokusai koryū* 66 (1995): 46–54.

Yamane, Hiroshi. "Nichibei bunka kōyū no honshitsu to bunka shisō kagaku sensen no mondai" [The true nature of U.S.-Japan cultural interchange and the problems of the fighting line on culture, thought, and science]. *Bunka hyōron* 7 (1962): 2–10.

Yonezawa, Yoshie. "Chōsen Dōran būmu" [The Korean War boom]. *Economist* 71, no. 21 (1993): 104–109.

Yoshida Shigeru Kinen Jigyō Zaidan, ed. *Ningen Yoshida Shigeru* [Yoshida Shigeru—A human being]. Tokyo: Chūō Kōron Sha, 1991.

Yui, Daizaburō. "Hikaku senryōshi kenkyū no kadai to hōhō" [The assignments and approaches of comparative studies in occupation history]. *Rekishigaku kenkyū* 600 (November 1989): 1–2.

———. *Mikan no Senryo Kiaku* [Unfinished occupation reforms]. Tokyo: University of Tokyo Press, 1989.

———. "Senryō kaikaku no seiji rikigaku" [Political dynamics of occupation reform]. In *Nihon dōjidaishi* [Japanese contemporary history], vol. 1, edited by Rekishigaku Kenkyūkai. Tokyo: Aoki Shoten, 1990.

Yui, Daizaburō, Nakamura Masanori, and Toyoshita Narahiko, eds. *Senryo kaikaku no kokusai hikaku—Nihon, Ajia, Yōroppa* [Comparative studies in occupation reforms—Japan, Asia, and Europe]. Tokyo: Sanseidō, 1994.

Index

Abe Osamu, 176, 315*n*94
Acheson, Dean, 63, 65, 97
Aldrich, Virgil C., 185, 198, 201, 202
All American Conference on Education concerning the Occupied Areas, 169
Allen, Charles M., 196
Allison, John M., 66, 79
"American Cultural Relations with Japan," 217
American literature in translation, 28–30
American Studies, 161–84; criticism of, 251; definition of, 161; and democratizing of Japanese higher education, 179–84, 248; formation of steering committee for, 171–72; founding of, 8–9, 99, 163–66; funding of, 166–67, 172, 248, 251; Japanese response to American initiative, 168–71; legacies of, 205–8; MacArthur's support for, 171; universities participating in, 207, 324*n*118. *See also* Amerika Gakkai; Kyoto American Studies Seminar; Tokyo-Stanford Seminars in American Studies
American views of Japanese culture, 148–55; conservatives on democracy in Japan, 219–23; on deference to authority, 115–16, 149, 223, 249; on democracy in Japan, 214, 218–29; on economic success of Japan, 254–55, 258–59; on inferiority of Japanese, 84, 249, 254, 287*n*92, 319*n*29; on Japanese scholars and intellectuals, 150–55, 251; and lack of knowledge about Japan, 26; liberals on democracy in Japan, 223–29; on nationalist resurgence, 60–63; on psychological disposition of Japanese, 149–50; and Rockefeller's concept of "two-way street," 103–6. *See also* racism
Amerika Gakkai (Japanese Association for American Studies), 9, 162, 163–66, 207, 249
Amerika kenkyū (Amerika Review), 164–65
Anglo-Japanese Alliance, 83
anti-Americanism: as aberration on part of Japanese, 83; of Japanese intellectuals, 155; and reverse course policy, 48; and Rockefeller's concept of "two-way street" to prevent, 103–6; and social policies, 58; and U.S. censorship, 32
anticommunism. *See* Cold War
Anti-Intellectualism in American Life (Hofstadter), 145
Ariga Tetsutarō, 191, 195
art, Japanese, 119
Aruga Tadashi, 9

359

Asahi Shimbun (newspaper): on cultural cold war, 26; use of phrase "by order of the occupation army," 275*n*106

Barzun, Jacques, 252
Bash, Wendell H., 203, 206
Battle Act (Mutual Defense Assistance Control Act), 76
Bellah, Robert N., 3–4
Benedict, Ruth, 2, 28, 116, 238
Benton, William, 138
Beplat, Tristan E., 62
Bevin, Ernest, 63
bilateral security treaty with Japan, 90–91, 92, 95, 289*n*128
biographies, promotion of, 156–58
Bisson, Thomas A., 61
Blakemore, Thomas L., 33, 38, 127, 275*n*110
Blue Stocking women's movement, 222
Bond, Niles W., 30, 89, 150
Borton, Hugh: on democracy in Japan, 218–19, 221; on Marxism in Japan, 122; on nationalist resurgence, 60; role in Council on Foreign Relations study group, 216–17; on U.S.-Japan relations, 62; work on Rockefeller report on cultural relations, 111
Bovenkerk, Henry, 226–27, 231, 232
Bowles, Gordon: biography of, 272*n*30; and cultural center development, 129, 130–31; meeting with Rockefeller, 127; on Stoddard education mission, 21
Bowman, Dean, 39
Bradford, Saxton E.: on cultural center development, 135; on cultural interchange, 81, 107; on cultural relations, 138; on international houses for students, 123; on Japanese intellectuals, 141, 146, 151–55, 162; on Japanese labor unions, 120; on promotion of American studies, 161, 162; working with Rockefeller, 99, 127
Britain: cultural relations with Japan, 108; and peace treaty with Japan, 110
Brown, Donald, 31–32, 33, 165, 183
Bryce, James, 165
Buddhism, 233
Bundy, McGeorge, 160
Burke, Edmund, 53
Burks, Ardath, 227, 228
Bush, George W., 1
business leaders: criticism of scholars and intellectuals by, 251; influential role of, 52, 116; purging of, 45; and trade with China, 76
Buss, Claude A.: and American Studies, 166–68, 170; on democratization process, 161; on Japanese scholars and intellectuals, 175; on Kishimoto's abilities, 172; on Korean War's effect, 173; on seminar attendance, 315*n*78

"Campaign of Truth": in Japan, 155–58; launch of, 27, 109, 139, 140–41, 247; Truman announcement of, 139, 247
Cardinal Principles of the National Polity, 57–58
CARE, 107
Cary, Otis, 121, 137, 144, 205–6, 230–31
Case, Everett, 216
censorship, 30–34, 45, 154, 164–65, 243
centralization vs. decentralization in government administration in Japan, 181–82
Charles E. Tuttle and Company, 36
charter of education, 20
China: communist takeover, 42; trade with Japan, 74–77, 88; U.S. trade policy toward, 76
Christianity, 150, 162, 229–33, 330*nn*89 & 98
The Chrysanthemum and the Sword (Benedict), 2, 28, 116
Civil Information and Education Section (CI&E): approval of Amerika Gakkai, 9, 171; creation and structure of, 20, 272*n*21, 292*nn*27 & 30; educational reform efforts of, 179, 180, 181, 247; information center (library) of, 24–25; Rockefeller's view of, 97; role of,

21–24, 246; translation programs, 25–36
Cohen, Jerome B., 28
Cohen, Theodore, 21–22, 153, 226, 228, 240, 243
Cold War, 4–5, 41–63, 245–47; and conservatism in Japan, 49–60; Dulles's view of, 65; and historical studies in Japan, 155–58; and NSC 13/2, 42; Peace Study Group's view of, 88; Radio Free Asia's activity in, 107–8; and resurgence of nationalism in Japan, 48–49; and reverse course in U.S. policy in Japan, 43–46, 58, 63, 140, 243; and role of Japan in Asia, 67, 92–94, 244; and scholarship on cultural relations, 258; Soviet vision for Japan in, 46–48; translations as informational tools in, 26–27; U.S. reaction to during Truman administration, 43, 66, 247. *See also* "Campaign of Truth"; cultural offensive
Colligan, Francis J., 102, 257
Cominform rebuke of Japan Communist Party, 46, 47–48
Committee for Free Asia, 107, 108
Committee of Japanese Educators, 21
Committee on the Seminar in American Studies, 171
communism: anticommunist titles, publication of, 27; and Japanese labor unions, 120; Japan's fear of, 144–46; Japan's vulnerability to, 115, 121–22, 142–44, 150, 244. *See also* Cold War; Japan Communist Party (JCP)
Confucianism, 56
Conlon Report: on American-Japanese alliance, 214; on influence of Japanese intellectuals, 115
Conroy, F. Hilary, 227, 228
consensus style of decision making, 220–21, 227
conservatism in Japan, 49–60; actions taken by conservatives, 59–60; conservative vision of Japan, 54–59;

Japanese conservative thought, 53–54; sources of, 51–53
constitution of Japan, 37, 88
consumerism, 214, 237–42
convergence theories, 258, 259
copyright issues for translations, 26, 34–36, 108
Council on Foreign Relations: conservative views on, 219–23; establishment and structure, 215–16, 325n1; liberal views on, 223–29; study group on Japan, 216–17, 237, 325–26n6, 326n7; War and Peace Studies, 267n3
Crew, Glenna, 31, 32, 35
cultural center: founding of, 324n119; funding of, 133–36, 301n104, 303n150; naming of, 25, 136–37; proposal for, 116, 122, 125, 127, 129–30; public image of, 130–31; purpose of, 122–23; Rockefeller's impatience with, 132–33
Cultural Center Preparatory Committee, 129–30, 132, 300–1n97, 301nn100 & 104
cultural exchange programs. *See* cultural interchange
cultural hegemony, 5, 8
cultural imperialism: sensitivity to, 5, 95, 105, 126, 268–69n14; U.S. exercise of, 6
cultural interchange, 6, 101–12; advantages of, 8, 102, 108–10; drafting Rockefeller report on, 110–12; Dulles' view of need for, 80–81; institutionalization of, 126–29; and joint U.S.-Japan enterprise, 106; methods for, 81–82; principles of, 102–8; and public and private coordination and cooperation, 106–8, 126; purpose of, 99, 101, 109, 286n81; Rockefeller's preliminary research for, 99–101; and "two-way street," 5, 103–6, 117. *See also* Rockefeller report on cultural relations
cultural offensive, 7, 18–19, 99–101, 138–60; and conditions in Japan, 142–44; and Japanese views of U.S.

cultural offensive (*continued*)
culture, 146–48; unintended consequences of, 247–53; and U.S. informational program, 139–42; and U.S. views of Japanese culture, 148–55. *See also* Cold War; communism
cultural relations: definition of, 5–7; and government—foundation—university interlock, 8–10; recognizing importance of, 62, 96, 245–47; and scholarship on U.S.-Japan relations, 257–62, 334n25; transfer from CI&E to USIE, 98–99; and treaty negotiations, 4, 80–82. *See also other headings starting with "cultural" or "culture"*
culture: and consumerism, 240–42; and decision making styles, 220–21; definition of, 6–7, 82, 269n18; and national traits, 221–22, 254

Dangerfield, Royden, 188, 192–93, 194
Davidson, W. Phillips, 105
Davis, Joseph S., 173, 175
Dean, Arthur H., 79
decision making differences between U.S. and Japan, 220–21
deference to authority, 115–16, 223, 238, 248–49
deficiency theory, 219
democratization of Japan, 2–5, 12, 214–43; and Christianity, 150, 162, 229–33; CI&E measures for, 22–24; conservatives on, 219–23; vs. consumerism in postwar Japan, 214, 237–42; and definition of democracy, 217–18; and duality of citizens, 326n10; evaluation of, 12, 150, 218–29; filling spiritual vacuum, 143, 229–30; as goal of U.S. occupation, 18, 19, 22–24; Japanese intellectuals' role in, 3, 22; Japanese views of, 22, 234–37; New Deal progressives on, 223–29; U.S. as model for, 4, 58
dependency of postwar Japan on U.S., 2,
8, 10, 12, 133, 212, 248–49, 254. *See also* deference to authority
The Development of the United States (Farrand), 165
divergence theories, 258, 259
Documentary History of the United States, 165
Dodge Line aimed to curb inflation, 278n15
Donovan, Eileen R., 111, 125
Donovan, William J., 159
Dooman, Eugene H.: on changing thinking of Japanese, 30; on democracy in Japan, 218–20, 221; on East Asian markets, 78; on occupation reforms, 44; on postwar social conditions in Japan, 222; work on Rockefeller report on cultural relations, 111
Dower, John W., 1–2, 222, 249, 327n34
Dōshisha University, 175–76, 196–98; involvement with Kyoto Seminar, 199–205; split with Kyoto University, 202–5. *See also* Kyoto American Studies Seminar
DuBois Cora, 159
Dulles, John Foster: appointment to treaty negotiations, 4, 65–68; on bilateral security treaty, 90; on continuous cultural exchange, 80–81; on economic prosperity needed to support democracy, 71–72, 78; on peace treaty, 64, 68, 95–96; on racial hierarchy, 83, 84, 85; response to Rockefeller report, 124, 125; on vulnerability of Japanese to communism, 143; working with Rockefeller on Peace Mission, 96, 97, 268n10
Dulles Peace Mission: arrival in Tokyo, 97–99; formation of, 95–97, 290–91n1; return to U.S., 110
Dunn, Frederick S., 66, 153, 283n11, 286n81
Dyke, Kenneth R., 20

economy of Japan: conservative viewpoint on, 55; and consumerism, 240, 241; Dodge Line aimed to curb inflation in, 278n15; geographical factors, 73; historical factors, 74–77; and MacArthur's shortcomings, 39; and peace negotiations, 71–79; structural factors, 77–79; and trade friction with U.S., 250–51, 254–55, 258–59. *See also* international trade
ECSAS (Executive Committee on the Seminar in American Studies), 172
educational exchange: English-language instruction, 117–18, 297n28; program for, 24, 109; Rockefeller report recommendations on, 116–19. *See also* cultural interchange
education reform: and Christianity, 232; of higher education in Japan, 179–84, 211, 247–48; importance of, 20, 21–22, 23–24; purging of teachers, 45; science and technology in, 55
Eelles, Walter C., 45
Eisenhower, Dwight D., 7, 329n65
Eisenhower, Milton, 102
elections in postwar Japan, 49, 50–51, 120, 280n38
elite. *See* business leaders; intellectuals and scholars
Ellis, Howard S., 154
Embracing Defeat (Dower), 222
Emery, Brooks, 226
Emmerson, John K., 97, 138, 143
Emperor Hirohito: meeting with Rockefeller, 100; and renunciation of divinity, 84, 142
Endō Shūsaku, 330n89
English Language Education Council Inc., 297n28
English-language instruction, 117–18, 297n28
equality: and Japanese conservatism, 56; and Western racism, 82–85, 287n92
Evans, Roger F., 187, 189, 190–91, 196
Exchange-of-Persons program for Japan, 24, 117. *See also specific exchange programs and foundations*
Executive Committee on the Seminar in American Studies (ECSAS), 172

Fahs, Charles B.: association with Kishimoto, 284n36; on censorship, 33; on cultural center development, 133; on cultural imperialism, 95; on cultural interchange, 106; on Japanese deference to authority, 115; on Japanese economy, 240; on Japanese historical studies, 157, 158; on Kyoto American Studies seminar, 185, 186, 187, 191–92, 193, 195, 196, 198; on lack of collaboration among Japanese universities, 202; on library and information center use, 24; on peace treaty, 89; relationship with Rockefeller, 96; on social sciences and humanities studies, 169; on Tokyo American Studies institute, 169–70, 171–72, 184; on transfer of leadership, 113; work on Rockefeller report on cultural relations, 111
Failure in Japan (Textor), 34
Farrand, Max, 165
films: American, effect on U.S. image, 147; Japanese, 119
Fine, Sherwood M., 79
Fisher, Sterling, 127, 129, 132
Folster, George Thomas, 36
France: cultural relations with Japan, 108; Japanese regard for literature and culture of, 27, 35, 148
Frankena, William, 197
freedom and free enterprise, 57
freedom of information, x–xi
Friedman, Thomas L., ix
Fukuda Tsuneari, 54
Fukuzawa Yukichi, 82
Fulbright program, 80, 81
Fulbright/Smith-Mundt grants, 118
Fundamental Law of Education (1947), 20, 180–81

Gayn, Mark, 28
Germany: information centers in, 305*n*22; popularity of, in Japan, 144; and scholarship on cultural relations, 257; and transfer of American values, 21, 269*n*23; translation of literature into Japanese, 27, 33
Gibney, Frank B., Sr., 222
Gienow-Hecht, Jessica C. E., 5, 269*n*23
Ginza section of Tokyo, 239
Goheen, John, 172, 175, 186, 187–89, 191
Gone with the Wind (Mitchell), 29, 147
government officials of postwar Japan, 51–52. *See also specific official by name*
Government Section, role of, 37
Gramsci, Antonio, 5
Grew, Joseph C., 97, 219
Grew Foundation, 286*n*80
Groot, Gerald, 22

Hall, John, 202
Hall, Robert, 197
Harada Tasuku, 232
Hatoyama Ichirō, 50, 76, 180
Hawley, Frank, 38, 230, 277*nn*146 & 156
hegemony: described, 5, 8, 91; U.S. role as hegemonic country, 15–17, 91, 92
Henderson, Gregory, 200
Henderson, Harold G., 104, 227
Hepburn Chair of American Constitution, History, and Diplomacy, 148
Hersey, John, 28, 29
Hidaka Daishirō, 210–11
higher education, reform of, 179–84, 211, 247–48
Hiroshima (Hersey), 28, 29
historical Japanese studies, 155–58; scholarship on U.S.-Japan postwar relations, 257–62, 334*n*25; and Shōwa history debate, 309*n*99
Hofstadter, Richard, 145
Holland, William L., 227
Hyūga Hōsai, 145

ICFTU (International Confederation of Free Trade Unions), 120
Ichimada Hisato, 134, 231–32
Ikeda Hayato, 93, 136, 241
information centers. *See* libraries
information dissemination by U.S.: fear of Japanese of losing, 100; funding for, 140; libraries, role of, 24–25, 100; during occupation of Japan, 9, 24–25; as part of cultural interchange, 109, 118–19; translation programs, 25–36. *See also* "Campaign of Truth"
in rem vs. *in personam* rights, 219–20
Institute for Education Leadership program, 23
institutionalization, defined, 269*n*26
institutionalizing cultural interchange, 122–24
intellectuals and scholars: and American Studies, 168–71, 174–75; anti-Americanism of, 162; approach of, 10–11, 150–55, 248–49; and communism, 47, 144–45; democratization role of, 3; and dependency on U.S., 248–49; and exchange programs, 80; fear of U.S. abandonment of Japan, 70–71; focus of during 1970s and 1980s, 331*n*121; and German academic thinking, 144; influential role of, 114–19, 287*n*98, 296*n*6; Peace Study Group formed by, 86–88, 288*n*105; and peace treaty negotiations, 85–86; pro-American liberal bent of, 8; programs targeting, 114–19, 141, 248–49; on SCAP censorship policies, 32–33, 154, 164–65; shirking role of moral leadership, 251–52; U.S. embassy's perceptions of, 150–55
interdisciplinary studies, promotion of, 159–60
International Christian University, 232
International Confederation of Free Trade Unions (ICFTU), 120
International House of Japan, 136–37, 208, 303*n*151. *See also* cultural center

international houses for students: proposal for, 116–17, 122, 125, 127, 130; purpose of, 123
international trade, 74–79, 75*t*, 88. *See also* economy of Japan
Iokibe Makoto, 260, 261, 262
Iraq, U.S. policy toward, 1–2
Ishikawa Tatsuzō, 19
Iwai Yūjirō, 116
Iwanami (Japanese publisher), 35, 86, 88, 165, 271*n*14, 287–88*n*99

Japan Communist Party (JCP), 44–45, 46–48, 152, 280*n*38
Japan Democratic Party, 50, 280*nn*38 & 44
Japan Diary (Gayn), 28
Japanese Association for American Studies. *See* Amerika Gakkai
Japanese Association of Political Science, 169
Japanese Economic Stabilization Board white papers, 74
Japanese Educational Reform Council, 180
Japanese viewpoints: and conservatism, 49–60; and deference to authority, 115–16, 223, 238, 248–49; of democracy, 234–37; and demoralization postwar, 19; and fear of Communism, 144–46; of higher educational system, 211; and nationalism, 48–49; of need to catch up to West, 82; and racism toward other Asians, 84–85, 128, 222–23; and Rockefeller's concept of "two-way street," 103–6, 117; of SCAP policy, 32, 59–60; of U.S. consumerism, 214, 237–42; of U.S. culture, 28, 66, 146–48, 161, 228; of western literature and culture, 27, 33, 147–48. *See also* anti-Americanism
Japan Liberal Party, 50, 76, 280*n*38
Japan Progressive Party, 50, 280*n*38
Japan relations with U.S. *See* cultural relations; U.S.-Japan postwar relations

Japan's Economy during and after the War (Cohen), 28
Japan Socialist Party, 49, 50, 120, 280*n*38, 280*n*42, 280*n*44
JCP. *See* Japan Communist Party
Jessup, Alpheus W., 36
Johnson, Charles S., 21
Jordan, Amos A., Jr., 62
Jorden, William J., 226, 242
journalists in Japan, 34, 99

Kabayama Aisuke: and cultural center development, 128, 129; meeting with Rockefeller, 100, 127; role of, 246
Kagawa Toyohiko, 145
Kaji Motoo, 313*n*64, 315*n*78
Kanō Hisaakira, 100, 127
Karitani Kōjin, 258
Katayama Tetsu, 50, 230
Keene, Donald, 225, 239
Kennan, George F., 39, 41–42
Kerlinger, F. N., 33
Kerr, George, 190
Kishimoto Hideo, 71, 171–72, 190, 284*n*36, 313*nn*61 & 64
Knoles, George H., 172, 175
Koizumi Shinzō, 54
Kokusai Bunka Kaikan. *See* cultural center
Kondō Rinji, 235–36
Korean War, 42, 43, 64, 74
Kōsaka Masaaki, 158
Kōza vs. Rōnō factions, 144, 145, 153
Kraft, Joseph, 215
Kuno Osamu, 326*n*10
Kyoto American Studies Seminar (1951–87), 185–213; continuation of funding after 1959, 208–10; effect of provincialism on collaboration with Dōshisha, 199–202; exploration of, 176; legacies of, 205–8; lining up sponsoring university, 188–89; and 1954 proposal to change approach of, 195–97; participants and faculty in, 265–66, 320*n*41, 321*n*67; reviews of, 192–94; rift with Dōshisha University,

Kyoto American Studies Seminar (*continued*)
202–5; rivalry with Tokyo, 184, 190–92; and Rockefeller Foundation, 186–88; topics of, 318*n*2, 321n67, 322*n*76; and University of Illinois, 187–89, 192, 194–95, 196; and University of Michigan, 194, 197–99

labor unions, 107, 120, 152
Ladejinsky, Wolf I., 240, 332*n*131
land reform, 119, 267*n*4
Langer, Paul, 157
The Last Chapter (Pyle), 28
Leonhart, William, 249
Levi, Jakev, 146
libraries: and American Studies institute, 183; condition of, 100; importance of, 24–25, 141–42, 305*n*22; U.S. provision of books to, 118
Loomis, Arthur K., 23

MacArthur, Douglas: arrival in Japan, 17–18; ban of Japan Communist Party, 45; and "Bataan boys," 37, 277*n*146; criticisms of, 38–39; on democratization and Christianity, 229, 230; and Dulles Peace Mission, 97, 98; on Japanese behavior and culture, 12, 104, 249; on organization of National Police Reserve, 44; on peace treaty, 41; recall from Japan, 70; support for American Studies in Japan, 164, 167, 170–71
MacArthur, Douglas, II, on Japanese behavior and culture, 329*n*65
Machlup, Fritz, 198, 200
MacLeish, Archibald, 218
Maeda Tamon, 127
Maeda Yōichi, 315*n*79
Magistretti, William L., 38
Mailer, Norman, 28
Mainichi shimbun on occupation orders of U.S., 224
Marshall Plan, 46

Maruyama Masao, 86, 87, 144, 235, 280–81*n*51, 287*n*98
Marxism, 46–47, 120, 122, 144–45, 153, 156, 247, 259. *See also* communism
Matsui Kiyoshi, 191
Matsui Shichirō, 122, 192, 197, 206–7, 235, 315*n*94
Matsukata Saburō, 32, 127, 235
Matsumoto Shigeharu: on American Studies, 161–62; and Amerika Gakkai, 164, 165, 166; and cultural center development, 127–28, 129, 131, 132–33, 246; on Japanese historical studies, 156–57, 309*n*99; meeting with Rockefeller, 100, 127; on peace treaty negotiations, 89
McLean, Donald, Jr., 125, 131, 132, 133–34
Meiji constitution and laws, 20, 220
militarism, elimination of, 20
military bases in Japan, 71, 77, 89, 90, 289–90*n*128
missionaries in Japan, 107, 126, 331*n*98
Mitchell, Margaret, 29
Mitsui Takakimi, 143
Modern Democracies (Bryce), 165
modernization theory, 52, 258, 280–81*n*51, 335*n*5
Mott, Rodney L., 196–97, 199–200, 201–2
movies. *See* films
Mutual Defense Assistance Control Act (Battle Act), 76

The Naked and the Dead (Mailer), 28
Namba Monkichi, 200
Nambara Shigeru: on American Studies institute, 169–73, 175–78, 182–83, 190, 315*n*78; on cultural center development, 128; and founding of Amerika Gakkai, 168; on legacy of American Studies, 207; meeting with Rockefeller, 100; on neutrality of Japan, 88–89; on political science studies, 169; on spiritual needs of Japan, 230; on teacher exchange, 117

nationalism in Japan: drop off in, 20, 271n15; of intellectuals, 85–86; resurgence of, 48–49, 106; U.S. response to, 60–63
national traits of Japanese, 221–22, 254
neutrality as possibility for Japan, 89
New Deal progressives on democracy in Japan, 223–29
Newsweek magazine in translation, 29
New York Times: on Japanese benefiting from troops stationed there, 77; in translation, 29
Niehuss, Marvin L., 197–98
Nihon kaigan (Cary), 231
Nippon Times: and nationalism, 106; on social sciences and humanities studies, 168
Nixon, Richard M., 287n92
Nosaka Sanzō, 47
NSC 13/2, 42
NSC-41, 76
NSC-68, 43
Nugent, Donald R.: on abandonment fears of Japanese, 100; authority of, 37–38; as CI&E chief, 20; on cultural interchange, 102; as Information Division member, 31; on Kyoto American Studies seminar, 186–87; on Tokyo American Studies institute, 171, 183; Typer's view of competence of, 33; working with Rockefeller, 127
Nye, Joseph S., 210

Obluck, Warren, 9, 11, 249–50
occupation of Japan, 15–40; availability of documents on, 260; and censorship, 30–34, 45, 164–65; and contact restrictions between Americans and Japanese, 224–25; as cultural offensive, 18–19, 237; democratization initiatives of, 18, 19, 22–24; effect of Cold War on, 43–46; elections during, 49, 50–51, 280n38; information dissemination by U.S., 24–25; Japanese participation in, 3; Japanese view of, 48–49; and MacArthur's arrival, 17–18; as model for future U.S. occupations, 1–2; political reforms of, 37–40; preparation for, 2; and Stoddard education mission, 21–22; translation programs, 25–36. *See also* Civil Information and Education Section (CI&E); Supreme Commander for the Allied Powers (SCAP)
Oda Makoto, 131
Office of Strategic Services (OSS), 159–60
Office of War Information (OWI), 139, 304n8
Ohara Keiji, 315n79
Ōhara Sōichirō, 214, 234, 240
Okamoto Harumi, 176, 315n94
Oka Yoshitake, 158, 313n61
Okinawa base. *See* military bases in Japan
Orr, Mark T., 33, 275n113
Ōshimo Kakuichi, 122, 203–4
OSS (Office of Strategic Services), 159–60
Ōtsuka Hisao, 280–81n51
Ōtsuka Setsuji, 186, 315n94
Ōuchi Hyōe, 86
"overcoming modernity," 59
Overton, Douglas W.: briefing Rockefeller for return trip to Japan, 125; on cultural center and international houses, 123; on follow up to Rockefeller report, 124–25; and founding of Amerika Gakkai, 164; work on Rockefeller report on cultural relations, 111
OWI. *See* Office of War Information

pacifism, 87–88
Paris Peace Conference (1919), 83
Passin, Herbert, 33, 127, 276n118
patriarchical family system, 56, 57–58, 60
Peace Study Group, 86–88, 288n105

peace treaty negotiations, 64–94; appointment of Dulles, 65–68; arrival of Dulles mission, 97–99; conditions underlying soft peace, 67, 69–85; and economic viability of Japan, 71–79; Japan's alternative to U.S. proposal, 85–90; principles of soft peace, 68–69; process of, 283n11; race as factor in, 82–85; and security and safety of Japan, 69–71; separate bilateral security treaty, 90–91, 92, 95, 289–90n128; treaty provisions, 90–94; U.S. provision of troops in side agreement to, 71; and U.S.-Japan cultural relations, 80–82. *See also* Dulles Peace Mission

Penrose, Ernest F., 78
Perle, Richard N., 1
Philippines and Japanese reparations, 78, 110
political reforms during occupation, 37–40, 45
political science studies, 169, 313n44
Popular Rights movement, 221–22
population of Japan, 331n99
Potsdam Declaration, 18, 41
Powell, Colin, 1
prefectures, 277n151
Program for Foreign Newsmen, 99
The Protestant Ethic and the Spirit of Capitalism (Weber), 252
public and private coordination for cultural interchange, 106–8, 126
Pyle, Ernie, 28, 84

racism: in American view of Japanese people, 146, 222–23, 287n92; as factor in peace negotiations, 82–85; Japanese view of other Asians, 84–85, 128, 222–23; of MacArthur, 104–5; U.S. practices of (generally), 146–47
Radio Free Asia, 107–8
Reader's Digest in translation, 29, 274n87
Reischauer, Edwin O., 96–97, 111, 115, 149

religious groups working in Japan, 107, 126, 232–33, 331n98
remilitarization of Japan, 44, 66, 89
reparations, waiver of, 78, 91, 110
reverse course in Japan in light of Cold War, 43–46, 58, 63, 140, 243
Rikkyō Gakuin University, 163–64
Rikkyō Institute for American Studies, 163–64, 207
Ritsumeikan University, 199–200
Rockefeller, John D., 3rd, 95–112; acquaintance with Dulles, 96, 268n10; on anti-Americanism as potential danger, 41; and cultural center development, 129–30, 132–33; on cultural imperialism, 5, 95; and cultural interchange, 82, 101–12, 126–29, 246; and cultural offensive, 99–101; D.C. meetings prior to departure for Japan, 97, 291n14; on democratization, 214, 228–29; on Japanese view of U.S., 15, 66, 242; on Japan-U.S. relations, 1, 65–66; as member of Dulles Peace Mission, 4, 96; on nationalism of Japanese, 61–62; on peace treaty, 64; on promotion of American studies, 161, 162; return to Japan after turning in report, 125, 126–29, 300n79; role in Council on Foreign Relations study group, 217. *See also* Rockefeller report on cultural relations
Rockefeller Foundation: activities in Japan, generally, 107; and cultural center development, 133–36; Japanese postwar view of, 98; and Kyoto American Studies Seminar, 186–88, 189, 191–92, 196; mandate of, ix; and promotion of American studies, 162, 166, 167, 171, 172, 177–78, 208–9; and promotion of area studies in U.S. and abroad, 158–60; and promotion of Japanese history, 156–58. *See also* Fahs, Charles B.; Kyoto American Studies Seminar; Tokyo-Stanford Seminars in American Studies

Rockefeller report on cultural relations, 108, 113–24; drafting of, 110–12; on institutionalizing cultural interchange, 113–14, 122–24; on intellectuals, 114–19; Japanese response to, 129–30; objectives of, 113–14; on social groups, 119–22; U.S. government response to, 124–26
Rōnō faction. *See* Kōza vs. Rōnō factions
Root, Elihu, Jr., 41, 44
Roseberry, William, 255
Rosenberg, Emily S., 6
Royall, Kenneth C., 41, 44, 69–70
rural population and cultural interchange, 119
Rusk, Dean: on alliance with Japan, 93; on American Studies institute, 175; briefing of Rockefeller by, 97; on cultural relations, 11, 113; on dangers of paternalism, 212, 252–53; on educational system, 161, 184; on follow up to Rockefeller report, 125; on Rockefeller Foundation aid, 133; on Rockefeller Foundation's mission, ix

Saitō Makoto, 142, 234
Sakanishi Shiho, 157, 235, 309*n*99, 315*n*79
Sakata Yoshio, 157
Salzburg Seminar in American Studies (1947), 166
Samuels, Richard J., 334*n*25
Sansom, George, 22, 111
Scalapino, Robert A., 77
SCAP. *See* Supreme Commander for the Allied Powers
scholars. *See* intellectuals and scholars
scholarship on U.S.-Japan relations, 257–62, 334*n*25
Schumpeter, Joseph A., 53
Schwantes, Robert S.: on Christianity in Japan, 232, 233; on Cold War importance of Japan, 62–63, 82, 247; on cultural interchange, 102, 110, 122; on democracy in Japan, 218; on goals of occupation, 243; role in Council on Foreign Relations study group, 217
Schwarts, Benjamin I., 158
science and technology, 55
security of Japan and peace negotiations, 69–71. *See also* bilateral security treaty with Japan
Sekai (periodical) on peace treaty, 86, 88, 287–88*n*99, 288*nn*101 & 108
Shepard, Merrill, 111
Shimada Masao, 26
Shintōism, 233
Shōwa history debate, 309*n*99
Simons, Walter, 77
Smith-Mundt Act, 268–69*n*14
social groups and cultural interchange, 119–22
social policies: breakdown in social morality postwar, 222; conservative views on, 56; U.S. failing as model for, 58
soft peace. *See* peace treaty negotiations
soft power: and creating dependence of Japan on U.S., 10–11, 243, 247–53; in occupied Japan, 2; perils of, 9–10, 210–13; in postwar U.S.-Japan relations, 4–5
Sōhyō, 120
Southeast Asian markets, 77–78
sovereignty of Japan, 69, 91
Soviet Union: copyright waiver from, 26, 108; and peace treaty negotiations, 88–89; translations of Russian materials, 35; vision for Japan in Cold War, 46–48. *See also* Cold War
Spinks, C. Nelson, 32, 38–40, 127, 277*n*158
spiritual void in Japan, 142–44
Stalin, Joseph, 228
Stanford University, role in American Studies, 167–68, 170, 171, 178, 186, 188. *See also* Tokyo-Stanford Seminars in American Studies
State Department cultural affairs officer, 123
Statham, Harlan R., 33

Sterling, John E., 167, 170
Steward, Julian H., 206
Stoddard, George D., 21, 188, 194, 307–8n62
Stoddard education mission, 21–22, 180
Strauss, Harold, 29, 30, 237
students: international houses for, 116–17; study and travel grants to, 118, 125; vulnerability to communism, 121. *See also* American Studies; *specific programs*
Suekawa Hiroshi, 199–200
Supreme Commander for the Allied Powers (SCAP): anticommunist campaign of, 44–45; democratization initiatives of, 20–24; goals of, 18, 243; on Japanese economy, 72, 78; Japanese view of policy of, 32, 59–60; reforms instituted by, 3, 267–68nn4–5; shortcomings of, 37–40; structure of, 37. *See also* Civil Information and Education Section (CI&E)
surrender. *See* unconditional surrender of Japan
Suzuki Daisetsu, 56
Suzuki Gengo, 51–52
Suzuki Shigetaka, 59

Taishō democracy, 222
Takagi Yasaka: on American Studies, 161–62; censorship of, 165; and cultural center development, 128, 131, 133, 246; on democratization and Christianity, 230; and founding of Amerika Gakkai, 164, 168; meeting with Rockefeller, 100, 127; and Tokyo-Stanford seminar, 313n61, 315n79; and treatment of Japanese intellectuals, 154
Takayanagi Kenzō, 32
Takemae Eiji, 22
Takeuchi Tatsuji, 70, 192–94, 195, 199
Takeyama Michio, 54
Takikawa Yukitoki, 206
Tanaka Kōtarō, 5, 54, 105, 269n15
Taniguchi Yoshihiko, 191

Teachers' Union, 181
Textor, Robert B., 34
Time magazine in translation, 29
Tokyo Imperial University, Hepburn Chair of American Constitution, History, and Diplomacy, 148
Tokyo-Stanford Seminars in American Studies, 166–68; follow up, 175–77; funding of, 107, 178; 1950 Seminar, 171–79; number of participants, 315n78; participants and faculty in, 173, 174–75, 263–64, 317n124; reviews of, 177–79; rivalry with Kyoto and other universities, 184, 190–92; schedule and content, 173–74; topics of, 314–15n77
Tokyo University: founding of Center of American Studies, 206–7, 324n119; graduates in government jobs, 51–52; library of, 183; prestige of, 181, 248. *See also* Tokyo-Stanford Seminars in American Studies
Torigai Risaburō: and Kyoto American Studies Seminar, 186; meeting with Rockefeller, 100
town meetings, 227
Tōyō keizai shimbun on trade with China, 76
traits of Japanese, 221–22, 254
translation programs, 25–36; and American books, 28–30; anticommunist titles, publication of, 27; and censorship, 30–34; copyright complications for, 34–36; Rockefeller proposal for, 126
treaty negotiations. *See* peace treaty negotiations
Truman, Harry: dispatch of Dulles Peace Mission by, 4; embargo against Sino-Japanese trade, 76; on foreign information and education programs, 138, 139; on peace treaty, 64; on religious needs of Japanese, 229. *See also* "Campaign of Truth"
Truman Doctrine, 46
Tsuda Sōkichi, 54

Tsurumi Kazuko, 100, 315*n*79
Tsuru Shigeto, 131, 145, 315*n*79
"two-way street" concept. *See* cultural interchange
Typer, Donald, 33

Ueno Naozō, 198, 201, 203
Umehara Sueji, 22
unconditional surrender of Japan, 2–5, 17–18
UNESCO (UN Educational, Scientific and Cultural Organization) on causes of war, 86
unions, 107, 120
United Mine Workers of America, 107
United States Foreign Policy: Asia. *See* Conlon Report
"United States–Japanese Cultural Relations." *See* Rockefeller report on cultural relations
universities and colleges, reform of, 179–84, 211, 247–48
University of Hokkaidō, 174
University of Illinois, 187–89, 192, 194–95, 196
University of Kyoto, 181. *See also* Kyoto American Studies Seminar
University of Michigan, 194, 197–99, 202
University of Tokyo. *See* Tokyo-Stanford Seminars in American Studies; Tokyo University
UN procurement, effect on Japanese economy, 77
Uramatsu Samitarō, 116, 235
U.S. embassy: and cultural center development, 131; Cultural Materials Section of, 27; and Japanese historians, 156; and Japanese intellectuals, 150–55; role of, 141, 246, 249
U.S. Information Agency (USIA), 80, 292*n*28
U.S. Information and Educational Exchange Act of 1948 (Smith-Mundt Act), 268–69*n*14
U.S. Information and Education Service (USIE): country papers on Japan, 29, 89, 110, 120, 121; creation and role of, 99, 139–40; on democratization of Japan, 224; response to Rockefeller report, 124, 126; target groups of, 141–42; transfer of cultural relations from CI&E to, 98–99
U.S. Information Service (USIS)–Japan, 27, 118
U.S. Initial Post-Surrender Policy, 18
U.S.-Japan Education Mission, 169
U.S.-Japan Friendship Commission, 251
U.S.-Japan postwar relations, 5, 210–13, 245–47; dependency of Japan on U.S., 2, 8, 248–49, 254; economic tensions in, 250–51, 254–55, 258–59; future of, 253–55; scholarship on, 257–62. *See also* cultural relations
U.S. postwar role in world, 15–17
USIE. *See* U.S. Information and Education Service

Valency, Maurice, 231, 307–8*n*62
venereal diseases, 225
Versailles, Treaty of, as lesson for negotiating peace treaty, 68
Voice of America, 99, 140

Wallerstein, Immanuel, 271*n*7
War and Peace Studies of the Council on Foreign Relations, 267*n*3
Ward, Dorothy R., 35, 100
Washington Naval Treaty of 1922, 245
Watkins, James T., 173
Weber, Max, 234, 252
Weeks, G. K., 245
Whitney, Courtney, 37, 277*n*146
Wilbur, C. Martin, 239
Willkie, Wendell L., 16
Willoughby, Charles A., 34, 277*n*146
Wilson administration's propaganda efforts, 304*n*8
Wolfowitz, Paul D., 1
women in Japan, 120–21, 222
"workshop of Asia" view of Japan, 286*n*69

world economies vs. world system, 17, 271*n*7

Yamamoto Yūzō, 98
Yanagida Kunio, 54
Yanaihara Tadao, 26, 86, 190, 313*n*61
YMCA/YWCA and cultural programs, 107, 126

Yomiuri newspaper: and nationalism, 106; and red purge, 45
Yoshida Shigeru, 50–51, 76–77, 84, 100, 260–61
youth as target group of U.S. information program, 121, 141

Zenrō, 120